FOURTH EDITION

♦

COUNSELING CHILDREN

Charles L. Thompson
The University of Tennessee, Knoxville

Linda B. Rudolph
Austin Peay State University

Brooks/Cole Publishing Company
I**T**P ™ An International Thomson Publishing Company

Pacific Grove ● Albany ● Bonn ● Boston ● Cincinnati ● Detroit ● London ● Madrid ● Melbourne
Mexico City ● New York ● Paris ● San Francisco ● Singapore ● Tokyo ● Toronto ● Washington

 A CLAIREMONT BOOK

Sponsoring Editor: Claire Verduin	Interior Design: Rita Naughton
Marketing Team: Nancy Kernal & Barbara Smallwood	Interior Illustration: Jeffrey Ricker
Editorial Associate: Patricia Vienneau	Cover Design: Kath Minerva
Production Coordinator: Penelope Sky	Art Coordinator: Mary Ackman
Service Coordinator: Anne Gassett	Typesetting: Graphic World Inc.
Manuscript Editor: Joy Matkowski	Cover Printer: Color Dot Graphics, Inc.
Permissions Editor: Lillian Campobasso	Printing and Binding: Quebecor/Fairfield

PHOTO CREDITS: 1. Mikki Ansin/Positive Images; 57. Bob Daemmrich/The Image Works; and 341. Rick Reinhard/Impact Visuals.

For more information, contact:

BROOKS/COLE PUBLISHING COMPANY
511 Forest Lodge Road
Pacific Grove, CA 93950
USA

International Thomson Editores
Campos Eliseos 385, Piso 7
Col. Polanco
11560 México D. F. México

International Thomson Publishing Europe
Berkshire House 168-173
High Holborn
London WC1V 7AA
England

International Thomson Publishing GmbH
Königswinterer Strasse 418
53227 Bonn
Germany

Thomas Nelson Australia
102 Dodds Street
South Melbourne, 3205
Victoria, Australia

International Thomson Publishing Asia
221 Henderson Road
#05-10 Henderson Building
Singapore 0315

Nelson Canada
1120 Birchmount Road
Scarborough, Ontario
Canada M1K 5G4

International Thomson Publishing Japan
Hirakawacho Kyowa Building, 3F
2-2-1 Hirakawacho
Chiyoda-ku, Tokyo 102
Japan

Printed in the United States of America

10 9 8 7 6 5 4 3 2 1

Library of Congress Cataloging-in-Publication Data
Thompson, Charles L.
    Counseling children / Charles L. Thompson, Linda B. Rudolph.—4th ed.
    p.   cm.
    Includes bibliographical references and index.
    ISBN 0-534-34002-4
    1. Child psychotherapy.   2. Children—Counseling of.   I. Rudolph, Linda B.
    II. Title.
RJ504.T49 1995
618.92′8914—dc20   95-39260
                                                                                    CIP

Dedicated to our families

Harriet
Charles, Marcia and Shane,
Cynthia and Randy

Bill
John and Emma, Steven and Sheila,
Andy and Tammy

and grandchildren

Robby and Jessy

Price, Ashley, and Bethany

A hundred years from now it will not matter what my bank account was, the sort of house I lived in, or the kind of car I drove . . . but the world may be different because I was important in the life of a child.

Author Unknown

About the Authors

Charles L. Thompson is a professor of counselor education and counseling psychology in the College of Education at The University of Tennessee at Knoxville. He received his bachelor's and master's degrees in science education and educational psychology from the University of Tennessee and his Ph.D. degree in counselor education and developmental and counseling psychology at The Ohio State University—where he held NDEA and Delta Theta Tau fellowships. Charles is a former teacher and counselor in grades 7 to 12. He holds memberships in the American Counseling Association and the American Psychological Association. He is a licensed psychologist and certified school counselor. His research interests are in counselor education and individual counseling. He has published articles in *The Journal of Counseling & Development, The Elementary School Guidance & Counseling Journal, The School Counselor, Counselor Education and Supervision,* and *The Journal of Counseling Psychology,* and has cowritten five books on counseling. He is coauthor of *Educational Psychology: For Teachers in Training* with Steven Banks. Charles has been editor of the IDEA Exchange in the *Elementary School Guidance & Counseling Journal* since 1979.

Linda Rudolph is a professor of psychology at Austin Peay State University, Clarksville, Tennessee. She earned undergraduate and master's degrees in psychology and holds a doctorate in counselor education with a cognate area in psychology. She has taught psychology for more than 15 years and has concentrated in the counseling field for more than 10 years. She is a licensed professional counselor in the State of Tennessee and has served as both vice president and president for the state licensing Board for Professional Counselors and Marital and Family Therapists. Linda holds membership in the American Counseling Association and in state and regional affiliations. She has been active in state, regional, and national counseling associations, presenting workshops on counseling with children as well as on her research into women's career choices. Her research has focused primarily on children of divorce, assessment, and the effects of women's backgrounds, values, and choices on their professional advancement. She has published numerous articles in professional journals and cowritten a chapter on women's career development in a textbook on counseling with women.

Linda is currently on a leave of absence from Austin Peay State University, and serves as Commissioner of the Tennessee Department of Human Services.

Contents

◆

◆

Part Two

Counseling Theories and Techniques: Their Application to Children   57

Chapter 3
Psychoanalytic Counseling   59

Chapter 9
Transactional Analysis   226

◆

Part Three

Counseling with Children: Special Topics   341

Chapter 12
Play Therapy   *343*

Preface

In *Counseling Children, Fourth Edition,* we put theory into practice for people preparing to work with children and for established professionals. Counselors, psychologists, teachers, and social workers will find the book useful in developing approaches for teaching children how to meet their own needs. We combine ideas from research and practice in straightforward, up-to-date methods for helping children with specific developmental, social, or behavioral problems. We have included specific suggestions for counseling children who are exceptional; who are experiencing divorce, death, abuse, homelessness, or alcoholism; or who are victims of AIDS, cults, or violence. Cross-cultural research is referred to regularly. Throughout, we emphasize the development of children.

This edition will be of help to mental health service providers as they work with managed health care programs. We discuss brief counseling theories, techniques, and interventions that are adaptable to the eight to ten sessions imposed by many insurers. The chapters on reality therapy, behavioral counseling, rational emotive behavioral counseling, individual psychology, and family counseling are particularly well-suited to short-term counseling treatments.

Any strategy for changing children's behavior depends on many variables, including the severity of the problem, the resistance or cooperation of the child and significant adults, and the orientation of the counselor. In this book we share the ideas and methods we have found useful in helping children become responsible, fully functioning persons.

ORGANIZATION

In this revision we have updated the theory and practice sections in each chapter, making the search for new literature our first priority and adding many new references. Our evaluation of current trends in counseling children resulted in the following modifications.

In Part One, we explain what causes children's problems, and briefly consider why some children seem to be resilient even when they are confronted with overwhelming difficulties. Exploring what effective counselors have in common, we conclude that counseling can be remedial, preventive, or developmental. We present Piaget's stages of cognitive development, Erikson's theory of social development, and Havighurst's developmental tasks. We define counseling and describe the counseling process, answering the practical questions often asked by new counselors. We also discuss ways of overcoming children's resistance to counseling.

In Part Two, we cover nine established counseling theories that may be used in working with children. Each chapter includes a biographical sketch, a philosophical statement by the theorist, discussion and application of the theory and methods used in practice, case histories that demonstrate application of these methods, and an updated summary of research. Part Two begins with psycho-analytic counseling, because Freud's work has been so influential. Reality therapy follows, because it provides counselors with a basic framework for working with children and their families. We have found that a blend of reality therapy and the person-centered approach of Carl Rogers is useful to beginning counselors who are developing their own styles. We go on to consider Gestalt, rational emotive, behavioral, cognitive behavioral, and transactional analysis theories. Each one offers a variety of interventions that can be used with the basic reality/person-centered model. We conclude Part Two with a family counseling section, emphasizing individual psychology and conjoint, strategic, structural, and family systems therapy. The chapter on family counseling has been completely reworked, as we define more clearly the differences between structural, strategic, and systems methods of counseling families. We have modified Part Two further by giving a more detailed description of how operant and classical methods are used in behavioral counseling. The chapter on individual counseling was reviewed by Harold Mosak, the foremost authority on Adlerian psychology; his research and suggestions have been incorporated.

Part Three begins with a new chapter on play therapy that includes two case illustrations. The chapter on consulting in school and mental health settings contains a new section on assessment as a consultative intervention. The chapter on group counseling with children has been updated with new material about group leadership skills. In two chapters the focus is on children with special concerns, including abuse, divorce, stepfamilies, and alcoholism; we also consider children who are affected by death, are exceptional, or belong to a non-mainstream culture. We address such issues as latchkey children, homelessness, suicide, cults, AIDS, and violence. Part Three concludes with the legal and ethical aspects of counseling children. We offer hypothetical situations that test readers' grasp of the subject, referring to the appropriate ACA, APA, and NASW ethical codes and explaining our own opinions.

Practicing counselors gave positive feedback about the interventions suggested in Appendixes A and B, which remain as a handy reference guide. We also include categories for classifying clients according to DSM-IV, for counselors in private practice or working in community agencies.

ACKNOWLEDGMENTS

We appreciate the encouraging support of our work from many people at our universities and in our communities, especially Richard Wisniewski at the University of Tennessee and John Butler at Austin Peay State University. We also acknowledge our reviewers, who were able to give expert advice and criticism while allowing us to maintain our self-esteem: Susan Anzivino, University of Maine at Farmington; Diane Frey, Wright State University; James Gumaer, Radford University; Harry Overline, California State University, Hayward; and Timothy Sewall, University of Wisconsin–Green Bay. Very special love and appreciation go to Claire Verduin, who guided and motivated us with expertise and warm encouragement through four editions. We wish her the same success in retirement that she experienced as editor and publisher at Brooks/Cole. We are grateful to our production editor, Anne Gassett, for her valuable assistance and support. Special thank-yous are due to Kirche Rogers, for manuscript preparation and editorial assistance, and to the following doctoral students, for proofreading and suggestions: Leigh Culpepper, Michael Nolan, Will Batts, Suzanne Holm, and Connie Sylve.

Finally, we offer our spouses, Harriet and Bill, our love and appreciation for their continuing patience, support, understanding, and encouragement. To our children, now adults of whom we are very proud, we extend our thanks for teaching us about children, parenting, and unconditional love. More recently, our education has been refreshed and enriched through the joys of grandparenting.

Charles L. Thompson
Linda B. Rudolph

PART ONE

◆

INTRODUCTION TO COUNSELING CHILDREN

Chapter 1

$\blacklozenge$

Introduction to a Child's World

The United States prides itself on being a child-oriented nation. Laws have been passed to prevent children from being misused in the workplace, to punish adults who physically or psychologically harm children, to provide means for all children to obtain an education regardless of their mental or physical condition, and to support programs for medical care, food, and clothing for children in need. Politicians have debated "save our children" issues such as educational reform, sex and violence on television, an adolescent girl's right to an abortion without parental consent, family-leave policies in the workplace, burdening our children and grandchildren with an increasing national debt, and ways of providing a more environmentally safe world for our children's future.

In sharp contrast, *Caring Connections: Helping Young People from Troubled Homes* (National School Boards Association and American School Counselors Association, 1994) reported that

- One in five children live in families with incomes below the poverty line.
- More than 1 million children are seriously abused each year.
- 12% of American children suffer from serious emotional disorders, but less than a third receive help.
- A child is murdered every 3 hours.

Bennett (1993) wrote that in 1940 teachers identified the top problems in America's schools as talking out of turn, chewing gum, making noise, running in the halls, cutting in line, dress code violations, and littering. In 1990, teachers identified the top problems of children as drug abuse, alcohol abuse, pregnancy, suicide, rape, robbery, and assault. Statistics included in this report indicated that "the fastest growing segment of the criminal population is our nation's children" (p. 4).

Achenbach and Howell (1993) analyzed whether the prevalence of children's problems had changed significantly from 1976 to 1989. They found that "parents and teachers judged American children to be functioning somewhat less well in

3

1989 than in 1976 and 1981 to 1982, respectively" (p. 1153). The researchers could identify no single cause for the change. They suggested that more children are receiving assistance for their problems, but more children are being identified as needing help and are *not* receiving treatment.

What is happening in the lives of our children? What is happening in American homes and society to cause approximately 9 million children to experience problems that require the help of mental health professionals?

The problems of children are increasing with serious rapidity and giving cause for grave concern. The factors that contribute to these statistics must be studied, and methods for individuals and society to help these children must be found.

Obviously, some children are born into warm and loving homes that provide excellent environments for growth and development. Many children pass successfully through the developmental stages of childhood and adolescence and become fully functioning or self-actualizing adults. Other children seem to be able to overcome the adversities of their childhoods and go on to lead productive and meaningful lives. These children have the resilience to carry them through neglect, abuse, poverty, and other unfavorable home conditions. Beardslee (1989) defined *resiliency* as unusually good adaptation in the face of severe stress; resilient children have learned to expect and cope with difficulties in their lives. Werner (1984) wrote that resilient children play vigorously, seek out novel experiences, lack fear, and are self-reliant. They are able to find help from adults and refuge when they need it.

Flach (1988) identified several traits of the resilient person:

- A strong sense of self-esteem
- Independence of thought and action
- Ability to give and take in personal interactions
- A high level of personal discipline and a sense of responsibility
- Open-mindedness
- Flexibility
- Insight into one's own feelings and those of others
- Ability to communicate feelings to others
- A high tolerance for distress
- A philosophical framework that gives meaning to life's experiences

Flach also suggested that faith in a higher power to which a person can turn in times of crisis can give a sense of purpose to life and therefore encourage survival. Since the children professionals work with need adult support to counter the chaos in their lives, Flach encouraged all who work with children to instill resilience by providing predictable and supportive structure.

Although some children do have the resiliency to survive a poor home environment, a growing number have emotional, behavioral, social, and other problems that warrant mental health treatment. Resources for counselors and others who work with children are increasing; however, clinical, agency, and school professionals have felt frustrated because information about specific counseling procedures for developmental, learning, and behavioral problems has been limited and difficult to obtain. This book provides people in clinical agency, school, and other counseling situations with suggestions for counseling children with specific learning or behavioral problems.

WHAT CAUSES OUR CHILDREN'S PROBLEMS?

Tommy is a fifth-grader referred for counseling because of "lack of motivation." He is a loner who does not seem to want friends. He appears unenthusiastic about life—nothing interests or excites him.

Rachel is a first-grader whose parents have recently divorced. Her mother and father have found other partners and in the excitement of their new lives have little time for Rachel. She is very confused about whom she can rely on and trust. At this very crucial point in her school life, she is floundering in an unstable world.

Stacie's family lives in abject poverty. Neither parent completed high school, and neither can hold a steady job. Stacie's few clothes are too small for her and sometimes not clean. She often does not have lunch or lunch money, and she complains about being hungry at home. At school, she seems to be in her own dream world.

Chris, a fourth-grader, has been acting out since the first grade, and no one has been able to work with him effectively. He comes from a "good" family, and his parents have tried to provide him with care and loving support. Chris is constantly in trouble for hitting, lying, and name-calling. He has now begun to fight in class, on the playground, and with children in his neighborhood. There are rumors about spouse abuse in his family.

Mike has been diagnosed as having attention deficit–hyperactivity disorder (ADHD), but his parents refuse to believe the diagnosis. They blame the school for Mike's learning and behavior problems. Mike is two grades behind in reading and a constant disruption in his classroom. The teacher has given up, saying that she cannot help Mike unless his parents cooperate with her educational plan.

A Changing World

As we approach the 21st century, predictions about future events and conditions abound. What will the new decade bring? One prediction all forecasters seem to make is that the world will continue to change rapidly. Naisbitt and Aburdene (1990) indicated (1) technological growth will continue; (2) the United States will move further from the Industrial Age into the Information Era; (3) "family" will be redefined to include many types of homes and relationships; (4) as more women enter the work force, more mothers of preschoolers and schoolage children will seek good child care; (5) although the divorce rate has leveled off, over half of all children will live in a single-parent household at some time during their lives; (6) international events will continue to have a strong influence on the United States, and children will need to learn about other cultures in order to live and work with others effectively; (7) concern about substance abuse and addiction will continue to have high priority; and (8) environmental issues will bring about changes in living patterns.

Crabbs (1989, p. 160) stated that it "is time to identify major social, political, educational, and economic influences that may have a direct impact on . . . the counselor's role in the year 2000." He encouraged counselors to identify "what is" in their counseling area and to plan for "what might be." Factors that Crabbs suggested be examined include

1. Violence on elementary and secondary school campuses
2. Experimentation with alcohol and drugs at young ages (approximately age 12)
3. Increasing prejudice
4. Gang membership
5. Physical and sexual abuse
6. A need for sex education due to increasing sexual activity
7. Increasing use of computer technology
8. Changing values and accompanying conflicts
9. Poor health practices in children (smoking, poor eating habits)
10. Poverty that limits potential
11. Continuing instability in the family structure
12. New ways to treat childhood fears of the 21st century (pp. 161–163)

We like to think our children are immune to the stressful complexities and troubles of the rapidly changing adult world. We see childhood as a carefree, irresponsible time, with no financial worries, societal pressures, or work-related troubles. Melton (1987) warned us that many adults who consider themselves child advocates do not understand children's perceptions. They do not believe a child's concerns matter much, and they believe that children are largely unaware of what is happening politically and economically. Melton's research evidence showed that schoolage children are effective decision makers and problem solvers and "political beings by reason of their living in a political society" (p. 363).

Normal child development involves a series of cognitive, physical, emotional, and social changes. Almost all children at some time experience difficulty adjusting to the changes, and the accompanying stress or conflict can lead to learning or behavior problems. Normal child development tasks include achieving independence, learning to relate to peers, developing confidence in self, coping with an ever-changing body, forming basic values, and mastering new ways of thinking and new information. Wertlieb, Weigel, and Feldstein (1987) reported that numerous factors in children's lives require them to adapt, including changes in home or school locations, death or divorce in the family, and major illnesses, as well as the usual "daily hassles." A high degree of stress has been found to be associated strongly with behavior symptoms. Add the stresses and conflicts of a rapidly changing society—which even adults find difficult to understand—to normal developmental concerns, and the child's world does not look so appealing.

The American Home

According to developmental psychologists, children need warm, loving, and stable home environments in order to grow and develop in a healthy manner. Years ago, children lived in large, stable, extended families. Fathers worked on the land, mothers in the home, and often grandparents or an unmarried aunt or uncle lived with the family. Thus, many adults were around when a child needed to talk or needed to feel special to someone. Decisions about social activities, careers, and marriage were relatively simple; the choices were restricted, and the expectations were clear.

In today's society the home is not so simple. Grandparents may live 3000 miles away and be almost unknown to their grandchildren. Aunts and uncles seldom live nearby; in any case, they are busy pursuing individual interests and careers. Fathers work long hours to provide financial security for their families and then are expected to attend meetings or other community events at night. A majority of mothers of schoolage children also work long hours to help support the family or for other reasons. Mothers still shoulder the primary responsibility for the care of the home, so they are often occupied at night with washing, ironing, or cleaning. And with the incidence of divorce in families remaining relatively high over the past few years, single parents are assuming the roles of both mother and father more frequently, doubling the burden on the parent, and leaving little time free for children. Thus, children may not be able to find someone to listen or to provide the care and guidance they need, even though adults are all around.

Gender Issues Affecting Children

Scher and Good (1990) pointed out that the influence of gender will be of great importance in the coming decade but that counselors are not as informed about the issue as they should be. Mintz and O'Neil (1990) wrote that "while gender roles have a profound effect on individuals in our culture, there has been a dearth of research on the impact of counselor and client gender roles on the therapy process" (p. 381). However, Scher and Good contended that beliefs about gender can have a powerful influence in counseling and that clients must be understood within the "context of their conceptions about gender" (p. 389).

What we do know is that children have been exposed to gender-biased books, toys, teachers, and school curricula, as well as to a society that shapes gender roles and behaviors. Unfortunately, counselors, too, have supported gender stereotypes in both personal and career counseling through their use and interpretation of tests and methods of helping young people make choices, learn new ways of interacting, or develop personal skills in other ways (Basow, 1986). Learned stereotypical attitudes and behaviors continue to influence the decisions and actions of individuals throughout their lives.

While researchers continue to debate what we do and do not know about the influence of sex and gender roles on a child's development and in the counseling environment, counselors can examine their own attitudes toward masculine and feminine roles and expectations. They should include discussion with colleagues about the issues, evaluation of their own counseling styles, and continuing education through reading and attending seminars and workshops. Scher and Good (1990) argued that "counselors must be aware of the impact of gender on the way in which our society is defined, organized, and functions in order to do the best possible job for our clients. Ignoring the impact of conceptions of gender on our work is an invitation to disaster" (p. 388). Counselors who work with children as they develop physically, psychologically, socially, and emotionally have an increased responsibility to concern themselves with their influence on their clients during the formative years.

Societal Crises

Not only do many children live in unstable homes but also they are continually confronted by conflict-ridden society. The media report the high cost of life's necessities—food, shelter, clothing—almost daily. Job markets change rapidly, and career planning is hampered by uncertainties about future demand for specific skills. Those adults with jobs are often dissatisfied. Crime seems to be everywhere, and many neighborhoods are no longer safe for children or adults. The cost of vandalism to schools and other private and public property is astronomical. People are increasingly cynical and distrustful of local, state, and federal government. Once-respected public figures and government agencies have engaged in criminal or highly unethical practices. Some experts predict economic disaster because of the high national debt and unbalanced budget. Finally, we live in a world full of tensions, war, and the threat of terrorism that can strike anywhere at any time.

Changing Values

Although change can be frightening or confusing, especially for a child, it can also be wondrous and exciting. It can bring new discoveries in medicine, new ideas for recreation, different jobs, new ways of living—all areas of life may be affected.

The children of today are forming values in a constantly and rapidly changing world. What is right or wrong seems to change daily or vary with the person we are talking to. Who is right concerning standards of sexuality, cohabitation, alternative lifestyles, or abortion? Are the various liberation movements good or bad? How does a person behave in a world with changing gender roles? Will drugs really harm a person? Should society condone mercy killing? Is capital punishment justified? Adults with mature thinking processes and years of life experience have trouble making rational judgments on such ethical and moral issues.

Children in today's world are expected to grow, mature, and make critical decisions at a very young age. Goodman (1990) lamented that a 5-year-old who cannot answer questions about what his or her parents do for a living, draw the missing parts of an incomplete man, name a certain number of animals in 1 minute, print his or her name, and count from 1 to 20 may be labeled "immature" and begin to believe that he or she is dumb. Counselors are now seeing psychosomatic symptoms—stomachaches, headaches, fevers, and other physical symptoms—in hurried children.

Obviously, some children enjoy secure childhoods that prepare them to meet the challenges of contemporary society. The purpose of presenting a pessimistic view is to discourage the idea that childhood is a carefree, irresponsible period and to encourage adults to investigate the increase in learning, behavioral, and emotional problems, drinking and drug abuse, runaways, suicides, lack of commitment, and the numerous other problems children face. Although every adult was once a child, as early as the days of Socrates and Aristotle adults felt that the younger generation was "going to the dogs." However, past generations did not have to deal with a gap in understanding so compounded by the complexities of today's society.

THE PERSONAL WORLD OF THE CHILD

The various social and cultural conditions we have been discussing can have a profound effect on the child's personal and psychological world.

Maslow (1970) believed we all have certain basic needs that must be met in order for us to become "self-actualizing" and to reach our potential in all areas of development. If our lower level basic needs are not met, we will be unable to meet higher order needs. His ideas suggest some possible reasons why our children are experiencing more learning and behavior problems.

The first level of Maslow's hierarchy is comprised of physiological needs for food, shelter, water, and warmth. We might be tempted to pass these needs by and believe that the children of today are fed well and have adequate shelter and clothes. However, we must consider the number of children who participate in breakfast programs in schools or who do not get breakfast either at home or at school, as well as the poor diet of some children who may consume an adequate quantity of food. We are just beginning to learn about the relationship between diet and academic/behavioral problems. Evidence supports the re-lationship of a poor diet and such problems as hyperactivity and inability to learn; recent research has suggested that an inadequate diet may contribute to mental illness in adolescents. Are we truly meeting the physiological needs of our children?

Maslow's second level is the need for safety. Again, we may be tempted to ignore this need at first glance. However, can we say that our children really feel safe, that they have little to fear? Some children feel afraid in their own homes for their very physical safety. Frustrated that their own needs are not adequately met, parents may take out their frustrations on the child through physical or psychological abuse. Some adults who would not think of hurting a child physically will psychologically abuse children with demeaning and damaging words. Children may receive similar treatment in school, where teachers may use children as a safe target for their personal or professional frustration. Children are afraid not only of adults; some are also afraid of their peers. Consider Tony, who is small for his age, is rather shy, and has few friends. As Tony enters school one morning, several bigger guys tell him they will be waiting to get him this afternoon. Tony cannot be expected to learn 6 × 6 with this problem weighing on his mind!

Tony's fear may not be limited to home and school. For some children, a high crime rate makes the neighborhood threatening. In addition, television news vividly portrays the dangers of natural disasters such as hurricanes, tornados, and earthquakes. The threat of war also seems ever-present.

Even if Tony feels safe and protected, his learning or behavior may be influenced by the need to feel loved and to belong—the first higher order need that emerges, according to Maslow, after physiological and safety needs have been met. Humans are social beings who want to feel part of a group, a need fulfilled in children's cliques, gangs, and clubs, as well as in the family. Wherever we are, most of us want to be loved and accepted and to fit in with the group. Tony may not be getting positive attention from adults or peers, and he may think that no one likes him. Children sometimes hide their feelings of rejection or compensate for the rejection with antisocial behavior; either defense can hurt learning and personal relationships.

Perhaps children have the most trouble satisfying their need for self-esteem— the fourth need in Maslow's hierarchy. Children are ordered, directed, commanded, criticized, devalued, ignored, and put down. An adult treated like a child feels annoyance, inferiority, defensiveness, and anger and may rebel, fight, or leave the scene. Such responses are not considered acceptable in children. All people—adults and children—need to be respected as worthwhile individuals, capable of feeling, thinking, and behaving responsibly. Children can be treated with the warmth and respect needed to encourage their learning within firm guidelines and expectations. Cruel and thoughtless remarks can be avoided; criticisms can be reduced; positive interactions can be accentuated to build self-respect and self-confidence.

The satisfaction of needs at the first four levels contributes to achievement of the fifth need in Maslow's hierarchy—self-actualization. Maslow stated that a self-actualized person is moving toward the fulfillment of his or her inherent potential. Fulfilling this need implies that the child is not blocked by hunger, fear, lack of love or feelings of belonging, or low self-esteem. The child is not problem-free but has learned problem-solving skills and can move forward to becoming all that he or she can be.

According to Glasser (1986), society is not meeting our children's needs and thus they are failing in school and in life, academically and behaviorally. He listed five needs of all persons: (1) the need to survive and reproduce, (2) the need to belong and love, (3) the need to gain power, (4) the need to be free, and (5) the need to have fun. Glasser stated that children's problems relate to the inability to fulfill these needs and emphasized teaching reality, right and wrong, and responsibility.

Adlerian psychologists believe that children often attempt to meet their needs in a mistaken direction. They suggest that adults examine the goals of misbehavior and redirect the behavior toward achieving more satisfying results.

Behavioral psychologists see academic and behavior problems as resulting from faulty learning. The child has learned inappropriate ways of behaving through reinforcement or from poor models. Unlearning or extinguishing inappropriate patterns and learning more appropriate behaviors help the child succeed.

Whatever the factors contributing to children's learning, behavioral, and social problems, parents, counselors, and other professionals must assist and support children as they grow and develop in this complex, changing world.

A Child's Cognitive World

Knowledge of the child's level of cognitive development is essential for success in counseling children (Table 1-1). The work of Piaget and Inhelder (1969) established that children aged 5 to 12 may function in as many as three stages of cognitive development. Although age is no guarantee of a child's stage of development, 5- and 6-year-olds are on the verge of moving from the preoperational to the concrete stage of cognitive development and that 11-year-old children are moving into the formal stage.

In the early stages of concrete cognitive thought, children face four blocks to further development of their thought processes:

1. *Egocentrism block:* inability to see another's point of view. Children believe that everyone thinks the same way and does the same things they do. The egocentrism block prevents children from questioning their own thoughts and behaviors, even in the face of conflicting evidence, and makes difficult the development of empathy.

2. *Centration block:* inability to focus on more than one aspect of a problem. For example, a child may perceive a long line of five coins as having more coins than a short line of six coins. The child's attention is focused on the lengthier line rather than the number of coins. The centration block makes problem solving in counseling more difficult; thus, the child needs more detail and explanation.

3. *Reversibility block:* inability to work from front to back and then back to front in solving a problem. Children may have difficulty in working such math problems as $17 - \_\_\_\_ = 8$. The reversibility block is also characterized as perception-bound. Children often lose track of quantity when the shape of a substance changes; for example, they may believe that a clay ball flattened into a pancake contained more clay when it was a taller ball. Children generally do not understand the concept of irreversibility before age 7; consequently, children's reactions to loss or death may seem uncaring or inappropriate.

4. *Transformation block:* inability to put events in the proper order or sequence. Children often cannot see the relationship between events, understand cause and effect, predict the consequences of their behavior, or evaluate the effect

TABLE 1-1 Piaget's four stages of cognitive development

Stage	Type of development	Age	Cognitive traits
Infancy	Sensori-motor	0–2	Children learn through their senses by touching, hitting, biting, tasting, smelling, observing, and listening. They begin to learn about the invariants in their environment (for instance, chairs are for sitting). Language begins to take form, habits develop, and children begin to communicate symbolically. Children make distinctions between self and other objects. They have the ability to think about things, and they engage in planned and purposeful behavior. At the midpoint of this stage, children achieve a sense of object permanence. Toward the end of this stage they begin to do some trial-and-error problem solving.
Childhood	Preoperational	2–7	Children are not able to conserve when solving problems, for example, account for the quantity of a solid or liquid when it changes shape. This is the period of greatest language growth. Children are trial-and-error problem solvers who tend to focus on only one stimulus at a time. They are able to classify objects more than one way (for instance, size, shape, color, and texture). They have trouble with reversible thinking and prefer to learn things in ascending order before descending order. They tend to be egocentric thinkers; play with other children helps overcome this egocentrism. Children are able to use mental images, imagination, and symbolic thought. They are capable of understanding simple rules; however, rules are regarded as sacred and unchangeable.

TABLE 1-1   Piaget's four stages of cognitive development (*continued*)

Stage	Type of development	Age	Cognitive traits
Preadolescence	Concrete	7–11	Children in this stage have conservation skills and can do reversible thinking. Reasoning is based on perception, which causes these children difficulty with abstract reasoning, but they are able to appreciate the viewpoint of others. Concrete objects, pictures, diagrams, and examples are helpful learning aids. Children move toward more logical thought and away from intuitive thinking and are less egocentric. Rules are regarded as changeable. Reality is distinguished from fantasy. Problem solving strategies are strengthened through a larger capacity for concentration, attention, and memory. Children are capable of understanding that distance equals rate times time.
Adolescence through adulthood	Formal	11+	These people do not need to manipulate objects to solve problems. They are capable of abstract thought and scientific experimentation, which includes generation of hypotheses and alternatives, plus the ability to design and implement a series of problem solving procedures. These people are capable of understanding ethical and moral principles and can apply this understanding to the establishment and revision of rules. They are also capable of self-reflective thought, high levels of empathic understanding, and a sense of what is best for society.

of their behavior on themselves and others. In addition, children faced with the transformation block have difficulty seeing gray areas; they view events as black or white, right or wrong, regardless of the situation.

The counselor must know the child's level of cognitive development, particularly the degree to which a child is able to engage in abstract reasoning, a characteristic of the formal thinking stage. Children in the concrete thinking stage need explicit examples, learning aids, and directions. The concrete thinker can walk through a series of directions but cannot draw a map of the same route.

Counseling methods need to be matched with the child's cognitive ability if counseling is to be effective. For example, a child limited by the egocentrism block has difficulty empathizing with another person's situation. Piaget characterized the preoperational child's behavior and thinking as egocentric; that is, the child cannot take the role of or see the viewpoint of another (see Wadsworth, 1989). Preoperational children believe that everyone thinks the same way and does the same things they do. As a result, preoperational children never question their own thoughts; as far as they are concerned, their thoughts are the only thoughts possible and consequently must be correct. When they are confronted with evidence that is contradictory to their thoughts, they conclude that the evidence must be wrong because their thoughts cannot be. Thus, from the children's point of view, their thinking is always logical and correct. This egocentrism of thought is not egocentric by intent; children remain unaware that they are egocentric and consequently see no problem in need of resolution.

Wadsworth (1989) added that not until around age 6 or 7, when children's thoughts and those of their peers clearly conflict, do children begin to accommodate others and egocentric thoughts begin to give way to social pressure. Peer group social interaction and the repeated conflict of the child's own thoughts with those of others eventually jar the child to question and seek verification of his or her thoughts. The very source of conflict—social interaction—becomes the child's source of verification. Thus, peer social interaction is the primary factor that acts to dissolve cognitive egocentrism. The work of Piaget suggests group counseling for children with the egocentrism block.

The Child's World for Social Development

Erikson (1963, 1968) and Havighurst (1961) have written extensively about the stages of human development. Erikson described eight stages of human development from birth through adulthood beyond the age of 50. Havighurst, in a similar vein, described expectations and developmental tasks over the life span. Effective counselors are well informed about human development and know how to incorporate this knowledge into their methods.

Using Erikson's (1963, 1968) and Havighurst's (1961) systems as a frame of reference, counselors can compare expectations, human needs, and developmental tasks of humans across the childhood years. Table 1-2 shows developmental

TABLE 1-2   Developmental tasks and interventions for the eight stages of human development

STAGE I: BIRTH TO AGE 1½
Basic Trust versus Basic Mistrust

TASK: Children need to develop trust in their environment and in their parents and caregivers. Through their trust, children learn that their world is a safe, secure, consistent, predictable, interesting, friendly place.

INTERVENTIONS: Children need parents and caregivers who help them achieve trust in their world and in others. Children need affectionate, consistent, predictable, and high-quality care to help them learn to bond with other people.

STAGE II: AGES 1½ TO 3
Autonomy versus Shame and Doubt

TASK: Children need to gain a sense of self-control as well as control over their environment.

INTERVENTIONS: Children need to experience success in doing things for themselves: expressing themselves, feeding, developing toilet behaviors, and performing various other motor tasks with hands and feet. Children often express their new feelings of autonomy by saying "no" to all requests and through frequent use of "me," "mine," and "I." They respond well to choices.

STAGE III: AGES 3 TO 6
Initiative versus Guilt

TASK: Children need to develop a sense of initiative, as opposed to feelings of guilt about never doing the right thing.

INTERVENTIONS: Children need to begin setting goals, taking leadership, and carrying out projects. Parents need to empower children and let them participate in family work activities and projects. When children's initiative carries them into unacceptable thoughts and behaviors, parents need to correct them in a loving, caring way as they teach their children what is and is not acceptable. Discipline based on logical consequences should help these children develop a sense of purpose and goal-directedness.

STAGE IV: AGES 6 TO 12
Industry versus Inferiority

TASK: Children need to learn a variety of skills that will help them find a place in the adult world. The necessary skills range from academic and social to physical and practical.

INTERVENTIONS: Children need large doses of encouragement and praise to help them achieve the competence they need to eventually find a place in the adult world. Academic, physical, social, and work skills are all important in developing healthy self-esteem. Children need nurturing adults to help them discover and develop their special talents and abilities.

Continued.

TABLE 1-2   Developmental tasks and interventions for the eight stages of human development (*continued*)

STAGE V: AGES 12 TO 18
Identity versus Role Confusion

TASK: Teenagers need to develop a self-image. They need to know who they are and how their roles will fit into their future.

INTERVENTIONS: Teenagers need to feel that they are accepted by others as they work toward self-acceptance and a sense of identity. Identity can be found in joining a group or cause. Another way to achieve a sense of identity is to find things they do well in work and play. It is often good to permit adolescents time-out periods for self-study and exploration before making commitments to further education or training, jobs, careers, and marriage.

STAGES VI, VII, AND VIII:
Adult Stages

TASK: The primary task in the young adult stage is to achieve intimacy through sharing in a close friendship or love relationship. Middle adulthood tasks revolve around proper care of children and a productive work life. Older adults are concerned with ego integrity, which involves an acceptance of past life, a search for meaning in the present, and continued growth and learning in the future.

INTERVENTIONS: Counseling interventions for adults are most effective when they match the client's learning style. As reported in Thompson and Campbell (1992), client preferences for interventions are nearly equally divided between affective, behavior, cognitive, and eclectic methods. Remember that age does not guarantee that any particular stage of development has been reached. Many adults use concrete rather than abstract reasoning in solving problems and making decisions. Issues in counseling often center on relationships, careers, and the search for meaning and purpose in life.

tasks and necessary interventions for each of the eight stages of human development. The two basic tasks are (1) coping with others' demands and expectations that conflict with people's own needs and (2) meeting these demands with the limited abilities they have in each developmental stage.

WHAT IS COUNSELING?

The American Psychological Association, Division of Counseling Psychology, Committee on Definition (1956), defined *counseling* as a process "to help individuals toward overcoming obstacles to their personal growth, wherever these may be encountered, and toward achieving optimum development of their personal resources" (p. 283). The National Conference of State Legislatures and the American Counseling Association (Glosoff & Koprowicz, 1990) defined counseling as "a process in which a trained professional forms a trusting relationship with a person who needs assistance. This relationship focuses on personal meaning of experiences, feelings, behaviors, alternatives, consequences, and goals. Counseling provides a unique opportunity for individuals to explore and express their ideas and feelings in a nonevaluative, nonthreatening environment" (p. 8).

How Does Counseling Differ from Psychotherapy?

Distinctions between counseling and psychotherapy may be superficial in that both processes have similar objectives and techniques. Pallone (1977) and Patterson (1986) have outlined some of the differences between counseling and psychotherapy; Table 1-3 summarizes these differences, which are often lost in the common ground they share. The key question about the domain of each process rests with counselors and therapists, who must restrict their practice to their areas of competence.

What Is an Appropriate Working Definition of Counseling?

Counseling involves a relationship between two people who meet so that one person can help the other resolve a problem. One of these people, by virtue of training, is the counselor; the person receiving the help is the client. The terms *counselor* and *client*, which some view as dehumanizing, can be replaced by words such as *helper* and *helpee, child, adolescent, adult*, or *person*. In fact, Carl Rogers referred to his client-centered counseling approach as *person-centered*. We see counseling as a process in which people learn how to help themselves and, in effect, become their own counselors. Counseling may also be a group process, in which the role of helper and helpee can be shared and interchanged among the

TABLE 1-3   Comparison of counseling and psychotherapy

Counseling is more for:	*Psychotherapy is more for:*
1. Clients	1. Patients
2. Mild disorders	2. Serious disorders
3. Personal, social, vocational, educational, and decision making problems	3. Personality problems
4. Preventive and developmental concerns	4. Remedial concerns
5. Educational and developmental settings	5. Clinical and medical settings
6. Conscious concerns	6. Unconscious concerns
7. Teaching methods	7. Healing methods

group members. The group counselor would then function as a facilitator as well as a counselor.

Coleman, Morris, and Glaros (1987) credit David Palmer of the Student Counseling Center at UCLA with the following definition of counseling:

> *To be listened to*
> *& to be heard . . .*
> *to be supported*
> *while you gather your*
> *forces & get your bearings.*
>
> *A fresh look at alternatives*
> *& some new insights;*
> *learning some needed skills.*
>
> *To face your lion—your fears.*
> *To come to a decision—*
> *& the courage to act on it*
> *& to take the risks*
> *that living demands (p. 282)*

WHAT COUNSELING CAN DO

Ask elementary classroom teachers to estimate how many of their students are experiencing learning, emotional, or behavioral problems. Then ask these teachers to predict how many of the approximately 30 students in each class will have serious trouble with the law or other adjustment problems in the future. Multiply these figures by the number of classrooms throughout the United States, and the estimates are overwhelming. We can change these statistics by becoming more effective professionals.

Counseling with children is a growing area of interest for people in the helping professions. Developmental theorists have studied children's growth and development and the effect of childhood experiences on the adult; child psychiatry has focused on seriously disturbed children. However, children with learning, social, or behavioral problems who are not classified as severely disturbed have been largely overlooked. Counseling can prevent "normal" problems from becoming more serious and resulting in delinquency, school failure, and emotional disturbance. It can create a healthy environment to help children cope with the stresses and conflicts of their growth and development. Counseling can also help children in trouble through appraisal, individual or group counseling, parent or teacher consultation, or environmental changes.

The principles of counseling with children are the same as those used with adults; however, the counselor needs to be aware of the world as the child sees it and adjust counseling procedures to suit the child's cognitive level, emotional and social development, and physical abilities. Each child is a unique individual with unique characteristics and needs.

Childhood should be a time for healthy growth, for establishing warm and rewarding relationships, for exploring a widening world, for developing confidence in self and others, and for learning and experiencing. It should contain some fun and carefree times, and it should also provide a foundation and guidance for the maturing person.

What Specific Types of Assistance Can Be Expected from the Counseling Session?

Counseling generally involves three areas: (1) the client's thoughts and feelings about life at present, (2) where the client would like to be in life, and (3) plans to reduce any discrepancy between (1) and (2). The emphasis given to each area varies according to the counseling approach used. Nevertheless, most counseling approaches seem to share the ultimate goal of behavior change, although they may differ in the method used to attain that goal.

Perhaps the most important outcome for counseling occurs when clients learn how to be their own counselors. By teaching children the counseling process, we help them become more skilled in solving their problems and, in turn, become less dependent on others. In our view, counseling is a reeducative process designed to replace faulty learning with better strategies for getting what the child wants from life. Regardless of the counseling approach, children bring three pieces of information to the counseling session: (1) their problem or concern, (2) their feelings about the problem, and (3) their expectations of the counselor. Failure to listen for these points makes further counseling a waste of time.

Most problems brought to the counselor concerning children can be classified in one or more of five categories:

1. *Interpersonal conflict, or conflict with others:* The child has difficulty relating with parents, siblings, teachers, or peers and is seeking a better way to relate with them.
2. *Intrapersonal conflict, or conflict with self:* The child has a decision-making problem and needs some help with clarifying the alternatives and consequences.
3. *Lack of information about self:* The child needs to learn more about his or her abilities, strengths, interests, or values.
4. *Lack of information about the environment:* The child needs information about what it takes to succeed in school or general career education.
5. *Lack of skill:* The child needs to learn a specific skill, such as effective study methods, assertive behavior, listening, or how to make friends.

In summary, counseling goals and objectives can range from becoming one's own counselor to positive behavior change, problem solving, decision making, personal growth, remediation, and self-acceptance. The counseling process for children often includes training in communication, assertiveness, and effective study; however, counselors choose the focus that seems most appropriate to the child and the child's situation. Some counselors prefer to work on developing meaning and purpose in everyday living, whereas others work toward solving specific problems (Figure 1-1). Of course, many counselors try to accomplish both ends. Conceivably, Child A could start at point −5 on both the x- and the y-axis and move toward +5 on both axes.

In counseling children in their middle childhood years (ages 5–12), for example, counselors may choose to work with problem areas in any or all of the quadrants represented in Figure 1-1. Some counselors prefer to work with the developmental and personal growth concerns found in Quadrant 1. The children in Quadrant 1 are solving their problems and seem to be finding purpose in living. They are sometimes referred to as stars because they get along well with their friends, teachers, and family. Quadrant 1 children seem to have a winner's script for achieving their goals in academic, athletic, social, and artistic endeavors. Working with these children is often a matter of staying out of their way, helping them develop their full potential, and ensuring they receive the appropriate teaching and parenting necessary for the development of their gifts and talents. This developmental model, emphasizing problem prevention over remediation, was pioneered by Herman J. Peters (Peters & Farwell, 1959), who encouraged counselors to focus on their clients' strengths as a way to facilitate their next steps

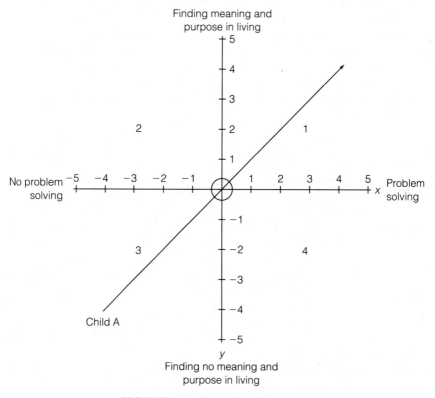

FIGURE 1-1   Counseling focus scale

up the developmental ladder. The developmental emphasis continues to be popular in counseling literature. Hoffman and McDaniels (1991) emphasized a developmental approach to career counseling for children. Parker and McDavis (1989) presented a personal developmental model with 34 activities designed to facilitate development of African American children's self-confidence, career development, social skills, work habits, problem-solving skills, and academic development. Myrick (1987, 1989) wrote extensively on the developmental model for counseling children. He said that better counselor time-management skills are the key to counseling children in school settings and described six counselor interventions for delivering developmental counseling services: individual and small group counseling, large group guidance, peer-facilitator training, consultation with teachers and parents, and guidance-activity coordination.

Quadrant 2 children find purpose in life but are not able to solve a lot of their problems. The counselor's role with these children is remedial in that counseling is directed toward establishing problem-solving strategies. Frequently these Quadrant 2 children have good interpersonal relationships but experience problems with academic achievement and self-concept. They lack the success identity found in Quadrant 1 children.

Quadrant 4 children do very well with their everyday problem solving but do not seem to find life exciting or challenging. Frequently these introverted children have little fun and few high points in their lives. A recent fourth-grade classroom discussion on the topic "My High Points from Last Week," led by one of the authors, revealed that 20% of the class had difficulty finding just one high point! Counseling plans for this group are more developmental than remedial in that they are directed toward building high points for each day of the child's life.

Quadrant 3 children represent the toughest counseling cases. They are not solving their problems, and they find little value in living their lives. Children in this group suffer from depression, have a very low self-concept, and may be potential suicides. Frequently no one really loves and cares about these children, and they have no one to love and care for in return. These children have experienced a world of failure at home and at school. Counseling with these children is a highly remedial process directed toward encouragement and, as in all counseling, establishing a positive, caring relationship between counselor and child. Once a helpful relationship has been established, the counseling focus can be directed toward building success experiences in the child's life.

WHO ARE THE MENTAL HEALTH PROFESSIONALS?

Those seeking help for children need to choose the counselor best suited to the child's and family's needs and the particular type of problem. Various people trained in the helping professions—counselors, school counselors, school psychologists, social workers, marriage and family counselors, counseling psychologists, clinical psychologists, rehabilitation counselors, child development counselors—work with children (Table 1-4). Their duties may include individual counseling, group counseling, and/or consultation in a school, agency clinic, hospital, criminal justice facility, or other institutional setting to assist children with their personal, social, developmental, educational, or vocational concerns; collecting and analyzing data (personality, interests, aptitude, attitudes, intelligence, and so on) about an individual through interviews, tests, case histories, observational techniques, and other means; and using statistical data to carry out evaluative functions, research, or follow-up activities. A counselor can serve in an administrative role as the director of a school guidance unit or the head of an institutional counseling division or can be engaged primarily in teaching or research. Wagner (1994) encouraged counseling psychologists to become more involved with children, pointing out that "by applying a developmentally based health-oriented model that recognizes sociocultural influences, counseling psychologists can, through their work with children, families, schools, and community, effect structural changes in the lives of young people and thereby facilitate more optimal development" (p. 394).

Some counseling positions require only a 4-year baccalaureate degree with a major in psychology, social work, or a related area; however, most positions require a master's or doctoral degree. Accreditation standards and state laws governing the certification and licensure of counselors and psychologists are moving toward requiring a 2-year master's degree, including a supervised practicum and internship. Doctoral programs, too, are raising their degree requirements to require additional supervised practicum and internship experiences. Doctoral programs generally require 5 years of study beyond the baccalaureate degree.

Many professionals use counseling skills in their jobs (for example, teachers use behavior modification procedures; ministers and nurses use active listening), but using these skills does not make them professional counselors, who have completed degree and credentialing requirements in their counseling specialty. Many states define and regulate the practice of counseling, psychology, and social work through certification (protection of title) and licensure (protection of practice).

The Council for Accreditation of Counseling and Related Educational Programs (CACREP), an accrediting body associated with the American Counseling Association (ACA), recommends a graduate training program including 48 semester hours of master's-level training and competency in such areas as human growth and development, social and cultural foundations, helping relationships, group work, lifestyle and career development, appraisal, research and evaluation, and professional orientation. Its recommendations for doctoral training build on these competencies and include additional internship experiences.

The National Board for Certified Counselors (NBCC) administers the National Counselor Examination (NCE) as a component of the NBCC national professional counselor certification program, according to the guide to the NCE. This booklet also states that the NCE "has been selected by the majority of state-level counselor credentialing agencies to serve as a part of their respective

TABLE 1-4   Mental health professionals

Professional	Minimum degree requirement	Work setting
Human service worker	Baccalaureate	Human service agencies
Juvenile justice counselor	Baccalaureate	Juvenile justice system
Child-development specialist	Master's	Community agencies
Clinical social worker	Master's	Private practice Community agencies Hospitals
Community agency counselor	Master's	Private practice Community agencies
Marriage and family therapist	Master's	Private practice Community agencies
Mental health counselor	Master's	Private practice Community agencies
Pastoral counselor	Master's	Churches Counseling centers Private practice
Rehabilitation counselor	Master's	Rehabilitation agencies Hospitals
School counselor	Master's	Elementary, middle, and secondary schools
Social worker	Master's	Community agencies Hospitals Schools
School psychologist	Educational specialist/ doctorate	Schools
Child psychologist	Doctorate	University Private practice Community agencies Hospitals
Clinical psychologist	Doctorate	University Private practice Community agencies Hospitals
Counseling psychologist	Doctorate	University Private practice Industry Community agencies Hospitals
Counselor educator	Doctorate	University Private practice Industry
Psychiatrist	Medical degree	Private practice Hospitals

licensure or registry processes" (1988, p. 3). The National Academy for Certification of Clinical Mental Health Counselors (NACCMHC), a branch of the ACA, publishes a registry of certified mental health counselors. Special credentialing associations provide information about the recognition of counselors in many specialties.

REFERENCES

Achenbach, T., & Howell, C. (1993). Are American children's problems getting worse? A 13-year comparison. *Journal of the American Academy of Child and Adolescent Psychiatry, 32*(6), 1145–1154.

American Psychological Association, Division of Counseling Psychology, Committee on Definition. (1956). Counseling psychology as a specialty. *American Psychologist, 11,* 282–285.

Basow, S. (1986). Gender stereotypes: Traditions and alternatives. In L. Mintz and J. O'Neil: Gender roles, sex, and the process of psychotherapy: Many questions and few answers. *Journal of Counseling and Development, 68,* 381–386.

Beardslee, W. (1989). The role of self-understanding in resilient individuals: The development of a perspective. *American Journal of Orthopsychiatry, 59,* 266–278.

Bennett, W. (1993). *The index of leading cultural indicators* (Vol. 1). Washington, D.C.: Empower America, Heritage Foundation, and Free Congress Foundation.

Coleman, J., Morris, C., & Glaros, A. (1987). *Contemporary psychology and effective behavior.* Glenview, IL: Scott, Foresman.

Crabbs, M. (1989). Future perfect: Planning for the next century. *Elementary School Guidance and Counseling, 24*(2), 160–166.

Erikson, E. (1963). *Childhood and society.* New York: Norton.

Erikson, E. (1968). *Identity, youth, and crisis.* New York: Norton.

Flach, F. (1988). *Resilience: Discovering a new strength at times of stress.* New York: Fawcett Columbine.

Glasser, W. (1986). *Control theory in the classroom.* New York: Harper & Row.

Glosoff, H., & Koprowicz, C. (1990). *Children achieving potential: An introduction to elementary school counseling and state-level policies.* Washington, D.C.: National Conference of State Legislatures; Alexandria, VA: American Association for Counseling and Development.

Goodman, E. (1990, May). Out from the start. *Parenting,* 104–110.

Havighurst, R. (1961). *Human development and education* (2nd ed.). New York: David McKay.

Hoffman, L., & McDaniels, C. (1991). Career development in the elementary school: A perspective for the 1990s. *Elementary School Guidance and Counseling, 25,* 163–171.

Maslow, A. (1970). *Motivation and personality* (2nd ed.). New York: Harper & Row.

Melton, G. (1987). Children, politics, and morality: The ethics of child advocacy. *Journal of Clinical Child Psychology, 16*(4), 357–367.

Mintz, L., & O'Neil, J. (1990). Gender roles, sex, and the process of psychotherapy: Many questions and few answers. *Journal of Counseling and Development, 68,* 381–386.

Myrick, R. (1987). *Developmental guidance and counseling: A practical approach.* Minneapolis: Educational Media Corporation.

Myrick, R. (1989). Developmental guidance: Practical considerations. *Elementary School Guidance and Counseling, 24,* 14–20.

Naisbitt, J., & Aburdene, P. (1990). *Megatrends 2000: Ten new directions for the 1990s.* New York: Morrow.

National Board for Certified Counselors. (1988). *Your guide to the National Counselor Examination: How to prepare.* Alexandria, VA: Author.

National School Boards Association and American School Counselors Association. (1994). *Caring connections: Helping young people from troubled homes.* St. Louis: Author.

Pallone, N. (1977). Counseling psychology: Toward an empirical definition. *Counseling Psychologist, 7,* 29–32.

Parker, W., & McDavis, R. (1989). A personal development model for black elementary school students. *Elementary School Guidance and Counseling, 23,* 244–253.

Patterson, C. (1986). *Theories of counseling and psychotherapy* (4th ed.). New York: Harper & Row.

Peters, H., & Farwell, G. (1959). *Guidance: A developmental approach.* Chicago: Rand McNally.

Piaget, J., & Inhelder, B. (1969). *The psychology of the child.* New York: Basic Books.

Scher, M., & Good, G. (1990). Gender and counseling in the twenty-first century: What does the future hold? *Journal of Counseling and Development, 68,* 388–390.

Wadsworth, B. (1989). *Piaget's theory of cognitive and affective development.* New York: Longman.

Wagner, W. G. (1994). Counseling with children: An opportunity for tomorrow. *Counseling Psychologist, 22*(3), 381–401.

Werner, E. (1984). Resilient children. *Young Children, 40,* 68–72.

Wertlieb, D., Weigel, C., & Feldstein, M. (1987). Stress, social support, and behavior symptoms in middle childhood. *Journal of Clinical Child Psychology, 16* (3), 204–211.

Chapter   2

◆

The Counseling Process

The type of help counselors offer children may vary according to the model of counseling used. Counseling theories often differ more in name and description than in actual practice. However, some counseling situations and some children are better suited to one approach than to another. Counseling is basically a learning situation, and people have favorite styles of learning.

WHICH APPROACHES TO COUNSELING ARE MOST EFFECTIVE?

Harper (1959) described 36 systems of counseling and psychotherapy. According to Corsini and Wedding (1995), by 1984, 250 systems were documented in the literature. Karasu (1986) wrote that the number of counseling systems exceeded 400. However, these myriad systems can generally be classified in four intervention categories: cognitive, behavior, affective, and some combination of categories, referred to as eclectic or integrative.

In comparison studies of the different systems of counseling and psychotherapy, no one system has emerged as consistently most effective (Glass & Kliegl, 1983; Luborsky, Singer, & Luborsky, 1975; Shapiro & Shapiro, 1982; Smith & Glass, 1977; Smith, Glass, & Miller, 1980; Stiles, Shapiro, & Elliott, 1986; Teasdale, 1985). Rather, various counseling approaches based on different theories and emphasizing different methods have been found effective for a wide range of people and their problems.

Training counselors in a variety of approaches has considerable support. Thompson and Campbell (1992), in a phenomenological study, surveyed 500 people on what type of self-help interventions they chose to alleviate mild depression. These interventions were spread fairly equally across affective, behavior, cognitive, and eclectic categories, with a slight but significant preference for affective remedies. The authors attributed these results to the preponderance of women in the sample and to their expressed preference for affective interventions. Men, by contrast, tended to favor cognitive interventions. The study indicates that effective counselors should be able to adapt to the client's preferred learning style rather than expecting the client to adapt to the counselor's preferred counseling style.

Further support for an eclectic approach to counseling came from Lewis (1985) and Dimond, Havens, and Jones (1978), who pointed out that an individualized counseling plan is superior but possible only when the counselor can draw on a vast array of theory and technique and is not bound by any single approach. Lazarus (1981, 1984, 1990) made essentially the same point in his argument that not only is behavior therapy not behaviorism but also neither behavior therapy nor behaviorism can account for all the events that occur in the counseling process. He recommended a multimodal, or comprehensive, eclectic framework for counseling that can be adapted to meet the needs of individual children. Lazarus developed his BASIC ID model to describe seven problem areas often treated in counseling.

B   Behavior:
    Fighting
    Disruption
    Talking
    Stealing
    Procrastination
A   Affect:
    Expression of anger
    Anxiety
    Phobias
    Depression
S   Sensation/School:
    Headaches, backaches, and stomachaches
    School failure
    Perceptual/motor problems
I   Imagery:
    Nightmares
    Low self-esteem
    Fear of rejection
    Excessive daydreaming and fantasizing
C   Cognition:
    Irrational thinking
    Difficulty in setting goals
    Decision-making problems
    Problem-solving difficulties
I   Interpersonal relationships:
    Withdrawing from others (shyness)
    Conflict with adults

Conflict with peers
Family problems
D   Drugs/Diet:
Hyperactivity
Weight-control problems
Drug abuse
Addictions

The Lazarus BASIC ID model covers most of the problems that counselors working with children, adolescents, or adults are likely to encounter.

Gerler (1990) and Gerler, Drew, & Mohr (1990) reviewed multimodal research, applications, and changes and cited considerable research support for this eclectic counseling method. Keat (1990a, 1990b) specialized his multimodal writing on counseling children. He converted the BASIC ID model into the acronym HELPING:

H refers to *health* issues (pain and sickness).
E stands for *emotions* (anxiety, anger, feeling down).
L is for *learning* problems (deficiencies, failing, and sensory shallowness).
P stands for *personal relationships* (adult and peer relationships).
I refers to *imagery* (low self-worth and poor coping skills).
N is the *need* to know (despair, faulty thinking, lack of information).
G stands for *guidance* of actions, behaviors, and consequences (behavior and
    motivation problems).

After identifying the problem areas, counselors design interventions to strengthen weak areas before they become more serious problems. The counseling approaches presented in this book offer possibilities for helping counselors work with one or more of the seven areas presented in the BASIC ID model.

CLASSIFYING COUNSELING THEORIES

In the first two editions of this book, we attempted to classify the counseling theories presented on a cognitive-affective continuum and explained away the behavior category by writing that considerable overlap exists among counseling theories; that put the behavior theories in the middle of our cognitive-affective ratings. A better way to classify counseling theories is to examine how the practitioners of each theory encounter their clients. Some counselors focus on the client's feelings, while others intervene with thinking or behavior. Change in any one of these three areas is likely to produce change in the other two. Therefore, rather than a two-dimensional continuum, we propose a model showing the integrative relationship that exists between thoughts, feelings, and behaviors (Figure 2-1).

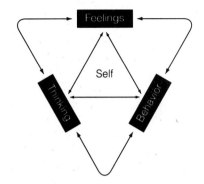

FIGURE 2-1   Classification of counseling approaches

By focusing on the point of intervention, we propose to classify the eight theories presented in this book as follows:

Affective (feeling)
      Person-centered counseling   *Rogers*
      Gestalt therapy
Behavior (behaving)
      Behavioral counseling
      Reality therapy   *Glasser*
      Individual psychology   *Adler*
Cognitive (thinking)
      Rational-emotive behavioral therapy   *Ellis*
      Cognitive behavioral therapy
      Psychoanalytic counseling   *Freud*
      Transactional analysis

Our intention is not to isolate feeling, thinking, and behaving. Failure to integrate feelings, thoughts, and behaviors is a symptom of schizophrenia, a diagnosis that describes a loss of contact with the environment, a split from reality, and a disintegration of personality. Rather, we attempt to describe how effective intervention in one of the three areas helps the individual integrate the other two areas into a more fully functioning lifestyle.

Counseling theories can also be classified as belonging to one of two broad categories. In the first, the focus is on observable events and data: behavior, antecedents to behavior, consequences of behavior, behavioral goals, and plans. The second category is focused on the unobservable events and data surrounding counseling: feelings, thoughts, motivation, and causes of behavior (Figure 2-2).

Category 1 counselors believe that if you feel bad at Point A (in Figure 2-2), the only way to feel better at Point B is to make a positive change in your behavior, which, in turn, leads to better feelings at Point B. Additional positive change in behavior leads to even better feelings at Point C.

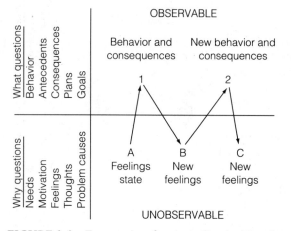

FIGURE 2-2   Focus points for counseling interventions

Category 2 counselors believe just the opposite. If you feel bad at Point A, you need to work through these feelings and/or thoughts with your counselor until you have sufficient strength to make a behavior change at Point 1. You then examine the resulting thoughts and feelings at Point B for meaning and significance, which help you gather sufficient strength to tackle the next behavior change.

Classifying the various approaches to counseling creates a framework for examining their similarities and differences. These approaches have a variety of techniques adaptable to learning style differences. The cognitive, affective, and behavior classifications should help counselors provide children with appropriate counseling methods.

WHAT DO EFFECTIVE COUNSELORS DO?

Effective counselors have many practices in common regardless of their specific orientations to counseling. A summary of these commonalities is presented in this section.

Preparing for the Interview

The counseling environment should contribute to a client's feelings of comfort and ease. A cluttered, stimulating, busy room can distract children, whose attention is easily drawn to interesting objects in the room and away from the counseling interaction. Restless, distractible children may be affected by brightly colored objects, mobiles, ticking clocks, outside noise, or even darting fish in an aquarium. Inasmuch as counselors are part of the environment, you should also check yourself for distracting jewelry, colorful ties, or patterns in clothing that may affect children.

The furniture in the counseling room should be comfortable for both adults and children. We suggest that the counselor not sit behind a desk or table that can act as a barrier between child and counselor. Children see people sitting behind desks as authority figures, such as teachers, principals, and caseworkers. Keep in mind that children prefer chairs that are low enough to allow them to keep their feet on the floor.

Counseling seems to work better if children can control the distance between themselves and the counselor. Adults are often too aggressive in trying to initiate conversations with children. Children prefer to talk with adults at the same eye level, so some care needs to be given to seating arrangements that allow for eye-to-eye contact and feet on the floor. Of the various possible seating arrangements (Figure 2-3), two seem to be *least* effective: (1) having a desk between the counselor and child and (2) having no barrier at all between counselor and child. The preferred seating arrangement (3) is to use the corner of a desk or table as an optional barrier that allows the child to retreat behind the desk or table corner or to move out around the corner when he or she feels comfortable doing so. A thick carpet, comfortable chairs, floor pillows, puppets, dollhouses, and other toys to facilitate communication are also recommended for the counseling room. Many counselors conduct all of their interviews with children on the carpet in a play therapy room (see chapter 12).

Effective counselors create a relaxed counseling environment and build rapport with their clients. Play media have developed a relaxed atmosphere with younger children and a few counselors have employed large, friendly dogs as icebreakers, with child and counselor sitting on a rug and playing with the dog

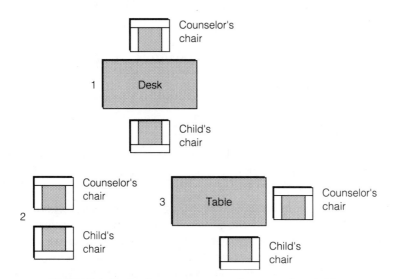

FIGURE 2-3 Seating arrangements for counseling children

during the session (Burton, 1995; Levinson, 1962; O'Brien, 1993; Trivedi & Perl, 1995).

Counselors should be models of promptness for scheduled sessions. Children (and adult clients) dislike being kept waiting. Tardiness may be interpreted as lack of interest or cause restlessness, fatigue, or irritability.

The counselor should be free from distracting worries and thoughts and ready to devote full attention to the child. Children are extremely sensitive to adult moods and can recognize insincerity or lack of concern quickly. Many counselors reschedule appointments when they do not feel well rather than risk hurting the counseling relationship. If you have a cold, headache, or other minor ailment, you may want to admit to the child that you are not feeling up to par rather than have the child misinterpret your behavior as a lack of interest.

What Are Some Things to Consider During the First Interview?

Children's Resistance to Counseling

Children who are clients are still children, with their own feelings, behaviors, problems, and expectations of counselors. Like adults, children have a fear of the unknown. To be frightened of new faces in new places with new activities and mystery outcomes is very natural. Children may not know why they are being taken to a counselor's office. In fact, parents or teachers may have given them misinformation that could result in mistrust of the counselor who does not meet a child's expectations. Questions children may have about counseling include

1. What is counseling, and why do I have to go there?
2. Did I do something wrong? Am I being punished?
3. Is something wrong with me?
4. Do Mom and Dad think something is wrong with me? Do they love me?
5. Will my friends think something is wrong with me? Will they make fun of me if they find out?
6. Will it hurt? Is it like going to the doctor?
7. How long does it take? When will I get to come home?
8. If I don't like it, will I have to go back?
9. What am I supposed to say and do? What if I say something wrong?
10. Should I tell bad things about my family?
11. Will the counselor tell anybody what I say?

Effective counselors understand the full range of fears, concerns, and questions children might have about visiting a counselor's office for the first time. In addition, children as well as adults naturally resist situations in which they might lose their autonomy or freedom to choose what they would like to say and do. When children are forced to do things, they become angry, resistant, and oppositional in an attempt to regain control. Children may also get angry because they view the trip to the counselor's office as unfair. They may think they are being blamed for the family's problems.

Children are generally not motivated to seek counseling. Children are drawn to pleasurable thoughts, feelings, and behavior and tend to avoid negative feelings, thoughts, and activities. A first visit to the counselor would ordinarily not be a favorite activity. The exception to the rule occurs in those elementary and middle schools that are fortunate enough to have talented counselors who lead regular group meetings with all of their children. Children will and do refer themselves to these trusted counselors.

Children do many of the same things adult clients do to resist counseling.

1. Refuse to talk, refuse to share anything of importance, deny there is a problem, or talk about irrelevant topics
2. Avoid eye contact
3. Are late for or miss their appointments
4. Exhibit negative body language and make hostile verbal comments
5. Act out and refuse to cooperate (e.g., hide behind the furniture)

This list is certainly not exhaustive. People can be very creative in devising ways to resist anything, and counselors ought to rely on their feelings as indicators of client resistance. Frustration and anger are common reactions counselors have to uncooperative clients. Counselors need considerable patience and high levels of frustration tolerance to work with difficult children. Their major task is to get on the same team with their child clients and try to help them find better ways to get what they want and need. Remember that resistant children are reacting normally, as anyone would do, to someone who is trying to change them. Many children are not self-referred, and counselors are often viewed as extensions of the system that has been unhelpful and even painful to them. Resistant children are protecting themselves from the counselor's agenda, which they are unwilling or scared to follow.

Steps to Overcoming Children's Resistance

The first step in the successful application of all counseling theories is the development of a good counseling relationship, a therapeutic alliance between counselor and client. The relationship-building process begins with the counselor as a person. *Friendly, warm, interested, genuine,* and *empathetic* are the key descriptive words used to define successful counselors. For children, such a person truly listens and understands how they think and feel about things. Children view effective counselors as caring, protective, safe, and on their side. "On the child's side" means the child's advocate rather than best friend. Taking the role of a child's advocate would not excuse the counselor from maintaining the empathy-objectivity balance requisite to successful counseling. Effective counselors are also able to strike a healthy balance between adult-adult and parent-child activities in the counseling session. From transactional analysis (see chapter 9), adult-adult activities are the problem-solving and decision-making parts of counseling; the parent-child activities are the nurturing and relationship-building parts of counseling. Finally, the counselor should offer children as many choices as possible to restore to them some of the control children thought they lost by coming to counseling.

As a second step, the counselor's office should seem like a friendly, comfortable, relaxed, safe place to be. Children find security in consistency, limits, and predictability. Counseling appointments should be regularly scheduled for the same time and day. Counseling time is the child's time and is not interrupted by phone calls or knocks on the door. Children should not be kept waiting for their appointments. Attention to these scheduling details makes children feel worthy and important. Behavioral limits should be set and enforced with logical consequences; for example, "the sand must stay in the sandbox, and sand play has to stop until the sand is swept up and put back in the box." Misbehavior is handled best by redirecting it to appropriate activity; for example, "People are not for hitting; punching bags are for hitting."

Third, children need to understand what counseling is and what they can expect from counseling. Some counselors prefer to ease the anxiety of the initial meeting by engaging in general conversation with the child for a few minutes. After initial introductions, the counselor may start to talk with the child about home, school, friends, hobbies, or other interests. For nonverbal or extremely anxious children, the first session or two may include play therapy. The counselor can begin to build a good relationship with the child while learning something about the child's world through these methods. Other counselors prefer to go directly to the problem: "Would you like to tell me why you have come to see me?" During the initial interview, a counselor may want to explain to the child the process of counseling and the counselor's expectations. The following is a sample dialogue for middle school children.

Counselor: Do you know what counseling is?

Child: No. [If the child answers yes, the counselor might say "Tell me your ideas about what counseling is."]

Counselor: Well, at some time during our lives, most of us have things that worry or upset us—things we would like to talk to someone about. It could be something about school that concerns us, like another student in our class or our teacher; it could be a problem at home with our brothers or sisters, or perhaps we feel that our parents don't really understand how we feel; it could be that we are having trouble with friendships; it could be that we have some thoughts or feelings that it would be helpful to discuss with someone. A counselor listens and tries to help the other person work these things out. A counselor tries to think with that person about ways to solve these worries. Your job is to tell me whatever is bothering you. My job is to listen carefully and try to help you find ways to solve these problems.

The preceding statement is too long and wordy for children under the age of 7. Boat and Everson (1986) suggested that counselors use sentences with only three to five more words than the number of words in the child's average sentence.

For children others have referred for counseling, the counselor can begin with a statement such as "Mrs. Jones told me that you were very unhappy since you moved here and that you might want to talk to me about it," or "Mr. Clifford told me that you would be coming by," and wait for the child to respond to tell what the trouble is.

In the first example, the counselor has informed the child that he or she is aware of the problem and is ready to discuss it. In the second example, the counselor is less directive, provides less structure, and allows the child to explain the problem, which may or may not be the one for which the child was referred. The counselor will want to consider the child's age, culture, and cognitive, social, and emotional development, as well as the type of presenting problem, before deciding which type of opening statement to use. The younger the child, chronologically and developmentally, and the more specific the problem, the greater the probability the child will respond more readily to a structured approach. Carlson (1990) preferred a direct approach for counseling "other-referred" children. For example, a counselor might say, "Let me tell you what your teacher shared with me that led to your being asked to see me." The counseling states the teacher's concern in a way that lets the child know that counselor is help and not punishment. The counselor could say, for example, "Mr. Thompson is concerned about your behavior in class. He is afraid you will not learn all you need to know if you don't change what you are doing."

Carlson (1990) also believed that counseling needs to be defined for "other-referred" children in language they can understand. For example, "Counseling is a time when you can talk to me about things that bother you. We can also talk about what we need to do to make things better."

Children need to know how much of what they say in counseling is confidential and what is not. Counselors are required by law to report any evidence of homicidal or suicidal ideation, child sexual or physical abuse, and child neglect. The counselor may also report any material clients give them permission to report. Counselors need to assure children that what they talk about is confidential or "just between you and me unless I have to stop someone from getting hurt. I will not tell anybody about anything else unless you say it is okay to tell something."

These examples of what counselors might say can be modified to fit the situation, the age and maturity level of the child, and the counselor's personality. The counselor may not think it necessary to define the counselor's role and the child's expectations, but many children and counselors feel more comfortable with structure.

First Interview Goals and Observations

The counselor's main task is to build bridges between the child's world and the counseling office. Friendly, confident counselors who seem in control help children feel safe and secure in the new counseling environment. Counselors can begin by asking children what name they want to be called. Fun activities are helpful in getting the first session off to a relaxing start. A child who feels anxious about separating from a parent can have the parent join the activity. Serving a snack, reading a favorite story, and playing a game are good ways to reach the child. A parent may be included in all of these introductory activities. Some children, having been told not to speak to strangers, need assurance from their parents that the counselor can be trusted and that it is okay to speak to the counselor. If parents oppose counseling, children may feel disloyal if they participate in counseling or cooperate with the counselor. These children need reassurance that it is okay for them to work with the counselor.

Children differ from adults in several ways that affect counseling and play therapy.

1. Children, lacking elaborate adult defenses, regress very quickly and easily into spontaneous and revealing play activities.
2. Children have rich fantasy lives that reveal their thoughts, feelings, and expectations.
3. Lacking adult formal thinking skills, insight, and verbal skills, children communicate through acting out their fantasies.

Once the relationship is established, the counselor can focus on how children conduct themselves in the counseling session. The counselor's work is to evaluate the climate of each counseling session. Was it happy, sad, pleasant, neutral, stormy, or productive? What seemed to set the tone? Next, counselors should look for patterns in the child's behavior or play. Hyperactive and attention deficit–disordered children act out their disorganization and impulsive behavior. Obsessive-compulsive children, by contrast, are rigid and structured in their play activities.

Children's choices of toys provide another rich area of data for counselors. Toys can be classified as passive or aggressive, masculine or feminine, and constructive or destructive; many toys may be neutral. Observe what the child does with each toy. Counselors search for themes and patterns in children's behavior and play therapy activities in the effort to learn the motivation directing their behavior. More important than the themes uncovered in counseling is the intensity with which these themes are played out in the sessions. The play themes of unstable or disturbed children are more variable and unreliable.

Counselors' accurate reflection of content, feelings, expectations, and behavior helps focus children's attention on their actions and stimulates the self-observation needed to gain insight about their lifestyle and motivational incentives.

Play therapy methods are presented in detail in chapter 12. The following six-step counseling model combines the best of reality planning with person-centered, active listening for children receiving general counseling or a combination of counseling and play therapy.

A GENERAL MODEL FOR COUNSELING

Diagnoses

Step 1. Defining the problem through active listening.   The way the counselor listens to the child is important in building rapport. An open, relaxed body posture is the best way to invite a child to talk. It is often helpful to suggest a time limit for your interview, which should vary according to the attention span of the child. One way to start might be to say, "Jimmy, we have 20 minutes today to talk about anything you'd like to discuss." In fact, several 20-minute periods might be used to build a friendship with Jimmy. Individualizing the counseling process to fit each child you counsel is very important.

When the child wishes to discuss a concern or problem with you, it is necessary to listen for three significant points: (1) a problem that has not been solved, (2) feelings about the problem, and (3) expectations of what the counselor should do about the problem. The counselor can assume the role of student and let the child teach these three topics; people learn best when they teach something to another person.

Counselors have the responsibility of letting the child know what they have heard and learned as their clients teach them. For example, the counselor should periodically respond with a statement such as "In other words, you are feeling _____ because _____ , and you want _____ ." This feedback to the child is referred to as *active listening;* it promotes better communication and lets the child know you are paying attention. The active listening process continues throughout the interview, but it is most important in helping to clarify the nature of the child's problem. When the child confirms your response as an accurate understanding of the problem, counseling can move to the next phase (see chapter 5 for a detailed explanation of the active-listening process).

Step 2. Clarifying the child's expectations.   Counselors also need to let children know if they can meet their expectations for counseling. The counselor probably cannot have an unpopular teacher fired, for example. However, counselors can inform children and their parents what they are able to do and let them determine if they want to accept or reject the service available. If the service is rejected, the counselor may want to explore other alternatives with the family about where or how the child can obtain the service.

Step 3. Exploring what has been done to solve the problem.   On looking at past attempts to solve the problem, remember that open-ended questions generally elicit the best responses. Closed questions that yield one-word answers such as *yes, no,* and *maybe* make the counselor's job much more difficult. As noted in this text, many approaches to counseling avoid heavy questioning, and others rely on a series of questions. Statements often work better than questions; they empower the client by letting the client maintain the pace and direction of the interview. For example, rather than asking the child, "What have you done to solve the problem?" the counselor would say, "If you feel ready, we could begin by looking at what you have tried to do to solve the problem."

In exploring the child's efforts to solve the problem, we find it helpful to have the client who can write make a list of these behaviors; otherwise, the child can dictate the answers to the counselor. The list becomes important if we want the child to make a commitment to stop behaviors that are not helping to solve the problem.

It is helpful to explore the possible rewards or payoffs the child derives from ineffective or unhelpful behaviors. Change is facilitated when both the pluses and the minuses are examined. A profit and loss statement can be prepared to see if the behavior is actually worth the cost the child is paying. If it is not, the child may discard the behavior in favor of a more productive alternative.

Step 4. Exploring what new things could be done to solve the problem.   The next step could be a brainstorming session in which the counselor encourages the child to develop as many problem-solving alternatives as possible. Judgment is reserved until the list is finished; quantity of ideas is more important than quality in this first step. Thompson and Poppen (1992) recommended drawing empty circles on a sheet of paper and then seeing how many circles the child can fill with ideas. If children are blocked from thinking of possible new ideas, the counselor can fill two circles with ideas as a way of encouraging the child to get started. The counselor thus allows the child to become a partner in the problem-solving process by choosing one of the counselor's two suggestions. Children seem to do best with a plan they have made or helped make. For example, if the plan involves learning a new skill such as assertion, effective study, or making friends, the counseling interview can be used for teaching and role-play rehearsal. After the brainstorming list is complete, children are asked to evaluate each alternative in light of its expected success in helping them get what they want.

Step 5. Obtaining a commitment to try one of the problem-solving ideas.   Building commitment to try a new plan may be difficult. Children must achieve success with their first plan because they may be quite discouraged by their previous failures to solve the problem. We suggest that the child not set impossible goals in this first attempt; the first plan should be achievable. Children do better if they are asked to report the results of their plan to the counselor. When plans do not work, the counselor helps the child write new ones until the child achieves success. Plans can include a program of reinforcement when the child succeeds in meeting daily or weekly goals.

Step 6. Closing the counseling interview.   A good way to close the interview is to invite the child to summarize or review what was discussed in the session; for example, the summary might include what progress was made and what plans were developed. Summarizing by the child is also helpful when the interview becomes mired and the child cannot think of anything to say. Because the process seems to stimulate new thoughts, summarizing at the close of the interview should be limited to 2 to 4 minutes. We also recommend asking the child to summarize the last counseling interview at the start of each new interview. These counselor requests to summarize teach children to pay attention in the session and to review counseling plans between sessions; they have the effect of an oral quiz without the threat of a failing grade. The summary also helps counselors evaluate their own effectiveness. Finally, the counselor and the child make plans for the next counseling interview or for some type of maintenance plan if counseling is to be terminated.

QUESTIONS COUNSELORS ASK

What Does the Counselor Need to Know About Counseling Records?

Most counselors keep some record of interviews with their clients. Notes that summarize the content of sessions and observations the counselor makes can assist in recalling previous information. Before deciding on a method of taking notes, counselors are wise to become knowledgeable about their state's laws regarding privileged communication and the regulations contained in the Buckley Amendment (the federal Family Rights and Privacy Act of 1974), which gave parents and young people of legal age the right to inspect records, letters, and recommendations about themselves. Personal notes do not fall under these regulations; however, for their own protection, counselors in institutional settings will want to become aware of the full requirements of the law.

Videotaping or audiotaping counseling sessions is also common practice. This procedure not only provides a record of the interview but also aids counselors in gaining self-understanding and self-awareness. Counselors can listen to or watch their tapes with another counselor and continue to grow and learn by evaluating their own work. In addition, listening to and discussing some sessions with the client may promote growth.

Permission to record should be obtained from the child and the parents before the procedure is begun. If the material is to be used for instruction or if anyone other than the counselor will hear the client, written permission should be obtained. Regarding use and storage of these records, reading state laws pertaining to privileged communication and the Buckley Amendment would be advisable.

When introducing a recording system to children, show them the recorder, perhaps allow them to listen to themselves for a minute, and then place the equipment in an out-of-the-way place. Occasionally, children are unable to talk when they are being recorded; most, however, quickly forget the equipment. Should a child resist being recorded, the counselor may wish to pursue the reasons for this resistance. If circumstances indicate that recording is inhibiting the counseling process, the counselor may choose to remove the equipment. At the other extreme, some children become so excited and curious about the taping equipment that counseling becomes impossible. Again, the counselor may prefer to remove the equipment, or a contract may be made with the child such as "After

30 minutes of the counseling work, Mickey may listen to the tape for 5 minutes." It is usually best to give as little attention to the recorder as possible after a brief initial explanation of its purpose and uses.

How Much Self-Disclosure
Is Appropriate for the Counselor?

Children are often interested in their counselors as people. They ask their age, where they went to school, where they live, and whether they have children, and counselors are faced with the perplexing problem of how much personal information to share. Counselors who refuse to answer any personal questions run the risk of hurting the counseling relationship or being viewed as a mysterious figure, bringing forth more questions. If counselors answer all personal questions, however, the interview time may center around the counselor rather than the client. With seriously disturbed or acting-out clients, revealing your address or where your children go to school could be bothersome or even dangerous. A general guideline might be to share some personal information (favorite sport or TV show, number of children) and, when the questions become too personal or continue too long, reflect to the child, "You seem to be very interested in me personally" and explore the child's curiosity and pursuit of the subject. Understanding the child's curiosity about the counselor could promote understanding the child as a person. Questioning the counselor can be a defense for children who wish to avoid discussing their own problems.

A second problem concerning self-disclosure relates to the counselor's feelings and emotions. Counselor training programs are founded on the assumption that people are unique, capable of growth, and worthy of respect. These programs focus on listening and responding to clients with empathic understanding and respect. The programs also emphasize being genuine; however, genuineness is often interpreted as showing only genuine *positive* emotions and feelings. Counselor trainees are sometimes quite surprised when their supervisors encourage them to admit to the client their negative feelings, such as frustration or anger. Obviously, admitting emotions does not mean attacking and degrading the client; rather, it means admitting that the counselor is a person with feelings and is frustrated or angry over what is occurring ("I am really frustrated that we seem to be talking about everything except what occurred with your friend today").

The counselor's proper level of self-disclosure is a controversial issue in the profession. Some feel comfortable being completely open and honest about their feelings (high levels of self-disclosure); others think such openness interferes with the counselor-client relationship and prefer low levels of self-disclosure. However, most counselors agree that self-disclosure is not "true confessions." Poppen and Thompson (1974) summarized the arguments on both sides of the issue. The principal arguments in favor of high levels of self-disclosure are as follows:

1. Counselors who are open and honest about their thoughts and feelings encourage similar behavior by their clients.

2. Knowing that the counselor has had similar adjustment problems helps clients feel more at ease to discuss their own.
3. Children learn by imitation and can learn to solve their own problems through hearing about the experiences of others.
4. Counselors could be models for behavior.

On the other side of the issue, those opposing high levels of self-disclosure claim the following:

1. Clients are in the counselor's office for help with their problems, not to hear about the counselor's problems.
2. Counseling could become a time for sharing gripes or problems rather than a working session for personal growth.
3. Counselors can lose objectivity if they identify too strongly with the child's concerns.

According to Poppen and Thompson (1974),

Self-disclosure is more beneficial when it takes a here-and-now focus—that is, when self-disclosure becomes an open and authentic expression of the counselor's or student's [child's] thoughts and feelings experienced at a particular time. Self-disclosure, when examined in the here-and-now context, means much more than dredging up the dark secrets of the past. (p. 15)

What Types of Questions Should the Counselor Use?

Adults often think they must ask children several questions in order to get the "whole story." Usually, these questions are of the "who," "what," "when," "where," and "what did you do next" variety. These questions may or may not be asked for the purpose of helping the child or for clarification; too often they arise out of general curiosity. Some questions may even be irrelevant and interrupt or ignore the child's thoughts and expressions. Questions can also be used to judge, blame, or criticize.

Child: The teacher called me a dummy in front of the whole class today!
Adult: (sarcastically) What did you say this time to make him call you that?

At that particular moment, the important fact is not what the child said but the fact that the child was embarrassed, hurt, and possibly angered. By listening and understanding feelings and expressions rather than probing for details of who said what and when, the adult will get the whole story eventually and maintain a much friendlier relationship with the child. Counselors who listen and respond with understanding learn the child's important thoughts or problems. In other words, questions rephrased as statements work better.

Some counselors, in their efforts to help the child, take over the counseling interview. Counselors who direct the interview risk missing important feelings and thoughts. The counselor may guide the conversation in a totally meaningless direction.

Child: I hate my brother.
Counselor: Why do you hate your brother?
Child: Because he's mean.
Counselor: How is he mean?
Child: He hits me.
Counselor: What do you do to make him hit you? [accusation]
Child: Nothing.
Counselor: Come on, now. Tell me about when he hits you—and what your mother does when he hits you.

This example sounds more like an inquisition than a counseling session. The hitting and what the mother does may or may not be what is really troubling the child. What could be more important is the feeling that exists between the child and her brother. Is it really "hate" because he hits her, or could there be other problems in the relationship that the counselor will miss by focusing on hitting rather than listening to the child tell about her relationship with her brother? It is also possible that "hating brother" could have been a test problem to see if the counselor really would listen and be understanding. A counselor who guides the interview by questions could overlook the true problem entirely.

In the preceding example the child answered the counselor's questions but offered no further information. Children easily fall into the role of answering adults' questions and then waiting for the next question. Rather than being a listener and helper, the counselor assumes the role of questioner. If this pattern has been established, the interview may die when the counselor runs out of questions.

Obviously, there are times in counseling when direct questions should be asked. The counselor may need factual information or clarification. However, counselors can probably get more information from children with open-ended questions. An open-ended question does not require a specific answer. It encourages the child to give the counselor more information about the topic but does not restrict replies or discourage further communication in the area. Suppose a counselor was interested in learning about a child's social relationships. Rather than asking the direct, closed question "Do you have friends?", the counselor might elicit more information about the child's social relationships by saying, "Tell me about what you like to do for fun—things that you enjoy doing in your free time." In this way, the counselor could learn not only about friends but possibly also about the child's sports interests, hobbies, and other activities (or lack of activities). Another open-ended question that might help the counselor understand what is going on in the child's life is "Tell me about your family," out of which could come answers to such unasked questions as "Do both your mother and father live in the home?", "How many people live in the household?", "What are your feelings about various members of the household?"

One further point should be made about questioning in counseling. Both Glasser (1969) and Benjamin (1987) cautioned adults about the use of "why" questions with youth because they are associated with blame; "Why did you do that?" is often interpreted in the mind of a child as "Why did you do a *stupid thing* like that?" These questions put people on the defensive; when asked why we acted a certain way, we feel forced to find some logical reason or excuse for our behavior. Glasser suggested that a better question might be a "what" question. Most of us are not really sure *why* we behaved a certain way, but we can tell *what* occurred. A "what" question does not deal with possible unconscious motives and desires but focuses on present behavior; the client and counselor can look at what is happening now and what can be done.

Garbarino and Stott (1989) reminded counselors that effective questions must be appropriate for the developmental level of their clients. They made the following suggestions for interviewing preschoolers:

- Use sentences that do not exceed by more than five words the number of words in a sentence the child uses.
- Use names rather than pronouns.
- Use the child's terms.
- Do not ask, "Do you understand?" Ask the child to repeat your message.
- Do not repeat questions children do not understand because they may think they have made errors and attempt to "correct" their answers. Rephrase the question instead.
- Avoid time-sequence questions.
- Preschoolers, being very literal, may give us answers that are easy to overinterpret.
- Do not respond to every answer with another question. A short summary or acknowledgment encourages the child to expand on his or her previous statement.

In summary, counselors learn more by listening and summarizing than by questioning. The habit of questioning is difficult to break. When tempted to question, counselors might first ask themselves whether the questions they ask will (1) contribute therapeutically to understanding the child and the child's problems or (2) inhibit the further flow of expression.

How Can Silences Be Used in Counseling?

Most of us are uncomfortable with silences. We have been socially conditioned to keep the conversation going; when conversation begins to ebb, we search through our thoughts for a new topic of interest to introduce to the group. Although silences can be very productive in a counseling interview, counselors often find them difficult to bear.

Benjamin (1987) suggested several productive uses of silences. A child may need a few moments of silence to sort out thoughts and feelings, and "respect for this silence is more beneficial than many words from the interviewer" (p. 42). The child may have related some very emotional event or thought and may need a moment of silence to think about this revelation or regain composure. Benjamin further stated that confusion can lead to brief periods of silence. The child or the counselor may have behaved or spoken in a confusing manner, and sorting things out may take time.

Then again, silence can be a way of resisting counseling. The child may be reluctant to open up and talk with this stranger who promises acceptance, or the child may not be willing to admit and deal with the problem. Techniques such as play therapy, role-playing, or confrontation may be necessary to establish a better relationship and deal with the resistance.

Finally, Benjamin pointed out, silences can be used productively for problem solving. At times all of us need a few moments to collect our thoughts so we can work out problems that confront us or express our thoughts and feelings more clearly.

Silences can be productive, but how long should the counselor allow the silence to last? Obviously, an entire session of silence between child and counselor is not likely to be helpful. The child may spontaneously begin to speak again when ready. Children's nonverbal behavior may provide counselors with clues that they are ready to begin. The counselor may test the water by making a quiet statement reflecting the possible cause of the silence: "You seem a little confused about what you just told me." The child's response to this reflection should indicate whether he or she is ready to proceed.

Should Counselors Give Advice?

The role of a counselor has often been interpreted as advice giver, and some counseling theorists advocate giving advice to clients. Their rationale is that the counselor, who is trained in helping and more knowledgeable, should advise the less knowledgeable client.

We prefer to view the role of the counselor as using skills and knowledge to assist another person in solving his or her own problems or conflicts. Counselors who believe in the uniqueness, worth, dignity, and responsibility of the individual and who believe that, given the right conditions, individuals can make correct choices for themselves are reluctant to give advice on solving life's problems. Instead, they use their counseling knowledge and skill to help clients make responsible choices of their own and, in effect, learn how to become their own counselor.

An illustration of the difference between giving advice and assisting in problem solving may clarify the point. Consider this example.

Tony was threatened by neighborhood bullies who were going to beat him up on the way home from school. Tony confided his fear of fighting to the counselor, who advised him to talk this over with his parents who, he said, will understand and probably talk to the neighborhood boys' parents, and everything will work out fine. Tony was reluctant to talk to his parents, but the counselor persuaded him they would understand and help. Tony returned later to relate that his father lectured him for being a "sissy" and instructed him to "go out and fight like a man." Tony was more terrified than ever because neither his parents nor the counselor understood his dilemma or could be counted on to support him. In this case, the counselor, not considering the client's home and culture, gave advice that intensified the problem. The counselor might have been more helpful by assisting Tony to think of ways of solving the problem—ways that Tony would choose.

Another possible disadvantage of counselors' advice is the problem of dependency. Counselors want their clients to become responsible individuals capable of solving their own problems. Children have a multitude of adults telling them how and when to act, but only a few assist them to learn responsible problem-solving behavior. In counseling, children learn the problem-solving process; they learn that they do not have to depend entirely on adults to make all decisions for them. The process can develop confident, mature, and independent individuals moving toward self-actualization.

Excessive advice-giving in counseling can foster dependency, overconformity, and low self-esteem. Counselors who encourage excessive dependency might investigate their own motivations and needs. Most counselors become extremely frustrated by clients who depend on them for decisions. A dependency relationship inevitably breeds hostility: the dependent person resents having to depend on the counselor; the counselor resents having to support the dependency of the client. This conflict is analogous to the typical adolescent struggle for independence.

Because many people see the counselor's role as that of advice-giver, some clients may become frustrated and angry when counselors will not give advice. When asked what they think they could do to work out the conflict or problem, children typically are unable to think of possible solutions. It is a new experience for many children to be involved in solving their own problems. When pressed to give advice, a counselor could reflect the feeling that the child is not sure what to do and would like to have an answer and then suggest again that they explore possibilities together. If the child is persistent and demands an answer, the counselor may wish to explore the reasons for this demand.

We need to point out, however, that counselors have a duty to protect their clients from any harm they might do to themselves as well as to prevent them from harming others. Therefore, counselors may need to give advice in emergency situations and to act on the advice they give.

Should Counselors Give Information?

Beginning counselors, believing that giving information is the same as giving advice, often give neither. Clients need good information to make good decisions, and counselors help clients by sharing what good information they have. For example, counselors should inform their clients of community and school resources where clients can receive assistance. The decision to seek assistance should be the client's. In other words, advice often takes the form of a suggestion to perform a certain behavior or to take some course of action. Information-giving, however, means providing data, facts, general knowledge, and, to some extent, alternatives. Remember, lack of information about self and the environment are two primary problem causes. The counselor's role is to help clients find the information they need to solve their problems. Once again, we believe the more actively clients seek their own information, the better their learning experience.

How Does the Counselor Keep the Client on Task During the Counseling Session?

Children soon discover that the counselor is a good listener who gives them undivided attention. Because many children are not listened to by adults, they often take advantage of the counseling situation to talk about everything except the reason for coming to counseling. With the least suggestion, the counselor may find the child rambling on about a TV show, last night's ballgame, a current movie, tricks a pet dog can do, or any number of other irrelevant topics. Children, like adults, can ramble excessively when they wish to avoid a problem. Talkative-ness then becomes a diversionary tactic either to avoid admitting what is troubling them or to avoid coping with the conflict. The conflict could be too traumatic or painful to face.

Another possible reason for losing focus in a counseling session is that children do not understand their role in the counseling interview. If the purpose of counseling and expectations of the people involved are clearly defined in the initial interview, pointless chatting is less likely.

Counselors who discover themselves being led into superficial or rambling conversations may want to bring the conversation back to the problem at hand by reflecting to the child, "We seem to be getting away from the reason for our time together. I wonder if you could tell me more about. . . ." If a child consistently wanders, state that you notice the wandering and then explore possible reasons for the avoidance. A tape recorder can be an excellent means of determining when, how, and why the distractions occur. A contract might be drawn up, such as *[The counselor]* and I will work on *[the problem]* for 25 minutes. I can talk to *[the counselor]* about anything else for the last 5 minutes."

What Limits Should Be Set in Counseling?

In training, most counselors are taught to be empathic, respectful, genuine, accepting, and nonjudgmental—characteristics that writers such as Carl Rogers and Robert Carkhuff defined as essential for a facilitative counseling relationship.

Counselors may follow many other theories during the counseling process, but most believe that establishing a therapeutic relationship based on these ingredients is a necessary first step for effective counseling. The characteristics of empathy, respect, and genuineness have been operationally defined by Carkhuff (1969), and many training institutions teach counselors these behaviors according to his model. To define the counseling attitudes and behaviors involved in being accepting and nonjudgmental may not be quite so easy.

Rogers (1961), van Kaam (1965), and Frankl (1962) concluded that acceptance is born of genuine concern for people. Acceptance implies that counselors believe individuals have infinite worth and dignity, the right to make choices and decisions for their lives, and responsibility for their own lives. Accepting an individual as a person of worth and potential is possible without accepting that person's behavior. Children should be viewed as unique and responsible individuals, capable of making wise choices; however, adults cannot totally accept all child behaviors. Acceptance does not imply total permissiveness. Respect for the rights of all individuals involved must accompany acceptance, and counselors cannot allow children to infringe on their rights as people or on the rights of other family members, friends, or acquaintances.

Being accepting and nonjudgmental can be difficult for some counselors, especially regarding moral and ethical issues. Counselors are human beings with their own attitudes, values, and beliefs. Remaining open-minded enough to really hear the client's entire story is difficult if the client's values and those of the counselor conflict.

Being nonjudgmental does not mean that anything goes. Rather, it is withholding those judgments we ordinarily make and allowing clients to tell the whole story without being threatened by the counselor's condemnation. Counselors attempt to refrain from blaming, accusing, criticizing, and moralizing, but they also attempt to teach responsible, reality-oriented behavior to their child clients. The counselor does not tell childen they are wrong; the counselor's job is to help children explore the consequences, advantages, and disadvantages of their choices and, perhaps, discover better methods of resolving the conflict. For instance, rather than sermonizing to Tony that fighting is wrong, the counselor might be more helpful by thinking with him about what would happen if he challenged the bully to a fight and whether he could gain his father's acceptance and respect in other ways.

In summary, accepting and nonjudgmental attitudes are essential for good counseling, but they must be combined with respect for the rights of others, the reality of the situation, and responsibility for one's own behavior.

What About the Issue of Confidentiality?

Most counselors have been taught that whatever is said in a counseling interview should remain confidential unless there is danger to the client, another person, or property. Many explain the principle of confidentiality to their clients during the first interview; others discuss confidentiality only if the child asks whether what is said will be told to parents or teachers. Should information indicating danger to a person or property be revealed during later interviews, counselors remind children of the counselor's obligation to report such danger to the proper authorities. Counselors do not have privileged communication in their counselor-client relationships unless they are licensed by a state regulatory board. Counselors' records can be subpoenaed, and counselors can be called to testify in court proceedings should the information they possess be deemed necessary for a court decision. If counselors think that revealing the information required in their testimony could harm the child, they can request a private conference with the judge to share both the information and their reasons for wanting to keep the information confidential.

Some counselors maintain that children and adults should be encouraged to communicate more openly and that the counselor can facilitate this process in the family counseling interview. They further contend that parents and other adults can provide insight and needed information about the child; the significant adult in the child's life can become a cocounselor. A signed contract with the parents to protect the confidentiality of the child's counseling sessions, although not legally binding, may help establish the interview content's confidentiality.

Careful evaluation of the child's presenting problem and the adults involved may help the counselor decide whether strict confidentiality should be maintained or if others should be included. To avoid misunderstanding and maintain the trust necessary for the counseling relationship, the decision to include others or share information should always be discussed with the child.

Is This Child Telling Me the Truth?

Another counseling problem is whether the child is telling the counselor the truth or enhancing or exaggerating to get attention or sympathy. Children often tell their counselors of seeing people shoot one another, raging fires, and robberies. Unfortunately, many of these stories are true; however, children have vivid imaginations, and it is difficult to know how much to believe. Counselors do not want to be gullible or deny the truth.

If counselors doubt the truth of what they are hearing, soliciting more details of the incident (for example, by saying, "Tell me more") may clarify whether the story is truth or fiction. When asked to give specifics, children may admit they were "only kidding" or "making it up." Counselors might also admit their genuine concerns: "I am really having trouble with this because I have never heard anything like it." An admission of this sort by a counselor expresses a genuine feeling and avoids labeling the child a liar or possibly denying a true story. It also provides the child with an opportunity to change the story while saving face.

However, Garbarino and Stott (1989) pointed out that in cases of suspected child sexual abuse, the most effective approach is to be willing to believe the child. They recommended recognizing that most child-initiated allegations are grounded in real experiences, even if these experiences in themselves do not constitute sexual abuse (see chapter 15).

What Can Be Done When the Interview Process Becomes Blocked?

In some counseling sessions the child does not feel like talking. It is possible that things have been going well for the past few days and the child really has nothing to discuss. There may be a lull before new material is introduced. One way to avoid these unexpected empty periods is to be prepared for a session. Some counselors have general goals for their client (for instance, to increase assertiveness) and also define specific short-term goals for each session as counseling proceeds. Whether the counselor prefers to define objectives or not, notes of the previous session can be reviewed and a tentative plan made for the coming interview. Obviously, this plan is subject to change, according to the content of the interview.

However, the best laid plans often go awry. When the child seems highly distracted, a short summary by the counselor or child of the previous conversation may stimulate further communication. If the child does not seem to want to talk, the techniques of play therapy (drawing, clay, games) may be beneficial. At times (illness, extreme excitability, or apathy) ending the session short of the designated time is best. The length of counseling sessions can vary from a few minutes to an hour, depending on the client's age and presenting problem.

When sessions become blocked, evaluate what is happening. Again, the tape recorder assists in assessing the lack of progress. Blocking may be a sign that the child is ready for the counseling to conclude. It could be resistance on the part of the child. It could come from the counselor's inadequate skills or lack of planning. Unproductive sessions occur occasionally with all counselors, but frequent periods of nonproductivity should signal the counselor to investigate what is happening.

When Should Counseling Be Terminated?

How does a counselor decide when to end counseling? Does the counselor or the client decide? How does either party know the client is ready to stand alone? If the counselor and client have clearly defined the problem brought to counseling and the goal to be accomplished, the termination time will be evident—when the goal is accomplished.

Termination may be difficult for children, who usually find the sessions to be a time when a caring adult gives them undivided attention. Deep friendships are often formed between counselor and child, and the child (and possibly the counselor) does not wish to end this pleasant relationship. In order to ease the break, client and counselor can discuss a possible termination date several weeks ahead of time. Plans can be made and rehearsed about how the child will react should problems recur. The child can be left feeling that the counselor still cares and will be available should trouble arise. Counselors may even consider building in a follow-up time when they ask their child clients to drop them a note or call to let them know how things are going. The counselor may want to schedule a brief follow-up visit. Any informal method of showing the child that a counselor's caring does not end with the last interview can signal the counselor's continued interest in the child's growth and development. Most successful counselors use a plan for maintaining the gains their clients have achieved during counseling. Such maintenance plans require periodic follow-up contacts, for example, 30 days, 6 months.

How Can Counseling Be Evaluated?

One method of evaluation is goal-attainment scaling, which has the double advantage of facilitating the counseling process and evaluating counseling outcomes. Goal-attainment scaling (Emmerson & Neely, 1988; Kiresuk, 1973, 1976; Kiresuk, Smith, & Cardillo, 1994; Smith, 1976) allows counselor and client the opportunity to establish counseling goals cooperatively. The counselor's task is to help the child clarify these goals in measurable terms as a way of evaluating the distance between "what I have" and "what I would like to have." The tabulation and calculation of the data are the counselor's responsibility. Generally one to five goals are set, with five levels of attainment defined for each goal (Table 2-1). In addition, each goal is given a weight to represent its importance to the client. Clients establish priorities for their goals and assign weights to the most important and least important. For instance, Goal 1 may be three times more important than Goal 2. Intermediate goals are assigned weights representing their relative importance to the client. For example, if the most important goal is three times as important as the least important goal, it would receive a weight of 30 compared to a weight of 10 for the least important goal. Intermediate goals are then weighted on a scale of 10 to 30.

Levels of attainment for each goal range from a +2 for the best anticipated success to a −2 for the least favorable outcome. A 0 value is assigned for the middle level of expected outcome success. Values of +1 and −1 represent "more than" and "less than" expected levels of success, respectively.

The goals are defined in measurable and observable terms, with the level of entry checked on the goal attainment follow-up guide. Following counseling, an

TABLE 2-1 Goal-attainment follow-up guide
Level at intake: ✓
Level at follow-up: ★

Scale attainment level	*Scale 1: Working on task W = 20*	*Scale 2: Disruptive behavior W₂ = 30*	*Scale 3: Punctuality W₃ = 25*	*Scale 4: Relationships W₄ = 30*	*Scale 5: Grade improvement W₅ = 10*
a. Most unfavorable counseling outcome thought likely (−2)	Daydreams, leaves desk; ignores assignments ✓	Pushes, hits, leaves room, talks without permission	Fails to set clock and oversleeps ✓	Child gets into three fights per day ✓	Child continues to fail ✓
b. Less than expected success with counseling (−1)	Completes one assignment per day	Talks without permission ✓	Shuts off alarm clock and goes back to sleep	Child gets into at least one fight per day	Child demonstrates "D" work
c. Expected level of counseling success (0)	Completes two assignments per day	Engages in appropriate behavior 75% of the time	Arises when alarm sounds	Child avoids all fights	Child demonstrates "C" work
d. More than expected success with counseling (+1)	Completes three assignments per day ★	Engages in appropriate behavior 85% of the time ★	Arises before alarm sounds; makes bed	Child develops one new friend ★	Child demonstrates "B" work ★
e. Best anticipated success with counseling (+2)	Completes four assignments per day	Engages in appropriate behavior 100% of the time	Arises in time to make bed and fix own breakfast ★	Child develops three new friends	Child demonstrates "A" work

*Percentage figures based on spot-check observations during the school day.

asterisk is placed on the guide indicating where the client is after counseling. Follow-up data can also be recorded periodically on the chart.

Goal attainment scores can be calculated for both the intake and follow-up levels. A follow-up goal attainment score of 50 or better is considered successful. Kiresuk and Sherman (1968) adopted a conventional T-score scale with the mean set at 50 and a standard deviation set at 10 for their goal attainment scale. The following formulas are used to derive the goal attainment scores for the guide in Table 2-1 (Kiresuk & Sherman, 1968).

Goal-Attainment Score Calculation: Level at Intake

$\overline{X}$ = mean $\qquad\qquad$ $\overline{X} = 50$

s = standard deviation $\qquad$ $s = 10$ (standard deviation)

p = probability $\qquad\qquad$ $p = .3$

w = weight value $\qquad\qquad$ $1 - p = .7$

x = scale value $\qquad\qquad$ $w = 10$ to 30

$\qquad\qquad\qquad\qquad$ $x = -2$ to $+2$

Goal-attainment score $(T) = 50 + \dfrac{10\Sigma w_1 x_1}{\sqrt{(.7\Sigma w_1{}^2 + .3(\Sigma w_1)^2}}$

$50 + 10[(20 \times -2) + (30 \times -1) + (25 \times -2) + (30 \times -2) + (10 \times -2)]$

$50 + \dfrac{10 \times -200}{\sqrt{.7(20^2 + 30^2 + 25^2 + 30^2 + 10^2) + .3(20 + 30 + 25 + 30 + 10)^2}}$

$50 + \dfrac{10 \times -200}{\sqrt{.7(2925) + .3(13225)}}$

$50 + \dfrac{10 \times -200}{\sqrt{6015}}$

$50 + \dfrac{10 \times -200}{77.56}$

$50 + \dfrac{(-2000)}{77.56}$

$50 + (-25.78)$

$T = 24.22$

z score $= \dfrac{50 - 24.22}{10} = 2.58$ standard deviations below the mean

Goal-Attainment Score Calculation: Level at Follow-Up

$\overline{X}$ = mean $\qquad\qquad\qquad$ $\overline{X}$ = 50

s = standard deviation $\qquad$ s = 10 (standard deviation)

p = probability $\qquad\qquad$ p = .3

w = weight value $\qquad\qquad$ $1 - p = .7$

x = scale value $\qquad\qquad$ w = 10 to 30

$\qquad\qquad\qquad\qquad\qquad$ $x = -2$ to $+2$

Goal-attainment score (T) = $50 + \dfrac{10\Sigma w_1 x_1}{\sqrt{(.7\Sigma w_1^2 + .3(\Sigma w_1)^2}}$

$50 + \dfrac{50 + 10[(20 \times 1) + (30 \times 1) + (25 \times 2) + (30 \times 1) + (10 \times 1)]}{\sqrt{.7(20^2 + 30^2 + 25^2 + 30^2 + 10^2) + .3(20 + 30 + 25 + 30 + 10)^2}}$

$50 + \dfrac{10 \times 140}{\sqrt{.7(2925) + .3(13225)}}$

$50 + \dfrac{10 \times 140}{\sqrt{6015}}$

$50 + \dfrac{10 \times 140}{77.56}$

$50 + \dfrac{(1400)}{77.56}$

$50 + (18)$

$T = 68$

z score = $\dfrac{68 - 50}{10} = \dfrac{18}{10} = 1.8$ standard deviations above the mean

Goal-attainment scaling (Dowd & Kelly, 1975) can be graphed to show weekly progress (Figure 2-4). The graph can also be used to chart the results of periodic follow-up checks on the maintenance of counseling gains.

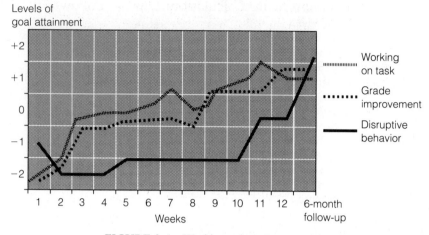

FIGURE 2-4   Weekly goal-attainment scale

REFERENCES

Benjamin, A. (1987). *The helping interview* (3rd ed.). Boston: Houghton Mifflin.

Boat, B., & Everson, M. (1986). *Using anatomical dolls: Guidelines for interviewing young children in sexual abuse investigations.* Unpublished manuscript.

Burton, L. (1995). Using a dog in an elementary school counseling program. *Elementary School Guidance and Counseling, 29* (3), 236–240.

Carkhuff, R. (1969). *Helping and human relations* (2 vols.). New York: Holt, Rinehart & Winston.

Carlson, K. (1990). Suggestions for counseling "other-referred" children. *Elementary School Guidance and Counseling, 24,* 222–229.

Corsini, R., & Wedding, D. (1995). *Current psychotherapies* (5th ed.). Itasca, IL: F. E. Peacock.

Dimond, R., Havens, R., & Jones, A. (1978). A conceptual framework for the practice of prescriptive eclecticism in psychotherapy. *American Psychologist, 33,* 239–248.

Dowd, E., & Kelly, F. (1975). The use of goal attainment scaling in single case study research. *Goal Attainment Review, 2,* 11–21.

Emmerson, G., & Neely, M. (1988). Two adaptable, valid and reliable data collection measures: Goal attainment scaling and the semantic differential. *Counseling Psychologist, 16,* 261–271.

Frankl, V. (1962). *Man's search for meaning: An introduction to logotherapy.* Boston: Beacon.

Garbarino, J., & Stott, F. (1989). *What children can tell us.* San Francisco: Jossey-Bass.

Gerler, E. (1990). Multimodal approaches to counseling in schools. *Elementary School Guidance and Counseling, 24,* 242.

Gerler, E., Drew, N., & Mohr, P. (1990). Succeeding in middle school: A multimodal approach. *Elementary School Guidance and Counseling, 24,* 263–271.

Glass, G., & Kliegl, R. (1983). An apology for research integration in the study of psychotherapy. *Journal of Consulting and Clinical Psychology, 51,* 28–41.

Glasser, W. (1969). *Schools without failure.* New York: Harper & Row.

Harper, R. (1959). *Psychoanalysis and psychotherapy: Thirty-six systems.* Englewood Cliffs, NJ: Prentice-Hall.

Karasu, T. (1986). The specificity versus nonspecificity dilemma: Toward identifying therapeutic change agents. *American Journal of Psychiatry, 143,* 688–695.

Keat, D. (1990a). Change in child multimodal counseling. *Elementary School Guidance and Counseling, 24,* 248–262.

Keat, D. (1990b). *Child muldimodal therapy.* Norwood, NJ: Ablex.

Kiresuk, T. (1973). Goal attainment scaling at a county mental service. *Evaluation,* Special Monograph 1, 12–18.

Kiresuk, T. (1976). *Guide to goals: Goal setting for children* (format two). Minneapolis: Program Evaluation Resource Center.

Kiresuk, T., & Sherman, R. (1968). Goal attainment scaling: A general method for evaluating comprehensive community mental health programs. *Community Mental Health, 4,* 443–453.

Kiresuk, T., Smith, A., & Cardillo, J. (1994). *Goal attainment selling: Applications, theory, and measurement.* Hillsdale, NJ: Erlbaum.

Lazarus, A. (1981). *The practice of multimodal therapy.* New York: McGraw-Hill.

Lazarus, A. (1984). Multimodal therapy. In R. Corsini (Ed.), *Current psychotherapies* (3rd ed.). Itasca, IL: F. E. Peacock.

Lazarus, A. (1990). Multimodal applications and research: A brief overview and update. *Elementary School Guidance and Counseling, 24,* 243–247.

Levinson, B. (1962). The dog as co-therapist. *Mental Hygiene, 46,* 59–65.

Lewis, C. (1985). *Listening to children.* Northvale, NJ: Aronson.

Luborsky, L., Singer, B., & Luborsky, L. (1975). Comparative studies of psychotherapies: Is it true that "everyone has one and all must have prizes"? *Archives of General Psychiatry, 32,* 995–1008.

O'Brien, M. (1993). Pets as counselors. *Elementary School Guidance and Counseling, 4,* 308.

Poppen, W., & Thompson, C. (1974). *School counseling: Theories and concepts.* Lincoln, NE: Professional Educators.

Rogers, C. (1961). *On becoming a person.* Boston: Houghton Mifflin.

Shapiro, D., & Shapiro, D. (1982). Meta-analysis of comparative therapy outcome studies: A replication of refinement. *Psychological Bulletin, 92,* 581–604.

Smith, D. (1976). Goal attainment scaling as an adjunct to counseling. *Journal of Counseling Psychology, 23,* 22–27.

Smith, M., & Glass, G. (1977). Meta-analysis of psychotherapy outcome studies. *American Psychologist, 32,* 752–760.

Smith, M., Glass, G., & Miller, T. (1980). *The benefits of psychotherapy.* Baltimore: Johns Hopkins University Press.

Stiles, W., Shapiro, D., & Elliott, R. (1986). Are all psychotherapies equivalent? *American Psychologist, 13,* 142–149.

Teasdale, J. (1985). Psychological treatments for depression: How do they work? *Behavior Research and Therapy, 23,* 157–165.

Thompson, C., & Campbell, S. (1992). Personal intervention preferences for alleviating mild depression. *Journal of Counseling and Development.*

Thompson, C., & Poppen, W. (1992). *Guidance activities for counselors and teachers.* Knoxville TN: Author.

Trivedi, L., & Perl, J. (1995). Animal facilitated counseling in the elementary school: A literature review and practical considerations. *Elementary School Guidance and Counseling, 29* (3), 223–234.

van Kaam, A. (1965). Counseling from the viewpoint of existential psychology. In R. Mosher, R. Carle, & C. Kehas (Eds.), *Guidance: An examination.* New York: Harcourt, Brace, & World.

PART TWO

◆

COUNSELING THEORIES AND TECHNIQUES
Their Application to Children

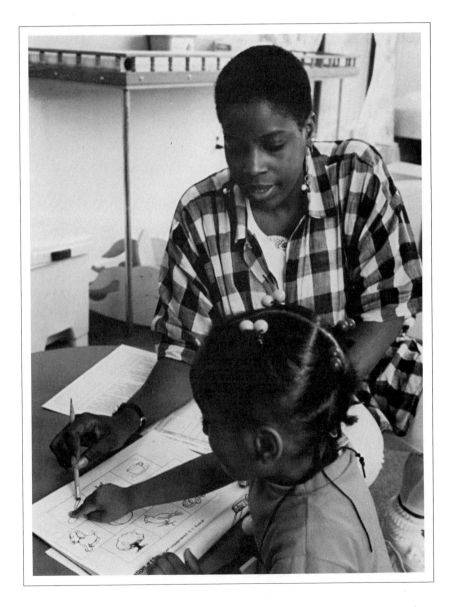

Chapter 3

◆

Psychoanalytic Counseling

SIGMUND FREUD

Sigmund Freud was born in Freiberg, Moravia, in 1856 and died in London in 1939. However, he is considered to have belonged to Vienna, where he lived for nearly 80 years. Freud was the firstborn of eight children by his father's second wife; he had two half-brothers more than 20 years his elder.

Freud graduated from the Gymnasium at 17 and, in 1873, entered the medical school at the University of Vienna. He became deeply involved in neurological research and did not finish his M.D. degree for 8 years. Never intending to practice medicine because he wanted to be a scientist, Freud devoted his next 15 years to investigations of the nervous system (Hall, 1954). However, the salary of a scientific researcher was inadequate to support the wife and six children he had by then. In addition, the anti-Semitism prevalent in Vienna during this period prevented Freud from achieving university advancement. Consequently, Freud felt forced to take up the practice of medicine.

Freud decided to specialize in the treatment of nervous disorders; at the time, not much was known about this particular branch of medicine. First, he spent a year in France learning about Jean Charcot's use of hypnosis in the treatment of hysteria (Stone, 1971). Freud (1925/1963) was dissatisfied with hypnosis because he thought its effects were only temporary and did not get at the center of the problem. Freud then studied with Joseph Breuer, learning the benefits of the catharsis (or "talking out your problems") form of therapy.

Noticing that his patients' physical symptoms seemed to have a mental base, Freud probed deeper and deeper into the minds of his patients. "His probing revealed dynamic forces at work which were responsible for creating the abnormal symptoms that he was called upon to treat. Gradually there began to take shape in Freud's mind the idea that most of these forces were unconscious" (Hall, 1954, p. 15). According to Stone (1971), this finding was probably the turning point in Freud's career. To substantiate some of his ideas, Freud decided to undertake an intensive analysis of his own unconscious forces in order to check on the material he had gathered from his patients. "On the basis of the knowledge he gained from his patients and from himself he began to lay the foundations for a theory of personality" (Hall, 1954, p. 17).

Freud's early support of Charcot and his new and revolutionary ideas cost him the support of most scholars and doctors. Eventually, however, Freud was accepted as a genius in psychotherapy. Many influential scientists, including Carl Jung, Alfred Adler, Ernest Jones, and Wilhelm Stekel, recognized Freud's theory as a major breakthrough in the field of psychology, however, these scientists broke with Freud early on. Freud's academic career with the University of Vienna began in 1883, however, he did not receive the rank of full professor until 1920. Freud's recognition by academic psychology came in 1909, when he was invited by G. Stanley Hall to give a series of lectures at Clark University in Worcester, Massachusetts.

Freud's writing career spanned 63 years, during which time he produced more than 600 publications. His collected works have been published in English in 24 volumes as *The Standard Edition of the Complete Psychological Works of Sigmund Freud* (1953–1964). Among his more famous works are *The Interpretation of Dreams* (1900) and *The Psychopathology of Everyday Life* (1901).

Freud seemed never to think his work was finished. "As new evidence came to him from his patients and his colleagues, he expanded and revised his basic theories" (Hall, 1954, p. 17). As an example of his flexibility and capability, at 70 Freud completely altered a number of his fundamental views: He revamped motivation theory, reversed the theory of anxiety, and developed a new model of personality based on id, ego, and superego.

Freud developed his psychoanalytic model of people over five decades of observing and writing. The major principles were based on the clinical study of individual patients undergoing treatment for their problems. Free association became Freud's preferred procedure after he discarded hypnosis.

Psychoanalysis includes theories about the development and organization of the mind, the instinctual drives, the influences of the external environment, the importance of the family, and the attitudes of society. As useful as psychoanalysis is as a therapeutic tool, its impact and value reach far beyond medical applications. It is the only comprehensive theory of human psychology. Psychoanalytic theory has proven helpful to parents and teachers in the upbringing and education of children.

Although psychoanalytic theory has been modified in some areas, its basic concepts remain. The fact that almost all counseling theories include some of the basic premises from the psychoanalytic method shows the influence and durability of the theory.

THE NATURE OF PEOPLE

The concept of human nature in psychoanalytic theory found its basis in psychic determinism and unconscious mental processes. Psychic determinism implies that mental life is a continuous manifestation of cause-related relationships. Mental processes are considered the causative factors in the nature of human behavior. Mental activity and even physical activity may be kept below the conscious level. Analysis on the basis of unconscious determinism is the base of psychoanalytic counseling. Counseling leading to catharsis then leads to confronting the unconscious mind in ways which promote learning, understanding, and growth in mental development and coping skills.

Freud viewed people as basically evil and victims of instincts that must be balanced or reconciled with social forces to provide a structure in which human beings can function. To achieve balance, people need a deep understanding of the forces that motivate them to action. According to Freud, people operate as energy systems, distributing psychic energy to the id, ego, and superego; human behavior is determined by this energy, by unconscious motives, and by instinctual and biological drives. Psychosexual events during the first 5 years of life are critical to adult personality development.

Sugarman (1977), in the belief that Freud's concept of human nature is often misinterpreted, presented a contrasting view of Freudian theory in which a humanistic image of people is recognized in the following eight ideas:

1. People have a dual nature, biological and symbolic.
2. People are both individuals and related to others simultaneously.
3. People strive for goals and values.
4. One of the strongest human needs is meaning in life.
5. One's internal world, including the unconscious, is more important than overt behavior.
6. People are social creatures whose need for interpersonal relationships is supreme.
7. People are always evolving, always in process.
8. People have a certain amount of autonomy within the constraints of reality.

In summary, according to psychoanalytic theory, the basic concepts of human nature revolve around the notions of psychic determinism and unconscious mental processes. Psychic determinism simply implies that our mental function or mental life is a continuous logical manifestation of causative relationships. Nothing is random; nothing happens by chance. Although mental events may appear unrelated, they are actually closely interwoven and dependent on preceding mental signals. Closely related to psychic determinism are unconscious mental processes, which exist as fundamental causative factors in the nature of human behavior. In essence, much of what goes on in our minds and hence our bodies is unknown, below the conscious level, so we often do not understand our feelings and/or actions. The existence of unconscious mental processes is the basis for much of what is involved in psychoanalytic counseling.

Freud believed that unresolved conflict, repression, and free-floating anxiety often go together. Painful and stressful conflicts that cannot be resolved in the conscious may be buried and forgotten in the unconscious. Later on, a person may experience anxiety that cannot be readily traced to any ongoing situation in the person's life. Relief from such anxiety may come only from accessing the unconscious and uncovering and resolving the original conflict. Recall and integration of repressed memories into one's conscious functioning often provide symptom relief from free-floating anxiety.

Freud also was interested in how people handled the tension of being pulled in opposite directions by the polarities in life. He saw people as born with the pleasure principle or the will to seek pleasure; however, people are confronted with an opposite force, the reality principle, which demands that the will to pleasure be bridled. The tension that results from being pulled in opposite directions by the pleasure principle and the reality principle becomes the essential, motivating force in one's life. People can either find productive ways to reduce the tension or give in to the tension and be destroyed by it. The task of humankind is to find a way to integrate the polarities into synergistic choices that neither compromise nor deny the opposing polarities. For example, taking your textbook to the beach on spring break may be an attempt to find a middle ground between doing what you want and what you should. A synergistic solution might be completing the work before leaving on the trip, which would likely result in higher

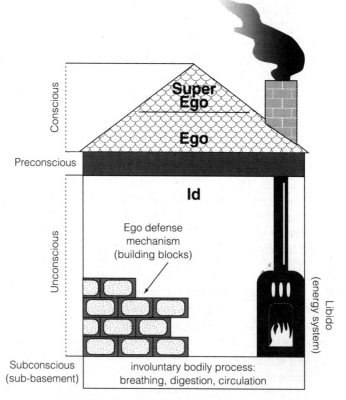

FIGURE 3-1 Freud's psychoanalytic model

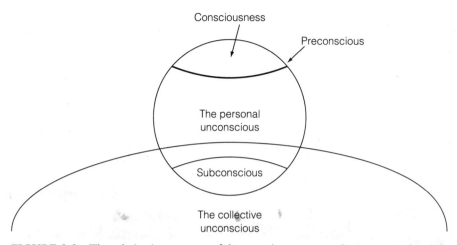

FIGURE 3-2   The relative importance of the conscious, preconscious, unconscious, subconscious, and collective unconscious

quality work and play. Living becomes a process of either mastering or succumbing to the tension resulting from life's polarities. A brief list of life's polarities is presented in chapter 6.

As noted in Figures 3-1 and 3-2, the *unconscious* holds about 85% of the material in our minds. The concept of the unconscious is the foundation of psychoanalytic theory and practice. It holds that, in a part of the mind that we are not aware of, drives, desires, attitudes, motivations, and fantasies exist and exert influence on how people think, feel, and behave in the conscious area of functioning. The *conscious* refers to the part of mental activity that we are aware of at any given time. The *preconscious* refers to thoughts and material that are not readily available to the conscious but can be retrieved with some effort. Students may struggle to find an answer to a test question lost in the preconscious. The *subconscious* refers to those involuntary bodily processes such as digestion and breathing that have been with the person since birth. Carl Jung's *collective unconscious* refers to the vast reservoir of inherited wisdom, memories, and insights that we share with all humankind (see Figure 3-2).

THEORY OF COUNSELING

Freud's concepts of personality form the basis of a psychoanalytic counseling theory. The principal concepts in Freudian theory can be grouped under three topic headings: structural, dynamic, and developmental. The structural concepts are id, ego, and superego. The dynamic concepts are instinct, cathexis, anticathexis, and anxiety. The developmental concepts are defense mechanisms and psychosexual stages.

Structural Concepts

Freud believed human behavior resulted from the interaction of three important parts of the personality: id, ego, and superego.

Id.   The id contains our basic instinctual drives, including thirst, hunger, sex, and aggression. These drives can be constructive or destructive. Constructive, pleasure-seeking (sexual) drives provide the basic energy of life (libido). In Freud's system, anything pleasurable is labeled sexual. Destructive, aggressive drives tend toward self-destruction and death. Life instincts are opposed by death instincts. The id, working on the pleasure principle, exists to provide immediate gratification of any instinctual need, regardless of the consequences. The id is not capable of thought but can form, for example, mental pictures of hamburgers for a hungry person. The formation of such images and wishes is referred to as *fantasy* and *wish fulfillment* (the *primary process*).

Ego.   Often called the "executive" of the personality, the ego strives to strike a balance between the needs of the id and the reality of the external world and transforms the mental images formed by the id (the hamburgers, for example) into acceptable behavior (purchasing a hamburger). These reality-oriented, rational processes of the ego are referred to as the *secondary process*. The ego, operating under the *reality principle*, is in line with environmental constraints and adjusts behavior to meet these constraints.

Superego.   Composed of two parts—the *ego ideal* (developed from the child's idea of what parents and significant others thought was good) and the *conscience* (what parents and significant others thought was bad)—the superego is, in essence, a personal moral standard. Often thought of as the judicial branch of the personality, the superego can act to restrict, prohibit, and judge conscious actions.

In summary, the id, the basic unit in Freud's personality structure, contains the basic human instincts plus each person's genetic and constitutional inheritance. As a result of interacting with reality, the id developed a liaison between itself and the environment that Freud labeled the ego. The ego's primary mission is self-preservation, which is accomplished by mediating the demands of the id (instinctual demands) with the realities of the environment. The well-functioning ego is able to achieve the right balance between seeking pleasure and avoiding the consequences of immoderate infringement on the societal rules and mores. As noted in Figure 3-3, children are generally dependent on their parents to a large extent during the first two decades of their lives. During this time, the ego develops a superego that continues the parents' influence over the remainder of the person's lifetime. Within the superego are two subsystems: the conscience and the ego-ideal. The conscience holds the parents' conceptions about what is bad; the ego-ideal holds the parents' conceptions about what is good. The ego is left with the task of mediating a balance between the demands of the id, superego, and reality.

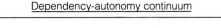

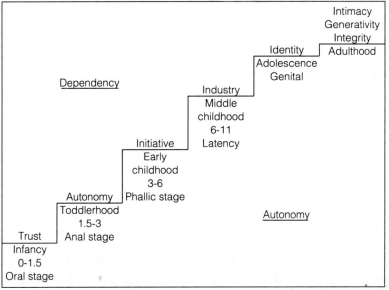

FIGURE 3-3   Developmental stages and the dependency-autonomy continuum

Dynamic Concepts

Instinct.   An instinct is an inborn psychological representation, referred to as a *wish,* which stems from a physiological condition referred to as a *need.* For example, hunger is a need that leads to a wish for food. The wish becomes a motive for behavior. Life instincts serve to maintain the survival of the species. Hunger, thirst, and sex needs are served by life instincts. Freud believed that human behavior is motivated by basic instincts.

Libido.   Libido is the energy that permits life instincts to work.

Cathexis.   Cathexis refers to directing one's energy toward an object that will satisfy a need.

Anticathexis.   Anticathexis refers to the force the ego exerts to block or restrain impulses of the id. The reality principle or superego directs this action of the ego against the pleasure principle emanating from the id.

Anxiety.   Anxiety refers to a conscious state in which a painful emotional experience is produced by external or internal excitation—a welling up of autonomic nervous energy. Closely akin to fear, but more encompassing, is the anxiety that originates from internal as well as external causes. Freud believed there were three types of anxiety: reality, neurotic, and moral. Reality anxiety results from real threats from the environment. Neurotic anxiety results from the fear that our instinctual impulses from the id will overpower our ego controls and get us into trouble. Moral anxiety results from the guilt we feel when we fail to live up to our standards.

Developmental Concepts

Defense Mechanisms

The ego protects itself from heavy pressure and anxiety with defense mechanisms. Patton and Meara (1991) pointed out that defenses are any operations of the mind that aim to ward off anxiety and depression. The healthy, high-functioning ego attempts to cope with anxiety, depression, and stress with effective, reality-based, task-oriented coping skills. When the load becomes too heavy, the ego may resort to defense-oriented coping methods that provide short-term relief but deny or distort reality and generally cause more problems in the long run.

Clark (1991) defined *defense mechanisms* as unconscious distortions of reality that reduce painful affect and conflict through automatic, habitual responses. Defense mechanisms are specific, unconscious, adjustive efforts used to resolve conflict and provide relief from anxiety. Counselors are generally able to detect their clients' defense mechanisms. Borrowing from Clark, we have provided examples of how an underachieving child might express a preference or lifestyle built around one, two, or a combination of defense mechanisms.

Identification.   Identification refers to the development of role models that people identify with or imitate. They may choose to imitate either a few traits of the model or the total person. Identification often occurs with the same-sex parent and may be born out of love or power, for example, "I love Dad so much I want to be just like him" or "If I can't beat him, I'll join him until I get big too." The underachieving child might say, "I know a high school student who dropped out and is making a lot of money. He says school is a waste of time."

Displacement.   Displacement means redirecting energy from a primary object to a substitute when an instinct is blocked. For example, anger toward a parent may be directed toward a sibling or another object because of the fear of reprisal from the parent. The underachieving child might say, "The stuff we study is so boring I'll never make good grades." The child may be redirecting hostile feelings from the teacher to the subject matter.

Repression and suppression.   Repression forces a dangerous memory, conflict, idea, or perception out of the conscious into the unconscious and places a lid on it to prevent the repressed material from resurfacing. In repression, the person unconsciously bars a painful thought from memory. Suppression is a conscious effort to do the same thing. An underachieving child might have repressed painful memories about failure in a prior school experience.

Projection.   Projection consists of attributing one's own characteristics to others or to things in the external world. For instance, a teacher may find it uncomfortable to admit he does not like the children in his class, so instead he says the children do not like him. Thus, he projects his dislike for his students onto the students. An underachieving child may say, "My teacher doesn't like me; he thinks I'm stupid."

Reaction formation.   Reaction formation refers to the development of attitudes or character traits exactly opposite to ones that have been repressed. Anxiety-producing impulses are replaced in the conscious by their opposites; for example, "I love booze" is replaced by "Liquor should be declared illegal." An underachieving child may say, "I don't want to be a nerd; nerds suck up to the teacher just to make good grades."

Rationalization.   Rationalization is an attempt to prove that one's behavior is justified and rational and is thus worthy of approval by oneself and others. When asked why they behaved in a certain manner, children may feel forced to think up logical excuses or reasons. An underachieving child may say, "I could finish my homework if my little brother would stop bothering me."

Denial.   Denial is a refusal to face unpleasant aspects of reality or to perceive anxiety-provoking stimuli. Children may deny the possibility of falling while climbing high trees. An underachieving child may say, "Things are going fine; my grades will be much higher this time." Counselors need to remember that denial is common in young children but is maladaptive for adolescents.

Fantasy.   Fantasy is a way of seeking gratification of needs and frustrated desires through the imagination. A fantasy or imagined world may be a more pleasant place than a child's real world. An underachieving child may say, "Just wait, one of these days I'll become a doctor and show that teacher. She'll be sorry she made fun of my bad test score."

Withdrawal.   Withdrawal means reducing ego involvement by becoming passive or learning to avoid being hurt; examples of withdrawn children include the shy child or school-phobic child. A withdrawn, underachieving child will probably not say much as he or she tries to avoid "risky" situations.

Intellectualization.   Intellectualization is the act of separating the normal affect, or feeling, from an unpleasant or hurtful situation; for example, a child whose dog has been hit by a car might soften his or her grief by saying, "Our dog is really better off dead; he was feeble and going blind." An underachieving child may say,

"I learn best from doing things outside school," or "I don't learn from the boring things we do at school."

Regression.   Regression is a retreat to earlier developmental stages that are less demanding than those of the present level. An older child may revert to babyish behavior when a baby arrives in the family. An underachieving child may say, "All we do is work; recess and lunch should be longer."

Fixation.   Fixation differs from regression in that the individual does not always regress to a more pleasant stage of development to avoid the pain or stress in a current developmental stage but rather might decide to remain at the present level of development rather than move to the next stage, which poses more difficulties and problems to solve. The tendency is to stay with a situation that is pleasurable and comfortable and in which the person has been successful. Counselors are often confronted with dependent, underachieving children who have a difficult time, first, in developing alternative problem solutions and, second, in making commitments to try their new alternatives.

Undoing.   Undoing is engaging in some form of atonement for immoral or bad behavior or for the desire to participate in such behavior. For instance, after breaking a lamp, a child may try to glue it back together. An underachieving child may say, "I get in a lot of arguments with my teacher, but I always try to do something to make up for it."

Acting out.   Acting out means reducing the anxiety aroused by forbidden desires by expressing them. The behavior of a revenge-seeking child is one example. An underachieving child may engage in violence, vandalism, or theft to express forbidden hurt feelings.

Compensation.   Compensation means covering up a weakness by emphasizing some desirable trait or reducing frustration in one area of life by overgratification in another area; for example, the class clown may compensate for poor academic performance by engaging in attention-getting behavior. An underachiever may be an attention-getting clown of the first order or may overachieve in another area to compensate for low grades (for example, sports, hobbies, or gang activities).

Sublimation.   Sublimation has often been referred to as the backbone of civilization. Through it, people redirect their libidinal desires and energy into productive and acceptable activities and outlets. Often the products of this redirected energy have resulted in significant advances in the arts, sciences, quality of life, and civilization in general. We might speculate that surgeons and butchers found more useful and acceptable outlets for their libidinal desires than did Jack the Ripper. Parents and teachers would do well to help children find productive outlets for their great energy. An underachieving child does not need a lot of unstructured time to fill with negative addictions such as television, gang activity, overeating, and drugs.

Psychosexual Stages

Freud (1940/1949) viewed personality development as a succession of stages, each characterized by a dominant mode of achieving libidinal pleasure and by specific developmental tasks. How well one adjusts at each stage is the critical factor in development. Freud believed that personality characteristics are fairly well established by the age of 6. Gratification of need during each stage is important if the individual is not to become fixated at that level of development. The key to successful adjustment in each stage is how well parents help their child adjust to the stage and make the transition to the next stage. The difficulty with Freud's system comes when counselors emphasize the extremes rather than the normal range of behaviors. The key seems to lie in maintaining a balance between extremes. The five developmental stages are oral, anal, phallic, latency, and genital.

Oral stage (birth–1½ years). The oral-erotic substage is characterized by the sucking reflex, which is necessary for survival. The child's main task in the oral-sadistic substage is to adjust to the weaning process and learn to chew food. The mouth is characterized as an erogenous zone because one obtains pleasure from sucking, eating, and biting. Adult behaviors, such as smoking, eating, and drinking, and the personality traits of gullibility, dependency (oral-erotic), and sarcasm (oral-sadistic) originate in the oral period.

Anal stage (1½–3 years). During this time, the membrane of the anal region presumably provides the major source of pleasurable stimulation. There are anal-expulsive and anal-retentive substages. The major hurdle is the regulation of a natural function (bowel control). Toilet training requires the child to learn how to deal with postponing immediate gratification. Again, the manner in which the parents facilitate or impede the process forms the basis for a number of adult personality traits. Stubbornness, stinginess, and orderliness (anal-retentive) and generosity and messiness (anal-expulsive) are among adult traits associated with the anal stage.

Phallic stage (3–6 years). Self-manipulation of the genitals provides the major source of pleasurable sensation, and the Oedipus complex occurs during this stage. The female version is sometimes referred to as the Electra complex. Sexual and aggressive feelings and fantasies are associated with the genitals. Boys have sexual desires for their mothers and aggressive feelings toward their fathers; girls develop hostility toward their mothers and become sexually attracted to their fathers. Attitudes toward people of the same sex and the opposite sex begin to take shape. Criticisms of Freud's castration complex concept range from labeling them ridiculous to calling them projections of his own fears. In any case, Freud believed that boys are afraid that their fathers will castrate them for loving their mothers. Girls' castration complexes were thought to take the form of penis envy; compensation for lacking a penis came with having a baby.

Latency stage (6–11 years).   Sexual motivations presumably recede in importance during the latency period as the child becomes preoccupied with developmental skills and activities. Children generally concentrate on developing same-sex friendships. Sexual and aggressive impulses are relatively quiet during this phase (As for aggression, Freud obviously never worked with a group of children in this age group).

Genital stage (Adolescence).   After puberty, the deepest feeling of pleasure presumably comes from heterosexual relations. The major task of this period is developing opposite-sex relationships, a risky task involving rejection and fear of rejection that has a tremendous impact on future heterosexual relationships.

Oral, anal, and phallic stages are classified as narcissistic because children derive pleasure from their own erogenous zones. During the genital stage, the focus of activity shifts to developing genuine relationships with others. The goal for the young person is to move from a pleasure-seeking, pain-avoiding, narcissistic child to a reality-oriented, socialized adult.

In summary, overgratification of the child's needs could result in the child becoming fixated at a particular stage; deprivation may result in regression to a more comfortable developmental stage. For example, a 3-year-old only child, suddenly finding a rival for his parents' attention in the form of a new baby sister, regresses to his pre–toilet training period in an effort to compete. Too much frustration in coping with a particular developmental stage could also result in fixating the child at that stage. Residue from regression and fixation may reappear in adult personality development.

Finding the healthy balance between unhealthy extremes is the key to mental health and a theme that runs throughout the book. Parents always have the difficult task of walking the thin line between too much and too little gratification of their child's needs. How much is too much or too little help in assisting a child in advancing to a new developmental stage? Perhaps the answer lies in the nurturing and preservation of the child's self-esteem, confidence, and trust.

Psychoanalytic counselors often search for repressed, traumatic events in the lives of their clients as possible causes for the symptoms and problems brought to counseling. Severe trauma is often associated with damaged egos, low self-esteem, and anxiety disorders; however, counselors can overlook the devastating effects on self-esteem of the daily onslaught of negative criticism heaped on some children throughout their developing years. Because such behavior falls short of legally being abuse and because it occurs in relatively small doses, it often goes unnoticed and unchecked. Therefore, we are presenting two systems for evaluating how well a child's self-esteem, mental health, and other personal needs are being cared for by the family and, to a great extent, by the school.

Simon (1988) presented six conditions for nurturing and maintaining self-esteem and mental health in children and adults. Self-esteem is a by-product of our productive activity and our relationships. It is not a goal that can be attained through self-affirmation activities. Programs designed to build self-esteem tend to fall short unless the participants take steps to improve their productivity and relationships. Freud believed that love and work are the keys to mental health. For children, the keys to mental health are their schoolwork and their relationships with family, peers, and other significant people.

Simon's (1988) six conditions complement the productivity and relationship equation for self-esteem.

Belonging: Children need to feel connected to their family or to a family of their own creation if the family of origin did not work out. As children grow older, they need to feel connected to a peer group.

Child advocacy: Children need at least one advocate who can be trusted to help them through crisis periods.

Risk management: Self-esteem increases as children are able to take risks and master challenging tasks. The difficulty is finding tasks that are challenging yet not impossible. Children need to believe that they are successful if they have given a task their best effort and that it is okay to take risks and fail.

Empowerment: Children need to exercise developmentally appropriate amounts of control over their own lives. Opportunities to make choices and decisions contribute to empowerment.

Uniqueness: Children need to feel they are special. Simon (1988) suggested that we work with children in constructing lists of 100 sentences validating their unique and positive qualities, which he calls "anti-suicide" lists.

Productivity: As children get things done, they feel better. Encouragement and reinforcement of productive activity can be useful in moving children toward finding intrinsic rewards in accomplishment.

Simon's six conditions are as relevant for adults as they are for children. Adding more risk to one's life can improve one's mental health, providing the risk falls within rational limits. Closely related to self-esteem is the degree to which children are meeting their other human needs.

Counseling children through Freud's five stages of development often requires an assessment of how well their basic needs are being met. A rating scale of 0 to 10 (0 for unmet needs and 10 for fully met needs) can be used to assess the child's progress in each level of Maslow's (1970) hierarchy, including self-esteem.

Child's Needs Assessment

	0	5	10
Physiological needs			
Nutrition, sleep, exercise, general health	0	5	10
Safety needs			
Safety within the family and peer group settings	0	5	10
Love and belonging needs	0	5	10
Affection shown to the child	0	5	10
Promises made and kept to the child			
Someone listens to the child	0	5	10
Family follows a dependable schedule	0	5	10
Child has own space, possessions, and a right to privacy	0	5	10
Someone is there when the child arrives home	0	5	10
Child is loved unconditionally	0	5	10
Self-esteem needs	0	5	10
Someone affirms the child's worth	0	5	10
Child is given the opportunity to achieve and accomplish tasks	0	5	10
Child is given the opportunity to make choices	0	5	10
Self-actualization needs	0	5	10
Child is not blocked by unmet needs in the previous four levels	0	5	10
Child is developing potential abilities and strengths	0	5	10
Child's problem-solving skills enable the child to engage in developmental rather than remedial activities	0	5	10

Problems in adult development are often traced to childhood frustration from failure to meet basic human needs during the developmental years. Psychoanalytic counseling can focus on the child's level of human needs attainment in past years as well as in the present. Questions of how children handle the pain of not getting what they want can be treated in psychoanalytic counseling. Are conflict and stress repressed in the unconscious or handled in the conscious area of functioning? Are depression and anxiety handled in task-oriented or defense-oriented ways? Both are good questions for psychoanalytic counselors to address.

Object Relations Theory

Love and work were important concepts in Freud's system. He believed that a quick assessment of mental health could be based on how well people were managing their relationships and careers. Object relations theory is a natural progression from his earlier work on how well children resolved the conflict surrounding competition with the same-sex parent for the love and attention of the opposite-sex parent. Object relations theory focuses on how early family relationships affect the type of relationships formed outside the family. For example, missing a solid father figure during her childhood years may motivate a woman to seek the love and attention she did not get from her father from older, fatherly types of men. Object relations theorists use the word *object* to refer to people other than the self. Family relationships that model appropriate and healthy models for future relationship development are the best assistance children can have in learning to build relationships outside the family. Children who receive proper nurturing during their dependent years do not seek parent figures in their adult relationships. Parents who facilitate their children's movement through the developmental stages toward the achievement of independence and identity provide them with blueprints for fulfilling and healthy adult relationships. As children begin differentiating themselves from their families, they carry their internalized view of how relationships operate to their peer group and eventually to their adult world. For example, a woman might carry a repressed image of her father as a hostile and rejecting person who did not provide the love and nurturing she needed and project this image of her father on all men in general. Seeing this hostile father image in her husband, she reacts accordingly, causing him to act out the hostile role of her father. Treatment for children educates parents to be better models of how to provide the right amounts of love and nurturing. Treatment for adults accesses the unconscious to find the history of the unresolved conflicts with their parents and to find out how the repressed conflicts contribute to their difficulties in establishing and maintaining the relationships they would like to have.

COUNSELING METHODS

The primary goal of counseling within a psychoanalytic frame of reference is to make the unconscious conscious. All material in the unconscious was once in the conscious. Repressed material that has been brought to the conscious level can be dealt with in rational ways by using any number of methods discussed in this book.

Several methods are used to uncover the unconscious. Detailed case histories are taken, with special attention given to the handling of conflict areas. Hypnosis, although rejected by Freud, is still used to assist in plumbing the unconscious. Analyses of resistance, transference, and dreams are frequently used methods, as are catharsis, free association, interpretation, and play therapy. All these methods have the long-term goal of strengthening the ego. The principal counseling methods discussed in this chapter are catharsis, free association, interpretation, analysis of transference, analysis of resistance, analysis of incomplete sentences, bibliocounseling, storytelling, and play therapy.

Catharsis

Freud, along with Breuer, first discovered the benefits of catharsis through hypnosis. Freud found that if, under hypnosis, hysterical patients were able to verbalize an early precipitating causal event, the hysterical symptoms disappeared. Freud soon discarded hypnosis because he was not able to induce in everyone the deep hypnotic sleep that enabled the patient to regress to an early enough period to disclose the repressed event. Freud discovered that for many people the mere command to remember the origin of some hysterical symptom worked quite well. Unfortunately, many of his patients could not remember the origin of their symptoms even upon command. Freud thus decided that all people were aware of the cause of their illness but that for some reason certain people blocked this knowledge. Freud believed that unless this repressed traumatic infantile experience could be retrieved from the unconscious, verbalized, and relived emotionally, the patient would not recover. Because not everyone had the ability to find this unconscious material, the analyst had to use more indirect means to gain access to the unconscious mind. Freud developed free association and interpretation to bring everyone to the emotional state of catharsis that was necessary for cure.

Free Association

In traditional psychoanalysis, the client lies on a couch with the analyst sitting at the head of the couch beyond the client's line of vision. The analyst then orders the client to say whatever comes to mind. Through this means, the unconscious thoughts and conflicts are given freedom to reach the conscious mind. A great struggle takes place within the client to keep from telling one's innermost thoughts to the analyst. The analyst must constantly struggle against this resistance. The fundamental rule of psychoanalytic counseling requires clients to tell the counselor whatever thoughts and feelings come into their minds, regardless of how personal, painful, or seemingly irrelevant.

While the client is trying to associate freely, the counselor must remain patient, nonjudgmental, and insistent that the client continue. The counselor must also look for continuity of thoughts and feelings. Although the client may appear to be rambling idly, psychoanalytic counselors believe there is a rational pattern to this speech. To interpret what the client is saying, the counselor must pay attention to the affect, or feeling, behind the client's verbalization, noting the client's gestures, tone of voice, and general body language during free association. The counselor, at this point, offers some interpretations of the client's statements to try to open another door for free association.

Interpretation

Free association, in turn, leads to another important technique—interpretation. Three major areas of interpretation are dreams, parapraxia, and humor.

Interpretation of dreams. To Freud, dreams expressed wish fulfillment. To correctly interpret the power of the id, the analyst must learn about and interpret the client's dreams. According to Freud, there are three major types of dreams: those with meaningful, rational content (almost invariably found in children), those with material very different from waking events, and those with illogical, senseless episodes. According to Freud, all dreams center around a person's life and are under the person's psychic control. Every dream reveals an unfulfilled wish. In children's dreams, the wish is usually very obvious. As the individual matures, the wish, as exposed in the dream, becomes more distorted and disguised. Freud said that the ego fights the initial conscious wish, which thus is pushed back to the unconscious mind; it brings itself back into the conscious mind by means of a dream.

According to Freud, the dream guards against pain, and humor serves to acquire pleasure. When people are sleeping, repressive defenses are lower, and forbidden desires and feelings can find an outlet in dreams. Freud referred to dreams as the royal road to the unconscious. The counselor's role is to listen to the client's dream and help the client by interpreting the dream's symbolism.

Freud's method of dream interpretation was to allow the client to free associate about the dream's content. Certain objects in dreams were universal symbols for Freud. For example, a car in someone's dreams usually represented analysis, the number 3 represented male genitals, jewel cases and purses were vaginas, peaches and twin sisters were female breasts, woods were pubic hair, trees and steeples were penises, and dancing, riding, and flying were symbols for sexual intercourse. Dreams about falling are related to fears about falling from one's moral standards.

Freud (1901/1952) believed every dream to be a confession and a by-product of repressed, anxiety-producing thoughts. Freud thought that many dreams represented unfulfilled sexual desires and that many expressed the superego's guilt and self-punishment. Nightmares result from the desire for self-punishment. Because we are consciously and unconsciously aware of those things that we fear most, we put these things into our nightmares to punish ourselves.

Parapraxia. Parapraxia, or "Freudian slips," are consciously excused as harmless mistakes, but through them the id pushes unconscious material through to the conscious. The counselor must be very aware of any slips of the tongue while dealing with a client. The Freudians also believe there are no such things as "mistakes" or items that are "misplaced." According to psychoanalytic thinking, everything we do—forgetting a person's name, cutting a finger while peeling potatoes—has unconscious motivation. The analyst must take all these unconscious mistakes and arrange them into a conscious pattern.

Humor.   Jokes, puns, and satire are all acceptable means for unconscious urges to gain access to the conscious. The things we laugh about tell us something about our repressed thoughts. One of the fascinations of humor, according to psychoanalytic theory, is that it simultaneously disguises and reveals repressed thoughts. Repressed thoughts, released by humor, usually generate from the id or superego. Because sexual thoughts are usually repressed, many jokes are sexually oriented; because aggressive thoughts are usually repressed, they are expressed in humor by way of satire and witticisms.

Again, the counselor must watch for patterns and themes. What does the client think is funny? How does the client's sense of humor fit into a pattern from the unconscious?

Analysis of Transference

Transference occurs when the client views the counselor as someone else. Freud was genuinely surprised when his patients first regarded him as someone other than an analyst, helper, or adviser. During the course of psychoanalytic counseling, clients usually transfer their feelings about some significant individual from the past to their therapist. Transference generally is a product of unfinished business with a significant person from the client's childhood. Clients commonly transfer their feelings, thoughts, and expectations about the significant other to the counselor. Counseling provides a stage for reenacting unresolved conflicts with the counselor, who can help clients deal with them in more effective and functional ways. Transference relationships can become a real battleground when love feelings directed toward the counselor are rejected and the client, in turn, rejects the counselor by resisting the counselor's every effort to be helpful. Both transference and resistance can be analyzed for cause-and-effect implications for the client's life. Countertransference occurs when the counselor begins to view a client as someone other than a client. Referral to another competent professional is recommended for a counselor who loses his or her balance on the objectivity-empathy continuum.

Analysis of Resistance

Freud was also surprised by the amount of resistance his patients mounted against his attempts to help them. Resistance took the form of erecting barriers to free association, thus breaking Freud's rule against censoring or holding back material; Freud's patients were often unwilling or unable to talk about some of their thoughts during free association or descriptions of their dreams. Resistance prevents painful and irrational content from reaching the conscious, and must be eliminated in order for the person to have the opportunity to face and react to these repressed conflicts in realistic and healthy ways. Therefore, the essential task of any counselor is building a trusting relationship with clients that undermines their need to resist the counselor's attempts to be helpful. Analysis of resistance can also provide valuable information regarding the client's need to withhold information from the counselor.

Analysis of Incomplete Sentences

Psychoanalytic counselors often use projective techniques such as the House/ Tree/Person or Children's Apperception Test in an attempt to understand their clients' thoughts, behaviors, and feelings. For counselors not trained in test interpretation, asking children to complete stimulus statements about likes, dislikes, family, friends, goals, wishes, and things that make the child happy or sad helps counselors understand children and find problem areas. This procedure may be especially helpful in assisting counselors to become acquainted with children and to establish better rapport with those who are anxious, fearful, or reluctant to talk.

Examples

The thing I like to do most is _____ .
The person in my family who helps me most is _____ .
My friends are _____ .
I feel happiest (or saddest) when _____ .
My greatest wish is _____ .
The greatest thing that ever happened to me was _____ .
I wish my parents would _____ .
When I grow up, I want _____ .
Brothers are _____ .
Sisters are _____ .
Dad is _____ .
Mom is _____ .
School is _____ .
My teacher is _____ .

Bibliocounseling

Bibliocounseling—reading and discussing books about situations and children similar to themselves—can help clients in several ways. Children unable to verbalize their thoughts and feelings may find them expressed in books. From selected stories, children can learn alternative solutions to problems and new ways of behaving; by reading about children similar to themselves, clients may not feel so alone or different.

In an article citing the benefits of bibliocounseling for abused children, Watson (1980) suggested that children may become psychologically and emotionally involved with characters they have read about. Vicarious experiences through books can be similar to the child's own thoughts, feelings, attitudes, behavior, or environment. Directed reading can lead to expression of feelings or problem solving. Watson listed the goals of bibliotherapy as (1) teaching constructive and positive thinking, (2) encouraging free expression concerning problems, (3) helping clients analyze their attitudes and behaviors, (4) looking at alternative solutions, (5) encouraging the client to find a way to cope that is not in conflict with society, and (6) allowing clients to see the similarity of their problems to those of others.

With bibliocounseling, discussion focused around characters' behaviors, feelings, thoughts, relationships, cause and effect, and consequences is more effective than just asking the child to relate the story. Discussion also clears up questions that arise from the reading. Counselors can guide children to see how the story applies to their own lives.

Bibliocounseling is also a means of educating children about certain areas of concern such as sex, physical disabilities, divorce, and death. Once children have enough information about a problem, their attitudes and behaviors tend to change. Books suggested for bibliocounseling with exceptional children and children with special concerns are listed at the end of chapters 15 and 16.

Storytelling

Richard Gardner developed the Mutual Storytelling Technique as a therapeutic means for working with children (Schaefer & Cangelosi, 1993). It uses a familiar technique to assist children in understanding their own thoughts and feelings and to communicate meaningful insights, values, and standards of behavior to children. The counselor sets the stage and asks the child to tell a story, which is recorded on tape. The counselor instructs the child that the story should have a beginning, a middle, and an ending and that the child will be asked to tell the moral (lesson) of the story at the end. The counselor may need to clarify some points of the story after the child has finished. The counselor then prepares a story using a similar theme and setting and including the significant figures from the child's story. The counselor's story, however, provides the child with better alternatives or responses to the situation.

We have found storytelling to be an excellent counseling technique to help children cope with feelings, thoughts, and behaviors they are not yet ready to discuss in a direct manner with the counselor. Storytelling has also been useful in helping children realize possible consequences of their behavior. (See the case study of Pete later in this chapter.)

In examining mutual storytelling as a viable therapeutic method, Kestenbaum (1985) presented three cases. In two cases, the child dictated the stories and the teacher wrote them down. In the third case, the child spoke into a tape recorder as though an original radio play were being produced. Transcripts from each case were typed, and the tapes were listened to during subsequent sessions. Story plots and characters were found to parallel events in the children's lives. The children's answers to questions about the characters, their backgrounds, and their motives were recorded for use in future sessions.

Lawson (1987) presented a helpful method of using a story within a story in working with an overweight 8-year-old girl who was acting out in an attempt to handle rejection by her peers. The therapist told a story about a similar girl who had no friends. No name was used in the story, but the counselor mentioned the client's name in nearly every sentence; for example, the counselor would say, "Ann, I once knew a little girl . . . ." Next, the counselor began another story within a story with the same theme: "Ann, this little girl had a dream about a little brown, black, and white puppy who had no friends because she was different than the other puppies who were all white, all black, or all brown." The second story worked out a solution around the theme that being different and special is good. When the girl wakes from her dream about the puppy, she is excited about being special and can hardly wait to take her new feelings to school because, as in the puppy story, what the other children thought about her did not matter as long as she felt special.

PLAY THERAPY AND THE EXPRESSIVE ARTS

Play is a universal activity that people of all ages need. Both spectator and participative play and recreation activities fill important human needs. Play provides needed change from our daily routines, whether they are in school or in the work world. Play provides opportunities to work through emotional problems and release pent-up emotions on the court or on the field in ways that are acceptable to society. Play allows rest for our bodies and minds. Play has been identified as preparation for adulthood in that it provides children with a medium in which to act out the roles they will live as or hope to live as adults: spouse, parent, hero, doctor, lawyer, and star athlete. The theory has even been advanced that play provides a theater for children to reenact the drama of the development of civilization. Young children begin learning about the "not me" world by biting, hitting, and pushing anything and anyone they can without regard to consequences and rules. Gradually, as children move through the socialization process, they do approximate, in brief form, the steps humankind took in moving from primitive to advanced civilizations.

From a Freudian view, play provides the medium for moving through the five psychosexual stages and the corresponding development of the ego and superego superstructures from the id structure. Exercise of the pleasure principle, such as hitting, biting, pushing others, and doing what one pleases, gradually comes up against the reality principle, which tells the child that games have rules and that sometimes it is necessary and even best to postpone pleasurable activities. Play is useful in working through healthy identification with the same-sex and opposite-sex parent. The development of relationships with same-sex peers and, eventually, with opposite-sex friends is facilitated through play activities.

For children, play therapy is the treatment of choice for bringing both conscious and unconscious material into the counseling session. Play is the natural mode of communication for children. Limited verbal ability prevents children from being able to verbally express their thoughts, feelings, and behavior. Play is the natural way for children to express themselves and to learn about their world. Many counseling techniques, including the expressive arts of painting, drawing, playing and singing music, and dancing, can be used with play therapy to adapt the process to the particular child's developmental level. Of course, most general theories of counseling can be adapted to fit the play therapy setting. Some counselors are beginning to use dogs and other pets in their play therapy and regular sessions (Burton, 1995; Levinson, 1962; O'Brien, 1993; Trivedi & Perl, 1995).

As is true with the counselor's office, children must perceive the play therapy room as a safe place to discuss anything they wish without fear of criticism or punishment. The counselor's role is to interpret the child's symbolic play in words that are meaningful to the child. Successful play therapy should result in higher levels of self-esteem, communication, trust, confidence, and problem-solving ability (See chapter 12 for a full discussion and presentation of play therapy).

In summary, Freud viewed the personal unconscious as the repository of "the primitive, the antisocial, and the evil within us." Repressed below the conscious area of functioning, these three forces tend to cause anxiety and tension through conflicts that affect our behavior in negative ways. The solution is to bring these three forces into conscious awareness.

Psychoanalytic counselors are interested in accessing the personal unconscious to bring these repressed conflicts into conscious awareness, where they can be treated. The most common means of returning unconscious content to the conscious are dream interpretation, free association, analysis of resistance, analysis of transference, hypnosis, meditation, journaling, reflection, and analysis of slips of the tongue, selective remembering and forgetting, and accidents. Play therapy, in combination with the expressive acts, provides the preferred treatment modality for any theoretical orientation for younger children.

◆ ◆ ◆

C A S E　S T U D I E S

Identification of Problem I*

Dennis, age 9, was considered a disturbed, slow, resistant boy who had to be pushed into doing everything he was supposed to be doing. He rarely participated

---

* Michael Gooch contributed the case of Dennis.

in any family activities and had no friends in the neighborhood. His school records listed such problems as regression, playing with much younger children, thumb-sucking, daydreaming, soiling, bullying, and tardiness. An excerpt from the first counseling session begins with Dennis entering the playroom.

Transcript

Dennis: Well, what are we going to do today?

Counselor: Whatever you'd like. This is your time.

Dennis: Let's talk.

Counselor: All right.

Dennis: Let's go back in history. We're studying about it in school. I'm going to be studying about Italy next week. I can't think of anything to talk about. I can't think of one thing to say. Can you?

Counselor: I'd rather discuss something you suggest.

Dennis: I can't think of a thing.

Counselor: We can just sit here if you like.

Dennis: Good. Do you want to read?

Counselor: Okay.

Dennis: You be the student, and I'll be the teacher. I'll read to you. Now you be ready to answer some questions. I don't like spelling. I like social studies, and I like history more than any other subject. I'd like being the teacher for a change. [Dennis asks counselor questions from a reading text.]

Counselor: You like to ask questions you think I'll miss.

Dennis: That's right. I'm going to give you a test next week. A whole bunch of arithmetic problems, and social studies, and other questions. Now, I'm going to read like my friend does . . . Notice how he reads?

Counselor: He seems to read fast without pausing.

Dennis: Yes.

Counselor: You'd like to be able to read like that.

Dennis: Not much. Let's name the ships in the books. [Dennis names each type of boat.] I have so much fun making up those names. That's what we'll do next week. [Dennis begins reading again.] Stop me when I make a mistake or do something wrong.

Counselor: I'd rather you stop yourself.

Dennis: The teacher always stops me.

Counselor: I'm a listener, not a teacher.

Dennis: Be a teacher, all right? [Dennis begins reading again.] That reminds me, I have three darts at home. The set cost me three dollars. Two have been broke. [The session is about to end. Counselor examines some darts and a board.] Oh boy, darts. Maybe we can play with them next week.

Counselor: You're making lots of plans for next time.

Dennis: Yeah.

Several counseling sessions followed this one. Dennis showed marked improvement at school and at home. Dennis's mother and teacher spoke more positively of him.

◆ ◆ ◆ ◆ ◆ ◆ ◆ ◆ ◆

Comments

The counselor gave Dennis his complete, undivided attention, participating in his games, tasks, projects, and plans. Here was someone with whom Dennis could talk and share his interests and ideas at a time when no one else would understand and accept him. He needed someone who would let him lead the way and be important in making decisions and plans. Dennis played the role of the initiator, the director, the teacher. He needed to have someone else know how it felt to be the follower who is told what to do, ordered into activity, and made to meet expectations. He needed to gain respect as well as confidence in his ability to face tasks and problems and see them through successfully. In short, he used the therapy experience to improve his relationships and his skills. He became a competent, self-dependent person by practicing behavior that gave him a sense of adequacy and self-fulfillment.

Identification of Problem II*

A family sought therapy for problems with Pete, their rebellious 12-year-old son. The boy and his younger sister had been adopted 5 years earlier after a series of foster care arrangements. The adopting couple had no children before the adoption.

A history-gathering first session with the adoptive parents revealed that Pete had been physically abused by his biological mother and by at least one subsequent foster mother. The parents described Pete as rebellious and disrespectful, especially toward his mother. During the second session, the counselor met separately with Pete to establish rapport and continue assessing the context of the presenting problem. Although the boy was 12 years old, his social and emotional development appeared to be more like that of a 6- or 7-year-old. The counselor wanted to help Pete feel comfortable, as well as to elicit more information about his inner thoughts. With these objectives in mind and in view of Pete's apparent developmental stage, the counselor asked him to draw a picture of a person. Pete drew a hypermuscular, threatening-looking young adult (Figure 3-4). Then the counselor asked Pete to make up a story about the picture. Pete then told the following story. Note how the story's themes metaphorically describe Pete's experiences and his frustrated efforts to cope with them.

---

* The case of Pete was contributed by Robert Lee Whitaker, Ph.D., and is reprinted by permission.

FIGURE 3-4   Pete's drawing (reprinted by permission)

Pete's Story

He was born in a hollow tree. His mom was a dog; his dad was a cat. He was green, and he was the strongest person who ever lived. People called him Starman. He could throw a car, and it wouldn't come down for a week.

Then one day he met a baby. The baby had a race with him in the Olympics and beat him. The baby asked if he thought he could beat him again. For 2 years, they competed, and the baby always won. So the guy trained for 2 more years to beat the baby, but by that time, the baby was so big his head went out of the earth. He could jump out of the earth. The guy knew he couldn't do anything about it, so he retired and went off to be a wimp and was never seen again. There were stories that he was beat up, killed, shot. And that was the last they saw of him.

A week later, the counselor asked Pete to tell the story of Starman's early life.

He lived in a jungle and helped his dad fight off the beasts that tried to attack his family. He's been alive 300 billion years. He was a god and a very powerful prince of the world then. His dad was the king. The prince made up the rules for the kingdom (which was communist). People could only work when the prince wanted them to work, and no family could have over $700. If so, they had to see him, and they couldn't leave the country.

The queen was named Laura. She was as skinny as a toothpick, and she was so powerful she could make it rain or snow or any kind of weather when she wanted. She could make people feel like they were dying and could make them grow old real fast. She could make them have nine lives or make them look ugly. She could change their bodies into beasts. She was very wicked.

The prince didn't like her because she was trying to overrule him and get all the power he had. So, the prince got all the other gods in all the world or universe and his dad and formed all their powers together and killed her. When she died, she turned into a planet called Saturn (her remains). The queen is dead now.

The prince grew up, and his dad died because of Zeus. Zeus gave him poison, and the prince was in charge from then on, except for Zeus (the god over all). The prince enforced all the laws the same way the lady did, and Zeus threatened to kill him. The lady had enforced the laws because Zeus threatened to kill her. The prince killed her because he didn't like the rules and what she was doing to the people, but he didn't know Zeus was making her do it by threatening to kill her.

The prince went on doing things the way Zeus wanted until he died. Now he is just a strong person.

Interpreting the Story

This story suggested to the counselor a need to explore issues of anger and powerlessness with Pete. "Starman," or "the prince," felt powerless against the exceptional power and influence of the queen and the baby. Queen "Laura" had absolute control over the environment and could make whatever kind of weather she wanted (usually bad), make people grow old quickly, make them experience a feeling of death, make them ugly, and even turn them into beasts. Leadership, no matter who was in power, was always threateningly authoritarian. The prince's battle for power or control is described as a violent act against the leader, made possible by combining the power of all oppressed victims.

The story appears to reflect the trauma of Pete's upbringing and the particularly negative feelings he has toward females with power over him. Further, the story seems to parallel closely his history of abuse and development into an aggressive person involved in a power struggle with his adoptive mother. The information elicited from the story alerted the counselor to Pete's experience of the reported historical events. It is unlikely that Pete could have conveyed the impact of his history and its present relevance to his life in a form more insightful and descriptively meaningful than the story he told.

Intervention

On the basis of the initial assessment interview with Pete's parents and the issues identified within the story, the counselor chose the following initial interventions: First, he decided to continue combining direct assessment procedures with picture-drawing and storytelling strategies to identify additional problematic areas for Pete. Second, the counselor began formulating a story to be used later about an abused person or animal who learned to adapt to a new environment by gradually learning to trust. Third, he asked Pete's permission to share with Pete's parents the story and the counselor's impressions of it. He then used the story to show the parents the relationship between Pete's present behavior and the trauma of his early experiences. The parents appeared to expect Pete to behave like any normal 12-year-old and not manifest any significant behavioral deficits related to the care he received during the first 7 years of his life. The counselor suggested that

Pete was attempting to cope with these early experiences and that Pete's parents might be able to help him and themselves by reconsidering the long-range impact of such an experience, adjusting their expectations, mutually deciding upon and concentrating on just a few rules, giving Pete choices within limits they could accept, and selecting the roles each of them wanted to serve in Pete's life in light of what the story might suggest. Finally, the counselor suggested they try an experiment to begin their exploration of the new roles they wished to assume in Pete's life by letting the mother have a vacation from her job as the primary disciplinarian.

Rationale

The therapeutic intentions of this plan were, first, to reinforce consistency in the parents' rules and expectations; second, to empower Pete with choices his parents could accept; third, to empower Pete's mother by providing more involvement and support from his father in parenting; fourth, to foster an expectation of trust rather than distrust ("I know he'll do the right thing" instead of "I know he'll do the wrong thing"); fifth, to focus less on punishment and more on logical consequences for Pete's misbehavior; and, finally, to do away with any "mystery" rules or consequences.

RESEARCH AND APPLICATIONS

Just as Sigmund Freud was the father of psychoanalysis, he was the grandfather of child psychoanalysis. His therapy with adults conducted at the Vienna Psychoanalytic Institute was continuous and lengthy, often requiring several years to complete. A school for children was established adjacent to the institute. Anna Freud, Sigmund Freud's daughter, began to take a great interest in these children and eventually devoted herself almost exclusively to the study of children. She stands today as the outstanding pioneer in the field. The institute also trained other prominent child analysts, most notable among them Peter Blos, Marianne Kris, and Erik Erikson. Erikson is best known for his theory of sequenced tasks as the means to develop one's identity.

Supporting research and literature summaries in the area of child psychoanalysis include the following topics: the relationship, childhood depression, and counseling methods.

The Relationship

Maenchen (1970) saw the differences in technique between adult and child analytical psychotherapy lessening. She saw less reliance on play therapy, more emphasis on the therapist interpreting "the moment" with the child, and more use of verbal games to elicit free association. She also saw more emphasis being placed on the relationship between child and counselor. Pothier (1976) agreed with Maenchen by designating a special category for relationship therapy in her list of counseling methods.

Zelman, Samuels, and Abrams (1985), in an investigation of the effect of long-term psychoanalytic treatment on children diagnosed as having oppositional disorder of childhood (DSM-III) and developmental delays of expressive language, found that 10 of 11 children were able to improve their overall IQ scores from a mean of 84.9 to 112.8. All children had received the cornerstone therapeutic-nursery approach of having an analyst work one-on-one with the child in the classroom in conjunction with the teacher. Weekly therapy sessions, consisting of interpretative interactions, averaged 521 visits over 54 months. The mean age of the children was 44 months at the time of admission.

Bouman, Blix, and Coons (1985) presented a case study of a 14-year-old girl who developed multiple personalities after a family history of intercourse with her father. The authors point out that children who are physically and/or sexually abused may develop multiple personalities. Dissociation provides an effective way to cope with strong affects evoked by abuse. Reintegration of the dissociative mechanism protecting the ego was the treatment goal, and therapy was conducted over 13 months. Initial steps were directed toward building trust in the therapeutic relationship. Trust was built by providing help with routine teenage problems. Efforts were made to strengthen the child's tolerance of affect, and communication among personalities was encouraged while dissociation was discouraged. Hypnosis was used in the end to fuse all personalities.

Childhood Depression

Orbach (1986), in an article related to determinants of suicidal behavior in children, discussed the "insolvable problem" as a primary factor in children's feelings of being trapped and incapacitated. The characteristics of the "insolvable problem" may include one or more of the following: (1) a problem beyond the child's ability to resolve that is deeply rooted and long-standing in the life of the entire family; (2) limitation of solution alternatives, by the parents, down to only one possibility that is undesirable to the child; (3) a problem situation in which every resolution creates a new problem; and (4) a family problem that is disguised from the entire family, which brings pressure to bear on the child to blindly fight this invisible enemy.

Rosenthal, Rosenthal, Doherty, and Santora (1986) constructed a profile of nine depressed, hospitalized preschoolers. The children, ranging in age from 3½ to 5½, were admitted to a psychiatric hospital for suspected suicidal behaviors, self-injury, serious aggression toward others, and/or fire setting. Individual diagnostic-play assessments were made to clarify the psychodynamic ramifications of the ideation and intentionality of their behavior. DSM-III criteria and the

Preschool Depression Scale were also used in the assessment. All the suicidal children demonstrated long-standing suicidal thoughts and repeated self-injurious behavior associated with angry feelings. Comparing inpatients with outpatients, inpatients tended to exhibit more attention-getting behaviors (such as setting fires and putting ropes around their necks), whereas outpatient suicidals tended to exhibit behaviors that might look like accidents (such as running into traffic and jumping from high places). Causes of the depression were linked to parents who tended to be depriving, punitive, rejecting, depressed, and drug abusers.

Nelson and Crawford (1990) point out that the stresses once identified with adolescence have now become prevalent in the lives of children. Increases in stress also increase anxiety, depression, and suicide ideation. The authors, surveying counselors in 123 elementary schools, found that counselors reported having made contact with 187 students who were considering suicide during the school year. Parental loss through separation or divorce was cited as the number one cause of childhood suicide. Herring (1990) echoes Nelson and Crawford in an article on suicide among children in the middle school years. He pointed out that 200 suicides are committed annually in the United States by children younger than 14. Mentioning many of the stressors children face, Herring stated that depression stands apart from other psychological disorders in that suicide is often its tragic outcome.

Hart (1991) cited studies that show a 20 percent rate of depression among school-age children (5 to 12) and a 33 percent rate for other school-age populations. A 51 percent to 59 percent depression rate was cited for child-psychiatric settings. Hart offers several theoretical models explaining depression. Traditional psychoanalytic theory would not allow for childhood depression because children lack a judging, controlling superego. Lack of guilt and self-blame does not lead to depression. From the contemporary psychodynamic view, the child's depressive difficulties relate to loss of self-esteem from feelings of helplessness or loss. Losses range from loss of contact with a primary caregiver to less traumatic losses, both actual and perceived. Children often respond to feelings of helplessness and loss by swallowing their anger. Depression is the result of anger turned inward.

COUNSELING METHODS

Sachs (1991) compared adult psychoanalysis to play, where successful outcomes depend on voluntary engagement and participation. He made the point that if play is not voluntary, it ceases to be play. Similarly, he viewed psychoanalysis as being difficult if the play element is not present. In fact, he stated that psychoanalysis is one of the few games that has maintained the play spirit. Free association depends on spontaneous, uncensored engagement in voluntary play, and working through transference is an exercise in imagination and a form of role playing. Metaphors are useful in describing how the unconscious works. The primary rule in analysis is free association. If censorship occurs the rule is broken and progress stops. Rather than expelling the client from the game, an interpretation of the censorship is made which helps the client gain insight. Solnit (1987) added that play therapy allows us to suspend reality, thus allowing children to direct a make believe gratification for those areas found wanting in their lives. Frederickson (1991) wrote that to work with delusions in therapy, a client must realize that the delusion can be worked or played with and can be analyzed. He viewed delusions as a failed form of play. The client cannot separate delusion (fantasy) from reality. Those clients do not know how to play and must be taught if treatment is to work.

Trustin (1987) discussed some difficulties in doing play therapy with autistic children who do not know how to play or to trust. Trustin recommended that sessions be structured to be effective. It is good to have the child wait for the appointment in the waiting room until the counselor comes to take the child to the playroom. These steps help set the tone that the environment has limits and that the child does not have complete control over the elements in the environment. What the child does with person-represented objects, such as dolls, is regarded as valuable insight into the child's mind. Once the child recognizes a structured environment, communication with something outside their created world is possible and play therapy can be effective.

Everson and Boat (1990), working with 223 children between the ages of 2 and 5 years old, found that use of anatomically correct dolls was effective in doing sexual abuse evaluations. The children were asked to identify the body parts and to state their function. Finally the children were asked to show what the dolls could do together. It was concluded that the dolls were not overtly suggestive to nonabused, sexually naive children.

Kapsch (1991) was successful in using play therapy with a 7-year-old girl who had a history of psychosis and emotional, physical, and sexual abuse. The basic approach was focused on building communication, trust, and the relationship. Limits were set as a way to decrease her aggressive behaviors as she gradually developed the strength to interact with others.

Knittel (1990) provided some helpful strategies for directing psychodrama with adolescents, particularly those who have lived in chaotic and dysfunctional families. First, provide very structured directions stated clearly in an exact manner, with little room for other interpretations. Second, take charge of the session with confidence and an attitude of knowing how to run things. Third, keep the drama in the first person so it is effective in working through personal concerns. Fourth, do not let the drama terminate prematurely before the important objectives have been achieved. Fifth, maintain realistic expectations about the amount of information that will be shared and the amount of time needed for sharing to occur.

Researchers have found considerable support for using play therapy and the expressive arts in psychoanalytic counseling. Both play and the expressive arts, including psychodrama, allow thoughts and feelings in the unconscious to return to the conscious, where they can be treated, especially in children who have limited verbal skills and ability to reason by nature of their stage of cognitive development, be it the preoperational or concrete stage.

SUMMARY

Freud (1918) identified the task of analysts as bringing to patients' knowledge their unconscious, repressed material and uncovering the resistances that oppose this extension of their knowledge about themselves. He believed that frustration made his patients ill and that their symptoms served them as substitute satisfactions. Freud (1918) clearly noted the harm that may come to patients who receive too much help and consolation from their therapists but also pointed out that many patients lack the strength and general knowledge to handle their lives without some mentoring and instruction, in addition to analysis, from their therapists.

Rutter (1975) pointed to four modifications in analytic approaches to children: (1) a move to briefer treatment, which encourages clearer focus on problems, the setting of definite goals, and more definite strategies; (2) greater attention to conscious conflicts and current environmental stresses; (3) a shift away from treatment of the individual toward a focus on the family as a group; and (4) less preoccupation with the interpretation of intrapsychic mechanisms and a greater reliance on the counselor-child relationship itself as the main treatment agent. This last trend seems to have consensus support from professionals in the field. To Rutter's list we would add a fifth: using play therapy and the expressive arts in counseling children.

Freud's theory continues to be criticized for its lack of sound research support. Freud considered his theory of repression to be the cornerstone of the entire structure of psychoanalysis. However, Grünbaum (1993) noted that more research is needed to validate the link between such things as repressed childhood molestation and adult neurosis. He pointed out that a first event followed by a second event does not prove causality between the events. The theories of dreams and parapraxia also suffer from lack of hard data to prove causality.

In Freud's defense, much of his data collecting was similar to what passes today for acceptable, phenomenological research. In fact, data collecting through free association has many similarities to the open-ended, phenomenological interviewing method in which participants are encouraged to free-associate about the topic under study. Moreover, much of what is being done in counseling today has its roots in his many contributions to the theory and practice of counseling.

REFERENCES

Bouman, E. S., Blix, S., & Coons, P. M. (1985). Multiple personality in adolescence: Relationship to incestual experiences. *American Academy of Child Psychiatry, 24,* 109–114.

Burton, L. (1995). Using a dog in an elementary school counseling program. *Elementary School Guidance and Counseling, 29*(3), 236–240.

Clark, A. (1991). The identification and modification of defense mechanism in counseling. *Journal of Counseling and Development, 69,* 231–236.

Everson, M., & Boat, B. (1990). Sexual dollplay among young children: Implications for the use of anatomical dolls in sexual abuse evaluations. *Journal of the American Academy of Child and Adolescent Psychotherapy, 29,* 736–742.

Frederickson, J. (1991). From delusion to play. *Clinical Social Work, 19*(4), 349–362.

Freud, S. (1918). *Lines of advance in psychoanalytic therapy.* Paper presented at the fifth International Psychoanalytic Congress, Budapest, Hungary.

Freud, S. (1949). *An outline of psychoanalysis* (J. Strachey, Trans.). New York: Norton. (Original work published 1940)

Freud, S. (1952). *On dreams* (J. Strachey, Trans.). New York: Norton. (Original work published 1901)

Freud, S. (1963). *An autobiographical study* (J. Strachey, Trans.). New York: Norton. (Original work published 1925)

Freud, S. (1965a). *The interpretation of dreams* (J. Strachey, Trans.). New York: Norton. (Original work published 1900)

Freud, S. (1965b). *New introductory lectures in psychoanalysis* (J. Strachey, Ed. and Trans.). New York: Norton. (Original work published 1933)

Freud, S. (1971). *The psychopathology of everyday life* (A. Tyson, Trans.). New York: Norton. (Original work published 1901)

Grünbaum, A. (1993). *Validation in clinical theory of psychoanalysis.* Madison, CN: International Universities Press.

Hall, C. (1954). *A primer of Freudian psychology.* New York: Mentor.

Hart, S. (1991). Childhood depression: Implications and options for school counselors. *Elementary School Guidance and Counseling, 25,* 277–289.

Herring, R. (1990). Suicide in the middle school: Who said kids will not? *Elementary School Guidance and Counseling, 25,* 129–137.

Kapsch, L. (1991). A culture of one: Case study of play therapy with an abused child. *Journal of Pediatric Nursing, 6,* 368–373.

Kestenbaum, C. J. (1985). The creative process in child psychotherapy. *American Journal of Psychotherapy, 39,* 479–489.

Knittel, M. (1990). Strategies for directing psychodrama with the adolescent. *Journal of Group Psychotherapy, Psychodrama and Sociometry, 43*(3), 116–120.

Lawson, D. (1987). Using therapeutic stories in the counseling process. *Elementary School Guidance and Counseling, 22,* 134–142.

Levinson, B. (1962). The dog as co-therapist. *Mental Hygiene, 46,* 59–65.

Maslow, A. (1970). *Motivation and personality* (2nd ed.) New York: Harper & Row.

Maenchen, A. (1970). On the technique of child analysis in relation to stages of development. *The Psychoanalytic study of the child, 25,* 175–208.

Nelson, R., & Crawford, B. (1990). Suicide among elementary school-aged children. *Elementary School Guidance and Counseling, 25,* 123–128.

O'Brien, M. (1993). Pets as counselors. *Elementary School Guidance and Counseling, 4,* 308.

Orbach, I. (1986). The "insolvable problem" as a determinant in the dynamics of suicidal behavior in children. *American Journal of Psychotherapy, 40,* 511–520.

Patton, M., & Meara, N. (1991). *Psychoanalytic counseling.* New York: Wiley.

Pothier, P. (1976). *Mental health counseling with children.* Boston: Little, Brown.

Rosenthal, P., Rosenthal, S., Doherty, M., & Santora, D. (1986). Suicidal thoughts and behaviors in depressed hospitalized preschoolers. *American Journal of Psychotherapy, 40,* 201–211.

Rutter, M. (1975). *Helping troubled children.* New York: Plenum.

Sachs, J. (1991). Psychoanalysis and the elements of play. *American Journal of Psychoanalysis, 51*(1), 39–53.

Schaefer, C., & Cangelosi, D. (Eds.). (1993). *Play therapy techniques.* Northvale, NJ: Aronson.

Simon, S. (1988). Six conditions for nurturing self-esteem. Paper presented at the American School Counselors Association Convention, Breckenridge, CO.

Solnit, A. (1987). A psychoanalytic view of play. *Psychoanalytic Study of the Child, 42,* 205–219.

Stone, I. (1971). *Passions of the mind.* New York: Doubleday.

Sugarman, A. (1977). Psychoanalysis as a humanistic psychology. *Psychotherapy: Theory, Research, and Practice, 14,* 204–211.

Trivedi, L., & Perl, J. (1995). Animal facilitated counseling in the elementary school: A literature review and practical considerations. *Elementary School Guidance and Counseling, 29*(3), 223–234.

Trustin, F. (1987). Psychotherapy with children who cannot play. *International Review of Psychoanalysis, 15,* 93–106.

Watson, J. (1980). Bibliotherapy for abused children. *School Counselor 27,* 204–208.

Zelman, A. B., Samuels, S., & Abrams, D. (1985). I.Q. changes in young children following long-term psychotherapy. *American Journal of Psychotherapy, 39,* 215–227.

Chapter 4

◆

Reality Therapy

WILLIAM GLASSER

William Glasser graduated from Case Institute of Technology as a chemical engineer in 1944, at the age of 19. He enrolled at Case Western Reserve University and, at 23, earned a master's degree in clinical psychology. At 28 he received a medical degree from the same institution. While serving his last year of residency at the University of California at Los Angeles School of Psychiatry and in a Veterans Administration hospital, Glasser discovered that traditional psychotherapy was not for him. Glasser voiced reservations about psychoanalysis to his last teacher, who reputedly responded, "Join the club," although such an attitude was not common or popular among his colleagues. Denied a promised teaching position because of his rebellion against Freudian concepts, Glasser said he would have made about $8,000 in the first 16 years of his practice if had relied on referrals from his alma mater, as most beginning psychiatrists do.

In 1956, Glasser became head psychiatrist at the Ventura School for Girls, an institution operated by the State of California to treat seriously delinquent adolescent girls. His first book, *Mental Health or Mental Illness?* (1961), laid the foundation for the techniques and concepts of reality therapy. For 12 years Glasser conducted a successful program at the Ventura School; the theory and concepts of reality therapy evolved out of this program. Glasser used the term *reality therapy* for the first time in April 1964 in a manuscript entitled "Reality Therapy: A Realistic Approach to the Young Offender." His widely read book *Reality Therapy* was published in 1965. In 1966, Glasser began consulting in California public schools for the purpose of applying reality therapy in education. These new ideas for applying reality therapy to teaching later became his third book, *Schools Without Failure* (1969).

In 1968, Glasser founded the Institute for Reality Therapy in Los Angeles. It offers training courses for physicians, probation officers, police officers, nurses, lawyers, judges, teachers, and counselors. Introductory and advanced courses and programs are offered on a regular and continuing basis. Following the publication of *Schools Without Failure*, the Educator Training Center, a special division of the Institute for Reality Therapy, was established in Los Angeles in 1971. In 1970, the William Glasser La Verne College Center was established at the University of La Verne in southern California to provide teachers with an off-campus opportunity to gain graduate and in-service credits while working within their own schools to provide an exciting educational environment for children.

The Schools Without Failure Seminars, sponsored by the Educator Training Center, drew large followings across the country. Glasser's books include *The Identity Society* (1972), *Positive Addiction* (1976), *Stations of the Mind* (1981), *Control Theory* (1984), *Control Theory in the Classroom* (1986), *The Quality School: Managing Students Without Coercion* (1990), and *The Quality School Teacher* (1993). Glasser has made approximately 75 speaking appearances a year in addition to television interviews, writing, and videotaping.

THE NATURE OF PEOPLE

Glasser believed that, despite varying manifestations, psychological problems are the result of one factor: inability to fulfill one's basic needs. Glasser (1965) saw a correlation between people's lack of success in meeting their needs and the degree of their distress. He maintained that all psychological problems can be summed up by people's denial of the reality of the world around them.

Borrowing from Maslow's hierarchy of human needs, Glasser focused his treatment plan on teaching people to love and be loved and to feel valued by oneself and others. Successful attainment of these two needs leads to a success identity (Figure 4-1). In fact, one's success in these two important areas can be a

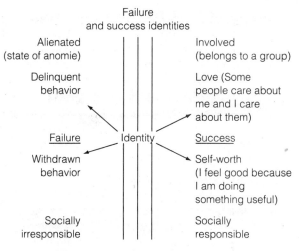

FIGURE 4-1   Failure and success identities

quick index of one's mental health. Both are key to healthy self-esteem; this theme runs through *The Social Importance of Self-Esteem* (Mecca, Smelser, & Vasconcellos, 1989). Kronick and Hargis (1990) echo the same points in their prescriptions for preventing school failure and school dropouts. They focus on teaching children basic social skills to help them interact more effectively with their peers and with adults in the school setting. Building a network of friends and supportive people puts a child on the road to achieving a healthy sense of self-esteem, a journey to be completed through success in the classroom. Kronick and Hargis also recommend treating children who have failure identities by teaching them time management and study skills as a way of ensuring their academic success. "Schools without failure" has been a principal theme throughout Glasser's work.

Sharing Rogers's optimistic view of human nature, Glasser believed that people can learn to fulfill their needs and to become responsible individuals. He based his system on what he called the "three Rs": responsibility, right and wrong, and reality. Glasser viewed adjusted people as those who are responsible and can fulfill their needs without infringing on the needs or rights of others. A primary product of becoming a responsible person is an increased feeling of self-worth.

THEORY OF COUNSELING

Glasser was reacting against some of the principles of psychoanalytic theory when he developed reality therapy. Reality therapy differs from traditional psychoanalytic therapy in six ways.

First, reality therapists discard the concept of mental illness in favor of the concept of responsibility. Traditionally, people behave irresponsibly because they are mentally ill, whereas Glasser believed that people become mentally ill because they behave irresponsibly.

Second, reality therapists focus on the moral issue of right and wrong—an issue often ignored in counseling because many believe that people already feel too guilty about various unresolved conflicts. In Freud's time, everyone talked about doing the right thing, so Freud thought it best to make psychotherapy a sanctuary free of moral judgments to avoid increasing his patients' feelings of guilt. In reality therapy, moral issues are addressed head on.

Third, reality therapists largely ignore the past in favor of dealing with the present and future. Most discussion in reality therapy evaluates how present behavior is helping to meet one's needs. If present behavior is not working, future alternatives are examined, and commitments to change are made.

A fourth difference involves transference. In traditional psychoanalytic practice, transference is frequently used as a therapeutic mechanism for living through unresolved conflicts. In reality therapy, the counselor relates to the client on a person-to-person basis and does not encourage the client to relate to the counselor as someone else; for example, the child does not relate to the counselor as a parent, teacher, or other authority figure.

Fifth, reality therapists largely ignore the unconscious, whereas it is generally the primary focus in psychoanalytic practice. According to Glasser, the unconscious is a fertile ground for excuses for misbehavior; the counselor is better off looking at *what* is going on than at *why*.

Perhaps the most significant feature of reality therapy distinguishing it from traditional practice is the aspect most dear to educators, whose philosophy is that the counseling performed with children is primarily a teaching-learning situation. Glasser said about reality therapy that it is a teaching process, not a healing process. Counselors are in the business of teaching children better ways to meet their needs. From the reality therapy point of view, counseling is a matter of learning how to solve problems—teaching children, in effect, to become their own counselors.

Control Theory

In *Control Theory* (1984), Glasser described methods for taking control of one's life. The theory is based on the idea that people are responsible for their own choices, decisions, and goals and the general degree of happiness in their lives. We are not controlled by external events and people unless we choose to let them take over. To a person who said, "Mary Sue hurt me when she rejected me, and I am too depressed to want to continue my life," Glasser would point out that the person is "depressing" (using *depression* as a verb) as a last, desperate, ineffective effort to regain control of a large part of his life that seems to be slipping away and recommend reframing the mental image of life to include something more than a relationship with Mary Sue as a raison d'être. This concept is similar to the methodology used in rational-emotive-behavior therapy and cognitive therapy, which focus on reframing thoughts, self-talk, and visualization as ways of treating undesired emotional states such as depression. In fact, many points Glasser raised are similar to those in Gestalt and existential theory regarding self-responsibility for living life. For example, rather than saying, "I have a cold," one would say, "I am doing a cold." Presumably, taking control over having a cold enables one to take control over stopping it. Two themes run through *Control Theory:* (1) We control our mental images or pictures. We can put them in, exchange them, add to them, or throw them out. We can also choose which picture or goal we can and want to satisfy. (2) Whenever we choose to depress or develop a psychosomatic illness, we have the option of choosing something more satisfying. The chapter on control theory and rearing children, in which Glasser integrates his control theory points into the standard steps of reality therapy, is particularly relevant for counseling children. Perhaps the greatest help to parents, counselors, and teachers is the idea that we need to empower rather than overpower children to win their cooperation when they grow too big to overpower.

The notion of empowering children is carried through to *Control Theory in the Classroom* (1986). In his best work for educators since *Schools Without Failure*, Glasser made a strong case for the teacher as manager, who motivates students by empowering them with the responsibility for learning. The principal motivation method is two- to five-member learning teams designed to meet student needs for belonging, power, friendships, and achievement. The team idea has been presented elsewhere (Thompson & Poppen, 1972) and found successful. Glasser's principal contribution in *Control Theory in the Classroom* is his parallel between successful managers in business and successful managers (teachers) in education. Glasser presented examples of the model with a sound explanation of why it works. He has been highly critical of stimulus-response (S-R) learning; however, the team-learning approach, if well designed, seems an excellent example of creating the proper stimulus conditions to foster the desired learning response. Much of the research and writing on reality therapy is related to the school environment because counselors and teachers find the theory and practice of reality therapy useful in working with student problems.

Glasser continued his *Control Theory in the Classroom* ideas in two other books: *The Quality School: Managing Students Without Coercion* (1990) and *The Quality School Teacher* (1993). The latter two books emphasize the business metaphor derived from Edward Deming's work with Japanese factories. The message is that managers and teachers have a lot in common in that the results depend on how people are treated. The book presented two managerial models: the boss manager and the lead manager. Boss managers motivate by punishment rather than reinforcement, tell rather than show, overpower rather than empower, and rule rather than cooperate. Lead managers do the reverse. In short, Glasser makes a case for democratic teachers rather than autocratic ones. The model works equally well in homes, schools, businesses, and government because, regardless of setting, people generally give·back, in full measure, what they receive.

The quality schools' principles, based on reality therapy and control theory, continue to be popular among educators. Renna (1993) outlined how reality therapy and control theory can be effective in mainstreaming disabled children into regular school programs. Reality therapy methods work well for students who have difficulty with abstract reasoning. Reality therapy is oriented toward action rather than insight. Students with cognitive disabilities learn best experientially. More important, the reality therapy attitude can help all students move toward filling the basic needs of achievement (work) and relationships (love).

Renna (1991) also detailed a control theory and reality therapy plan for working with students who are out of control from crisis situations. The out-of-control person is usually behaving without thinking and without focus. Cognitive hooks can be used to redirect irrational behavior with questions or statements that are unrelated to the situation, for example, "Would you help me move these two chairs?" The client is then asked to do many of the things we have suggested under crisis management in chapter 14.

Edens (1993) presented several reality therapy and quality schools ideas for working with junior high school children. Lead management, rather than boss management, was the key factor in the program. Lead manager-teachers engage students in discussions, show what is expected, request student input, encourage exploration, and assist students in evaluating their work. Edens found that school suspensions, office referrals, fighting, and truancy were reduced by 50% under this plan.

One successful application of reality therapy and control theory to educational settings has been classroom meetings and cooperative learning teams as described in Glasser's books on schools. Omizo and Cubberly (1983) found classroom meetings helpful in working with learning-disabled children. Sullo (1990) outlined steps for introducing control theory and reality therapy into cooperative learning groups. McDonald (1989) described how she taught control theory in grades 1 through 3.

Reality therapy has also been applied to higher education settings. Fried (1990), in one such application, described a method for teaching college students the concepts of reality and self-control in decision making and problem solving.

Parish, Martin, and Khramtsova (1992) attempted to increase congruence between the real and ideal selves of 23 students by using control theory in a class conducted on an interactive, closed-circuit, communications network. The treatment consisted of 12 semiweekly sessions of 2½ hours each focused on self-understanding and methods for taking more responsibility for controlling their own lives. The control theory treatment was successful in developing more congruence between real and ideal selves. Students who learned how to develop alternative behaviors had more choices in moving toward behaving like their ideal self-images.

Edens and Smryl (1994) combined reality therapy with Glasser's quality schools principles in an effort to reduce off-task and disruptive behaviors during a seventh-grade physical education class in an inner city school. Students were given leadership responsibilities over triad groups, control theory was taught, students chose their own teams based on equal skill levels for each team, and reality therapy was used when students were disruptive. Disruptive behaviors decreased from 31 in Week 1 to 7 in Week 4.

COUNSELING METHOD

The practice of reality therapy follows eight steps. Step 1 is building good relationships with children clients. Glasser calls this first step becoming involved, although *involvement* may not be the best word to describe this stage of counseling because it implies entangled or complex rather than positive, honest, open, unencumbered relationships. Any approach to counseling children tries to build the kind of trust and climate in which children feel free to express their innermost fears, anxieties, and concerns.

In Step 2, children describe their present behavior. In Step 3, children evaluate what is going on in their lives and how they are helping themselves. In other words, is their behavior helping them get what they want from life? If not, the counselor asks, "Do you want to change what is going on?" Glasser believed that the only way for a person who feels bad to feel better is to make a positive change in behavior (see Figure 2-2). Reality therapy focuses on working with observable content, including behavior, plans, and goals. "What" questions are preferred to "why" questions, which encourage people to find excuses for irresponsible behavior.

During the fourth step in reality therapy, the counselor and child begin to look at possible alternatives for getting what the child wants in life. In Step 4, a brainstorming format is used in which the children look at better ways of meeting their needs. In Step 5, children select alternatives for reaching their goals. The child then makes a commitment to try the alternative. A key process in counseling children is helping them make commitments. When they are able to carry out present commitments, counselors can help them build on these successes to get more from life. Therefore, children are first asked to make a relatively small commitment; they can then achieve success and have a basis on which to build.

In Step 6, counselor and client examine the results of the commitment. Often children returning for a second interview say, "Well, I made a commitment to turn in one homework paper a day, and I did not meet my commitment" and begin to list all the reasons why they failed. Reality therapists do not dwell on rationalizing "whys." At this point, the counselor and child discuss writing a new contract the child can handle; maybe one homework paper per day is too much for now, and a less demanding contract is needed. Counselors do not accept excuses if children do not meet the commitments they made. Excuses are designed to avoid punishment, and when children learn they will not be punished for not meeting a commitment and for talking about what they do, they have no need for excuses.

In Step 7, logical consequences are used—for example, a lower grade for failing to turn in a homework paper. Additional penalties that are not logical or natural consequences of failing to turn in the paper, such as paddling, are considered neither effective nor humane; however, logical and natural consequences are not permissively removed.

In Step 8, perseverance is required. How long should counselors stick with children who seem bent on destroying their self-concepts? Glasser recommends working with such children three or four times longer than they expect. "Never give up" does not mean a lifelong commitment but rather building on whatever relationship has been established in Step 1 and continuing to build this relationship through the entire eight-step process.

The three key terms in reality therapy are *reality, responsibility,* and *right and wrong. Reality* is generally defined as willingness to accept the logical, natural consequences of one's behavior. Trying to avoid these consequences denies reality and makes people prone to act irresponsibly. Glasser defined *responsibility* as the ability to meet one's needs without infringing on other people's rights to meet their needs. The third term is difficult to define, and Glasser's definition is on somewhat shaky ground. Glasser defined *right and wrong* as something people know by how they feel; feelings are good indicators of responsible and correct behavior. For example, if we feel good about what we are doing and most other people also feel good about it, then we are probably doing the right thing. One problem with defining right and wrong in terms of others' opinions is that mass criticism is not always right. In essence, Glasser defines the right behavior as behavior you would like done to or for you (the Golden Rule). The question becomes, How should these three concepts be treated in counseling children, adolescents, and adults? Piaget (1973) described three broad stages of moral development, which match his stages of cognitive development:

1. Preconventional (preoperational stage)
2. Conventional (concrete stage)
3. Postconventional (formal stage)

Kohlberg (1981) expanded Piaget's three stages to six by defining two substages within each of Piaget's stages. The questions on which people make their moral judgments, choices, and decisions are listed for each substage.

Preconventional morality

Stage 1   Will I get caught?
Stage 2   What is in it for me?

Conventional morality

Stage 3   What will the neighbors think?
Stage 4   What is the rule or law?

Postconventional

Stage 5   What is best for society?
Stage 6   What is best for humankind?
           Is human life at risk?

A strong case can be made that most problems brought to counseling are actually disorders of responsibility. Neurotic individuals assume too much responsibility; people with character disorders assume too little. Most people find themselves, at times, doing a little of both, depending on the situation. Sometimes knowing how much responsibility to take is difficult. Perhaps Glasser's answer would be to consult your feelings as reliable indicators of what you should do.

Gordon (1995) pointed out the need to link the concepts of freedom and responsibility in counseling children and adolescents. The basic framework of reality therapy is evaluating one's behavior against the responsibility criterion of how it affects other people. Gordon also summarized how the exercise of freedom with responsibility can lead to increased self-esteem, as children and adolescents successfully complete their reality therapy commitments and homework assignments developed in counseling sessions.

The Reality Therapy Process

The first step—one that must continue throughout the counseling process—is to build a warm relationship. Next, a series of five questions is often asked in reality therapy: (1) What are you doing? (2) Is what you are doing helping you get what you want? (3) If not, what might be some other things you could try? (4) Which idea would you like to try first? (5) When? The following dialogue is an example.

Counselor: Mary, can you tell me a little bit about your life right now here at school?

Mary: What do you mean?

Counselor: Well, Mary, it seems as though you get sent to the office a lot to talk to me about problems you're having with your teachers. Tell me what you're doing, and let's talk about it.

Mary: Well, I guess I talk out of turn in class too much sometimes. But my classes are so boring.

Counselor: Okay, so you talk out a lot in class, and the teachers don't like what you're doing. Do you do anything else that seems to get you in trouble with Mr. Thompson and Mrs. Rudolph?

Mary: No, I don't think so.

Counselor: Are you happy with what happens to you when you do these things?

Mary: I do the same old things that keep getting me in trouble, but I feel good for the moment.

Counselor: I know you do feel better for a while. Are the good feelings worth the price you have to pay for them?

Mary: I guess not, because I'm sure tired of spending so much time in the office.

Counselor: Would you like to work on a better plan?

Mary: Okay. Why not?

Counselor: Let's start by thinking of some things you could do to get along better in your classes and some ways to make them less boring, too.

Mary: Well, I could stop talking out of turn! I know the teachers would like that.

Counselor: Stopping unhelpful things is usually a good way to start. What about some things you could begin doing in class?

Mary: Doing more assignments would please the teachers, but I don't like all the work.

Counselor: Your two suggestions will probably help you with the teachers, but they won't do much to make the class more enjoyable for you. Can you think of something to help you like school more?

Mary: Some of the kids get free time or get to go to the library when they turn in their work. Could I do this, too?

Counselor: We can ask your teachers about that today. That might be a way to please both you and the teachers. Can you think of other ideas to try?

Mary: I guess that's about all for now.

Counselor: Okay, Mary, how many of these ideas do you want to try?

Mary: I think I can do all of them if I can get free time, too.

Counselor: When do you want to start?

Mary: Today, if I can.

Counselor: We can try. Can you go over these with me one time before we leave?

Mary: I think so. No more talking out of turn, and do enough work to earn some free time.

Counselor: That sounds good to me. Do you want to shake hands and make this an agreement between you and me?

Mary: Okay.

Counselor: Good. I'd like to talk with you a little each day to see how your plan is working. If it doesn't work, we'll have to make another plan. See you tomorrow?

Mary: Okay, see you.

This is a typical reality therapy interview. Identifying and evaluating present behavior are followed by making a plan and building a commitment to follow through on it. Each step in the reality therapy process is supported by a relationship of trust, caring, and friendship between the counselor and the child.

As mentioned in chapter 2, the counseling process works better when the counselor uses statements rather than questions. Questioning moves the interview from a dialogue toward a teacher-student question-and-answer session that develops the counselor's plan rather than one for which the child feels ownership. More important, statements by the counselor allow the client more options in shaping the direction of the interview. As Carl Rogers said, given the opportunity to take charge of the counseling interview, clients may gradually begin to take charge of their lives outside the counseling session as well. Examples of questions changed to reality therapy statements follow.

1. What are you doing to solve the problem?
   If you are ready to do this, we can begin by looking at what you have been doing to solve the problem.
2. How is what you have been doing helping? Is your behavior getting you what you want?
   It might be helpful to evaluate your behavior to see how each method is working for you if you feel ready to move to the next step.
3. If what you have been trying is not working, what are some things you could do that would help?
   We could look at some new alternatives to try when you are more comfortable about moving toward a plan.
4. Which of these new alternatives would you like to try?
   You have several alternatives listed. I am not sure what you think about committing yourself to any of them.
5. When can we meet again to find out how well your plan worked out?
   It might be helpful to schedule a time for a follow-up of your plan. [Shake hands and sign a written plan if necessary.]

For each theory presented in part 2 we have included a transcript from a case brought to a counselor as a way of demonstrating how the theory can be put into practice.

CASE STUDY

Identification of the Problem

Wendy Smith is a 12-year-old girl in the seventh grade at White Oak School. She was referred to the counselor because she cheated on a mathematics test.

Individual and Background Information

Academic.   School records indicate that Wendy is a high achiever, with an overall "A" average on her elementary school record. She also has an "A" average for the first two grading periods in the seventh grade. During the third grading period, which is almost over, Wendy has had some erratic test scores in mathematics. The test she was caught cheating on was an important test that could have brought up her low grades, had she done well on it.

Family.   Wendy is the only child of older parents, both of whom are professionals. Teachers have indicated that the parents seem to expect Wendy to make the highest grades in her class.

Social.   According to teachers' reports on cumulative records, Wendy was well liked by most of the children in her classes in elementary school. She did not seem to have a close friend then, but this year she has developed a close friendship with a girl in her class. A sociogram done in her sixth-grade class last fall shows she is well accepted by her peers.

Counseling Method

The counselor used the reality therapy counseling method to help Wendy evaluate her behavior and identify some things she could do to meet more of her needs socially and emotionally without creating problems in other areas of her life.

   The five basic steps followed by the counselor in this case are (1) establishment of a relationship, (2) identification of present behavior (what is being done or has been done), (3) evaluation of present behavior (is it helping the client get what he or she wants?), (4) development of plans that will help, and (5) commitment from the client to try at least one of the plans.

Transcript

   Counselor: Wendy, I understand that there has been a problem in your math class. Would you like to talk about it?

Wendy: I guess so.

Counselor: You're feeling somewhat embarrassed about the problem and uncomfortable about talking with me.

Wendy: Yes, I am, but I know I need to talk about it.

Counselor: Would you like to tell me what happened?

Wendy: Miss Waters caught me cheating on my math test. I have some bad grades in math this period. I knew I had to do well on this test, but I wasn't ready for it.

Counselor: How did you see cheating as helping you?

Wendy: I was feeling a lot of pressure because I wasn't prepared, and my parents expect me to do well.

Counselor: Can you tell me what you've been doing that kept you from being prepared for the test?

Wendy: I'm just getting to know Susan, and I've been spending a lot of time talking with her and not enough time studying.

Counselor: Susan's friendship is very important to you.

Wendy: Yes. I've never had a really close friend before.

Counselor: What might be some ways you could still be friends with Susan and also keep up with your studies?

Wendy: Well, I guess I could spend less time talking to her and more time studying.

Counselor: You believe that you can spend less time with Susan and still be close friends?

Wendy: Yes, I'm sure she'd understand.

Counselor: What are some other things you could do that might help?

Wendy: Maybe we could spend time together studying instead of talking so much.

Counselor: Would you like to try one of these plans for the next week and see how it works?

Wendy: Okay. I'd like to try studying with Susan.

Counselor: All right. Let's meet next Tuesday at one o'clock and see how well your plan worked.

◆ ◆ ◆ ◆ ◆ ◆ ◆ ◆ ◆

As pointed out in chapter 1, counselors must adapt their counseling style and language to their clients' the developmental levels. A suggested format for counseling younger children follows.

1. What did you do?
2. What is our rule about this?
3. Was what you did against our rule?
4. What were you supposed to do?
5. What are you going to do next time?
6. Do you want to write your plan for next time, or do you want me to write it?

7. Let's check tomorrow to see if your new plan is working. [Shake hands and sign names.]

Next is an outline of basic reality therapy for older children and teenagers who are capable of formal reasoning and abstract thinking.

1. Let's begin by talking about what you have been doing to solve the problem.
2. It would be helpful if you could give me an idea of how all of what you have been doing has been helping you or the situation. We may want to consider some questions: Is your behavior in touch with *reality*? Is your behavior the *responsible* thing to do? Is your behavior the *right* thing to do? From a cost-analysis point of view, is your behavior cost-effective?
3. If your behavior is not getting you what you want, what would you like to do differently?
4. What plan would you like to develop?
5. When can we follow up on your plan?

As suggested in these questions, much of reality therapy becomes a cost-analysis procedure of helping clients determine if their behavior is giving them fair value for the price they are paying. A good question to investigate is "Are you getting your money's worth?" Dennis (1990) developed a life-equity ledger sheet to help people analyze the cost and return on investment of their behavior. When people grow to like themselves and others, take good care of their physical well-being, and begin to define their self-worth internally as opposed to defining it by some outside standard such as financial worth, Dennis pointed out, they are well on the road to living a healthy, balanced life.

Oz (1994) presented a reality-based intervention that can facilitate discussion during any stage of the divorce process. Briefly, her method provides a cost-analysis system of the benefits and costs of each alternative related to a particular problem. Following a brainstorming session for generating a list of alternatives for solving a problem, the client moves to evaluate each alternative in light of the costs the client is willing and prepared to pay. How costs can be reduced for selected alternatives is considered. After narrowing the choices to the most cost-effective alternative, the client may be asked to role-play the situation with the chosen alternative. Likely impediments and worst-case scenarios are considered in the client's implementation plan. A secondary advantage accrues to the client in reframing "cowardly" alternatives as the least expensive and most cost-effective choices.

REALITY THERAPY AND BRIEF COUNSELING

Reality therapy has much in common with theories in the brief counseling category. It is designed as a short-term counseling method focused on goal setting and behavior change. Bruce (1995) summarized brief counseling approaches and identified four components that are shared with reality therapy.

1. Development of a working alliance in which the counselor and client work together in attacking the problem and its causes
2. Identification of clients' strengths as foundations on which to build their confidence in their ability to make positive changes in their lives
3. Implementation of active, eclectic counseling strategies and interventions, including role-playing, homework assignments, confrontations, interpretations, visualization, and reframing, to help clients achieve their goals
4. Establishment of clear, concrete, measurable goals that serve to help counselors and clients evaluate their progress

Reality therapy and brief counseling are both focused on present behavior and future plans and goals. Both methods include assessment of previous and current attempts to solve the problem.

Brief counseling differs from reality therapy in the heavier emphasis in brief counseling on concrete word pictures to describe the problem and problem setting. Clients are asked to describe exactly what happens, who is there, and what is said and done. The brief counseling practitioner takes a more directive role in actually prescribing interventions. Bruce (1995) detailed four useful intervention tasks:

1. "Do something different" for the client who tends to repeat the same ineffective reaction in problem situations.
2. "Pay attention to what you do when you overcome the urge to . . . " for the client who has trouble controlling impulsive behaviors.
3. "Tell me about a time when you had a good day at school" for clients who have taken on the victim mentality of believing that nothing good ever happens to them.
4. "Observe and take notes" for clients who have trouble avoiding problem situations and interactions. The observations help the client identify the good and bad things that happen in the problem setting; however, the most beneficial outcome is the client's role shift from interactor to observer. A role shift by one person in a group leads to role shifts by the other interacting members.

Paradoxical intention and dereflection (Frankl, 1962) are additional brief counseling methods often used with resistant clients and with problems resistant to change. Paradoxical strategies often involve prescribing the symptom. For clients who have trouble sleeping, the prescription is to stay awake, perhaps even set a world record for staying awake. Tantrum-throwing children are instructed to schedule their tantrums, for example, at 2 p.m. in a time-out area. Dereflection strategies reduce the anxiety surrounding certain events in a client's life. To relieve test anxiety, common to many students, the pressure to do well is removed. Students deliberately fail several practice tests just to get themselves accustomed to taking tests. Test-anxious students generally improve when the pressure to pass or make a certain grade is removed.

THE 10-STEP REALITY THERAPY CONSULTATION MODEL

The 10-step reality therapy consultation model (Thompson & Poppen, 1992) is an effective tool for counselors to use with teachers and parents who seek the counselor's assistance with their children's behavior and motivation problems. The 10 steps are divided into three phases, each with a special objective. Phase I, consisting of three steps, is designed to assist a teacher or parent in building a better relationship with the child.

Step 1. List what you have already tried with the child that does not help. Stopping these ineffective interventions often stimulates a positive change in the child's behavior.

Step 2. If Step 1 is unsuccessful, make a list of change-of-pace interventions to disrupt the expected interactions between the adult and the child. For example, catch the child behaving appropriately; act surprised when the child repeats the same old irritating behavior; ask yourself what the child expects you to do and then do *not* do it; try a paradoxical counseling strategy, such as asking the child to increase the behavior you would like to eliminate.

Step 3. If Step 3 is necessary, make a list of things you could and would do to help the child have a better day tomorrow. For example, give the child at least three, 20-second periods of your undivided, positive attention; ask the child to run an errand for you; give the child some choices in how to complete a task or an assignment; ask the child's opinion about something relevant to both of you; give the child an important classroom or household chore; negotiate a few rules (fewer than five) that you and the child think are fair to both of you.

Phase II, consisting of three steps, is devoted to counseling the child. In most cases we find that successful interventions happen in the first phase. When this does not occur, we ask the adult to move to Step 4.

Step 4. Try one-line counseling approaches such as the following:
   a. Ask the child to stop the undesirable behavior. Use as few words as possible, relying instead on nonverbal gestures. Do not use threats.
   b. Try the "Could it be?" questions recommended by the practitioners of individual psychology (see chapter 10).
   c. Acknowledge the child's cooperative efforts, but do not thank the child for behaving responsibly as if this behavior is a favor to you.

Step 5. Use reality therapy questions that emphasize the rules on which agreement was reached in a previous negotiation.

a. What did you do?

b. What is our rule?

c. What were you supposed to do?

d. What will you do?

Step 6. Use the standard reality therapy questions that end with a written contract or a handshake.

a. What did you do?

b. How did it help you?

c. What could you do that would help you?

d. What will you do?

Have the child dictate or write and sign a contract; have a follow-up meeting. If the contract is broken, have the child write or dictate a contract that he or she can meet. Eliminate punishment in favor of letting the child experience the logical consequences of appropriate and inappropriate behavior.

Phase III, consisting of four steps, is designed for children whose behavior makes teaching and learning difficult for everyone else in the classroom. In the home setting, Phase III is used when the child's behavior infringes on the rights of other family members. We hope to solve our consultant problems in the six steps before Phase III, in which the primary intervention is isolation.

Step 7. In-class time-out is recommended. A quiet corner, study carrel, or private work area may be used. Time-out should not be in a punishment area or a "dunce's corner." The child has two choices: be with the group and behave or be outside and sit. When the misbehavior occurs, send the child to the quiet area firmly with no discussion. The rest of the group does not have to be aware of the intervention. Have the child make a plan before returning to the group. The child's room may be used for time-out at home.

Step 8. Some children may require a time-out outside the classroom. The procedure is basically the same one described in Step 7. Some schools use a time-out room, and others use an in-school suspension room. Contracts or plans for making a successful return to the classroom group can follow the questions employed in the reality therapy method.

Step 9. Some children have difficulty getting through the entire school day without disrupting the class. Individual educational plans (IEPs) for these students may list four or five expectations or rules that the school has for all students. If the child fails to meet one of these rules, have the child's parents remove the child from school for the remainder of the day. Allow the child to return the next day and remain as long as he or she follows the rules. Community agencies have been used when home isolation was not possible. Once again, no punishment in addition to the logical consequence of isolation needs to be administered. Such IEPs require the input of teachers, parents, administrators, the child, and the counselor.

Step 10. Step 10 often involves taking the child on a field trip to juvenile court to observe the probable consequences of continuing present behavior patterns. Interviews with the judge, other court officials, counselors, teachers, and inmates increase the child's awareness of logical consequences existing outside the home and school settings. Failure to meet consultation goals with a child who has not reacted positively to the 10-step method may mean that the child should be referred to a community agency better equipped to solve the child's problem.

Chance (1985); Dempster and Raff (1989); Engelhardt (1983); Fuller and Fuller (1982); Gang (1976); Hart-Hester, Heuchert, and Whittier (1989); Heuchert (1989); Johnson (1985); and Thompson and Cates (1976) have all reported success in using the 10-step RT consultation model to help teachers teach discipline and manage student behavior and motivation problems. The basic consultation model can be adapted to any situation in which the counselor is consulting with a client about how to work with a third person. (See chapter 13 for more information about consultations.)

RESEARCH AND APPLICATIONS

The research, reactions, and applications section for each counseling approach contains a summary of the literature regarding how the approach is used to work with children. Because it is difficult to work with children without knowing how to work with their families, we have also included some literature on families, adolescents, and adults. We have as well included literature on general topics related to each theory because we believe such related material aids in generalization of the theory and approach to other case settings.

Perhaps the best validation of reality therapy is Glasser's success at the Ventura School for Girls. Before his tenure, the school's recidivism rate approached 90%; in a relatively short time, this rate fell to 20%. What was the secret of changing the orientation of these young women into success identities? Glasser gave them the experience of personal responsibility and success by assigning them tasks they could handle and by making each girl responsible for her own behavior. He discarded punishment in favor of logical consequences, gave generous amounts of praise, and showed sincere interest in each girl's welfare. Regardless of one's theoretical outlook, it would be difficult to argue with Glasser's formula for success. In fact, most counseling approaches are effective under Glasser's conditions, as described earlier in the chapter.

Cross-Cultural Applications of Reality Therapy

Reality therapy has worked with a wide variety of clients and cultures. Ford (1983) wrote that reality therapy is a recommended counseling approach for minority adolescents because the RT process is directed toward developing reason and logic to meet one's needs of love and self-worth without depriving others of the means to meet their own needs. McCrone (1983) found RT to be an effective method for rehabilitation counselors to use as they try to assist their deaf clients in making choices and plans that lead toward the clients' career development. In addition to being straightforward and to the point, RT is easier to communicate than many other approaches.

Applications of Reality Therapy to Community Settings

The practice of reality therapy has also been widely accepted in various community settings. Cohen and Sorda (1984) found RT effective with adult offenders; Yarish (1985), Ross (1984), and Thatcher (1983) successfully counseled juvenile offenders with RT. Chance, Bibens, Crowley, Pouretedal, Dolese, and Virtue (1990) found the RT-based lifeline program useful in treating drug and alcohol addiction in prisons. Honeyman (1990) used RT with addicts in a residential treatment program.

Poppen and Welch (1976) demonstrated RT's effectiveness as a group-counseling strategy for weight loss in adolescent women. Dolly and Page (1981), in a study of the effects of RT and behavior modification on the behavior of emotionally disturbed, institutionalized adolescents, helped their clients achieve significant, positive behavior changes.

Geronilla (1985), also in a hospital setting, recommended reality therapy for working with adult and youth patient noncompliance. The practice of RT should create an atmosphere in which treatment goals are negotiated rather than dictated and in which value judgments of personal behavior are left to the patient. Responsibility must be given to noncompliant patients in order to win their cooperation in writing productive plans and making commitments to follow their plans.

Applications of Reality Therapy to Marriage and Family Counseling

Reality therapy is often used in marriage and family counseling. Bassin (1976) developed a theory of marriage counseling called *IRT therapy,* which represents a combination of integrity, reality, and transparency theories. Bassin leans heavily on the ideas that a person must (1) love, be loved, and feel worthwhile and (2) meet personal needs without depriving others of their needs. Emphasizing Glasser's methods, he states that the focus should be on current evaluation of behavior in terms of its contribution to a satisfactory marriage and on working out plans to correct any apparent deficiencies.

Connor (1988) presented another RT-based model for helping troubled marriages. The model is based, in part, on the idea that negative feelings toward a person can be changed through positive behavior experiences with that person.

Thatcher (1988) discussed how reality therapy can be used with survivors of spouse abuse. Once again, the treatment focused on evaluating the helpfulness of present behaviors in moving the client toward desired outcomes and goals.

Glasser (1995), in his book *Staying Together*, wrote how the principle of control theory can be applied to creating and maintaining a successful marriage. Special consideration is given to meeting your own and your partner's basic needs of survival, love and belonging, power, freedom, and fun.

Applications of Reality Therapy and Control Theory to Group Counseling

Claggett (1992) described a successful application of reality therapy for counseling adolescent groups in wilderness camps for juvenile delinquents. Considerable decision making and planning were delegated to the groups, which also resolved conflicts and evaluated the success and failure of each day's activities. Plans for the next day were based on improving the previous day's performance. Six-month follow-up studies of the program revealed that graduates were 85% crime-free.

Williamson (1992) used group reality therapy to increase the self-esteem of four adolescent girls with relationship and performance problems. The focus of the group sessions was meeting the five basic needs in the reality therapy and control theory system: survival, belonging and love, empowerment, freedom, and fun. The success of the group increased in direct proportion to the behavior changes the girls made. Self-esteem, a by-product of meeting basic needs, likewise increased.

Comiskey (1993) researched the effectiveness of group reality therapy on at-risk ninth graders' self-esteem, locus of control, academic achievement, school attitude, attendance, and classroom behavior. Three groups of 15 students each formed treatment Groups 1 and 2 plus a control group. Group 1 received counseling, Group 2 received counseling and a school-within-a-school program, and Group 3 (the control group) participated in career education. Group 2 made the most gains, with significant differences in achievement, self-esteem, school attitude, and attendance. Locus of control and classroom behavior showed no significant differences.

Peterson and Woodward (1993) researched the effectiveness of the CHOICE drug education program in raising self-concepts and locus of control levels in sixth-grade students. The 9-month program focused on helping students develop alternatives for solving problems. Based on several reality therapy principles, the program is designed to increase students' options in the face of decisions and problems. The treatment group had significant gains in self-esteem, but changes in locus of control for the treatment group were not significantly greater than those for the control group.

Cobb, Rose, and Peterson (1992) cited the advantages of using day-long, quality-school insight classes as part of a drug prevention program for students in grades 7 to 12. The program objectives included making choices, accepting responsibility, providing self-help tools, building self-confidence, building relationships, developing personal plans, and setting goals. Parent involvement in the program proved to be a positive factor; however, periodic follow-up is needed to make the RT process work.

SUMMARY

The focus of articles supportive of RT over the past 30 years ranges from the counselor-client relationship to the helpfulness of the RT process in decision making, problem solving, and behavior planning.

Not all of the literature supports RT. Masserman (1975) wrote that RT may offer only illusory comfort to clients. Kovel (1976) saw RT as a system for manipulating people into conformity to the established order. Moravec (1965) attacked Glasser for his emphasis on right and wrong, and Wahler (1965) criticized Glasser's strict emphasis on behavior change. Barr (1974) wrote that Glasser's originality is marginal and that Glasser's work echoes that of Alfred Adler, B. F. Skinner, Norman Vincent Peale, Mary Baker Eddy, Thomas Szasz, and Horatio Alger. We might also include Abraham Maslow in this list. In many ways, Glasser does seem to have reinvented the wheel. To his credit, as Barr pointed out, Glasser's ideas are his own in the sense that he personally discovered them, put them together on his own, and created a system that works well for counselors and clients in many different settings. Glasser would, of course, object to any link to Skinner's behaviorism. Johnson (1989), in an article comparing the theories of Glasser and Skinner, stated that, despite these theories' differences, significant similarity and overlap exist. She concluded that the degree to which one sees a Skinnerian influence in RT depends on the degree to which one subscribes to the existence and relevance of the "inner person" and the freedom of choice.

In interviews with Glasser, Evans (1982) and Cockrum (1989) noted several points familiar to practitioners of reality therapy: First, reality therapy is simple and easy to understand but difficult and demanding to implement. The key is helping people accept responsibility for what they are doing now. Second, a pessimistic counselor cannot be a successful reality therapist. Considerable effort, persistence, and optimism are required from both the client and the counselor who wish to make the reality therapy process work. Third, the definition of behavior should expand to include feelings and thoughts, as well as what we actually do. The focus remains on what we can change about these three behavior components.

As is true with all counseling approaches, reality therapy has its supporters and critics. As might be expected, Glasser continues to find his greatest following among counselors, educators, psychologists, and social workers.

REFERENCES

Barr, N. (1974, February). The responsible world of reality therapy. *Psychology Today, 104,* 64–67.

Bassin, N. (1976). IRT therapy in marriage counseling. In A. Bassin, T. Bratter, & R. Rachin (Eds.), *The reality therapy reader* (pp. 64-67). New York: Harper & Row.

Bruce, M. (1995). Brief counseling: An effective model for change. *School Counselor, 42*(5), 353-363.

Chance, E., Bibens, R., Crowley, J., Pouretedal, M., Dolese, P., & Virtue, D. (1990). Lifeline: A drug/alcohol treatment program for negatively addictive inmates. *Journal of Reality Therapy, 9*(3), 33–38.

Chance, E. W. (1985). *An overview of major discipline programs in public schools since 1960.* Unpublished doctoral dissertation, University of Oklahoma, Norman.

Claggett, A. (1992). Group-integrated reality therapy in a wilderness camp. *Journal of Offender Rehabilitation, 17,* 1–18.

Cobb, P., Rose, A., & Peterson, A. (1992). A quality day . . . the insight class. *Journal of Reality Therapy, 11*(12), 12–16.

Cockrum, J. (1989). Interview with Dr. William Glasser. *Journal of Human Behavior, 26,* 13–16.

Cohen, B., & Sorda, I. (1984). Using reality therapy with adult offenders. *Journal of Offender Counseling, Services, and Rehabilitation, 8,* 25–29.

Comiskey, P. (1993). Using reality therapy group training with at-risk high school freshmen. *Journal of Reality Therapy, 12*(2), 59–64.

Connor, R. (1988). Applying reality therapy to troubled marriages through the concept of permanent love. *Journal of Reality Therapy, 8*(1), 13–17.

Dempster, M., & Raff, D. (1989). Managing students in primary schools: A successful Australian experience. *Journal of Reality Therapy, 8*(2), 19–23.

Dennis, B. (1990). Living a balanced life. *Journal of Reality Therapy, 9*(2), 118–132.

Dolly, J., & Page, D. (1981). The effects of a program of behavior modification and reality therapy on the behavior of emotionally disturbed institutionalized adolescents. *Exceptional Child, 28,* 191–198.

Edens, R. (1993). Strategies for quality physical education: The Glasser approach to physical education. *Journal of Reality Therapy, 13*(1), 46–52.

Edens, R., & Smryl, T. (1994). Reducing disruptive classroom behaviors in physical education: A pilot study. *Journal of Reality Therapy, 13*(2), 40–44.

Engelhardt, L. (1983, April). *School discipline programs that work.* Paper presented at the convention of the National School Boards Association, San Francisco.

Evans, D. (1982). What are you doing? An interview with William Glasser. *Personnel and Guidance Journal, 60,* 460–465.

Ford, R. (1983). *Counseling strategies for ethnic minority students.* Unpublished manuscript.

Frankl, V. (1962). *Man's search for meaning: An introduction to logotherapy.* New York: Washington Square.

Fried, J. (1990). Reality and self-control: Applying reality therapy to student personnel work in higher education. *Journal of Reality Therapy, 9*(2), 60–64.

Fuller, G., & Fuller, D. (1982). Reality therapy: Helping LD children make better choices. *Academic Therapy, 17,* 269–277.

Gang, M. (1976). Enhancing student-teacher relationships. *Elementary School Guidance and Counseling, 11,* 131–134.

Geronilla, L. (1985). Handling patient non-compliance using reality therapy. *Journal of Reality Therapy, 5*(1), 2–13.

Glasser, W. (1961). *Mental health or mental illness?* New York: Harper & Row.

Glasser, W. (1965). *Reality therapy.* New York: Harper & Row.

Glasser, W. (1969). *Schools without failure*. New York: Harper & Row.

Glasser, W. (1972). *The identity society*. New York: Harper & Row.

Glasser, W. (1976). *Positive addiction*. New York: Harper & Row.

Glasser, W. (1981). *Stations of the mind*. New York: Harper & Row.

Glasser, W. (1984). *Control theory*. New York: Harper & Row.

Glasser, W. (1986). *Control theory in the classroom*. New York: Harper & Row.

Glasser, W. (1990). *The quality school: Managing students without coercion*. New York: Harper & Row.

Glasser, W. (1993). *The quality school teacher*. New York: Harper Collins.

Glasser, W. (1995). *Staying Together*. New York: Harper Collins.

Gordon, B. (1995). A responsible solution. *Adolescence, 8*(2), 32–35.

Hart-Hester, S., Heuchert, C., & Whittier, K. (1989). The effects of teaching reality therapy techniques to elementary students to help change behaviors. *Journal of Reality Therapy, 8*(2), 13–18.

Heuchert, C. (1989). Enhancing self-directed behavior in the classroom. *Academic Therapy, 24,* 295–303.

Honeyman, A. (1990). Perceptual changes in addicts as a consequence of reality therapy based group treatment. *Journal of Reality Therapy, 9*(2), 53–59.

Johnson, E. (1985). Reality therapy in the elementary/junior high school. *Journal of Reality Therapy, 5*(1), 16–18.

Johnson, E. (1989). The theories of B. F. Skinner and William Glasser: Relevance to reality therapy. *Journal of Reality Therapy, 8*(2), 69–73.

Kohlberg, L. (1981). *The philosophy of moral development: Moral stages and the idea of justice*. New York: Harper & Row.

Kovel, J. (1976). *A complete guide to therapy: From psychoanalysis to behavior modification*. New York: Pantheon.

Kronick, R., & Hargis, C. (1990). *Dropouts: Who drops out and why—and the recommended action*. Springfield, IL: Charles C. Thomas.

Masserman, J. (1975). *Current psychiatric therapies*. New York: Grune & Stratton.

McCrone, P. (1983). Reality therapy with deaf rehabilitation clients. *Journal of Rehabilitation of the Deaf, 17*(2), 13–15.

McDonald, A. (1989). Me and my shadow: Teaching "control theory" in elementary school. *Journal of Reality Therapy, 8,* 30–32.

Mecca, A., Smelser, N., & Vasconcellos, J. (Eds.). (1989). *The social importance of self-esteem*. Berkeley and Los Angeles: University of California Press.

Moravec, M. (1965, May 1). Letter to the science editor. *Saturday Review,* p. 64.

Omizo, M., & Cubberly, W. (1983). The effects of reality therapy classroom meetings on self-concept and locus of control among learning disabled children. *Exceptional Child, 30,* 201–209.

Oz, S. (1994). Decision making in divorce therapy: Cost-cost companions. *Journal of Marital and Family Therapy, 20*(1), 77–81.

Parish, T., Martin, P., & Khramtsova, I. (1992). Enhancing convergence between our real and ideal selves. *Journal of Reality Therapy, 11*(2), 37–40.

Peterson, A., & Woodward, G. (1993). Quantitative analysis of the CHOICE drug education program for sixth grade students. *Journal of Reality Therapy, 13*(1), 40–45.

Piaget, J. (1973). *The moral judgment of children*. New York: Free Press.

Poppen, W., & Welch, R. (1976). Work with adolescent girls. In A. Bassin, T. Bratter, & R. Rachin (Eds.), *The reality therapy reader* (pp. 337–344). New York: Harper & Row.

Renna, R. (1991). The use of control theory and reality therapy with students who are "out of control." *Journal of Reality Therapy, 11*(1), 3–13.

Renna, R. (1993). Control theory and persons with cognitive disabilities: A neuropsychological perspective. *Journal of Reality Therapy, 13*(1), 10–26.

Ross, R. (1984, April). *Education of the young offender: A dynamic approach.* Paper presented at the annual convention of the Council for Exceptional Children, Washington, DC.

Sullo, R. (1990). Introducing control theory and reality therapy principles in cooperative learning groups. *Journal of Reality Therapy, 9*(2), 67–70.

Thatcher, J. (1983). *The effects of reality therapy upon self-concept and locus of control for juvenile delinquents.* Unpublished doctoral dissertation, Kent State University, Kent, OH.

Thatcher, J. (1988). Spouse violence: Survivors. *Journal of Reality Therapy, 7*(2), 2–7.

Thompson, C., & Cates, J. (1976). Teaching discipline to students in an individual teaching-counseling approach. *Focus on Guidance, 9,* 1–12.

Thompson, C., & Poppen, W. (1972). *For those who care: Ways of relating to youth.* Columbus, OH: Merrill.

Thompson, C., & Poppen, W. (1992). *Guidance activities for counselors and teachers.* Knoxville, TN: University of Tennessee.

Wahler, H. (1965, May 1). Letter to the science editor. *Saturday Review,* p. 64.

Williamson, R. (1992). Using reality therapy to raise self-esteem of four adolescent girls. *Journal of Reality Therapy, 11*(2), 3–11.

Yarish, P. (1985). *The impact of a treatment facility utilizing reality therapy on the locus of control and subsequent delinquent behavior of a group of juvenile offenders.* Unpublished doctoral dissertation, Florida State University, Tallahassee.

Chapter 5

◆

Person-Centered Counseling

CARL ROGERS

Carl Rogers (1902–1987) was born in Illinois, the fourth of six children. His early home life was marked by close family ties, a strict religious and moral atmosphere, and an appreciation of the value of hard work. During this period, Rogers thought his family was different from others because they did not mix socially. In fact, Rogers had only two dates during his high school years.

When Rogers was 12, his parents moved to a farm to remove the young family from the "temptations" of suburban life. From raising lambs, pigs, and calves, Rogers learned about matching experimental conditions with control conditions and about randomization procedures, and he acquired knowledge and respect for the methods of science. Rogers's thinking was influenced by teachers who encouraged him to be original in his thought.

Rogers started college at the University of Wisconsin to study scientific agriculture. After 2 years, however, he switched his career goal to the ministry as a result of attending some emotionally charged religious conferences. In his junior year, he was chosen to go to China for 6 months for an international World Student Christian Federation conference. During this period, two things greatly influenced his life. First, at the expense of great pain and stress within his family relationships, he freed himself from the religious thinking of his parents and became an independent thinker, although he did not abandon religion entirely. Second, he fell in love with a woman he had known most of his life. He married her, with reluctant parental consent, as soon as he finished college so they could attend graduate school together.

Rogers chose to go to graduate school at Union Theological Seminary, where Goodwin Watson's and Marian Kenworthy's courses and lectures on psychology and psychiatry interested him. He began to take courses at Teachers College, Columbia University, across the street from Union, and found himself drawn to child guidance while working at Union under Leta Hollingsworth. He applied for

115

a fellowship at the Institute for Child Guidance and was accepted; he was well on his way to a career in psychology.

At the end of his internship at the Institute for Child Guidance, Rogers accepted a job in Rochester, New York, at the Society for the Prevention of Cruelty to Children. He completed his Ph.D. at Columbia Teachers College and spent the next 12 years in Rochester. His son and daughter grew through infancy and childhood there. Rogers once said that his children taught him far more about the development and relationships of individuals than he ever learned professionally.

Rogers spent his first 8 years in Rochester immersed in his work, conducting treatment interviews, and trying to be effective with clients. Gradually, he began teaching in the sociology department at the University of Rochester. He was also involved in developing a guidance center and writing a book, *The Clinical Treatment of the Problem Child* (1939). At this time, Otto Rank's work influenced Rogers's belief in people's ability to solve their own problems, given the proper climate.

In 1940, Rogers accepted a full professorship at The Ohio State University. Realizing he had developed a distinctive viewpoint, he wrote the then-controversial *Counseling and Psychotherapy* (1942), in which he proposed a counseling relationship based on the warmth and responsiveness of the therapist. Rogers believed that, in such a relationship, clients would express their feelings and thoughts. This first truly American system was a radical change in the field of psychotherapy, which had been dominated by psychoanalysis and directive counseling. He and his students at Ohio State made detailed analyses of counseling sessions and began to publish cases in "client-centered therapy." The theory developed as Rogers and his colleagues began to test the hypotheses they formed from their case studies.

In 1945, Rogers moved on to the University of Chicago, where he organized the counseling center and spent the next 12 years doing research. While he was associated with the University of Chicago he wrote his famous *Client-Centered Therapy,* published in 1951. Rogers described his years at Chicago as very satisfying but accepted an opportunity at the University of Wisconsin, where he was able to work in both the departments of psychology and psychiatry; he had long wanted to work with psychotic individuals who had been hospitalized.

Rogers moved to the Western Behavioral Science Institute in La Jolla, California, in 1966. In 1968, he and several colleagues formed the Center for Studies of the Person, also in La Jolla. Through the 1970s and into the 1980s, Rogers spent most of his time working with and writing about person-centered therapy with groups. As noted in chapter 2, Rogers came to prefer the term *person-centered* to *client-centered* in writing about his approach.

THE NATURE OF PEOPLE

Carl Rogers and his person-centered school of thought view people as rational, socialized, forward-moving, and realistic beings. Negative, antisocial emotions are only a result of frustrated basic impulses; this idea is related to Maslow's hierarchy of needs. For instance, extreme aggressive action toward other people results from failure to meet needs of love and belonging. Once people are free of their defensive behavior, their reactions are positive and progressive.

People possess the capacity to experience—that is, to express rather than repress—their own maladjustment to life and move toward a more adjusted state of mind. Rogers believed that people move toward actualization as they move toward psychological adjustment. Because people possess the capacity to regulate and control their own behavior, the counseling relationship is merely a means of tapping personal resources and developing human potential. People learn from their external therapy experience how to internalize and provide their own psychotherapy.

In summary, a person-centered counselor believes that people

- Have worth and dignity in their own right and therefore deserve respect
- Have the capacity and right to self-direction (self-actualization) and, when given the opportunity, make wise judgments
- Can select their own values
- Can learn to make constructive use of responsibility
- Have the capacity to deal with their own feelings, thoughts, and behavior
- Have the potential for constructive change and personal development toward a full and satisfying life (actualization)

Perhaps Rogers's view of human nature is best revealed by a quote from him:

> *One of the most satisfying experiences I know—is just fully to appreciate*
> *an individual in the same way that I appreciate a sunset. When I look*
> *at a sunset . . . I don't find myself saying, "Soften the orange*
> *a little on the right hand corner, and put a bit more purple*
> *along the base, and use a little more pink*
> *in the cloud color. . . ." I don't try to control a sunset.*
> *I watch it with awe as it unfolds.* (1994, p. 189)

THEORY OF COUNSELING

Rogers (1992), in a reprint of his classic 1957 article, addressed the question, "Is it possible to state in clearly definable and measurable terms what is needed to bring about personality change?" Accepting the behaviorists' challenge, Rogers proceeded to answer in descriptive terms. His six conditions for personality change, having passed the test of time, have become the classic conditions for person-centered counseling.

1. Two persons are in psychological contact.
2. The client is in a state of incongruence.
3. The therapist is congruent and involved in the relationship.
4. The therapist experiences unconditional positive regard for the client.

5. The therapist experiences empathetic understanding of the client's frame of reference.
6. The communication of empathetic and positive regard is achieved.

Rogers believed that each condition is necessary to create optimal opportunity for personality change. Condition 6, the basis for trust between counselor and client, is especially vital to the therapy process. We agree with Rogers that the six conditions, which need not be limited to the person-centered method of counseling, provide a sound foundation for most standard methods of counseling children and adults.

Rogers first called his process *nondirective therapy* because of the therapist's encouraging and listening role. Later he adopted the term *client-centered,* because of the complete responsibility given to clients for their own growth, and then *person-centered,* in hopes of further humanizing the counseling process.

Reflecting Rogers's view of human nature, if the counselor creates a warm and accepting climate in interviews, people trust the counselor enough to risk sharing their ideas about their lives and the problems they face. During this sharing with a nonjudgmental counselor, people feel free to explore their feelings, thoughts, and behaviors as they relate to their personal growth, development, and adjustment. Such explorations should, in turn, lead to more effective decision making and to productive behavior. Rogers (1951) wrote that the counselor operates from the point of view that people have the capacity to work effectively with all aspects of their lives that come into conscious awareness. Expansion of this conscious awareness occurs when the counseling climate meets Rogers's standards and clients realize that the counselor accepts them as people competent to direct their own lives.

Person-centered counseling deals primarily with the organization and function of self. The counselor becomes an objective, unemotional "mirror" who reflects the person's inner world with warmth, acceptance, and trust. This mirroring allows people to judge their thoughts and feelings and begin to explore their effects on behavior. Thus, people are enabled to reorganize their thoughts, feelings, and behaviors and function in a more integrated fashion.

The Rogerian model for helping, as modified by Carkhuff (1973), involves three general stages through which the client proceeds. In the first phase, self-exploration, people are encouraged to examine exactly where they are in their lives, including a type of self-searching in which people question themselves concerning their status at the present moment. In the second phase, people begin to understand the relationship between where they are in life and where they would like to be. In other words, they move from a type of discovery in self-exploration to an understanding. The third phase involves action. In this context, action is goal-directed; people engage in some program or plan in order to reach the point where they want to be. The only exception to the logical order of these three stages might be in helping children; their movement through the process may be more meaningful if action is followed by understanding and then self-exploration. Children find moving from the concrete to the abstract easier in problem solving, and in Rogers's system self-exploration is the most abstract area of the process.

One can think of person-centered counseling in two dimensions: responsive and facilitative, which includes attending, observing, and listening; and initiative, which includes initiating, personalizing, and responding. The counselor must remain in control of the counseling process, becoming an "expert" in creating the nonthreatening environment vital to the counseling process. Empathy, respect, warmth, concreteness, genuineness, and self-disclosure all facilitate change in client behavior. The process works best when the counselor lets the client direct the interview—a first step in teaching clients how to direct their lives. The client is the expert whose task is to teach the counselor about the client's life situation. Clients thereby learn more about themselves, as teaching generally helps the teacher learn. This factor may be the main reason that person-centered therapy helps many people.

The main goal of person-centered therapy is assisting people in becoming more autonomous, spontaneous, and confident (Rogers, 1969). As people become more aware of what is going on inside themselves, they can cease fearing and defending their inner feelings. They learn to accept their own values and trust their own judgment rather than live by the values of others. Expectations of person-centered therapy include the discussion of plans, behavioral steps to be taken, and the outcome of the steps; a change from immature behavior to mature behavior; fewer current defensive behaviors; more tolerance for frustration; and improved functioning in life tasks (Poppen & Thompson, 1974).

The ultimate goal of person-centered therapy is to produce fully functioning people who have learned to be free. According to Rogers, learning to be free is the essential goal of education "if the civilized culture is to survive and if individuals in the culture are to be worth saving" (1969, p. 12). People who have learned to be free can confront life and face problems; they trust themselves to choose their own way and accept their own feelings without forcing them on others. Such individuals prize themselves and others as having dignity, worth, and value.

COUNSELING METHOD

The counselor as a person is vital to person-centered counseling. The conditions the counselor models become the ultimate counseling goals for all clients. Optimally, effective person-centered counselors must possess openness, empathic understanding, independence, spontaneity, acceptance, mutual respect, and intimacy. After clients move through the immediate counseling goals of self-exploration and subgoals such as improving a math grade or making a new friend, they begin to work toward achieving the ultimate counseling goals.

Perhaps the strongest techniques in the person-centered counselor's repertoire are attitudes toward people: *congruence* (genuineness), *unconditional positive regard* (respect), and *empathy*. Congruence implies that the counselor can maintain a sense of self-identity and can convey this identity to clients. In other words, the counselor is not playing an artificial role. Unconditional positive regard implies that the counselor accepts clients as people who have the potential to become good, rational, and free. Because people have self-worth, dignity, and unique traits as individuals, they require individualized counseling approaches. Thus, people direct their own counseling sessions. For the process to succeed, clients must feel they can reveal themselves to the counselor in an atmosphere of complete acceptance. Empathy is the attitude that holds the counseling process together. By attempting to understand, the counselor helps convince people that they are worth hearing and understanding.

In general, the person-centered counselor refrains from giving advice or solutions, diagnosing, interpreting, moralizing, and making judgments, which would defeat the plan for teaching clients how to counsel themselves and imply that the counselors know and understand their clients better than the clients know themselves—an assumption totally out of line with Rogers's view. Instead, person-centered counselors use the methods of (1) active and passive listening, (2) reflection of thoughts and feelings, (3) clarification, (4) summarization, (5) confrontation of contradictions, and (6) general or open leads that help client self-exploration (Poppen & Thompson, 1974).

The major technique for person-centered counseling is active listening, which lets the client know that the counselor is hearing and understanding correctly all that the client is saying. As we said in chapter 2, active listening is especially important for counseling children. If the counselor fails to receive the correct message, the child attempts to reteach it to the counselor. Once counselor and child agree that the counselor has the story straight and that the counseling service will be helpful, counseling can continue.

Carkhuff (1973, 1981) has systematized Rogers's concept of active listening (reflection) into a highly understandable, usable model (Table 5-1). Carkhuff believes that counselors typically respond on any one of five levels relating to the

TABLE 5-1   Five levels of communication

Levels	Phase I	Phase II	Phase III
	Thoughts and feelings about where you are now	*Thoughts and feelings about where you would like to be*	*Plans for getting from where you are to where you would like to be*
1			
2			X
3	X		
4	X	X	
5	X	X	X

NOTE: The Xs indicate which phase of counseling is treated by each of the five levels of communication.

three phases of counseling: (I) where you are now in your life, (II) where you would like to be, and (III) planning how to get from Phase I to Phase II. He classifies Levels 1 and 2 as harmful, Level 3 as break even, and Levels 4 and 5 as helpful. It is often assumed that the worst thing that can happen in counseling is that clients show no change. However, this is not true. Clients who receive a preponderance of Level 1 and 2 responses could grow worse as the result of counseling.

Level 1 and 2 responses in Carkhuff's model also appear in Gordon's (1974) "dirty dozen" list of responses that tend to close or inhibit further communication:

1. Ordering; directing
2. Warning; threatening; stating consequences
3. Moralizing; shoulds, oughts
4. Advising; giving suggestions and solutions
5. Messages of logic; counterarguments
6. Judging; criticizing
7. Praising; buttering up
8. Name-calling; ridiculing
9. Psychoanalyzing
10. Reassuring; giving sympathy; consoling
11. Probing: "who, what, when, where, why?"
12. Humor; distracting; withdrawing

Level 1 responses tend to deny a person's feeling and thinking with statements such as the following:

- "Oh don't worry about that. Things will work out."
- "If you think you have a problem, listen to this."
- "You must have done something to make Mrs. Jones treat you that way."

As such, Level 1 responses do not help with any of the three counseling phases in Table 5-1.

Level 2 responses are messages that give advice and solutions to problems. These responses are relevant in Phase III, but they are not considered helpful because they do not allow the counselor and the client to fully explore the problem situation. Ignoring the active-listening process deprives clients of the opportunity to work out their own solutions to their problems. Level 2 responses keep clients dependent on the counselor's authority and prevent clients from learning to counsel themselves. Typical Level 2 responses include the following:

- "You need to study harder."
- "You should eat better."
- "You should be more assertive."
- "Why don't you make more friends?"
- "How would you like to have your brother treat you the way you treat him?"

Even though the advice may be excellent, the client—child or adult—may not have the skill to do what you suggest. Moreover, rebellious children may work especially hard to show that your advice is ineffective to receive the satisfaction of knowing that an "expert" counselor is no more successful than they are in solving day-to-day problems.

Level 3 responses are classified as break-even points in the counseling process—neither harmful nor helpful. However, these responses provide bridges to further conversation and exploration in the counseling process; they are the door openers and invitations to discuss concerns in more depth.

Level 3 responses reflect what the client is thinking and feeling about the present status of the problem, for example, "You are feeling *discouraged* because *you haven't been able to make good grades in math.*" Such responses are checkpoints for counselors in determining if they are hearing and understanding the client's problem. Either the client acknowledges that the counselor has understood the message correctly, or the client makes another attempt to relate the concern to the counselor. At this point in counseling, clients are teaching the counselors about their problems and are thereby learning more about their problems themselves.

According to Carkhuff's model, an aid to counselors in making Level 3 responses is to ask themselves if the client is expressing pain or pleasure. The next task is to find the correct feeling word to describe the pain or pleasure. Below are listed seven feeling words. To build your counseling vocabulary, add three synonyms of your own under each word. In reflecting the client's feeling and thoughts, do not parrot the exact words of the client. Time-out for a summary is often helpful; say to your client, "Let's see if I understand what you have told me up to now."

Strong	*Happy*	*Sad*	*Angry*	*Scared*	*Confused*	*Weak*
___	___	___	___	___	___	___
___	___	___	___	___	___	___
___	___	___	___	___	___	___

Level 4 responses reflect an understanding of Phases I and II in Carkhuff's model; for example: "You are feeling *discouraged* because *you haven't been able to make good grades in math,* and you want *to find a way to do better.*" Rephrase the responses in your own words as you summarize the client's thoughts and feelings.

Level 5 responses are appropriate when the client agrees that the counselor understands the problem or concern. Now it is time to assist the client in developing a plan of action. Reality therapy provides a good framework for planning after person-centered counseling has helped the client relate the concern to the counselor. An example of a combined Level 5 response would be the following:

Person-centered therapy: You feel _____ because _____, and you want

_____ .

Reality therapy: Let's look at what you have been doing to solve your problem.

PC and RT: You feel *discouraged* because you *haven't been able to make good grades in math,* and you want to *find a way to do better.* Let's look at what you have been trying to do *to make good grades in math.*

The entire counseling interview cannot be accomplished in one response. Several sessions of Level 3 and 4 responses may be necessary before the problem is defined well enough for solving.

Because the success of the person-centered approach to counseling depends so much on the relationship between counselor and client, this approach may be *unsuccessful* with young children. Not every adult is capable of establishing true empathy with children or even of liking children. Children, to a greater degree than adults, are sensitive to the real feelings and attitudes of others. They intuitively trust and open up to those who like and understand them. Phony expressions of understanding do not fool a child for very long. A good example of a person-centered counseling method used with play therapy is presented in Virginia Axline's *Dibs: In Search of Self* (1964).

To help children effectively, the counselor must provide a warm, caring environment in which children can explore their emotions and verbally act out the consequences of alternative means of expressing these emotions. Together, counselor and child—or the child alone if he or she possesses sufficient maturity— can evaluate the alternatives and select the one most likely to be appropriate and productive.

In using the person-centered approach with young children, the counselor may have to assume a more active role. Still, even young children can distinguish between positive and negative behaviors and are able to choose the positive once the counselor has established an open dialogue in which feelings and emotions can be aired and conflicts resolved.

Again, the counselor needs active listening to deal with children, and the child needs an opportunity to release feelings without feeling threatened by the counselor. Listening carefully and observing the child increase the counselor's ability to understand what the child is trying to communicate. All clients convey both verbal and nonverbal messages, and the counselor needs to be alert to them. Because a child's verbal skills may be limited, nonverbal messages may be the most important clue to what the child is really feeling and trying to communicate.

We contend that the person-centered approach is most successful when clients take the role of teaching their counselors about their problem situations. The counselor's job, as the "student" being taught, is to take periodic oral quizzes (counseling summary/reflection statements) to let the client (teacher) know how well the subject matter is being understood. The subject matter consists of the problem, type and depth of feelings about the problem, and expectations the client has for its solution.

Lacking the verbal skills of most adults, children can benefit from bibliocounseling, storytelling, and play therapy (see chapter 12), as aids to teaching about their problem situations.

◆ ◆ ◆

CASE STUDY*

Identification of the Problem

Ginger Wood, an 11-year-old girl in the sixth grade at Hill Middle School, was referred to the school counselor because her grades had recently fallen and she seemed depressed.

Individual and Background Information

Academic.   School records show that Ginger is an "A" student who was chosen to be in an advanced group in third grade. On her last report card, however, her grades dropped to a "C" average.

Family.   Ginger is the elder of two children; her younger brother is 9. Her mother is an elementary school teacher, and her father is a systems analyst; they have recently separated.

Social.   Ginger is approximately 30 pounds overweight. She has a friendly personality, and teacher reports do not show that she has a problem relating to her peers.

Counseling Method

The counselor chose to use Rogers's (1965) person-centered counseling method. The counselor believes that Ginger's problem originates from emotional blocks. Her goal is to establish a warm relationship with Ginger, aid her in clarifying her thoughts and feelings, and enable her to solve her problems.

In this method, the counselor uses five basic techniques:

1. Unconditional positive regard
2. Active listening
3. Reflection
4. Clarification
5. Summarization

---

* The case of Ginger was contributed by Anne Harvey.

Transcript

Counselor: Hi, Ginger. I'm Susan Morgan. Your teacher, Ms. Lowe, told me that you might come to talk to me.

Ginger: Yeah, I decided to.

Counselor: Do you know what a counselor's job is?

Ginger: Yeah, Ms. Lowe told me that you help people with their problems.

Counselor: That's right. I try to teach people how to solve their own problems. Do you have something on your mind that you'd like to talk about?

Ginger: Well, I haven't been doing so well in school lately.

Counselor: Yes, Ms. Lowe said you are normally an "A" student.

Ginger: I used to be, but not now. I made "C's" on my last report card. My mom was really upset with me; she yelled at me and then grounded me.

Counselor: It sounds as though she was angry with you because your grades went down.

Ginger: Well, not so much angry as unhappy. She looked like she was about to cry.

Counselor: So she was disappointed that you weren't doing as well in school as you usually do, and this made you feel bad too.

Ginger: I guess so. She probably blamed herself some, too, and that could have made her feel worse.

Counselor: You mean that she felt responsible for your grades going down.

Ginger: Well, maybe. Things aren't going so well at home. Mom and Dad aren't living together right now, and they may get a divorce. She hasn't had a lot of time for us lately. I guess she's really been worried.

Counselor: The problem at home has made it tougher for you to do well at school because you're worried about what's happening.

Ginger: Yeah, I think about it a lot. It's harder to study when I'm worrying about it.

Counselor: It would be for me too. This must be a very hard situation for you to go through.

Ginger: It sure is; everybody's mad. My little brother doesn't understand what's going on, and he cries a lot. Mom does, too.

Counselor: So the whole family is upset.

Ginger: Well, I guess so. My dad doesn't seem to be, but why should he be? It's all his fault. He's getting what he wants.

Counselor: I guess he's the one who wants the divorce. It doesn't seem fair to the rest of you.

Ginger: Yeah. He's got a girlfriend. My mom didn't even know anything about her until Daddy said he was leaving. I hate him! [Starts to cry.] And that makes me feel even worse cause I know I shouldn't hate my father. I wish he were dead!

Counselor: [Handing her a tissue] So you're all torn up between the way you feel and the way you think you should feel.

Ginger: Yeah. It's so hard to sort everything out. Do you think that makes me a bad person for me to hate my father?

Counselor: I think you are a good person who doesn't know what to do with all of her feelings right now. I'm wondering if you think you are a bad person.

Ginger: No, I guess not. I mean, I think most of my friends would feel about the same way I do if they were in my shoes.

Counselor: Sure, it's a tough thing to handle.

Ginger: And I guess they're not all bad people. Thanks, Ms. Morgan. I'm glad we talked about it. I feel a little better now.

Counselor: I'm glad, Ginger. It sounds like you're beginning to work out your problems. Would you like to make another appointment to talk with me?

Ginger: Okay. Could I come back during free time next week?

Counselor: That will be fine. You can see me any day when you want to talk.

Ginger: Bye, Ms. Morgan, and thanks.

Counselor: You're welcome.

◆ ◆ ◆ ◆ ◆ ◆ ◆ ◆ ◆

INTEGRATING SELF-CONCEPT DEVELOPMENT INTO LIFE SKILLS*

Self-concept development (or, more specifically, self-esteem development within the context of self-concept) has been a centerpiece of person-centered counseling. Building self-esteem in children is receiving increasing emphasis. Our position is that self-esteem is a by-product of achievements and relationships and that self-esteem can be increased by helping clients improve these two important areas in their lives.

Radd (1987) developed a process to integrate self-concept development into life skills education, a theme consistent with the application of person-centered theory to education. The process includes a series of activities that focus on teaching children about self-concept and ways of applying that information to daily living. (See chapter 5 in the study guide.)

The activities each have three steps. The counselor may choose to teach these statements in the first person or in the format given. The counselor begins by saying:

1. "All people are special and valuable because they are unique." This statement is discussed to teach the concept of unconditional valuing of people simply because they are people. For children in kindergarten through fourth grades, the words "special and different" are effective. "No matter what you do,

---

* Tommie R. Radd, professor in the College of Education, University of Nebraska at Omaha, contributed this section.

you are still special because you are a person." For children in grades 5 through 8, variations of the words "unique and valuable" are effective. "If everyone were the same, it would be boring." "It is impossible for people to be better than other people because everyone is unique." In other words, "I'm the best me there is." The counselor continues:

2. "Because people are special and unique, they have a responsibility to *help* and *not hurt* themselves. People *show* if they remember that they are important by the way they *choose* to act. If people choose to hurt themselves or others, they are forgetting that they are special. Likewise, if people choose to help themselves or others, they are remembering that they are special. What is special to you? How do you treat it? Do you *help* or *hurt* the things you think are special? Are your toys and computer games more important to you than people? Toys and games can be replaced, but people are different and not replaceable. If you are remembering that you are as special as your toys, will you help or hurt yourself? When people help others, they are helping themselves. People hurt themselves when they hurt other people by forgetting that all people are special and unique. Possible consequences of hurting others include feeling bad about oneself and losing positive relationships, which result in self-concept erosion. What people give is generally what they receive. The point we want to teach is that if we like ourselves, we do not hurt ourselves or others." The counselor continues:

3. "People are responsible for 'watching' their actions to determine if they are remembering the *truth* that they are special. People are 'with' themselves at all times and are accountable for remembering to treat themselves as important people. When people blame others for their actions, they are forgetting their responsibility to value themselves. Who is with you all the time? Who will live with you forever? Who decides what happens to you? Who is the only one you can change?"

Integrating Self-Concept Activities with the Child's Life

After the self-concept activities are introduced into all environments children experience, the concepts are related to the children's daily life experiences and associated with various situations, interactions, and other skills such as decision making, self-control, and group cooperation.

The continuing process of relating self-concept activities to a child's life is the *self-concept series weave*. Picture the self-concept activities being introduced to children. After this information is taught and processed, the children experience the integration of these concepts into their daily life experiences. The weaving process makes the concepts about self alive and relevant for children.

The self-concept series weave process is implemented consistently regardless of counseling approach or setting. The self-concept activities and weave can become the core of classroom group guidance, small-group counseling, individual counseling, and positive behavior management. The self-concept activities are introduced and taught. Then, each subsequent session begins with a brief review of the self-concept activities and a weave of the self-concept activities into the process of the group or individual session.

An example of the self-concept series weave process follows. Although it is part of the second individual counseling session with a third-grade student, the same process is used in classroom group guidance, in small group counseling, and within the classroom behavior plan.

In the first session, the self-concept activities were introduced and woven throughout the session. Bill was referred to counseling because of his problems with work completion.

Bill: I'm still in trouble with my teacher this week.

Counselor: You are not feeling very good about this.

Bill: I think my teacher doesn't like me. She thinks I'm dumb.

Counselor: Your feeling bad comes from what your teacher thinks about you. I'm wondering how this fits in with what we talked about last week.

Bill: You said that I am special, no matter what I do, because no one else is like me anywhere in the world.

Counselor: It seems this week you are feeling as though you're not special.

Bill: I don't know. My teacher doesn't think so.

Counselor: So you think you are not important or special because you think your teacher does not think you are special.

Bill: Yeah. I know you think I'm special, but it is hard for me to think so when my teacher doesn't like me.

Counselor: You may be showing that you forget you are special by the way you have been acting in your class. You and your teacher told me you have been deciding not to complete your work. I'm wondering if you have been hurting yourself with your choices.

Bill: I've been hurting myself because I'm not doing my work. But other people aren't doing their work, and they don't get picked on.

Counselor: It sounds as though you feel cheated because the teacher likes the other children better than you and does not treat you fairly. Let's see if we can figure this out with the ideas we learned last week.

Bill: Okay.

Counselor: I wonder if you remember what we said about whom children hurt when they choose not to do their work.

Bill: I think they are hurting themselves.

Counselor: So, we could take a look at what happens to you when you don't do your work.

Bill: I guess it hurts me.

Counselor: If you want to, we can think of some ways to help you stop hurting yourself.

Bill: Okay. Maybe. I can ask the teacher for help when I get lost on my work, or I can get a friend to help me. I can ask for help remembering the homework, too.

Counselor: These ideas might help you. We need to know which ones you want to try.

Bill: I guess I just need to do what it takes to turn in all my assignments.

Counselor: Next week we can see if you've been remembering to do all those things you need to do to help yourself. Maybe you could show me the work you get done each day.

Bill: Okay.

The process of integrating self-concept with life skill development is most effective if it becomes the focus and foundation of group guidance, group counseling, behavior management, and individual counseling (Radd, 1990). The consistent exposure of children to self-concept activities related to life experiences clarifies and personalizes these difficult concepts so they become part of the children's knowledge base. Once again, however, self-esteem development is best served by helping children improve their academic performance and develop more friendships.

RESEARCH AND APPLICATIONS

Counseling Process

Numerous studies of counseling process involving adults have lent support to person-centered counseling. One of the most productive contributions to validating the approach was the process scale, originally developed in 1958 by Rogers and Rablen (1979), which provided seven progress stages descriptive of the counseling process. Studies using the process scale showed significant behavior variations discernible over the course of counseling. Walker, Rablen, and Rogers (1960) and Tomlinson and Hart (1962) showed that counseling cases prejudged as more successful were highly distinguishable when ratings were made on the process scale; this indicates a positive correlation between counselor ratings and the process scale.

Rogers (1967b), by listening to numerous recordings of successful person-centered cases, also noted a consistent pattern of change in clients: The most successful clients moved from a rather rigid and impersonal type of functioning to a level marked by change and acceptance of personal feelings. Corsini and Wedding (1995) have documented similar support for person-centered counseling in their review of Rogers's work over the past 55 years.

Mercier and Johnson (1984) used neurolinguistic programming to determine if therapists track or accommodate their language usage with that of their clients. The study involved training judges to a 75% agreement level in identifying both predicate and representational systems used by counselors and clients. The judges reviewed and analyzed the film series *Three Approaches to Psychotherapy* (Shostrom, 1965) and transcripts of the films and found that the three therapists (Rogers, Perls, and Ellis) differed in the frequency of their use of representational systems (RSs): Rogers used the kinesthetic RS most often, while Perls and Ellis used the auditory RS most often. Rogers's session with the client (Gloria) had the fewest differences in RS predicates. Perls's session with Gloria varied during the first two thirds of the interview; however, Perls used the kinesthetic RS more frequently during the last third of the session. Ellis and Gloria used the most different RSs. The study suggests that the person-centered approach lends itself to the client's style rather than molding the client to fit the counselor's style.

Mahrer, Stalikas, Fairweather, and Scott (1989) found significant relationships between intensity of feeling and categories of "good moments" of client movement, progress, or change during the counseling process. In fact, the maintenance of relatively low-intensity levels of feeling were found sufficient for maintaining the "good moments."

Williams and Lair (1991) presented a strong case for using person-centered methods with children with disabilities, who often lack self-esteem and self-acceptance. The authors noted a large discrepancy between the intent and impact of Public Law 94-142, which was a mandate for "a learning environment compatible with individual and developmental characteristics of students who have disabilities." Most children with disabilities have been failing to complete the educational requirements needed for gainful employment. Person-centered counseling and teaching can help children who have difficulty in resolving the conflicts between who they are, what others expect them to be, what they should be, and what they want to be. Williams and Lair stressed the importance of Rogers's three conditions (counselor genuineness, unconditional acceptance and caring, and deep empathic understanding) to help build self-acceptance in those who have disabilities.

In a similar vein, Foreman (1988) recommended Rogers's three conditions for work with parents of handicapped children. She argued that these parents should be viewed in light of their potential for growth rather than as "in need" and lacking in skills and resources.

Lindt (1988) presented an argument for using holding as a person-centered method to restore contact between parent and child. Holding is one way to communicate Rogers's three conditions. It provides safety and abreaction; it helps break down imbalance in the division of power between parent and child. The Lindt article included a case study about holding a boy, age 7, who exhibits autistic-like behavior.

Ellinwood (1989) made a similar case for ensuring that Rogers's process conditions were present for every member of the family if person-centered counseling was the treatment of choice. She was especially concerned that children might be omitted from the conditions. Ellinwood based her argument on the experiences she has had with children (age 8 and 9) in family therapy.

Karlsberg and Karlsberg (1994) incorporated reciprocal empathy into couple-centered therapy as a means of promoting better communication and emotional sharing between partners. The goal of couple-centered therapy is affectionate bonds between partners. Reciprocal affectionate bonds, accompanied by empathetic attitudes between partners encourage more self-acceptance, trust, and self-disclosure of feelings and thoughts.

Barrineau (1992) proposed a process model for working with dreams while using a person-centered approach. Although Rogers did not discuss working with dreams, he stated that the unconscious mind can sometimes be wiser than conscious thought. The locus of control or expertise resides within the client in the person-centered method. Barrineau distinguished between content expertise, which rests with the client, and process expertise, which rests with the therapist in working with dreams. He pictured the person-centered therapist as a co-inquirer using most of the standard nondirective Rogerian methods of clarification and reflection of content and feelings associated with the dream. The client is left with the task of interpreting the content, meaning, and significance of the dream.

Counseling Outcomes

Although published outcome studies on person-centered counseling are not as numerous as process studies, several have been reported. Of outcome studies conducted in school settings, one involved Rogers himself. He (1967a) applied person-centered principles in an educational institution that was seeking positive and productive change. Small groups, including parents, faculty, students, and administrators, met on an intensive basis. The results showed

- A loosening of the categories of student, faculty, and administrator enhanced communication.
- There was more student participation in decision making at all levels, and more student-centered teaching occurred.
- More experimentation and innovation took place.

Bayer's (1986) study also supported a nondirective counseling approach. Two approaches to affective education (a directed condition versus a facilitated condition) were compared on the two dimensions of self-concept gains and student ratings of interest and value attached to the program. This well-designed experiment took place in 12 sessions with seventh graders over 3 weeks. One hypothesis was confirmed: The facilitated experimental group showed a significantly greater gain in self-concept. However, no significant difference was found between the two groups on perception of interest and value of the sessions.

Omizo and Omizo (1988), applying Rogerian principles of self-concept and interpersonal relationship development, found that group counseling enhanced self-concept and interpersonal relationship development with learning-disabled children ages 9 to 11. The group sessions were designed to accomplish both ends.

Kazdin, Bass, Siegel, and Thomas (1989) compared cognitive-behavior therapy with relationship therapy for children referred for antisocial behavior. Children receiving person-centered relationship therapy remained at pretreatment levels of functioning; however, the cognitive-behavioral problem-solving skills group reduced antisocial behavior and increased prosocial behavior.

Outcome studies on person-centered counseling cover topics ranging from the effects of the counseling relationship, counselor or therapist personality, empathy, and expectations for counseling outcomes to the effects of various person-centered methods on educational and training outcomes. Perhaps the most conclusive support for Rogers's method comes from a study that compared psychotics (schizophrenics), neurotics, and normals (Rogers, 1967b). Rogers compared these three groups to see how effective person-centered counseling would be with each. Although the findings were complex, they included the following:

1. Counselors' empathic understanding and schizophrenics' perception of them as genuine were associated with involvement and constructive personality changes in clients.
2. Both psychotics and normals had more realistic perceptions of the therapeutic relationship than the counselor did.
3. The same qualities in the counseling relationship were facilitative for the schizophrenic and the neurotic.
4. The qualities of client in-therapy behavior that indicated progress were identified.
5. The process of change involved a chain of events. The quality of the therapeutic relationship facilitated improved inner integration in the client, which facilitated a reduction in pathological behavior, which, in turn, facilitated an improvement in social adjustment.
6. Early assessment of the relationship qualities provided a good indicator of whether constructive change would result.

Knox (1992) presented two case studies of combining person-centered counseling and rational-emotive-behavior therapy to work with children who had been victims of bullying incidents. Person-centered counseling was used to create a trusting counseling environment conducive to sharing feelings about being bullied; REBT was used to help the victims put their bullying experience in a realistic frame of reference that is not so devastating to their self-esteem. The bully in the first case was the bullying victim in the second case. The combination therapy was useful in helping the children handle bullies and find ways to relate better to their peers.

Cogswell (1993) described a "walking in one's shoes" method to enhance the nonjudgmental, empathetic approach to person-centered therapy. The therapist observes the client, reflects the client's feelings and thoughts, and, while walking around the room, summarizes to the client exactly what is happening in the client's life. In a sense, the counselor is metaphorically taking a "walk in the client's shoes." The method was reported to have been successful in six cases.

One can draw several conclusions from the literature on person-centered counseling.

1. Consistent patterns of change are discernible over the course of therapy: Successful people move from rigid functioning to more flexible functioning.
2. Person-centered therapy can be helpful in educational settings.
3. People increase their positive evaluation of self as a result of therapy.

4. Improved versus unimproved people show more relief from symptoms and more insight into self.
5. Reflection of feelings leads to continued self-exploration.
6. Significant decrements in anxiety as well as increased adjustment result from successful therapy.
7. The success of therapy rests partly with the ability of the person and the therapist to perceive their relationship in similar terms.
8. A case is less likely to be successful if the person is seen for a short time.
9. Successful therapists understand themselves as well as other people.
10. A combination of person-centered counseling and other methods is often effective.
11. Different theories and procedures for schizophrenics may be unnecessary. They responded constructively to person-centered therapy.

MULTICULTURAL COUNSELING

Person-centered counseling has enjoyed wide acceptance across many cultures. The emphasis on individual freedom and self-directed thinking and behavior featured in person-centered counseling is quite popular with people who, because of their cultures, have not always been free to make choices and speak their minds.

Follensbee, Draguns, and Danish (1986) studied the differential effects of affective responses and closed questions on adult client responses in an analog counseling setting. Affective responses were superior to closed questions in facilitating client verbalizations focusing on the present, the client, and the client's feelings. This finding held true for African American, Puerto Rican, and Anglo American clients.

In an attempt to evaluate person-centered counseling across cultures, Usher (1989) examined person-centered counseling against 10 possible problems with cultural bias arising from the method. The point is made that, although not a perfect method for all cultures, person-centered counseling has some advantages. There is less risk of being judged by the dominant culture's definition of normality because the client defines the goals and evaluates the process in person-centered counseling. Rogers also allowed for circularity of thinking, which allows culturally different clients to express feelings and thoughts within an open, nonjudgmental setting. Possible cross-cultural disadvantages of person-centered counseling include an emphasis on individualism that fails to accommodate the healthy dependencies on family members fostered in other cultures. Focusing on the self, subjective experience, and the "here and now" may be truly foreign or offensive to other cultures. The level of abstraction required in person-centered counseling conducted in English may also be too difficult to be helpful.

Waxer (1989), in an effort to research the multicultural implications for person-centered counseling, compared Cantonese and Canadian college students' reactions to Rogers and Ellis in *Three Approaches to Psychotherapy* (Shostram, 1965). The Canadians preferred Rogers, and the Cantonese chose

Ellis. Although both groups of students viewed Ellis as more directive, paternalistic, and authoritarian than Rogers, the Cantonese students did not rate him as harshly as the Canadians did. The Asian preference could be for counselors who are more autocratic, paternalistic, and directive; North Americans may view counseling as an open, exploratory, and democratic process.

Nevertheless, Hayashi (1992) reported that person-centered counseling is viewed in a positive light in Japan. Person-centered counseling and theory are highly regarded by students in the Japanese university system; however, cultural differences have deterred full understanding of Rogerian theory, and the Japanese Focusing Institute has been established to provide insight and self-help through person-centered therapy. In addition to university settings, in Japan the approach is used in schools, hospitals, and companies.

A significant indicator of person-centered counseling as a viable cross-cultural counseling method was Rogers's work with South Africans. In an interview with Carl Rogers shortly before his death in 1987, Hill-Hain (Hill-Hain & Rogers, 1988) explored some of the basic challenges involved in a large-scale, cross-cultural application of person-centered group work with white and black South Africans that Rogers had started in 1986. Rogers believed that the facilitator must not only accept a great deal of responsibility for learning about the culture of the participants but also must be ready for surprises. Rogers also stressed the goal of relinquishing any attempt to control the outcome of the group experience, direction, or mood. However, group members were not to physically or psychologically abuse other group members. Rogers reported that his method seemed to accomplish its goals. The interview ended with Rogers posing the question: "Can I really be open to any little clue that might open up doors of new understanding?" That is how Rogers worked with individuals and groups.

Stipsits and Hutterer (1989) detailed another account of person-centered approaches in another culture. They found that after two decades of experience with person-centered approaches, Austrian professionals and their clients were moving toward this U.S. system of working with people. One survey revealed that 35 percent of the professionals in Austria who work in psychosocial areas have a person-centered orientation, and 40 percent of all clients in Austria had been in person-centered therapy. The person-centered numbers are most impressive when considered in light of the fact that they were compiled in the homeland of psychoanalysis, individual psychology, and logotherapy. Finally, Combs (1988), in writing about current issues in person-centered therapy, summarized Rogers's work in cross-cultural settings by pointing out how people from groups with supposedly irreconcilable differences and prejudices apparently learned to appreciate and communicate with one another in Rogers's encounter groups.

Rogers was actively working on world peace projects at the time of his death in 1987. Soloman (1990) points out that Rogers devoted the last 15 years of his life to working on ways to bring emotional honesty and personal congruence into international dialogue. Rogers firmly believed that the methodology of person-centered theory could be successfully applied to the negotiation process needed to achieve peace among people and nations.

SUMMARY

Criticisms of person-centered counseling call it too abstract for young children and for adults who have not attained the ability to do formal thinking. The perfect clients for person-centered counseling have often been described as having the "YAVIS" syndrome; that is, they are young, attractive, verbal, intelligent, and sensitive. Such people may not need much counseling. Who, then, we might ask, will counsel tough, nonverbal children? Others criticize the person-centered approach as one that becomes mired in feelings and does not move quickly enough into planned behavioral change. Another criticism is Rogers's distaste for diagnostic tools and tests; critics argue that valuable data may be lost to counselors who do not use diagnostic methods. Hand in hand with Rogers's refusal to use diagnostic tests went his equally strong aversion to prognostication and prescription. Critics of person-centered counseling hold that counselors are experts who can dispense valuable advice as well as predict future behavioral patterns and personality development in their clients.

In rebuttal, Rogers (1977) pointed out how person-centered counseling relates to a wide variety of individual and group concerns that span diverse populations, including the areas of family counseling, couple relationships, education, politics, government, and business administration.

Quinn (1993) challenged the person-centered approach of Carl Rogers as being too soft to provide the motivation clients often need to move ahead in their lives. Further, according to Quinn, the person-centered method does not allow the confrontation needed to help clients see the contradictions and inconsistencies in their thinking and behavior. Quinn stated that people develop best when they interact with and confront their environment and that counselors should provide the same opportunities. Person-centered counselors, he argued, avoid interactive confrontation with their clients. We believe that Quinn missed the point that Rogers, in his method, was trying to create a counseling environment in which clients felt safe and could begin directing their own lives within the context of the therapy setting. Rogers's hope was that, given the opportunity to direct their lives within the counseling session, this inner-directed behavior would generalize to life outside the counseling interview. Counselors who take an active and directive role in counseling deprive their clients of the opportunity to practice directing their own lives.

In a response to Quinn, Graf (1994) wrote that Quinn did not understand Rogers's approach to genuineness. Graf argued that Quinn's recommendation on what genuineness should be was actually what Rogers intended it to be: counselor and therapist communicating their thoughts and feelings honestly and openly. According to Graf, Rogers never intended to restrict person-centered counseling to active listening and expression of empathy.

Herman (1990) and Aspy (1988) discussed Rogers's contribution to teachers and learners and how person-centered theory and practice can humanize education. Hutterer (1990) has presented the same type of summary regarding application of Rogers's philosophy to conducting research. In an article on developing a more human science of the person, Rogers (1985) recommended several new scientific models that promise new research alternatives. These models include phenomenological research, heuristics, and hermaneutics. Rogers believed these introspective models have some common elements: (1) Traditionalists are beginning to accept them. (2) The methods are appropriate for answering difficult questions about an inexact science. (3) The approaches require the scientist to indwell the perceptions, attitudes, feelings, experiences, and behaviors of the participants. (4) Participants are viewed as coresearchers, not subjects. Once again we see Rogers's humanizing philosophy reflected in all parts of his work, whether in counseling, teaching, or research.

REFERENCES

Aspy, D. N. (1988). Carl Rogers' contributions to education. *Person-Centered Review, 3,* 10–18.

Axline, V. M. (1964). *Dibs: In search of self.* Boston: Houghton Mifflin.

Barrineau, P. (1992). Person-centered dream work. *Journal of Humanistic Psychology, 32*(1), 90–105.

Bayer, D. L. (1986). The effects of two methods of affective education on self-concept in seventh-grade students. *School Counselor, 34,* 123–134.

Carkhuff, R. (1973, March). *Human achievement, educational achievement, career achievement: Essential ingredients of elementary school guidance.* Paper presented at the National Elementary School Guidance Conference, Louisville, KY.

Carkhuff, R. (1981, April). *Creating and researching community based helping programs.* Paper presented at the American Personnel and Guidance Association Convention, St. Louis.

Cogswell, J. (1993). Walking in your shoes: Toward integrating sense of oneness. *Journal of Humanistic Psychology, 33*(3), 99–111.

Combs, A. W. (1988). Some current issues for person-centered therapy. *Person-Centered Review, 3,* 263–276.

Corsini, R., & Wedding, D. (1995). *Current psychotherapies* (5th ed.). Itasca, IL: F. E. Peacock.

Ellinwood, C. (1989). The young child in person-centered family therapy. *Person-Centered Review, 4,* 256–262.

Follensbee, R. W., Jr., Draguns, J. G., & Danish, S. J. (1986). Impact of two types of counselor intervention on Black American, Puerto Rican, and Anglo-American analogue clients. *Journal of Counseling Psychology, 33,* 446–453.

Foreman, J. (1988). Use of person-centered theory with parents of handicapped children. *Texas Association of Counseling and Development Journal, 16*(2), 115–118.

Gordon, T. (1974). *Teacher effectiveness training.* New York: Wyden.

Graf, C. (1994). On genuineness and the person-centered approach: A reply to Quinn. *Journal of Humanistic Psychology, 34*(2), 90–96.

Hayashi, S. (1992). The client-centered therapy and person-centered approach in Japan: Historical development, current status, and perspective. *Journal of Humanistic Psychology, 32*(2), 115–136.

Herman, W. E. (1990). Helping students explore the motives, medium, and message of Carl R. Rogers. *Person-Centered Review, 5,* 30–38.

Hill-Hain, A., & Rogers, C. (1988). A dialogue with Carl Rogers: Cross-cultural challenges of facilitating person-centered groups in South Africa. *Journal for Specialists in Group Work, 13,* 62–69.

Hutterer, R. (1990). Authentic science: Some implications of Carl Rogers' reflections on sciences. *Person-Centered Review, 5,* 57–76.

Karlsberg, J., & Karlsberg, R. (1994). The affectionate bond: The goal of couple-centered therapy. *Journal of Humanistic Psychology, 34,* 132–141.

Kazdin, A. E., Bass, D., Siegel, T., & Thomas, C. (1989). Cognitive-behavioral therapy and relationship therapy in the treatment of children referred for antisocial behavior. *Journal of Consulting and Clinical Psychology, 57,* 522–535.

Knox, J. (1992). Bullying in schools: Communicating with the victim. *Support for Learning, 7*(4), 159–162.

Lindt, M. (1988). Holding and the person-centered approach: Experience and reflection. *Person-Centered Review, 3,* 229–240.

Mahrer, A. R., Stalikas, A., Fairweather, D. R., & Scott, J. M. (1989). Is there a relationship between client feeling level and categories of "good moments" in counseling sessions? *Canadian Journal of Counseling, 23*(3), 219–227.

Mercier, M., & Johnson, M. (1984). Representational system predicate use and convergence in counseling: Gloria revisited. *Journal of Counseling Psychology, 31,* 161–169.

Omizo, M. M., & Omizo, S. A. (1988). Group counseling's effect on self-concept and social behavior among children with learning disabilities. *Journal of Humanistic Education and Development, 26,* 109–117.

Poppen, W., & Thompson, C. (1974). *School counseling: Theories and concepts.* Lincoln, NE: Professional Educators.

Quinn, R. (1993). Confronting Carl Rogers: A developmental-interactional approach to person-centered therapy. *Journal of Humanistic Psychology, 33*(1), 6–23.

Radd, T. R. (1987). *The Grow with Guidance system section: Classroom behavior management.* Canton, OH: Grow with Guidance.

Radd, T. R. (1990). *The Grow with Guidance video: A powerful system for maximizing youth potential.* Canton, OH: Grow with Guidance.

Rogers, C. R. (1939). *The clinical treatment of the problem child.* Boston: Houghton Mifflin.

Rogers, C. R. (1942). *Counseling and psychotherapy.* Boston: Houghton Mifflin.

Rogers, C. R. (1951). *Client-centered therapy.* Boston: Houghton Mifflin.

Rogers, C. R. (1965). *Client-centered therapy: Its current practice, implications, and theory.* Boston: Houghton Mifflin.

Rogers, C. R. (1967a). A plan for self-directed change in an educational system. *Educational Leadership, 24,* 717–731.

Rogers, C. R. (1967b). *The therapeutic relationship and its impact: A study of psychotherapy with schizophrenics.* Madison: University of Wisconsin Press.

Rogers, C. R. (1969). *Freedom to learn.* Columbus, OH: Merrill.

Rogers, C. R. (1977). *Carl Rogers on personal power: Inner strength and its revolutionary impact.* New York: Delacorte Press.

Rogers, C. R. (1985). Toward a more human science of the person. *Journal of Humanistic Psychology, 25,* 7–24.

Rogers, C. R. (1992). The necessary and sufficient conditions of therapeutic personality change. *Journal of Consulting and Clinical Psychology, 60,* 827–832.

Rogers, C. R. (1994). Rogers's quote. *Journal of Humanistic Education and Development, 32*(4), 189.

Rogers, C. R., & Rablen, R. A. (1979). A scale of process in psychotherapy. In R. Corsini (Ed.), *Current Psychotherapies*. Itasca, IL: F. E. Peacock.

Shostrom, E. (Producer). (1965). *Three approaches to psychotherapy* [Film]. Orange, CA: Psychological Films.

Soloman, L. N. (1990). Carl Rogers' efforts for world peace. *Person-Centered Review, 5,* 39–56.

Stipsits, R., & Hutterer, R. (1989). The person-centered approach in Austria. *Person-Centered Review, 4,* 475–487.

Tomlinson, T. M., & Hart, J. T. (1962). A validation study of the process scale. *Journal of Consulting Psychology, 26,* 74–78.

Usher, C. H. (1989). Recognizing cultural bias in counseling theory and practice: The case of Rogers. *Journal of Multicultural Counseling and Development, 17,* 62–71.

Walker, A., Rablen, R., & Rogers, C. (1960). Development of a scale to measure process changes in psychotherapy. *Journal of Clinical Psychology, 16,* 79–85.

Waxer, P. H. (1989). Cantonese versus Canadian evaluation of directive and non-directive therapy. *Canadian Journal of Counseling, 23*(3), 263–271.

Williams, W., & Lair, G. (1991). Using a person-centered approach with children who have a disability. *Elementary School Guidance and Counseling, 25,* 194–203.

Chapter 6

◆

Gestalt Therapy

FRITZ PERLS

Fritz Perls's estranged wife, Laura, once referred to him as half prophet and half bum; Perls considered this description accurate. In his autobiography, *In and Out the Garbage Pail* (1971), Perls wrote that, at the age of 75, he liked his reputation of being both a dirty old man and a guru. Unfortunately, he continued, the first reputation was on the wane and the second ascending.

Born in a Jewish ghetto on the outskirts of Berlin on July 8, 1893, Friedrich Salomon Perls was the third child of Amelia Rund and Nathan Perls. He later Anglicized his first name to Frederick but is remembered more commonly as Fritz.

Perls disliked his eldest sister, Else. He thought of her as a clinger and was uncomfortable in her presence. Else also had severe eye trouble, and Perls disliked the thought that he might have to take care of her someday. He did not mourn much when he heard of her death in a concentration camp. Shepard (1975) speculates that Perls resented the extra attention and favor his mother offered Else because of her partial blindness. He did seem to like his second sister, Grete.

After a difficult first few weeks of life, Perls seems to have led a happy and healthy life for his first 9 years. Around the age of 10, Perls became rebellious. His parents were having bitter fights, and his father was away from home quite often. Perls even began to doubt his paternity and suspected that his biological father was a much-respected uncle; this question remained open for Fritz until his death. His marriage was not much happier than his childhood, although he and Laura remained married and worked together in the development of Gestalt therapy. Perls came to realize that the roles of husband and father gave him little satisfaction.

After some hard times in Europe, Perls found success as a training analyst in Johannesburg, South Africa. While there, he founded the South African Institute for Psychoanalysis. He learned to fly and got his pilot's license. During this time, in 1936, he flew to Czechoslovakia to deliver a paper to the Psychoanalytic Congress. He intended to meet with his hero, Sigmund Freud, but he was given only a cool 4-minute audience while he stood in Freud's doorway. Perls experienced another disappointment when most of the other analysts gave his paper an icy reception. From then on, Perls challenged the assumptions and directions of Freud and the psychoanalysts. In his final years, many people began to listen. Perls thought he had four main "unfinished situations" in his life: not being able to sing well, never having made a parachute jump, never having tried skin diving, and never having had the opportunity to show Freud his mistakes.

Perls spent 12 years in South Africa, during which time he formulated all the basic ideas underlying what he would later call Gestalt therapy. At 53, he moved his family to New York, where the "formal birth" of Gestalt therapy took place. The people involved debated what to call the new theory. Perls held out for *Gestalt,* a German term that cannot be translated exactly into English, but the meaning of the concept can be grasped:

> a form, a configuration or a totality that has, as a unified whole, properties which cannot be derived by summation from the parts and their relationships. It may refer to physical structures, to physiological and psychological functions, or to symbolic units. (English & English, 1958, p. 225)

In late 1951, Perls's *Gestalt Therapy* was published. Perls is listed as author, although Ralph Hefferline wrote nearly all of the first half of the book and Paul Goodman the second. At first, the new therapy had almost no impact. Perls began traveling to cities such as Cleveland, Detroit, Toronto, and Miami to run groups for professionals and lay people interested in the new idea. As he traveled about the country, he discovered that he was received far better on the road than he was in New York. At the end of 10 years in New York, Perls decided to leave that city, and his wife, for the warmth of Miami. Laura Perls's interpretation of Fritz's reason for leaving was that he was not the leading psychotherapist—nor even the leading Gestaltist—in New York.

Miami was very important to Perls because there he met "the most significant woman in my life," Marty Fromm. In Florida he also found LSD and became involved in the drug subculture. He then moved to California, eventually Big Sur, where he became widely known. At the Esalen Institute, he had to compete with people such as Virginia Satir, Bernard Gunther, and Will Schutz. Perls contended that the techniques Gunther and Schutz employed used other people's ideas and offered "instant joy." Perls, who opposed quick cures and respected only originality, established his own Gestalt Institute of Canada at Cowichan on Vancouver Island in British Columbia.

Nine months after the center in Canada was begun, Fritz Perls died. Two biopsies the doctors had taken during a long operation came back negative, but an autopsy disclosed that he had suffered from advanced cancer of the pancreas. Perls died as he had lived. On the last evening of his life, March 14, 1970, Perls was attempting to get out of bed against the wishes of his nurse. "Don't tell me what to do," he said to her, fell back, and died.

Perls viewed Gestalt theory as being in progress at the time of his death. Perls thought that theory development, like human development, was a process of becoming. He was not one to close the book on his theory and treat it as gospel. Rather, Perls revised the theory to fit his observations of human behavior.

THE NATURE OF PEOPLE

According to Gestalt theory, the most important areas of concern are the thoughts and feelings people are experiencing at the moment. Normal, healthy behavior occurs when people act and react as total organisms. Many people fragment their lives, distributing their concentration and attention among several variables and events at one time. The results of such fragmentation can be seen in an ineffective living style, with outcomes ranging from low productivity to serious accidents. The Gestalt view of human nature is positive: People are capable of becoming self-regulating beings who can achieve a sense of unity and integration in their lives.

Perls (1969) saw the person as a total organism—not just as the brain. His saying that people would be better off losing their minds and coming to their senses meant that our bodies and feelings are better indicators of the truth than our words, which we use to hide the truth from ourselves. Body signs such as headaches, rashes, neck strain, and stomach pains may indicate that we need to change our behavior. Perls believed that awareness alone can be curative. With full awareness, a state of organismic self-regulation develops, and the total person takes control.

Mentally healthy people can maintain their awareness without being distracted by the various environmental stimuli that constantly vie for our attention. Such people can fully and clearly experience their own needs and the environmental alternatives for meeting these needs. Healthy people still experience their share of inner conflicts and frustrations, but, with their higher levels of concentration and awareness, they can solve their problems without complicating them with fantasy elaborations. They likewise resolve conflicts with others when it is possible and otherwise dismiss them. People with high levels of awareness of their needs and their environment know which problems and conflicts are resolvable and which are not. In Perls's theory, the key to successful adjustment is the development of personal responsibility—responsibility for one's life and response to one's environment. Much of the Perls's doctrine is summarized in his famous Gestalt Prayer (Perls, 1969):

I do my thing and you do your thing.
I am not in this world to live up to your expectations,
And you are not in this world to live up to mine.
You are you and I am I
And if by chance we find each other, it's beautiful.
If not, it can't be helped. (p.4)

The healthy person focuses sharply on one need (the figure) at a time while relegating other needs to the background. When the need is met—or the Gestalt is closed or completed—it is relegated to the background, and a new need comes into focus (becomes the figure). The smoothly functioning figure-ground relationship characterizes the healthy personality. The dominant need of the organism at any time becomes the foreground figure, and the other needs recede, at least temporarily, into the background. The foreground figure is the need that presses most sharply for satisfaction, whether the need is to preserve life or is related to less physically or psychologically vital areas. For individuals to be able to satisfy their needs, close the Gestalt, and move on to other things, they must be able to determine what they need, and they must know how to manipulate themselves and their environment. Even purely physiological needs can be satisfied only through the interaction of the organism and the environment (Perls, 1976).

Perls defined neurotic people as those who try to attend to too many needs at one time and, as a result, fail to satisfy any one need fully. Neurotic people also use their potential to manipulate others to do for them what they have not done for themselves. Rather than running their own lives, they turn them over to those who will take care of their needs. In summary, people cause themselves additional problems by not handling their lives appropriately in the following six categories:

1. *Lacking contact with the environment:* People may become so rigid that they cut themselves off from others or from resources in the environment.

2. *Confluence:* People may incorporate too much of themselves into others or incorporate so much of the environment into themselves that they lose touch with where they are. Then the environment takes control.

3. *Unfinished business:* People may have unfulfilled needs, unexpressed feelings, or uncompleted situations that clamor for their attention. (This situation may manifest itself in dreams.)

4. *Fragmentation:* People may try to discover or deny a need such as aggression. The inability to find and obtain what one needs may be the result of fragmenting one's life.

5. *Topdog/underdog:* People may experience a split in their personalities between what they think they "should" do (topdog) and what they "want" to do (underdog) (see Passons, 1975).

6. *Polarities (dichotomies):* People tend to flounder at times between existing, natural dichotomies in their lives, such as body-mind, self-external world, emotional-real, infantile-mature, biological-cultural, poetry-prose, spontaneous-deliberate, personal-social, love-aggression, and unconscious-conscious (Sahakian, 1969). Much of everyday living seems to be involved in resolving conflicts posed by these competing polarities.

Assagioli (1965) has identified five types of polarities:

1. *Physical:* masculinity-femininity and parasympathetic-sympathetic nervous system
2. *Emotional:* pleasure-pain, excitement-depression, love-hate

3. *Mental:* parent-child, eros (feeling)-logos (reason), topdog-underdog
4. *Spiritual:* intellectual doubt-dogmatism
5. *Interindividual:* man-woman, black-white, Christian-Jew

THEORY OF COUNSELING

Any adaptation of Perls's system to counseling children would incorporate the five layers of neuroses proposed by Perls (1971; see also Fagan & Shepard, 1970). Perls devised these five layers to depict how people fragment their lives and prevent themselves from succeeding and maturing. The five layers form a series of counseling stages, or benchmarks, for the counseling process; in fact, they could be considered as five steps to a better Gestalt way of life.

1. *The phony layer:* Many people are trapped in trying to be what they are not. The phony layer is characterized by many conflicts that are never resolved.

2. *The phobic layer:* As people become aware of their phony games, they become aware of their fears that maintain the games. This experience is often frightening.

3. *The impasse layer:* This is the layer people reach when they shed the environmental support of their games and find they do not know a better way to cope with their fears and dislikes. People often become stuck here and refuse to move on.

4. *The implosive layer:* People become aware of how they limit themselves, and they begin to experiment with new behaviors.

5. *The explosive layer:* If experiments with new behaviors are successful, people can reach the explosive layer, where they find much unused energy that had been tied up in maintaining a phony existence.

Perls believed that progress through the five layers of neuroses is best achieved by observing how psychological defenses might be associated with muscular position, or what he called *body armor*. He believed the client's body language would be a better indicator of the truth than the client's words and that awareness of hidden material could be facilitated by acting out feelings. Perls asked people to project their thoughts and feelings upon empty chairs representing significant people in their lives. People were often asked to play several roles in attempting to identify who was experiencing conflict. Perls expanded on Rogers's idea of feedback as a therapeutic agent by including body posture, voice tone, eye movements, feelings, and gestures.

Gestalt therapists emphasize direct experiences. They focus on achieving awareness of the here and now and frustrating the client in any attempt to break out of this awareness. As an experiential approach, Gestalt therapy is not concerned with symptoms and analysis but rather with total existence and integration. Integration and maturation, according to Perls, are never-ending processes directly related to a person's awareness of the here and now. A "Gestalt" is formed in a person as a new need arises. If a need is satisfied, the destruction of that particular Gestalt is achieved, and new Gestalts can be formed. This concept is basic in Gestalt therapy. Incomplete Gestalts are referred to as "unfinished situations."

Perls (1969) wrote that the aim of his therapy was to help people help themselves to grow up—to mature, take charge of their lives, and become responsible for themselves. The central goal in Gestalt therapy is deeper awareness, which promotes a sense of living fully in the here and now. Other goals include teaching people to assume responsibility for themselves and facilitating their achievement of personal integration. These goals are consistent with those of most counseling systems.

The aim of integration is to help people become systematic, whole persons whose inner state and behavior match so that little energy is wasted within the system. Such integration allows people to give their full attention and energy to meeting their needs appropriately. The ultimate measure of success in Gestalt therapy is the extent to which clients grow in awareness, take responsibility for their actions, and move from environmental support to self-support.

COUNSELING METHOD

The function of the Gestalt counselor is to facilitate the client's awareness in the "now." Awareness is the capacity to focus, to attend, to be in touch with the now. The Gestalt counselor is an aggressive therapist who frustrates the learner's attempts to break out of the awareness of here and now. The counselor either stops, retreats into the past and jumps into the future or relates them to the immediate present.

Miller (1989) pointed out that Perls often used sarcasm, humor, drama, and shock to rouse people from neurosis. For Perls, Gestalt therapy was a search for a workable solution in the present. The counselor's job would be to assist the client in experimenting with authentic new behaviors rather than to explain and maintain the unhelpful or harmful behaviors of the past. Dolliver (1991), attacking "inconsistencies" in Perls's philosophy and style in the often-reviewed *Three Approaches to Psychotherapy* (Shostrom, 1965), concluded that none of the counselor's objectives in Miller's statement were met with Gloria. Miller and others, no doubt, disagree, and the controversy over the film will continue in the 21st century. Fritz Perls—in person or on film—never left anyone feeling neutral; he made everyone think and react.

Gestalt Techniques

Several language, game, and fantasy methods may be used to maintain the present-time orientation of the counseling interview. Helpful resources available to the counselor include books by Lederman (1969), Passons (1975), and Fagan and Shepard (1970). We and our students have used some of the following techniques with 5- to 12-year-old children.

"I" language. Encourage the use of the word *I* when the client uses a generalized *you* when talking, for example "*You* know how it is when *you* can't understand math and the teacher gets on *your* back." When *I* is substituted for *you*, the message becomes, "*I* know how it is when *I* can't understand math and the teacher gets on *my* back." The client tries on such substitutions of *I* for *you* like a pair of shoes to see how they fit. They help children take responsibility for their feelings, thoughts, and behaviors.

Substituting *won't* for *can't*. Again, the client tries on the "shoes" for comfort: "I *won't* pass math" rather than "I *can't* pass math." How much of the responsibility the child will own is the question to be answered.

Substituting *what* and *how* for *why*. "*How* do you feel about what you have just done?" "*What* are you doing with your foot as we talk about your behavior?"

No gossiping. If the child must talk about someone not present in the room, let the talk, all in the present tense, be directed to an empty chair. For example, the child might say, "I think you treat me unfairly, Ms. Clark. I wish you would be as nice to me as you are to the other kids." The child can then move to the other chair and answer for Ms. Clark. "Joan, I would find it easier to like you if you would be more helpful to me during the day." The dialogue between Joan and Ms. Clark would continue until the child finished her complaint and the anticipated responses from her teacher. Person-to-person dialogues not only update the material into the present but also increase the child's awareness of the problem. Side benefits include a better picture of the situation for the counselor and rehearsal time for the child, who may wish to discuss the problem later with the teacher. Some appreciation for the teacher's side of the conflict may also emerge from the dialogue.

Changing questions into statements. This method has the effect of helping children to be more authentic and direct in expressing their thoughts and feelings. For example, rather than "Don't you think I should stop hanging around those guys?" The child should say "I think I should stop hanging around those guys" or "I think you want me to stop hanging around those guys." Perls believed that most questions are phony in that they are really disguised statements.

Taking responsibility. Clients are asked to fill in sentence blanks as another way of examining personal responsibility for the way they manage their lives. For example, "Right now I'm feeling _____, and I take _____ percent responsibility for how I feel." The exercise is quite an eye-opener for those clients who tend to view outside sources as the total cause of their good and bad feelings.

Incomplete sentences. These exercises, like the exercise on taking responsibility, help clients become aware of how they help and hurt themselves. For example, "I help myself when I _____" or "I block or hurt myself when I _____."

Bipolarities. Perls applies the term *differential thinking* to the concept of thinking in terms of opposites. Much everyday life appears to be spent resolving conflicts posed by competing polarities.

Topdog Versus Underdog

One of the most common bipolarities is what Perls (1969) labeled *topdog* and *underdog*. The topdog is righteous, authoritarian, and knows best. The topdog is a bully and works with "you should" and "you should not." The underdog manipulates by being defensive or apologetic, wheedling, and playing crybaby. The underdog works with "I want" and makes excuses such as "I try hard" and "I have good intentions." The underdog is cunning and usually gets the better of the topdog because the underdog position appeals to the pleasure-seeking side of our personality.

Two chairs can be used to help children resolve "I want" versus "I should" debates. Label one chair topdog (I should), and the other chair underdog (I want). Children are asked to present their best "I should" argument while sitting in the topdog chair and facing the empty underdog chair. Upon completing the first "I should" point, the child moves to the underdog chair to counter with an "I want" argument. The debate continues back and forth until the child completes all arguments from both points of view. Processing the activity often reveals in which chair (or on which side of the argument) the child feels that the greatest integration of shoulds and wants occurs, thus allowing the client to have the best of both sides.

The topdog-underdog technique works for individuals and groups. To use the technique in a group, the counselor can divide the clients into two subgroups, the topdogs and the underdogs. The topdog group members list reasons they *should* do a certain thing, while the underdog group members think of reasons they *want* to do something. The lists generally lead to much discussion. Children respond very well to this activity.

The best outcomes from the topdog-underdog debate occur when children can identify areas in their lives where the "I shoulds" and "I wants" agree. For example, "I love to read, and I should read." These synergistic solutions help children integrate the polarities.

The Empty Chair Technique

The Gestalt technique of the empty chair is often used to resolve a conflict between people or within a person. The child can sit in one chair and play his or her own part; then, sitting in the other chair, the child can play out a projection of what the other person is saying or doing in response. Similarly, a child may sit in one chair to discuss the pros of making a decision and then argue the cons of the decision while sitting in the opposite chair.

For example, Sharon was having trouble deciding whether to tell of her friend's involvement in destruction of property. She thought her friend had behaved wrongly and should not let other children take the blame for the incident, yet she was reluctant to tattle on the friend and get her in trouble. The counselor suggested that Sharon sit in one chair and talk about what would happen if she did tell on her friend and then move to the other chair to describe what would happen if she did not. The technique helped Sharon to look at the consequences of both acts and make her decision.

Thompson and Poppen (1992) suggest a variation of the empty chair. A problem can be explored in an individual or group situation by introducing the empty chair as a hypothetical person with behaviors and characteristics similar to those of the child and his or her particular problem. It is sometimes easier for children to discuss a hypothetical child and how this child feels or could change than to discuss their own feelings and behaviors. While discussing an imagined person, children learn about themselves.

My Greatest Weakness

In another exercise, clients are asked to name their greatest weakness and write a short paragraph on how this weakness is really their greatest strength, for example, "My greatest weakness is procrastination, but I'll never give it up because by putting things off I create the motivation I need for completing unpleasant tasks."

Once clients realize that their greatest weakness may, in fact, be the greatest strength they have going for them, they begin to realize that they control the weakness rather than vice versa. Clients also realize that the counselor who uses this technique is not pushing them to fix their weakness.

Resent, Demand, and Appreciate

Another exercise involves listing the three people the client is closest to and, for each of the three, having the client think of one thing he or she resents about each person, one thing that is demanded, and one thing that is appreciated.

Name	I resent	I demand	I appreciate
John	that you don't spend enough time with me	more time	your company and friendship
Mary			
Sue			

Such an exercise helps clients become more aware of the mixed feelings they have about others, how it is possible to resent and appreciate a person at the same time, and how opposing thoughts and feelings can be integrated.

The purpose of working with these bipolarities, or splits in the personality, is to bring each side into awareness so a reorganization can take place that does not exclude either side. Gestalt therapy is directed toward making life easier by integrating the splits in existence; each side is necessary and has its place in the well-integrated personality.

Fantasy Games

Fantasy games can be great fun for children of all ages and can let them become aware of their feelings right now. As a group activity, the children choose an animal they would like to be and then move around as they think this animal would. The children sit down in pairs and discuss what they would feel if they were this particular animal. As a culmination to the activity, they write stories about how they would feel if they were actually the animal. By the end of the exercise, children should have a real awareness of how they feel and be able to discuss their feelings with the counselor, teacher, or parent.

Fantasy games can be devised from almost any object or situation. The rosebush and wise-person fantasies are two favorites. In the first, the client pretends to be a rosebush and then considers the following points:

1. Type of bush—strong or weak?
2. Root system—deep or shallow?
3. Number of roses—too many or too few?
4. Number of thorns—too many or too few?
5. Environment—bad or good for growing?
6. Does your rosebush stand out?
7. Does it have enough room?
8. How does it get along with the other plants?
9. Does it have a good future?

The wise-person fantasy involves asking a fantasized source of wisdom one question, which the wise person ponders for a few minutes before answering—speaking through the client, of course. Both question and answer should add some awareness and understanding to the client's life. For example, a client might ask, "What should I do with my life?" and answer, as the wise person, "Develop all your talents and skills as much as you can."

Clients are asked to discuss their fantasies in depth with the counselor in individual sessions and with groups of two to four if a group is meeting. A good follow-up procedure for clients is to complete the statement "I learned that _____ " after each exercise. The fantasy games are enhanced if clients lie down and participate in relaxation exercises before the experience and continue to lie down in a comfortable spot during the fantasy exercises.

Heikkinen (1989) wrote a helpful article on reorienting clients from altered states of consciousness (ASC), used in Gestalt and other therapies, in a way that avoids uncomfortable aftereffects such as unusual cognitive or emotional functioning and atypical body reactions. As clients may experience an ASC during activities such as the rosebush or wise-person fantasies, these activities should end with the counselor counting backward slowly from 10 or in the direction opposite to that used to reach the ASC. Imagining a walk up steps, a swim to the top of the lake, or a return from a journey is a useful method for reorienting clients. Directing clients in a group setting to look slowly around the area and become reacquainted with their environment is also effective.

Dreamwork

Dreaming is a way of becoming aware of the world in the here and now. Because awareness is the dominant theme of Gestalt, dreaming and Gestalt seem to work well together. Dreaming is a guardian of one's existence because the content of dreams always relate to one's survival, well-being, and growth; therefore, Gestalt therapists have helped clients overcome impasses in their lives through serious consideration of dreams. The Gestalt approach to dreams is helpful not only to people suffering from dilemmas in their lives but also to the average "healthy" person. Most people spend many of their waking hours out of touch with the here and now by worrying compulsively about the future or doting on memories of failure or past pleasures.

Spontaneity is an important feature of Gestalt therapy, and, according to Perls, dreams are the most spontaneous expression of the existence of the human being. The Gestalt approach is concerned with integration rather than analysis of dreams. Such integration involves consciously reliving a dream, taking responsibility for being the objects and people in the dream, and becoming aware of the messages the dream holds. According to Perls, all parts of the dream are fragments of the dreamer's personality that must be pieced together to form a whole. These projected fragments must be reowned; thus, hidden potential that appears in the dream is also to be reowned. As clients play the parts of all the objects and persons in the dream, they may become more aware of the message the dream holds. They may act out the dream until two conflicting roles emerge—for instance, the topdog and the underdog. This want-should conflict is essentially the conflict from which the dreamer suffers.

Gestaltists believe that dreams have hidden existential messages that, once discovered, can fill the voids in people's personalities. In the Gestalt framework, dreamwork holds many possibilities for solving the problems of life or for developing a better self-awareness.

Variations of the dreamwork method can be used with children. A volunteer can describe a dream, and other students can role-play the objects and people in the dream by expressing their thoughts and feelings. The volunteer can direct the dream enactment. The therapist's task in the integration of dreams is to concentrate on what clients are avoiding in their present existence and help them act out painful situations and reintegrate the alienated parts of their personality into their lives. Gestalt dreamwork is very effective in stopping recurring nightmares.

Gestalt Activities Adapted for Children

Polster and Polster (1973) discussed contact functions that highlight everyday communication. *Contact* usually implies touching in the physical sense. However, the seven processes of contact functioning—looking, listening, touching, talking, moving, smelling, and tasting—are not all directly physical; contact can also be made through space; for example, seeing is being touched by light waves, and hearing is being touched along the basilar membrane by sound waves. Although physical contact is one of the most obvious ways of reaching people, the opportunities for reaching people through space are certainly more available and can be very effective. Application of the contact function can be useful in the elementary school classroom. Children can become more aware of their present actions and feelings by participating in activities that bring about contact functioning. Listening activities are particularly appropriate for creating a classroom atmosphere conducive to learning.

Mullen (1990) suggested that Gestalt therapists familiarize themselves with the principles of developmental psychology to tailor Gestalt therapy methods to fit the developmental levels of their clients. Understanding developmental principles would also help Gestalt therapists understand differences in how clients construe reality as they grow and move through the various stages of development. Mullen cites the importance of Jean Piaget's work, as we do in chapter 1. The developmental theories of Erik Erikson and Robert Havighurst, also presented in chapter 1 are important, as are Freud's psychosexual stages, presented in chapter 3. Knowledge of developmental stages is a prime requisite for successful counseling.

Music

Teachers or counselors can play a melody on the piano or a tape. They ask the children to listen carefully to it and then to write down how the music makes them feel, what they think of when they hear it, and whether they like it. Different children read their papers and discuss their reactions. This exercise allows children to get in touch with their present feelings and evaluate what they hear and think as well.

Musical Instruments

Musical instruments can help emotions come forth that might otherwise be repressed. The counselor may choose a shy child to sit in the center of a circle of the other children and select one of several noisy instruments, such as cymbals or drums, for leading the group in lively, strong-sounding music. The other children may either also play instruments or clap hands and stamp their feet in time to the music. The shy child may become lost in the activity and, by banging away, express some emotions he or she usually hides. Leading the group may also enhance the child's self-confidence. This activity can also be used to elicit the opposite effect on a hyperactive or overaggressive child. The child could lead the group with a quiet instrument (perhaps the triangle) and play it during a soft song or lullaby. The counselor can encourage the rest of the group to close their eyes, think of peaceful things, and sway slowly to the music, which may give the child the experience of feeling peaceful and soothed.

Tone of Voice, Body Movement

This activity involves the contact functions of listening and looking. The counselor asks the children to select partners for role-playing certain emotions or feelings. The activity can be initiated as a result of some altercation between two youngsters. The group can discuss what emotions the two children were feeling or even role-play the incident. The counselor asks the children to notice not only the words spoken but also the tones of voice and body movements that express the emotion. After working out the bad feelings between the two children involved, the counselor can ask the children to think of other emotions and practice role-playing with their partners. When they have had a few minutes to practice a short scene to display an emotion, the counselor can select different partners to demonstrate for the class, each time making the class aware that emotion is expressed in many ways and that we need to learn to recognize how people show their feelings.

Awareness-Enhancing Activities

1. *Feelings awareness.* Give children the following directions: "For 5 minutes or so, focus your attention on the way things feel on your skin . . . the way you feel as your weight presses on the chair . . . the feel of your feet in your shoes and against the floor . . . the places where clothing is tight. . . . Can you feel any draft? Are some places warmer or colder than others? Now reach out and touch different things." Have a variety of objects and textured surfaces available for touching. The children can be asked to verbalize descriptions ("I don't like this, it feels squishy," "This feels rough," and so on).

2. *Taste time.* Have several bite-sized bits of different foods available— carrots, apples, turnips, meat, and so on—and give children the following directions: "For 5 minutes or so, focus your attention on the way several mouthfuls of food feel, change, and taste. Try not to talk to yourself as you do this. Feel the texture of the food with your tongue, lips, teeth, and mouth. Try the difference between bland, soft foods and crisp, strong-tasting foods. Toward the end of the exercise, take one bite of food and chew it, focusing

your awareness on it all the time until it is liquefied. Don't swallow it until it is absolutely liquefied."

3. *Mirror, Mirror.* Bring a good-sized mirror to the group and have the children look into it one at a time. Have each child look without any comment at all for 30 seconds or so, then ask the child to tell you what he or she sees. Ask for more and more description. Be gentle but persistent. When the child cannot come up with any more comments, shift to another child. Polaroid snapshots, videotaping, and even movies can be used in the same way to build self-awareness.

4. *Now.* Give children the following directions: "As you sit quietly, make statements to yourself about exactly what you are aware of at this very moment. Make every statement begin with 'Now I. . . .' Be aware of as many things as you can. Try writing things down. Then just talk to yourself. Finally, try to be aware without talking to yourself."

Art Activities

For disturbed children who cannot verbalize emotions, many art media can be used. The child can smear fingerpaint with hands or feet, create and destroy images with clay, and draw or paint pictures to express confusing feelings. When appropriate, the child can be encouraged to verbalize after the artwork is completed. ("Tell me about your picture.") See Chapter 12 for further elaboration on using the expressive arts in counseling.

Activities That Build Self-Confidence

1. *Touching games.* Children need to be touched, to touch others playfully and affectionately, and to realize the difference between "good" touch and "bad" touch. Hugs, pats on the back, and handshakes of various types should be a part of the counselor's reinforcement and encouragement repertoire. In addition, several touch games can be used with children's groups. "Group sitdown" requires that children form a circle with both hands on the shoulders of the person in front of them and then sit down on the lap of the person behind them. No chairs are used, and if done correctly, the circle maintains itself without anyone falling on the floor. In another touching game, the group forms two parallel lines with children sitting on the floor back to back. With arms interlocked with their back-to-back partner's, each person attempts to stand up. Good teamwork brings about good results in both activities. Shoulder massages are also popular and can be done in a group setting with children standing in a circle massaging the shoulders of the person in front of them. The "trust fall" often introduces the topic of trusting others not to let you down. Partners take turns catching each other as they fall with their backs toward their partners. The various touch games promote teamwork, trust, and experience with the good touch of nonsexual caring for one another.

2. *Applause! Applause!* The group gathers and sits in a circle with space cleared in the center of the floor. One at a time, children go to the cleared space and say their names aloud. At this, the rest of the group loudly cheers, claps, shouts "bravo!" and so forth. Children acknowledge the applause in whatever way they choose.

3. *Confidence courses.* This gentle form of obstacle course, designed to build confidence, uses combinations of pit jumps, incline balances, boxes, barrels, ladder climbs, rope slides, and the like. (Children can also be involved in constructing such a course.) As children attain better motor coordination and balance, they form better self-images, a feeling of mastery, and an "I can do it" attitude about themselves. They begin to feel they can solve problems and deal with their world competently.

◆ ◆ ◆
C A S E   S T U D I E S

Many short-term counseling sessions can be conducted with children using the empty chair technique. For example, consider the following method for working with anger.

Child: I hate my dad. He's mean. I hate his guts.

Counselor: Let's pretend your dad is sitting in that empty chair. What do you want to say to him? You can walk over there and say whatever you want.

Child: Get off my back! Leave me alone! I cleaned my room just as good as I could.

Counselor: Now sit in the other chair. Pretend to be your dad.

Child: I've told you and told you that this room looks like a pigpen.

Counselor: Now be yourself again.

Child: I cleaned my room good, Dad! Then you came in and said it still isn't good enough. Nothing was left out in the room but my toys!

Counselor: Now be your dad.

Child: This is the last time I'm telling you, Son. The room better be finished when I get back. That means toys, too.

Counselor: Now be you.

Child: You don't care about me! You don't care about how I feel. You just worry about the house being messed up. You get mad when I get out my toys. Kids are supposed to have toys! It's MY ROOM! Quit buggin' me! [accompanied by much nonverbal expression of anger as well as the overt angry verbal content]

The child has expressed his strong thoughts that his room should be his territory, that it should be okay to have his toys out. A global "hatred" for the father has been reduced to anger about a specific recurring problem (the differing standards for the room held by the parent and the child). After release of the built-up anger, some problem solving could achieve a compromise about the room situation.

Another sample counseling session involves the topdog-underdog debate, using an empty chair for each "dog." This technique is useful when the child has a decision-making problem. Most decision-making problems involve a debate between the inner voice of "I should do . . ." (topdog) versus "Yes, but I want to do . . ." (underdog). An empty chair is assigned to each point of view.

Identification of the Problem

Susan is experiencing a conflict over whether to live with her mother or with her father when their divorce is final.

Individual and Background Information

Susan Adams is a 10-year-old in the fourth grade. Her mother and father are getting a divorce, and she has to decide whether to live with her mother or her father. Susan is the second of three children. This marriage was the second for Susan's mother and the first for Susan's father. Her elder brother is not her father's son. Both parents work in factory jobs, but their income seems to be limited by the fact that Susan's father drinks up most of his paycheck. Susan is an average student in school; she is quiet and has never been a behavior problem. She gets along well with her peers at school. Susan's physical health is good, but she has a vision problem that requires a new pair of glasses, which her parents parents say they do not have the money to buy.

Transcript

Counselor: Susan, we have the next 30 minutes for our talk. Where would you like to start?

Susan: Well, you know my problem about having to decide whether to live with Mom or Daddy after their divorce is final. I just don't know what I'm going to do.

Counselor: I know that when we talked about this the other day, you were feeling really upset about this situation of having to choose between your mom and dad. I can tell you still feel this way.

Susan: Yes, I do. I did all the things we talked about—like talking to both of them. That made it even harder to decide because they both want me. I still don't know what to do. I wish they would stop the divorce.

Counselor: Well, it's a good feeling to know that they both want you, but a bad feeling to know you have to choose. You would really like to have them stay together.

Susan: Yes, I really would, but that's impossible! I've tried every way I can to keep them together.

Counselor: Susan, would you try an exercise with me that might help clarify your thinking about this decision?

Susan: I'll try anything to help.

Counselor: [explains and demonstrates the topdog-underdog technique] So, when you are in the topdog chair, you say "I should . . ." and when you are in the underdog chair, you say "I want. . . ." Okay?

Susan: Okay [goes to the topdog chair first].

Topdog: I should go with Daddy because he'll be all alone.

Underdog: Yes, but I want to stay with Mom because I hate to give up my room, and I want to stay with my sister.

Topdog: What is Daddy going to do without anyone to cook for him and clean house?

Underdog: Why can't he hire a maid, and I can visit him a lot, too?

Topdog: If I don't live with Daddy, he won't have anybody, because he doesn't want Jake, and Sally is too young to move away from Mom.

Underdog: Well, Daddy goes out and drinks a lot with his friends, and sometimes he gets sick and is not nice to be around when he gets drunk.

Topdog: I think I should take care of him when he gets sick.

Underdog: I think it is better not to be near him when he drinks. I would like to visit him when he is not drinking.

Topdog: How can I live with Mom and help Daddy, too?

Underdog: I just know things will be better if I live with Mom in my room and see Daddy as often as I can.

Counselor: Do you think you've finished with this argument, Susan?

Susan: Yes, I've said all I can think of.

Counselor: I'm wondering what you learned from doing this exercise.

Susan: Well, I think things will be better if I stay where I am with Mom. But I'll need to see a lot of Daddy—as much as I can. I love them both so much [starts to cry].

Counselor: I know this has to be a sad and rough time for you. It really hurts, doesn't it?

Susan: It sure does. I need to be brave about this and not let it make me so sad.

Counselor: Its okay to feel sad about this. You can always come in here to talk to me when you want to.

[Counselor terminates the interview and schedules another session for the next day.]

◆ ◆ ◆ ◆ ◆ ◆ ◆ ◆ ◆

RESEARCH AND APPLICATIONS

Fritz Perls took pride in the fact that Gestalt therapists were doers, not researchers and writers. One of his pet four-letter, descriptive terms was reserved for the material turned out by researchers and writers on the topic of psychotherapy. In spite of Perls, the literature on Gestalt therapy continues to grow; however, little of it is research.

Noting the lack of research on Gestalt therapy, Skolnick (1990) warned against enshrinement of current philosophy and theory. Instead, he suggested Gestalt therapy and theory need to be revitalized through good research. Miller (1989) stated an opposite concern, that Gestalt therapy may lose its identity because it is being absorbed into other systems as others rediscover the obvious, just as Perls did.

Agreeing with Miller, Laura Perls (1992) discussed her concerns about the misconceptions surrounding Gestalt therapy. She noted that many therapists who had attended Fritz's workshops began to attach Gestalt therapy to whatever they happened to be working on at the time. People began holding workshops on such topics as sensitivity training and Gestalt therapy or transcendental meditation and Gestalt therapy. Laura Perls noted that Gestalt therapy has been useful in working with a variety of subject areas and client treatment programs. However, she pointed out that Fritz Perls realized that Gestalt methods were not effective in working with every type of disorder and would not work with people who had paranoid or schizoid disturbances.

Laura Perls discussed other misconceptions about Gestalt therapy. Contrary to popular belief, Gestalt therapy is not limited to treating the here-and-now aspects of the client's life. The focus of Gestalt therapy is on the here-and-now present occurring within the therapy session; however, a person's past and present life outside therapy are also valued by Gestalt therapists. Fritz Perls believed that the past is very real in defining our life experiences and memories.

Laura Perls reminded her readers that Fritz Perls thought that tension was too valuable to waste. Tension is an indicator that something in a person's life is not working or that some unfinished business needs attention. Yet, many therapists use Gestalt methods to rid their clients of tension. Tension, as a resource, can provide the motivation and energy to make adjustments and changes in one's life.

Further misconceptions surround the use of Gestalt methods for quick and exciting results, whereas Gestalt therapy was developed as a lengthy, time-consuming process. Effective practitioners of Gestalt therapy use small steps to help clients heighten their own awareness. Too much awareness too soon can have an adverse effect on clients. Clients cannot be expected to drop elaborate defenses and "walk without these crutches" after just a few sessions. Living without defenses requires considerable rehearsal and practice within the therapy session.

Others are concerned about the misuse of popular Gestalt techniques with fragile clients who cannot handle the emotional intensity these methods generate. Fagan and Shepard (1970) offered words of caution regarding the Gestalt approach with severely disturbed or psychotic clients. They recommended caution, sensitivity, and patience. In the initial stages of therapy, they preferred to limit therapeutic activity to procedures that strengthen clients' contact with reality, their confidence in their own being, and their faith in the counselor's goodwill and competence, rather than involving them in role-playing or reenactment of past experiences of pain or conflict. This advice seems sensible. Fagan and Shepard endorsed activities that increase sensory, perceptual, and motor capacities toward self-support. Such activities could be useful adjuncts to many other therapies with children and could be employed in a wide variety of settings.

Greenberg (1989) echoed similar concerns about using traditional Gestalt therapy with people who have borderline personality disorder. He recommended interactive group therapy over talking to a dead parent in an empty chair and "hot-seat" confrontations. Therefore, the question of who should receive Gestalt therapy is as important as the skill, training, experience, and judgment of the therapist. A counselor who uses this approach must be neither afraid nor inept in allowing the client to follow through and finish the experience of grief, rage, fear, or joy. Without such skill, the counselor may leave the client vulnerable (Fagan & Shepard, 1970).

Aylward (1988), in an attempt to give readers a better understanding of Gestalt therapy, presented a transcript of a session complete with commentary on breakthroughs made toward helping the client overcome a decision-making block. This article is especially helpful in understanding the counseling process from a Gestalt viewpoint.

Another issue hinges on the questions of when, with whom, and in what situations Gestalt therapy should be used. In general, Gestalt therapy is most effective with overly socialized, restrained, constricted individuals. Less organized, more severely disturbed clients require long-term counseling. Limiting activities at first to those that strengthen a client's contact with reality is preferable to role-playing situations further removed from the here and now. Individuals whose problems lie in lack of impulse control, acting out, and delinquency require a different approach. For these people, Gestalt therapy can reinforce the activities that are causing the problems.

Gestalt Methods with Children

Greater optimism for using Gestalt methods, particularly with children, is found in the writings of Oaklander (1978, 1993) and Owmby (1983).

Oaklander described several Gestalt techniques she adapted for children. She recommended projection through art and storytelling as a way of increasing the child's self-awareness and cited fantasy and imagery, such as the wise-person fantasy, as good ways to tap intuitive thought in children and adults. Oaklander has also used the empty chair method frequently, as a helpful way to handle unfinished business, frustration, and anger.

Owmby (1983), in another article on Gestalt therapy with children, described adaptations of the topdog-underdog technique, as well as projection and retroflection. The author suggested the topdog-underdog method for angry children who can talk to their angry self in another chair and find out why they are so upset, as well as projection for the child who is afraid of an ugly monster. The child can become the monster and allow that creature to explain its motives for scaring children. Retroflection is giving voice to that part of the body that is exhibiting muscular tension. The counselor may ask a child who tightens up his or her mouth to say what the mouth would like to say.

Allan and Crandall (1986) found that the use of relaxation and visual imagery, drawing, and postdrawing inquiry to identify coping and noncoping students was accurate about 80% of the time for counselors trained in projective techniques. The study was conducted with fourth- and fifth-grade students. The authors suggested that the rosebush visualization could identify sexually abused children.

Alexander and Harman (1988) reported a successful application of a Gestalt approach to group counseling with middle school classmates of a student who committed suicide. Using the empty chair, writing, and artwork, children said goodbye and discussed their own fears and anxieties about suicide.

Outcome Research

Outcome research in Gestalt therapy is mostly in the categories of training and treatment. Simkin (1976), working with experienced therapists, found that training in Gestalt therapy could be successfully condensed into a 3-month period. Greenberg and Sarkissian (1984) had similar success in teaching Gestalt counseling methods such as the two-chair dialogue to counselors in training. Simkin (1979) found that residential patients rated Gestalt therapy workshops as more helpful than individual and group therapy. The nine-to-one preference for the workshops is a favorable point for conducting counseling as an educational enterprise.

Frew (1988) surveyed Gestalt therapists to ascertain the nature, frequency, and usefulness of group work in Gestalt therapy. They ranked group skills second in importance to individual therapy skills by 9 percentage points. Many therapists reported using individual methods within the group setting.

Holiman and Engle (1989) conducted observational studies on Gestalt training through group supervision, with trainees role-playing therapist, client, and observer. The trainees were taught to attend first to the content of the client's story, second to the process, and third to the integration of content and process. Holiman and Engle recommended group Gestalt training in which trainees play all three roles and receive feedback from the group.

Several outcome studies on treatment with Gestalt methods have also been documented. Conoley, McConnell, Conoley, and Kimzey (1983), working with college students, found both the empty chair technique of Gestalt therapy and the ABC technique of rational-emotive-behavior therapy (see chapter 7) to be effective in anger reduction; reflective listening was less effective.

Clarke and Greenberg (1986), working with adult clients, compared the Gestalt two-chair intervention with a cognitive-behavioral intervention for treating decision-making conflicts. The two-chair intervention proved superior to the cognitive-behavioral intervention as well as to the no-treatment control group. The cognitive-behavioral group outperformed the control group in resolving indecision.

Greenberg and Webster (1982) used the Gestalt two-chair dialogue in a study with adolescents and adults on the process and outcome of resolving decision-making conflicts. Such conflicts, arising from underlying splits between the client's standards and values on the one hand and personal wants and needs on the other, were resolved through the two-chair method. The study also revealed two basic groups of clients—resolvers and nonresolvers—based on a pattern of in-session progress indicators. Resolvers reported greater resolution, less discomfort, greater mood change, and greater goal attainment than nonresolvers.

Serok and Zemet (1983) increased the reality perception of adult schizophrenic patients by using Gestalt therapy methods. In one exercise, they asked patients to recall (with eyes closed) who sat next to whom and what each person wore to enable participants to better perceive concrete elements in their environment. Miming was also used to help the participants perceive events occurring in a series.

Serok and Bar (1984), working with graduate students, compared a Gestalt group with a t-group and a lecture group on posttreatment gains in self-concept. The Gestalt group outgained the other groups in decisiveness, general adaptation, and self-criticism and self-concept. No group differences were found for self-identification or self-acceptance.

In a discussion of paradoxical counseling strategies in transactional analysis and Gestalt therapy, Wathney (1982) proposed that paradoxical strategies give clients control over their problem behavior. The theory that forced change can actually inhibit change is basic to most counseling theories. Proponents of Gestalt theory contend that clients must be allowed to change spontaneously. Paradoxical counseling strategies allow spontaneous change. For example, a client wants to be rid of grief over the loss of a loved one; instead of providing relief, the counselor encouraged the person to experience the grief more fully. The human tendency to rebel may, in fact, provide the relief. Wathney presented another application example, a male adolescent suffering from insomnia. He was told to stay up past his usual bedtime so he could work on an unpleasant task (math homework) and then do a relaxation exercise. Success in sleeping was immediate; no report was given of his math grade.

Halfond (1989) employed Gestalt counseling with adolescent and adult male stutterers. Participants experienced increased social interaction and expression of affect. Although the decrease in stuttering was minimal, the participants expressed increased interest in working with a speech therapist.

Hill, Beutler, and Daldrup (1989) attempted to study the relationship of process to outcome in Gestalt therapy. Two therapists conducted 18 sessions with 6 white women who suffered from rheumatoid arthritis. The authors found that all patients improved in positive feelings. However, the therapist rated higher by patients for session smoothness (process) had patients who experienced lower levels of dependency and global severity (outcome).

SUMMARY

Saner (1989) voiced concerns about possible cultural bias in U.S. Gestalt therapy. He suggested several ways to make Gestalt therapy valid across cultures: Drop the ethnocentric emphasis on the individual in favor of stressing reciprocal interaction by all participants in a social setting, use psychodrama in group therapy rather than the hot-seat method of individual therapy within the group setting, and incorporate contributions from other disciplines in Gestalt theory and practice.

Enns (1987) made a similar argument for integrating the self-responsibility and individualism of Gestalt therapy with the feminist values of interrelatedness and interdependence. She considered Gestalt therapy helpful in meeting three important goals of feminist therapy: (1) definition of the self and empowerment, (2) awareness and constructive use of anger, and (3) discovery of alternatives.

Because Gestalt techniques facilitate discovery, facing, and resolution of the client's major conflict, often in a dramatically short time, the inexperienced therapist, observer, or client might assume that Gestalt therapy offers an "instant cure." Even experienced counselors are tempted to push the client to a stance of self-support too fast, too soon. Group Gestalt therapy is common, but frequently it amounts to individual counseling in a group setting. Another hazard is the counselor's assumption of excessive responsibility for the direction of the group by too much activity, thus fostering client passivity and defeating the goal of client self-support. Extensive experience with Gestalt therapy may actually make clients less fit for or less adjusted to contemporary society; at the same time, however, they may be motivated to work toward changing the world into a more compassionate and productive milieu in which human beings can develop, work, and enjoy their full humanness.

Perls seems to have done well in his attempt to establish the philosophy and practice of Gestalt therapy. The approach is well grounded in and consistent with the principles of human behavior. By removing the mystique of professional jargon, he made Gestalt therapy comprehensible to the general public. Many counselors, while choosing not to become true believers or disciples of Gestalt therapy, use many of the procedures reported in the Gestalt literature. Most notable among these techniques are the two-chair dialogue, visualization, fantasy, and projection.

REFERENCES

Alexander, J., & Harman, L. (1988). One counselor's intervention in the aftermath of middle school student's suicide: A case study. *Journal of Counseling and Development, 66*, 283–285.

Allan, J., & Crandall, J. (1986). The rosebush: A visualization strategy. *Elementary School Guidance and Counseling, 21*, 44–51.

Assagioli, R. (1965). *Psychosynthesis.* New York: Viking Press.

Aylward, J. (1988). A session with Cindy. *Gestalt Journal, 11*(1), 51–61.

Clarke, K., & Greenberg, L. (1986). Differential effects of the Gestalt two-chair intervention and problem solving in resolving decisional conflict. *Journal of Counseling Psychology, 33,* 11–14.

Conoley, C., McConnell, J., Conoley, J., & Kimzey, C. (1983). The effect of the ABCs of rational emotive therapy and the empty chair technique of Gestalt therapy on anger reduction. *Psychotherapy: Theory, Research and Practice, 20,* 112–116.

Dolliver, R. (1991). Perls with Gloria re-reviewed: Gestalt techniques and Perls's practices. *Journal of Counseling and Development, 69,* 299–304.

English, H., & English, A. (1958). *A comprehensive dictionary of psychological terms.* New York: Longmans, Green.

Enns, C. Z. (1987). Gestalt therapy and feminist therapy: A proposed integration. *Journal of Counseling and Development, 66,* 93–95.

Fagan, J., & Shepard, I. (1970). *Gestalt therapy now.* Palo Alto, CA: Science and Behavior Books.

Frew, J. (1988). The practice of Gestalt therapy in groups. *Gestalt Journal, 11*(1), 77–94.

Greenberg, E. (1989). Healing the borderline. *Gestalt Journal, 12,* 11–55.

Greenberg, L., & Sarkissian, M. (1984). Evaluation of counselor training in Gestalt methods. *Counselor Education and Supervision, 23,* 328–339.

Greenberg, L., & Webster, M. (1982). Resolving decisional conflict through Gestalt two chair dialogue: Relating process to outcome. *Journal of Counseling Psychology, 29,* 468–477.

Halfond, M. (1989). Gestalt therapy with stutterers. *Folia Phoniatrica, 41,* 173.

Heikkinen, C. (1989). Reorientation from altered states: Please, more carefully. *Journal of Counseling and Development, 67,* 520–521.

Hill, D., Beutler, L., & Daldrup, R. (1989). The relationship of process to outcome in brief experiential psychotherapy for chronic pain. *Journal of Clinical Psychology, 45,* 951–956.

Holiman, M., & Engle, D. (1989). Guidelines for training in advanced Gestalt therapy skills. *Journal for Specialists in Group Work, 14,* 75–83.

Lederman, J. (1969). *Anger and the rocking chair: Gestalt awareness with children.* New York: McGraw-Hill.

Miller, M. (1989). Introduction to Gestalt therapy verbatim. *Gestalt Journal, 7*(1), 5–24.

Mullen, P. (1990). Gestalt therapy and constructive developmental psychology. *Gestalt Journal, 13,* 69–90.

Oaklander, V. (1978). *Windows to our children.* Moab, UT: Real People Press.

Oaklander, V. (1993). From meek to bold: A case study of Gestalt therapy. In T. Kottman & C. Schaefer (Eds.) *Play therapy in action: A casebook for practitioners* (pp. 281–300). Northvale, NJ: Aronson.

Owmby, R. L. (1983). Gestalt therapy with children. *Journal of Gestalt Therapy, 6,* 51–58.

Passons, W. (1975). *Gestalt approaches in counseling.* New York: Holt, Rinehart & Winston.

Perls, F. (1969). *Gestalt therapy verbatim.* Moab, UT: Real People Press.

Perls, F. (1971). *In and out the garbage pail.* New York: Bantam Books.

Perls, F. (1976). *The Gestalt approaches and eye witnesses to therapy.* New York: Bantam Books.

Perls, F., Hefferline, R., & Goodman, P. (1951). *Gestalt therapy.* New York: Julian Press.

Perls, L. (1992). Concepts and misconceptions of Gestalt therapy. *Journal of Humanistic Psychology, 32*(3), 50–56.

Polster, E., & Polster, M. (1973). *Gestalt therapy integrated: Contours of theory and practice*. New York: Brunner/Mazel.

Sahakian, W. (Ed.). (1969). *Psychotherapy and counseling: Studies in technique*. Chicago: Rand McNally.

Saner, R. (1989). Culture bias of gestalt therapy: Made-in-U.S.A. *Gestalt Journal, 12,* 57–71.

Serok, S., & Bar, R. (1984). Looking at Gestalt group impact on environment. *Small Group Behavior, 15,* 270–277.

Serok, S., & Zemet, R. M. (1983). An experiment of Gestalt group therapy with hospitalized schizophrenics. *Psychotherapy: Theory, Research and Practice, 20,* 417–424.

Shepard, M. (1975). *Fritz*. New York: Saturday Review Press.

Shostrom, E. (Producer). (1965). *Three approaches to psychotherapy: Part 2. Fredrick Perls* [Film]. Orange, CA: Psychological Films.

Simkin, J. (1976). *Gestalt therapy mini-lectures*. Millbrae, CA: Celestial Arts.

Simkin, J. (1979). Gestalt therapy. In R. Corsini (Ed.), *Current psychotherapies* (pp. 273–301). Itasca, IL: F. E. Peacock.

Skolnick, T. (1990). Boundaries, boundaries, boundaries. *Gestalt Journal, 13,* 55–68.

Thompson, C., & Poppen, W. (1992). *Guidance activities for counselors and teachers*. Knoxville, TN: The University of Tennessee.

Wathney, S. (1982). Paradoxical interventions in transactional analysis and Gestalt therapy. *Transactional Analysis Journal, 12,* 185–189.

Chapter 7

◆

Rational-Emotive-Behavior Therapy* and Cognitive-Behavior Therapy

ALBERT ELLIS

Albert Ellis is currently executive director of the Institute for Advanced Study in Rational Psychotherapy in New York, a community agency chartered by the regents of the State University of New York. He is widely known as the founder or developer of rational-emotive therapy, which he has recently renamed rational-emotive-behavior therapy (REBT) (A. Ellis, personal communication, 1994).

For the past 5 decades, Ellis has given individualized remedial instruction— what he calls *emotional education*—to several thousand adults, adolescents, and children. In addition, he has conducted group therapy with more than 3,000 adults and adolescents.

Ellis was born in Pittsburgh in 1913 and grew up in New York City. In spite of a difficult childhood, he managed to earn a degree in business administration from the City University of New York in 1934. He earned his living during the Depression first by working with his brother in a business that located matching pants for still-usable suit coats. Later he worked as the personnel manager in a gift and novelty firm.

Ellis's ambition was to write, which he did in his spare time. He collected material for two books on sexual adjustment that were eventually published: *The American Sexual Tragedy* (1954) and *The Case for Sexual Liberty* (1965). His friends began to regard him as an expert on the subject and often asked his advice. He discovered he enjoyed counseling people as much as writing and decided to return to school. In 1942, Ellis entered the clinical psychology program at Columbia University and in 1947 was awarded his doctorate.

---

* Albert Ellis has changed the name of his Theory/Therapy from Rational-Emotive Therapy (RET) to Rational-Emotive Behavior Therapy (REBT).

Ellis's early professional work as a therapist in state institutions in New Jersey employed classical psychoanalytic methods, but Ellis has set psychoanalysis aside completely. His change in philosophy came about when he discovered that clients treated once a week or even every other week progressed as well as those he saw daily. Ellis found that a more active role, interjecting advice and direct interpretation, yielded faster results than passive psychoanalytic procedures. His own theory of counseling, however, did not emerge until after he had received his doctorate from Columbia and later received training as a traditional psychoanalytic therapist. Consequently, some of the origins of REBT can be traced to Freud and some to disillusionment with Freudian psychoanalysis.

After discovering that rationalist philosophy fit his temperament and taste, Ellis began concentrating on changing people's behavior by confronting them with their irrational beliefs and persuading them to adopt more rational ones. He now considers himself a philosophical or educational therapist and sees REBT as uniquely didactic, cognition-oriented, and explicative. He believes that REBT places people at the center of the universe and gives them almost full responsibility for their fate.

More than 400 books and articles, in addition to his Institute for Rational Living, have proceeded from Ellis's conceptualization of REBT. From its early days to the present, he has modified REBT. Writing in 1977, Ellis noted that REBT, once a limited rational-persuasive therapy, had grown into a therapy that consciously used cognitive, emotive, and behavioral techniques to help clients (Ellis, 1977). In 1957, he published his first REBT book, *How to Live with a "Neurotic"* (1957/1975), and in 1960 his first really successful book, *The Art and Science of Love* (1960/1969a).

Dryden (1989a), in an interview with Albert Ellis, explored four topics—Ellis's early years, women and marriage, his personal characteristics and reflections on his professional career—that provided insights into Ellis's personal and professional life.

THE NATURE OF PEOPLE

Ellis based rational-emotive-behavior therapy on the philosophy of Epictetus (ca. A.D. 55–135): "What disturbs men's minds is not events, but their judgment of events." Generally speaking, very young children and animals have limited emotional repertoires and tend to express emotions in a quick, unsustained manner. When children grow old enough to use language effectively, they acquire the ability to sustain their emotions and possibly keep themselves emotionally upset. Rather than concentrating on past events, REBT practitioners emphasize present events and how one reacts to them. The theory of REBT stresses that, as human beings, we have choices. We control our ideas, attitudes, feelings, and actions, and we arrange our lives according to our own dictates. We have little control over what happens or what actually exists, but we do have both choices and control over how we view the

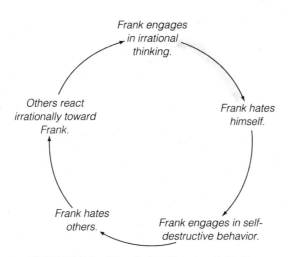

FIGURE 7-1   The circle of irrational thinking

world and how we react to difficulties, regardless of how we have been taught to respond.

People are neither good nor bad if they respond to others with a rational belief system, according to REBT theory. If individuals react with irrational beliefs, however, they view themselves and others as evil, awful, and horrible whenever they or others fall short of their expectations. Ellis (1987) viewed humans as naturally irrational, self-defeating individuals who need to be taught to be otherwise. They think crookedly about their desires and preferences and escalate them self-defeatingly into musts, shoulds, oughts, and demands. In assimilating these irrational beliefs, people become emotionally disturbed and feel anger, anxiety, depression, worthlessness, self-pity, or other negative feelings that lead to destructive behavior. However, Ellis also stated that people can be "naturally" helpful and loving *as long as they do not think irrationally.* In other words, Ellis described a circular process, as depicted in Figure 7-1. Irrational thinking leads to self-hate, which leads to self-destructive behavior and eventually to hatred of others, which, in turn, causes others to act irrationally toward the individual and thus to begin the cycle again.

Ellis wrote that some of our irrational thoughts are biological in origin, but the majority stem from our upbringing (parents, teachers, and clergy). Ellis has described three areas in which people hold irrational beliefs: They must be perfect, others must be perfect, or the world must be a perfect place to live. The following examples describe in a nutshell what people tell themselves when they interpret events with an irrational belief system. A more rational replacement thought follows each irrational self-message.

1. Because it would be highly preferable if I were outstandingly competent, I absolutely should and must be; it is awful when I am not, and I am therefore a worthless individual.

- *Alternative:* It would be nice if I were outstanding in whatever I do, but if I am not, it is okay, and I will try my best anyway.

2. Because it is highly desirable that others treat me considerately and fairly, they absolutely should and must, and they are rotten people who deserve to be utterly damned when they do not.

- *Alternative:* I would prefer people to treat me considerately. However, I realize they will not always, so I will not take it personally when they do not, *and* I will make it my business to be considerate.

3. Because it is preferable that I experience pleasure rather than pain, the world should absolutely arrange this outcome, and life is horrible and I can't bear it when the world doesn't.

- *Alternative:* I realize that in life there are both pleasurable moments and painful moments. Therefore, I will try to make the painful moments positive learning experiences so I can endure trials and even benefit from them.

THEORY OF COUNSELING

When interpreting daily events with one or more irrational philosophies, the individual is likely to feel angry or hostile toward others or to internalize these feelings with resulting anxiety, guilt, or depression. In essence, REBT theory holds that people are primarily responsible for their feelings about themselves, others, and the environment and for whether they want to be perpetually disturbed by them.

In their *A New Guide to Rational Living*, Ellis and Harper (1975) wrote that, because humans naturally and easily think crookedly, express emotions inappropriately, and behave self-defeatingly, it seems best to use all possible educational modes dramatically, strongly, and persistently to teach them how to do otherwise. Ellis and Harper compiled a list of irrational beliefs that cause people trouble.

1. It is a dire necessity for people to be loved or approved by almost everyone for virtually everything they do.
2. One should be thoroughly competent, adequate, and achieving in all possible respects.
3. Certain people are bad, wicked, or villainous, and they should be severely blamed and punished for their sins.
4. It is terrible, horrible, and catastrophic when things are not going the way one would like them to go.
5. Human unhappiness is externally caused, and people have little or no ability to control their sorrows or rid themselves of their negative feelings.
6. If something is or may be dangerous or fearsome, one should be terribly occupied with and upset about it.
7. It is easier to avoid facing many life difficulties and self-responsibilities than to undertake more rewarding forms of self-discipline.

8. The past is all-important, and because something once strongly affected one's life, it should do so indefinitely.
9. People and things should be different from the way they are, and it is catastrophic if perfect solutions to the grim realities of life are not immediately found.
10. Maximum human happiness can be achieved by inertia and inaction or by passively and uncommittedly enjoying oneself.
11. My child is delinquent [or emotionally disturbed or mentally retarded]; therefore, I'm a failure as a parent.
12. My child is emotionally disturbed [or mentally retarded]; therefore, he or she is severely handicapped and will never amount to anything.
13. I cannot give my children everything they want; therefore, I am inadequate.

Goodman and Maultsby (1974) constructed a list of 26 consequences that may result from irrational thinking, which include the following:

1. High degree of interpersonal difficulties
2. Persisting in emotionalism in reacting to daily problems
3. Desiring what one cannot have or is unlikely to get
4. Not wanting or appreciating what one has or could get
5. Tending to attribute all one's difficulties to others
6. Tending to see oneself as worthless
7. Pursuing contradictory goals or behavior inconsistent with professed goals
8. Tolerating bad situations rather than taking steps to rectify or improve them
9. Remaining dependent on others past the point when it is necessary
10. Remaining angry or hurt past a reasonable period of time
11. Demanding perfection in one's own behavior or in that of others
12. Indulging in behavior that injures one's body or mind or impedes one's functioning
13. Needlessly tormenting self over past events or presumed failures
14. Chronic or intermittent states of depression or anxiety
15. Unreasonable fears
16. Excessive anger

Crawford and Ellis (1989) provided further information on irrational beliefs and their consequences in their dictionary of 36 self-defeating feelings accompanied by their corresponding rational and irrational beliefs. In the listing, the rational beliefs appear first and are often followed by sequential irrational beliefs to form a chain of irrational beliefs. Crawford and Ellis classified each irrational belief into one of five categories: (1) *self-defeating* beliefs that interfere with basic goals and drives, (2) highly rigid and *dogmatic* beliefs that lead to unrealistic preferences and wishes, (3) *antisocial* beliefs that cause people to destroy their social groups, (4) *unrealistic* beliefs that falsely describe reality, and (5) *contradictory* beliefs that originate from false premises.

In "What Rational-Emotive Therapy Is and Is Not," Ellis (1974) made the following points:

1. Anxiety is not "irrational" but an inappropriate feeling that stems largely from irrational ideas. Feelings should not be confused with ideas.
2. Clients have almost full or complete responsibility for their ideas and consequently for their feelings.
3. Clients mainly—not early environment or conditioning or contemporary conditions—choose to create their irrational ideas and consequent feelings. They can choose to change their ideas.
4. Do not blame, damn, denigrate, or condemn people for choosing irrational ideas, inappropriate feelings, or defeating behaviors.
5. Discourage absolutes, such as *must, should,* and *ought,* in clients' thinking. There are no absolutes (pun intended).
6. Therapists definitely do not determine whether clients' ideas or behaviors are rational or irrational.

The goal of rational-emotive-behavior therapy is to teach people to think and behave in a more personally satisfying way by making them realize they have a choice between self-defeating, negative behavior and efficient, enhancing, positive behavior. It teaches people to take responsibility for their own logical thinking and the consequences or behaviors that follow it.

COUNSELING METHOD

In the past, counselors concentrated on either the developmental events in one's life or one's feelings about these events. Ellis did not believe these two main methods were totally erroneous, but he did not find either approach very effective. Neither approach explained why some people are rather well adjusted (that is, not too unhappy too much of the time, regardless of the passage of events) and others are emotionally dysfunctional much of the time with the same passage of events.

Ellis theorized that individuals' belief systems predicate their responses or feelings toward the same events. These individual belief systems are what people tell themselves about an event—in particular, an unfortunate incident. For example, 100 people may be rejected by their true loves. One of these people may respond: "I can't go on; I've lost my purpose in life. Because I've been rejected by such a wonderful person, I must really be a worthless slob. My only solution for getting rid of the unbearable pain I feel is to kill myself." Another may respond: "What a pain in the neck! I had dinner reservations and tickets for the show. Now I have to get another date for Saturday night. This surely sets me back. What an inconvenience!" Between these two extreme reactions are several other degrees of bad feelings growing from the various self-messages of the rejected

100. Such a wide variety of reactions to the same basic event suggests that one's view of the event and consequent self-message provide the key to the counseling strategy. The same process happens to children who experience bad feelings from school failure, peer conflicts, and conflicts with adults.

In the development of REBT, Ellis postulated, among other things, a system of inherently irrational beliefs or philosophies common to our culture that are conducive to maladjustment. Jones (1968) developed an instrument to measure these beliefs. He concluded on the basis of his data that his Irrational Beliefs Test was sufficiently reliable and valid as a measure of irrational beliefs for use in both research and specific clinical situations. The results of the study substantially confirmed Ellis's theoretical position with respect to irrational beliefs.

Stoltenberg, Pace, and Maddux (1986) found that thinking-type students, as measured on the Myers-Briggs Type Indicator, tended to show a stronger preference than feeling types for the REBT cognitive style of counseling. The finding is consistent with research on successful counseling resulting from counselor-client personality similarity.

Thebarge (1989), differentiating REBT from behavior modification, systematic desensitization, and traditional psychoanalysis, pointed out that REBT treats underlying causes (irrational beliefs) of symptoms and not the symptoms themselves. Therefore, successful REBT generates none of the symptom substitution that may occur when treatment is focused on symptoms only. Behavior modification and systematic desensitization are two therapies that are directed toward symptom removal.

Dryden (1989b) discussed four types of chains people use to turn irrational beliefs into bad feelings and destructive behaviors. *Inference* chains occur when inferences are chained together and trigger emotions and irrational beliefs. The key to treatment is to find the most relevant inference. *Inference-evaluative belief* chains occur when a person holds an evaluative belief about each inference in the chain. The key to repairing this chain is to identify the earliest irrational belief that creates increasingly distorted beliefs. *Disturbance-about-disturbance* chains relate to how people become more upset by becoming upset about disturbances. In these cases, the client chooses the starting point in the chain. *Complex* chains are too difficult to handle by starting at the end of the chain. Clients are encouraged to start at the beginning and replay the entire process in slow motion to see the process of chain development.

DiGiuseppe (1990) detailed a method for using inference chaining as a technique for helping children reevaluate their automatic irrational beliefs. Children were asked to imagine or think about what would happen next if the automatic thought (for example, "I am stupid") were true and what it would mean to them. DiGiuseppe also recommended deductive interpretation with children. In this method, the counselor and the child form and test hypotheses concerning the irrational belief. Both methods allow self-discovery by the child.

The main goal of REBT is to increase happiness and decrease pain. In order to achieve a prevailing happier state, REBT has two main objectives. The first is to show the emotionally disturbed client how irrational beliefs or attitudes create dysfunctional consequences. These consequences might include anger, depression, or anxiety. The second objective is directively and intellectually teaching clients how to dispute or crumble their irrational beliefs and replace them with rational beliefs. Once counselors lead the clients to dispute the irrational ideas, they guide them into adopting new expectations for themselves, others, and the environment. Ellis reasoned that if the irrational, absolute philosophies and resultant feelings are replaced with more rational, productive thoughts, clients will no longer be trapped in a repetitious cycle of negative feelings. When children are no longer incapacitated by dysfunctional feelings, they are free to choose behaviors that eliminate the problem or at least lessen its disappointing impact.

Rational-emotive-behavior therapy is often referred to as the "A, B, C, D, and E" approach to counseling. "A, B, C" shows how problems develop. "D, E" are the treatment steps.

A   is the activating event: "I failed my math test."
B   is how you evaluate the event.
    B_1—irrational message: "I failed the test; therefore, I'm a total failure as a person."
    B_2—rational message: "I failed the test. This is unpleasant and inconvenient, but that is all it is. I need to study more efficiently for the next exam."
C   represents the consequences or feelings resulting from your self-message at the B stage. The B_1 message will cause you to feel very depressed. The B_2 message won't make you feel great, but it will not be so overwhelming as to inhibit your performance on the next test.
D   represents the disputing arguments you use to attack the irrational self-messages expressed in B_1. The counselor's function is to help you question these irrational self-messages once they have been identified.
E   represents the answers you have developed to the questions regarding the rationality of your B_1 self-messages.

For example, counseling would proceed through the following steps:

A—something unpleasant happens to you.
B—you evaluate the event as something awful, something that should not be allowed to happen.
C—you become upset and nervous.
D—you question your B self-message:
  1. Why is it awful?
  2. Why shouldn't it be allowed to happen?
E—you answer:
  1. It's a disappointment.
  2. It's a setback, but not a disaster.
  3. I can handle it.
  4. I would like things to be better, but that doesn't mean I'm always supposed to get things done my way.

Ellis provided another example of REBT in action in "Teaching Emotional Education in the Classroom." A student named Robert is so anxious about reciting in class, even though he knows the material, that he anticipates the event (A) and already feels the blocking and nervousness (C) just by anticipating the event (A). At point B_2 he tells himself: "It would be unfortunate if I did not recite well because the other children might think I did not know my lesson. They might even think I am a dummy, and I would not want that." At B_1, however, Robert usually adds another statement to his rational message: "It would be awful if I failed. No one would like me, and I would be a bum." The great anxiety felt at C caused by the B_1 message would sabotage Robert's efforts to recite in class the next time the teacher called on him.

Rational-emotive-behavior therapy is direct, didactic, confrontational, and verbally active counseling. Initially, the counselor seeks to detect the irrational beliefs that are creating the disturbance. Four factors help to detect irrational thinking:

1. Look for "awfulizing."
2. Look for something you think you cannot stand.
3. Look for absolute uses of *should, must, ought, always,* and *never.*
4. Look for damning of yourself and others.

Once the irrational beliefs are recognized, the counselor disputes and challenges them. Ultimately, the goal is for children to recognize irrational beliefs, think them through, and relinquish them. As a result of this process and therapy, children, it is hoped, reach three insights. First, the present neurotic behavior has antecedent causes. Second, original beliefs keep upsetting children because they keep repeating these beliefs. Third, they can overcome emotional disturbances by consistently observing, questioning, and challenging their own belief systems.

People hold tenaciously to their beliefs, rational or not; consequently, the counselor vigorously attacks the irrational beliefs in an attempt to show the children how illogically they think. Using the Socratic method of questioning and disputing, the counselor takes a verbally active part in the early stages of counseling by identifying and explaining the child's problem. If counselors guess correctly, which often happens, they argue with and persuade the child to give up the old philosophical view and replace it with a new, essentially existentially oriented, philosophy.

Ellis (1962) suggested that, to the usual psychotherapeutic techniques of exploration, ventilation, excoriation, and interpretation, rational therapists add techniques of confrontation, indoctrination, and reeducation. Counselors are didactic in that they explain how children's beliefs (which intervene between an event and the resultant feelings), rather than events themselves, cause emotional disturbances. Because the counselor honestly believes that children do not understand the reason for their disturbance, the counselor enlightens and teaches. Counselors frequently assign homework—reading, performing specific tasks, and taking risks—for the child as an integral part of therapy.

There is little transference in REBT. Contrary to classical psychoanalysis, the counselor serves as a model of rational thinking and behavior and urges children to resolve problems with significant people in their lives.

In addition, the counselor sometimes uses conventional methods such as dream analysis, reflection of feeling, and reassurance and employs all these methods together, with the end result that the child's irrational thinking—which has led to irrational behavior—is destroyed, and a saner belief system replaces it.

Rational-emotive-behavior counselors believe that the development of a person's belief system (which is defined as the meaning of facts) is analogous to the acquisition of speech. Just as children learn language by imitation and modeling, they learn a belief system. Therefore, the belief system and attitudes children acquire are largely a reflection of the significant people in their lives. Furthermore, the belief systems incorporated into children's minds determine whether they think rationally about facts. Continuing the analogy, just as one continues to add vocabulary and modify one's speech, one can also change or replace one's belief system.

For children, REBT is modified because its style depends so much on verbal and abstract conceptualization skills. Working on the premise that people feel the way they think, the therapist attempts to change overt behavior by altering internal verbalization. A major disadvantage in using REBT with children is that studies have shown that children do not generalize well from one situation to another; that is, the improved behavior is limited to the specific circumstances. Furthermore, Piaget's research indicated that children in the preformal stages of cognitive development (see chapter 1) might have difficulty relating to the REBT counseling method.

Role reversal is one very effective technique with children. In this technique, the child describes the activating event and the emotional consequences. Next, the counselor explains that thoughts are upsetting the child. Then they role-play the activating event, with the counselor playing the child. While acting out the event, the counselor demonstrates the appropriate behavior while uttering rational self-statements aloud. The roles are reversed again, with the child trying on new thoughts and being rewarded, preferably with social approval, as reinforcement for rational statements and behaviors. The child may need rewards for successive approximations.

Rational-Behavior-Emotive Education

An offspring of REBT is rational-emotive-behavior education (REBE). Its objectives are to teach how feelings develop, how to discriminate between valid and invalid assumptions, and how to think rationally in "antiawful" and "antiperfectionist" ways.

One study reported by Knaus (1974) illustrated quite effectively the results of reinforcing rational verbal expressions with disturbed children. The children became more rational not only in their verbal expressions and belief systems but also in their behaviors. The following are examples of beliefs that were reinforced by writing statements:

I don't like school, but I can stand it.
I did something bad, but I'm not a bad person.
I don't like being called insulting names, but being insulted is not awful.
Just because someone calls you a "dum-dum" does not mean you are one.

Some children in the experiment improved in their rational behaviors to the extent that they were recommended for dismissal from treatment.

Ellis said that all children act neurotically simply because they are children. He stated that childish behavior cannot be differentiated from neurosis until the age of 5. At this point, many children have integrated into their belief system the irrational belief that one should be thoroughly competent, adequate, and achieving in all possible respects to be considered worthwhile. Ellis, Moseley, and Wolfe (1972) listed several strategies for undermining this philosophy in children.

1. Teach children the joy of engaging in games that are worthwhile because they are fun. Deemphasize the importance of winning at all costs by teaching children that you do not have to win to have fun and be a worthwhile person.

2. Teach children that significant achievements rarely come easily and that nothing is wrong with working long and hard to achieve one's goals.

3. Teach children that they are not bad people when they do not meet their goals. Children must like themselves during periods of failure, even when they may not be trying their best to achieve their goals. Children also need to learn the difference between wants and needs. Wanting something we cannot get is not the same as not getting what we absolutely need.

4. Teach children that, although striving for perfectionism in performance is good, perfection is not required to be a worthwhile person. Making mistakes is not only okay but also a good way to learn why certain things happen and how to prevent them from happening again.

5. Teach children that popularity and achievement are not necessarily related, that to be liked by all people at all times is very difficult, and that being a worthwhile person does not require 100% popularity.

6. In summary, teach children not to take themselves and situations too seriously by turning minor setbacks into catastrophes. Balance constructive criticism with positive reinforcement in evaluating children's performances.

Rational-emotive-behavior education for children in the elementary school setting interests those who want to teach children to think rationally about events before they are programmed to react irrationally. Several anecdotal studies have supported the view that the principles of REBT can be effective with both disturbed and "normal" children. Omizo, Cubberly, and Omizo (1985) presented the results of a 12-week study designed to evaluate the impact of REBE on self-concept and locus of control of children with learning disabilities. The REBE objectives of the experimental group were (1) learn the ABCDE format, (2) acquire basic problem-solving skills, (3) demonstrate that feelings are influenced by thoughts, (4) understand that feelings are not expressed in identical ways, (5) transfer learning to real life, (6) develop rational coping skills, (7) learn expression of feelings rather than generalities, (8) be empathic to other group members, and (9) learn to dispute irrational thoughts. The experimental group differed significantly in a positive direction from the control group on three of five self-concept subscales and on the locus-of-control measure.

Roush (1984) proposed a version of REBT for use in institutional settings with younger children and other children having limited cognitive abilities. He noted three basic processes that are necessary for an effective REBT intervention: (1) the ability to discriminate between rational and irrational beliefs; (2) possession of a working knowledge of core irrationalities; and (3) development of a usable system for identifying and disputing the components of irrational thinking. Roush developed four approaches geared to the readiness level of children and youth with lower levels of cognitive development.

Zoints (1983) proposed a strategy for implementing REBE in the classroom: teach students how their disturbing emotions develop from their thinking or belief systems and also disputation techniques to change the irrational beliefs that cause the disturbing emotions. Zoints recommended a problem-solving, group discussion format, with the teacher taking an active-directive role; for example, the teacher would challenge the students with such questions as "How does failing a test make you a dumb jerk?"

Voelm, Cameron, Brown, and Gibson (1984) reported on the effects of REBE on acting-out and socially withdrawn adolescents' self-concepts, academic achievements, classroom behavior, and abilities to comprehend and remember REBE concepts over time. Compared with a transactional analysis group and a control group, the REBE group (1) showed a dramatic increase in self-concept scores, (2) showed a significant increase in survey of rational concepts scores, (3) scored significantly lower on an excessive anxiety scale, and (4) were rated by their teachers as less aggressive, less resistant, and having control over anger and impulses.

Omizo, Lo, and Williams (1986) reported success in using REBE with learning-disabled adolescents. The treatment group emerged with lower levels of anxiety and higher levels of aspiration, leadership, initiative, and internal locus of control.

Vernon (1990) designed a program for using REBE with children and teachers, including a workshop outline for teaching teachers how to use REBE in the classroom. Joyce (1990) and Bruner (1984) presented two different approaches for using REBE with parent education and consultation.

Gossette and O'Brien (1993) examined the research on the efficacy of REBE with children in creating behavior change through discovery and alternation of irrational beliefs. They analyzed 33 unpublished dissertations, reporting a total of 278 comparisons of REBE treatment with other treatments. Support for REBE was rather weak, with only about 25% of the studies showing benefits from the treatment. Children who were already troubled seemed least likely to benefit from REBE.

Contrasting with that study was Hajzler and Bernard's (1991) review of 21 REBE outcome studies done with children and adolescents in the following schools-aged populations: nonclinical, learning disabled, "high risk," low self-esteem, anxious, and a mixed group of single-subject studies. The studies revealed significant decreases in irrationality 88% of the time, increases in internal locus of control 71% of the time, self-esteem increases 57% of the time, and student behavior positively modified 56% of the time. Decreases in anxiety occurred in 80% of the studies. Rational-emotive-behavior education was most effective with learning-disabled students in strengthening their internal locus of control and least effective in reducing interpersonal anxiety in highly anxious students. A common finding across all studies of counseling intervention was that better results were obtained with longer treatment periods. The authors identified the REBE interventions that were critical to the studies: imagery, behavioral rehearsal, and counseling homework.

Finally, Forman (1990) provided a literature review of REBT strategies and training programs designed to help teachers become better managers of their own stress. Managing teacher stress might be a good way to manage student stress.

REBT OUTCOME RESEARCH

Glass and Smith (1976) reviewed 375 outcome studies in psychotherapy, 35 of which were conducted with REBT. In a ranking of 10 types of therapy, REBT placed second to systematic desensitization in outcome success, with behavior modification a close third. The other theories ranked were Gestalt, psychodynamic, transactional analysis, Adlerian, person-centered, implosion, and eclectic.

Ricketts and Galloway (1984) compared the effectiveness of three 1-hour approaches—relaxation training, REBT, and study skills—to reducing test anxiety among college students. Relaxation training was found to reduce test anxiety best, followed by REBT, study skills, and the placebo treatment, in that order. However, the sessions did not improve academic achievement.

Conoley, McConnell, Conoley, and Kimzey (1983) compared the ABCs of REBT with the Gestalt empty chair method for effectiveness in achieving anger reduction. Systolic blood pressure and a feelings questionnaire were the dependent variables. A control group received active listening. Sixty-one undergraduate females were asked to discuss an anger-producing situation with a counselor. Both the REBT and Gestalt participants outperformed the control group in anger reduction. There was, however, no significant difference between the REBT and Gestalt groups.

Maxwell and Wilkerson (1982) found that weekly REBT sessions over 10 weeks reduced the anxiety of 24 female participants as measured by the Sixteen Personality Factor Questionnaire. Thurman (1983) studied the effects of REBT on type-A behavior among college students. Following treatment, the experimental group significantly reduced self-reported levels of type-A speed and impatience, hard-driving and competitive behavior, high self-expectation, anxious overconcern about the future, and perfectionism.

Sklare, Taylor, and Hyland (1985) recommended an emotional control card (ECC) to facilitate the use of rational-emotive-behavior imagery outside the counseling session. Recognizing that imagery has been a helpful tool in REBT, the authors believed it could be improved because clients may forget to apply newly learned imagery skills in real-life situations. The proposed ECC lists various situations and matches problem emotional responses with words to describe a more realistic or rational picture that leads to a less drastic emotional response. The ECC would provide the client with varied and numerous life situations in which to practice imagery. The authors presented three successful case applications using the emotional control card.

Ellis (1989) presented a case-study report of REBT for crisis intervention during a single interview with a suicidal client. The client, a 27-year-old woman, was a successful resident in obstetrics and gynecology who was contemplating suicide after the loss of her last three lovers. Ellis described how he used REBT, humor, contracting, and the homework assignment of singing some of Ellis's rational humor songs 3 times daily.

Dash, Hirt, and Schroeder (1989) reviewed and conducted a meta-analysis on 48 studies examining the effects of self-statement modification (SSM) in the treatment of child behavior disorders including attention-deficit hyperactivity disorder (ADHD), phobias, shyness, and behavior. Although the evidence for the effectiveness of SSM is not conclusive, the data were most supportive of using SSM with adolescents and preadolescents and with 5- to 7-year-old children. Children aged 8 to 10 did not fare as well.

Raynor (1992) researched the effectiveness of REBT with three 7-year-old children who had low self-esteem and difficulty dealing with anger. The two boys and one girl were hyperactive and depressed, with histories of troubled peer relationships, difficulty with self-expression, and suicidal thoughts. Treatment lasted only five sessions, but each child exhibited an improvement in verbal self-expression. Although most 7-year-olds have not reached the formal thinking stage of cognitive development (the ability to do critical thinking and complex problem solving), the children were able to recognize their own thought patterns and problem-solve in role-play situations involving anger.

Barry (1993) compared the effectiveness of an REBT treatment program with conduct disorder (CD) and ADHD adolescents. The treatment program, following a lecture, discussion, and video format, taught goal setting, time management, positive thinking, self-esteem, self-confidence, self-motivation, anxiety management, and relationship building. The author noted substantial changes in the CD group but not for the ADHD group. The CD group's trait anger and irrational thinking decreased because they overcame their learned helplessness and increased their responsibility for their anger. They reduced their need to blame others, their past, and external factors for their problems and were able to decrease their irrational thinking about the necessity to be wholly competent and achieving and to always have things their own way. Problem-solving skills also increased for the CD group. The REBT treatment program was not successful in modifying the thinking of ADHD students. However, the treatment did seem to follow the standard classroom teaching format, which is almost never effective for the ADHD population.

COGNITIVE-BEHAVIORAL THERAPY

The movement toward integrative approaches to counseling is documented in the literature. These integrative approaches often involve the combination of two or more standard approaches into one treatment modality. We suggest that this has been happening in practice since the beginning of the counseling movement, and only now is the profession feeling sufficiently secure to admit that many practitioners have been integrative all along. One such integrative combination is represented by the unification of cognitive and behavioral approaches into cognitive-behavioral therapy (CBT). The practice of cognitive-behavioral therapy combines behavior-change methods with thought-restructuring methods to produce behavior and feeling change in clients. Such a marriage between two approaches results from deficiency in one or both of the methods in bringing about the desired counseling outcomes. The terms *cognitive restructuring, cognitive behavior modification,* and *stress inoculation* all represent current descriptions of Ellis's original work and some related work by Beck (1976), Maultsby (1984), and Meichenbaum (1977, 1985). These techniques combine various cognitive and behavioral approaches (Bernard, 1990). Stress-inoculation methods combined with role-playing provide an example of a cognitive-behavioral technique. In cases of test anxiety, the client might be asked to practice the following examples of self-talk: (1) "Tests are no fun, but all I want is to do the best I can." (2) "Though it would be nice to make an 'A,' it is not required for me to be a good and worthwhile person." (3) "All I need to do is prepare for the test and do the best I am able to do. If I fail, it will be inconvenient and no fun at all, but that is all it will be. For the moment, I just will not be getting what I want." Combining the self-talk with taking practice tests and visualization practice of the steps in the client's test-taking stimulus hierarchy (systematic desensitization) represents a typical cognitive-behavioral treatment plan.

Other stress-inoculation techniques include relaxation training, deep-breathing exercises, and reframing exercises that help children replace their anxiety with relaxation. Such reframing exercises help children perceive anxiety-provoking situations in a less threatening light. Rather than having the child focus on school as a place of potential failure and frightening teachers, for example, the counselor teaches the child to focus on the friends and fun available at school.

Ritter (1985), in a review of cognitive therapies, summarized the stress-inoculation training program designed by Meichenbaum (1977, 1985). The skills taught were four categories of coping self-statements designed to help people master difficult or highly stressful situations:

1. *Preparation for a stressor:* "What is it you have to do? You can develop a plan to deal with it. Don't worry."
2. *Confrontation and management of a stressor:* "One step at a time; you can handle the situation. Relax, you are in control. Take a slow, deep breath."
3. *Coping:* "Don't try to eliminate fear totally; just keep it manageable. Keep the focus on the present; what is it you have to do?"
4. *Reinforcing self-statements:* "It worked; you did it. It wasn't as bad as you expected. It's getting better each time."

Winnett, Bornstein, Cogswell, and Paris (1987) developed a CBT model for treating childhood depressive disorders. The model consists of four levels of treatment: (1) behavioral procedures, such as contingent reinforcement, shaping, prompting, and modeling, to increase social interaction; (2) CBT interventions, which included pairing successful task completion with positive self-statements and reinforcement for those self-statements; (3) cognitive interventions, which are used with social-skills training, role-playing, and self-management; and (4) self-control procedures, such as self-evaluation and self-reinforcement.

Watkins (1983) has adapted Maultsby's (1976) rational self-analysis format to fit the developmental level of children (Table 7-1). In Step 1, children write down what happened ("Jimmy called me a name because he doesn't like me"). In Step 2, children are asked to write, from the vantage point of a video camera, what they would see and hear ("Jimmy didn't like it when I didn't choose him for my team"). With the increased objectivity obtained in Step 2, children are then asked in Step 3 to write down their thoughts about what happened ("It's terrible when people talk mean to me," or "If people get angry at me, I'm a bad person"). In Step 4, children are asked to write how they felt (hurt, angry) and what they did ("I hit him"). In Step 5, children are asked to find out if they have been thinking "smart" thoughts by testing their thoughts with the five questions listed in Step 6 (for example, "Does my thought help me stay out of trouble with others?"). The answers are tabulated in the Step 5 box. If no wins, the children go to Step 7 and list some of the feelings they want to feel (for example, a child may prefer to feel sad or disappointed instead of hurt, irritated, or angry). In Step 8, children are asked to write "smarter" thoughts that would help them feel better feelings ("I don't like it when others get upset with me, but things could be worse, and I don't have to let others control how I act"). Step 9 is reserved for a plan of action children can use the next time somebody does something to make them feel bad.

◆ ◆ ◆

CASE STUDY

Jeff is a quiet, serious, 12-year-old seventh-grader at Smith County Middle School. He was referred to the counselor because a failing grade on a language arts

TABLE 7-1 Rational self-analysis for children

Step 1. Write down what happened.	**Step 2.** Be a video camera. If you were a video camera and recorded a videotape of what happened, what would you see and hear?	**Step 3.** Write down your thoughts about what happened. What did you think? A. B. C.

Step 4.
A. How did you feel?
 	
B. What did you do?
	Step 5. Decide if your thoughts are "smart." To do this, look at each thought you had and ask yourself the five questions in Step 6. Answer yes or no to each question and write your answers below.
	A. 1. B. 1. C. 1.
	    2. 2. 2.
	    3. 3. 3.
	    4. 4. 4.
	    5. 5. 5.
		Step 6. How do you know if you're thinking "smart" thoughts? Ask
		1. Is my thought really real, say if I were a video camera, what would I see?
		2. Does the thought help me stay alive and in good physical shape?
		3. Does the thought help me get what I want?
		4. Does the thought help me stay out of trouble with others?
		5. Does the thought help me feel the way I want to?

Step 7. How do you want to feel?	**Step 8.** Write down thoughts you could have that would be "smarter" than those listed. A. B. C.	**Step 9.** What do you want to do?

SOURCE: Watkins, 1983; adapted from Maultsby, 1976.

test left him very upset. After the test, Jeff seemed to be firmly convinced that he would fail the class.

Individual and Background Information

Academic. School records indicate that Jeff is a high achiever. He had excellent grades ("B" and above) in all his classes for the first two grading periods of the year. Except for the "F" on the last test, he has also maintained an above-average grade in language arts this grading period.

Family.   Jeff is the youngest of three sons. His father is retired, and his mother works as a grocery store cashier. Both of Jeff's older brothers, one a high school senior and the other a college sophomore, are excellent students. The family expects (or appears to expect) Jeff to excel also.

Social.   Jeff seems to get along well with his peers. He participates in group efforts and is especially good friends with one other student, John, also a good student with a quiet personality.

Counseling Method

The school counselor used rational-emotive-behavior therapy as a counseling method to help Jeff recognize and evaluate the erroneous messages he was giving himself (and which upset him) about his low grade in language arts. The counselor also taught Jeff to replace the erroneous messages with "sane" messages and to recognize "insane" messages when he encountered them again. The basic steps the counselor used included having Jeff examine each step along the way to becoming upset and look at the real message he was telling himself at each step.

Transcript*

Counselor: Jeff, why do you think you're going to fail language arts?

Jeff: Because I failed the last test.

Counselor: You mean if you fail one test, you're bound to fail the next one?

Jeff: Well, I failed that test, and I'm stupid!

Counselor: What are you telling yourself about your performance on that test?

Jeff: I remember thinking it was a really bad grade—not at all the kind I was used to getting. Then I thought how terrible it would be if I failed language arts and how my mom and dad and brothers would hate me and would think I was lazy and dumb!

Counselor: It would be unpleasant and inconvenient if you failed language arts, but would this make you a hateful and dumb person?

Jeff: It makes me really worried about passing the next test that's coming up. . . .

Counselor: I can understand how you would be worried about the next test, but does a bad grade make someone a bad or hated person?

Jeff: No, but it's not the kind of grade I usually get.

Counselor: Okay, so a bad grade is unpleasant, and you don't like it, but it does not make you a bad person.

---

* The case of Jeff was contributed by Sharon Simpson.

Jeff: *My* grade was an "F" and most of the other kids made "A's," so it made me look dumb.

Counselor: Okay, it *was* a bad grade compared to the rest of the class, but does this mean you are the dumbest kid around?

Jeff: No, I make mostly "A's," a few "B's." One bad grade does not make me a dumb kid.

Counselor: So, compared to your usual grade and the class's grades, this *was* a bad grade, and that is all it is, right?

Jeff: Yeah.

Counselor: What else are you telling yourself about the low test grade?

Jeff: Well, like I said, I immediately thought how terrible it would be if I failed language arts, and. . . .

Counselor: Stop there for just a minute, Jeff. Suppose you did fail language arts, even with your other high grades. It would be a bad experience, but would it be the end of the world?

Jeff: No, I guess I'd have to repeat the class, that's all.

Counselor: Right, it would be inconvenient and maybe embarrassing. It would not be pleasant, but you would go on living.

Jeff: Well, I guess that's right.

Counselor: Are you beginning to see what you told yourself about the consequences of *one* bad grade?

Jeff: Yeah, I guess I believed that one bad grade was awful—the end of the world—and that I shouldn't even try any more because I would fail the class anyway.

Counselor: Was that the correct information to give yourself about your grade?

Jeff: No!

Counselor: Okay! Let's look at the rest of the message you gave yourself after you got that bad grade. Remember what was next?

Jeff: I think I thought my family would hate me and think I was dumb and lazy because I failed that test and would probably fail language arts.

Counselor: Do you think your family's love depends on your grades?

Jeff: No, Jimmy made an "F" on a chemistry test the first part of the school year, and nobody hated him.

Counselor: What did your parents do?

Jeff: Let's see. Oh, yeah, they got him a tutor—a friend of Dad's knew a student who was majoring in chemistry.

Counselor: What did your brother in college do when Jimmy failed the test?

Jeff: He offered to help Jim on weekends. He's a brain—a physics major!

Counselor: So when your brother failed a test, your family helped him out. They didn't say he was "dumb" or "lazy" or that they hated him for it!

Jeff: No, they didn't. And I guess they wouldn't say it to me, either; in fact, Dad and Jim ask every night if I need help with my homework. I can usually do it okay by myself.

Counselor: Okay. Let's go back over some of these bad messages you've been giving yourself about your bad grade.

Jeff: I got a bad grade. I thought I would fail language arts no matter what I did. I decided my family would hate me and think I was dumb and lazy.

Counselor: Do you *still* believe those "crazy" messages you told yourself about failing and the way your family would react?

Jeff: No!

Counselor: Next time you mess up on something—maybe a ball game, maybe a test—what message will you give yourself?

Jeff: Well, I'm not exactly sure what I'll say, but I *won't* tell myself that it's a disaster and I'll never be able to do anything else. I'll probably say that I don't like what happened and that I'm not happy about it. That's all. Now I guess I'll go study and try to ace that next language arts test. Thanks a lot!

CBT OUTCOME RESEARCH

Maultsby (1971) has significantly modified Ellis's basic system by focusing on homework assignments for clients. He refers to his system as *rational-behavior therapy.* In a study of 87 psychiatric outpatients receiving homework therapy for 10 weeks, Maultsby found that 85% of the patients who were judged most improved rated the homework as effective in their treatment.

Bernard, Keefauver, and Kratochwill (1983) combined REBT with a behavioral intervention to eliminate chronic hair pulling in a female client. The treatment consisted of REBT with self-instructional training. Used alone, REBT produced partial success. The addition of self-instructional training, including a self-monitoring program, produced complete success.

Gilchrist and Schinke (1983) found that young people given cognitive-behavioral treatment about sex and contraception possessed more sex education knowledge and held more positive attitudes toward contraception than a control group receiving information on the topic. They also were observed to engage in more effective problem solving and communication skills in videotaped role-plays.

Deutschle, Tosi, and Wise (1987) have successfully applied cognitive-experiential therapy (CET), or rational stage-directed hypnotherapy (RSDH), to the treatment of impulsivity in children. This treatment modality combines hypnosis, relaxation imagery, and cognitive restructuring. The technique is further enhanced through the use of metaphors designed to help children develop an objective, nonthreatening identification with the elements of their experiential themes.

Bor, Dadds, Gordon, Morrison, Rebgetz, Sanders, and Shepard (1989) found CBT effective in treating recurrent nonspecific abdominal pain in children. Treatment included training in coping skills for self-managing pain, progressive muscle relaxation, self-monitoring of pain, and activities for redirecting children after a pain complaint. Mothers completed the eight sessions of training with their children.

Lochman and Lampron (1988) found CBT effective for aggressive boys in the 10 to 12 age range. A goal-setting component was added to the cognitive-behavioral interventions.

Warren, McLellarn, and Ponzoha (1988) found both REBT and CBT effective in treating low self-esteem and related emotional problems. The authors conclude that REBT needs to be combined with other methods, such as skills training, for optimum effectiveness.

Kendall (1993) addressed the issue of how best to intervene to reduce or remediate cognitive, behavioral, and emotional difficulties in childhood that are associated with present psychological distress and later psychopathology. Specifically, Kendall presented a status report on the effectiveness of cognitive-behavioral therapies (CBT) in treating children in four diagnostic categories: aggression, anxiety, depression, and ADHD.

Aggression

Kendall emphasized that aggressive children suffer from both distortions and deficiencies in their cognitive processing. Cognitive distortions result from dysfunctional thinking. Cognitive deficiencies result from insufficient cognitive activity in situations requiring cause-effect reasoning or the ability to visualize consequences of behavior. Kendall found support for the effectiveness of CBT treatments with aggressive psychiatric children in reducing their aggressive behavior. The treatments included problem-solving skills training and self-monitoring with self-instruction for monitoring their arousal states.

Anxiety

Kendall found support for using muscle relaxation, deep breathing, and cognitive imagery (systematic desensitization) to reduce anxiety in anxious children. Anxious children exceed the norm by a significant margin with thoughts of being scared, hurt, and in danger. The same is true for self-critical thoughts.

Depression

Depressed children suffer from distortions in attributions, self-evaluation, and perceptions of past and present events. They exhibit more external locus of control (an indication that they feel less capable) and low self-esteem, resulting from a perceived inability to succeed academically and socially. Effective help for depressed children included training in self-control, self-evaluation, assertiveness, and social skills. Social skills training included initiating and maintaining interactions and conflict resolution; specific CBT included relaxation, imagery, and cognitive restructuring.

Attention-Deficit Hyperactivity Disorder

Children with ADHD show deficiencies in the mechanisms that govern (1) sustained attention and effort, (2) inhibitory controls, and (3) the modulation of arousal levels to meet situational demands. Kendall proposed CBT with medication to treat ADHD. Stimulant medication should improve attention, and CBT should improve cognitive functioning.

Lochman (1992) studied the effects of CBT on the behavior of 145 aggressive 10- to 12-year-old boys. The CBT interventions, ranging from watching video training tapes to role-playing social problem-solving situations, had a long-term effect on some behaviors of aggressive boys. The most notable area of change was lower levels of substance abuse over a 3-year follow-up period. It did not prove to have as strong an impact on decreasing deviant behavior.

Davis and Boster (1993) proposed using CBT in combination with expressive interventions in working with aggressive and resistant youth. They viewed the combined approach as a way to modify the dysfunctional cognitive, affective, behavioral, and problem-solving skills seen in aggressive youth and considered several multimodal treatment interventions. Logbooks of perceptions were recommended as helpful for recording thoughts and reinforcing nonviolent appraisals. Art therapy techniques such as cartoons without captions helped to frame nonviolent appraisals. Art therapy, as well as the other expressive arts of music and movement, was also effective with violent clients, who are likely to be limited in requisite verbal skills and creative resources for expressing and testing alternative appraisals of life events. Instruction in social skills and conflict resolution was also recommended for the multimodal package for treating aggressive youth.

Ronen (1992) discussed cognitive therapy with children and its suitability for children's needs and ability levels. She listed the most frequent behavior problems of children (from most common to least common): loss of temper, hyperactivity, fears, restlessness, sleep disorders, enuresis, food intake, nail biting, tics, and stuttering. Her review of the literature revealed that children with behavior problems such as hyperactivity, impulsivity, and aggression tend to (1) generate fewer alternative solutions to interpersonal problems, (2) focus on ends or goals rather than on the intermediate steps toward obtaining them, (3) see fewer consequences associated with their behavior, (4) fail to recognize causes of others' behavior, and (5) be less sensitive to interpersonal conflict. Ronen then outlined some successful applications of CBT such as self-assessment, self-instruction, self-reinforcement, and self-punishment. Cognitive treatments require children's active participation in learning to identify irrational thoughts, initiate internal dialogues, halt automatic thinking, change automatic thoughts to mediated ones, and use CBT to changing unwanted behavior. Ronen responded to the question of whether children have developed sufficient cognitive skills to benefit from a cognitive approach by citing the similarity in difficulty between early childhood tasks and understanding CBT; she compared changing one's behavior to learning to ride a bicycle, use computers, read, and write. Three keys to such learning were identified: (1) the knowledge of how to do it, (2) the desire to learn and practice, and (3) time to practice. Basically, our position is that good counselors should be able to teach children almost any skill they can break down into mediating steps that children can understand and find meaningful to the events in their everyday lives.

Jay, Elliot, Woody, and Siegel (1991) investigated the effectiveness of CBT in combination with diazepam (Valium) for children undergoing painful medical procedures. The study was done with 83 children ages 3 to 12 who were suffering from leukemia. The purpose of the study was to find ways to reduce the anxiety and distress caused by the medical tests and procedures required to treat their disease. One group received CBT and one group received CBT plus Valium. The CBT techniques included modeling, breathing exercises, imagery, positive incentives, and behavior rehearsal. The results showed that Valium did not increase the efficacy of CBT as hypothesized. In fact, the data, though not statistically significant, supported the possibility that Valium may impair the learning process of CBT. Used alone, CBT was found to decrease distress and to increase the children's rate of reporting their fears.

Duffy and Spence (1993) researched the effectiveness of cognitive self-management as an adjunct to behavioral interventions for childhood obesity. The study was done with 29 children ages 7 to 13. The traffic light system, which classified foods into three categories—green (eat freely), amber (eat in moderation), and red (stop, danger)—was used in behavior therapy (BT). The BT group also received training in exercise, and their parents were trained to use goal-setting and positive reinforcement strategies for facilitating behavior change. The CBT component included monitoring negative thoughts, restructuring negative or maladaptive thoughts, problem-solving skills, self-instructional training, and self-reinforcement. The results of the study confirmed the effectiveness of behavioral programs in the reduction of obesity in some children. The addition of CBT component did not add significantly to the BT approach.

As we have noted throughout the book, counseling children and adults who do not view themselves as having a problem is difficult. Such was true with children in this obesity reduction study.

Webb (1993) endorsed CBT as a valuable method for school counselors to use with children of alcoholics (COAs). The principal benefit of CBT for COAs was help in dealing with situations beyond their control and thus help in avoiding responsibility for family issues that are, in reality, the responsibility of other family members. Moreover, CBT provided a client the means for taking control of his or her life and for improving those areas that are in the client's control.

Beck, Sokol, Clark, Berchick, and Wright (1992) found that cognitive therapy was more effective than person-centered therapy for helping clients suffering from panic disorders. Cognitive strategies were used to break down the panic cycle. Person-centered strategies were nondirective and did not focus on the panic symptoms. Cognitive therapy resulted in a 71% rate of effectiveness in ending panic attacks, whereas only 25% of the person-centered participants succeeded. Clients could elect to cross over to the other treatment group. Crossover clients to cognitive therapy were successful in 79% of the cases. Readers should know that Aaron Beck is a cognitive therapist and researcher.

RESEARCH AND APPLICATIONS

Research relating to rational-emotive-behavior therapy began with Ellis's (1957) review of his own casework employing three different methods of psychotherapy. Ellis found that with orthodox psychoanalysis 13% of his patients improved considerably, 37% showed distinct improvement, and 50% showed little or no improvement; with analytically oriented therapy, the figures were 18%, 45%, and 37%, respectively. Ellis found his system (then called *rational therapy*) to be the most successful, with figures of 44%, 46%, and 10%. In addition, Ellis found his system to be effective in one to five sessions rather than the longer periods of therapy required for the other two approaches.

A study by Berkowitz and Alioto (1973) demonstrated that activating events were not necessarily the causes of aggressive consequences. Rather, anger originated in human cognitions. However, an article by Zajonc (1980) challenged this assumption by presenting evidence for emotion occurring without cognition.

Berkowitz's (1970) comprehensive review of the literature on aggression pointed out the futility and danger of "acting out" aggressive impulses as a way of relieving these emotions. Aggression apparently begets more aggression; therefore, a more productive system for treating aggression is needed.

Finally, in a reply to articles critical of rational-emotive-behavior therapy, Ellis (1981, 1984) wrote that REBT remains within the field of science while resting on some evaluative assumptions. For example, the REBT concept of unconditional humanistic self-acceptance is still valid even though it requires an operational definition. The REBT philosophy does not conflict with all religions, only with those that are absolutist and sabotage human health and happiness. Human nature has the potential to be both rational (scientific approach) and irrational (departure from science). The REBT concept of self-acceptance means that a person is more than a set of behaviors; that is, people are better off negating specific behaviors without labeling their entire selves as good or bad.

SUMMARY

Albert Ellis (1993a) traced the development of his rational-emotive-behavior therapy from 1955 to the present and suggested directions where REBT might be taken in the future. He pointed out that in 1955 REBT, the first of today's cognitive-behavioral therapies, was highly cognitive, largely positivist, and very active-directive. Its ABC theory of human disturbance held that people experience undesirable activating events (A), that they have rational and irrational beliefs (B) about these events, and that they create *appropriate* emotional and behavioral *consequences (aC)* with their *rational beliefs (rB)* or they create *inappropriate* and dysfunctional *consequences (iC)* with their *irrational beliefs (iB)*. Thus, REBT is directed to the client's belief system, which is the cause of the problem, not the activating event.

Ellis made a distinction between general REBT, which he viewed as synonymous with general cognitive-behavioral therapy, and preferential REBT, which he described as a unique type of cognitive therapy that is distinctly constructivist and humanistic. He listed 10 points defining the unique style of preferential RET.

1. People, learning their expectations, preferences, and goals for success and culture, feel appropriately frustrated and disappointed when they fail and are disapproved. People make themselves neurotic by their innate tendencies to construct absolutist "musts" and demands on themselves, others, and their environments.

2. People make themselves more disturbed by creating exaggerated derivatives of their "musts" and demands. For example, "She absolutely must like me!" and when she ignores me, I rashly conclude and devoutly believe that (a) "She hates me!" (b) "It's awful that she hates me!" (c) "I'm worthless because she hates me!" and (d) "No decent person will ever like me!"

3. REBT contains the information to prevent people from making themselves neurotic.

4. REBT is multimodal and used in conjunction with a variety of cognitive, emotive, and behavioral methods including imagery, shame-attacking exercises, coping statements, role-playing, encouragement, and humor.

5. People are biologically predisposed to hold on strongly to their irrational beliefs. Therefore, REBT is designed to teach clients to think, feel, and act against these beliefs.

6. REBT tends to be more heavily behavioral than some of the other cognitive-behavioral therapies. Behavioral methods used in REBT include behavioral homework with reinforcements and penalties, in vivo desensitization, implosive counterphobic procedures, and response prevention.

7. REBT has always been psychoeducational and consequently includes a number of instructional and teaching methods to help people learn to survive within a dysfunctional system and change the system.

8. People are faced with two opposing creative tendencies: (a) to make themselves disturbed and dysfunctional or (b) to change and actualize themselves to reduce their self-disturbing tendencies and thus enjoy happier lives.

9. REBT opposes dogma, rigidity, "must-urbation," and one-sidedness in favor of science, empiricism, and logic in constructing a healthy, rational belief system. The preceding statement defines *mental health* for Ellis.

10. Once people upset themselves, their emotional reactions of panic, depression, and self-hatred are so strong that they require an active-directive REBT approach to provide the instruction and guidance people need to pull themselves out of the hole they have dug.

In summary, Ellis's objective for all people is that they rate their performance in relation to the goals they have set. It is *healthy* to believe "It is good when I succeed and am loved" or "It is bad when I fail and am rejected." It is *unhealthy* to believe "I am good for succeeding" and "I am bad for getting rejected." Regarding unconditional positive regard, Ellis pointed out that REBT therapists try to give this type of acceptance to all clients but also teach them how to give it to themselves. Ellis (1993) envisioned the main future of REBT in psychoeducational applications to the millions of people who do not have access to counseling services. In spite of some contradictory evidence, rational-emotive-behavior education still has promise as a preventive intervention for children inclined to exaggerate negative events.

REFERENCES

Barry, M. (1993). A rational-emotive treatment program with conduct disorder and attention-deficit hyperactivity disorder adolescents. *Journal of Rational-Emotive and Cognitive Behavior Therapy, 11*(3), 123–124.

Beck, A. (1976). *Cognitive therapy and emotional disorders.* New York: International Universities Press.

Beck, A., Sokol, L., Clark, D., Berchick, R., & Wright, F. (1992). A crossover study of focused cognitive therapy for panic disorder. *American Journal of Psychiatry, 149*(6), 778–783.

Berkowitz, C. (1970). Experimental investigations of hostility catharsis. *Journal of Consulting and Clinical Psychology, 35,* 1–7.

Berkowitz, L., & Alioto, J. (1973). The meaning of an observed event as a determinant of its aggressive consequences. *Journal of Personality and Social Psychology, 28,* 206–217.

Bernard, M. (1990). Rational-emotive therapy with children and adolescents: Treatment strategies. *School Psychology Review, 19,* 294–303.

Bernard, M., Keefauver, L., & Kratochwill, T. (1983). The effects of rational emotive therapy and self instructional training on chronic hair pulling. *Cognitive Therapy and Research, 7,* 273–280.

Bor, W., Dadds, M., Gordon, A., Morrison, M., Rebgetz, M., Sanders, M., & Shepard, R. (1989). Cognitive behavioral treatment of recurrent nonspecific abdominal pain in children: An analysis of generalization, maintenance and side effects. *Journal of Consulting and Clinical Psychology, 57,* 294–300.

Bruner, G. (1984). Rational-emotive education for parent study groups. *Individual Psychology Journal of Adlerian Theory, Research and Practice, 40,* 228–231.

Conoley, C., McConnell, J., Conoley, J., & Kimzey, C. (1983). The effect of the ABCs of rational emotive therapy and the empty chair technique of Gestalt therapy on anger reduction. *Psychotherapy: Theory, Research and Practice, 20,* 112–116.

Crawford, T., & Ellis, A. (1989). A dictionary of rational-emotive feelings and behaviors. *Journal of Rational-Emotive and Cognitive-Behavioral Therapy, 7,* 3–28.

Dash, D., Hirt, M., & Schroeder, H. (1989). Self-statement modification in the treatment of child behavior disorder: A meta-analysis. *Psychological Bulletin, 106,* 97–106.

Davis, D., & Boster, L. (1993). Cognitive-behavioral expressive interventions with aggressive and resistant youth. *Residential Treatment for Children and Youth, 10,* 55–67.

Deutschle, J. Jr., Tosi, D., & Wise, P. (1987). *The use of hypnosis and metaphor within a cognitive experiential framework: Theory, research, and case applications with impulse control disorders.* Paper presented at a meeting of the American Society for Clinical Hypnosis, Las Vegas, NV.

DiGiuseppe, R. (1990). Rational-emotive assessment of school aged children. *School Psychology Review, 19,* 287–293.

Dryden, W. (1989a). Albert Ellis: An efficient and passionate life. *Journal of Counseling and Development, 67,* 539–546.

Dryden, W. (1989b). The use of chaining in rational-emotive therapy. *Journal of Rational-Emotive and Cognitive-Behavior Therapy, 7,* 59–66.

Duffy, G., & Spence, S. (1993). The effectiveness of cognitive self-management as an adjunct to a behavioral intervention for childhood obesity: A research note. *Journal of Child Psychology and Psychiatry, 34,* 1043–1050.

Ellis, A. (1954). *The American sexual tragedy.* New York: Twayne.

Ellis, A. (1957). Outcome of employing three techniques of psychotherapy. *Journal of Clinical Psychology, 13,* 334–350.

Ellis, A. (1962). *Reason and emotion in psychotherapy.* New York: Lyle Stuart.

Ellis, A. (1965). *The case for sexual liberty.* Tucson, AZ: Seymour Press.

Ellis, A. (1969a). *The art and science of love* (2nd ed.). New York: Lyle Stuart/Bantam.

Ellis, A. (1969b). Teaching emotional education in the classroom. *School Health Review, 1,* 10–13.

Ellis, A. (1972). Emotional education in the classroom. *Journal of Clinical Psychology, 1,* 19–22.

Ellis, A. (1974). What rational-emotional therapy is and is not. *Counselor Education and Supervision, 14,* 140–144.

Ellis, A. (1975). *How to live with a "neurotic"* (rev. ed.). New York: Crown.

Ellis, A. (1977). *How to live with—and without—anger.* New York: Reader's Digest Press.

Ellis, A. (1981). Science, religiosity and rational emotive psychology. *Psychotherapy: Theory, Research and Practice, 18,* 55–58.

Ellis, A. (1984). Rational emotive therapy and pastoral counseling: A reply to Richard Wessler. *Personnel and Guidance Journal, 62,* 266–267.

Ellis, A. (1987). The impossibility of achieving consistently good mental health. *American Psychologist, 42,* 364–375.

Ellis, A. (1989). Using rational-emotive therapy (RET) as crisis intervention: A single interview with a suicidal client. *Individual Psychology Journal of Adlerian Theory, Research and Practice, 45,* 75–81.

Ellis, A. (1993a). Reflections on rational-emotive therapy. *Journal of Consulting and Clinical Psychology, 61*(2), 199–201.

Ellis, A. (1993b). *Rational emotive therapy.* Paper presented at the convention of the American Psychological Association, Toronto, Ontario.

Ellis, A., & Harper, R. (1975). *A new guide to rational living.* Englewood Cliffs, NJ: Prentice-Hall.

Ellis, A., Moseley, S., & Wolfe, J. (1972). *How to raise an emotionally healthy, happy child.* North Hollywood, CA: Wilshire Books.

Forman, S. (1990). Rational-emotive therapy: Contributions to teacher stress management. *School Psychology Review, 19,* 315–321.

Gilchrist, L., & Schinke, S. (1983). Coping with contraception: Cognitive and behavioral methods with adolescents. *Cognitive Therapy and Research, 7,* 379–388.

Glass, G., & Smith, M. (1976, June). *Meta-analysis of psychotherapy outcome studies.* Paper presented at the annual meeting of the Society for Psychotherapy Research, Boston.

Goodman, D., & Maultsby, M. (1974). *Emotional well-being through rational behavior training.* Springfield, IL: Charles C. Thomas.

Gossette, R., & O'Brien, R. (1993). Efficacy of rational-emotive therapy with children: A critical re-appraisal. *Journal of Behavior Therapy and Experimental Psychiatry, 24*(1), 15–25.

Hajzler, D., & Bernard, M. (1991). A review of rational-emotive education outcome studies. *School Psychology Quarterly, 6*(1), 27–49.

Jay, S., Elliot, C., Woody, P., & Siegel, S. (1991). An investigation of cognitive-behavior therapy combined with oral Valium for children undergoing painful medical procedures. *Health Psychology, 10*(5), 317–322.

Jones, R. (1968). *A factored measure of Ellis' irrational belief systems with personality and maladjustment correlates.* Unpublished doctoral dissertation, Texas Technological University, Lubbock.

Joyce, M. R. (1990). Rational-emotive parent consultation. *School Psychology Review, 19,* 304–314.

Knaus, W. (1974). *Rational emotive education: A manual for elementary school teachers.* New York: Institute for Rational Living.

Knaus, W., & Boker, S. (1975). The effect of rational emotive education on anxiety and self-concept. *Rational Living, 10,* 7–10.

Kendall, P. (1993). Cognitive-behavior therapies with youth: Guiding theory, current status, and emerging developments. *Journal of Consulting and Clinical Psychology, 61,* 235–247.

Lochman, J. (1992). Cognitive-behavioral intervention with aggressive boys: Three-year follow-up and preventive effects. *Journal of Consulting and Clinical Psychology, 60*(3), 426–432.

Lochman, J., & Lampron, L. (1988). Cognitive-behavioral interventions for aggressive boys: 7-month follow-up effects. *Journal of Child and Adolescent Psychotherapy, 5*(1), 15–23.

Maultsby, M. (1971). Systematic written homework in psychotherapy. *Psychotherapy, 8,* 195–198.

Maultsby, M. (1976). *Rational self-analysis format.* Lexington, KY: Center for Rational Behavior Therapy and Training, University of Kentucky.

Maultsby, M. (1984). *Rational behavior therapy.* Englewood Cliffs, NJ: Prentice-Hall.

Maxwell, J., & Wilkerson, J. (1982). Anxiety reduction through group instruction in rational therapy. *Journal of Psychology, 112,* 135–140.

Meichenbaum, D. (1977). *Cognitive behavior modification: An integrative approach.* New York: Plenum.

Meichenbaum, D. (1985). *Stress-inoculation training.* New York: Pergamon Press.

Omizo, M., Cubberly, W., & Omizo, S. (1985). The effects of rational emotive education groups on self-concept and locus of control among learning disabled children. *Exceptional Child, 32,* 13–16.

Omizo, M., Lo, G., & Williams, R. (1986). Rational-emotive education, self-concept, and locus of control among learning-disabled students. *Journal of Humanistic Education and Development, 25,* 58–69.

Raynor, C. (1992). Managing angry feelings: Teaching children to cope. *Perspective in Psychiatric Care, 28*(2), 11–14.

Ricketts, M., & Galloway, R. (1984). The effects of three different one-hour single-session treatments for test anxiety. *Psychological Reports, 54,* 115–120.

Ritter, K. (1985). The cognitive therapies: An overview for counselors. *Journal of Counseling and Development, 64,* 42–46.

Ronen, T. (1992). Cognitive therapy with children. *Child Psychiatry and Human Development, 23,* 19–30.

Roush, D. (1984). Rational emotive therapy and youth: Some new techniques for counselors. *Personnel and Guidance Journal, 62,* 414–417.

Sklare, G., Taylor, J., & Hyland, S. (1985). An emotional control card for rational-emotive imagery. *Journal of Counseling and Development, 64,* 145–146.

Stoltenberg, C., Pace, T., & Maddux, J. (1986). Cognitive style and counselor credibility: Effects on client endorsement of rational emotive therapy. *Cognitive Therapy and Research, 10,* 237–243.

Thebarge, R. (1989). Symptom substitution: A rational-emotive perspective. *Journal of Rational-Emotive and Cognitive-Behavior Therapy, 7,* 93–97.

Thurman, C. (1983). Effects of a rational treatment program in type A behavior among college students. *Journal of College Student Personnel, 24,* 417–423.

Vernon, A. (1990). The school psychologist's role in preventative education: Applications of rational-emotive education. *School Psychology Review, 19,* 322–330.

Voelm, C., Cameron, W., Brown, R., & Gibson, S. (1984, April). *The efficacy of rational emotive education for acting-out and socially withdrawn adolescents.* Paper presented at the annual meeting of the American Education Research Association, New Orleans, LA.

Warren, R., McLellarn, R., & Ponzoha, C. (1988). Rational-emotive therapy vs. general cognitive-behavior therapy in the treatment of low self-esteem and related emotional disturbances. *Cognitive Therapy and Research, 12,* 21–38.

Watkins, C. E. (1983). Rational self-analysis for children. *Elementary School Guidance and Counseling, 17,* 304–306.

Webb, W. (1993). Cognitive behavior therapy with children of alcoholics. *The School Counselor, 40,* 170–177.

Winnett, R., Bornstein, P., Cogswell, K., & Paris, A. (1987). Cognitive-behavioral therapy for childhood depression: A levels-of-treatment approach. *Journal of Child and Adolescent Psychotherapy, 4,* 283–286.

Wolkersheim, J., & Bugges, I. (1982). Effect of rationales for therapy on perceptions of clinical depression. *Psychological Reports, 50,* 314.

Zajonc, R. (1980). Feeling and thinking: Preferences need no inferences. *American Psychologist, 35,* 151–175.

Zoints, P. (1983). A strategy for understanding and correcting irrational beliefs in pupils: The rational emotive approach. *The Pointer, 27,* 13–17.

Chapter 8

◆

Behavioral Counseling

DEVELOPERS OF BEHAVIORAL COUNSELING

Important contributors to behavioral counseling include Ivan Pavlov, John B. Watson, Edward L. Thorndike, Edward C. Tolman, Clark L. Hull, John Dollard, Neal E. Miller, H. J. Eysenck, L. Krasner, L. P. Ullman, Joseph Wolpe, Arnold Lazarus, and John Krumboltz. However, the name best known to the general public, as well as most controversial, is B. F. Skinner. Although he did not develop new principles of behaviorism, Skinner did the most to translate the theories and ideas of other behaviorists into methods that are widely used today by psychotherapists, educators, counselors, and parents.

Burrhus Frederic Skinner (1904–1990) was born in Susquehanna, Pennsylvania. He majored in literature at Hamilton College in Clinton, New York, with the goal of becoming a writer. After a few years with little success, Skinner regarded himself a failure as a writer. Reflecting later on this time in his life, Skinner commented that he failed because he had nothing to say. Giving up on writing, he entered Harvard University to study psychology. The behavior of humans and animals was of special interest to him. He received a master's degree in 1930 and a Ph.D. in experimental psychology in 1931. Following graduation, Skinner began his most productive career as a teacher and researcher at the University of Minnesota, after which he was appointed chairman of the psychology department at Indiana University. He later returned to Harvard to accept a professorship, which he held until his death.

As he began to generate things to say in the field of behaviorism, Skinner's flair for writing returned. His numerous books include the following:

The Behavior of Organisms (1938)
Walden Two (1948)
Science and Human Behavior (1953)
Verbal Behavior (1957)

Schedules of Reinforcement (coauthored by C. Ferster, 1957)
The Technology of Teaching (1968)
Beyond Freedom and Dignity (1971)
About Behaviorism (1976)
Particulars of My Life (1976)
Reflections on Behaviorism and Society (1978)
The Shaping of a Behaviorist: Part II of an Autobiography (1979)
Skinner for the Classroom (1980, edited by R. Epstein)
A Matter of Consequences: Part III of an Autobiography (1983)
Upon Further Reflection (1987)

Skinner's contribution to knowledge is not strictly confined to the laboratory. He made considerable contributions to solving educational problems. He developed and advanced the concepts of programmed instruction, operant conditioning in classroom management, behavioral counseling, and the teaching machine (first developed by Sidney Pressey in 1923). Perhaps the most controversial of Skinner's works is *Beyond Freedom and Dignity,* which pictures a society where behavior is shaped and controlled by a planned system of rewards.

Skinner (1990a), in an article he completed the evening before his death, attacked those who would use introspection or brain analysis as methods for analyzing behavior. He asserted that behavior is the product of three types of variation and selection: natural selection, operant conditioning, and modeling. Skinner had little use for cognitive psychology because it has not contributed, as behavior analysis, to the design of better environments for solving existing problems and preventing future problems. Summing up his 62 years in the profession, Skinner (1990a) said that the point he tried to make is that it can be demonstrated that people choose behavior based on anticipated consequences. According to Skinner, this selection by consequences has negative implications for the world and its future unless some vital changes are made. He concluded by saying that "any evidence that I've been successful in that [fostering needed changes] is how I should like to be remembered" (Skinner, 1990a).

Skinner's death in 1990 ended 6 decades of significant contributions to behavioral psychology that began with the publication of his first paper in 1930. During his 60-year career, citations of Skinner's name in the literature exceeded those of the previous leader, Sigmund Freud (Banks & Thompson, 1995; Cook, 1991; Lattal, 1992).

THE NATURE OF PEOPLE

A broad statement of the behaviorist view of the nature of people is Skinner's (1971) belief that things that happen to children influence and change them as biological entities. He believed the idea that the child of our past is still contained within us was a form of animism that served no useful purpose in explaining present behavior. Behaviorists view human beings as neither good nor bad but merely as products of their environment. People are essentially born neutral (the blank slate or tabula rasa idea), with equal potential for good or evil and for rationality or irrationality.

Behaviorists view people as responders. They reject self-directing, mentalistic concepts of human behavior. Behaviorists contend that people can make only those responses they have learned, and they make them when the stimulus conditions are appropriate.

Behavioral counselors, then, view individuals as products of their conditioning. The stimulus-response paradigm is the basic pattern of all human learning. People react in predictable ways to any given stimulus according to what they have learned through experience. Humans react to stimuli much as animals do, except that human responses are more complex and organized on a higher plane.

Skinner regarded the human being as an organism who learns patterns of behavior, catalogues them within a repertoire, and repeats them at a later date. More specifically, the organism learns a specific response when a satisfying condition follows an action. The number of these responses mounts as time passes and satisfying conditions are repeated. The behaviorist's interest is in the science of behavior as it relates to biology. Skinner believed that

> a person is a member of a species shaped by evolutionary contingencies of survival, displaying behavioral processes which bring him under the control of the environment in which he lives, and largely under the control of a social environment which he and millions of others like him have constructed and maintained during the evolution of a culture. The direction of the controlling relation is reversed: a person does not act upon the world, the world acts upon him. (1971, p. 211)

Because human behavior is learned, any or all behavior can be unlearned and new behavior learned in its place. The behaviorist is concerned with observable events that, when they become unacceptable behaviors, can be unlearned. The behavioral counselor is concerned with this unlearning or reeducation process. Behavioral counseling procedures can be developed from social learning theory.

THEORY OF COUNSELING

Behavioral counseling is a reeducation or relearning process. Counselors reinforce adaptive or helpful behavior and extinguish maladaptive or unhelpful behavior. The counselor's role is, through reinforcement principles, to help clients achieve the goals they have set for themselves.

Behavioral counseling includes several techniques based on principles of learning employed to manage maladaptive behavior. Today, behavioral counseling is used with covert processes (cognitions, emotions, obsessive ideation) as well as with traditional, overt behavior problems. Behavioral counseling involves two types of behavior: operant and respondent.

In operant conditioning, *operant behavior* refers to behavior that operates on and changes the environment in some manner. It is also referred to as *instrumental behavior* because it is instrumental in goal achievement. People who

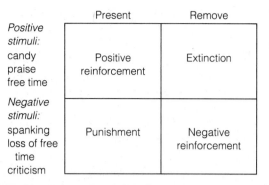

FIGURE 8-1 Examples of operant conditioning

use operant conditioning wait until the desired behavior or an approximation of the desired behavior occurs and then reinforce it with a rewarding stimulus known as *positive reinforcement* (praise, money, candy, free time, and the like). *Negative reinforcement* (different from punishment) occurs when the operant behavior is reinforced by its capacity to stop an aversive stimulus. For example, rats learn to press a bar to shut off an electric shock, and children take their seats at school to shut off the aversive sound of their teacher's scolding. *Punishment,* like positive reinforcement, occurs after the behavior is emitted but tends to decrease its occurrence. *Extinction* is the process of eliminating a learned behavior by ignoring the behavior or by not reinforcing it through attention and other rewards. Figure 8-1 explains these four terms.

Behavior Analysis

Why People Behave as They Do

People behave in ways that maintain or enhance their self-images. They also behave in ways to achieve goals that meet the following hierarchy of needs (Maslow, 1970):

- Self-fulfillment (the need to develop skills, interests, and talents)
- Self-esteem (feeling worthwhile)
- Social (belonging to a group, giving and receiving love)
- Security (safety, shelter)
- Physiological (food, sleep, oxygen, water)

Steps in Behavior Analysis

Principles of behavior

1. Behavior consists of three phases:
   - *Antecedent:* the stimulus or cue that occurs before behavior that leads to its occurrence

TABLE 8-1   Determining causes of and solutions to performance problems

What category of problem?	*Is it a problem of:*	*Is it due to:*	*Approach it by:*
Performing a task	Being unable*	Lack of knowledge about what, when, how	Providing training
		Obstacle in the environment	Removing the obstacle
Dealing with people	Being unwilling*	Lack of knowledge about why something needs to be done	Providing information/feedback
		Simple refusal	Changing the balance of positive and negative consequences

NOTE: *Could he or she do it if his or her life depended on it?" No = unable; yes = unwilling.

- *Behavior:* what the person says or does (or doesn't)
- *Consequence:* what the person perceives happens to him or her (positive, neutral, and negative) as a result of the behavior
2. Behavior problems are usually rooted in antecedents or consequences.
3. People usually prefer behavior for which the consequences are known to behavior for which the consequences are uncertain.

A behavior analysis designed to determine causes of and solutions to performance problems requires four steps: (a) identify the problem category, (b) identify the problem type, (c) determine the cause of the problem, and (d) select a problem solution (Table 8-1). If the problem solution involves changing the balance of positive and negative consequences, the counselor needs to determine what reinforces the undesired behavior and what punishes the desired behavior. The counselor then must decrease or eliminate reinforcement of the undesired behavior and punishment of the desired behavior while reinforcing performance of the desired behavior (Figure 8-2).

Schedules of Reinforcement

Changing the balance of positive and negative consequences requires selecting an appropriate schedule of reinforcement. Banks and Thompson (1995) identified two schedules of reinforcement for the acquisition and establishment of a new behavior: continuous and intermittent. *Continuous reinforcement,* the reinforcement of each successful response, is best when the new behavior is first being learned. Once the new behavior has been learned, continuous reinforcement has

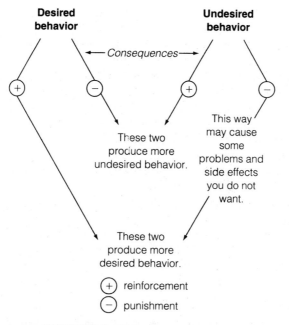

FIGURE 8-2   Balancing consequences

the effect of extinguishing the behavior by satiating the learner. Reinforcement should be switched to one of four intermittent schedules: fixed interval, variable interval, fixed ratio, and variable ratio.

Fixed Interval Schedule

Reinforcement is provided on the first response after a fixed time has elasped. The interval could be set at, for example, 30 seconds.

Variable Interval Schedule

Reinforcement is provided on the first response after some average period of time. For instance, intervals could range from 15 to 45 seconds, averaging 30 seconds over several successful responses.

Fixed Ratio Schedule

The participant is reinforced, for instance, for every 5, 10, or 20 correct responses. The reinforcement rate is fixed at the same rate (e.g., every fifth correct response is reinforced).

Variable Ratio Schedule

Participants are reinforced on a schedule varying, for example, from 5 to 25 correct responses, with an average number of responses between reinforcements falling somewhere in midrange between 5 and 25.

As with most counseling, the ultimate goal of behavioral counseling is teaching children to become their own counselors for changing their behavior to better meet their needs. All behavior change, internal and external, can be attempted through behavioral counseling. Specific techniques reduce and eliminate anxiety, phobias, and obsessive thoughts, as well as reduce inappropriate, observable behaviors.

The goals of a behavioral counselor fall into three main categories (Krumboltz & Hosford, 1967):

1. Altering maladaptive behavior
2. Teaching the decision-making process
3. Preventing problems

A fourth goal, teaching new behaviors and skills, could also be added. Krumboltz (1966) has summarized the criteria for any set of goals in counseling children.

1. Individualize the goals of counseling for each child.
2. Make the counseling goals for each child compatible with, although not necessarily identical to, the values of the counselor.
3. Make each child's degree of goal attainment observable and measurable.

After the problem has been identified and the desired behavior change agreed on by counselor and child, the behavioral counselor is apt to employ a variety of counseling procedures to help the child acquire the behaviors necessary to solve the problem. The ultimate outcome of behavioral counseling is to teach children to become their own behavior-modification experts—in other words, to program their own reinforcement schedules (self-management). Encouraging children to move from extrinsic to intrinsic reinforcement—to please themselves with their behavior rather than constantly seek the approval of others—would be even more desirable. Training in self-management skills is a successful application of behavioral principles to counseling children.

Because behavioral counseling differs from traditional counseling principally in terms of specificity, the behavioral counselor prefers to state goals as overt changes in behavior rather than as hypothetical constructs. The basic counseling function involved in behavioral counseling is defined as discrimination—differential responding to different situations (individuals, groups, institutions, and environmental settings). In behavioral counseling, continuing assessment of the effects of each counseling procedure on outcomes determines effectiveness.

COUNSELING METHODS

When using behavioral counseling (BC) methods with children, the counselor needs to match reinforcement to the child's developmental level and to reward preferences. Social development is one good predicator of effective reinforcers. Egocentric children in the preoperational stage of development probably do not find sharing toys with siblings or friends to be a priority reward. Preoperational-stage children find playing alone with favorite toys or playing a game in which they can make up all the rules much more reinforcing.

Contingency Contracts

Contracts are effective for children if they have a voice in writing the terms. Contract language must be simplified for understanding, and the goals should be quite clear, with as few steps as possible to meet the goals. Reinforcement should be immediate when the target behavior is being established. Readily available cost-free and developmentally appropriate rewards are preferable—being first in line, doing a favorite classroom job, being a student helper, running errands, tutoring a classmate—if they are reinforcing to the child.

The contingency contracting process can be broken down into six steps:

1. The counselor and the child identify the problem to be solved.
2. The counselor collects data to verify the baseline frequency rate for the undesired behavior.
3. The counselor and the child set mutually acceptable goals.
4. The counselor selects specific counseling techniques and methods for attaining the goals.
5. The counselor evaluates the techniques for observable and measurable change.
6. If the selected counseling techniques are not effective, the counselor repeats Step 4. If the techniques prove effective, the counselor develops a maintenance plan for the new behavior changes.

For example, Jerry completed no assignments in any of his school subjects. His teacher is lowering his grades because of his unwillingness to complete these assignments. He is referred to the counselor.

Step 1. The counselor talks with Jerry about the problem. Jerry is not happy with his grades but still has trouble concentrating on completing his work. He would like to do better on these assignments and make better grades.

Step 2. A 5-day period is set aside to determine the exact amount of work Jerry completes. The record verifies the teacher's report that Jerry does not complete any assignments, even though he starts about half of them.

Step 3. Jerry and the counselor agree that a good goal for a start would be to complete one assignment each day.

Step 4. For each assignment completed, Jerry will receive 10 points to be applied toward a total of 100 points, which can be exchanged for 30 minutes of free time during the school day.

Step 5. Evaluation of the contingency contract indicates that Jerry completed four assignments the first week, earning 40 points, and six assignments the second week, for a total of 100 points. He then received his 30 minutes of free time. The following week he earned 100 points and received a second 30 minutes of free time. He was also successful during Week 3.

Step 6. The counselor and Jerry agree that continuing with the point system is not necessary. Jerry's grades are improving and everyone seems happier—the teacher, Jerry, and his parents. As a maintenance procedure, Jerry agrees to check in with the counselor each Friday afternoon for reports on his completed assignments for the week, which he records on a pocket-sized scorecard. Of course, a good teaching procedure would be to continue to allow Jerry and his classmates to earn free time when they complete assigned work.

Ayllon and Azrin (1965) demonstrated that contingency contract tokens, when delivered contingent on specific behaviors, could have profound effects on the behavior of institutionalized psychotics. Many other applications have also been demonstrated (Rimm & Masters, 1974).

The results of a study by Blechman, Kotanchik, and Taylor (1981) indicate that school-based contingency contracts written by families help to inspire inconsistent students to become more consistent in classroom performance, thus achieving the primary aims of home-school collaboration: better work and a more self-confident child.

Williamson, Williamson, Watkins, and Hughes (1992) researched the differential effectiveness of two reinforcement contingencies (independent group-oriented versus individual) for improving cooperation among students in solving a mathematics estimation task. A total of 371 students in second through fifth grades in two schools were asked to guess the correct number of cubes in a glass jar. One school had an individual reinforcement plan in which there would be one winner from each class. The other school was on a group reinforcement plan that stated that everyone in the class would get a prize if anyone in the class guessed the right number. The group reinforcement plan resulted in superior estimation accuracy and was associated with a higher degree of cooperation among students.

Brantley and Webster (1993) studied the effectiveness of a group contingency management system for decreasing the disruptive classroom behaviors of 25 fourth-grade students. Three rules were posted on a classroom chart: (1) Pay attention and finish your work, (2) get permission before speaking, and (3) stay in your seat without touching others. Classroom time was divided into 45-minute sessions. Students completing the requirements of two or more rules during a session received a check by their names on the chart; five checks were the maximum number of checks a student could earn during the week. Rewards were chosen at the beginning of the week from a list generated and ranked by the students. The authors noted significant decreases in targeted, disruptive behaviors.

Self-Management

An adaptation of the six-step contingency contract method, the self-management plan is for children who can take more responsibility for their behavior. These plans also follow a step-by-step process: defining a problem in behavioral terms, collecting data on the problem, introducing a treatment program based on behavior principles, evaluating the effectiveness of the program, and appropriately changing the program if the plan is not working. The major difference between self-management and other procedures is that children assume major responsibility for carrying out their programs, including arranging their own contingencies or reinforcement when they have the skills to do so.

Steps in developing a self-management plan are as follows:

1. Choose an observable and measurable behavior you wish to change.
2. Record for at least 1 week (a) your target behavior, (b) the setting in which it occurs, (c) the antecedent events leading to the behavior, and (d) the consequences resulting from the behavior.
3. Set a goal you can achieve.
4. Change the setting and the antecedent events leading up to the target behavior.
5. Change the consequences that reinforce the target behavior.
6. Keep accurate records of your target behavior—your successes and failures.
7. Arrange a plan to maintain the goals you have reached.

Self-management contracts are generally not effective for younger children unless the plan is managed by the child and an older person. Self-tracking and self-rewarding are usually difficult for children younger than 11. Children can set goals and choose consequences but need an adult monitor for tracking and reinforcing behavior.

Genshaft (1982) used cognitive behavior therapy effectively to reduce math anxiety in seventh-grade girls. Three groups were included in the study: a tutoring group, a tutoring group with training in self-instruction, and a control group. The group receiving self-instructional training was the only one that showed a significant improvement in computations and reported improved attitudes toward math.

Christie, Hiss, and Lozanoff (1984) found self-recording beneficial in changing the classroom behavior of hyperactive children. The teacher decreased inattentiveness and other unacceptable behavior by having children record their own behavior at varying time intervals convenient for the teacher.

Andrews and Feyer (1985) found behavioral therapy effective in treating stuttering behavior, as demonstrated in both posttreatment and 13-month follow-up evaluations. Clients maintained gains in fluency, rate, and positive personal feelings about their progress.

Kane and Kendall (1989), working with children who had anxiety disorders, found a variety of behavioral and cognitive interventions effective in reducing anxiety. The children were given 16 to 20 1-hour treatments that included modeling, role-play, relaxation training, and coping strategies.

Working with 4- and 5-year-old children who were experiencing mild peer rejection, Mize and Ladd (1990) were successful in training the children to perform useful social skills. Treatment included instruction, rehearsal, practice, and feedback. Hand puppets were used to model the target skills.

In a study on children's school-refusal behavior, Silverman and Kearney (1990) found that school refusal stemmed from four causes: fear, escape from social situations, attention getting, and various types of positive reinforcement. The authors, in developing successful treatment programs for school refusal, made a case for basing treatment on the causes of the behavior (behavior analysis).

In researching a method for teaching self-management to children, Kahn (1989) reported that self-observation with an external feedback group outperformed a control group, an external feedback group, and a self-observation group. The dependent variable was staying on task during arithmetic classes.

Wurtele (1990), in a study designed to measure the effects on 4-year-old children of teaching safety skills to prevent sexual abuse, found no differences between the treatment and control groups on parent and teacher observation scales, children's attitudes toward their private parts, and a personal safety questionnaire. The positive finding from the study is that the program did not seem to have any negative effects on the children.

Wolfe, Gentile, and Wolfe (1989), studying the impact of sexual abuse on children, conducted behavior analyses on 72 children (age 5 to 16) who had been referred for sexual abuse assessment. Mothers rated sexually abused children as showing relatively high levels of internalizing and externalizing symptoms, as well as high levels of posttraumatic stress disorder (PTSD) symptoms. However, the children did not report elevated levels of negative affect. Younger children showed more symptomatology, were more distressed by sex-related situations, and were more likely to report stigmatization and anxiety.

Shaping

The basic operant technique of shaping is a general procedure designed to induce new behaviors by reinforcing behaviors that approximate the desired behavior. Each successive approximation of the behavior is reinforced until the desired behavior is obtained. To administer the technique, the counselor must know how to skillfully use (1) looking, (2) waiting, and (3) reinforcing. The counselor looks for the desired behavior, waits until it occurs, and reinforces it when it does occur. In essence, the counselor is catching the child in good behavior—a much more difficult task than catching the child in bad behavior. Shaping of successful approximations of the target behavior works well with children if the program is administered correctly. Small steps need to be reinforced immediately each time they occur. Shaping offers a method for teaching complex behaviors to children because mediating steps are identified and rewarded. Extrinsic reinforcers are more likely to be effective with children. Sugar-free candy, stickers, trinkets, and "good behavior" ink stamps on the hand all work well. Pairing intrinsic rewards with extrinsic rewards is always good practice to help children move away from the need for extrinsic rewards.

Harrop and McCann (1984) showed that shaping can increase third-year creative writing students' use of fluency, elaboration, and flexibility. The counselors explained and shaped the skills through awarding points and positive teacher comments.

Chirico (1985) described three guidance programs in Providence, Rhode Island, that have built self-esteem and decreased problem behavior and poor school attitudes. The programs included behavior management in addition to student-of-the-week, group guidance, and puppetry programs.

Rosen and Rosen (1983), using stimulus control with a 7-year-old boy, extinguished his chronic stealing. The child's items were marked with green circles and checked at 15-minute intervals. They reinforced possession of marked items, and punished possession of unmarked items (stolen goods). The boy could use points earned at the classroom store.

Darveaux (1984) found that a good behavior game plus merit points was effective in improving the behavior and motivation of two second-grade boys who were labeled as high risk for placement in a behaviorally impaired program. Using a two-team approach, with one boy on each team, the teacher recorded marks on the board when any team member violated a rule. Merit points were awarded for assignment completion and positive classroom participation. Merit points could be used to eliminate the "bad" marks on the board.

Assessing the impact of a parent/child training program that employed positive reinforcement on families from different socioeconomic levels (Wahler, Winkel, Peterson, & Morrison, 1965), Holden, Lavigne, and Cameron (1990) found that program dropouts and difficulty in program completion occurred primarily in families who had a greater number of problems, families from a lower socioeconomic level, and families from minority populations. One could conclude that parent training that focuses on "catching" children in cooperative behavior might need some adjustments to meet such families' needs.

Biofeedback

In biofeedback, a machine accomplishes the three behaviors of looking, waiting, and reinforcing. Brain waves, muscle tension, body temperature, heart rate, and blood pressure can be monitored for small changes and fed back to the client by auditory and visual means. The more the child relaxes, the slower and lower the beeping sound on the monitor. Biofeedback methods have been successful in, for example, teaching hyperactive children to relax. The equipment may provide feedback with electric trains and recorded music. Both stop when the child stops relaxing and restart when the child takes the first small step toward relaxing again. An understanding of cause and effect by the children would enhance biofeedback methods but is not a necessity.

Modeling

Modeling consists of exposing the child to one or more individuals, either in real life or in film or tape presentations, who exhibit behaviors to be adopted by the child. Counselors may be the models to demonstrate certain behaviors to the child, or peers of the child may be used.

Peers are an important part of a child's world, and their influence can help children change. Children usually imitate the behaviors of people they like. A model may be presented to the child through the use of television, films, videotapes, or books. Other models include friends, classmates, adults, and the counselor.

For example, Charlene mentioned a friend, Patty, a number of times during the counseling sessions. She indicated that she would like to be like Patty because Patty had a lot of friends, made good grades, and got along well with parents and teachers. The counselor asked Charlene to observe Patty's behaviors closely for 1 week and to write on an index card those she particularly liked and wanted to imitate. The next week Charlene brought back her list of six behaviors. The counselor and Charlene selected the most important one for Charlene (giving compliments) and began to work on that behavior. Role-playing and behavior rehearsal were included in the counseling to help Charlene learn the new behaviors. The observed behaviors were practiced and modified until they were appropriate for Charlene. As counseling progressed, Charlene continued to observe her model and to practice new behaviors until she became more like her idealized self.

Modeling is a process for teaching children voluntary behaviors through observation and replication of desired behaviors. Modeling and shaping could be done in combination for younger children. Negative reinforcement is effective here if a new behavior is learned to avoid a consequence such as peer ridicule.

Lazarus (1966) compared the effectiveness of three treatments: behavior rehearsals, reflection interpretation, and advice giving. Behavior rehearsal included modeling by the therapist, practice by the client, and relaxation induction at the first sign of anxiety. He found that 92% of the behavior rehearsal subjects showed improvement, compared with 44% and 32% improvement rates, respectively, for the other two groups.

Epstein and Borduin (1984) studied the effect of a children's feedback game with reinforcement on increasing the skill and frequency of giving and receiving positive and negative feedback to one another in a group therapy setting. The positive study results were maintained through practice and modeling of the group leader's behavior.

Barlow, Hay, and Hay (1981), employing covert modeling procedures in the treatment of a 10-year-old boy with gender-identity confusion, corrected target behavior in five areas. These behaviors were maintained throughout the 6-month follow-up and generalized to the home environment.

Celiberti and Harris (1993) studied the effects of modeling correct behavior for playing with autistic children. The purpose of the study was to find out if children could acquire behavioral skills that could lead to creative play with their siblings who were diagnosed as autistic. Three sibling dyads participated in the study; the younger siblings were the autistic children in each dyad. All three autistic children displayed typical autistic behaviors: being unfocused and preoccupied, grabbing, having tantrums, and verbally rejecting any attempt at sibling interaction. Three areas of behavior were modeled for the older siblings: (1) appropriate play and related language, (2) praise of appropriate responses and prompting responses when the autistic child did not respond, and (3) correcting incorrect responses. All three normal siblings made significant gains in the three targeted areas of behavior after the training and modeling treatment.

Token Economies

Token economies are used on a group basis, as in a school classroom. The children earn tokens or points for certain target behaviors. These behaviors are classified as either on task or socially appropriate. Children also lose tokens or points for off-task and socially inappropriate behaviors. Children may periodically cash in tokens or points earned for rewards like free time, game time, trinkets, and sugarless candy. Some teachers use token economies for their classroom groups. An empty jar sits on the teacher's desk. Everytime something good happens in the classroom, the teacher drops some marbles in the jar. The marble noise becomes an auditory reinforcement to go with the visual image of the jar filling up. A full jar means all students get free popcorn during the lunch period. The case study on Sue in this chapter is an example of how to use a token economy contract.

Behavior-Practice Groups

Behavior-practice groups have some advantages in counseling children. They provide a relatively safe setting for the child to practice new behaviors before trying them out in real-life situations. These groups are also useful in supporting and reinforcing children as they attempt new behaviors and reach goals. Behavior-practice groups may focus on any of several behavior changes, including the following:

- Weight loss
- Study habits
- Assertiveness training

- Communication skills
- Negative addictions such as drugs, alcohol, and smoking

In working with behavior-practice groups, the counselor needs to develop a lesson plan with behavioral objectives, instructional methods, reinforcement, and evaluation. A good lesson plan would maintain a balance among three teaching strategies: (1) tell me, (2) show me, and (3) let me try it. For example, a lesson plan in assertiveness training might have the following objective: After 10 weekly group meetings, each child in the group will have demonstrated in at least three real-life settings the ability to do the following:

1. Make an effective complaint
2. Give negative feedback
3. Give positive feedback
4. Make a reasonable request
5. Say no to an unreasonable request

Role-Playing

Role-playing is a counseling technique not restricted to one theory. Many counseling professionals use it. Behavioral counselors often find that role-playing facilitates clients' progress in self-management programs; for example, it can help clients see their behaviors as others see them and obtain feedback about these behaviors. Role-playing can also provide practice for decision making and exploring consequences.

Negative role-playing or rehearsal can be helpful in identifying what *not* to do. Role-playing negative behaviors and their consequences may help children evaluate objectively what is happening and the consequences of their behavior.

Role-playing can help children learn about cause and effect and experience the consequences of their behavior in a relatively safe setting. Role-playing is useful to children who are working toward developing a sense of empathy and beginning to modify their egocentric views of the world. Children can usually act out a problem scenario better than they can describe it.

Role-playing to define a problem

Children often have trouble describing exactly what occurred in a particular situation, especially one involving interpersonal problems with parents, teachers, or peers. Moreover, they may be unable to see clearly how certain behaviors have evoked an unwanted response or consequence. For example, suppose Jerome tells the counselor that he and his mother are in constant conflict. She is unfair and never allows him to do *anything* he asks. Role-playing could provide some insight into what occurs when Jerome asks for permission.

Counselor: I'll be your mother, and you show me exactly how you ask your mother to allow you, for instance, to have a birthday party. Talk to me exactly as you would to your mother if you were to ask her for the party.

Jerome: Mom, you never let me do anything! You always say no to anything I want. I want a birthday party, and you'll be mean if you don't let me have one this year!

The counselor can now readily see that if a conflict already exists between mother and child, this demand will increase the conflict and is unlikely to get Jerome his birthday party.

Children having trouble with peers might be asked to describe what happened and then to role-play one or more persons in the incident. Verbal and nonverbal behaviors not adequately described in relating the incident often become more apparent when they are role-played.

Role reversal

When conflicts occur between children, adults frequently ask one child, "How would you feel if he hit you like that [said that to you, bit you, and so on]?" The purpose of this admonition is to have the child empathize with the other. However, many cognitive theorists, especially Piaget, emphasized that young children up through the preoperational stage (2 to 7 years old) lack the cognitive development to be able to put themselves in another person's place. Because children understand better what they see, hear, or experience directly, role-playing other children's positions could promote a better understanding than a verbal admonition.

Counselor: Barbara, I understand from your sister that you hit her on the head quite often. Would you agree that this is what happens?

Barbara: Yeah, I can really make her move if I threaten to hit her good on the head!

Counselor: Would the two of you describe to me what happened the last time you hit Judy? [The girls describe the incident.] Now Barbara, I wonder if you would mind playing Judy and saying and doing exactly what Judy did. I would like Judy to say and do exactly what you did. [Remind the girls that hitting hard is not allowed in the role playing because people are not for hitting.]

The purpose of this role reversal is to help Barbara experience Judy's feelings when Barbara hit her in the hope that Barbara will then want to explore better methods of relating to Judy.

Role reversal can be effective when communication breaks down between parents and children, between teachers and children, between peers, or between counselors and their clients. Each player can gain increased knowledge of the other's point of view.

Role-playing used as behavior rehearsal

Most adults rehearse a speech before presenting it to an audience to refine the speech and ensure a smooth presentation. Children, too, may feel more comfortable about trying a new behavior if they can practice it before actually facing the real world.

Dave is a shy little boy who has no friends. In an effort to help Dave make friends, the counselor may want to help him decide exactly how to approach another child and what to say to the child after the opening "hello." To build confidence, the counselor could first role-play another child and allow Dave to practice his new behaviors in a safe atmosphere. When Dave feels secure in role-playing with the counselor, another child can be involved in the role-play situation to help Dave gain more realistic experiences in meeting other children.

Counseling Homework Assignments

Homework assignments may be given to children in counseling for a variety of reasons. Homework can build continuity between sessions and facilitate counseling by encouraging "work" on the child's problems between sessions. A homework assignment could be a commitment by the child to keep a record of some particular feeling or behavior, to reduce or stop a present behavior, or to try a new behavior. Homework assignments provide the child with an opportunity to try out new or different behaviors and discuss the consequences with the counselor. For example, after Dave (in the preceding example) has rehearsed approaching a new person within the counseling session, the counselor might ask him to approach one new person during the coming week and try out this new behavior. Dave could evaluate whether the new behavior was effective for him and discuss the results with the counselor; if it was not effective, they could explore other methods.

Assertiveness Training

Some children's typical response to everyday interactions is withdrawal. Some of these children may have poor self-concepts and feelings of inferiority that inhibit them; others, having experienced negative consequences as a result of speaking out, are inhibited from doing so by their anxiety. Children who are withdrawn and passive need to be encouraged to recognize their rights as people as well as accept the rights of others.

Tim and Charles were close friends. However, Tim always took from Charles whatever he wanted or needed—toys, pencils, food, and so on. Charles responded passively, always allowing Tim to have his way. The counselor asked Charles to describe in detail the latest incident in which Tim had taken Charles's new bike, ridden it all afternoon, and brought it back scratched. The counselor encouraged

Charles to formulate an assertive statement such as "I want to ride my new bike. Would you go and get your bike to ride?" Charles and the counselor took several incidents from the past, and Charles was encouraged to state (1) his needs and (2) what he would like to have happen in each situation. They then used behavior rehearsal to give Charles an opportunity to practice his assertiveness.

After several sessions, Charles made a commitment to try out his new response. He reported that he told Tim "I want to use my Magic Markers now. Would you get your own?" and that it had worked. The counselor worked for several months on helping Charles learn how to become appropriately assertive. Each new situation was discussed and practiced in the counseling sessions before Charles actually tried it in daily living.

A word of caution is necessary to counselors teaching assertiveness to children. The adults in the child's life must be prepared for the child's new behavior. Parents who discipline children by authoritarian methods may not tolerate assertiveness on the part of their child. In order to avoid unpleasant consequences, the counselor has to determine the effect of the child's behavioral change on the child's significant others or on the child's culture and environment before teaching the child this new skill.

CLASSICAL CONDITIONING METHODS

Respondent behavior is associated with classical conditioning, in which learning occurs when a stimulus that already elicits a response (an unconditioned stimulus) is presented along with a neutral stimulus that elicits no response or a different response. With repeated pairings of the two stimuli, the neutral stimulus begins to elicit the same response as the unconditioned stimulus. In the case of Pavlov's dogs, for example, Pavlov paired the unconditioned stimulus of food with the neutral stimulus of a bell. The response to the unconditioned stimulus was salivating. The neutral stimulus (the bell) became the conditioned stimulus, and the response to the conditioned stimulus became the conditioned response (salivating).

Systematic Desensitization

Systematic desensitization, developed by Wolpe (1958, 1969) from earlier work by Jacobsen (1938), is a procedure used to eliminate anxiety and fear. A response incompatible with anxiety, such as relaxation, is paired with, first, weak and then progressively stronger anxiety-provoking stimuli. The approach is based on the principles of counterconditioning; that is, if all skeletal muscles are deeply relaxed, one cannot experience anxiety at the same time.

A child may be experiencing anxiety related to specific stimulus situations such as taking tests, performing in front of a group, being in high places, or seeing some animal. The first step is to develop a hierarchy of scenes related to the fear or phobia, with mildly aversive scenes at the bottom and progressively more aversive scenes at the top. The counselor then teaches the child the process of deep muscle relaxation and asks the relaxed child to visualize the various scenes in the hierarchy.

The relaxation exercises consist of successively tensing and relaxing 19 different muscle groups at 6-second intervals until a high level of relaxation is achieved. The process is usually performed with the child in a recliner-type chair or stretched out on a soft rug. The child is asked to go as high as possible on the hierarchy without feeling anxiety. When the child feels anxiety, he or she signals the counselor by raising one finger, and the counselor reverts to a less anxiety-provoking scene. Behavior practice facilitates the process. A child may successively practice giving a short speech in front of a mirror, with an audiotape recorder, with a videotape recorder, in front of a best friend, in front of a small group, and so on, until the child can give the speech in front of a class of 25 students. The child's stimulus hierarchy might look like this:

0. Lying in bed in your room just before going to sleep—describe your room
1. Thinking about speech alone in your room 1 week before you give it
2. Discussing the upcoming speech in class a week before it's due
3. Sitting in class while another student gives a speech 1 week before your speech
4. Writing your speech at home
5. Practicing your speech alone in your room or in front of your friend
6. Getting dressed the morning of the speech
7. Eating breakfast and thinking about the speech before going to school
8. Walking to school on the day of your speech
9. Entering the classroom on the day of the speech
10. Waiting while another student gives a speech on the day of your presentation
11. Standing in front of your classmates and looking at their faces
12. Presenting your speech before the class

The technique consists of asking the child to relax, imagine, relax, stop imagining, relax, and so on until, after repeated practice, the child learns to relax while visualizing each stage of the stimulus hierarchy.

Several relaxation exercises can be used with children. Following are two types of exercises frequently used.

1. Consciously "let go" of the various muscle groups, starting with your feet and moving to your legs, stomach, arms, neck, and head as you make yourself as comfortable as you can in a chair or lying down.
   a. Stop frowning; let forehead relax.
   b. Let hands, arms, and so on relax.
   c. Tighten 6 seconds, relax; tighten again 6 seconds, relax.
2. Form mental pictures.
   a. Picture yourself stretched out on a soft bed. Your legs are like concrete, sinking down in the mattress from their weight. Picture a friend coming

into the room and trying to lift your concrete legs, but they are too heavy and your friend cannot do it. Repeat with arms, neck, and so on.

b. Picture your body as a big puppet. Your hands are tied loosely to your wrists by strings. Your forearm is connected loosely by a string to your shoulder. Your feet and legs are also connected with a string. Your chin has dropped loosely against your chest. All strings are loose, your body is limp and just sprawled across the bed.

c. Picture your body as consisting of a bunch of rubber balloons. Two air holes open in your feet and the air begins to escape from your legs. Your legs begin to collapse until they are flat rubber tubes. Next a hole is opened in your chest, and the air begins to escape until your entire body is lying flat on the bed. Continue with heads, arms, neck, and so on.

d. Imagine the most relaxing, pleasant scene you can remember—a time when you felt really good and peaceful. If you remember fishing in a mountain stream, pay attention to the little things, such as quiet ripples on the water and leaves on the trees. What sounds were present? Did you hear the quiet rustling of the leaves? Is your relaxing place before an open fireplace with logs crackling, or is it the beach, with warm sun and breeze?

Continued practice facilitates achievement of these mental pictures and relaxation levels.

Systematic desensitization, a classical conditioning technique, could be too complex for younger children, who are not always capable of handling sequential behaviors. Conscious relaxation and visualization may also be difficult for younger children, who benefit more by actual practice of the steps in the stimulus hierarchy. For example, the following systematic desensitization program could be used to help a 6-year old child who is experiencing school phobia: The child indicates that he would like to work toward getting a favorite video game. A chart is drawn up with spaces to star each day he followed the program and earned a dollar toward the purchase price of his video game. Steps in the hierarchy were small enough not to overwhelm the child. Each session lasted 30 minutes.

Step 1. Child and his mother working together alone in the school room, the child reading or talking to his mother.

Step 2. Child, mother, and friend of the child in the school room with the child talking to his friend.

Step 3. Child, mother, friend, and familiar adult (not on the school staff) together in the school room with child talking while playing.

Step 4. Child, mother, friend, and teacher in the school room, the child talking with the teacher; mother leaves them; friend leaves.

Step 5. Child and teacher together in the school room talking to each other.

Step 6. Child and teacher move to the classroom and talk to each other.

Step 7. Child joins the classroom for half a day.

Step 8. Child spends an entire day in the classroom.

In extreme anxiety, desensitization methods may need to be paired with appropriate medication to help the child relax. Going off the medication and performing the task becomes the final step in the hierarchy.

Classical conditioning and operant conditioning usually occur at the same time. A child is given after-school detention for disrupting her class. Detention has the operant effect of preventing the child's disruptive behavior; however, detention may also cause a classical conditioned response of hating school because more school is used as punishment. School time becomes associated with punishment. Associating being in school with a privilege would be much better. When the child misbehaves, she loses the privilege of being in class and has to spend her class time working in a time-out area or in the in-school suspension room. Additional school time (detention) would not be used as a punishment or consequence.

In summary, the technique of desensitization is based on a principle of learning referred to as *reciprocal inhibition;* that is, an organism cannot make two contradictory responses at the same time. If we assume that all responses are learned, relearning or reconditioning can extinguish them. Therefore, relaxation, being more rewarding than anxiety, can gradually replace anxiety as the response to the anxiety-evoking situation.

Wolpe (1989), attacking those who would practice cognitive therapy, made the point that if a habit has been acquired by learning, the logical approach is to treat it by a method based on learning principles. He wrote that the real difference between true behavior therapy and cognitive therapy is the cognitivists' failure to deny the possibility that some fears may be immediately triggered by a particular stimulus without the mediation of an idea of danger. Wolpe also criticized cognitive therapists for dispensing with the behavior analysis required for successful treatment of neurotic suffering.

Lang and Lazovik (1963) published the first controlled experiment that found greater reduction in the behavioral measure of snake avoidance for a desensitization group than for the no-treatment controls, who showed almost no change. Moreover, no evidence of symptom substitution appeared in a 6-month follow-up.

Morris and Kratochwill (1985) reviewed the literature to find what behaviorally oriented fear-reduction methods had been used with children. They found systematic desensitization to be the most frequently mentioned behavioral therapy. Variations of the method included contact desensitization, which combines elements of modeling and desensitization; it proved to be the most effective treatment of animal phobias. Morris and Kratochwill also encountered some use of self-controlled desensitization, which involves training children in developing coping skills. Contingency management, using positive reinforcement both alone and in combination with other operant procedures, was effective, as was shaping, in decreasing fears and increasing approach behavior. Contingency-management procedures were most often used for social withdrawal, school phobia, and selective mutism. Modeling, in addition to being used for treating animal phobias, was also used for test anxiety and dental and surgical treatment. Self-control methods, under the labels of cognitive-behavior or rational-emotive-behavior therapy, involve the development of helpful thinking skills and were cited in both the behavioral and rational-emotive-behavior therapy literature as treatment methods for children's fears.

Fundudis (1986), in describing a case of anorexia nervosa in a preadolescent girl, found that a focused approach to treatment was likely to be more effective than a nonspecific or general management approach. A combination of behavioral and cognitive-behavioral methods was used, including cognitive restructuring, environmental stimulus control (for example, no exercising before completion of a group activity), and systematic desensitization for anxiety generated about the ingestion of food.

Glasscock and MacLean (1990) reported success with a 6-year-old girl suffering from dog phobia and an associated generalized fear of the outdoors because a dog had attacked her outdoors. To use systematic desensitization, they developed and used a 10-step stimulus hierarchy. The steps ranged from the least to most fearful outdoor exposure to a dog. They continued the program over a 9-month period to provide for the maintenance of gains made in her outdoor play behavior.

Flooding

Flooding, the opposite of desensitization, begins with the most feared stimulus in the stimulus hierarchy rather than the weakest or least feared. It is diving into cold water rather than getting used to it gradually. The clients are exposed to their strongest fears by putting themselves into the situation repeatedly over a short period of time. For example, a client might make several public speeches over a period of 2 weeks. The constant, concentrated approach has the effect of literally wearing out the stimulus. Flooding conducted during visualization exercises is referred to as *implosion*.

Flooding, also referred to as *reactive* or *internal inhibition,* is a process in which an anxiety-evoking stimulus is presented continuously, leading to fatigue and eventual unlearning of the undesirable response. When a parent told you to get back on your bike after a crash, you were exposed to the flooding technique. Another application might involve taking a child with a fear of riding in cars on a 4-hour trip. The initial response would be high anxiety or panic, which would, after a while, wear itself out as a stimulus. For example, the next time you find your eyelid blinking involuntarily when you are under too much stress, try blinking your eyelid 100 times without stopping (flooding). If the blinking continues, try again with 200 blinks of your eyelid.

Hypnosis

A technique that incorporates deeper forms of relaxation, hypnosis has long been controversial; however, researchers have found that it can be a useful tool for working with children. Children seem to be fascinated with the procedure and, therefore, are usually easier to hypnotize than adults. Hypnotherapy has been used successfully with children experiencing anxiety, high blood pressure, asthma, and psychosomatic pain and to overcome such habits as nail biting, thumb sucking, tics, insomnia, and sleepwalking.

The danger of hypnotherapy, of course, comes when untrained persons attempt to use the procedure. Counselors may wish to investigate the availability of training in this area. Hypnotherapy appears to be a highly effective counseling tool for working with repressed conflicts, including memories of child sexual abuse.

Counterconditioning

In counterconditioning, a stronger pleasant stimulus is paired with a weaker aversive stimulus as a procedure for overcoming the anxiety the aversive stimulus evokes. For example, a child may be given his or her favorite candy while sitting in the classroom. If the candy is sufficiently rewarding to the child, the anxiety evoked by the classroom should be diminished.

Aversive Conditioning

Aversive conditioning is the application of an aversive or noxious stimulus, such as a rubber-band snap on the wrist, when a maladaptive response or behavior occurs. For example, children could wear rubber bands around their wrists and snap them each time they found themselves daydreaming instead of listening to the teacher. Opportunity for helpful behavior to occur and be reinforced is recommended with this technique.

Blakemore, Thorpe, Barker, Conway, and Lavin (1963) reduced transvestism by applying electric shock while the client was putting on women's clothing.

Ashcraft, Jensen, Preator, and Peterson (1984) found that inappropriate touching in an autistic child can be reduced by overcorrection that is topographically related to and incompatible with appropriate behavior. The addition of question-asking to overcorrection pointed out the effectiveness of enhancing aversive techniques with alternate appropriate behavior.

Silber and Haynes (1992) compared two methods for treating nail biting. Twenty-one participants were randomly assigned to one of three groups: control group, aversion therapy, and competing response therapy. The aversion therapy group applied a bitter substance to their nails twice a day, and the competing response therapy required the participants to clench their fists each time they wanted to bite their nails. Both treatment groups showed significant improvement over the control group.

The following diagrams represent each of the four classical conditioning methods presented:

Key: ⊕ pleasant stimulus; ⊖ aversive stimulus

1. Desensitization

    where ⊖ is giving a speech.

   The aversive stimulus is handled in small steps by visualization or relaxation and by practice until increasingly larger steps can be handled.

2. Flooding (Internal inhibition)

   ⊖ ⊖ ⊖ ⊖ ⊖ ⊖ ⊖ ⊖ ⊖ ⊖, where ⊖ is getting back on the bike after falling off.
   The aversive stimulus is continually repeated until the fear response wears itself out.

3. Counterconditioning

   ⊕ and ⊖, where ⊕ is a candy bar and ⊖ is going to school.
   The larger pleasant stimulus overcomes the anxiety or fear evoked by the smaller aversive stimulus.

4. Aversive conditioning

   ⊖ and ⊕, where ⊖ is a snap of a rubber band on the wrist and ⊕ is daydreaming during class.
   The more painful stimulus overcomes the smaller reward gained from daydreaming in class.

◆ ◆ ◆

CASE STUDY

Identification of the Problem

Sue is a 9-year-old in the fourth grade. She has exhibited some behavior problems in her classroom. She does not complete her classroom assignments, tells lies about her work and about things she does at home and at school, and is reported to be out of her seat constantly.

Individual and Background Information

Academic.   Sue has an above-average IQ. She is an excellent reader and has the ability to do any fourth-grade assignment.

Family.   Sue is an only child. Sue's parents are in their 30s. Sue comes from an upper-middle-class family; her father and mother manage their own business.

Social.   Sue seems to get along relatively well with the other children but has only one close friend, Marie. Sue has been caught telling lies by the other children, and they tell her they do not like her lies. She brings money and trinkets to share with Marie and lets her wear her nice coats, sweaters, and jewelry. Sue has no other children to play with and is mostly around adults who let her have her own way.

Counseling Method

The counselor in this case used a behavioral counseling technique to help Sue evaluate her behavior problems and to teach her to counsel herself. When using this method, a counselor has to determine carefully just how much right one has to influence the client's choices in modifying behavior. The criteria for determining when to use behavioral counseling are based on the frequency of the maladaptive behavior and the degree to which the behavior hinders the child's healthy development and that of the others in the class.

In this case, the counselor used the following steps:

1. Established a warm, talking relationship (therapeutic alliance).
2. Wrote out the problems on paper.
3. Listed rewards and consequences of the plans.
4. Obtained a commitment from the client on the plan of action that would most likely help.
5. Used a behavior contract with positive reinforcement in the form of a social reward (praise) for desirable behavior and token reinforcement (points to exchange for fun time activities). Positive reinforcers were withdrawn (by loss of points) when undesirable behavior occurred.
6. Drew up plans for a behavior contract. These plans were discussed with, agreed upon, and signed by the client, counselor, teacher, and parents because the child was exhibiting some of the undesirable behavior at home by not completing assigned tasks and telling her parents lies.

Transcript

Counselor: Sue, your teacher sent you to me because you seem to be having some problems in class. Would you like to tell me what kind of problems you seem to be having? I'll write them down in a list so we can see what could be done to help you here and at home.

Sue: I just can't seem to get my work done or turned in on time.

Counselor: How do you stop yourself from doing this?

Sue: I just can't seem to be able to sit still long enough to finish, and then time is always up before I finish.

Counselor: Who else is affected by your getting out of your seat?

Sue: I guess I'm keeping the others from working when I go to their seats, and it bothers my teacher because she stops what she is doing and tells me to sit down and get busy.

Counselor: What happens when you don't finish your work?

Sue: Well, nothing really happens, except I try to get out of being fussed at and being kept in during play period for not doing my work.

Counselor: What do you mean, Sue?

Sue: I make up stories about I can't find my paper or somebody took it when I really hadn't even started it, or I hide what I have started in my desk or notebook and take it home and do it and then turn it in the next day and say I found it.

Counselor: What do you tell your mom and dad about your work for the day when they ask you?

Sue: Well, I tell a story to them, too. I tell them I did all my work, and usually the same things I tell the teacher I tell them, too.

Counselor: How do you feel about telling untrue stories?

Sue: I don't really feel good about it, but I want Mom and Dad to be proud of me and I really do want to do my work, but I just can't seem to do it, so I just tell a story.

Counselor: Okay, Sue, you say you want to change, so let's look at the list of things you want to change and see what you and I can work out together.

Sue: Okay, I'd like that.

Counselor: Let me read your contract terms to you. If you think there is anything you can't live with, we'll change it until we get it the way we think will help you the most. This contract tells you what will happen when you are able to finish your work. Your teacher, your mom and dad, you, and I will all sign it to show you we are all willing to help you live up to the terms. Will you go over it with your mother and father and see if there is anything that needs to be changed?

Sue: I think it's okay just the way it is.

Counselor: Okay, you and I will sign first, and I will send copies to your teacher and your parents to sign. We will try this for a week, and then you and I will meet at the same time next week to see how you are doing and if any changes need to be made.

Sue: Okay.

Contract for Behavior and Learning

Positive behaviors	Tokens
1. Bringing needed materials to class	5
2. Working on class or home assignment until finished	5
3. Staying in seat	5
4. Extra credit (reading SRA or laminated task sheets)	1, 2, 3, 4, 5

You may exchange tokens earned for positive behavior for time to do "fun" activities.

Fun activities	*Tokens*
1. Writing on the small chalkboards	15
2. Playing Phonic Rummy	15
3. Playing with the tray puzzles	15
4. Getting to be the library aide for a day	15
5. Getting to use the cyclo-teacher	15
6. Playing Old Maid with classmates	10
7. Using the headphone and tape recorder to hear a story from tapes	15
8. Using clay, finger paints, and other art supplies	10

I, _____, agree to abide by the terms set forth in this contract. It is my understanding that tokens earned will depend on my classroom work and behavior.

_____

Signature

We, your teacher, your parents, and your counselor, agree to abide by the conditions specified in the contract. It is our understanding that we will assist you in any way we can with your tasks and behavioral problems.

_____

Teacher

_____

Parents

_____

Counselor

Behavioral counseling helps individuals look at what they are doing and what happens when they do it. The contract helps children try different behaviors to see which ones work for them. It encourages parents to adhere to the terms of the contract and positively reinforce all desirable behaviors at home. If the child continues to receive positive reinforcement for socially desirable and classroom-adaptive behavior, the counselor gradually implements a self-reinforcement system to help the child develop a sense of intrinsic reinforcement.

RESEARCH AND APPLICATIONS

Behavioral counselors have more supporting data available than counselors of any other school. As noted previously, behavioral counselors must collect accurate data if their procedures are to operate with maximum efficiency. Therefore, behavioral counselors have done a thorough job of validating their claims of success.

The purpose of behavioral counseling is to change the client's overt and covert responses (cognitions, emotions, physiological states). Bandura (1974) reacted to the oft-repeated dictum "Change contingencies and you change behavior," by adding the reciprocal side: "Change behavior and you change the contingencies . . . since in everyday life this two-way control operates concurrently" (p. 866). Behavioral counselors work with behavior that is objective and measurable. Behavioral counseling methods, not confined to one stimulus-response theory of learning, are derived from a variety of learning principles.

London (1972) declared that the distinguishing features of behavioral counseling include the functional analysis of behavior and the development of the necessary technology to bring about change. Thus, behavioral counseling is the application of specified procedures derived from experimental research to benefit an individual, a group, an institution, or an environmental setting.

Supporting research includes studies emphasizing a number of behavioral-counseling methods.

Punishment and Response Cost

Little and Kelley (1989), studying the effects of response cost procedures for reducing children's noncompliance with parental instructions, found removal of reinforcers to be effective.

In a study on delayed punishment, Abramowitz and O'Leary (1990) reported that immediate reprimands were superior to both delayed reprimands and a combination of immediate and delayed reprimands in reducing interactive off-task behavior by hyperactive children in Grades 1 and 2.

Stratton (1989), in an attempt to assess consumer satisfaction with three cost-effective parent-training programs for children with conduct problems, found that parents favored the "time out" program over both the "ignore and play" and the "rewards and commands" programs.

Whelan and Houts (1990), in a study on the effects of an hourly waking schedule on primary enuretic children with full-spectrum home training (FSHT), reported that the waking schedule did not shorten the time required to achieve success. The program requires the child to change bed linens, clean urine-alarm pads, remake the bed, and reset the alarm after each wetting. The child receives prearranged monetary rewards for success in postponing urination. Following 14 dry days, overlearning starts by having the child drink 16 ounces of water before bedtime. Success is defined as 14 dry nights.

Applying similar response cost procedures with positive reinforcement for the treatment of childhood encopresis, Gumaer (1990) successfully treated the problem with a response cost contract. Briefly, punishment included washing dirty clothes, bathing immediately after soiling, doing extra chores, or losing privileges. Positive reinforcement included spending time in favorite activities with parents or receiving a toy or money.

Extinction

Richman, Douglas, Hunt, Lansdown, and Levere (1985) reported a 77% success rate in treating sleep disorders in children ages 1 to 5. The specific behavior techniques used included extinction, positive reinforcement, and consistent parental behaviors.

France and Hudson (1990) found similar success in using extinction to treat sleep disorders in children aged 20 months to 8 years. Basically, parents consistently ignored their children's crying during a 4-week treatment period. Children with health problems that could cause sleep disturbances were excluded from the study.

Eating Disorders

Behavioral counseling has been effective in treating eating disorders. Response prevention has been used to treat bulimia, in which eating is followed by vomiting or purging, which relieves the anxiety produced by eating and sustains the habit of binge eating because it removes the consequence of feeling guilty. The treatment plan is designed to allow the client to eat but not purge. The client is forced to tolerate the resulting anxiety and guilt by locking all nearby bathroom doors and remaining in the presence of other people, in front of whom the client is ashamed to vomit. This rather harsh treatment should be accompanied by plans to teach the client how to eat in moderation until eating produces less anxiety and the client can eat normal amounts of food without vomiting.

Anorexic clients need positive reinforcement (social activities and visiting privileges) and negative reinforcement (isolation, bed rest, and tube feeding) to encourage eating and gaining weight. Friends and family often reward undesired behaviors with their attention and sympathy and need to be instructed how to reward the helpful and lifesaving behaviors of eating and gaining weight.

Multimodal Approaches

Boster and Davis (1992) recommended a multimodal treatment plan for working with aggressive and violent youths, who present a wide range of learning styles and complex personalities that cannot be treated effectively with a single approach for everyone. We believe that the same argument holds true for all people. Suggested interventions for aggressive and resistant youths include CBT, the expressive arts, stress management, modeling of social skills, and the conflict resolution skills of negotiation and compromise. Interventions for unwilling clients include (1) frequent group therapy with individual therapy as a contingency for refusal to participate in the group, (2) options for clients to terminate therapy after a set number of sessions, and (3) allowing them to know as much as possible about their cases by sharing case records and tapes of their counseling sessions, along with the privilege of sitting in on their own case conferences. Many of the recommendations rest on the assumption that aggressive and violent people are fascinated with themselves and that sharing their case data with them may draw them into the treatment process by making them active participants.

Kettlewell, Mizes, and Wasylyshyn (1992) found moderate success with a cognitive-behavioral group treatment program for bulimia. Thirteen women with an average age of 24 participated in the study. Eight weekly 90-minute sessions focused on consequences of bulimia, goal setting (2 weeks), functional analysis of the antecedents and consequences in the binge-purge cycle, selection of an appropriate weight, coping strategies, benefits and risks of striving for thinness, and maintenance of progress. The participants had weekly homework assignments related to each topic.

SUMMARY

We find the same eclectic theme running through the current literature on behavioral counseling that we find in all approaches to counseling. A balanced view of behavioral counseling can be found in Lazarus's "Has Behavior Therapy Outlived Its Usefulness?" (1977). Lazarus suggested that behavioral counseling methods by themselves are inadequate to treat the full range of human problems and that a more eclectic approach, such as his multimodal counseling, discussed elsewhere in this book, is preferable. However, he saw behavioral methods as valuable tools in the counselor's repertoire of methods.

Levine and Fasnacht's "Token Rewards May Lead to Token Learning" (1974) made the point that reinforcement methods may serve to extinguish desired behavior when the reward or token replaces any intrinsic reward a person might receive from engaging in the desired behavior. For example, if parents reward or reinforce a child's piano practice, the message to the child may be that piano playing is not worth doing without pay and therefore is not worthwhile in itself.

Finally, Shapiro and Goldberg (1986) found that children prefer independent group contingencies over interdependent and dependent group contingencies. Independent group contingencies require the same response of all individuals in the group, but access to reinforcement is based only on each individual's response (for example, everyone scoring 90% gets a reward). Interdependent contingencies depend upon the collective performance of the group (for example, the entire group receives a reward if the group mean equals 90% or better). Dependent group contingencies are based on the performance of a selected member or selected members of the group (for example, if a paper drawn at random from a box containing all group members' test papers has a score of 90% or better, everyone receives a reward). Considerable evidence exists in the literature to support behavioral methods that use self-control, self-determination, and personal responsibility as motivators and reinforcers.

Behavioral counseling (BC), like most other counseling methods, is moving toward multimodal or integrative approaches that use BC in combination with other counseling approaches. However, behavioral counselors do share several commonalities. Their work is based on research in experimental and social psychology. Like most of the other counseling orientations presented in this book, BC is focused more on present than past concerns and more on actions than on personality. Behavioral counselors operationalize terms referring to subjective states listed under such diagnostic categories as depression, anxiety, paranoia, shyness, obsession, and compulsion by describing these conditions as specific patterns of observable actions. For example, *depression* might be defined as loss of adequate reinforcement. Behavioral counselors are committed to defining problems precisely by breaking them down into observable and countable components of behavior. Behavioral goals are set in advance and systematically evaluated throughout the treatment process and follow-up period. Behavioral counselors view their work as reeducative rather than healing and reject diagnostic labels for behavior analysis. Often BC begins with a written contract outlining what the client is going to do and what outcomes are to be expected. Counseling begins with the behavior that is easiest to change, with accurate records maintained throughout the counseling experience. Counselors discard ineffective interventions in favor of new intervention plans.

REFERENCES

Abramowitz, A., & O'Leary, S. (1990). Effectiveness of delayed punishment in an applied setting. *Behavior Therapy, 21,* 231–239.

Andrews, G., & Feyer, A. (1985). Does behavior therapy still work when the experimenters depart? An analysis of a behavioral treatment program for stuttering. *Behavior Modification, 9,* 443–457.

Ashcraft, P., Jensen, W., Preator, K., & Peterson, P. (1984). Overcorrection and alternate response training in the reduction of an autistic child's inappropriate touching. *School Psychology Review, 13,* 107–110.

Ayllon, T., & Azrin, N. (1965). The measurement and reinforcement of behavior of psychotics. *Journal of the Experimental Analysis of Behavior, 8,* 357–383.

Bandura, A. (1974). Behavior therapy and the models of man. *American Psychologist, 29,* 859–869.

Banks, S., & Thompson, C. (1995). *Educational psychology: For teachers in training.* St. Paul, MN: West.

Barlow, D., Hay, L., & Hay, W. (1981). Using covert modeling in a boy with gender identity confusion. *Journal of Consulting and Clinical Psychology, 49,* 388–394.

Blakemore, C., Thorpe, J., Barker, J., Conway, C., & Lavin, N. (1963). The application of paradic aversion conditioning in a case of transvestism. *Behavior Research and Therapy, 1,* 29–34.

Blechman, E., Kotanchik, N., & Taylor, C. (1981). Families and schools together: Early behavioral intervention with high risk children. *Behavior Therapy, 12,* 308–319.

Boster, L., & Davis, D. (1992). Cognitive-behavioral-expressive interventions with aggressive and resistant youths. *Child Welfare, 71,* 557–573.

Brantley, C., & Webster, R. (1993). Use of an independent group contingency management system in a regular classroom setting. *Psychology in the Schools, 30,* 60–66.

Celiberti, D., & Harris, S. (1993). Behavioral interventions of siblings of children with autism: A focus on skills to enhance play. *Behavior Therapy, 24,* 573–599.

Chirico, J. (1985). Three guidance programs in Providence, Rhode Island. *School Counselor, 32,* 388–391.

Christie, D., Hiss, M., & Lozanoff, B. (1984). Modification of inattentive classroom behavior: Hyperactive children's use of self-recording with teacher guidance. *Behavior Modification, 8,* 391–406.

Cook, D. (1991). B. F. Skinner: The man with pigeons and persistence. *Bostonia,* 56–58.

Darveaux, D. (1984). The good behavior game plus merit: Controlling disruptive behavior and improving student motivation. *School Psychology Review, 14,* 84–93.

Epstein, R. (Ed.). (1980). *Skinner for the classroom.* Champaign, IL: Research Press.

Epstein, Y., & Borduin, C. (1984). The children's feedback game: An approach for modifying disruptive group behavior. *American Journal of Psychotherapy, 1,* 63–71.

Ferster, C., & Skinner, B. F. (1957). *Schedules of reinforcement.* New York: Appleton-Century-Crofts.

France, K. G., & Hudson, S. (1990). Behavior management in infant sleep disturbance. *Journal of Applied Behavior Analysis, 23*(1), 91–98.

Fundudis, T. (1986). Anorexia nervosa in a pre-adolescent girl: A multimodal behavior therapy approach. *Journal of Child Psychology and Psychiatry, 27,* 261–273.

Genshaft, J. (1982). The use of cognitive behavior therapy for reducing math anxiety. *School Psychology Review, 11,* 32–34.

Glasscock, S., & MacLean, W. (1990). Use of contact desensitization and shaping in the treatment of dog phobia and generalized fear of the outdoors. *Journal of Clinical Child Psychology, 19,* 169–172.

Gumaer, J. (1990). Multimodel counseling of childhood encopresis: A case example. *School Counselor, 38,* 58–64.

Harrop, A., & McCann, C. (1984). Modifying creative writing in the classroom. *British Journal of Educational Psychology, 54,* 62–72.

Holden, G., Lavigne, V., & Cameron, A. (1990). Probing the continuum of effectiveness in parent training: Characteristics of parents and pre-schoolers. *Journal of Clinical Child Psychology, 19,* 2–8.

Jacobsen, E. (1938). *Progressive relaxation.* Chicago: University of Chicago Press.

Kahn, W. (1989). Teaching self-management to children. *Elementary School Guidance and Counseling, 24,* 37–46.

Kane, M., & Kendall, P. (1989). Anxiety disorders in children: A multiple-base-line evaluation of a cognitive-behavioral treatment. *Behavior Therapy, 20,* 499–508.

Kettlewell, P., Mizes, S., & Wasylyshyn, N. (1992). A cognitive-behavioral group treatment of bulimia. *Behavior Therapy, 23,* 657–670.

Krumboltz, J. (1966). Behavioral goals for counseling. *Journal of Counseling Psychology, 13,* 153–159.

Krumboltz, J., & Hosford, R. (1967). Behavioral goals for counseling in the elementary school. *Elementary School Guidance and Counseling, 1,* 27–40.

Lang, P., & Lazovik, A. (1963). Experimental desensitization of a phobia. *Journal of Abnormal and Social Psychology, 66,* 519–525.

Lattal, K. (1992). B. F. Skinner and psychology. *American Psychologist, 47(11),* 1269–1272.

Lazarus, A. (1966). Behavioral rehearsal vs. nondirective therapy vs. advice in effective behavior change. *Behavior Research and Therapy, 4,* 209–212.

Lazarus, A. (1977). Has behavior therapy outlived its usefulness? *American Psychologist, 32,* 550–554.

Levine, F., & Fasnacht, G. (1974). Token rewards may lead to token learning. *American Psychologist, 29,* 816–820.

Little, L., & Kelley, M. (1989). The efficacy of response cost procedures for reducing children's noncompliance to parental instructions. *Behavior Therapy, 20,* 525–534.

London, P. (1972). The end of ideology in behavior modification. *American Psychologist, 27,* 913–926.

Maslow, A. (1970). *Motivation and personality* (2nd ed.). New York: Harper & Row.

Mize, J., & Ladd, G. (1990). A cognitive-social learning approach to social skill training with low status pre-school children. *Developmental Psychology, 26,* 388–397.

Morris, R., & Kratochwill, T. (1985). Behavioral treatment of children's fears and phobias: A review. *School Psychology Review, 14,* 84–93.

Richman, N., Douglas, J., Hunt, H., Lansdown, R., & Levere, R. (1985). Behavioral methods in the treatment of sleep disorders: A pilot study. *Journal of Child Psychology and Psychiatry, 26,* 581–590.

Rimm, D., & Masters, J. (1974). *Behavior therapy: Techniques and empirical findings.* New York: Academic Press.

Rosen, H., & Rosen, L. (1983). Elementary stealing: Use of stimulus control with an elementary student. *Behavior Modification, 7,* 56–63.

Shapiro, E., & Goldberg, R. (1986). A comparison of group contingencies for increasing spelling performance among sixth grade students. *School Psychology Review, 15,* 546–557.

Silber, K., & Haynes, C. (1992). Treating nailbiting: A comparative analysis of mild aversion and completing response therapies. *Behaviour Research and Therapy, 30,* 15–22.

Silverman, W., & Kearney, C. (1990). A preliminary analysis of a functional model of assessment and treatment for school refusal behavior. *Behavior Modification, 14,* 340–363.

Skinner, B. F. (1938). *The behavior of organisms.* New York: Appleton-Century-Crofts.

Skinner, B. F. (1948). *Walden two.* New York: Macmillan.

Skinner, B. F. (1953). *Science and human behavior.* New York: Macmillan.

Skinner, B. F. (1957). *Verbal behavior.* Englewood Cliffs, NJ: Prentice-Hall.

Skinner, B. F. (1968). *The technology of teaching.* Englewood Cliffs, NJ: Prentice-Hall.

Skinner, B. F. (1971). *Beyond freedom and dignity.* New York: Knopf.

Skinner, B. F. (1976a). *About behaviorism.* New York: Random House.

Skinner, B. F. (1976b). *Particulars of my life.* New York: Beekman.

Skinner, B. F. (1978). *Reflections on behaviorism and society.* Englewood Cliffs, NJ: Prentice-Hall.

Skinner, B. F. (1979). *The shaping of a behaviorist: Part II of an autobiography.* New York: Knopf.

Skinner, B. F. (1983). *A matter of consequences: Part III of an autobiography.* New York: Knopf.

Skinner, B. F. (1987). *Upon further reflection*. Englewood Cliffs, NJ: Prentice-Hall.

Skinner, B. F. (1990a). Can psychology be a science of mind? *American Psychologist, 45,* 1206–1210.

Skinner, B. F. (1990b, August). *Cognitive science: The creationism of psychology*. Keynote address presented at the meeting of the American Psychological Association, Boston.

Stratton, C. (1989). Systematic comparison of consumer satisfaction of three cost-effective parent training programs for conduct problem children. *Behavior Therapy, 20,* 103–115.

Wahler, R., Winkel, G., Peterson, R., & Morrison, D. (1965). Mothers as behavior therapists for their own children. *Behavior Research and Therapy, 3,* 113–124.

Whelan, J., & Houts, A. (1990). Effects of a waking schedule on primary enuretic children treated with full spectrum home training. *Health Psychology, 9,* 164–176.

Williams, C. (1959). The elimination of tantrum behavior by extinction procedures. *Journal of Abnormal and Social Psychology, 59,* 269.

Williamson, D., Williamson, S., Watkins, P., & Hughes, H. (1992). Increasing cooperation among children using dependent group-oriented reinforcement contingencies. *Behavior Modification, 16,* 414–425.

Wolfe, V., Gentile, C., & Wolfe, D. (1989). The impact of sexual abuse on children: A PTSD formulation. *Behavior Therapy, 20,* 215–228.

Wolpe, J. (1958). *Psychotherapy by reciprocal inhibition*. Stanford, CA: Stanford University Press.

Wolpe, J. (1969). *The practice of behavior therapy*. New York: Pergamon Press.

Wolpe, J. (1989). The derailment of behavior therapy: A tale of conceptual misdirection. *Journal of Behavior Therapy and Experimental Psychiatry, 20,* 3–15.

Wurtele, S. (1990). Teaching personal safety skills to four-year-old children: A behavioral approach. *Behavior Therapy, 21,* 25–32.

Chapter 9

◆

Transactional Analysis

ERIC BERNE

Eric Lennard Bernstein was born May 10, 1910, in Montreal. His family consisted of his father, a general practitioner; his mother, a professional writer and editor; and a sister 5 years younger than he. Eric respected his father a great deal and was permitted to make house call rounds with him. He was 10 years old when his father died from tuberculosis, at which time his mother assumed responsibility for supporting the two children.

After receiving his medical degree from McGill University at the age of 25, Berne moved to the United States and began a psychiatric residency at Yale University. He became a citizen around 1938 and shortly thereafter changed his name to Eric Berne. Following service with the armed forces from 1943 to 1946, he began working to earn the title of psychoanalyst. His first book, *The Mind in Action,* was published in 1947. In this same year, Berne began analysis with Erik Erikson.

Each of Berne's three marriages ended in divorce. He had seven children from his first two marriages; he found the role of parent rewarding and loved his children very much. He was said to be overly permissive and more nurturing than authoritarian or critical. One of the major rejections of his life occurred when, in 1956, the Psychoanalytic Institute denied his application for membership and recommended that he continue through 4 more years of personal analysis and then reapply for the coveted title. This action greatly discouraged Berne but at the same time motivated him, and he immediately began work on a new approach to psychotherapy.

Although Berne first published information on the three ego states in "The Nature of Intuition" (1949), he formed the core of transactional analysis (TA) in 1954. At that time, Berne was involved in the psychoanalysis of a successful middle-aged lawyer he was treating by classic Freudian principles. During a session, the patient suddenly said, "I'm not a lawyer, I'm just a little boy," sparking the idea that each of us contains a child ego state accompanied by parent and adult ego states. After listening to his patients relating "games" for some 30 years, Berne decided to gather certain of these breezily named games into a catalogue. Three years after its publication, *Games People Play* (1964) had been on the nonfiction best-seller list for 111 weeks—longer than any other book that decade. Some reviewers called the book psychiatric gimmickry, emphatically denying that it would ever be regarded as a contribution to psychological or psychiatric theory. Other reviewers found the book a real contribution to psychology and suggested that Berne had offered a thesaurus of social transactions with explanations and titles. In 1967, Berne attributed the book's success to the recognition factor—some of us recognize ourselves in it, and some recognize other people.

Poker was Berne's favorite game because people play it to win. He had little patience with losers and said you might as well play to win if you are going to play. He saw losers as spending a lot of time explaining why they lost. In the final years of his life, Berne shifted his emphasis from games to life scripts.

Berne published 8 books and 64 articles in psychiatric and other periodicals and edited the *Transactional Analysis Bulletin*. In an article in the *New York Times* magazine in 1966, Berne renounced the therapeutic value of shock treatment, hypnosis, and medication in favor of his easy-to-understand approach to psychotherapy. Today TA is an international organization with more than 10,000 members. Eric Berne died in 1970.

THE NATURE OF PEOPLE AND THEORY OF COUNSELING

The nature of people and the theory of counseling are covered together in this chapter because the TA theory of counseling is basically a statement describing the human personality.

Berne had a positive view of the nature of people. He believed children were born princes and princesses, but shortly thereafter their parents and the environment turned them into frogs. He believed people had the potential to regain their royal status, providing they learned and applied the lessons of transactional analysis to their personal lives. Berne believed that the early childhood years were critical to personal development. During these early years, before children enter school, they form their basic life script and develop a sense of being either "OK" or "not OK." They also arrive at conclusions about other people's "OK-ness." In Berne's view, life is very simple to live. However, people upset themselves to the point that they invent religions, pastimes, and games. These same people complain about how complicated life is, while persisting in making life even harder. Life is a series of decisions to be made and problems to be solved. Berne believed that people have the rationality and freedom to make decisions and solve their own problems.

Shahin (1995) took a less than positive view of human nature and of the "I'm okay, you're okay" position. He wrote that the 1990s version of the "I'm okay, you're okay" message is "I'm a jerk, you're a jerk. And that's okay." In fact, Shahin found this message reassuring, that jerks have always been among us and ever shall be—an eternal truth amid the storms of constant change. However, Shahin expressed dismay with a society that defines bullies as just people with low self-esteem, meanies as misunderstood, and liars as insecure and acting out. To him, these people are jerks.

The TA theory of human nature and human relationships derives from data collected through four types of analysis:

1. Structural analysis, in which an individual's personality is analyzed
2. Transactional analysis, which is concerned with what people do and say to each other
3. Script analysis, which deals with the specific life dramas people compulsively enjoy
4. Game analysis, in which ulterior transactions leading to a payoff are analyzed

Structural Analysis

In explaining the TA view of human nature and the difficulties people encounter in their lives, we begin with the structural analysis of personality. Each individual's personality is divided into three separate and distinct sources of behavior, the ego states: Parent, Adult, and Child, or P, A, and C, for short. The ego states represent real persons who now exist or once existed and had their own identities. Therefore, the conflicts among them often cause inconsistencies as well as flexibility in people.

The Parent, Adult, and Child ego states Berne proposed are not concepts like the superego, ego, and id of Freud but rather phenomena based on actual realities. They each represent skeletal-muscular and verbal patterns of behavior and feeling based on emotions and experiences perceived by people in their early years.

Parent

The Parent aspect of personality contains instructions, attitudes, and behaviors handed down mostly by parents and significant authority figures. It resembles a recording of all the admonitions, orders, punishments, encouragement, and so on experienced in the first years of life. Parents can take two different attitudes, depending on the situation: (1) Nurturing Parent manifests itself in nurturing or helping behavior, and (2) Critical Parent provides criticism, control, and punishment. The Parent feels and behaves as the one who raised you did—both critical and nurturing. The Parent admonishes, "you should" or "you should not," "you can't win," "boys will be boys," or "a woman's place is in the home." The Parent, wanting to be in control and to be right, acts with superiority and authority, but the Parent is also responsible for giving love, nurturance, and respect to the Child in you.

Adult

The Adult ego state operates logically and nonemotionally, providing objective information by using reality testing and a computerlike approach to life. Your Adult uses facts as a computer does to make decisions without emotion. The Adult says, "This is how this works" with mature, objective, logical, and rational thinking based on reality. The Adult ego state is not related to age. A child is also capable of dealing with reality by gathering facts and computing objectively.

Child

All the childlike impulses common to everyone are in the Child state. The Child is an important part of personality because it contributes joy, creativity, spontaneity, intuition, pleasure, and enjoyment. The Child has two parts: (1) Adaptive Child emerges as a result of demands from significant authority figures and is marked by passivity, and (2) Natural or Free Child represents the impulsive, untrained, self-loving, pleasure-seeking part of the Child.

The Child part of us is an accumulation of impulses that come naturally to a young person and of recorded internal events or responses to what is seen and heard. It has an element of immaturity but also deep feeling, affection, adaptation, expression, and fun. Figure 9-1 presents the ego states and their divisions in graphic form.

The well-adjusted person allows the situation to determine which ego state is in control, striking an even balance among the three. A common problem is allowing one ego state to assume predominant control. For example, the Constant Parent is seen as dictatorial or prejudiced; the Constant Adult is an analytical bore; the Constant Child is immature or overreactive. No age is implied by any of these states, as even the young child has Adult and Parent states, and senior citizens can evince a Child response.

Research on Ego States

Goldberg and Summerfield (1982) tested the assumption that personality depends on the amount of time a person spends in a given ego state. Two hypotheses were tested: (1) Observers' judgments on neuroticism and extrover-

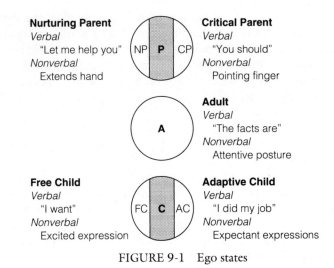

Nurturing Parent
Verbal
   "Let me help you"
Nonverbal
   Extends hand

Critical Parent
Verbal
   "You should"
Nonverbal
   Pointing finger

Adult
Verbal
   "The facts are"
Nonverbal
   Attentive posture

Free Child
Verbal
   "I want"
Nonverbal
   Excited expression

Adaptive Child
Verbal
   "I did my job"
Nonverbal
   Expectant expressions

FIGURE 9-1   Ego states

sion depend on the ego state of the videotaped stimulus person, and (2) managers and students significantly differ on the judgments stated in the first hypothesis. The Child ego state was rated significantly more extroverted than the Parent ego state. The Parent ego state was rated more neurotic and less extroverted. No significant differences between managers' and students' ratings were found in the videotaped ratings. Gilmore (1981), in an attempt to go beyond the clinical observation of ego states, measured physiological responses to the three ego states. Subjects were to respond orally to a questionnaire composed of questions designed to evoke Child, Adult, or Parent ego states. Each category required answers to 15 questions. Ego State 1 compared Child and Adult, Ego State 2 compared Child and Parent, and Ego State 3 compared Adult and Parent. Monitors recorded skin temperature, respiration, and heart rate. Significant changes occurred in half the comparisons made. A significant change was detected in skin surface temperature and respiration rate with Ego States 2 and 3. There was also a significant difference between heart rate and skin conductance for Ego State 1.

White (1983) proposed a three-chair version of the Gestalt topdog-underdog debate. The client would be asked to speak from chairs representing Parent, Child, and Adult. Presumably the same "I should" versus "I want" debate would still take place until the Adult ego state takes over, evaluates the data, and makes a decision.

Kleinewiese (1980) compared two methods for teaching TA to children. One method employed visual models of the ego states, and the other was the traditional lecture approach. The visual model group required an average explanation time of 3.75 minutes on each of the ego states. The other group required 10.75 minutes to accomplish the same task. Visual aids are always superior for teaching and counseling children who have not attained formal thinking skills.

Bala (1986) described a TA treatment method for autistic children and offered a four-step plan: (1) attachment (developed on a physical level, followed by an emotional level, by nurturing the child), (2) Child ego state (work on body image and a sense of "me" and "not me" by increasing contact with the outside world), (3) Adult ego state (special-education classes in perception, language, communication, and motor ability), and (4) Parent ego state (after language skill develops, the child can integrate good and bad objects). For example, TA with play therapy can be used to integrate the child's perception of mother as sometimes good and sometimes dangerous. The counseling session can be used to work on new responses to the mother's behavior.

Manning and Manning (1988), in an attempt to study the quantity and content of the private self-talk of preservice teachers, found that 65% of the self-talk characterized the Adult ego state, 55% indicated an external locus of control, and negative self-talk exceeded positive self-talk. The increased levels of stress involved in teaching would be better handled by positive self-talk, an internal locus of control, and adult problem-solving logic.

In describing five driver responses as mediators of stress, Hazell (1989) crossed over into REBT territory. The five drivers, or self-messages, are Be Pleasing, Be Perfect, Be Strong, Hurry Up, and Try Harder. As is the case with most irrational thoughts, these driver responses usually get their user exactly what they try to avoid. Extremes of each driver parallel a variety of personality disorders. Be Pleasing, associated with seeking love while avoiding rejection, relates to histrionic, avoidant, and dependent disorders. Be Perfect, associated with gaining respect while avoiding looking bad, is linked with obsessive-compulsive and narcissistic disorders. Be Strong, associated with hiding feeling, is related to schizoid disorders. Hurry Up, associated with gaining control, is compared to impulse-control disorders. Try Harder, associated with avoiding being controlled, is linked to passive-aggressive, antisocial, and paranoid personality disorders.

Craig and Olson (1988), in researching changes in ego states following treatment for drug abuse, found that ego states, as measured by the Adjective Checklist, changed from the Adaptive Child to the Adult. Before treatment, the participants were characterized by higher needs for succorance, abasement, heterosexuality, exhibitionism, deference, nurturance, and change. Following treatment, the participants' scores were higher for achievement, dominance, endurance, and orderliness.

Transactional Analysis

The second type of analysis—the study of the transaction—is the heart of TA. Any time a person acknowledges the presence of another person, either verbally or physically, a transaction has taken place. A *transaction* is often defined as a unit of human communication or as a stimulus-response connection between two people's ego states.

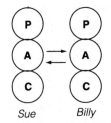

FIGURE 9-2   Complementary transaction

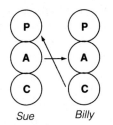

FIGURE 9-3   Crossed transaction

Transactions are grouped into three categories:

1. Complementary transactions, which Berne describes as "the natural order of healthy human relationships," occur when a response comes from the ego state to which it was addressed (Figure 9-2).

Sue: Billy, have you seen my bike?
Billy: Yes, it is in the backyard.

2. Crossed transactions break communications. They occur when a response comes from one of the other two ego states (Figure 9-3).

Sue: Billy, would you help me find my bike?
Billy: Can't you see I'm watching my favorite program?

3. Covert, or ulterior, transactions involve more than one ego state of each person and are basically dishonest. On the surface, the transaction looks and sounds like number 1 or 2, but the actual message sent is not spoken (Figure 9-4). For example, the ulterior message being sent in number 1 could be on a social or overt level:

Sue: Billy, why don't you help me find my bike so we can go riding?
Billy: Okay, it's a good day for a ride!

Or the ulterior message could be on a psychological, covert, or ulterior level:

Sue: I wish you would be my boyfriend.
Billy: I hope you like me better than the other boys.

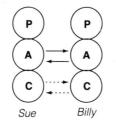

FIGURE 9-4   Covert transaction

Script Analysis

The nature of people can be further described by script analysis. A psychological script is a person's ongoing program for a life drama; it dictates where people are going with their lives and the paths that will lead there. The individual—consciously or unconsciously—acts compulsively according to that program. As mentioned before, people are born basically OK; their difficulties come from bad scripts they learned during their childhood.

Berne (1961) developed the theory of scripts as part of TA theory from its inception. A life script is that life plan your Child selected in your early years, based mostly on messages you received from the Child in your parents. For example, at the request of her mother, a little girl takes it upon herself to save her alcoholic father. The same script may emerge once again later in life as she tries to save an alcoholic husband in an attempt to regain some of the payoffs from the original experience. Although the Parent and Adult of your mother and father may have told you sensible things such as "Be successful," the unspoken injunction from the Child in your parents may communicate the message "You can't make it" (Figure 9-5). Injunctions are prohibitions and negative commands usually delivered from the parent of the opposite sex. Injunctions are seldom discussed or verbalized aloud. Values we hold as guidelines for living may have come from injunctions. These injunctions determine how we think and feel about sex, work, money, marriage, family, play, and people. ·

The best way to learn about scripts is to examine how we spend our time and how we relate (transactions) with others. Scripts have main themes, such as martyring, procrastinating, succeeding, failing, blaming, distracting, placating, and computing, and three basic types: winner, loser, and nonwinner. A small percentage of people seem to be natural winners; everything they touch turns to gold. Conversely, a slightly larger percentage seem to be natural losers; everything turns out badly for them. The majority, perhaps 80% or 85%, follow the nonwinners' script. Nonwinners are identified by a phrase they often use: "but at least . . ." ("I went to school and made poor grades, *but at least* I did not flunk out").

Transactional analysis borrows heavily from fairy tales for its terminology and analogies. For example, the Cinderella script is not an especially healthy plan because a prince or prize does not come to one who sits around waiting. Even martyrdom, as Cinderella did for her stepmother and stepsisters, does not help.

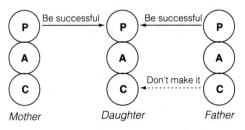

FIGURE 9-5   Life script: injunctions

The Santa Claus script is based on a similar myth. Because life scripts are formed in early childhood, selecting children's stories requires considerable care. We have included a comprehensive list of books in this text that we believe to be helpful to children and their families (see chapters 15 and 16).

In summary, Berne believed that scripts have five components: (1) directions from parents, (2) a corresponding personality development, (3) a confirming childhood decision about oneself and life, (4) a penchant for either success or failure, and (5) a pattern for behavior.

Research on Script Analysis

Stapleton and Murkison (1990), in a study with implications for career development, found evidence of early scripting in college business majors. More than 50% of the business students studied entertained their first entrepreneurial fantasies and thoughts during their middle teens. Comparing students to actual entrepreneurs, they found that only 35% of the entrepreneurs had experienced similar fantasies and thoughts before age 19. Those people whose entrepreneurial fantasies appeared after age 21 had fewer business failures.

Writing on borderline disorders, Price (1990) emphasized the role the family plays in these cases. Borderline disorder is defined as inability to integrate the good and bad aspects of self and others. Things are either all good or all bad, with no gray areas or in-betweens. This all-or-nothing approach to living, which can shift immediately from one extreme to the other, results in an inability to acquire a coherent sense of self and others. Price lists four causal family factors of borderline disorders: (1) rewarding Child behavior and punishing independent, assertive Adult behavior; (2) stressing the importance of the family myth (for example, in cases of child sexual abuse, the abuse is justified or denied); (3) sending double-bind messages that force the child to deny or distort the truth (for example, the reality of abuse and its cover-up); and (4) activating the child's "protect my parent" defense mechanism, in which the child protects and preserves the idealized image of the abusive parent. With a "perfect" parent, any problem must be the fault of the "bad" child victim.

In an article on treating adult survivors of sexual abuse, Olia (1989) focused on memory retrieval. She pointed out that approximately 27% of women and 16%

of men have been victims of sexual abuse and that many victims have handled the trauma by denial or dissociation. *Denial* is defined as blocking the event from consciousness. *Dissociation* allows victims to desensitize their bodies or remove themselves altogether from the event. Memory work for survivors is similar to that done for amnesiacs, for whom loss of knowledge, rather than of memory, is the problem. Asking clients to "guess" or "tell a story" often helps them regain the lost knowledge. Two other methods are also used: (1) recall, requiring a client to consider a stimulus possibility before determining its familiarity, and (2) recognition, determining whether a stimulus seems familiar to the client. Olia provided some guidelines for recognizing adult survivors of sexual abuse. Although the indicators are not sure signs of childhood sexual abuse, most survivors suffer depression, phobias, anxiety disorders, sexual dysfunction, and difficulty maintaining close, intimate relationships.

Osnes and Rendack (1989), in a related article on abuse survivors, stated that we live our lives in four script areas: body, mind, emotion, and spirit. Childhood abuse affects each area's function and development. Bodies may be neglected by excessive eating or physical illness. Minds may be affected by faulty reasoning. Emotional lives may be disjointed, and spiritual involvement may run from hyperreligiosity to complete atheism. The recommended treatment is ego-state education, in which the Parent and Adult ego states are aligned with the counselor as advocates of the not-OK Child ego state. Trust building and maintenance, although important in all counseling, are especially critical to success in counseling abuse survivors.

In an article on how to move from Karpman's Drama Triangle (DT) to the Winner's Triangle (WT), Choy (1990) made the point that the persecutor, rescuer, and victim of the drama triangle correlate to the respective assertive, caring, and vulnerable roles in the winner's triangle. "Vulnerable" is distinguished from "victim" in that the vulnerable person, maintaining contact with the adult's logical problem-solving capability, works out a solution to the problem. Assertive people see negotiation as a viable part of problem solving and have no interest in punishing or cheating others. Persecutors, by contrast, satisfy personal needs by discounting the victim's importance and feelings. People in both the rescuer and the caring roles act out of genuine concern; however, the rescuer's motivation is the need to feel superior or reassured that "I'm OK." Counselors can avoid the rescuer role if they maintain adult-to-adult communication in counseling interviews. Active listening, coupled with no advice giving, should also help the counselor avoid the rescuer role.

Game Analysis

Unfortunately, most people, in following their scripts, learn how to use ulterior transactions. In other words, they play games. A game is an ongoing series of complementary ulterior transactions progressing to a well-defined, predictable outcome. Like every ulterior transaction, all games are basically dishonest, and they are by no means fun. One of the first games a child learns is "Mine is better than yours." Its relatively benign outcome could range, in later years, to considerably more serious games. *Games People Play* (Berne, 1964) offers a vastly entertaining, chilling overview of what might happen to a not-OK child.

However, Bary and Hufford (1990) stated that game playing offers six advantages that facilitate mental health. Berne (1964) believed that the general advantages of a game are its stabilizing (homeostatic) functions. He defined *homeostasis* as the tendency of an individual to maintain internal psychological equilibrium by regulating his or her own intrapsychic processes. Thus change is difficult for people who automatically accept only what reinforces or confirms their personal prejudices, values, and views. As such, many people are not open to new data. Game playing functions to maintain homeostasis in biological, existential, internal psychological, external psychological, internal social, and external social areas.

Bary and Hufford (1990) suggested a standard treatment approach for recalibrating the unhealthy and out-of-balance psychological systems. Clients are ready to terminate counseling when their self-esteem is in order and they are able to exchange honest strokes from an "I'm OK, you're OK" view of human nature. In addition, fully functioning clients do confront and master the appropriate development tasks for age and stage. The ease with which children can understand TA concepts makes it a valuable approach for problem prevention.

Research on Games

Douglas (1986) reviewed the current literature on adolescent suicide in an attempt to find support for the theory that it is a third-degree game in the TA system. (The third-degree game is a magnification of inflexible, tenacious, and intense game patterns that constitute mental disturbance. The victims in the game include family and friends who must suffer when the teenager commits suicide.) Some conclusions reached in the review were that (1) adolescent suicide attempts, whether successful or not, are attempts to gain strokes from others; (2) suicide attempts are often preceded by rebelling, withdrawing, or running away; (3) parent-child relationships are not good in these situations and are often characterized by too much parental control or no control at all; (4) parent-child relationships often lack closeness; and (5) the third-degree game requirements are met.

Zalcman (1990), in an update of Berne's concepts of game and racket analysis, reemphasized that games undermine the stability of relationships. Strokes are the motivation for games, and the need for strokes often turns an honest transaction into a game. Rackets are described as ego-state switches within the intrapsychic structure of an individual. Game analysis deals with transactions between two people. A racket could be the procrastination racket of "I'll do it tomorrow," in which the child masquerades as the adult. An example of a game is "Why don't

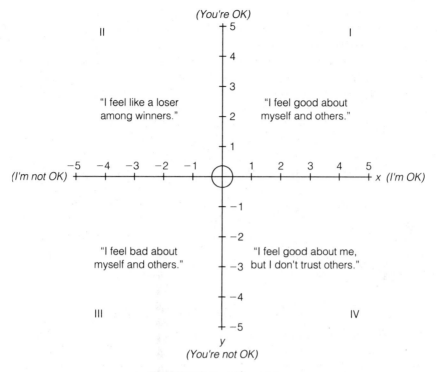

FIGURE 9-6   Life positions

you; yes but," in which a person says, "Help me," the helper gives advice, and the helpee says, "Yes, but that won't work."

Life Positions

On the basis of the transactions and scripts, children develop life positions that summarize their concepts of self-worth and the worth of others. The four life positions (described by Harris, 1969) are as follows:

1. *I'm OK—You're OK.* This position of mentally healthy people enables them to possess realistic expectations, have good human relationships, and solve problems constructively. It is a "winner's" position, defined as that of an authentic being. The extreme of this position would be represented by a +5 on both the *x*- and *y*-axes in quadrant I of Figure 9-6.

2. *I'm not OK—You're OK.* The universal position of childhood represents the introjective position of those who feel powerless. Adults in this position often experience withdrawal and depression. The extreme of this position would be represented by a −5 on the *x*-axis and +5 on the *y*-axis in quadrant II of Figure 9-6.

3. *I'm not OK—You're not OK.* This life position is the arrival point of the child who cannot depend on parents for positive stroking (discussed later in this chapter). Already not OK, the child perceives Mom and Dad as not OK, too. Adults in this category are losers who go through a series of helpless, disappointing experiences and may even become suicidal or homicidal. The extreme of this position would be represented by a −5 on both the x-and y-axes in quadrant III of Figure 9-6.

4. *I'm OK—You're not OK.* The individual feels victimized in this position. The brutalized, battered child ends up here, the position of the criminal, the psychopath. Whatever happens is someone else's fault. The extreme of this position is a +5 on the x-axis and a −5 on the y-axis in quadrant IV of Figure 9-6.

Games Clients Play

Among the many games Berne identified, some are to be especially avoided in the counseling interview.

1. *Why don't you; yes, but. . . .* The counselor's Adult is tricked into working for the client's Child or Parent when the counselor gives advice.

Counselor: Why don't you ask your teacher to give you some extra help with math?
Client: Yes, but what if she says she doesn't have time?

The payoff comes to the client in spreading bad feelings, as in the misery-loves-company game: "I am not okay, and you aren't either because you can't help me solve my problem."

2. *I'm only trying to help you.* Counselors sometimes play this game with their clients. The message to the client is "You are not okay, and I know what is good for you." The payoff is for the counselor, who holds the faulty belief that "If I straighten my client out, then maybe I can get my own life in order." A truly helpful counselor offers help when it is requested but believes that help can be accepted or rejected. When help fails or is rejected, the helpful counselor does not respond derogatorily, "Well, I was only trying to help you."

3. *Courtroom.* The courtroom game puts the counselor in the position of judge and jury if two clients can manipulate the counselor into placing blame. The payoff is bad feelings for all—persecutor, victim, and rescuer—because the rescuer (counselor) usually ends up being victimized by the other two players.

4. *Kick me and NIGYYSOB.* Counselors may find that some clients enjoy playing "kick me" with the counselor, just as they do with their bosses, colleagues, and spouses. They seem to enjoy being victimized and work at getting themselves rejected. They even work at getting themselves terminated from counseling before any gains have been made. Kick-me players manipulate others into playing NIGYYSOB (now I've got you, you son of a bitch) when they react to the bids for the negative attention the kick-me players make.

The NIGYYSOB game is played by itself if a person tries to trap others in a double bind: damned if you do and damned if you don't.

Mother: Johnny, do you love me?
Johnny: Yes, I do.
Mother: How many times have I told you not to talk with your mouth full!

5. *Gossiping.* Gossiping refers to talking about people who are not present. In a counseling interview, the counselor may wish to have clients role-play dialogue between themselves and a missing person, as was suggested in chapter 6. For example, a child complaining about a teacher could role-play a conversation between the two of them, with the child playing the role of the teacher and then responding as he or she would in the classroom. The technique uses an empty chair to represent the missing person. Role-playing and role-reversal methods have a way of limiting gossip while creating greater awareness of the problem situations and proper assignment of responsibility for the problem.

6. *Wooden leg.* The wooden-leg game is a display of the inadequacy pattern described in chapter 10. Clients playing wooden-leg games work to increase their disabilities as a way of avoiding responsibility for taking care of themselves. These clients are experts at making people give up on them. Children are adept at convincing parents that they cannot handle certain chores and school subjects.

Paradoxical strategies, which are at times effective with these clients, focus on harnessing their rebellion into productive activity. The counselor might say, for example, "Frank, you've got me convinced that you really can't make it." The rebellious client, Frank, often rises to the occasion to show that the counselor is a total idiot and begins to succeed in the face of the prediction that he could not.

For clients who are really defeated and not rebellious, we stick to our advice of offering large doses of unconditional encouragement. Counselors of welfare and rehabilitation clients often find themselves in the wooden-leg game. The payoff goes to the client, who justifies not getting better, or even getting worse, as a way of increasing their benefits.

7. *If it weren't for you.* Related to the wooden leg, this game is another way of avoiding the assumption of responsibility for life and its unsolved problems. The client says, for example, "If it weren't for you and your good cooking, I could lose 10 pounds." The counselor may want to examine with the client the payoffs of being overweight and even develop a rationale of how being fat may be the preferred and "best" lifestyle for the client.

The Pursuit of Strokes

Human beings need recognition; in order to obtain it, they exchange what Berne called *strokes*. In acknowledging the presence of another person, people give a stroke, which can be either positive or negative. Which is which is usually obvious, except in the case of ulterior transactions. Young children receive positive or negative physical strokes when they are cuddled or spanked, whereas adults obtain primarily symbolic strokes in conversations or transactions with others. Positive strokes, such as compliments, handshakes, open affection, or uninterrupted listening, are the most desirable, but negative strokes, such as hatred or disagreement, are better than no recognition at all. A middle ground is maintenance strokes, which keep transactions going by giving recognition to the speaker but neither positive nor negative feedback. All these strokes can be either conditional or unconditional—that is, given as a result of some specific action or given just for being yourself. Unconditional regard—"I like you"—has more positive stroke value than conditional acceptance—"I like you when you are nice to me."

The pattern of giving and receiving strokes an individual uses most is determined by the person's life position, as explained in the section on life positions. How people view themselves and others controls their ability to give and receive conditional and unconditional positive and negative strokes.

People engage in transactions to exchange strokes. According to Berne (1964), people have an inherent psychological hunger for stimulation through human interactions and stroking, and any act implying recognition of another's presence is a means of satisfying these hungers. Failure to fulfill these needs may cause a failure to thrive in infants (James & Jongeward, 1971) and feelings of abandonment and not-OK-ness in both children and adults. Satisfied hunger yields feelings of OK-ness and release of creative energy (Phillips & Cordell, 1975). Awareness of psychological hungers and satisfaction of them are important.

Negative strokes, such as lack of attention, shin kicking, and hatred, send "You're not OK" messages. Diminishing, humiliating, and ridiculing strokes all treat people as though they are insignificant.

Positive strokes are usually complementary transactions. They may be verbal expressions of affection and appreciation, or they may give compliments or positive feedback; they may be physical, like a touch, or they may be silent gestures or looks. Listening is one of the finest strokes one person can give another (James & Jongeward, 1971). All yield reinforcement to the "I'm OK—you're OK" position. Maintenance strokes, although lacking in meaningful content, at least serve to give recognition and keep communication open.

Horwitz (1982), using a sample of 52 female and 27 male adult subjects who had applied for counseling services, studied the relationship between positive stroking and self-perceived symptoms of distress. Distress was defined as a self-reported lapse of memory, lower back pains, headaches, low self-esteem, bad temper, or loss of desire for physical encounters. The author hypothesized that people who frequently get positive strokes by asking for them show fewer symptoms of distress than those who view themselves as recipients of infrequent positive strokes. Self-reported symptoms of distress were found to decrease as receipt of positive strokes increased.

Writing on stroking and its relationship to biological well-being, Allen and Allen (1989) pointed out that lack of strokes may not shrivel up anyone's spinal cord, but it could relate to other biological conditions as well as to depression and failure to thrive. The authors argued that, for TA to continue to "thrive," it must be a framework in developmental and longitudinal research on real children, and it must be integrated with current developments in biological research.

Structuring Time

People have six options for structuring their time in pursuit of strokes.

1. *Withdrawing,* in which no transaction takes place. It involves few risks, and no stroking occurs.
2. *Rituals,* which involve prescribed social transactions such as "Hello" and "How are you?" These transactions are fairly impersonal.
3. *Pastimes,* which provide mutually acceptable stroking. Pastimes are a means of self-expression but often involve only superficial transactions or conversations. Examples are baseball, automobiles, shopping, or other safe topics of conversation.
4. *Activities,* in which time is structured around some task or career. Activities are a way to deal with external reality.
5. *Games,* in which the need is met in a crooked way. Intense stroking is often received, but it may be unpleasant. Games are considered destructive transactions.
6. *Intimacy,* which provides unconditional stroking. It is free of games and exploitation.

Obviously, some of these ways of structuring time are good and some are bad, depending on the time and energy given to each. One of the goals of TA therapy is to help people learn productive ways of structuring their time.

Withdrawing may be the Adult's decision to relax or be alone, the Parent's way of coping with conflict, or the Child's adaptation to protect itself from pain or conflict. It is fairly harmless unless it happens all the time or when a person needs to pay attention. Withdrawing into fantasy may allow one to experience good stroking when the present setting does not appear to hold any.

Harris (1969) observed that a ritual is a socially programmed use of time in which everybody agrees to do the same thing. Brief encounters, worship rituals, greeting rituals, cocktail party rituals, and bedroom rituals may allow maintenance strokes without commitment or involvement. The outcome is predictable and pleasant, but most people need more intense stroking.

James and Jongeward (1971) stated that pastimes are, as they imply, ways to pass time. They are superficial exchanges without involvement that people use in order to size up one another. Conversations concerning relative gas mileage, the weather, or potty training may yield minimal stroking at the maintenance level while allowing one to decide whether to risk a more intimate relationship.

Doing work or activities, according to Phillips and Cordell (1975), is time spent dealing with realities of the world. It is getting something done that one may want to do, need to do, or have to do. Activities allow for positive strokes befitting a winner.

Berne (1964) defined games as an ongoing series of complementary ulterior transactions progressing to a well-defined, predictable outcome. One who sends an ulterior message to another person, for some hidden purpose, is playing a game. The Adult is unaware that the Child or Parent has a secret reason for playing or wanting to play. Harris (1969) believed all games derive from the Child's "mine is better than yours" attempt to ease the not-OK feeling—to feel superior while the other feels put down. Games are differentiated from rituals and pastimes in two ways: (1) their ulterior quality and (2) the payoff. Games are a way, too, of using time for people who cannot bear the stroking starvation of withdrawal and yet whose not-OK position makes the ultimate form of relatedness—intimacy— impossible (Berne, 1964; Harris, 1969).

James and Jongeward (1971) defined *intimacy* as a deep human encounter stemming from genuine caring. Steiner (1974) viewed intimacy as the way of structuring time when there is no withdrawal, no rituals, no games, no pastimes, and no work. Conditions favorable for intimacy include a commitment to the "I'm OK—you're OK" position and a satisfying of psychological hungers through positive strokes.

Rackets

Some people find themselves involved in what is known in TA theory as a "stamp-collecting enterprise," in which they save up archaic bad feelings until they have enough to cash in for some psychological prize. The bad-feelings racket, or stamp collecting, works in much the same way that supermarket stamp collecting works. People save brown stamps for all the bad things others have caused them to suffer and gold stamps for all the favors others owe them. Gray stamps refer to lowered self-esteem, red stamps symbolize anger, blue stamps mean depression, and white stamps connote purity (James & Jongeward, 1971). The filled-up bad-feelings stamp books may be cashed in for such things as a free divorce, custody of children, nervous breakdown, blowup, drunken binge, depression, tantrum, runaway, or love affair. Good-feelings stamps are used to justify playtime, relaxation, and breaks from work. According to McCormick and Campos (1969), stamp collecting is a racket learned from parents. The collector uses the stamps as excuses for behavior and feelings, and the suppliers may not even be aware they are giving them out. "I'm OK—you're OK" people do not need stamps because they need no excuses.

COUNSELING METHOD

Transactional analysis is the ideal system for those who view the counseling process as teaching. As is evident from this chapter, TA abounds with terms, diagrams, and models. Clients are taught the TA vocabulary so they can become proficient in identifying ego states, transactions, and scripts. The counselor's role includes teaching and providing a nurturing, supportive environment in which clients feel free to lift or eliminate restricting injunctions, attempt new behaviors, rewrite scripts, and move toward the "I'm OK—you're OK" life position. Contracting between counselor and client is a large part of the TA process.

TA practitioners teach the principles of transactional analysis to participants and then let them use these principles to analyze and improve their own behavior. TA concepts have been taught to people of all ages and ability levels, from the very young to the very old and from mentally retarded children to gifted children. The following TA points are most useful in counseling children:

1. Definition and explanation of ego states
2. Analysis of transactions between ego states
3. Positive and negative stroking (or "warm fuzzies" and "cold pricklies")
4. I'm OK, you're OK
5. Games and rackets
6. Scripts

Put simply, the primary goal in transactional analysis is to help the person achieve the "I'm OK—you're OK" life position. Various methods and techniques can accomplish this aim. Because children can easily learn and understand the terms and concepts of TA, the approach has become popular in helping school-age children.

The "I'm OK—you're OK" life position is one the child chooses to take. The other three positions more or less evolve of themselves; the child feels no sense of free choice in the matter. According to Harris (1969), the first three positions are based on feelings, and the fourth position—"I'm OK—you're OK"—is based on thought, faith, and initiation of action. The first three have to do with "why"; the fourth has to do with "why not." No one drifts into a new position; it is a decision a person makes. The graph in Figure 9-6 enables plotting a person's progress in moving from one quadrant to another, providing each step on the number axis is defined in operational terms. The *x*-axis refers to gains and losses in self-esteem; the *y*-axis indicates the same for relationships with others.

Ideally, the role of a transactional analyst is teacher. Once children have been taught how to speak the language of TA, the counselor can help them analyze their own transactions and see how their behavior affects others and vice versa. Children learn to identify the source of the reasoning that goes into their decisions; that is, they learn how to use their Adult in dealing with the demands of their Parent and Child.

Probably the most important concept to remember when dealing with children is that everyone grows up feeling not OK. Children function on the basis of the OK-ness they see in their parents. If Mommy frequently responds to the child with *her* not-OK Child, the stage is set for the establishment of the "I'm not OK—you're not OK" position. In the case of the severely abused child, the extreme "I'm OK—you're not OK" position is a real possibility. One of the best ways for youngsters to develop strong Adult ego states is to observe their parents use their Adults in handling inappropriate responses from the demanding Parent or Child.

Posters, pictures, humorous role-playing, and other tools can teach TA principles to children. Alvyn Freed and Margaret Freed have given examples in their books *TA for Kids* (1974a) and *TA for Tots* (1974b). The kids learn how to be "prinzes" instead of "frozzes." They also learn how to give and get warm fuzzies (positive strokes) and how to avoid giving and getting cold pricklies (negative strokes). Of course, in getting strokes, one must not play games.

As mentioned before, the goal of TA counseling with children is to help them learn to control their responses with their Adult, thereby achieving the "I'm OK—you're OK" life position. However, strengthening a child's Adult causes his or her family role to shift. The child becomes no longer as active in playing the destructive games that dominate many families. Other family members' roles of necessity shift also. For this reason, the child's parents must be included in the counseling process to achieve lasting results.

Children can learn all about warm fuzzies and cold pricklies, but because of the tremendous influence of their parents, it is next to impossible, without effective intervention, for them to reverse a "loser" life script if their parents have given it to them. Everything parents do and say to children tells them they are OK or not OK, depending on what life position the parents themselves occupy. People attract not what they want but what they are. People also rear not the children they want but children who reproduce the parents.

Positive stroking and respect are two things everyone needs to build a winner's script. The child needs positive strokes, both conditional ("We'll have some ice cream after you put away your toys") and unconditional ("I love you no matter what"). Children come to see themselves as OK because their parents treat them that way.

As a positive stroke, respect is hard to beat. The conclusion a child reaches is this: If my OK parents think I'm OK, then I really must be OK.

Another useful TA principle for both teachers and parents is to teach "do" and not "don't." Parents' and other adults' attempts to teach appropriate behavior by catching children in inappropriate behavior baffle children. Because Mommy is OK, a child thinks, "It must be all my fault, and I must be not OK."

A slightly different aspect of the same idea is that children who are counseled and taught to "do more" or "do better" must also know *what*. The Parent in everyone admonishes "do better"; the Adult supplies the "do *what* better."

As children and their families become better acquainted with the whys of their relationships, they learn to avoid undesirable ways of structuring time. Again, the goal of TA is to help the individual learn to lead a full, game-free life, and everyone has that choice. The usefulness of the P-A-C model comes in creating awareness of how the Parent, Adult, and Child function in decision making.

As mentioned earlier, several techniques can teach TA to children. The concepts of positive and negative stroking have been taught with smiling and frowning faces as well as with fuzzy yarn balls and sharp, prickly plastic objects to connote warm fuzzies and cold pricklies. The warm fuzzy, cold prickly fairy tale (Steiner, 1975) was written for the Child in everyone.

> There once existed a town where people shared their warm fuzzies without fear of running out of their supply of fuzzies. One day a wicked witch appeared and planted the idea that people should hoard their fuzzies in case there happened to be a shortage of fuzzies. When the townspeople did this, their backbones began to shrivel up. The witch cured the shriveling backbones by giving everybody a bag of cold pricklies to share. The sharing of cold pricklies continued until a good witch arrived and put the townspeople back on the right track, sharing their warm fuzzies.

Counselors and teachers can follow the story by bringing a bowl of sugar-free candy to class and telling the children that they can have a piece of candy only if someone gives them a piece. The counselor or teacher serves as a model in the exercise to make sure that each child receives a piece of candy.

Posters can be made with representations of the various ideas of TA (stroking, ego states, "I'm OK—you're OK," lists of games with appropriate illustrations, lists of scripting phrases, and so on). Puppets, dolls, and make-believe stories can be successful with younger children who cannot yet read.

A three-step process is effective in teaching TA to any child: First, explain the principle by using a story, a poster, puppets, or other age-appropriate methods. Second, ask the children to "read" back what they understand of the TA principle (correcting them as they go along). Third, ask the children to give examples of the principle from their own experience ("What positive strokes have you received today?") or to identify examples of the principle from the explanation ("What ego state does 'You must always go to bed early' come from?").

Teach children who are having interpersonal conflicts new stroking patterns. They first need to analyze the other person's behavior. What response does parent, teacher, or friend give to the child's positive or negative strokes? What strokes does the other person like? Teach children new ways of stroking from among these categories:

1. *Self-stroking:* doing nice things for yourself
2. *Physical strokes:* hugs, kisses, pats, backrubs, handshakes, "high fives" (be sure to distinguish between good and bad touching)
3. *Silent strokes:* winks, nods, waves, smiles
4. *Verbal strokes:* "I like you," "Good job," "Thanks"

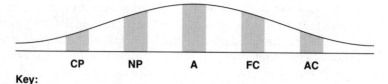

Key:

P The Parent refers to a person's values, beliefs, and morals.

    CP The Critical Parent finds fault, directs, orders, sets limits, makes rules, and enforces one's value system. Too much CP results in dictatorial or bossy behavior.

    NP The Nurturing Parent is empathic and promotes growth. The NP is warm and kind, but too much NP becomes smothering, and children will not be able to learn how to take care of themselves.

A The Adult acts like a computer. It takes in, stores, retrieves, and processes information. The A is a storehouse of facts and helps you think when you solve problems, but too much Adult is boring.

C The Child can be fun, expressive, and spontaneous, and sometimes it can be compliant and a follower of rules.

    FC The Free Child is the fun and spontaneous part of the child. When you cheer at a ballgame, you are in the Free Child part of your personality. However, too much FC might mean that you have lost control of yourself.

    AC The Adapting Child is the conforming, easy-to-get-along-with part of your personality. Too much AC results in guilt feelings, depression, other bad feelings, and robotlike behavior.

FIGURE 9-7   Ego-gram

5. *Rewards or privileges:* letting younger siblings go with you, playing with them, doing something for parents

Young children (up to 7 years) may not be able to symbolize stroking and ego states as well as older ones, and less technical language may be necessary. Young children can understand "warm fuzzy" if a stroke feels good and "cold prickly" if they feel bad after someone says or does something to them. They may need permission to ask for a warm fuzzy instead of manipulating for a cold prickly when they feel bad. Likewise, small children can understand "my bossy part," "my thinking part," "my angry part," or "my happy part" rather than the ego states, which they sometimes confuse with actual people.

Ego-grams are bar graphs showing children "how much" of each ego state they use (Figure 9-7). An ego-gram can indicate what changes might be made. A child who thinks that he or she wants to make a change can work on strengthening low ego states by practicing appropriate behaviors. See if the child thinks the ego-gram differs in various situations—at home, at school, playing with friends.

Once children understand ego states, they can learn to distinguish complementary, crossed, and ulterior transactions. If they bring in a situation that illustrates one of these, have them diagram it. In the case of crossed or ulterior transactions, encourage children to use their Adult to figure out ways to obtain a more successful result.

Some other methods for teaching the various TA techniques are described in the following list.

1. Talk about the feelings and behaviors that go with each ego state. Have children identify their own and others' ego states, by relating the ego states to what children say about their experiences.

Child: My brother always tells me what to do. He's not my father.
Counselor: You feel rebellious when your brother acts like a bossy parent.

As children become aware of their ego states and can discriminate them, their Adult can gain control of which ego state is expressed and give them permission to replace destructive ideas with constructive ones.

2. The OK Corral diagram is useful in helping children identify how they feel and think about themselves and other people. Children are able to discuss what OK-ness and not-OK-ness mean to them in terms of specific behaviors.

3. Games intrigue children. Once they have the concept, they can readily pick up on games in themselves and others and describe them. Any time children describe a pattern of games or recognize that "this always happens to me," the counselor can introduce the concept of games as a way of getting negative strokes to replace the positive strokes children think they cannot get: "You seem to mess up a lot. How do you manage that?" "What does this mean about you?" "How did it feel after it happened?" "What do you really want? How could you get it better?" "What 'bad' (scary) thing does this game prevent?" Children can also identify the three game roles of persecutor, rescuer, and victim and learn to stay out of them. The persecutor role can be demonstrated by having the child try to "put someone down" by pressing straight down on his or her shoulders. Putting people down this way is difficult unless they lean over or bend their knees. One can demonstrate the rescuer role by trying to pick up a limp person (of about the same size). Holding up a person who does not want to stand is also difficult. The victim role is demonstrated in relation to the other two by the partner's "giving in," lying down, and staying limp.

4. Racket feelings can be discussed in terms of stamp collecting. Children can usually identify the bad feelings they save up and the prize they get. Hypothetical situations such as the following create bad feelings: "Did you ever have a rotten day? Your mom yells at you at breakfast, your teacher catches you

talking, the other guys play keep-away with your hat, and you drop your books in the mud when your dog jumps on you because he's so glad to see you home. All day long you have felt mistreated and hurt, and that is the last straw. So you pick a fight with your little sister." Talk about how cashing in stamps feels and how getting dumped on feels. As small people, children are often the target when stamps are cashed in. Awareness can help children stop collecting stamps (child abuse is the worst form of stamp cashing) by learning to talk about bad feelings with someone they can trust and asking for and receiving the positive strokes they need.

5. For counselors working with script issues, useful questions for figuring out a child's script include many of the same questions used in the Adlerian lifestyle interview (chapter 10):

What are the "hurt" points in your family? (G)
Who is in your family? (BP)
What are the people in your family like? (BP)
Has anyone else ever lived with you? (BP)
What were they like? (BP)
Who is boss in your family? (PI, P)
What is your mother's (or father's) favorite saying? (PI, CI)
Describe yourself in three words. (BP, D)
What words would other people in your family use to describe you? (PI, CI, BP)
What bad feeling do you have a lot? (R)
What good feeling do you have a lot? (BP)
Who is your mother's favorite? (PI, CI)
Who is your father's favorite? (PI, CI)

The preceding questions are coded to fit parts of the life script.

BP—Basic life position regarding how I feel about myself and others
PI—Parental injunction (message from parent's Child): "Don't do as I do"
CI—Counterinjunction (message from parent's Parent): "Do at least try"
G—Games (getting strokes at others' expense)
R—Racket (bad feelings)
D—Decision (how I have chosen to live my life)
P—Program (how to obey injunctions)

6. Most people have kept a diary or journal at some time during their lives in which they have recorded their innermost feelings, thoughts, and other events. Children respond well to a homework assignment of keeping a diary. The diary provides the counselor and child with a record of feelings, thoughts, and life script to be explored. Keeping a journal or diary may also provide the child with a feeling of closeness to the counselor between sessions.

7. What *not* to do: The counselor who is not in a position to protect a child from negative consequences, ought not interfere with script behavior that still serves a purpose in the family. Do not ask children to give up their games or rackets

before they learn more appropriate ways to get strokes. Do not decide for children what they "should" do. Do not encourage children to play TA counselor with people who have power over them and may not appreciate their comments.

All the preceding exercises can be used in group and family counseling as well as in individual counseling. Role-playing and acting-out games are very effective group techniques. Families in TA counseling come to recognize where their transactions become crossed, how and when scripting occurs, and how stroking behavior can change family feelings.

◆ ◆ ◆

CASE STUDIES *

Transcript I

Jim, age 5, is being seen by the school counselor because Jim has been fighting with other children in his kindergarten class. Jim has only recently started this.

Counselor: Jim, remember when I came to your class and read the story about the warm fuzzies and the cold pricklies? [Jim nods.] Well, everybody, kids and grown-ups, needs to get some of these to live. Sometimes people do things to get cold pricklies like slaps or frowns, or being yelled at. Would you like to find out how to give yourself and other people nice warm fuzzies like smiles and hugs, and get them back from others?

Jim: Yes. Everybody doesn't like me now.

Counselor: What do you do to get hugs and smiles from your mommy?

Jim: I don't do anything, she just gives them to me. Or sometimes I hug her first or say "I love you."

Counselor: Sometimes mommies are busy. What do you do to get her attention then?

Jim: Well, I get a hug from Grandma. But if I can't get one, I make my little sister yell. Then somebody comes to see what's happening.

Counselor: If you can't get a warm fuzzy, you get them to give you a cold prickly?

Jim: Yeah.

Counselor: What do kids in your class have to do to get a hug?

Jim: They hug you if you fall down. But I don't fall down, so nobody hugs me.

Counselor: If you can't get a hug or other warm fuzzy when you want one, what do you do to get attention?

Jim: I make one of the other kids yell.

Counselor: Sometimes getting yelled at is better than nothing, huh?

Jim: Yeah.

---

* The case study transcripts and several teaching ideas in the "Counseling Method" section were contributed by Mary Wells Holbrook (Transcript II) and Jean Wycoff (Transcript I).

Counselor: Do you think any of your teachers would give you a warm fuzzy?

Jim: Miss Sally has a nice face.

Counselor: So when you feel bad inside and need a warm fuzzy, you could get one from Miss Sally?

Jim: Yeah, like when I miss my mommy. I could tell Miss Sally that and ask her to hug me.

Counselor: That sounds like a good plan, Jim. And if you feel bad, or sad, or lonely, or angry, and need to talk about it, you can come here and talk to me about it.

Jim: Okay.

Counselor: [gives Jim a hug] I give warm fuzzies, too.

Counselor feedback to Jim's teacher should include talking about giving Jim some strokes when he is being good and not making a bid for negative feedback.

Transcript II

The child in this interview is a 10-year-old boy.

Counselor: Christopher, you've read the Freeds' book about stroking. Can you explain to me what they mean by strokes?

Christopher: Stroking is when somebody does some type of action, physical or verbal, that makes you feel either good or not so good.

Counselor: I think that's a very good definition. Can you give me some examples of a positive stroke?

Christopher: Patting somebody, or hugging them, or saying something nice.

Counselor: Like what?

Christopher: You really did well today.

Counselor: Can you think of a positive stroke you've given someone today?

Christopher: Not really.

Counselor: How about when I came in, and you looked up and smiled?

Christopher: I guess. I smiled at most everybody in the class today.

Counselor: You have to remember that they don't have to be verbal; just a smile is a positive stroke. Can you think of any negative strokes you've given anyone today?

Christopher: No.

Counselor: That's good. Of course, the same holds true for negative strokes—if, without realizing it, you looked at someone and gave them a hard frown or something, that could be a negative stroke that you didn't realize you gave.

Christopher: I don't see why I would have given any, even by accident. There wasn't any reason to give any.

Counselor: Well, good. Can you think of any positive strokes anyone gave you today?

Christopher: When I got 100 on our test today, Mrs. Kincaid said that that was very good.

Counselor: I'm glad. Any negative strokes?

Christopher: No.

Counselor: Well, I told you your hands and face were dirty and I didn't like you coming downtown like that, right? You think you've got the idea about how positive and negative strokes work?

Christopher: Yes.

Counselor: How would you use stroking?

Christopher: Well, whenever I thought somebody did a good job on something, I could tell them.

Counselor: You know, there's such a thing as giving strokes that are not asked for, strokes that you just offer freely. Can you give an example of one of those, maybe?

Christopher: Just saying something nice when they don't even really need it . . . well, they do need it. Just saying it, but just saying it even if they haven't done anything.

Counselor: Be more specific.

Christopher: Well, if you meet somebody, you can say, "I like your shoes," or "Your hair looks nice," or something like that.

Counselor: Yes, those would be nice to hear. Can you tell me how you might use nonverbal positive strokes?

Christopher: By patting somebody, or smiling at them, or giving them a hug.

Counselor: How do you think you would feel if you started giving more positive strokes and getting more positive strokes?

Christopher: All covered over with strokes.

◆ ◆ ◆ ◆ ◆ ◆ ◆ ◆ ◆

RESEARCH AND APPLICATIONS

Kenny and Lyons (1980) researched the usefulness of TA as a model for school consultation with a 14-year-old girl in a class for students with learning disabilities and her teacher as subjects. Following consultation with the teacher on how to use and practice using the Nurturing Parent and Free Child ego states with the student, the student's oppositional behavior declined. The increased use of the two ego states in interactions with the student remained through a 5-day follow-up period. The TA interventions have the immediate goal of rebalancing the ego states.

Kenny (1981), in a follow-up effort, studied the effect of problem students on teacher ego states. Two teachers, each with an identified problem student, were the subjects in this study. Three teacher ego-state behaviors were targeted and monitored on the days the students were present and absent. The three ego states were Nurturing Parent (approval, praise, rewards), Critical Parent (disapproval, punishment), and Free Child (laughter, surprise, pleasant excitement). Both teachers exhibited more Nurturing Parent behaviors and Free Child behaviors with their classes when the problem student was absent. The teachers' Critical Parent behaviors toward the class increased when the problem student was present.

Tudor (1991) discussed a developmental framework that integrated TA concepts with the Gestalt contact cycle for educational and therapeutic work with children in groups. An international group of children, age 5 to 14, participated in the workshop. The TA concepts of ego states were used with the Gestalt exercises. *Parent* was defined as "looking after," *Adult* as "thinking," and *Child* as "feeling." Children also received help on giving and receiving strokes without collecting and cashing in stamps. Permissions and injunctions were two other TA concepts used in the workshop. The Gestalt contact cycle referred to feel, to think, to do/or to act, to make it, to enjoy, and to let go. The workshop relied heavily on role-playing to help the children learn the skills they need to reach emotional literacy.

Veevers (1991) suggested that social workers can use the theory of injunctions and associated permissions to identify the emotional needs of an adoptive child. She suggested that the child's needs can be matched with the adoptive parents most likely to be able to supply the emotional strengths the child needs. The new parents can then receive training on how to reparent the child. Many adopted children bring destructive, defeating scripts to their new family. Frequently, these children have been given the wrong injunctions and lack the permissions necessary for effective living. Typical injunctions from troubled homes include "Don't be important," "Don't be yourself," "Don't think," "Don't feel or express emotions," "Don't be a baby," "Don't belong," and "Don't trust or feel safe." Veevers used the case of a 7-year-old child to illustrate her thesis.

Parent Education

Bredehoft (1986) studied the effect of TA parent education on family members' self-esteem, adaptability, cohesion, and conflict. The classes were conducted in 10 2-hour sessions. Fathers who attended the class perceived their families as more adaptable and were more satisfied with family cohesion. Significant changes occurred in both average family empathy and the mother's empathy with the father. No significant changes were recorded in the area of self-concept.

The Glen family (1982) described an interesting family-counseling technique incorporating TA techniques to improve their family-system functioning. Basically, they agreed to spend one half-day period practicing role reversal, in which the two children could select parent roles while the parents took the children's roles. The roles came complete with duties. The parent role included setting limits for the children, cooking, and putting the children to bed. Role reversal offers a good way to exchange positive and negative feedback, as well as to build empathy for the other family members. The role reversal facilitated communication and interaction.

Bredehoft (1990) researched the effectiveness of a TA parent-training program on the self-esteem and communication skills of abusive parents. The program was successful in building self-esteem; however, there was no evidence that communication skills improved.

Self-Esteem

Golub and Guerriero (1981), in a study of the effects of TA training on the self-concepts of learning-disabled boys from grades 2 to 4, found that 18 sessions of 30 minutes each helped the boys achieve a significant positive change in their Coopersmith Self-Esteem Inventory scores. Role-playing and practice sessions gave the learning-disabled students the opportunity to demonstrate application of their TA understanding.

Relationships

In a study on reactions to emotions, Gormly and Gormly (1984) found that the most likely reaction to anger, anxiety, or happiness is to seek out others. For depression, the most likely reaction is avoiding people. Their results have implications for counselors using transactional analysis.

Nykodym, Rund, and Liverpool (1986) investigated whether TA training would be an effective strategy to improve communication skills before beginning quality circles. An experimental group received six half-day sessions of TA training. Two hypotheses were affirmed: (1) TA training improves perception of coworker communication, and (2) interaction of group members improves after TA training. A control group showed no change on either dimension.

Reparenting

Wilson, White, and Heiber (1985) compared the TA technique of "reparenting" with traditional psychotherapy in treating adolescent and young adult schizophrenics. The hospital patients in both groups received five 2-hour sessions per week. The reparenting patients were held and fed by bottles and allowed to regress to earlier developmental stages when proper nurturance was not available to them. Pretreatment and posttreatment data were collected on the Minnesota Multiphasic Personality Inventory (MMPI) and DSM-III evaluations. The reparenting group made significant positive changes in mental condition and level of adaptive functioning. The authors rated the reparenting group slightly higher than the traditional treatment group in both areas.

Smith (1989) conducted a study of clinicians who use regressive work in their therapy. Regressive work is based on the TA concept of reparenting, in which new parent messages replace old, counterproductive messages as a new, healthy life script begins to take shape. Results of the survey indicated that regressive work is most effective with adults 18 to 40 and is seldom used with children under 12. Regression therapy was rated to be 30% effective with adolescents. Women seemed to benefit from it more than men, 74.6% to 54.1%.

Moroney (1989) described five reparenting strategies for providing clients with new parent messages to replace the inadequate or dysfunctional ones they received in childhood. Total regression reparenting is a 24-hour, comprehensive approach in which the client lives with the therapist throughout treatment. Through regression to early childhood periods of conflict, the client is provided with a nurturing and protective environment until he or she reaches psychological adulthood. The Child's needs are met, and a complete change in the client's unhealthy Parent ego state results. Reparenting with time-limited regression can take place in a series of 2-hour group sessions. Spot reparenting is a focused approach targeted toward less severely disturbed patients and toward traumatic incidents rather than developmental periods. Self-reparenting does not attempt to replace the entire Parent ego state. Instead, the counselor affirms the positive aspects of the client's Parent ego and gives the Child ego comfort and support. Reparenting using parents of origin involves the client in playing the reparenting role. Here, the dysfunction of the defective Parent ego resulted from defective communication rather than from bad parenting.

Clarkson and Fish (1988) discussed "rechilding" as creating a new past in the present as a support for the future. The individual regresses to a younger age, in which development deficits occurred. There, deficit periods are recreated in ways that allow clients to react with positive, healthy responses. Briefly, when stressed, a person may move from the Adult to either the Child or Parent ego state. If neither can support the stressed Adult, script regression may occur. Reparenting and rechilding allow the Adult to find greater stability under stress.

SUMMARY

The practitioners of transactional analysis continue to enjoy wide popularity for improving relationship and communication skills between individuals and within groups of various types. However, Douglass (1990), in a survey of TA literature available to college students, found that Gestalt therapy is represented more often than TA. Students had a 37% chance of studying TA and a 66% chance of studying Gestalt. Douglass was also concerned that TA is not well defined and that its techniques are not properly integrated with theory. In fact, many authors had difficulty agreeing on where to place TA in relation to philosophical orientation. Douglass recommended that standards and guidelines on TA information be developed in an effort to ensure TA's survival and proper professional presentation.

REFERENCES

Allen, J., & Allen, B. (1989). Stroking: Biological underpinnings and direct observations. *Transactional Analysis Journal, 19*, 26–31.

Bala, J. (1986). "Mama stop doing MMMMMMM": TA in the treatment of autistic children. *Transactional Analysis Journal, 16*, 234–239.

Bary, B., & Hufford, F. (1990). The six advantages to games and their use in treatment. *Transactional Analysis Journal, 20*, 214–220.

Berne, E. (1947). *The mind in action.* New York: Simon & Schuster.

Berne, E. (1949). The nature of intuition. *Psychiatric Quarterly, 23*, 203–226.

Berne, E. (1961). *Transactional analysis in psychotherapy.* New York: Grove Press.

Berne, E. (1964). *Games people play.* New York: Grove Press.

Bredehoft, D. (1986). An evaluation of self-esteem: A family affair. *Transactional Analysis Journal, 16*, 175–181.

Bredehoft, D. J. (1990). Self-esteem: A family affair. *Transactional Analysis Journal, 20*, 111–116.

Choy, A. (1990). The winner's triangle. *Transactional Analysis Journal, 20*, 40–45.

Clarkson, P., & Fish, S. (1988). Rechilding: Creating a new past in the present as a support for the future. *Transactional Analysis Journal, 18*, 51–59.

Craig, R., & Olson, R. (1988). Changes in functional ego states following treatment for drug abuse. *Transactional Analysis Journal, 18*, 43–48.

Douglas, L. (1986). Is adolescent suicide a third degree game and who is the real victim? *Transactional Analysis Journal, 16*, 165–169.

Douglass, H. (1990). Transactional analysis in American college psychology textbooks. *Transactional Analysis Journal, 20*, 92–109.

Freed, A., & Freed, M. (1974a). *TA for kids.* Sacramento, CA: Freed.

Freed, A., & Freed, M. (1974b). *TA for tots.* Sacramento, CA: Freed.

Gilmore, J. R. (1981). Psychological evidence of ego states. *Transactional Analysis Journal, 11*, 207–212.

Glen, R., Glen, O., Glen, L., & Glen, A. (1982). Upside-down day: A family role reversal experience. *Transactional Analysis Journal, 12*, 277–279.

Goldberg, H., & Summerfield, A. (1982). The perception of Parent and Child ego states. *Transactional Analysis Journal, 12*, 223–226.

Golub, S., & Guerriero, L. (1981). The effects of a transactional analysis program on self-esteem in learning disabled boys. *Transactional Analysis Journal, 11*, 244–246.

Gormly, A., & Gormly, J. (1984). A psychological study of emotions. *Transactional Analysis Journal, 14*, 74–79.

Harris, T. (1969). *I'm OK—you're OK.* New York: Harper & Row.

Hazell, J. (1989). Drivers as mediators of stress response. *Transactional Analysis Journal, 19*, 212–222.

Horwitz, A. (1982). The relationship between positive stroking and self-perceived symptoms of distress. *Transactional Analysis Journal, 12*, 218–221.

James, M., & Jongeward, D. (1971). *Born to win.* Reading, MA: Addison-Wesley.

Kenny, W. (1981). Problem-student effects on teacher ego state behavior. *Transactional Analysis Journal, 11*, 252–253.

Kenny, W., & Lyons, B. (1980). A TA model of school consultation: An empirical analysis. *Transactional Analysis Journal, 10*, 264–269.

Kleinewiese, E. (1980). TA with children: Visual representation model of the ego states. *Transactional Analysis Journal, 10*, 259–263.

Manning, B., & Manning, P. (1988). Analysis of private self-talk of preservice teachers. *Educational Research Quarterly, 12,* 46–50.

McCormick, P., & Campos, L. (1969). *Introduce yourself to transactional analysis.* Stockton, CA: San Joaquin Transactional Analysis Study Group.

Moroney, M. (1989). Reparenting strategies in transactional analysis therapy: A comparison of five methods. *Transactional Analysis Journal, 19,* 35–41.

Nykodym, N., Rund, W., & Liverpool, P. (1986). Quality circles: Will transactional analysis improve their effectiveness? *Transactional Analysis Journal, 16,* 182–187.

Olia, A. (1989). Memory retrieval in the treatment of adult survivors of sexual abuse. *Transactional Analysis Journal, 19,* 93–99.

Osnes, R., & Rendack, S. (1989). Therapy with long-term abuse survivors. *Transactional Analysis Journal, 19,* 86–91.

Phillips, P., & Cordell, F. (1975). *Am I OK?* Niles, IL: Argus.

Price, R. (1990). Borderline disorders of the self: Toward a reconceptualization. *Transactional Analysis Journal, 20,* 128–133.

Shahin, J. (1995). Hey, ya jerk. *American Way, 28*(6), 32, 37–38.

Smith, S. (1989). A study of clinicians who use regressive work. *Transactional Analysis Journal, 19,* 75–79.

Stapleton, R., & Murkison, G. (1990). Scripts and entrepreneurship. *Transactional Analysis Journal, 20,* 193–197.

Steiner, C. (1974). *Scripts people live.* New York: Grove Press.

Steiner, C. (1975). *Readings in radical psychiatry.* New York: Grove Press.

Tudor, K. (1991). Children's group: Integrating TA and gestalt perspectives. *Transactional Analysis Journal, 21*(1), 12–19.

Veevers, H. (1991). Which child—which family? *Transactional Analysis Journal, 21,* 207–211.

White, A. (1983). Three-chair parenting. *Transactional Analysis Journal, 13,* 110–111.

Wilson, T., White, T., & Heiber, R. (1985). Reparenting schizophrenic youth in a hospital setting. *Transactional Analysis Journal, 15,* 211–215.

Zalcman, M. (1990). Game analysis and racket analysis: Overview, critique, and future developement. *Transactional Analysis Journal, 20,* 4–19.

Chapter 10

◆

Individual Psychology*

ALFRED ADLER

Alfred Adler, the founder of individual psychology, was born in Vienna on February 7, 1870, the second of six children. When Adler was 10 years old, he was such a poor math student that his teachers suggested he be removed from school and assigned as an apprentice to a cobbler. As often happens with paradoxical counseling strategies, the boy became angry, studied harder, and placed first in his class. As a child, Adler suffered from rickets, pneumonia, and several accidents. The resulting frequent contact with doctors influenced Adler to study medicine.

Adler spent his entire youth in Vienna and received his medical degree from its university in 1895. In addition to medicine, Adler was also knowledgeable in psychology, philosophy, the Bible, and Shakespeare. Two years after his graduation, Adler married Raisa Timofeyeuna Epstein, an intellectual and friend of Freud's who had come from Russia to study at the University of Vienna (Alexander, Eisenstein, & Grotjahn, 1966).

In the fall of 1902, Adler joined Sigmund Freud's discussion group, which was to become the first psychoanalytic society. Adler was not a proponent of Freud's psychosexual theory, and his writings about "feelings of inferiority" in 1910 and 1911 initiated a break with Freud. In 1910, in an attempt to reconcile the gap between himself and the Adlerians, Freud named Adler president of the Viennese Analytic Society and coeditor of a journal published by Freud. Nevertheless, Adler continued to disagree with Freud's psychosexual theory. Adler was the first psychoanalyst to emphasize human nature as being fundamentally social. Upon Freud's demand that his entire staff accept his theory without any conditions, Adler resigned, along with seven others, and founded

---

* We owe appreciation to Harold Mosak, PhD, of the Adler School of Professional Psychology in Chicago for his contributions and his review of this chapter.

the Society for Free Psychoanalytic Research. In 1912, Adler changed the name to the Society for Individual Psychology (Orgler, 1965).

After World War I broke out, Adler served for 2 years as a military doctor and later was appointed to head a large hospital for the wounded and shell-shocked. In 1926, Adler accepted a visiting professorship at Columbia University in New York, and in 1935 he moved his family to the United States. His children, one son and one daughter, became psychiatrists and worked with the principles of individual psychology. On May 28, 1937, while giving a series of lectures in Scotland, Adler suddenly collapsed on the street and died of heart failure.

Adler's achievements included founding *Zeitschrift für Individual Psychologie* (1912), introducing the term *inferiority feelings,* and developing a flexible, supportive psychotherapy to direct those emotionally disabled by inferiority feelings toward maturity, common sense, and social usefulness.

Adler originated (1919) the network of child-guidance clinics called *Erziehungsberatungsstellen,* which means literally "places to come for questions about education"—parent-education centers. Their staffs included physicians, psychologists, and social workers. Because of his idea of group discussions with families, many people believe Adler to have been 50 years ahead of his time; the present-day emphasis on group counseling and parent education supports this claim.

Rudolf Dreikurs contributed perhaps the most helpful adaptations and development of Adler's work. A leading proponent of individual psychology until his death in 1972, Dreikurs was a pioneer in music therapy and group psychotherapy, which he introduced into private psychiatric practice in 1929. His most significant contribution to counseling children was his ability to translate theory into practice. Dreikurs developed many of Adler's complex ideas into a relatively simple applied method for understanding and working with the behavior of children in both family and school settings.

THE NATURE OF PEOPLE

If Freud had done nothing more than stimulate thinking and reactions in other theorists, he would have made a significant contribution to counseling and psychotherapy. Like many others, Adler reacted against Freud's ideas and developed a new theory. Freud attempted to interpret all behaviors and problems as extensions of sex, pleasure, and the death instinct; Adler believed that all people develop some sense of inferiority because they are born completely helpless and remain that way for a rather long childhood. Such feelings of inferiority may be exaggerated by body or organ defects (real or imaginary), by having older and more powerful siblings, or by parent neglect, rejection, or pampering. One way to cope with feelings of inferiority is compensation or gaining power to handle the sense of weakness. The effects of organ inferiority are reduced through development of skills, behaviors, traits, and strengths that replace or compensate for these thoughts of weakness and powerlessness. Mosak (personal communication,

July 21, 1992) pointed out that Adler introduced the theory of organ inferiority in 1907, when Adler was a Freudian and that Freud complimented Adler on a major addition to Freudian theory. Although it is not a part of Adlerian theory today, Adlerians and others have observed that some people with organ inferiorities do compensate for them.

Adler viewed human behavior as falling on a continuum between his concepts of masculinity, representing strength and power, and femininity, symbolizing weakness and inferiority. What he called *masculine protest,* a striving for power, was common to both sexes, especially women. Adler replaced Freud's concept of sexual pleasure as the prime motivator of behavior with the search for power.

According to Adler, personality development progresses along a road paved with evidence of either personal superiority or inferiority. As infants—small, helpless, inexperienced—we are especially subject to others' whims and vulnerable to inferiority feelings. As we grow older, both family and society emphasize the advantages of size, beauty, and strength. Therefore, our wishes and dreams for superiority, our attempts to achieve it, and the social realities that make us feel inferior are in continual conflict. This striving for power (masculine protest) occupies a place in his theory similar to that of the Oedipus situation in Freudian theory. A person develops into a normal, neurotic, or psychotic adult as the result of this struggle between the masculine protest and social reality.

Freud believed that love and work were the two important indexes of mental health in that a person's mental health depends on how well these two areas are progressing. In a similar vein, Adler believed that problems brought to therapy reside in the areas of career (occupation), love relationships (intimacy), and friendships (Kern, Hawes, & Christensen, 1989).

The Need for Success

Adler was struck by the importance of the hunger for success in human life—the ways people seek power and prestige and strive for goals associated with social approval. He was very concerned with the problems of competition, blocked ambition, feelings of resentment and hostility, and impulses to struggle and resist or to surrender and give in. Adler shifted his clinical attention from a primary focus on clients' psychosexual history to an examination of their success-failure pattern, or style of life. Adler's term *style of life* emphasizes the direction in which the individual is moving. Style-of-life analysis involves an assessment of children in terms of their habitual responses to frustration, to assumption of responsibility, and to situations that require exercising initiative.

Goals of Behavior

Adler's individual psychology emphasizes the purposive nature of human strivings. All behavior, including emotions, is goal directed. According to

Adlerian theory, the issue is not the cause of the behavior but determining what children want to accomplish, either in the real world or in their own minds. Behaviors do not continue over time unless they "work" for children. By looking at the consequences of children's behavior, adults can determine their goals. Adler's conception was that people are guided by a striving for ideal masculinity. Adler described what Horney (1950) termed the *neurotic search for glory:* Neurotics are characterized by an unrealistic goal of masculinity and mastery that they strive to overcome or attain. He also anticipated later psychoanalytic groups in his emphasis upon the social as well as the constitutional determinants of one's style of life. To Adler, the term *individual psychology* emphasized the unity of personality as opposed to Freud's emphasis on instincts common to all people. An individual builds a style of life from interactions between heredity and environment; these lifestyle building blocks fit a person into life as that person perceives it.

Lifestyle

Adler believed that a person's behavior must be studied from a holistic viewpoint. Usually by the age of 4 or 5, children have drawn general conclusions about life and the "best" way to meet the problems life offers. They base these conclusions on their biased perceptions of the events and interactions that go on around them and form the basis for their lifestyle. The style of life, unique for each individual, is the pattern of behavior that will predominate throughout that person's life. Only rarely does a person's lifestyle change without outside intervention. Understanding their lifestyle—that is, the basic beliefs they developed at an early age to help organize, understand, predict, and control their world—is important for adults, but children who have not reached the formal stage of cognitive development are incapable of understanding their lifestyles. Therefore, in working with children, Adlerians focus on the immediate behavior goals rather than on long-term goals. Socratic questioning methods help children learn their current lifestyle and goals through self-discovery.

Stiles & Wilborn (1992) developed a lifestyle instrument for children that describes children who responsibly cope with and solve problems and those who engage in social interest activities that help others. Based on Adler's four lifestyle types, the scale reflected six lifestyle themes: pleasing, rebelling, getting, controlling, being inadequate, and being socially useful. They found that boys (age 8 to 11) scored higher than girls of the same age on rebelling; girls scored higher on pleasing.

Social Interest

A person's amount of social interest is, according to Adler, a good barometer of mental health. Social interest is a feeling for and cooperation with people—a sense of belonging and participating with others for the common good. Ansbacher (1992) described how social interest and community feeling differ. He defined *social interest* as the more active of the two terms because it relates to how the individual handles the life tasks of love, friendship, and work in the social context. *Social interest* is the more concrete, workable term, whereas *community feeling* deals with the spiritual, universal order of a person's life.

Everyone has a need to belong to a group. Although social interest is inborn, it does not appear spontaneously but must be encouraged and trained, beginning with the relationship between the newborn infant and the mother. Children who feel they are part of a group do useful things that contribute to the well-being of that group; those who feel left out—and therefore inferior—do useless things in order to prove their own worth by gaining attention. From this concept comes the idea that misbehaving children are discouraged children—children who think that they can be known only in useless ways. Because children behave within the social context, their behavior cannot be studied in isolation. The study of human interaction is basic to individual psychology.

Many of life's problems center around conflicts with others. Solutions for these problems involve cooperating with people in the interest of making society a better place to live. A strong point in Adler's theory is his understanding of the implications of the social structure of life. Because every individual depends on other people for birth and growth, for food and shelter and protection, for love and companionship, a great web of interdependence exists among people. Thus the individual, Adler points out, owes a constant debt to society. Each person is responsible to the group, and those who do not learn to cooperate are destroyed. Adler believed that a person cannot violate the love and logic that bind people together without dire consequences for the health of one's personality. Pronounced egocentricity (the opposite of social interest) leads to neurosis, and the individual becomes healthy again only when this egocentricity is renounced in favor of a greater interest in the well-being of the total group. Reimanis (1974) found that young criminals compared with other youths showed higher levels of anomie and more childhood-experience memories suggesting interference with development of social interest.

Critics of Adlerian theory who hold a less positive view of human nature point out that people know they should cooperate but ordinarily do not do so until forced. Cross-cultural research evidence exists to support this view. However, Hjelle's (1975) research supported the hypothesis that high social interest, internal locus of control, and high self-actualization are positively related.

Barkley, Wilborn, and Towers (1984), in an attempt to foster social interest in a peer-counseling training program, selected 20 adolescent student volunteers for a study group that met 45 minutes per day, 5 days per week, over an 18-week period. The students received training in communication skills, and the sessions stressed the importance of caring for and helping others. Following 9 weeks' training, the students worked in a helping relationship with two other people drawn from an elementary school, junior high school, or nursing home population. A social interest index was administered at the beginning, middle, and end of the program to both experimental and control groups. Although females outperformed males in the experimental group, all members of the experimental group were observed to have improved their social interest skills and behaviors.

In studying relationships between sexual and love attitudes and social interest, Leak and Gardner (1990) reported that high social interest was related to a companion love style, nonpermissive sexual attitudes, and characteristics of mature love. Eros was not found to be a characteristic of people high in social interest.

Fish and Mozdzierz (1988) found that the Sulliman Scale of Social Interest (SSSI) as did the Social Interest Index and the Social Interest Scale, correlated directly with measures of adjustment and inversely with measures of maladjustment. However, the SSSI did not appear to be more accurate than the Social Interest Index and the Social Interest Scale.

Meunier and Royce (1988), using the Social Interest Scale, demonstrated that social interest continues to increase with age at the same rate for elderly persons as for younger persons. Inasmuch as mental health and personal adjustment directly relate to social interest, we can conclude that older adults have high levels of personal adjustment.

Leak and Williams (1989b) found social interest to be positively correlated to positive perceptions of one's family. Social interest was also linked to multicultural orientation and a sense of religion or morality. Leak and Williams (1989a) also found a positive correlation between social interest and the psychological hardiness areas of commitment and control. They found a negative correlation between social interest and feelings of alienation.

Ostrovsky, Parr, & Gradel (1992) discussed three factors that inhibit learning social interest: substance abuse, family breakdown, and poverty. The family unit once developed interest; with the dissolution of the family unit, the authors recommended that schools assume yet another job, providing social interest instruction, and providing guidelines for working with moral and social interest development.

Adler believed that social interest was exhibited through such qualities as friendliness, cooperation, and empathy. Social-interest development, being associated with so many good things, seems a worthwhile pursuit for clients of all ages.

Environment

Three environmental factors affect the development of a child's personality: family atmosphere, family constellation, and the prevalent methods of training. Through the family atmosphere, children learn about values and customs and try to fit themselves into the standards their parents set. Children also learn about relationships by watching how their family interacts and about sex roles by seeing the patterns adopted by their parents. The family constellation is important in that children formulate personalities based on how they interpret their positions in the family relative to other siblings: The firstborn child dethroned by a new baby tries very hard to maintain the position of supremacy and seeks recognition by whatever means possible. The second child feels inadequate because someone is always ahead and seeks a place by becoming what the older child is not; this child may feel squeezed out by a third child and adopt the position that life is unfair. The youngest child may take advantage of being the youngest and become outstanding in some respect, good or bad, even by becoming openly rebellious or helpless.

In summary, Adler believed that the principal human motive, a striving for perfection, could become a striving for superiority and thus an overcompensation for a feeling of inferiority. Children are self-determining persons able to create a style of life in the context of their family constellation. By trial and error and observation, children form their own conclusions about life and their place in it.

THEORY OF COUNSELING

Adler (1938/1964) held that four ties create reality and meaning in people's lives:

1. People are on earth to ensure the continuance of the human species.
2. Our survival depends on our need to cooperate with our fellow human beings.
3. Human beings each live in two sexes—the masculine, powerful side of our nature and the feminine, weak side of our nature.
4. Human problems can be grouped into three categories: social, occupational, and sexual.

Adler viewed the counselor's job as helping the child substitute realistic goals for unrealistic life goals and instilling social interest and concern for others.

As with most approaches to counseling, the goal of establishing a positive sense of self-esteem is primary. To achieve this feeling of self-esteem, children need to feel good about finding a place in life and about their progress in overcoming the unpleasant sense of inferiority associated with the dependence, smallness, and vulnerability introduced in early childhood. In the Adlerian view, the ideal or well-adjusted child exhibits the following qualities:

1. Respects the rights of others
2. Is tolerant of others
3. Is interested in others
4. Cooperates with others
5. Encourages others
6. Is courteous
7. Has a strong, positive self-concept

8. Has a feeling of belonging
9. Has socially acceptable goals
10. Exerts genuine effort
11. Is willing to share with others
12. Is concerned with how much "we" can get rather than how much "I" can get

In response to the specific pattern of inferiority feelings experienced by a child in a specific home situation, one unitary way of coping with the problem is discovered, one fundamental attitude is developed, and one mode of compensation is achieved. Thus, a person forms a style of life early in childhood—a style that is unitary, dependable, and predictable.

Adler recognized two fundamental styles of life: direct and indirect approaches to the good things, through strength and power or through weakness. A person usually tries power first; if power is blocked, a person chooses another road to the goal. The second road is paved with gentleness and bids for sympathy. If both roads fail, secondary feelings of inferiority arise. These secondary inferiority feelings, which Adler considered more serious than the primary, universal inferiority feelings, are ego problems, which can be the most burning problems of all. The focus of counseling, therefore, is harnessing this drive to compensate for weakness so that positive, constructive behavior results. Freud held that the backbone of civilization was sublimation. Adler thought that talent and capabilities arise from the stimulus of inadequacy. Adlerians believe that people are pulled by their goals and priorities. Knowledge of these goals is a major key to understanding behavior. For example, Kfir (1989) and Dinkmeyer, Pew, and Dinkmeyer (1979) identified four priorities that relate to the need to belong:

1. *To please others:* The main objective of pleasing others is to avoid rejection. Although other people may find a "me last" person quite easy to accept, the price for this behavior may be the rejection the person is trying to avoid. The "me last" position may also limit a person's growth and opportunities for learning, personal development, and general success in life. The pleasing attitude is supported by the faulty belief that "my meaningfulness and survival depend on whether I am loved by all," or that "Life is good when my approval rating is high and bad when it is not."

2. *To be superior:* The main objective of trying to be superior is to avoid meaninglessness. Such an attitude of superiority tends to make others feel inadequate. The price for superiority may be an overloaded lifestyle. Children may become overly responsible and perfectionistic, with all the resulting worry and anxiety when things are not perfect. People holding superiority as their number one priority attempt to avoid insignificance by influencing others through high achievement, leadership, and martyrdom. The superiority priority is supported by the faulty belief that "I am meaningful and therefore can survive only if I am better, am wiser, or know more than others."

3. *To control:* The main objective of trying to control oneself, others, and the

environment is to avoid unexpected humiliation. Controlling others tends to make them feel challenged, with the resulting price of increased social distance. Too much self-control results in a very structured life with little spontaneity. Control people are best described as uptight and their faulty belief is that "I am meaningful and therefore can survive only if I can control my life and the events and people who are part of my life."

4. *To be comfortable:* Avoidance of stress and pressure are the main objectives of those holding comfort as their number one priority. At their extreme, comfort seekers specialize in unfinished business and unresolved problems and conflicts. They adopt a reactive rather than proactive stance toward life. Delayed gratification is not one of their strengths; they often give way to the self-indulgent attitude of "I want what I want now." The comfort-seeking priority is supported by the faulty beliefs that "I am meaningful and therefore can survive only if I am left alone, unpressured, and free to move" and "Life is bad when I am uncomfortable."

Each priority has a price. As is done in the practice of reality therapy, the counselor can confront children and adults with a cost analysis of their chosen priorities. Because people are often reluctant to give up their number one priority, counseling may focus on cost reduction by exploring how clients can manage their priorities in more cost-efficient ways. As is done in the practice of rational-emotive-behavior therapy, the counselor can ask clients to modify their faulty beliefs that meaningfulness and survival rest solely on the total and constant fulfillment of their number one priority.

The Family Constellation

One goal of counseling is to construct a picture of the family dynamics and the child's place in the family constellation. *Ordinal position* (the exact order in which the child was born, e.g., second or fourth) in the family constellation is a key to the lifestyle pattern being developed by the child, and it may have a significant effect on how that child perceives reality. Although certain characteristics are associated with each child's *birth order* (one of the Adlerian birth positions: first, second, middle, youngest, and only), there are many exceptions; not all firstborns are alike. Mosak (Shulman & Mosak, 1977) has pointed out that the study of birth order and ordinal position has limited value because of the confounding variables of family size and number of children; for example, the second-born is the youngest child in a two-child family and the middle child in a three-child family.

However, in an effort to find their special place in the family, children tend to select different roles, behaviors, and interests. In general, some stereotypic behaviors based on birth order have been catalogued by Adlerians over the past 90 years. Some of these generalizations are summarized in the following paragraphs.

The Only Child

The only child enjoys some intellectual advantages by not having to share mother and father with any siblings. Language development is usually accelerated because the child learns adult language patterns. However, the reverse is sometimes true in an extremely child-centered home where everyone talks baby talk. Only children may experience difficulties outside the home when peers and teachers do not pamper them, or only children may be skillful in getting along with adults but not in making friends with other children. They enjoy being the center of attention. Observing how they gain the approval and attention to maintain their center-stage position can help a counselor understand these children. Have they developed skills, do they elicit sympathy by being helpless, or do they act shyly? Only children are more likely to have problems with the egocentrism block. They are usually interested only in themselves and may resort to tantrums and uncooperative behavior if their requests are not granted. They may depend too much on adults because they have not learned to do things on their own. Exceptions to the rule are those only children who learn to play ball and other games by themselves when they have not had an opportunity to be around friends. Shulman (Shulman & Mosak, 1977) wrote that only children never have rivals and that peers tend to be curiosities rather than rivals. Only children may not have learned how to share.

Firstborn Children

Often considered the special child by the family, especially if male, firstborns enjoy their number-one ranking but often fear dethronement by the birth of a second child. Firstborns work hard at pleasing their parents. They are likely to be conforming achievers, defenders of the faith, introverted, and well behaved. Twenty-three of the first 25 astronauts were firstborn males. The National Aeronautics and Space Administration (NASA) was interested in recruiting high-achieving followers for the space program; it had no need for "creative astronauts" who might decide to take the scenic route home. Firstborns often find themselves functioning as substitute parents in larger families. Shulman (Shulman & Mosak, 1977) believed that firstborn children, having had it all at one time, still prefer to be first and foremost.

Second-Born Children

Second-born children may be those extroverted, creative, free-thinking spirits that NASA was trying to avoid. More often than not, second-borns look at what is left over in the way of roles and behavior patterns that the firstborn child has shunned; picking another role is easier than competing with an older sibling with a head start. Second-borns may get lower grades in school even if they are brighter than number one. Parents are often easier on second-born children and show less concern with rules. In fact, second-borns may be the family rebels—with or without a cause! In any case, a second-born is usually the opposite of the first child. Second-borns are easily discouraged by trying to compete with successful, older, and bigger firstborns. The more successful firstborns are, the more likely second-borns are to feel unsure of themselves and their abilities. They may even feel squeezed out, neglected, unloved, and abused when the third child arrives.

Middle Children

Some of the idiosyncrasies common to the middle-child position may affect second-born children. Middle children are surrounded by competitors for their parents' attention. They have the pace-setting standard-bearers in front and the pursuers in the rear. Middle children often label themselves as squeezed children. However, many younger children increase their skill development in academic, athletic, and other pursuits through competition with older siblings.

The Youngest Child

Often referred to as Prince or Princess Charming, the youngest child could find a permanent lifestyle of being the baby in the family. Youngest children often get a lot of service from all the other family members. They may become dependent or spoiled and lag in development. Youngest children readily develop real feelings of inferiority because they are smaller, less able to take care of themselves, and often not taken seriously. The really successful charmers may learn how to boss subtly or to manipulate the entire family. They decide either to challenge their elder siblings or to evade any direct struggles for superiority. Then again, the path is marked and the trail is broken for the youngest child. Family guidelines are clear, and the youngest children always retain their position. Perhaps the downside is the child's perception that a lot of catching up is necessary to ever find a place in the family.

When a 5-year difference exists between two children in a family, the situation changes. With this large a gap, the next-born child often assumes the characteristics of a firstborn; apparently, the 5 years remove the competitive barriers found between children who are closer in age.

Extreme behavior patterns are often observed in children who find themselves the only boy or girl among siblings of the opposite sex. They may tend to develop toward extremes in either masculinity or femininity. Sex roles children assume often depend on roles perceived as most favored in our culture.

Large families appear to offer some advantages in child rearing by making it tough for parents to overparent each child. Children in large families frequently learn how to solve their own problems, take care of themselves, and handle their conflicts because their parents cannot give personal service and attention to each and every problem. Large families are probably good training grounds for learning how to be independent.

Many factors enter into the perceptions children have of their particular roles in their family:

1. The parents may have a favorite child.
2. The family may move.
3. Parents become more experienced and easygoing as they grow older.
4. Some homes are single-parent homes.
5. The children may have a stepparent living in the home.
6. The family climate changes with each addition to the family.
7. Chronic illnesses or handicaps may be a problem in the family.
8. A grandparent may live in the home.

Birth Order Research

Research on birth order has not supported clear-cut differences between birth positions. Some commonalities in birth order were reported in the 1970s.

Horn and Turner (1975), in a study of unwed mothers, found a higher incidence of firstborn women reporting premarital sexual intercourse—a finding that was interpreted to mean that firstborn women are more likely than later-born women to model the wife-mother role. Nystul (1974) found no significant effect of birth order on Oregon State University students' self-concept as measured by the Tennessee Self-Concept Scale. Fakouri (1974) found a relationship between birth order and achievement but no significant relationship between birth order and dogmatism.

Other research on birth order has not supported fixed birth order. In fact, exceptions seem to be the rule. Phillips, Bedeian, Mossholder, and Touliatos (1988) found no relationship between firstborn and laterborn accountants on managerial potential, work orientation, achievement by independence, and sociability. Firstborns did, however, score slightly higher on the California Personality Inventory (CPI) in dominance, good impressions, and achievement by conformity.

Stein, DeMiranda, and Stein (1988) researched the relationship between substance abuse, criminality, and birth order by correlating firstborn, intermediate-born, and last-born substance abusers on the three dimensions. Being a firstborn male was significantly correlated with substance abuse and criminality, but the authors identified no other relationships.

Harris and Morrow (1992) used the California Psychological Inventory (CPI) to determine the relationship between birth order and self-perceptions of responsibility and dominance. They found that gender (not birth order) influenced self-perception of responsibility, but there was an interactive effect on birth order and gender regarding dominance.

Bloser and Thompson (1996) researched the common belief that married people who had the same birth order might have more adjustment problems than couples from different birth orders. They found no significant difference in marital adjustment between couples from the same and different birth orders.

Poston and Falbo (1990) studied the difference between Chinese only children and Chinese children from other birth orders. They found that urban only children outperformed their peers who have siblings in math and verbal achievement, but rural Chinese children did not have the same only child advantage.

Wilson, Mundy-Castle, and Panditji (1990) questioned the belief that intelligence diminishes as a function of birth order because the addition of more children to the family dilutes the intellectual atmosphere of the family environment. The Cattell Children's B scale of general intelligence was given to 1,143 Zimbabwean children ranging from firstborn to eighth-born. Their average age was 11.5 years. The results supported earlier findings by Zajonc and Marcus (1975) that the number of siblings in a family dilutes the intellectual climate in the family. Test scores decreased as birth order increased, a finding that contradicted a Davis, Cahan, and Bashi (1977) study.

Rule (1991) found one advantage of being a later-born child. He asked 116 college students to circle a number from 1 (extremely strict) to 7 (extremely permissive) that best reflected their memories of their parents' strictness or permissiveness. Firstborns regarded both parents as much stricter than did later-borns. Most of the difference originated from the high ratings accorded fathers' strictness by firstborn women.

In summary, too much emphasis on birth order and ordinal position works in opposition to the Adlerian principle of free choice. Members of birth order positions may share some commonalities with people in the same position but are not predestined to turn out the same.

The Family Atmosphere

Dewey (1971) examined the importance of the family atmosphere in the development of the child. Whereas the family constellation is a description of how family members interact, the family atmosphere is the style of coping with life that the family has modeled for the child.

The following 12 family atmospheres indicate how a negative family atmosphere can adversely affect children.

1. *Authoritarian.* The authoritarian home requires unquestioned obedience from the children. Children have little or no voice in family decisions. Although these children are often well-behaved and mannerly, they also tend to be more anxious and outer-directed. What was once a shy child may turn into a rebel with a cause in later life.

2. *Suppressive.* In tune with the authoritarian home is the suppressive family atmosphere, in which children are not permitted to express their thoughts and feelings. Expression of opinion is limited to what the parents want to hear.

Frequently, children from such a family cannot express their *feelings* when they are allowed in situations outside the home, such as counseling. This type of family atmosphere does not encourage close relationships.

3. *Rejective.* Children feel unloved and unaccepted in this family atmosphere. Some parents do not know how to show love and frequently cannot separate the deed from the doer. Children and parents need to know and understand that love can be unconditional and not tied to unacceptable behavior: "I love you, but I am still angered by your irresponsibility." A child can easily become extremely discouraged in the rejective family.

4. *Disparaging.* A child criticized by everyone else in the family often turns out to be the "bad egg" everyone predicted. Too much criticism generally leads to cynicism and inability to form good interpersonal relationships.

5. *High standards.* Children living in the high-standards atmosphere may think such things as "I am not loved unless I make all 'A's.'" Fear of failure leads to the considerable distress perfectionist people experience. The tension and stress these children experience often prevent them from performing as well as they are able.

6. *Inharmonious.* In homes with considerable quarreling and fighting, children learn the importance of trying to control other people and keep others from controlling them. Power becomes a prime goal for these children. Discipline may be inconsistent in these homes and depend on the mood of the parents.

7. *Inconsistent.* Inconsistent methods of discipline and home routines are often sources of confusion and disharmony in the home. Lack of self-control, low motivation, self-centeredness, instability, and poor interpersonal relationships are often attributed to inconsistency in parenting practices.

8. *Materialistic.* In this type of home, children learn that feelings of self-worth depend on possessions and on comparisons to what peers own. Interpersonal relationships take a backseat to accumulating wealth.

9. *Overprotective.* These homes often prevent children from growing up because parents do too much for them. They protect the children from the consequences of their behavior and, in doing so, deny the reality of the situation. This parental overindulgence leads to a child who feels helpless and dependent. Dependent children fall into the class of outer-directed people who rely on others for approval.

10. *Pitying.* Like overprotectiveness, pitying also prevents children from developing and using the resources they have for solving their problems. Such may be the case with handicapped children, especially, who may be encouraged to feel sorry for themselves and to expect favors from others to make up for their misfortunes.

11. *Hopeless.* Discouraged and "unsuccessful" parents often pass on these attitudes to their children, who make hopelessness a part of their lifestyle. A pessimistic home atmosphere may be due to economic factors, especially if the breadwinners lack financial resources.

12. *Martyr.* People suffering from low self-esteem, hopelessness, and discouragement may have another pessimistic viewpoint, martyrdom. Once again, children may learn that life is unfair and that people should treat them better; martyrdom is a breeding ground for dependency.

Remember that atmosphere is not the total cause of behavior. Behavior is most influenced by the child's biased perceptions of the family climate.

Goals of Misbehavior

As children grow and interact with their environment, they gradually develop methods for achieving their basic goal, belonging. Several factors, including the child's place in the family, the quality of parents' interaction with the child, and the child's creative reaction to the family atmosphere, are critical in the development of coherent patterns of behaviors and attitudes.

Dreikurs and Soltz (1964) made an especially insightful and useful analysis of the immediate goals by which children attempt to achieve their basic goal of belonging. Children with no pattern of misbehavior have an immediate goal of cooperation and constructive collaboration. They find their place and feel good about themselves through constructive cooperation. They generally approach life with the goal of collaborating, and their usual behavior is socially and personally effective. By contrast, children with a pattern of misbehavior are usually pursuing one of four mistaken goals: attention, power, revenge, and inadequacy or withdrawal. Understanding the goal for which a misbehaving child is striving helps put the behavior in perspective and provides a basis for corrective action.

Attention

All children seek attention, especially those of preschool age. However, excessive attention-getting behavior should diminish in the primary school years before it becomes a problem to teachers, parents, and peers. The child's goal is to keep an adult busy, and the natural reaction is to feel annoyed and provide the service and attention the child seeks. Attention getting appears in four forms:

1. *Active constructive.* This child may be the model child, but with the goal to elevate self, not to cooperate. This is the successful student whose industrious and reliable performance is for attention only.

2. *Passive constructive.* This charming child is not as vigorous as the active-constructive child about getting attention. This child is a conscientious performer and a prime candidate for teacher's pet.

3. *Active destructive.* This nuisance child is the prime candidate for the child most likely to ruin a teacher's day—the class clown, show-off, and mischief-maker.

4. *Passive destructive.* This lazy child gets a teacher's attention through demands for service and help. This child often lacks the ability and motivation to complete work.

Power

These children have an exaggerated need to exercise power and superiority. They take every situation, debate, or issue as a personal challenge from which they must emerge the winner; otherwise, these children think they have failed. The child's goal is to be the boss. A teacher's reaction ranges from anger to feeling threatened or defeated. The child acts in a stubborn, argumentative way and may even throw tantrums; this child leads the league in disobedience. The power struggle takes two forms:

1. *Active destructive.* This child is the rebel who has the potential of leading a group rebellion.
2. *Passive destructive.* This child is stubborn and forgetful and could also be the lazy one in the group.

Revenge

These children feel hurt and mistreated by life. Their goal is to get even by hurting others. They achieve social recognition, although they usually make themselves unpopular with most other children. The child's goal, then, is to even up the score, and the adult's reaction is usually to feel hurt. Revenge has two forms:

1. *Active destructive.* This child is violent and resorts to stealing, vandalism, and physical abuse to extract revenge. This child is a candidate to become a gang leader.
2. *Passive destructive.* This child is also violent but in a passive way: the quiet, sullen, defiant child. Both revenge types believe their only hope lies in getting even.

Inadequacy or Withdrawal

These children often feel inferior and think they are incapable of handling life's problems. Their deficiencies may be real or imagined. By giving up, they hope to hide their inferiority and to prevent others from making demands on them. The child's goal is to be left alone, and the adult's reaction is helplessness and giving up. Inadequacy has only one form: *passive-destructive.* These children are usually described as hopeless. They often put on an act of being stupid just to discourage the teacher from asking them to recite and do work. They may have an unwritten contract with their teachers that says, in effect, "I'll leave you alone if you leave me alone."

Manly (1986) adapted the four goal questions into an informal inventory for use with students who have been referred to her for behavior or attitude problems. Manly tells her students that the inventory will help her know them better and know what they think. The inventory may be taken as a pencil-and-paper client list or as an interview between counselor and client. Students are asked to indicate which of the following sentences are true for them.

Goals Inventory

Attention

___ I want people to notice me.
___ I want people to do more for me.
___ I want to be special.
___ I want some attention.

Power

___ I want to be in charge.
___ I want people to do what I want to do.
___ I want people to stop telling me what to do.
___ I want power.

Revenge

___ I think I have been treated unfairly.
___ I want to get even.
___ I want people to see what it is like to feel hurt.
___ I want people to feel sorry for what they have done.

Display of inadequacy

___ I want people to stop asking me to do things.
___ I want people to feel sorry for me.
___ I want to be left alone. I can't do it anyway.
___ I know I'll mess up, so there's no point in trying.

The questions may be intermixed or administered in these groupings. The four goal labels are not meant to be included on the inventory.

Research and Theory on the Goals of Misbehavior

Mattice (1976) found that teachers and children considered the four goals of misbehavior a reasonable explanation of human behavior. She also found that children formulated interpersonal goal statements about misbehavior better than did teachers. School psychologists had difficulty categorizing the misbehavior goals.

Nystul (1986) recommended that counselors look beyond the goals of children's misbehavior to the special reasons for misbehavior. He makes three assumptions about people:

1. Human nature is positive.
2. The child's most basic psychological need is positive relationships with significant others.
3. The child has four life choices: to be a "good somebody," a "good nobody," a "bad somebody," or to have severe mental health problems (a "bad nobody"?).

Adlerians have long stated that asking children why they misbehave is not helpful. In Porter and Hoedt's (1985) study of fourth- and fifth-grade students from inner city schools, 70% of the children replied "I don't know" when asked why they misbehaved. Focusing on the goal of misbehaviors (for example, asking "Could it be that you want to be the boss?") was more effective when combined with action plans that increased children's understanding of the goals.

Brannon and Jacques (1989) studied the goals of misbehavior for 150 male adolescent offenders committed to a state facility. The percentage for each goal was as follows: attention, 28; power, 32; revenge, 24; and inadequacy, 14.

Kottman and Stiles (1990) described how mutual storytelling can be incorporated into Adlerian counseling. They provided a useful framework for developing stories about how children use various misbehaviors to achieve the four goals. The stories also include ways to achieve goals with acceptable, responsible behavior.

Kottman (1992), Kottman and Warlick (1989), and Kottman and Johnson (1993) adapted play therapy to the Adlerian model.

Phase I: Building a democratic relationship with the child
    a. Tracking behavior ("I see you are building a house")
    b. Restatement of content
    c. Reflection of feeling
Phase II: Exploring the child's lifestyle through the parents, child, observation, and drawings
    a. Family atmosphere
    b. Family constellation
    c. Early recollections
Phase III: Allowing the child to gain insight about relationships and behavior
    a. Four goals of misbehavior ("Could it be . . .")
    b. Lifestyle ("Let's look at how others feel when you blow up")
    c. Parallels of behavior inside and outside the playroom

Phase IV: Reorienting the child toward better ways to achieve goals
  a. Alternative behaviors
  b. Encouragement
  c. Consultation with parents

COUNSELING METHOD

Adler based the counseling methods he pioneered on his experience and philosophy about the nature of people. Later Adlerians, including Rudolf Dreikurs, Heinz Ansbacher, Harold Mosak, and Don Dinkmeyer, have used and modified many of Adler's original ideas.

Adlerian counseling makes no distinction between conscious and unconscious material. The counselor uses dreams, for example, to discover the lifestyle of adult clients—that is, the type of defense used to establish superiority. Many counselors use questions similar to adult lifestyle interviews with children as a means of assessing how well things are going for them. Although organ inferiority is not a part of modern-day Adlerian theory, counselors frequently analyze the inferiority feelings that stem from real or fancied personal deficiencies, particularly so-called organ deficiencies (such as defective vision) or organic inferiority (weak heart), some form of which everyone is assumed to possess. Next, the counselor proceeds to examine the client's academic, extracurricular, and social adjustments to see how the client has maintained or achieved superiority in each of these major areas of life and to examine the inferiority feelings that may plague the client. A primary goal of Adlerian counseling is to point out to the client the overcompensation and defensive patterns the client is using to solve problems and to find more successful ways of solving problems related to school, play, and other social concerns.

The establishment of the counselor-client relationship is the key step in the process. The counselor's job is to reeducate children who have developed mistaken ideas about some concepts of their lives. The counseling relationship assumes that the counselor and child are equal partners in the process and that the child is a responsible person who can learn better ways to meet personal needs. The positive view of human nature is indicated through the counselor's faith, hope, and caring attitude toward the child.

Adlerians believe that lives are holistic. Dinkmeyer, Pew, and Dinkmeyer (1979) refer to *teleoanalytic holistic theory,* which regards any troubled or troublesome behavior as a reflection of one indivisible, unified, whole organism moving toward self-created goals. The foremost task of Adlerian counselors is to prove this unity in people, in their thinking, feeling, and behavior—in fact, in every expression of their personality (Ansbacher & Ansbacher, 1956). Adlerians believe that children are the artists of their own personalities and are constantly moving purposefully toward self-consistent goals. An information interview based on questions used in the adult lifestyle analysis helps to reveal the pictures children have painted of their lives and their current personality development. The information interview consists of present and past (early) recollections of the children themselves and their families, how they fit into the family constellation, and how they perceive siblings and parents in relation to themselves. Questions often used include those in the following structured, interview guide:

Information interview guide

1. What type of concern or problem would you like to discuss, and how did this problem develop?
2. On a 5-point scale, how are things going for you? (Great 1 or 2, medium 3 or 4, poor 5)
   In school?_____
   With your friends?_____
   With your hobbies?_____
   With your parents?_____
   With your brothers and sisters?_____
   With your fun times?_____
3. Can you tell me about your mother and father? (Separate the answers for mother and father or for any other parent figures living at home.)
   What do they do?
   What do they want you to do?
   How do you get along with them?
   How are you like your parents?
   How are you different from your parents?
4. What things in your family would you like to be better?
5. Can you tell me about your brothers and sisters? (Make a list of children in the family, from eldest to youngest, with their ages.) Of all your brothers and sisters, who is:
   Most like you? How?
   Most different from you?* How?
6. What kind of child are you?
7. What kind of child did you used to be?
8. What scares you most?
9. What used to scare you most?
10. Have any of your brothers or sisters been sick or hurt?
11. What does each of the children in your family do best?
12. Who is the smartest?
    Best athlete?
    Mother's favorite?
    Father's favorite?
    Hardest worker?
    Best behaved?
    Funniest?
    Most spoiled?

---

* The sibling most different from the client usually has the greatest influence on the client's lifestyle.

Best in mathematics?*
Best in spelling?*
Best in penmanship?*
Most stubborn?
Best looking?
Friendliest?
Strongest?
Healthiest?
Best musician?
Best with tools?

The counselor uses these and other questions initially to explore the pictures children have painted of their lives. The information is also helpful in assessing how children are developing their lifestyles. The interview can also help older adolescents and adults understand their lifestyles.

Terner and Pew (1978) recommended examining the client's personality structure (the lifestyle). They divided the counseling process into four phases.

Phase I: The first phase includes an examination of the formative years of the person in his or her family constellation. For younger children, this phase is an ongoing or current event; it is an early recollection of an older adolescent or an adult.

Phase II: The second phase is focused on collecting early recollections (ERs) from the client's past, which are detailed in the next section of this chapter.

Phase III: The third phase's objective is to illustrate for clients what they are doing in their lives and the principles under which they are operating. Clients are confronted with the goals they are attempting to reach.

Phase IV: The fourth phase is reorientation toward living through an encouragement process designed to build clients' self-confidence. The counselor assesses strengths within clients in lieu of the problems that need to be solved and attends to how clients make themselves sick and what they need to recover. The counselor identifies discouragement, the loss of self-confidence, as the root of all deficiencies.

Early Recollections (ERs)

Counselors use early recollections to understand the child's earliest impressions of life and how the child felt about them. They ask children to remember as far back as they can, particularly recollections of specific incidents, as detailed as possible, including the child's reaction at the time. "If we took a snapshot when that happened, what would we see? How did you feel?" Three to six of those early

---

* These three school subjects relate to the child's personality development. Good mathematics students are good personal problem solvers. Good spellers and good writers (good in penmanship) are generally well-behaved children who follow rules and cooperate with the social order.

recollections help to show a pattern in the lifestyle. These recollections tend to reflect a prototype that is apparent in the lifestyle analysis. Although the occurrences children relate may not be factually accurate, they are true insofar as they reflect the children's memories and feelings. The counselor then has a clearer idea of the child's basic view of life and how some attitudes may have mistakenly crystallized. Examples of themes that may appear in these recollections and the child's accompanying mistaken beliefs include the following:

1. *Early dangers:* Be aware of the many hostile aspects of life.
2. *Happy times with adults around:* Life is great as long as many people praise and serve me.
3. *Misdeeds recalled:* Be very careful that they do not happen again.

Myer and James (1991) presented useful guidelines on ERs as an assessment technique to discern children's behavior patterns. A nonverbal child can produce ERs as drawings and other types of play media. Counselors can make ERs a memory game or a "make up a story about when you were small" game. Modeling what the child is to do may be helpful. At least three ERs are needed to find a child's pattern of behaviors. The process should not be rushed. The counselor's job is to help the child teach the counselor about his or her situation by summarizing content and feelings. Open-ended statements are good if the counselor is not leading the child into one of the counselor's own ERs. Myer and James recommend paying attention to context (for example, a child alone may indicate isolation), content (for example, recurring topics such as food, water, animals, and wearing boots have special significance for the child), persons (for example, family members left in and out of the story), movement (for example, passivity and compliance may indicate discouragement), and feelings (for example, hot and cold feeling words tell much about the child's outlook on life). The counselor must be careful to avoid overinterpreting or underinterpreting ERs in planning interventions for children.

Understanding. Counselors must be very understanding with children. No matter what they are doing, they are probably doing the best they can at the moment. Ways of relieving some anxiety and conflict include helping them interpret what is happening and giving the problem, child, or action a "handle." Use encouragement. Change negative situations to positive ones by telling fables where appropriate: "The Miller and the Donkey" helps children understand they can never please everyone, even by absurdly attempting the impossible. "The Frogs in the Milk" tells about two frogs who jumped into a barrel of milk and simply paddled until they made butter; they were then able to jump out easily.

Confrontation. When children are unable to change the mistaken ideas behind their behavior, confrontation is necessary (Myer & James, 1986). A counselor can confront children with educated guesses about the goals they are trying to achieve at others' expense. Be aware also of the child who sees the counselor as an obstacle and is using depreciation. Typically, the child is unwilling to move in a direction indicated by the counselor and attempts avoidance or wastes time. Counselors are advised to stay out of these power struggles.

Stages. Actual changes in children's perspectives occur in stages. First, children are limited to afterthoughts of insight: They can clearly see what they are doing to cause mistaken ideas or unhappiness to persist, but only after they have misbehaved. In the second stage, children become able to catch themselves in the act of misbehaving. Added awareness enables them to sensitize themselves to inappropriate behavior. In the next stage, children have developed a heightened sense of awareness that enables them to anticipate the situation and plan a more appropriate behavior or response.

Research and Theory on Early Recollections

Lord (1982), in a study of the validity of early recollections for clinical use, asked 10 children (age 6½ to 8) to write one early recollection each; 10 graduate students were asked to do the same. The recollections were rated according to 13 variables: success/failure, active/passive, we/I, confident/inferior, praise/ blame, participant/observer, obedient/defiant, benevolent/hostile, reward/ punishment, secure/jeopardize, pampered/mistreated, cheerful/depressed, and pleasure/pain. Any of these categories voted as not appearing in the recollection were rated as neutral (absence ratings). Two hypotheses were tested: (1) Children do not have sufficient thematic apperceptions to use in lifestyle analysis. (2) Children's thematic apperceptions vary so much in clinical interpretation that the content cannot be communicated as well as that of adults. Both hypotheses were proven false, indicating that counselors can use ERs in analyzing children's lifestyles and behavior goals.

Further support for using ERs appears in a study by Kopp and Der (1982). They compared the early recollections of two groups of adolescents who had been referred for counseling. The two groups, classified as active and passive, were asked to rate six early recollections on the Role/Activity Scale in Early Recollections, which indicates the degree to which a person is active in memory and if the person is an initiator or a responder. The active group had significantly higher scores on the Role/Activity Scale, indicating support for early recollections analysis as a viable method for examining present lifestyle.

Investigating early recollections and criminal behavior in mentally ill homeless men, Grunberg (1989) found that very few of their ERs were positive. Most ERs (before age 8) involved conflict, loneliness, defiance of authority, or victimization. Of those participants who reported negative ERs, 92% had been convicted of a crime. The ERs might be more reflective of a person's present rather than past condition, but that is not a problem when counselors try to obtain a picture of how their clients view life.

Coram and Hafner (1988) found that hypnosis produced ERs that contained more themes about mothers, misdeeds, hostility, motor activities, and mastery. It also led to qualitatively different recollections, with more detail, but did not affect productivity.

Jorgensen and Newlon (1988), analyzing the lifestyle themes of 10 unwed, pregnant adolescents who chose to keep their babies, found that all felt a lack of self-esteem and a need for positive attention. Pregnancies were hypothesized to be deliberate attempts to gain closeness and excitement. Birth order, found not to be a determinant in who would deliberately become pregnant, was a factor in how pregnancy was handled. The ERs of firstborns and only children focused on life's "shoulds" and responsibilities; ERs of later-born children emphasized being the center of attention and blaming others for their behavior.

Studying Vietnam veterans with posttraumatic stress disorder (PTSD), Hyer, Woods, and Boudewyns (1989) found that their ERs contained more negative themes and less social interest than the average range of responses.

Lingg and Kottman (1991) have used visualization to work with ERs. Visualization of the ER scenario allows the client to go back to the situation and repair damage done or to protect and reassure self and others who might have been harmed. More important, the client has the opportunity to reprogram any faulty self-messages that originated from the early recollection situation.

Finally, Bishop (1993) recommended upgrading the validity and reliability of the interpretations of ERs. He proposed that ER interpretations be integrated into systematic, psychometric evaluations with categories for analyzing and classifying ERs. Then researchers could obtain normative data on ERs.

Interventions for the Four Goals of Misbehavior

The four goals of misbehavior are intended to help parents, teachers, and counselors understand that *how they feel* about what the child is doing most clearly explains the *child's* mistaken goal. (Dreikurs & Soltz, 1964) analysis and description of the four mistaken goals, (attention, power, revenge, and withdrawal), the ways of identifying them, and the methods of correction have resulted in an impressive array of guidance and counseling approaches to help discouraged children and their discouraged families. The steps he outlines for determining a child's mistaken goals—learning the adult's corrective response to misbehavior and the child's reaction to the correction—are both penetrating and simple. The counselor who understands the child's goal can, through counseling with the child and parents, help the child develop a constructive goal and appropriate behavior.

In describing and analyzing specific immediate goals, Dreikurs and his colleagues have focused primarily on preadolescents. Dreikurs notes that, in early childhood, the children's status depends on the impression they make on adults. Later, they may develop different goals to gain social significance in their peer group and, later still, in adult society. These original goals can still be observed in people of every age. However, they are not all-inclusive; teenagers and adults have other goals of misbehavior based on irrational self-messages (see chapter 7). Dreikurs reminds us that people can often achieve status and prestige more easily through useless and destructive means than through accomplishment.

Dreikurs advocates modifying the motivation rather than the behavior itself. When the motivation changes, more constructive behavior follows automatically.

The "four-goal technique" requires the following steps:

1. Observe the child's behavior in detail.
2. Be psychologically sensitive to one's own reaction.
3. Confront the child with the goal of the behavior.
4. Note the recognition reflex.
5. Apply appropriate corrective procedures.

Remember that misbehaving children are discouraged children trying to find their place; they are acting on the faulty logic that their misbehavior will give them the social acceptance that they desire. Goal 1, attention getting, is a manifestation of minor discouragement; Goal 4, display of inadequacy is a manifestation of deep discouragement. Sometimes a child switches from one kind of misbehavior to another, which is often a signal that the discouragement is growing worse.

To identify young children's goals, the counselor's own immediate response to their behavior is most helpful. It is in line with their expectations. The following four examples of behaviors show how the adult may feel, what the child may be thinking, what alternate behaviors exist, and what questions may come to mind about the child's behavior.

Attention

You are annoyed; you begin coaxing, reminding.
Charlie thinks he belongs only when he is noticed.
You can (1) attend to the child when he is behaving appropriately; or
(2) ignore misbehavior (scolding reinforces attention-getting behavior).
You can ask: Could it be that you want me to notice you?

Power

You are angry, provoked, and threatened.
Linda thinks she belongs only when she is in control or the boss.
You can withdraw or "take your sail out of her wind" by leaving the room.
You can ask: (1) Could it be that you want to be the boss?
(2) Could it be that you want me to do what you want?

Revenge

You are deeply hurt and want to get even.
Sally thinks her only hope is to get even.
You can (1) use group and individual encouragement; and
(2) try to convince her she is liked.
You can ask: Could it be that you want to hurt me?

Inadequacy

You are feeling helpless and don't know what to do.

Tom thinks he is unable to do anything and that he belongs only when people expect nothing of him.

You can show genuine faith in the child and use encouragement.

You can ask: Could it be that you feel stupid and don't want people to know?

A counseling interview that uses the four "Could it be?" questions might go as follows:

Counselor: Alice, do you know why you did (the misbehavior)?

Alice: No. (This may be an honest response.)

Counselor: Would you like to work with me so that we can find out? I have some ideas that might help us explain what you are trying to get when you do _____ . Will you help me figure this out?

Alice: Okay.

Counselor: (using one question at a time, in a nonjudgmental, unemotional tone of voice):

1. Could it be that you want Mr. Jones to notice you more and give you some special attention?
2. Could it be that you would like to be boss and have things your own way in Mr. Jones's class?
3. Could it be that you have been hurt and you want to get even by hurting Mr. Jones and others in the class?
4. Could it be that you want Mr. Jones to leave you alone and to stop asking you all those questions in math?

The counselor always asks all four of these questions sequentially, regardless of the child's answers or reflex because the child may be operating on more than one goal at a time. The counselor observes the body language and listens carefully for the response in order to catch the "recognition reflex." An accurate disclosure of the child's present intentions produces a recognition reflex such as a "guilty" facial expression, which is a reliable indication of his or her goal, even though the child may say nothing or even say "no." Sometimes the confrontation itself helps the child change. Another indication of the child's goal is the child's response to correction. Children who are seeking attention and get it from the teacher stop the misbehavior temporarily and then repeat it or do something similar. Children who seek power refuse to stop the disturbance or even increase it. Those who seek revenge respond to the teacher's efforts to get them to stop by switching to some more violent action. Instead of cooperating, a child with Goal 4 remains entirely passive and inactive.

Once the counselor suspects the goal of the child's misbehavior, confronting the child is most important. The purpose of this confrontation is to disclose and confirm the mistaken goal of the child. The emphasis is on "for what purpose," not "why."

The next step after identifying the goal of misbehavior is to choose and use appropriate corrective procedures, which may range from encouragement to logical consequences.

Encouragement

Dreikurs and Soltz (1964) wrote that encouragement implies faith in and respect for children as they are. One should not discourage children by having extremely high standards and ambitions for them. Children misbehave only when they are discouraged and believe they cannot succeed by other means. In fact, one evaluation of counseling is how far the child has moved from feeling discouraged toward feeling encouraged. Children need encouragement as plants need water and sunshine. Telling children they can be better implies they are not good enough as they are.

Problems with Dreikurs's ideas on encouragement arise when parents ask how they are supposed to *not* expect children performing below their ability levels to do better. The answer seems to be in loving children unconditionally in spite of their behavior and performance. One does not have to love their misbehavior or pretend to love it.

Encouragement is advocated in place of praise and reinforcement; bribery is strongly discouraged. Adlerians see praise as a message that tells children that, under conditions determined by the adult, they are okay. Praise focuses on the product. Encouragement, however, accepts children where they are; it focuses on the process. Encouragement occurs *before* the child completes a task or even starts it.

- "I am proud of you."
- "That's a rough one, but I think you have what it takes to work it out."
- "I know you can do it; let me help you get started."

Praise

Praise (reinforcement) occurs *after* the child performs a behavior or completes a task.

- "You certainly did a good job."
- "That was great work you did in math."
- "I like the way you handled that."
- "You played a good game."

Bribery

Bribery occurs *during* the child's misbehavior.

- "If you quiet down, I'll give you a candy bar."
- "I'll buy you a surprise if you stop fighting."
- "If you stop bothering me, you won't have to help with the dishes."

Adlerian counselors believe that extrinsic reward and illogical punishment have detrimental effects on the development of the child, particularly in the democratic atmosphere that prevails today. Only in an autocratic society are these reward and punishment systems an effective and necessary means of obtaining conformity; they presuppose a certain person is endowed with superior authority. Children may see rewards as one of their rights and soon demand a reward for everything they do if they are trained under this system. Children may interpret punishment as their right to punish others. In fact, children often are hurt more by their retaliation than they are hurt by the punishment. They are experts in knowing how to hurt their parents, whether by getting into trouble or by making low grades. Therefore, Adlerians reject reward and punishment methods that focus on extrinsic reinforcement in favor of encouragement, intrinsic reinforcement, and logical consequences.

To discover children's preference for praise or encouragement, Pety, Kelly, and Kafafy (1984) administered the Praise/Encouragement Preference Scale to 277 students in Grades 4, 6, 8, and 10. *Praise* was defined as emphasizing the worth of the child (for example, "Good boy" or "Good job"). *Encouragement* was defined as emphasizing nonjudgmental observations of achievement, improvement, or appreciation (for example, "You must be very proud of yourself"). Children in the fourth through eighth grades preferred receiving praise, but as children matured they began to prefer encouragement to a greater degree. Boys more than girls preferred praise over encouragement.

Rathvon (1990), studying the effects of encouragement on off-task behavior and academic performance of children, found that encouragement decreased off-task behavior for all five first-grade children in the study but failed to increase academic performance in 6 of 10 measures. The author used two types of encouragement with approximately equal success: *proximal,* defined as encouraging remarks given within approximately 1 meter of the student when the student was engaging in off-task behavior; and, *distal,* defined as the same treatment delivered from approximately 7 meters from the off-task child. Examples of encouragement included "You can do it," "Keep trying," "If you get stuck on one question, try the next," and "Keep it up."

Morawski (1992) presented an excellent idea to help students who have difficulties with reading and writing. The reading and writing question (TRWQ) is an adaptation of Adler's "The Question." Teachers ask students, "How would your life be different if you did not have any trouble with reading and/or writing?" Responses to the question are classified as: (a) functional, (b) not related to the school subject, or (c) organic. Data collected from TRWQ help teachers design corrective procedures that address the students' specific needs.

Natural and Logical Consequences

Natural and logical consequences are Adlerian techniques favored over reward and punishment because they allow children to experience the actual consequences of their behavior.

Natural consequences

Natural consequences are a direct result of children's behavior. Careless children who touch the hot stove get burned and become more careful of stoves in the future.

Natural consequences of irresponsible behavior are unfavorable outcomes that occur naturally without any prearranged plan or program. For example, if Sue leaves her baseball glove outside and it is ruined in a rainstorm, she has experienced a natural consequence. If I am late in making my airline reservation, I may find I cannot take the flight I want. Natural consequences to irresponsible behavior happen on their own, or naturally, without being planned and administered by others.

Logical consequences

Logical consequences, established through rules and family policy, are fair, direct, consistent, and logical results of a child's behavior. For example, if Frank comes home late for dinner, his family has assumed that he would have been home on time to eat or would have called if he were hungry. Therefore, they removed his plate from the table. He is allowed to fix any food he can as long as he cleans up after himself.

As another example of a logical consequence, if Mary breaks someone's window, she is asked to repair the damage or pay to have the damage repaired. If Mary does not have the cash or skill required to repair the damage, she could work off her debt by performing other jobs. In school, if John interferes with someone's right to learn, he is moved to a place where he cannot continue to do so (some form of isolation). In other words, the consequence fits the misbehavior; it is a logical consequence. Punishment, as defined by Adlerians, is any illogical consequence for irresponsible behavior. For example, if Frank is late for dinner, he gets paddled and sent to bed. The punishment or consequence does not match the crime, but it teaches children that bigger people get to overpower smaller people. Children reared under a punishment-by-power system become very impressed with power and use it whenever they can to get what they want.

Both natural and logical consequences allow children to experience the results of their behavior instead of arbitrary punishment exercised through the parent's personal authority. These two techniques direct children's motivation toward proper behavior through personal experience with the social order in which they live. We are not recommending, however, that adults *not* protect children in dangerous situations, for example, teaching children about the dangers of street traffic through personal experience!

Natural and logical consequences focus on the Adlerian belief that people are responsible and capable of leading full, happy lives. Consequences allow the child to understand an inner message that is more likely to be remembered than punishment, which can harm the relationship with a child.

Natural and logical consequences give children the message that they are capable of making their own decisions. They have an opportunity for growth through weighing alternatives and arriving at a decision. Given overly severe limits, however, the child is deprived of making decisions that foster self-respect and responsibility. Children need to do for themselves what they are capable of doing.

◆ ◆ ◆

C A S E   S T U D Y

Identification of the Problem

J. B., a 9-year-old boy in the fourth grade at Spoonbill Elementary School, was referred to our group by the teacher because of his classroom behavior. J. B. repeatedly leaves his seat and does not complete his work.

Individual and Background Information

Academic. According to J. B.'s teacher, J. B. does less than average work. Most of his grades are "U." He does not usually complete his assignments; when he does, he hurries and commits many errors. His teacher believes that he is not working up to his potential in many areas: His test scores support her view that J. B. is an underachiever, and J. B. loves to read. His teacher reported that J. B.'s behavior sometimes annoyed her, and at other times made her angry. She mentioned that she was discouraged about his schoolwork.

Family. J. B. is the youngest son of an older father and stepmother. The sibling closest to his age is 19. He came to live with his father last year after spending time in a home for boys because of his abusive mother. Recently his stepmother threatened to send him back to the home for boys if he did not behave in school.

Social. J. B. has a friendly personality and seems to relate well with his peers.

Counseling Method

The counselor used the Adlerian counseling method to help J. B. identify the goals of his behavior and how well he was meeting his goals. They spent considerable time on helping J. B. understand what he did to get himself in trouble at school and what he could do to make his life more pleasant at school and home. They looked at ways J. B. could meet his goals without getting into trouble.

Transcript

Counselor: Well, J. B., it is good to see you again. We need to check up on how things are going with you in Ms. Johnson's room.

J. B.:   Did she tell you I have been bad?

Counselor: She feels discouraged about your schoolwork.

J. B.:   Sometimes it is just too hard.

Counselor: So sometimes you feel discouraged too.

J. B.:   Yeah, I sure do.

Counselor: It is sort of like sometimes you don't get the help you need.

J. B.:   She won't look at me when I raise my hand to get her to help.

Counselor: That must be frustrating to you. Do you know what I mean by frustrating?

J. B.:   Yeah, I get mad and go up by her desk, and she tells me to get back in my seat.

Counselor: So a lot of bad things seem to happen, one right after another one, and you just keep getting angrier.

J. B.:   That's right!

Counselor: Well, J. B., we've got some work to do. We need to figure out what you are trying to get and if you are getting what you want.

J. B.:   What do you mean?

Counselor: If we can find out what goals you are trying to reach we will be able to figure out what you need to do to get what you want without getting into trouble.

J. B.:   I'm not trying to get anything.

Counselor: Could be; let's check it out.

J. B.:   Okay, I guess.

Counselor: J. B., could it be when you do your work poorly or don't do it at all, you want to get Ms. Johnson to leave you alone?

J. B.:   What do you mean?

Counselor: Maybe if you convince her you can't do the work, she and your parents will get off your back about making better grades.

J. B.:   Sometimes I really do try to do it all.

Counselor: So, you really haven't given up on making better grades.

J. B.:   Oh, no, I haven't.

Counselor: Well, could it be you would like to have Ms. Johnson pay more attention to you, and the way to do that is break rules about talking out of turn and leaving your seat?

J. B.:   Yeah, sometimes she really loses it and everybody laughs.

Counselor: So, you end up getting a lot of attention, some good and some bad.

J. B.:   Yeah, but it's worth it.

Counselor: You seemed pleased with having the attention and don't mind the consequences or bad stuff that happens to you.

J. B.:   Well, I do wish I could move back to my old seat. I don't like sitting right in front of the teacher's desk.

Counselor: So attention is important to you, but sitting close to the teacher is not what you want.

J. B.:   You got that right! Can you get me moved?

Counselor: You and I can work on it. We might be able to figure out how.

J. B.:   Let's go for it!

Counselor: We have to figure out how to convince Ms. Johnson that you can be trusted to follow the class rules and do your work when you are sitting away from her desk.

J. B.:   How?

Counselor: Well, Joey, you know her a whole lot better than I do. I would like to know what you think would work.

J. B.:   Maybe I can make a deal. She likes deals.

Counselor: How would that work?

J. B.:   Well, I could ask her if I stay out of trouble and turn in all of my work for a whole week, could I move to my old seat?

Counselor: I wonder what she will say about how well your work needs to be done.

J. B.:   I could tell her that I will make at least a "B" in everything.

Counselor: Well, I guess you could try that. I wonder what she should do if you go back to your old seat and the old behavior comes back.

J. B.:   I guess I would have to go back to my old seat.

Counselor: Could be. Tell you what. If Ms. Johnson agrees to your plan, would you come by the office each day on your way home and give me the word on how your day went?

J. B.:   Sure.

Counselor: If it doesn't work out, come back tomorrow and we'll try to write a plan that will work.

J. B.:   See you.

Counselor: Let's shake hands on this deal. Hope it works out. See you tomorrow.

As noted in the interview transcript, the Adlerian counseling method works well in concert with many of the other counseling approaches discussed in the text. Gamble and Watkins (1983) presented an excellent case for combining the best of individual psychology and reality therapy in designing intervention plans for children. Using a case-study approach, they integrated motives, goals, and logical consequences with client self-evaluation, classroom meetings, and written contracts to design a successful intervention for a 12-year-old boy experiencing problems with school attendance, stealing, and peer relationships.

Pepper and Roberson (1983) integrated individual psychology and behavioral approaches in working with eight males (ages 12 to 14) in special education classes. They described the students as disruptive and engaging in power struggles with others. Encouragement, group discussions, and logical consequences were used with shaping (positive reinforcement and extinction) to bring about positive behavior change.

ADLERIAN FAMILY COUNSELING

Adlerian methods are well suited for counseling the entire family. The following interview guide is suggested:

1. Interview the parents on the following topics (while their children are observed in a playroom situation):
   a. Describe your children—their respective ordinal positions, schoolwork, hobbies, athletics, and so on.
   b. How does each child find his or her place in the family?
   c. What problems revolve around getting up? mealtime? TV? homework? chores? bedtime?
   d. Does something in your family need to be better?
   e. Would you like to make a change? (Before the counselor gives suggestions, it is preferable that the parents admit they are bankrupt in child-rearing ideas; that is, nothing has worked in improving the particular family concern.)
2. Interview the children on the following topics with the parents not present. (Use "Could it be?" questions when appropriate. Ask who is in charge of discipline.)
   a. Do you know why you are here today?
   b. Does anything bother you in the family that you would like to change?
   c. How can we make things better at home?
   d. Who is the good child?
   e. Who is Father's favorite?
   f. Who is Mother's favorite?
   g. Who is best in sports?
   h. What does each of you do best?
   i. Which are your best school subjects?*
   j. Which are your worst school subjects?*
3. Interview the entire family. Summarize plans for the coming week, clarifying roles, behaviors, and expectations. Recommendations for each family generally include the following:
   a. Provide individual parent time for each child, each day.
   b. Have one family conference per week.
   c. Do one family activity per week.
   d. Each family member does chores.

---

* For students who have the ability to do better and are not handicapped by a particular learning or perceptual disability, good math students are good personal problem solvers, and children good at spelling and penmanship are well behaved, follow the rules, and cooperate with the social order.

To evaluate the outcome of Adlerian family counseling, Croake and Hinckle (1983) followed a family study group model. They administered the MMPI, Child-Rearing Practice Scale, and Attitudes Toward the Freedom of Children Scale as pretest and posttest measures of the family counseling experience. They found significant positive changes on each of the scales, with married parents scoring the highest.

Berry (1983) used a case-study approach in Adlerian family counseling with two families having difficulty adjusting to rearing a handicapped child. The emphasis was on each child's strength and increased family involvement through the encouragement process.

Watkins (1984) presented a model for Adlerian family counseling as a viable alternative for treating crimes committed within the family (such as child abuse). Watkins applied two major Adlerian principles: (1) offering nothing for the client to resist and (2) building on family and personal strengths rather than focusing on weaknesses. Specific counseling steps included (1) breaking down the resistance between client and counselor, (2) discovering family strengths, and (3) planning and implementing activities that focus on family strengths.

Kern and Carlson (1981) suggested four Adlerian constructs for counselors to understand and implement in their work with families: (1) All problems are social problems; interpersonal relationships are more important than intrapersonal factors. (2) All behavior is purposeful; misbehavior has a way of maintaining the family at its present level. (3) Knowledge of the family constellation is necessary, as is how children perceive their position in the constellation. (4) Each family member strives to move from an inferior position to one of competence.

Nicoll (1984) provided a rationale for school counseling programs to provide family counseling services: (1) Referred families rarely follow through with counseling. (2) Counseling in the school setting may be less threatening. (3) Family counseling is more effective and economical than individual or group counseling. (4) The school counselor is able to add perceptions and input from the child's school behavior.

Casper and Zachary (1984) pointed out that cases of anorexia nervosa, bulimia, and obesity may result from a family's inability to solve problems or conflicts effectively. Eating disorders may communicate symbolically a failure to learn skills that enable the child to live effectively with others. Casper and Zachary provided checklists of effective family and coparenting goals to help family members recognize their role behavior and the family reactions to these roles.

Main and Oliver (1988) researched complementary, symmetrical, and parallel personality priorities as indicators of marital adjustment. Symmetric relationships occur when spouses' first priorities match; complementary relationships are defined as "opposites attract"; parallel relationships are a mixture of symmetric and complementary. Based on the Langenfeld Inventory of Personality Priorities and the Dyadic Adjustment Scale, couples with parallel relationships had significantly higher marital adjustment scores than did couples in complementary relationships.

Dinkmeyer (1988) based "marathon family counseling" on Adlerian psychology. The process, completed in one 8-hour day, focuses on family constellation, mutual respect, encouragement, and taking responsibility for one's behavior. Dinkmeyer described four stages:

Stage I: Orientation and organization
    a. Determine if this type of counseling is suitable for the family.
    b. Obtain family background information.
    c. Arrange for family members to participate.
Stage II: Exploration
    a. Give overview and summary of Stage I.
    b. Obtain an overview of the family's life circumstances.
    c. Explore problems in more depth.
Stage III: Action
    a. Encourage family members to commit to doing something to improve the family situation.
    b. Confront family members who are reluctant to change.
    c. Encourage family members to take responsibility for their own behavior.
Stage IV: Termination
    a. Have family members talk about their commitments to change and how they will accomplish their goals.
    b. Thank family members for participating in the session.
    c. Talk individually with family members who want more counseling.

Pew (1989) outlined another method for conducting brief marriage therapy, Adlerian style, that may extend over several sessions.

1. The counselor and couple discuss why the couple is seeking counseling.
2. The counselor and couple discuss the couple's goals for counseling.
3. The counselor shares expectations.
4. The counselor draws a family constellation for each person and uses this and ERs to construct a lifestyle form for each client.
5. The couple works on the basic marriage skills of conflict resolution, communication, and doing fun things together.
6. The couple uses the paradoxical strategies of practicing at home those things that annoy each partner.
7. The couple keeps daily journal entries of feelings, thoughts, and behaviors.

Freeman, Carlson, and Sperry (1993) conducted a descriptive study of adapting Adlerian family counseling to middle-income couples coping with economic stress. The Adlerian emphasis on skill building, problem solving, goal setting, and rational thinking helped the couples deal with economic stress and its side effects on their marriages: hostile interaction, reduced self-esteem, and decreased supportive behavior. They followed Dinkmeyer's (1988) four-stage conflict-resolution model.

Parent Education

Parent education has been a significant part of Adler's system from the beginning. Several parent education packages have been published and used successfully over the past several years. In addition, parent education groups meet regularly around the country.

Weaver (1980) and Pelley (1980), in separate studies, have shown the effectiveness of the Adlerian method in training parents to parent more effectively. Both studies employed the Dinkmeyer and McKay (1976) Systematic Training for Effective Parenting (STEP) kit for use with parent groups. Weaver found the method more effective with mothers from middle socioeconomic levels and somewhat less effective with mothers from lower socioeconomic levels. Pelley found the method more effective in stimulating group interaction in parent groups using the materials than in groups not using the materials. Both studies supported the transferability of group learning to the home setting.

Bundy and Poppen (1986) reviewed research on the effectiveness of elementary school counselors as parent educators. In eight successful studies with parents, four counselors used Adlerian psychology, three used parent effectiveness training, and one used a multimodal approach.

Comparing research on behavioral, Adlerian, and communications approaches to parent training, Krebs (1986) found the Adlerian approach fostered more democratic parenting practices. The STEP approach, based on the Adlerian model, was effective with both parents and children. Children became more responsible and considerate and better problem solvers. The author saw behavioral programs, based on rewards and punishment, as more difficult to implement and too heavily focused on behavior as opposed to courses of behavior. The author found the communications approach, similar to parent effectiveness training (PET), effective in moving parents away from a power model to a cooperation model of parenting. However, as Dembo, Switzer, and Lauritzen (1985) warned, parent training programs are not well researched.

In summary, Adler favored efforts directed toward prevention of mental illness through parent education programs. He recognized the difficulty of undoing in adulthood the wrongs done to children.

Kottman and Wilborn (1992) compared counselor-led parent groups and parent-led parent groups and found that both were equally effective except that the counselor-led groups performed better on causation of children's behavior. The parent group leaders were trained in the Adlerian method by an experienced counselor. Breaking the cycle of bad parenting practices that were passed from one generation to the next was the cornerstone of Adler's parent education program.

SUMMARY

Watkins (1992) found research activity on Adlerian theory quite active. Since 1981, birth order had received the most attention (25 studies), followed by early recollection (23), social interest (21), lifestyle (7), and other related topics (27), for a total of 103 studies.

Critics of the Adlerian system agree that, although it explains much of our behavior, it tends to oversimplify some of the complex human behaviors brought to the counseling interview. Not everyone can be sorted into a birth-order category or a particular goal of misbehavior. Many Adlerian assumptions are nothing more than broad generalizations. Are we not all motivated by power and the drive to compensate for our inferiority as we seek to find a place in this world? Furthermore, the Adlerian system has a contradiction. On one hand, the basis of learning potential is striving to compensate for feelings of inferiority; on the other hand, the pessimist or the one who poses the greatest learning problem is characterized by deep feelings of inferiority. Adlerian counseling, like psychoanalytic counseling, puts the child on the spot: the child is wrong, and the counselor is right. Mosak (1991) disagreed, however, pointing out that Adlerian psychology prides itself on being a growth psychology. Treatment has focused on reeducation rather than healing. In fact, the current trend is away from the concept that the child is wrong and the adult is right. Parents, teachers, and counselors are often wrong, and many times counseling and consulting interventions with children involve change in the adult's behavior.

The Adlerian counseling system offers a wealth of techniques for counseling children and families. Many other counseling theorists have borrowed, both knowingly and unknowingly, from Adler's work. His commonsense ideas on effective counseling have been with us since the early 1900s. Perhaps Adler's most significant contribution was demystifying psychotherapy and making it practical and available to the general public.

REFERENCES

Adler, A. (1964). *Social interest: A challenge to mankind.* New York: Capricorn. (Original work published 1938.)

Alexander, F., Eisenstein, S., & Grotjahn, M. (1966). *Psychoanalytic pioneers.* New York: Basic Books.

Ansbacher, H. (1992). Alfred Adler's concepts of community feeling and social interest and the relevance of community feeling for old age. *Individual Psychology: The Journal of Adlerian Theory, Research, and Practice, 48,* 402–412.

Ansbacher, H., & Ansbacher, R. (1956). *The individual psychology of Alfred Adler: A systematic presentation in selections from his writings.* New York: Basic Books.

Barkley, H., Wilborn, B., & Towers, M. (1984). Social interest in a peer training program. *Individual Psychology: The Journal of Adlerian Theory, Research, and Practice, 40,* 295–299.

Berry, J. (1983). Adlerian family counseling: A strengths approach. *Individual Psychology: The Journal of Adlerian Theory, Research, and Practice, 39,* 419–424.

Bishop, R. (1993). Applying psychometric principles to the clinical use of early recollections. *Individual Psychology, 49,* 153–164.

Bloser, E., & Thompson, C. (1996). *Birth order and marital adjustment.* Manuscript in preparation.

Brannon, J., & Jacques, R. (1989). The mistaken goals of adolescence in residential group treatment of juvenile offenders. *Individual Psychology: The Journal of Adlerian Theory, Research, and Practice, 45,* 376–380.

Bundy, M., & Poppen, W. (1986). School counselors' effectiveness as consultants: A research review. *Elementary School Guidance and Counseling, 20,* 215–222.

Casper, D., & Zachary, D. (1984). The eating disorder as a maladaptive conflict resolution. *Individual Psychology: The Journal of Adlerian Theory, Research, and Practice, 40,* 445–452.

Coram, G., & Hafner, J. (1988). Early recollections and hypnosis. *Individual Psychology: The Journal of Adlerian Theory, Research, and Practice, 44,* 472–479.

Croake, J., & Hinckle, D. (1983). Adlerian family counseling education. *Individual Psychology: The Journal of Adlerian Theory, Research, and Practice, 39,* 247–258.

Davis, D., Cahan, S., & Bashi, J. (1977). Birth order and intellectual development: The confluence model in the light of cross-cultural evidence. *Science, 196,* 1470–1472.

Dembo, M., Switzer, M., & Lauritzen, P. (1985). An evaluation of group parent education: Behavioral, PET, and Adlerian programs. *Review of Educational Research, 55,* 155 200.

Dewey, E. (1971). Family atmosphere. In A. Nikelly (Ed.), *Techniques for behavior change: Applications for Adlerian theory.* Springfield, Ill: Thomas. pp. 41–47.

Dinkmeyer, D. (1988). Marathon family counseling. *Individual Psychology: The Journal of Adlerian Theory, Research, and Practice, 44,* 210–215.

Dinkmeyer, D., Pew, W., & Dinkmeyer, D., Jr. (1979). *Adlerian counseling and psychotherapy.* Monterey, CA: Brooks/Cole.

Dreikurs, R., & Soltz, V. (1964). *Children: The challenge.* New York: Hawthorn/Dutton.

Fakouri, M. (1974). Relationships of birth order, dogmatism, and achievement motivation. *Journal of Individual Psychology, 30,* 216–220.

Fish, R., & Mozdzierz, G. (1988). Validation of the Sulliman Scale of Social Interest with psychotherapy outpatients. *Individual Psychology: The Journal of Adlerian Theory, Research, and Practice, 44,* 307–315.

Freeman, C., Carlson, J., & Sperry, L. (1993). Adlerian marital therapy strategies with middle income couples facing financial stress. *American Journal of Family Therapy, 21,* 324–332.

Gamble, C., & Watkins, C., Jr. (1983). Combining the child discipline approaches of Alfred Adler and William Glasser: A case study. *Individual Psychology: The Journal of Adlerian Theory, Research, and Practice, 39,* 156–164.

Grunberg, J. (1989). Early recollections and criminal behavior in mentally-ill homeless men. *Individual Psychology: The Journal of Adlerian Theory, Research, and Practice, 45,* 289–299.

Harris, K., & Morrow, K. (1992). Differential effects of birth order and gender on perceptions of responsibility and dominance. *Individual Psychology, 48,* 109—117.

Hjelle, L. A. (1975). Relationship of social interest to internal-external control and self-actualization in young women. *Journal of Individual Psychology, 31,* 171–182.

Horn, J. M., & Turner, R. G. (1975). Birth order effects among unwed mothers. *Journal of Individual Psychology, 31,* 71–78.

Horney, K. (1950). *Neurosis and human growth.* New York: Norton.

Hyer, L., Woods, M., & Boudewyns, P. (1989). Early recollections of Vietnam veterans with PTSD. *Individual Psychology: The Journal of Adlerian Theory, Research, and Practice, 45*, 300–312.

Jorgensen, J., & Newton, B. (1988). Lifestyle themes of unwed, pregnant adolescents who chose to keep their babies. *Individual Psychology: The Journal of Adlerian Theory, Research, and Practice, 44*, 466–471.

Kern, R., & Carlson, J. (1981). Adlerian family counseling, *Elementary School Guidance and Counseling, 15*, 301–306.

Kern, R., Hawes, E., & Christensen, O. (1989). *Couples therapy: An Adlerian perspective.* Minneapolis: Educational Media Corporation.

Kfir, N. (1989). *Crisis intervention verbatim.* New York: Hemisphere.

Kopp, R., & Der, D. (1982). Level of activity in adolescents' early recollections: A validity study. *Individual Psychology: The Journal of Adlerian Theory, Research, and Practice, 38*, 213–222.

Kottman, T. (1992). Billy, the teddy bear boy. In Golden, L., & Norwich, M. (Eds.), *Case studies in child counseling.* New York: Macmillan.

Kottman, T., & Johnson, V. (1993). Adlerian play therapy: A tool for school counselors. *Elementary School Guidance and Counseling, 28(1)*, 42–51.

Kottman, T., & Stiles, K. (1990). The mutual storytelling technique: An Adlerian application in child therapy. *Individual Psychology: The Journal of Adlerian Theory, Research, and Practice, 46*, 148–156.

Kottman, T., & Warlick, J. (1989). Adlerian play therapy: Practical considerations. *Individual Psychology: The Journal of Adlerian Theory, Research, and Practice, 45*, 433–446.

Kottman, T., & Wilborn, B. (1992). Parents helping parents: Multiplying the counselor's effectiveness. *School Counselor, 40*, 10–14.

Krebs, L. (1986). Current research on theoretically based parenting programs. *Individual Psychology: The Journal of Adlerian Theory, Research, and Practice, 42*, 375–387.

Leak, G., & Gardner, L. (1990). Sexual attitudes, love attitudes, and social interest. *Individual Psychology: The Journal of Adlerian Theory, Research, and Practice, 46*, 55–60.

Leak, G., & Williams, D. (1989a). Relationship between social interest, alienation, and psychological hardiness. *Individual Psychology: The Journal of Adlerian Theory, Research, and Practice, 45*, 369–374.

Leak, G., & Williams, D. (1989b). Relationship between social interest and perceived family environment. *Individual Psychology: The Journal of Adlerian Theory, Research, and Practice, 45*, 362–367.

Lingg, M., & Kottman, T. (1991). Changing mistaken beliefs through visualization of early recollections. *Individual Psychology, 47*, 255–260.

Lord, D. B. (1982). On the clinical use of children's early rehabilitations. *Individual Psychology: The Journal of Adlerian Theory, Research, and Practice, 38*, 198–206.

Main, R., & Oliver, R. (1988). Complementary, symmetrical, and parallel personality priorities as indicators of marital adjustment. *Individual Psychology: The Journal of Adlerian Theory, Research, and Practice, 44*, 324–331.

Manly, L. (1986). Goals of misbehavior inventory. *Elementary School Guidance and Counseling, 21*, 160–161.

Mattice, E. (1976). *Dreikurs' goals of misbehavior theory: Child and teacher generation of a neo-Adlerian construct.* Unpublished doctoral dissertation, University of Tennessee, Knoxville.

Meunier, G., & Royce, S. (1988). Age and social interest. *Individual Psychology: The Journal of Adlerian Theory, Research, and Practice, 44,* 49–52.

Morawski, C. (1992). "The reading and writing question" as a classroom therapeutic intervention. *Individual Psychology, 48,* 203–217.

Mosak, H. (1973). *Alfred Adler: His influence on psychology today.* Park Ridge, NJ: Noyes Press.

Mosak, H. (1991). Where have all the normal people gone? *Individual Psychology, 47(4),* 437–446.

Myer, R., & James, R. (1986, February). *Confrontation: A strategy for counseling.* Paper presented at the Tennessee Association for Counseling and Development State Conference, Gatlinburg.

Myer, R., & James, R. (1991). Using early recollections as an assessment technique with children. *Elementary School Guidance and Counseling, 25,* 228–232.

Nicoll, W. (1984). School counselors as family counselors: A rationale and training model. *School Counselor, 31,* 279–284.

Nystul, M. S. (1974). The effects of birth order and sex on self concept. *Journal of Individual Psychology, 30,* 211–215.

Nystul, M. S. (1986). The hidden reason behind children's misbehavior. *Elementary School Guidance and Counseling, 20,* 188–193.

Orgler, H. (1965). *Alfred Adler: The man and his work.* New York: Capricorn.

Ostrovsky, M., Parr, G., & Gradel, A. (1992). Promoting moral development through social interest in children and adolescents. *Individual Psychology, 48,* 218–225.

Pelley, A. (1980, March). *Family involvement in guidance programs.* Paper presented at the American Personnel and Guidance Association Convention, Atlanta.

Pepper, F., & Roberson, M. (1983). The integration of Adlerian behavioral approaches in the classroom management of emotionally handicapped children. *Individual Psychology: The Journal of Adlerian Theory, Research, and Practice, 39,* 165–172.

Pety, J., Kelly, F., & Kafafy, A. (1984). The praise-encouragement preference scale for children. *Individual Psychology: The Journal of Adlerian Theory, Research, and Practice, 40,* 92–101.

Pew, M. (1989). Brief marriage therapy. *Individual Psychology: The Journal of Adlerian Theory, Research, and Practice, 45,* 191–200.

Phillips, A., Bedeian, A., Mossholder, K., & Touliatos, J. (1988). Birth order and selected work-related personality variables. *Individual Psychology: The Journal of Adlerian Theory, Research, and Practice, 44,* 492–501.

Porter, B., & Hoedt, K. (1985). Differential effects of an Adlerian counseling approach with pre-adolescent children. *Individual Psychology: The Journal of Adlerian Theory, Research, and Practice, 41,* 372–385.

Poston, D., Jr., & Falbo, T. (1990). Academic performance and personality traits of Chinese children: Onlies vs. others. *American Journal of Sociology, 96,* 433–451.

Rathvon, N. (1990). The effects of encouragement on off-task behavior and academic productivity. *Elementary School Guidance and Counseling, 24,* 189–199.

Reimanis, G. (1974). Anomie, crime, childhood memories, and development of social interest. *Journal of Individual Psychology, 30,* 53–58.

Rule, W. (1991). Birth order and sex as related to memory of parental strictness-permissiveness. *Psychological Reports, 68,* 908–911.

Shulman, B., & Mosak, H. (1977). Birth order and ordinal position: Two Adlerian views. *Individual Psychology, 33,* 114–121.

Stein, S., DeMiranda, S., & Stein, A. (1988). Birth order, substance abuse, and criminality. *Individual Psychology: The Journal of Adlerian Theory, Research, and Practice, 44,* 500–506.

Stiles, K., & Wilborn, B. (1992). A lifestyle instrument for children. *Individual Psychology, 48,* 96–105.

Terner, J., & Pew, W. (1978). *The courage to be imperfect: The life and work of Rudolf Dreikurs.* New York: Hawthorn.

Watkins, C. E. (1992). Research activity with Adler's theory. *Individual Psychology, 48,* 107–108.

Weaver, C. (1980, March). *The STEP program: A comparison of its effectiveness with middle and lower socio-economic status mothers.* Paper presented at the American Personnel and Guidance Association Convention, Atlanta.

Wilson, D., Mundy-Castle, A., & Panditji, L. (1990). Birth order and intellectual development among Zimbabwean children. *Journal of Social Psychology, 130(3),* 409–411.

Zajonc, R., & Markus, G. (1975). Birth order and intellectual development. *Psychological Review, 82(1),* 74–78.

Chapter 11

◆

Family Counseling

HOW DOES FAMILY COUNSELING DIFFER FROM INDIVIDUAL COUNSELING?

The principal difference between family and individual counseling is that the focus in family counseling is on the family and its members' interactions and relations. Often, individual counseling tends to separate individuals and their problems from the family setting. Family counseling or family therapy, by contrast, almost always involves interventions to alter the way an entire family system operates. The family counseling and therapy label covers a wide variety of arrangements; it may be individual, husband and wife, parent and child, or the entire family including all who live in the home.

Another key difference between individual and family counseling is problem diagnosis. Family therapists use a circular causality diagnosis, whereas individual therapists tend to rely on linear causality. For example, a linear causality diagnosis might be as follows: Alice fails to turn homework into her teacher and therefore suffers a lower grade; a circular causality diagnosis might include how the teacher's reaction to Alice then influences how Alice reacts to her teacher as well as to her parents. Mom nags Alice about not doing her homework; Alice, in turn, gets the attention, albeit negative, that she wants. The teacher sends home a failing note to Alice's parents, who, in turn, both start to nag Alice, who resists homework even more than before. In other words, a circular causality diagnosis involves the roles each family member plays. In fairness to all the theorists discussed in the previous chapters, however, they all believed their own approaches to be effective for working with families.

WHAT DEFINES A FAMILY?

Definitions of family range from the nuclear family of breadwinner father, homemaker mother, and two children to multiple families living together.

Between the two extremes are at least eight types of families: extended, blended, common-law, single-parent, communal, serial, polygamous, and cohabitational (Goldenberg & Goldenberg, 1991; Swartz, 1993; Thomas, 1992).

Families are also defined by their organizational structure, characterized by degrees of cohesiveness, love, loyalty, and purpose. High levels of shared values, interests, activities, and attention to the needs of its members serve to distinguish the functional family group from other organizational groups and teams.

How Does General Systems Theory Relate to Families?

Systems are organized wholes or units made up of several interdependent and interacting parts. The whole unit is greater than the sum of its parts, and change in any part affects all other parts. Any family member's graduation from high school or hospital admission has effects on all other family members. Family therapists choose to view the family as a system in which each member has a significant influence on all other members. For significant positive change in an identified client, therefore, family members have to change the way they interact. Most family therapists work with present family relationships rather than with past family relationships and conflicts.

A key point of interest to all family therapists is the balance families maintain between the several sets of bipolar extremes that characterize dysfunctional families. For example, families may struggle to find a healthy balance between overinvolvement in each others' lives *(enmeshment)* and too much detachment from each other *(disengagement)*. A family could be viewed as a canoe full of people heading into the current of a river. Some canoes are balanced and stable, but maintaining this balance requires each family member to assume a very uncomfortable position, and a shift by one person necessitates a shift by everyone else for the canoe to remain upright. Other families are paddling balanced canoes while sitting comfortably, allowing them to adapt to the changes all families face as they go through the stages of family development; still other canoes are capsized, with family members hanging on this side just trying to survive. Family therapists see their job as righting capsized canoes and making family members comfortable in their canoe-paddling roles. Staying with the canoe metaphor, family therapists see an obvious advantage in working with the whole crew as a group rather than focusing on the identified problem member of the family.

THE SYSTEMS APPROACH TO FAMILY THERAPY

Family therapy roots reach back to the turn of the century, beginning with Alfred Adler's parent groups and developing through various parent, family, and couple education groups within each decade until the 1950s, when family therapy as we know it today was born. Murray Bowen, an early theorist on family relationships, focused on how family members could maintain a healthy balance between being enmeshed and being disengaged. He believed each family member should develop an individual identity and independence separate from family identity, while also maintaining a sense of closeness and a feeling of togetherness with their families. The task for Bowen was to help people integrate the opposing forces of seeking independence from the family while maintaining a sense of family membership and closeness (Bowen, 1976, 1978).

Often functioning like an educator or coach, Bowen emphasized the cognitive side of the therapeutic equation. He focused on (1) relationship between the spouses, (2) detriangulation of self from the family emotional system, (3) knowledge of emotional systems, and (4) differentiation models.

The Spousal Relationship

Bowen and his followers pay attention to defining and clarifying the relationship between couples: How well do they move in and out of the various roles healthy couples play? Do they care for and nurture each other? Do they solve problems and make decisions well? Do they play well together? Do they work well together? Do they parent well together? Are they able to differentiate themselves as individuals apart from the couple? Do they enjoy time alone? Do they maintain individual relationships and friendships outside the marital dyad? Do they pursue individual goals, interests, and careers? Most important, how well do individuals handle differentiation within themselves and between other family members?

Differentiation within oneself refers to the ability to separate feelings from thoughts. For example, in crises does the person put rational thinking on hold and react emotionally to the situation? Lack of differentiation between persons refers to the degree to which people introject the thoughts and feelings of others or do the opposite by automatically reacting against these thoughts and feelings.

Detriangulation of Self from the Family Emotional System

Triangulation, another important concept in Bowen's theory, refers to the practice of two family members bringing a third family member into conflictual situations. Therapists attend to the extent a husband or wife involves one of their children in a problem situation that the two of them should handle. Another example of triangulation is involvement of a person outside the marital dyad, such as a lover, to fill unmet needs in the marriage. A form of triangulation was discussed in chapter 9 in reference to games and the roles people play in those games; for example, one family member may take the role of prosecutor, another the victim, and the third a rescuer. All three roles are needed to maintain the game, and a shift in role by any one of the three alters the roles of the other two. Many of these dysfunctional interactions are similar to dances where it takes two people to keep the dance going and one to stop it.

Emotional Systems of the Family

Understanding family emotional systems and how they work is also central to Bowen's theory. Once again, failure to achieve differentiation between family members results in unhealthy family relationships that recycle from one generation to the next unless some helpful intervention interrupts. Bowen might well have envisioned himself as a cycle breaker, which is not a bad role for a counselor to take. In fact, Bowen often assumed the role of educator in teaching people about family emotional systems. Once again, when the family of origin lacks differentiation, children have either totally absorbed their parents' feelings and emotions or have totally detached themselves. These children often seek out mates who are also undifferentiated, thus providing fertile ground for future family conflict and discord. Undifferentiated people typically do not develop close, lasting relationships. They do not solve problems or resolve conflicts, and they often develop psychosomatic symptoms in an attempt to meet their needs. In addition, undifferentiated people tend not to take responsibility for their behavior. Many of these consequences are in concert with what Glasser (chapter 4) has written about people who have not developed or have not had healthy and caring relationships in their lives.

Modeling Differentiation

Bowen favored modeling for teaching differentiation to his patients. He did this by using "I" statements and taking ownership of his own thoughts, feelings, and behaviors; for example, "I think the best thing for me to do is to confront my colleague about his behavior, but thinking about doing it gives me an uneasy feeling." In addition to owning one's thoughts and feelings, this statement lends some help for separating feelings and thoughts.

STRUCTURAL FAMILY THERAPY

Structural family therapy is closely related to Bowen's family systems theory. Structural family therapists also operate on the assumption that the individual client should be treated within the context of the family system. The therapist does not see the client as a sufficient source of information about the problems brought to counseling or the only source of causes of the problem. Changes resulting from individual counseling are not stable enough to stand against the pressures a dysfunctional family brings to bear. Therefore, the overall goal of structural family therapists is to alter the family structure to empower the dysfunctional family to move toward functional ways of conducting or transacting family business and family communications.

Structural family therapy is also based on the assumption that families are evolving, hierarchical organizations with rules and behavior patterns for interacting across and within the family subsystems. Families get into trouble when their members either become overly enmeshed in each other's business or totally disengaged. Family members should feel a sense of belonging to the family that does not destroy their sense of being unique individuals within and outside the family context. In other words, functional families are characterized by each member's success in finding the healthy balance between belonging to a family and maintaining a separate identity.

One way to find the balance between family and individual identity is to define and clarify the boundaries that exist between the subsystems; for example, a family may have a spousal subsystem, a sibling subsystem, and a parent-child subsystem. Each subsystem contains its own subject matter that is private and should remain within that subsystem. Spouses have matters they need to discuss that do not belong in the context of the parent-child and child-child subsystems. Such topics might include their sex life, financial concerns, and interpersonal conflicts. Dysfunctional families often discuss and play out these topics in an open family forum. Boundaries between subsystems range from rigid to diffuse. Private subject matter from one subsystem that leaks out to other subsystems indicates diffuse, poorly established boundaries. Diffuse boundaries can lead to family members becoming overly enmeshed in the private business of other family members; rigid boundaries allow too little interaction between family members, resulting in disengagement from the family. Once again, the secret to developing functional families is finding the right boundary balance between too rigid and too diffuse; boundaries need to be clearly defined. For example, parents need to provide, on the one hand, enough love and support and, on the other hand, enough room for children to develop independence. A parent-child subsystem and a sibling subsystem also have communications and subject matter that belong to and are unique to those systems. Families who understand and respect differences between healthy and unhealthy subsystem boundaries and rules function successfully; families who do not understand and respect these differences find themselves in a dysfunctional state of conflict, either disengaged from or enmeshed in the family business. Structural family therapy is directed toward changing the family organizational structure as a way of resolving the presenting problem or changing a family member's behavior patterns. For example, in a particular session, Dad might be asked to give up being in charge of the children's homework assignments. The structural therapist actively directs the session and participates as a family member. The therapist may even take over the *family ruler* role as a way of sidetracking the dominant family member.

Salvador Minuchin's Contributions to Structural Family Therapy

Salvador Minuchin is considered the founder of structural family therapy as it is practiced today. He was born in 1921 to Russian Jewish parents in a small

Argentinian town. According to Simon (1984), Minuchin benefited from a multicultural childhood and became an activist early in life. As a university student, he joined a Zionist organization and was arrested for taking part in a protest against Juan Perón in 1943. After spending 3 months in jail, Minuchin was expelled from the university and studied in Uruguay for a time. Later he completed his medical degree in Argentina. Next came a residency in child psychiatry and an 18-month tour of duty as a doctor in the Israeli 1948 war. Minuchin came to the United States with the intention of working with Bruno Bettelheim in Chicago's Orthogenic School; however, he met Nathan Ackerman in New York and eventually decided to work in Ackerman's child-development center. Minuchin sandwiched in 3 years of work with African and Asian immigrant children in Israel before receiving more analytic training and becoming director of family research at the Wiltwyck School for Boys in New York.

Minuchin's best training did not come from books and classes. As so many therapists have soon noticed, traditional psychoanalytic methods do not often work with populations such as delinquent boys. The recidivism rate seemed to be close to 100%, with the young men repeating their delinquent behaviors upon their release. Noticing that some families produced several delinquent children, Minuchin concluded that families must be making a significant contribution to the problem. Therefore, Minuchin began to develop an approach for working with families who did not have the verbal skills for traditional psychotherapy, focusing on the nonverbal communication, a standard practice in individual, group, and family therapy.

Much of what Minuchin learned about families was by observation through a one-way glass and in collaboration with his colleagues at the school. In an approach similar to the Adlerian method for working with families, Minuchin and his colleagues developed a three-step approach: Two counselors met with the entire family; then one counselor met with the parents, and the other with the children. The process culminated in a final stage in which everyone gathered to share information and plans for change. Further observation and study led to a language for describing family structure and a system of interventions designed to change unhelpful and even harmful patterns of family organization. Just as Glasser wrote his first successful book based on his experience at the Ventura School for Girls, Minuchin wrote *Families of the Slums* (1967) based on his experiences at Wiltwyck.

Minuchin's next project was transforming the Philadelphia Child Guidance Clinic into a model family therapy center. He had a flair for the dramatic and was highly critical of seminar case presentations that did not meet his standards. As a practicing family therapist, he set the family scene, assigned roles, started and stopped the action, and took a leading or supporting role himself.

Working with Jay Haley, Minuchin developed the clinic's family orientation and the Institute for Family Counseling, which was designed to train para-professionals. Perhaps his most notable accomplishment during this period was the treatment he developed for psychosomatic families, particularly those of anorexics. He wrote *Families and Family Therapy* (1974) during his 10 years as director of the clinic. After stepping down as director, Minuchin served as head of the training center until 1981. His next book, *Psychosomatic Families,* was published in 1978. Since then, Minuchin continued family research with "normal" families, wrote several plays, and wrote a book for the lay public, *Family Kaleidoscope* (1984).

Minuchin has been praised for rescuing family therapy from intellectuality and mystery. His pragmatic approach contributed both to understanding how families function and to productive interventions for correcting malfunctions in the family system. As Papp (1986) pointed out, Minuchin worked with children and families written off by the psychiatric community as unsuitable for treatment. His achievements are rooted in his philosophy of putting clients first and in his total commitment to their cases.

Once Minuchin diagnosed a flaw in the family system, he appeared willing to go to any length to bring about a needed change. His techniques ranged from gentle persuasion to outright provocation and confrontation. He viewed psychosomatic illness as a symptom brought on and maintained by the family and successfully treated eating disorders, asthma, and uncontrolled diabetes. As mentioned previously, the Minuchin's structural family therapy approach is directed toward changing the family structure or organization as a way of modifying family members' behavior. The counselor makes interventions by becoming an active "family" member.

Marcus (1977), quoting Minuchin, described traditional psychotherapy as a magnifying glass and structural family therapy as a zoom lens that can focus on the entire family or zoom in for a close-up of any family member. Leaving the family belief system in place, the structural therapist works with this belief system to effect behavior changes between people. Rule changes may be the immediate goal as the family explores three questions: (1) How do family members relate to one another? (2) Who is allied with whom against whom? (3) What is the nature of the parental dyad? The idea is to change the immediate context of the family situation and thereby change the family members' positions. The cognitive dissonance principle operates much the same way.

For example, Minuchin (1978) described the case of an asthmatic 12-year-old girl with psychosomatically triggered asthma. She had a history of heavy medication, missed school, and several trips to the emergency room. During the first family interview, the counselor directed the family's attention to the eldest sister's weight problem, and the family's concern then shifted to the newly identified patient. The result for the asthmatic was fewer symptoms, less medication, and no lost school time.

Minuchin referred to the preceding case as the foundation of family therapy. The family structure had changed from two parents protectively concerned with one child's asthma to two parents concerned with one child's asthma and one child's obesity. The asthmatic child's position in the family changed, and that changed her experience.

As with all counseling approaches, the counselor's first step is to establish a trusting relationship with the family. Minuchin recommended three ways: (1) *tracking,* or demonstrating interest in the family by asking a series of questions about the topics they bring up; (2) *mimicry,* or adapting your communication style to fit the family's; and (3) *support,* which includes 1 and 2 plus acceptance of the problem as presented by the client.

Minuchin's style was to get the family to talk briefly until he identified a central theme of concern and the leading and supporting roles in the theme. At this point, he operated like a play director or group dynamics consultant in determining the roles being played, what is interrupting the flow, what is silencing communication, and what diverting maneuvers are blocking family interaction.

Next, the counselor examines boundaries or family rules, which define (1) who participates in what and how, (2) areas of responsibility, (3) decision making, and (4) privacy (Lewis, 1986). When rules have been broken, the family works on them with the help of "stage directions." The counselor may ask a family member to observe the family interaction but not interfere. Minuchin paced the family by adopting their mood and tempo and gradually changing it as the interview proceeded. He asked questions in the enactive mode: not "Why doesn't your mother talk to you?" but "See if you can get your mother to talk to you" (Ferber, Mendelsohn, & Napier, 1970).

The counselor might assign tasks related to the manipulation of space, such as ask a child to move his chair so he cannot see his mother's signals or ask a husband to sit next to his wife and hold her hand when she is anxious. Assigned tasks can dramatize family transactions and suggest change.

Minuchin (1974) shared a case about an anorexic girl and her family to illustrate how he conducts family therapy. Once again, like a play director, he sets the stage. The family of six and Minuchin sat down at the table to have lunch.

Minuchin began to develop the crisis in the family by announcing that Sally must eat or soon die. He assigned her father the task of helping her eat. The father tried bribery with ice cream and a soft drink, to no avail, and was "rewarded" by a minor tantrum from Sally.

Next, having received the assignment to help Sally eat, the mother's pleas, guilt inducements, and lectures go unheeded except for more tantrum behavior in the corner of the room (including slapping the mother).

Minuchin began a new stage in the process by standing up and ordering Sally to sit at the table. At this point, the family is exhausted and searching for a way to solve the problem. The reality therapy philosophy that no one stops any behavior until thorough disgust sets in may come into play at this stage.

The therapist offered a way out of the trap: a negotiation model that allowed Sally to negotiate with a pediatric resident, who presented several choices from all the required food groups from which Sally was to select her daily meals. The therapist blocked any attempt by the parents to intervene in the process and developed a separation between Sally and her parents and a therapeutic dyad between Sally and the therapist. The one rule of the game remained: Sally must eat. The strategy of offering alternatives empowered Sally with control over her life that she had attempted to achieve through not eating. In 1 month, she returned to her normal weight.

Structural Family Therapy: Research and Applications

Kurtines (1989) researched the differential effects of structural family therapy and psychodynamic child therapy on problematic Hispanic boys age 6 to 12; a recreational group served as a control group for the study. Structural family therapists saw the families conjointly, with emphasis on modifying maladaptive patterns of interaction. Individual psychodynamic child therapists saw the child in a playroom and also saw the mother briefly, with emphasis on feelings, limit setting, transference interpretations, and insight as a mechanism to change. Both treatment groups outperformed the recreational group and were basically equal in decreasing the boys' behavioral and emotional problems. Although both approaches used the corrective experience approach, the structural family approach helped parents change their own behaviors and become the source of the corrective experience.

Fish (1989) compared structural, strategic, and feminist-informed therapies to determine whether family therapists consider feminist and gender issues in their therapy. The structuralists attempt to restructure a family's present organization in order to achieve their goals of broadening the family's resources to cope; strategists focus on solving the presenting problem; feminist-informed therapists want to broaden sex roles for men and women. Survey results from the three groups revealed that men have been discouraged from participating in family life and that women should give up being the sole emotional support in the home. Structuralists solve the problem by unbalancing, creating a crisis, boundary making, restructuring, and escalating stress; strategists use reframing, positive connotation, and indirect techniques; the feminist-informed approach emphasizes coresponsibility in the family.

Regarding integration of family systems and feminist concepts, Enns (1988) wrote that the strategic techniques of reframing and restraining can be compatible with a feminist perspective. Reframing vulnerability, neediness, and helplessness as sensitivity to others and the power of empathy may help clients realize that they do have strengths on which to build a better life.

In summary, Minuchin's approach to structural family therapy was both active and directive. The first task is to shift the family focus from the identified client to the therapist, which allows the identified client to begin the process of rejoining the family as a regular family member. The shift in focus to the therapist occurs when the therapist joins the family and becomes part of the family system. When treatment is complete, the therapist moves outside the family structure and leaves

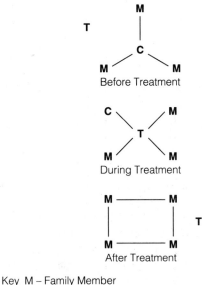

Before Treatment

During Treatment

After Treatment

Key M – Family Member
     C – Identified Client
     T – Therapist

FIGURE 11-1   Stages of Structural Family Therapy

the family intact and connected without the loss of individual family member identities (see Figure 11-1).

STRATEGIC FAMILY THERAPY

Following the popularity of structural family therapy in the 1970s, strategic family therapy dominated the 1980s, led by Milton Erickson, Jay Haley, and Cloe Madanes.

Strategic family therapy is based on the assumption that family member behavior, which is ongoing and repetitive, can be understood only in the family context. The family's ineffective problem solving develops and maintains symptoms. The counselor's role is to design a strategy for solving the presenting problem. Haley (1973) defined strategic family therapy as any therapy in which the therapist initiates what happens in therapy and designs a plan for solving each problem. It is characterized by its brief duration, generally no more than 10 sessions. The therapist takes on a very high activity level by giving specific directives for behavior change that are carried out as homework assignments. Many of the therapists' directives are paradoxical interventions, as introduced by Frankl (1960; and Watzlawick, Weakland, & Fisch, 1974).

Paradoxical Interventions

Paradoxical interventions harness the strong resistance clients have to change and to taking directives from the therapist. Rather than working against the client's resistance, the therapist uses the client's resistance to bring about the changes in behavior needed to correct the problem and repair the family system. The client is in the double-bind position of either obeying the therapist, which the client does not want to do, or stopping the problematic, "uncontrollable" behavior. The client soon discovers that the behavior is controllable and stops the undesirable behavior. For example, the counselor tells an insomniac to see how long the person can go without sleep, maybe even enter a stay-awake contest or go for the world's record, or a tantrum-throwing child to have more tantrums and the child's parents to provide a private room for the tantrums. The counselor might also tell children who lose their tempers and commit aggressive acts to do so between 4 p.m. and 5 p.m. daily in a room equipped with a punching bag and their parents to remind the children when it is time to vent their anger.

In another paradoxical intervention, the counselor takes a "one-down" position, encouraging the client not to do too much too soon. Clients often play the wooden leg game, described in chapter 9, which highlights the client's disabilities and the reasons why the client cannot function properly. In the one-down position, the counselor emphasizes all that the client is already doing despite problems and suggests that the client must have great inner strength even to show up for counseling.

Counselors tell clients who handicap themselves through anticipatory anxiety over activities such as making speeches, taking tests, or meeting new people are directed to practice all the symptoms they fear, such as blushing, speaking in a trembling voice, stuttering, passing out, or completely failing the test. They often tell test-anxious people to take practice tests and fail each one.

Madanes (1981) often asked children to pretend doing the symptom the family was trying to prevent. The other family members were directed to play along with and encourage the child to act out the symptoms. Counselors often treat displays of inadequacy and learned helplessness with directives to the child to act more helpless more often and with directives to other family members to overhelp by providing too much service.

Although strategic or brief therapy is directed toward symptom removal, counselors distinguish between first-order and second-order changes. First-order change occurs when the symptom is temporarily removed, only to reappear later because the family system has not been changed. Haley (1976) pointed out that the behaviors of family members do not occur in isolation. Rather, family behaviors occur in a sequence in which one member's behavior is both the result of and the catalyst for other members' behaviors. Fixing the symptom while failing to fix the system does not fix the family. First-order change is typical for dysfunctional families who work very hard to maintain the status quo.

Second-order change occurs when symptom *and* system are repaired, and the need for the symptom does not reappear. For example, Mom and Dad quarrel, the children start a fight, Mom and Dad stop their quarrel to deal with their children, and a period of family peace is achieved. Until Mom and Dad find a better way to resolve conflicts, the sequence repeats frequently and the peace is only temporary. Healthy families with an adaptive facility for repairing the family system when it is broken engage in second-order change.

Contributions of Milton Erickson, Jay Haley, and Cloe Madanes to Strategic Family Therapy

Jay Haley, director of the Family Therapy Institute of Washington, D.C., was a longtime colleague and student of Milton Erickson. He described Erickson as his mentor and major source of ideas about therapy. Since Erickson's death in 1980, Haley perhaps has been his best interpreter. Haley also worked closely with Salvador Minuchin at the Philadelphia Child Guidance Clinic. For the past several years, Haley's work has been closely associated with that of his wife, Cloe Madanes. They founded the Family Therapy Institute and now conduct lectures and workshops on strategic family therapy.

To strategic family therapists, *strategic* refers to the development of a specific strategy, planned in advance by the therapist, to resolve the presenting problem as quickly and efficiently as possible. Erickson promoted the idea that insight, awareness, and emotional release are not necessary for change. Rather, people need to solve their immediate problems and eliminate bothersome symptoms in order to move ahead with their lives. Followers of Erickson's approach do not have the client's personal growth and development as a primary therapeutic goal. Problem solving through minimal intervention is the key goal for the strategic group.

According to Feldman (1985), Erickson's approach incorporated three principles in addition to discounting the importance of achieving insight: (1) The therapist uses the client's reality rather than attempting to fit the client to the views of the world, or even to those of the therapist; (2) both the therapist and client play active roles in the action-oriented process; and (3) minimal change must occur in one or more areas of the client's life for change to result in the family system. Eclecticism is alive and well in family therapy practice as the therapist works to construct strategies to implement the needed changes.

Erickson and Zeig (1985) presented one of Erickson's cases concerning a mother and her 61-pound anorexic daughter, Barbie, who was limiting her daily diet to one oyster cracker and a glass of ginger ale. Initial treatment began with routine questions for Barbie, which her mother answered. Erickson allowed the mother's behavior to continue for 2 days as a way of building rapport and establishing a pattern before initiating an intervention. The next stage began with Erickson's scolding the mother in front of Barbie for answering all of Barbie's questions. Barbie developed a new perspective on her mother. The next step was to punish Barbie for keeping her mother awake at night with her whimpering. The punishment was forcing Barbie to eat scrambled eggs—acceptable to her because she viewed eating as punishment. In the next stage, Erickson used storytelling as a way of indirectly replacing Barbie's maladaptive behavior patterns with good associations of food in various social settings. He altered her role as victim by placing her in other roles in the stories, such as rescuer or persecutor. Barbie's treatment was successful and remained so during a lengthy follow-up period.

Haley (1976) described a young boy's fear of dogs. A problem of family dynamics was that the boy was close to his mother but disengaged from his father. Haley's first step was to get father and son to interact by having them talk about the dangers of dogs in the neighborhood. When the mother tried to interrupt, Haley neutralized her by explaining that this was Dad's area of expertise. The second step was to get a dog into the home to help in three areas: (1) to continue the father-son interaction, (2) to achieve systematic desensitization of the dog phobia, and (3) to stimulate change in the family dynamics. Haley accomplished step 2 by asking the boy to pick out a dog who was afraid and to work with his father on teaching the dog not to be afraid.

The preceding case illustrates a common malfunction in a child-centered family structure. Generally one or more overinvolved dyads exist, one of which usually includes the "problem" child. Haley (1973) described three ways to handle the overinvolved dyad: (1) act on the relationship between the child and his mother (neutralize mother); (2) modify the relationship between father and child (interact about the dog); and (3) change the relationship between spouses (bring the dog into the home for the son to care for and teach with the father's help).

Stone and Peeks (1986) provided another application of the same three steps with a method Haley (1984) refers to as "ordeal therapy." The case concerned a 17-year-old male with seriously disruptive behavior in one class at school. After individual counseling had failed to resolve the problem, the counselor presented the following plan to the family:

> When Frank misbehaves at school, he will be sent to me with a note of explanation. I will call you, Dad, at your office to pick up Frank, take him home, and supervise his digging of a 3- by 3- by 3-foot hole in your flower bed. Upon completion of the digging, Frank is to place one of his record albums or tapes in it, fill the hole, tramp it down, clean the shovel, and return the shovel to the garage. You will then return Frank to me, and I will return him to his class. At the end of the day, you, Dad, are to have a talk with your wife about Frank's behavior for that day.

The treatment plan solved both problems: The son's behavior improved both at school and at home.

Strategic Family Therapy: Research and Applications

Bergman (1983) explored paradoxical interventions or invariant prescriptions with two families displaying dysfunctional symptoms of fusion in their family systems. The specific symptoms differed for the two families: suicidal depression in one family and refusal to attend school in the other. Intense criticism between parents and children characterized both families. Failing to overcome resistance to change with structural techniques, the author prescribed parental criticism in an attempt to shift the fusion in each family to a more functional reorganization of family dynamics. The presenting symptoms of dysfunctional fusion in both families disappeared and remained absent through a 1-year follow-up period. The prescribed parental criticism blocked the ongoing parental criticism and led to more functional patterns of family interactions. The therapist succeeded in harnessing family resistance to work for change rather than against it.

McColgan, Puch, and Pruitt (1985) reported successful treatment of a 9-year-old boy (diagnosed with primary encopresis) and his family. Treatment consisted of an initial family assessment interview, six family sessions, and five individual 10-minute prefamily sessions with the boy. The therapist made structural changes, forming an alliance with the disengaged stepfather, which unbalanced the system by increasing the stepfather's authority. This change blocked the boy's attempt to detour marital conflict with his encopresis. The therapist conducted the strategic intervention in the 10-minute sessions with the boy, which focused on allowing him to take complete and private responsibility for his toilet habits and any cleanup that might occur after an accident. The family agreed not to interfere with his encopresis. Three- and 18-month follow-up reports revealed only occasional episodes of encopresis.

Mirkin (1983) presented a successful family treatment approach for anorexia nervosa, which the therapist viewed as an illness that stemmed from an overprotective family, leading to suppression of autonomy in the adolescent, Cathy, and surfacing in the form of an illness rather than outward rebellion. The therapist used two interventions: (1) Cathy's refusal to eat was termed "disobedient behavior" and was dealt with as unacceptable by the parents, and (2) parental intervention in her eating habits was prevented. Cathy's defiance of the parental rules surfaced in her eating habits. She controlled the family by manipulating her eating behavior. Therapy with the entire family focused on discussing, negotiating, and resolving difficult family issues. The children gained more autonomy and responsibility for their decisions, and the parents spent more time with each other. Any weight gain Cathy showed was reinforced by allowing her more autonomy. Weight loss was punished by loss of new privileges. In other words, Cathy's eating behavior now controlled only her own autonomy and the number of privileges available to her.

DeShazer and Molnar (1984) described a useful team approach for prescribing four common interventions in their practice of brief family therapy. The therapy hour is divided as follows: (1) a 40-minute interview with the family, (2) a 10-minute consultation time with the team, and (3) a 10-minute delivery of the intervention message and closing of the session. The first intervention, designed for families who focus on the perceived stability of their problem pattern, requires family members to observe one another between sessions so that "you can tell us next time what happens in your family that you want to continue to have happen." The second intervention is for families who are bankrupt of ideas about how to solve the problem. The therapist requests that they "do something different."

The third intervention is for clients who believe their problem is out of their control. The therapist asks them to "pay attention to what you do when you overcome the temptation or urge to _____ ." The fourth intervention works well for clients who are convinced they are doing the only logical thing. The therapist's response is, "A lot of people in your situation would have _____ ." All four interventions are designed to help clients experience changing.

Morgenson (1989) presented an excellent example of strategic methods used with children. Morgenson met with parents of a 7-year-old girl who was described as whiny, argumentative, and stubborn. The parents viewed this behavior as bad behavior, but the daughter did not. Without the child's recognition that the behavior was bad, the door was open for the counselor to use the age-metaphor technique. The girl was brought into the office with the parents, and the counselor asked her age.

After the child told him she was 7, the counselor looked incredulously at the mother and father. He shook his head and said to the parents, "This can't be, for this girl is 7 and this is the behavior of a 5-year-old." With a puzzled look, the counselor asked the girl how old she was on her last birthday and how old she would be on her next birthday. The counselor noted that the behavior she was exhibiting during the session was that of a 7-year-old, and he asked the parents to keep a log of the child's behavior for 1 week. This direct challenge of age appeals to children's desire to look their age or older.

Chasin, Roth, and Bograd (1989), in an article on action methods in strategic therapy, described a counseling method that would be quite at home in Gestalt counseling. In an approach to therapy that involves deemphasizing the problems, their main focus was on looking for clients' strengths and using various action strategies to open up new perspectives and discussions. The authors provide a five-step outline:

1. Therapists and clients contract to promote safe, voluntary participation. The clients have the right to disclose at the level they choose and can refuse to answer any question or participate in any activity.

2. Each participant is invited to list his or her individual strengths and the strengths of the relationship.

3. Participants enact three dramatizations. First, the couple enacts what would happen if the goals for the relationship were reached. Second, each client enacts a painful past experience. Third, each client enacts the painful past experience "as it should have been." The partner's roles in this enactment are preventive, protective, and/or resolving.

4. Each participant states what he or she perceives to be the problem in the relationship.

5. The therapist recommends the next step (homework, follow-up appointment, and so on) based on what happened during the session.

Writing on eclectic strategic practice, Duncan, Parks, and Rusk (1990) emphasized a theme that runs throughout this book—counselors adapting to their clients rather than vice versa. The eclectic strategies offer a fuller menu for setting a context for change and empowering clients to independently discover better alternatives to meet their needs.

Duncan and Solovey (1989), in an attempt to integrate strategic brief therapy with insight-oriented therapy, restated that therapists are more similar than dissimilar and that they should not close themselves off from potentially helpful methods in other systems. The authors believed that considerable overlap exists between reframing and therapist-ascribed meaning (interpretation) designed to achieve insight. Reframing refers to changing the framework of a situation to make it more workable and manageable.

Writing on resistance in existential-strategic marital therapy, Coche (1990) defined *resistance* as all those behaviors in the therapeutic system that interact to prevent the system from achieving the family's goals for therapy. Strategists intervene by encouraging resistance, thereby making the resistance "cooperative." Four stages for handling resistance were presented: (1) the halo effect and cynical disbelief (clients bring considerable cynicism and doubt to counseling); (2) joining the couple and reframing the problem; (3) pulling for despair (despair is used as a change agent—a person could have the assignment of deliberately experiencing despair for 2 days); and (4) turning the corner when the decision is made not to live unhappily ever after.

Peeks (1989) supported the use of behavior metaphors in solving children's problems. One example, entitled *straightforward reorganizations,* corrects a problem by altering the usual course of action the family takes. A young girl, unable to walk, suffered from a swollen leg that was diagnosed as psychosomatic. The therapist advised the mother to disengage herself from taking care of her widowed father to give structure back to her marriage. The therapist viewed the girl's swollen leg as a metaphor of her mother's situation. The reorganization of the family resulted in a rapid cure of the swollen leg.

Breit, Im, and Wilner (1988) provided examples in defense of strategic therapy. One case concerned a 10-year-old girl who was driving her parents to high levels of stress by constant talk about dirt and feces. The therapists told the parents to set aside 30 minutes to listen to their daughter talk about this topic. If approached outside the time frame, they told their daughter to hold the dirt and feces talk until the scheduled time. The problem disappeared in a few days because the child was caught between disobeying her parents by not talking about feces or obeying her parents and talking about it with their blessing. She chose to "disobey" and not talk about feces at any time.

In summary, the job of the strategic family therapist is fourfold: First, the hierarchical structure of the family must be identified. "Who is in charge of whom and what?" and "What role does each family member play?" are the critical questions to be answered. Confusion about who is in charge and about role identity is characteristic of dysfunctional families. Second, the sequence of behaviors that causes and maintains the problem symptom needs to be identified. For example, what is the presenting problem, and what family conditions create and maintain the problem? Third, the therapist develops an intervention plan to serve as a directive for how family members are to change certain behaviors.

Fourth, the therapist and family evaluate the plan's effectiveness in removing the symptom and repairing the family system. Haley (1976) distinguished between advice and directives. Giving advice is telling people what they ought to do, what job to take, or what person to marry. Giving a directive is like assigning behavior homework or writing a behavior prescription designed to alter family interaction sequences.

Haley (1976) described four stages of a typical strategic therapy first interview.

1. Stage one, the *social stage,* accomplishes three tasks: building rapport, observing family communication patterns and alliances, and forming tentative hypotheses about how the family functions.

2. In Stage two, the *problem stage,* the main task is obtaining a clear statement of the problem that meets with each family member's agreement. Haley suggested involving reluctant participants first in the problem discussion and the identified client last, a procedure followed in most family therapies to bring everybody into the discussion without focusing on the identified client as the scapegoat for the family's dysfunction.

3. Stage three, the *interaction stage,* accomplishes two tasks: Everybody should discuss the problem and everybody should interact with all other family members. During Stage 3, the therapist does not become personally involved in the family interaction because the family interaction patterns require full attention. The therapist directs the family to discuss their disagreements and to role-play or act out a typical family problem such as deciding who does what family chores. We prefer to observe how a typical family meeting might operate, even if the family is not accustomed to holding them. All these interactions provide valuable information about problem sequences, communication patterns, and the lines of authority in the family hierarchy.

4. In Stage 4, *goal setting,* the obvious task is to define the goal for therapy in concise, observable, behavioral terms. For example, in a family that does not discuss family conflicts, an acceptable goal might be weekly 30-minute family meetings to clear the air of conflicts. The therapist could add a paradoxical directive encouraging the family not to resolve any of the conflicts during the meetings. Again, complete clarity and agreement on the goals are necessary if the family is to have ownership in the therapy process and the resulting cooperation and commitment to make therapy work.

THE COMMUNICATIONS APPROACH TO FAMILY THERAPY

Our discussions of systems, structural, and strategic approaches to family therapy have highlighted several commonalities and overlap between methods as well as specific differences. Perhaps the common thread that unites the field of family therapy is the focus on how family members communicate. Communication is the very heart of the two methods presented next in our discussion: John Gottman's behavioral family therapy and Viriginia Satir's conjoint family therapy.

John Gottman's Behavioral Interview Method

Gottman's behavioral family therapy (1979, 1990) has much more in common with traditional family therapy than it does with the behavioral counseling and therapy discussed in chapter 7. The therapist in Gottman's system functions more as an educator than healer, as is true for most of the practitioners of the theories and systems presented in this book.

Family therapists following a communications approach to family therapy naturally hold the view that accurate communication is the key to solving family problems. All families are faced with problems; however, some families solve more of their problems than other families. Good problem-solving families hold several traits in common. They communicate in an open and honest manner rather than relying on phony or manipulative roles when trying to meet their needs or resolving family crises. In addition, these family members match the intent and impact of their communication. For example, a wife may want more cooperation from her husband on household chores. She stated her request in clear terms and listened empathetically to her husband's response about his needs; the intent of her communication achieved the desired impact. Had she been sarcastic, the impact of her message may have resulted in less cooperation from her husband. Dysfunctional families have low success rates in matching the impact with the intent of their communications.

Gottman built his approach around matching intent and impact of communication (Gottman, 1979, 1994; Gottman, Notarius, Gonzo, & Markman, 1976). He designed his behavioral interviewing method to teach people about what they are doing that is not working and to help them correct the situation by learning how to get the impact they want from their communication.

Stage I: Exploration of how a couple or family made the decision to seek therapy is done. The therapist also determines the level of commitment to therapy and who, if anyone, might be a reluctant client. The dynamics give the therapist an opportunity to view the family interaction pattern firsthand. Areas of family or couple agreement and disagreement surface during this stage.

Stage II: Identification of the goals each person has for therapy, some of the fears they have about coming to therapy, and fears about what could go wrong is done. The therapist asks clients what their situation would be like if all their goals were attained; in other words, how would they be behaving differently, and how would an observer know they had met their goals? More specifically, what would their typical day be like if they achieved their goals? Couples in counseling often state their goals (for treatment) in terms of what they want for each other; a better focus is the goals the couple wants for the partnership. The therapist can facilitate goal setting by presenting each client with a list of possible goals—improve communication, have more fun, do more things together, become more of a team, become better parents, end fighting, manage finances better, improve love-making, cooperate more on household jobs—and instructing them to select just one goal each. The clients then elaborate on their choices and explain why the goal is important to them. The second task in Stage II is to identify any fears or inhibitions the couple might have about counseling. A good introduction to the subject is asking the couple the worst possible thing that could happen from counseling. The therapist can use this opportunity to explain how treatment is conducted and the roles of the therapist and clients. If the couple is having a problem with finances, for example, the therapist's role is not to solve the money problem per se; rather, the therapist focuses on the couple's communications. Better and more effective communication should provide the means to solve problems more efficiently, including handling finances better.

Stage III: The counselor asks the couple to articulate their perceptions of their marital issues or problems. Again, the couple completes a checklist of several marital issues and rates each issue for its severity on a scale of 1 to 10, with 10 being most severe. The typical list of issues approximates the goals list used in Stage II: for example, house and yard chores, fighting, finances, sex, in-laws, communication, cooperation, parenting, time together, and addictions. Again, the couple's discussion of their marital issues affords the therapist another opportunity to observe the couple's communication pattern.

Stage IV: The therapist asks the couple to select one issue to discuss, just as they might try to resolve it at home, and then observes the free interaction to note of how well the intent of each communication is getting the desired impact.

Stage V: A play-by-play analysis of the couple's interaction focuses on miscommunications in which the intent of the speaker's message did not get the desired impact. In fact, the miscommunication often gets an effect opposite the intended meaning. The intent might be to get a partner to help out around the house more, but the result is that the other partner is helping even less than before. After pointing out the differences between intent and impact for a series of communications, the therapist might ask one partner to assume the role of a play director to describe how the other partner could have responded better to the statement just made. Then the couple compares the desired response with the one actually made. As in reality therapy, the couple can decide whether what they are doing is getting the desired response, and they can stop or change what they are doing. The receiver of the message can validate the impact of the sender's message, and the sender then analyzes the receiver's return message for intent and impact. Step V might require the therapist to lecture on the intent and impact equation. Good communication occurs when intent equals impact. The therapist explains that choice of words, nonverbal communications, and the sender's and receiver's value filters can distort the intent of the message and lead to an undesired impact. Oftentimes restating and clarifying the sender's message before reacting helps. In other words, the couple may have to pass the message back and forth before the receiver understands it the way it was intended. Even with a clear message, the sender may not get the intended impact of the message and need to alter it to get the desired response. The receiving partner can help by stating how he or she wishes to be approached on the presenting issue.

Stage VI: The therapist concludes the session by negotiating a contract with the couple on what goal(s) they will try to achieve and the method of treatment they will use. The clients' job is to decide on the objective, and the therapist's job is to supply the process. Again, as is true with most counseling approaches, the principal goal is to teach people a communication process that enables them to solve more of their problems.

The Communications Approach to Family Therapy: Research and Applications

Studying the characteristics of close personal relationships, Gottman (1990) found three patterns: (1) More negative affect exists among dissatisfied couples than among satisfied couples. (2) A higher level of reciprocity of negative affect exists in dissatisfied couples. (3) The interactions of satisfied couples are less structured than those of dissatisfied couples.

Ponzetti and Long (1989), reviewing the literature on healthy family functioning, found strong spousal relationships to be the most prominent indicator of healthy families. Other universal healthy traits include mutual interests, effective communication, problem-solving capability, adaptability to change, the ability to have fun together, mutual respect, and shared responsibilities.

In a study of how strong families use humor, Wuerffel, DeFrain, and Stinnet (1990) found that stronger families use wit, fun, and jokes to the benefit of their family and seldomly use put-down humor. Strong families reported negative effects when humor was used to put down other family members.

Koch and Ingram (1985) found that the two components of behavioral marital therapy (behavior exchange and communication/problem-solving training), offered independently, were initially effective during posttest evaluation, as was a combination of the two approaches. However, the combination-approach client group continued to improve on follow-up evaluation while the other two client groups declined. Although the behavior-exchange group had the best posttreatment gains, it also showed the greatest decline at follow-up. The communication and problem-solving group, which had significant but smaller gains at posttest, showed only minimal decline at follow-up.

VIRGINIA SATIR'S CONJOINT FAMILY THERAPY

When Virginia Satir (1916–1988) was 5 years old, she decided to become a detective to help children figure out parents. She was not sure what she would be looking for, but even at this age she knew that more strange things were going on in families than met the eye. More than half a century later, after working with thousands of families, Satir reported that she still found a lot of puzzles in families.

Satir viewed family life as an iceberg. Most people are aware of only a 10th of what is happening in the family—the 10th that they can see and hear. Like the ship that depends on the captain's awareness of the total iceberg, the family must depend on the total awareness of the family structure to survive. Satir referred to the hidden 90% as the family's needs, motives, and communication patterns. In four books, Satir shared some of the answers she found to the puzzles over the years: *Conjoint Family Therapy* (1967), *Peoplemaking* (1972), *Helping Families to Change* (Satir, Stachowiak, & Taschman, 1975), and *Step by Step* (Satir & Baldwin, 1983). According to Satir, she embellished some of the early concepts in *Conjoint Family Therapy* as a result of her work with the Gestalt concepts presented by Fritz Perls and the body-awareness work of Bernard Gunther.

Virginia Satir earned excellent qualifications as a parent detective: formal academic training in psychological social work at the University of Chicago and work as a teacher, consultant, and practitioner in psychiatric clinics, mental hospitals, family service centers, growth centers, and private practice. In 1959, she joined with two psychiatrists to form the initial staff of the Mental Research Institute in Palo Alto, California. She also served as the first director of training at the Esalen Institute in Big Sur, California, and lectured in most parts of the world. She was a visiting professor to at least 10 universities and a consultant to the Veterans Administration and to several other agencies and schools. As is true about many theorists presented in this book, she was more effective demonstrating her methods than lecturing about them.

Satir cited several contributors to the development of her system—including Harry Stack Sullivan's interpersonal theory of the 1920s (an individual's behavior is influenced by his or her interaction with another) and the growth of group therapy, whose major contributors were J. L. Moreno and S. R. Slavson, also during the 1920s. Gregory Bateson and Murray Bowen began to look at families to discover why individuals became "schizophrenic." They believed that one person could represent the family situation.

Bateson, of the Mental Research Institute, contributed the idea of the double bind, communications that occur when one person sends a conflicting, double message to another person; for example, Mom says, "Jane, if you really loved me, you would make better grades at school."

Much of Satir's theory has roots not only in classic theories of clinical psychology and psychiatry but also in her past research at the Mental Research Institute and the National Institute of Mental Health. Satir synthesized older with newer theories and added original techniques.

The Nature of People

Satir had a positive view of human nature. After studying 12,000 families in depth, she was convinced that, at any time, whatever people are doing represents the best they are aware of and the best they can do. She believed that people are rational and have the freedom and ability to make decisions in their lives. Although Satir viewed people as basically free, she considered the extent of their knowledge as the biggest limitation on personal freedom. People can learn what they do not know and change their ways of interacting with others. People can also make themselves healthier by freeing themselves from the past. Like Maslow, Satir believed that people are geared to surviving, growing, and developing close relationships with others. Although some behavior may be labeled psychotic, sick, or bad, Satir saw it as an attempt to reach out for help.

Self-esteem plays a prominent role in Satir's system. She believed that self-esteem and effective communication beget one another. Conversely, low self-esteem and dysfunctional communication are also correlated. Satir saw self-esteem—the degree to which people accept both their good and their bad points—as the basic human drive. Self-esteem is a changing variable that fluctuates within a healthy range, depending on the amount of stress one is experiencing. It is related to one's participation in the family interaction. When individual family members experience stress, their ability to communicate openly, give and receive feedback, and solve problems depends on the collective self-esteem of the family. Family members may try to block communication in order to protect their own self-esteem under stress or in crises. Family members with low self-esteem are likely to create disturbances to make the others feel as bad as they do. For example, parents guilty of child abuse often have low self-esteem and may unconsciously internalize: "One way to punish myself for my wasteful ways is to punish that same behavior in one of my children."

Behavior, according to Satir, is directly related to one's family position and view of that position. Good or bad feelings about ourselves are probably communicated to others. Satir viewed people as mature and functional when they behave in acceptable and helpful ways and take responsibility for their actions. Satir (as well as Adler and Glasser) saw irresponsibility and poor communication as symptoms of a low self-concept.

Satir made the point that a person needs a high degree of self-esteem to qualify as a good marriage partner. People with healthy self-concepts view their partners as enhancing their own self-esteem. However, people who have low self-esteem look to their partners as extensions of themselves. A marital relationship is dysfunctional if one partner looks to the other to supply what is missing in the self. In this dysfunctional couple relationship, a person sees the marriage or partnership as a place for getting and not giving. For example, someone may marry as a type of therapy for strengthening an inadequate personality. However, the general outcome of a "taking" relationship is disappointment and an even lower sense of self-esteem.

By the same token, parents with low self-esteem may compensate for feelings of inferiority by having a child. The child may be used to demonstrate the parents' worth to the community and their self-worth as parents, as well as an extension of themselves. Unconsciously they seem to be thinking, "If I did not fulfill many of my life's aspirations, perhaps I can relive them through my child." In such situations, parents never see children as individuals with separate worth, value, and identities. Children of parents deficient in self-esteem have a heavy, difficult burden to bear: live out their parents' fantasies. They see success and failure from the vantage point of the parent. Children who show individuality and different points of view may be accused of not loving their parents: "After all I have done for you, how could you do this to me?" "If you loved me, you would practice the piano more."

Satir (1967) held that children are the third angle of the family triangle. As such, their position may be intolerable, similar to the persecutor-victim-rescuer triangle described in transactional analysis (chapter 9). Parents in conflict consider any direction the child turns as a turn for or against one of the parents. Given this state of affairs, Satir wrote, children who seem to side with one parent run the risk of seeming not to love the other parent. Because children need both parents, making such a choice inevitably hurts them. Both parents have interlocking roles to play in the process of educating children emotionally, and failure of one angle of the family triangle (one parent) disturbs the entire system; frequently the result is disturbed children.

A further complication in the triangle is that the child has already established an identity with the same-sex parent, and the hurt of taking sides is further compounded by the stunted or stifled psychosexual development that may occur. Children need the opposite-sex parent to admire, respect, and love and the same-sex parent as a good role model. When the parents are divided, arguing, and fighting, children cannot achieve these identity and interpersonal goals. In a family with no parental coalition—cooperation between father and mother to fulfill their respective roles as man and woman and husband and wife—the child may need counseling to fulfill unsatisfied wishes. Satir conceptualized this child as the *identified client,* even though the entire family is counseled.

Satir did not believe in the concept of triangular relationships; that is, she believed there is no such thing as a relationship "among" three people, only shifting two-person relationships, with the third member in the role of observer. The building blocks of Satir's system are two-person, interacting relationships. The key to success or failure in this system is the relationship between husband and wife. If the system is dysfunctional and they are not acting in parental coalition, then both mates may look to the child to satisfy their unmet needs.

According to Satir, children who are triangled into a marital situation in the role of "ersatz mate"—an ally who is wooed seductively by the parent of the opposite sex—are not happy. The child has loyalties to and needs for both parents. Although a child may appear closer to one parent, such an alliance is illusory. Children cannot unambivalently side with either parent.

Satir wrote that people develop self-esteem in the early childhood years. Besides the obvious physical needs, children need a warm, ongoing, predictable mastery over their world and validation of themselves as distinct and worthwhile people. They also require a sense of what it is to be male or female and an acceptance of this role. If parents consistently show that they consider their children masterful, sexual people and demonstrate a gratifying, functional male-female relationship, their children acquire self-esteem and become in- creasingly independent. In every way, self-esteem, independence, and indi- viduality go together.

Satir viewed mature people as those who are fully in charge of their feelings and who make choices based on accurate perceptions of themselves and others. The mature person takes full responsibility for choices that have been made. In summary, Satir regarded mature people as (1) being in touch with their feelings, (2) communicating clearly and effectively, and (3) accepting differences in others as a chance to learn.

Theory of Counseling

Satir believed that four components in a family situation are subject to change and correction: the members' feelings of self-worth, the family's communication abilities, the system, and the rules of the family. The rules are the way things are accomplished in the family. They are the most difficult component to uncover during therapy sessions because they usually are not verbalized or consciously known to all members of the family. Satir wanted all members of a family to understand the rules that govern their emotional interchanges, including (1) freedom to comment, (2) freedom to express what one is seeing or hearing, (3) freedom to agree or disapprove, and (4) freedom to ask questions when one does not understand. The family unit becomes dysfunctional when members do not understand the unwritten rules. Satir told families who were having problems with a member that families have no bad members who cause pain, only bad rules. She believed that what goes on at a given moment is the natural consequence of the experience of one's own life; consequently, anything can change. However, Satir believed that change is not a "have to" but rather one possibility among several. She believed in taking risks, controlling the counseling process, and leaving the outcome to the family.

In family systems theory, the main idea is that the family functions as a unit, with certain rules, expectations, and emotions. Members of the family unit are interdependent; therefore, stress applied to one part of the system or to one family member is felt throughout the system by all members in varying degrees. The family system has both the potential to share and deal with the stress in a healthy, open, and productive way and the potential to close the communication process by focusing blame for the stress on one family member (the identified client).

To bring about changes in a family's functioning, analyzing the interaction processes between the family members and the family system is as important as analyzing the communications content. Questions of who is right and who is wrong border on value judgments that have no place in the process of family growth and further development. The focus is on discovering how individuals can adjust to the various events within the family to achieve satisfaction and avoid withdrawing problems.

Satir emphasized the necessity of developing trust before any meaningful change process can begin. Given willingness to take a risk, trust can be assumed. The second step is developing awareness, or knowing what one is doing. With awareness comes understanding and applying this new understanding to effective decision making. At this point, the new decision-making behavior can be put to use. The underlying theme is the development of self-worth and the freedom to comment.

Satir believed that whether a family grows is primarily the responsibility of counselors and their input. They must be able to put clients in touch with themselves at a feeling level. The counselor assumes the role of teacher to reeducate the family to new ways of thinking, feeling, and communicating.

Communication, the most important factor in Satir's system, is the main determinant of the kinds of relationships people have with one another and of how people adjust to their environment, as well as the tie that binds the family together. When a family is operating smoothly, communication among family members is open, authentic, assertive, and received. Conversely, when a family system is in trouble, communication is blocked or distorted in a futile attempt to ward off anxiety and tension.

Fear of rejection is a common source of anxiety. Because people fear rejection, they resort to one response pattern or to a combination of patterns to communicate with others. These universal response roles are the placater, the blamer, the computer, the distractor, and the leveler. The last response, leveling, helps people develop healthy personalities; all the others hide real feelings for fear of rejection. In such situations, people feel and react to the threat of rejection, do not want to reveal "weakness," and attempt to conceal it. Satir (1971) agreed with Gestalt theory on nonverbal behavior: the body expresses your whole integration. Each response pattern is accompanied by a unique body posture and nonverbal behaviors.

> *Placater.* These people placate so others do not get angry. Their motto is "peace at any price." They talk in ingratiating ways to try to please, or they apologize. They never disagree and even take on the air of a yes person. They have low self-esteem. They cannot negotiate solutions of mutual benefit because the process is too threatening. In other words, placaters negate self in the interest of serving others and staying within the context of the situation. Nonverbal behaviors of the placater send the message that "Whatever you want is okay with me; I am just here to make you happy."
>
> *Blamer.* These people are the faultfinders, directors, and bosses. They also do not feel good about themselves. They may feel lonely and unsuccessful and attempt to compensate by trying to coerce others into obeying them so they can feel that they amount to something. Blaming is also a good way to create

distance and prevent others from getting too close. The blamers are good guilt inducers: "After all I have done for you, how could you do this to me?" Blamers negate others while focusing on the context of the situation and on themselves. Nonverbal behaviors from the blamer send the message that "You never do anything right. What is the matter with you?"

Computer. These people are calm, correct, show no feelings, and speak like a recording. They pretend there is no conflict when there is. Computers are the superreasonable people. Their bodies reflect their rigid personalities. They negate self and others to concentrate on context. They cover up their vulnerability with big words to establish self-worth. Nonverbal behaviors from the computer send messages that "I am cool, calm, and collected." They may also take the position of "see it my way" at the expense of others and of the context of the situation.

Distractor. These people make completely irrelevant statements. They change the subject and never respond. Their strong point is evading the issue. They may even resort to withdrawing from the situation to avoid a crisis. Distractors negate all three elements of reality: self, others, and the context of the situation. Nonverbal behaviors from distractors send messages that "Maybe if I do this long enough, the problem will really go away."

Leveler. These people communicate their honest thoughts and feelings in a straightforward manner that addresses self, others, and the context of the situation. Their verbal messages and nonverbal body posture are consistent. Leveling occurs when all aspects of communication are congruent: body, vocal tone, context, and facial expression. Levelers do not cover up or put other people down in the name of being open and honest. They are not phonies. Levelers tell the truth about what they are thinking, feeling, and doing, and they allow others to do the same. Their relationships are free and honest, with few threats to self-esteem. The leveling response is the truthful message for a particular person at a given time. It is single and straight. There is an openness and a feeling of trust in interactions with a person who is leveling. This response allows people to live as complete persons in touch with their behavior, thinking, and feelings. Satir (1972) stated that being a leveler allows a person to have integrity, commitment, honesty, intimacy, competency, creativity, and the ability to solve real problems. The other four forms of communicating result in doubtful integrity, commitment by bargain, dishonesty, loneliness, incompetence, strangulation by tradition (inability to change traditional patterns), and destructive ways of dealing with fantasy problems.

Our society does not encourage leveling responses. Although people would like to be honest, they are afraid and instead play games. Satir outlined a variety of experiences to help family members become aware that they can choose to change their responses and understand how they can do so. Levelers can choose one of the other four response patterns if they are willing to accept the consequences, but for them such responses would not be the automatic response of people locked into a particular pattern. Levelers can choose to placate, blame, compute, or distract; the difference is that they know what they are doing and are prepared to accept the result of their behavior.

The message of the leveler is consistent. If a leveler says "I like you," the voice is warm and the eye contact and body speak the same message. If the leveler is angry, the voice is harsh, the face is tight, and the words are clear: "I am mad as hell at you!"

Satir pointed out that every person she has seen with a behavior or coping problem was a member of a family in which all significant communication was double level—that is, phony or hidden (Satir et al., 1975). If people learn to recognize harmful communication patterns and level with their family members, then the family has a chance to make its members' lives better and to solve problems more efficiently. As mentioned previously, Satir's system is based on two-person, interacting relationships. However, every couple has three parts: you, me, and us. For the relationship to continue and love to grow, each part has to be recognized and not dominated by the other two. Although love as a feeling begins a marriage, the process makes it work. The process is the "how," which is what Satir taught her clients.

Satir divided all families into two types: nurturing and troubled. Each type has varying degrees. Her main objective for her clients was recognition of their type and then change from either troubled to nurturing or from nurturing to more nurturing. The nurturing family helps its members develop feelings of self-worth, whereas the troubled family diminishes these feelings. In every family, factors to be considered include feelings of self-worth, communication, rules, and links to society.

According to Satir (1972), aliveness, honesty, genuineness, and love mark nurturing families. These families have the following characteristics:

1. People are listened to and interested in listening to others.
2. People are not afraid to take risks because the family understands that mistakes are bound to happen when taking risks.
3. People's bodies are graceful, and their facial expressions are relaxed.
4. People look at one another and not through one another or at the floor.
5. The children are friendly and open, and the rest of the family treats them as people.
6. People seem comfortable about touching one another and showing their affection.
7. People show love by talking and listening with concern and by being straight and real with one another.
8. Members feel free to tell one another how they feel.
9. Anything can be discussed—fears, anger, hurt, criticism, joys, achievements.
10. Members plan, but if something does not work out, they can adjust.
11. Human life and feelings are more important than anything else.

12. Parents see themselves as leaders and not as bosses. They acknowledge to their children their poor judgment as well as their good judgment, their hurt, anger, or disappointment as well as their joy. Their behavior matches their teaching.
13. When nurturing, parents need to correct their children. They rely on listening, touching, understanding, and careful timing and are aware of children's feelings and their natural wish to learn.
14. Nurturing parents understand that children learn only when they are valued, so they do not respond in a way that makes the child feel devalued.

Counseling Method

The counseling method of conjoint family therapy involves the entire family and is based on communication, interaction, and general information. The approach Satir taught to families was both physical and emotional. Counselors who prefer to work less with emotions and more with behavior find the Adlerian method more comfortable.

Satir's goals for family counseling were to establish the proper environment and to assist family members in clarifying what they want or hope for themselves and for the family. She wanted them to explore the present state of the family and who plays which roles. She sought to build everyone's self-esteem. Satir also worked to help families operationalize their definitions of words like *respect* and *love*. For example, she asked clients, "What would be happening that would let us know you were getting the respect and love you desire?" or "What must be done for you to make you feel respected and loved?" Satir also used reframing to turn negatives into positives and thus allow clients to view difficult situations in a better light and see possibilities for cooperation, conflict resolution, and change.

Satir led the family in role-playing both family situations and each other's actions and reactions to the happenings in a typical day. She used some Gestalt techniques of "sculpting" a family argument or interaction; she believed that the body is often a more honest reflection than the verbal message. Satir used videotape replay to teach communication, and her role-play dramas used various props, such as ropes and stepladders, to demonstrate and analyze the types of family interactions. She staged these dramas to help family members learn how to level with each other, express their emotions, and use honest, direct language. Satir examined the family history by drawing family trees to look at how past and immediate family styles are passed on from parent to child. She used ropes to demonstrate the complicated process of communication between parents and children.

Even with a multitude of techniques, Satir proposed no formula for therapy because therapy involves human feelings and the ability to respond on a human level. Satir viewed the family as a "people-making factory" in which people are made by a process that is crude at best and destructive at worst.

An Example of Satir's Method

A 40-year-old woman sits in a fetal position on the floor, hiding behind a sofa. Her husband, sitting in a chair, points an accusing finger at her from across the room. One daughter, with arms outstretched, tries to make peace. Two children sit with their backs to the group, and a fourth child rubs his mother's back. Satir breaks the silent role-play, rests her hand on the father's shoulder, and asks how he feels right now. She has asked the family to act out silently how they each feel during a family argument. This sculpting method is excellent in creating awareness of personal feelings as well as awareness of the feelings of other family members.

Satir reported research data that showed that blood pressure, galvanic skin response, and electroencephalographs were significantly affected when people changed their stance and body posture and held them for at least 10 seconds during role-play demonstrations with double-level communication. For example, assuming the blamer posture caused a physiological response as well as an emotional response after 10 seconds. In other words, people engaging in harmful role behavior over a period of time make themselves sick.

The Importance of Including Children

Including children is imperative for family counseling success in Satir's system. Satir advocated inclusion of all the children, not just the child who has a problem, because all are part of the family homeostasis—a process by which the family balances forces within itself to achieve unity and working order. Satir operated from the assumption that all members feel dysfunction within the family in some way. Therefore, the counselor works with all members of the family to help them redefine their relationships. Family members have their own perceptions of what is going on in the family, and each member's input is vital in building a functional family. The counselor works with the family's interpersonal relationships to discover how the members interact so they can strengthen their bonding.

Satir suggested meeting with the marital pair before bringing the children in. She made the couple aware of themselves as individuals as well as mates and parents. She also suggested preparing the parents in the initial interview for bringing the children into the counseling sessions. After the parents agreed that the children's role in family counseling was important the children were included.

Working with children means the counselor needs to be fully aware of the children's capabilities and potential. The counselor can plan the length of sessions according to the children's ages. Children have short attention spans, and the counseling process must hold their interest. Counselors confronted with these obstacles can work within them and make the counseling process beneficial, productive, and enjoyable for all.

The counselor should begin by recognizing all the children and repeating their names, ages, and birth order to let the children know they are being heard. The counselor also sets rules for the sessions; for example, no one may destroy property within the room, no one may speak for the others, all must speak so they can be heard, and everyone must enable others to be heard. When the ground rules have been established, in-depth discussion can begin.

The counselor should set the mood by asking questions in a warm, specific, matter-of-fact way. The setting should encourage people to take the risk of looking clearly and objectively at themselves and their actions. Satir suggested many questions, but questions the children are able to answer. During this time, the counselor must be sure the children understand what is happening and what the family is striving to gain. The children need to feel comfortable and be aware of themselves as individuals who are different from one another. They need to know the importance of communicating with one another—for example, to feel free to agree or disagree with other family members, to say what they think, and to bring disagreements out in the open. The children need to know that the counselor will treat them as people with perceptions and feelings.

The counselor should demonstrate individuality by speaking to each child separately, differentiating each child, and restating and summarizing what each child says. Counselors need to convey their sincerity by honoring all questions from each child and demonstrating that questions are not troublemaking and illegitimate—that all should ask questions about what they do not know or are unsure about. Counselors who convey their expectations of the children increase the likelihood that the children will rise to meet them. Children listen, are interested, and contribute to the discussions.

The counselor has to ask the children their ideas about why they are in counseling and then repeat what each child says to make sure the child's meaning is understood. The counselor may proceed by asking the children where they got their ideas about why they are there, who told them, and what was said. From this exchange, the counselor can gain insight into communication within the family. The counselor encourages the children to talk about themselves and their feelings in relation to each family member. The counselor also helps the children express frustration and anger and has the children ask their family members for answers to any questions they may have. The counselor may use confronting questions to provoke thought in the child. As the counseling sessions advance, questions concerning family rules and roles arise. After establishing good rapport and a comfortable atmosphere, the counselor may begin to bring out underlying feelings and confront people concerning the family's dysfunction. The basis for further probing and confronting must be established between counselor and parent, counselor and child, parent and child, and counselor, parent, and child in the initial interviews. From the initial interviews, the counselor must gain the child's confidence in order to move forward.

The counselor wants to see each child's place in the family unit. In the beginning, to build the children's self-esteem, the counselor focuses on them—not ignoring the parents, but having the parents respond intermittently. Counselors help children understand their parents as parents and people and themselves as children and people.

Three Keys to Satir's System

Satir's approach to family counseling focused on three key ingredients:

1. Increase the self-esteem of each family member by facilitating their understanding of the family system and teaching them to implement changes toward open systems and nurturing attitudes and behaviors.

2. Help family members better understand and analyze their encounters with each other and learn the leveling response so that they can improve and open communication patterns.

3. Use experiential learning techniques in the counseling setting to help the family understand present interactions and encourage family members to take personal responsibility for their own actions and feelings.

Satir viewed the counselor as a facilitator, a change agent who assists in the process of moving toward a more open family system and a more nurturing family. The counselor is not the expert but one who helps family members become the experts on the family's problems and growth.

Satir's Technique

Family therapists use a variety of techniques to assist the family in self-discovery. Satir's method was designed to help family members discover what patterns do not work and how to better understand and express their feelings in an open, level manner. Rather than have them rehash past hurts, Satir had the family analyze its "systems" in a present interaction in the counseling setting. Among the many ways to accomplish this analysis are the following:

1. The counselor asks the family to describe a situation that causes the difficulties that have brought them to counseling or asks them to describe a typical situation from their recent experience that usually results in the problem. Family members enact the situation.

2. The counselor has the family sit in a circle in chairs to simulate a family decision, such as deciding where to go on their next vacation.

3. The family participates in a family sculpture, as in the example presented earlier. The counselor asks someone to describe a typical family argument and then has that person "sculpt" the argument by placing each family member in appropriate positions—complete with gestures, facial expressions, and touching. The counselor might then ask each of the other members how he or she would

change it and allowing each make the changes. Next, discussion aimed at leveling and participation by each family member follows.

4. Each family member takes some long ropes, one for each of the others in the family, and ties all of them around his or her waist. Next, the counselor instructs each of them to tie one rope to each of the other family members. Discussion of the resulting tension and mass of ropes can help the family better understand its complex relationships and crossed transactions.

5. Role-playing and reverse role-playing stimulate family discussion.

6. Videotaped family sessions and discussions help family members achieve a better understanding of all members' reactions and responses.

7. Games include (a) the simulated-family game, (b) the systems game, and (c) communication games.

Satir's games, which are used for counselor training as well as family therapy, are based on her definition of *growth model,* which assumes that an individual's behavior changes as a process that is represented by transactions with other people. People function fully when they are removed from the maladaptive system or when the system is changed to promote growth. This model differs greatly from the *sick model,* which proposes that the individual's thinking, values, and attitudes are wrong and therefore must be changed, and from the *medical model,* which purports that the cause of the problem is an illness located in the patient.

Satir developed games to deal with the family's behavior when family members operate within these three models. All family members are present during the family counseling process, including the games.

The Simulated Family Game

In the simulated family game, various family members simulate each other's behavior; for example, the son plays the mother. The therapist may also ask family members to pretend that they are a different family. Following this enactment, the counselor and family members discuss how they differ from or identify with the roles.

Systems Games

Systems games are based on either open or closed family systems; learning and insight can be obtained from both family types. Satir believed that emotional and behavioral disturbances result directly from a member's being caught in a closed family system. The closed system does not allow any individual the right to honest self-expression. The family views differences as dangerous, and the overriding "rule" is to have the same values, feelings, and opinions. In the open-system family, honest expression and differences are received as natural occurrences, and open negotiation resolves such differences by "compromise," "agreeing to disagree," "taking turns," and so on.

One set of games entails having family members take roles revolving around the five interactional patterns of behavior discussed earlier: (1) the placater, (2) the blamer, (3) the distractor, (4) the computer, and (5) the leveler. On the basis of these interactional patterns, various games have been constructed.

1. *Rescue game.* Behaviors 1, 2, 3, and 4 are played. Who plays each role is variable, but each member must remain in this role throughout the session.
2. *Coalition game.* Behaviors 1 and 2 are played. Two people always disagree and gang up on a third person.
3. *Lethal game.* Behavior 1 is used. Everyone agrees.
4. *Growth vitality game.* Each person includes himself or herself and others by honest expression and by permitting others to express themselves (leveling).

These techniques can be broadened beyond the initial family triad by incorporating all family members into a prescribed family situation and assigning various roles to each member. These sessions are extremely vital for younger children who have been ruled by the adage "children should be seen but not heard." The games aid families in understanding the nature of their own family system. They also allow family members to experience new interactional patterns through identification of their current behavior and insight into possible alternatives. By using the growth vitality game and the leveling role, families can experience movement from a pathological system of interaction to a growth-producing one.

Communication Games

These games are aimed at establishing communication skills. Satir believed that an insincere or phony message is almost impossible to deliver if the communicator has skin contact and/or steady eye contact with the listener. One communication game involves having two members sit back to back while they talk. Next they are turned around and instructed to stare into each other's eyes without talking or touching. Satir (1967) reported that this type of interaction leads to many insights concerning the assumptions that each makes about the other's thoughts and feelings. Next, the participants continue to stare and then touch each other without talking. This process continues in steps until each partner is talking, touching, and "eyeballing" the other. Assuming these positions, they are asked to disagree, which Satir found was nearly impossible. People either enjoy the effort or are forced to pull back physically and divert their eyes to get angry.

The counselor's role is an important part of these games. Throughout and after each session, the counselor intervenes and discusses each member's responses, feelings, and gut reactions to himself or herself and to other family members.

The Counselor's Role

In Satir's approach to family counseling, the counselor is a facilitator who gives total commitment and attention to the process and the interactions. The counselor does not take charge and must be careful not to manipulate the participants' reactions and verbalizations. By careful and sensitive attention to each family member's interactions, transactions, and response (or lack of response), the counselor can intervene at certain points to ask whether the messages are clear and correct and how a particular person is feeling. Each person thus has a chance to interact or make corrections. For example, the counselor might interrupt the dialogue when one person makes a statement about how another feels or thinks by asking the second person if the statement is accurate and how he or she feels at that moment.

In short, the counselor intervenes to assist leveling and taking responsibility for one's own actions and feelings. The counselor also intervenes to give quieter family members permission to talk and be heard. Analyzing a present interaction in the counseling setting should help family members understand past hurts and problems. Understanding what patterns produced the trouble also helps family members. With experience in openness and leveling, family members can change their communication, and growth can occur. The family is then better able to continue the discussions, come to new insights, and implement appropriate changes.

◆ ◆ ◆

C A S E   S T U D I E S

People's ability to assume other roles in the family group situation supports the idea that people can change their response roles and that families can change their ways of interacting and solving problems. Family members need to learn to share both positive and negative feedback in ways that do not hurt or belittle others. The following is a family role-play transcript in which the leveling response is omitted:

Don [father/husband, blaming]: Why isn't our dinner ready?

Sandy [mother/wife, blaming]: What are you yelling about? You've got as much time as I have.

Bill [son, blaming]: Aw, shut up. You two are always yelling. I don't want any dinner, anyway.

Don [blaming]: You keep your trap shut. I'm the one who makes the rules around here because I'm the one who makes the money.

Sandy [blaming]: Says who? Besides, young man, keep your nose out of this.

Don [placating]: Maybe you'd like to go out to dinner for a change?

Sandy [computer]: According to the last issue of *Woman's Day*, they say eating out is cheaper than cooking the same things at home.

Don [placating]: Whatever you would like to do, Dear.
Bill [placating]: You always have good ideas, Mother.
Sandy [computer]: That's right. I have a list of the restaurants offering specials this week.

Perhaps one good leveling response by any of the family members could have helped these short exchanges. Perhaps Sandy could have said that she needed a rest from a long, hard day and would like to have dinner out. Don could have made a statement rather than asking a phony question. Perhaps a leveling remark by Don might have informed Sandy that he was wondering what she wanted to do about dinner tonight. Bill could have changed his remark to "I really worry when we argue and fight in this family, and I would like this to stop." The counselor's job is to rehearse these leveling responses until the problem is solved in the role-playing setting and then make plans to try the leveling response in real life.

In a second family session with the counselor present, the Frazier family is seated clockwise around the counselor: Jody, the wife-mother, 43 years old; Frank, the 11-year-old son; Larry, the husband-father, 44 years old; Joyce, the 14-year-old daughter; and Kathy, the 16-year-old daughter.

Kathy: Mom, just say yes or no. Am I going to be allowed to go out on weekdays or not?
Jody: Why don't you do what you want? You always do anyway.
Counselor [to Kathy]: How does this make you feel?
Kathy: Angry. I'd like to be able to do what the rest of the kids are doing, but I know Mom and Dad don't approve.
Counselor: That sounds funny because I heard your mom say it was up to you. [To Jody] Is that what you said? Maybe it was the expression on your face and the way you spoke your message to Kathy that made her think you didn't really mean "Do what you want to do."
Kathy: Yes, her stern face said "no."
Counselor: What did she do with her face to tip you off?
Kathy: Well, she squinted her eyes and wrinkled up her nose.
Counselor: It's hard to read your mom's mind, but I am guessing that she thinks nobody listens to her very much. We can check this with her later. But I'm wondering if you have ever felt this way.
Kathy: Sometimes.
Counselor [to Jody]: Do you ever have this feeling?
Jody: I think maybe we've hit on something new.
Counselor: Do you think no one listens to you?
Jody: I have a rough day just keeping house for this family. Larry comes home from work too tired to talk, and all I ever talk to the children about are their fights and arguments. I have to handle all the family problems.
Larry: Well, my job is all I can handle.
Jody: See, no one listens to my side of the story.

Counselor [to Larry]: Were you aware of what Jody was saying when she said that? What did it feel like, Larry?

Larry: It irritates me that everybody thinks it's my fault that things don't go better in our family.

Counselor: Hold it one minute. Frank is doing something over here.

Larry [to Frank]: Settle down over there and shape up.

Counselor: Let's take some time out and find out what's going on with Frank. I haven't been paying much attention to Frank and Joyce. [To Frank] How did you feel about what was going on over here?

Frank: Well, I, uh. . . .

Joyce [blaming Frank]: You weren't even paying attention.

Kathy: Frank, if you move over here with me, we can get along better.

Jody [to Larry]: Can't you do anything to make him mind me? It's all your fault he acts like he does.

Counselor [to Kathy and Larry]: An interesting thing happened before Frank started acting up. I was wondering, Kathy, how you felt when your father said to your mother, "It's all my fault that things don't go better in our family."

In this short segment, the counselor attempts to look at present communication patterns and the feelings these patterns conceal. After achieving awareness of the communication blocks, the family can begin to practice leveling as an alternative way of communicating.

Virginia Satir's method could fit very well into a systems, structural, or communications approach for counseling families. She focused on developing better family communication by making family members aware of how others in the family react to their communication styles. Satir saw improved communication skills as leading to better family conflict resolution and problem solving.

Conjoint Family Therapy: Research and Applications

Taylor (1984) developed a seven-stage, structural, conjoint family therapy approach to use in spouse abuse cases. The treatment schedule is directed toward relearning about anger and appropriate expression of anger, positive self-talk, awareness of anger and stress levels, enhanced self-image and marriage image, and learning autonomy, assertiveness, and decision-making skills. Five major topic areas are targeted: (1) stress and anger management, (2) positive expression of anger through assertion, (3) problem solving, (4) positive interaction and relationship climate, and (5) values, expectations, and jealousy.

Gentry and Eaddy (1980) proposed a similar method that uses a family systems approach for spouse-abusive families. They recommend a therapeutic-educational program that focuses on safety, long-term planning, child guidance, children's fears, relationship skills, and conflict management.

Pevsner (1982) divided into two groups 15 families with children age 5 to 13. One group received individual treatment, and the other group received both individual and group family treatment. Those with the additional treatment did better on posttest instruments that measured knowledge of behavioral principles, but every family showed fewer targeted behaviors. A 9-month follow-up revealed that every one of the participating families maintained their gains in targeted behaviors.

Szapocznik, Kurtines, Foote, Perez-Vidal, and Hervis (1986) presented evidence that one-person family therapy can be done successfully with the problem-source individual in the family. Drug-abusing adolescents were the problem-source people in the 35 families under study. Half the families received conjoint family therapy and the other half one-person family therapy; the researchers found the treatments equally effective in reducing family discord.

Gurman and Kniskern (1986), in a review of literature on the comparative effectiveness of individual versus conjoint family therapy, found more support for conjoint family therapy. Specifically, they concluded that there is (1) very little acceptable evidence of the inefficacy of individual marital therapy; (2) no evidence, acceptable or otherwise, of the efficacy of individual marital therapy; and (3) a large body of acceptable evidence of the efficacy of conjoint marital therapy.

Brach and O'Leary (1986) compared the effectiveness of conjoint behavioral marital therapy and individual cognitive therapy for couples experiencing discord and depression (by the wife). Comparing a conjoint treatment focusing on social learning with a cognitive treatment focusing on self-talk, the researchers found the behavioral approach significantly superior to the cognitive approach and the control-group waiting list in reducing marital discord and depression.

Rosenthal and Glass (1990) conducted a longitudinal study to assess the impact of day treatment and family therapy as alternatives to placement of 93 children age 12 to 17. The alternative treatments reduced the incidence of placement outside the home. The most significant factor related to family therapy was a great reduction in the amount of money spent per child. The amount of delinquency following the alternative treatments was also lower, but school performance changed very little, and parents reported less satisfaction with the in-home treatments than the control group did with out-of-home services. Szykula and Fleischman (1985) conducted a similar study with children age 3 to 12. They found family interventions more effective than placement in 50% of the cases and also cited tremendous cost benefits in family interventions as opposed to placement.

Shortly before her death, Satir contributed to an article on family reconstruction and sculpting in group counseling (Satir, Bittner, & Krestensen, 1988). The therapists created a drama around each group member, with members starring in their own dramas. Scripts for each drama were developed from family maps, family life fact chronologies, and the family wheel of influence. Core moments of each member's family drama were reenacted in a psychodrama with group members as family players in the drama. Role-players enacted verbal and nonverbal behaviors of the family members in each person's family.

Yaccarino (1993) presented some helpful guidelines for adapting Minuchin's structural family therapy to cultural differences in families. Using Italian-American families as an example, he detailed several points defining family norms for this culture. For example, individuality is secondary to family obligations; family roles are clearly defined with the husband-father earning the money, wife-mother maintaining the home, and children working to help with the family finances; and acceptance by the family is a measure of one's accomplishment. He described Italian-American families as tending toward enmeshment, which could support unhealthy symptoms within the family system.

As with any counseling method, family therapists must have thorough knowledge of cultural family norms and communication patterns to be effective in their assessment and treatment of families from unfamiliar cultures. Tamura and Lau (1992) made many of these same points in their research of Japanese families, as did Szapocznik, Kurtines, Santisteban, and Rio (1990) in their research on Hispanic families. Soto-Fulp and Delcampo (1994) unsuccessfully applied structural family to Mexican-American families.

Considerable research exists on the consequences of structural defects within the family. Stewart, McKenry, Rudd, and Gavazzi (1994) found depression in rural adolescents associated with poor communication with parents, lower levels of family cohesion, and larger numbers of life events. Gavazzi (1993) studied the relationship between family differentiation levels and the severity of presenting problems in adolescents and found that highly differentiated families displayed the lowest average number of problems. Stack and Wasserman (1993) researched the linkage among marital integration, alcohol consumption, and suicide. Low marital integration increased the odds of heavy drinking and thereby increased the odds of suicide. The authors found unmarried people more likely to be heavy drinkers than married people.

Gerson, Hoffman, Sauls, and Ulrici (1993) have constructed frames in marital therapy that relate family-of-origin information from genograms to current family interactional processes. The frames describe the roles played in dyadic situations within the family context: pursuer and distancer, overfunctioner and underfunctioner, blamer and placater. Coping frames describe how someone learned to reduce anxiety, and modeling frames describe how somebody learned a behavior from a family member. Loyalty frames illustrate how the family of origin experienced coalitions, triangles, and loyalty issues and how they might be passed on to the current family.

Concerning work done in child-focused family therapy, Sayger, Szykula, and Sudweeks (1992) compared behavioral and strategic family therapy in treating families with children presenting as the identified patients. A follow-up of treatment effects was conducted with 100% of the mothers who participated in behavioral family therapy, and 68% of the mothers in strategic family therapy reported satisfaction with treatment outcomes.

Kuehl (1993) and Fauber and Long (1991) supported the idea of individual sessions with the child in addition to regular family therapy sessions in order to balance the attention given to the child and the family. Children often use behavior to communicate their dislike for the way things are going at home. Frequently, improvement in the child's behavior helps the marital relationship and vice versa. Sayger, Horne, and Glaser's (1993) study also supported the positive relationship between marital satisfaction and improvement in child conduct problems.

Several family therapists have described incorporating techniques and methods from other counseling theories. Early (1994), Villeneuve and LaRoche (1993), and Stoddard, Wilberger, and Olafson (1993) integrated play therapy and family therapy into a family systems treatment. Play therapy has the advantage of helping children communicate their story to the therapist. Engaging the family in play therapy activities offers a rich observational field for evaluating the family system in action. A principal therapeutic effect from play therapy is the opportunity to help children move from dysfunctional enmeshment with a parent to functional individualization. Likewise, overly rigid family boundaries might be relaxed to allow for a healthy sense of family cohesion.

Similar breakthroughs in family therapy with children have been reported for storytelling, art therapy, and outdoor adventure programs. Sedney, Baker, and Gross (1994), Becvar and Becvar (1993), and Schnitzer (1993) have described storytelling in their work with families. Storytelling helps the family talk about the painful topics that are disrupting the continuation of the larger family story. Loss of a family member through death or divorce is a painful event that is difficult to talk about, yet talking is a great healing method. Storytelling can provide the means to speak the unspeakable. Many therapists use storytelling to assess the family system before and after treatment; people think in metaphors and in storytelling formats, and, as we all know, people listen better to stories than to lectures. Riley (1993) makes some of the same points for art therapy as a means of illustrating the family story. From a social constructivist position, art therapy can be used to obtain each family member's invented reality of the family and the world. Art therapy can be a method of assessment, treatment, and evaluation. It provides an opening into unspoken thoughts, feelings, and perceptions and can be a bridge across cultural and perceptual boundaries.

SUMMARY

Although this chapter is focused on differences among the schools and proponents of the various family therapies, similarities do exist. First, all agree that families are like engines with interdependent parts. When one part malfunctions, the total engine is adversely affected; that is, one malfunction may cause other parts to break down as well. For lasting behavior change, therefore, the entire family may need to change. Second, (to change the analogy) the family is like a canoe floating downstream—that is, maintaining its balance only because one member of the family is leaning way out over the right side and two other members are tilted slightly to the left. In other words, the canoe *is* balanced, but uncomfortably so. The goal of family therapy is to relieve the pain by finding a more comfortable balance without upsetting the canoe. Families often say, "Stabilize us, but do not change anything." Third, to bring about successful change, the counselor may need to tip the canoe; the counselor's job is to ensure that the emergency process is a safe one. Fourth, all family therapy approaches borrow heavily from the material discussed in the previous chapters as well as from sources outside the present text. Once again, as with other theories, eclectic and integrative themes continue in the current literature on family therapy.

Piercy and Sprenkle (1990) reviewed the trends of marriage and family therapy during the 1980s. The strategic family therapies and the Milan systemic therapy underwent the most significant changes. Family therapy branched out to include more nontraditional problems, including delinquency, anxiety disorders, schizophrenia, mood disorders, family violence, family abuse, and addictive disorders. Traditionally, family therapists had been mainly concerned with marital, sexual, and child concerns.

The authors predicted that the next 10 years will see increased societal awareness in family therapy, a trend certainly welcomed by the Adlerians, who have had social interest as a primary theme over the past century, and offered the following conclusions in support of the effectiveness of family therapy. Nonbehavioral marital and family therapies were effective in about 67% of the reported studies. Marital therapy was significantly more effective when both spouses were involved conjointly in therapy. Positive results in family therapy typically occur in 1 to 20 sessions. Finally, family therapy is more than holding its own when compared for effectiveness with individual counseling and psychotherapy.

REFERENCES

Becvar, D., & Becvar, R. (1993). Storytelling and family therapy. *American Journal of Family Therapy, 21,* 145–160.

Bergman, J. S. (1983). Prescribing family criticism as a paradoxical intervention. *Family Process, 22,* 517–521.

Bowen, M. (1976). Theory in the practice of psychotherapy. In P. J. Guerin, Jr. (Ed.), *Family therapy: Theory and practice* (pp. 42-89). New York: Gardner Press.

Bowen, M. (1978). *Family therapy in clinical practice.* New York: Aronson.

Brach, S. R., & O'Leary, K. D. (1986). The treatment of depression occurring in the context of marital discord. *Behavior Therapy, 17,* 43–49.

Breit, M., Im, W., & Wilner, R. S. (1988). In defense of strategic therapy. *Contemporary Family Therapy: An International Journal, 10,* 169–181.

Chasin, R., Roth, S., & Bograd, M. (1989). Action methods in systemic therapy: Dramatizing ideal futures and reformed pasts with couples. *Family Process, 28,* 121–136.

Coche, J. M. (1990). Resistance in existential-strategic marital therapy: A four-stage conceptual framework. *Journal of Family Psychology, 3,* 236–250.

DeShazer, S., & Molnar, A. (1984). Four useful interventions in brief family therapy. *Journal of Marital and Family Therapy, 10,* 297–304.

Duncan, B. L., Parks, M. B., & Rusk, G. S. (1990). Eclectic strategic practice: A process constructive perspective. *Journal of Marital and Family Therapy, 16,* 165–178.

Duncan, B. L., & Solovey, A. D. (1989). Strategic-brief therapy: An insight-oriented approach? *Journal of Marital and Family Therapy, 15,* 1–9.

Early, J. (1994). Play therapy as a family restructuring technique: A case illustration. *Contemporary Family Therapy, 16,* 119–130.

Enns, C. (1988). Dilemmas of power and equality in marital and family counseling: Proposals for a feminist perspective. *Journal of Counseling and Development, 67,* 242–248.

Erickson, M., & Zeig, J. (1985). The case of Barbie: An Erickson approach to the treatment of anorexia nervosa. *Transactional Analysis Journal, 15,* 85–92.

Fauber, R., & Long, N. (1991). Children in context: The role of family in child psychotherapy. *Journal of Consulting and Clinical Psychology, 59*(6), 813–820.

Feldman, J. (1985). The work of Milton H. Erickson: A multi-system model of eclectic therapy. *Psychotherapy, 22,* 154–161.

Ferber, A., Mendelsohn, M., & Napier, A. (1970). *The book of family therapy.* New York: Aronson.

Fish, L. S. (1989). Comparing structural, strategic, and feminist-informed family therapies: Two delphi studies. *American Journal of Family Therapy, 17,* 303–314.

Frankl, V. (1960). Paradoxical intention: A logotherapeutic technique. *American Journal of Psychotherapy, 14,* 520–533.

Gavazzi, S. (1993). The relation between family differentiation levels in families with adolescents and the severity of presenting problems. *Family Relations, 42,* 463–468.

Gentry, C. E., & Eaddy, V. B. (1980). Treatment of children in spouse abusive families. *Victimology: An International Journal, 5,* 240–250.

Gerson, R., Hoffman, S., Sauls, M., & Ulrici, D. (1993). Family-of-origin frames in couples therapy. *Journal of Marital and Family Therapy, 19*(4), 341–354.

Goldenberg, I., & Goldenberg, H. (1991). *Family therapy* (3rd ed.). Belmont, CA: Brooks/Cole.

Gottman, J. (1979). *Marital interaction: Experimental investigations.* New York: Academic Press.

Gottman, J. (1990). Finding the laws of close personal relationships. *Methods of Family Research, 1,* 249–263.

Gottman, J. (1994). *What predicts divorce?* Hillsdale, NJ: Lawrence Erlbaum.

Gottman, J., Notarius, C., Gonso, J., & Markman, H. (1976). *A couple's guide to communication.* Champaign, IL: Research Press.

Gurman, A., & Kniskern, D. (1986). Commentary: Individual marital therapy—Have reports of your death been somewhat exaggerated? *Family Process, 25,* 51–62.

Haley, J. (1973). *Uncommon therapy.* New York: Norton.

Haley, J. (1976). *Problem-solving therapy.* New York: Harper & Row.

Haley, J. (1984). *Ordeal therapy: Unusual ways to change behavior.* San Francisco: Jossey-Bass.

Koch, A., & Ingram, T. (1985). The treatment of borderline personality disorder within a distressed relationship. *Journal of Marital and Family Therapy, 11,* 373–380.

Kuehl, B. (1993). Child and family therapy: A collaborative approach. *American Journal of Family Therapy, 21*(3), 260–266.

Kurtines, W. (1989). Structural family versus psychodynamic child therapy for problematic Hispanic boys. *Journal of Consulting and Clinical Psychology, 57,* 571–578.

Lewis, W. (1986). Strategic interventions with children of single parent families. *School Counselor, 33,* 375–378.

Madanes, C. (1981). *Strategic family therapy.* San Francisco: Jossey-Bass.

Marcus, M. (1977, January). The artificial boundary between self and family. *Psychology Today, 10*(8) 66–72.

McColgan, E. B., Puch, R. L., & Pruitt, D. B. (1985). Encopresis: A structural/strategic approach to family treatment. *American Journal of Family Therapy, 13,* 46–53.

Minuchin, S. (1967). *Families of the slums.* New York: Basic Books.

Minuchin, S. (1974). *Families and family therapy.* Cambridge, MA: Harvard University Press; London: Tavistock.

Minuchin, S. (1978). *Psychosomatic families.* Cambridge, MA: Harvard University Press.

Minuchin, S. (1984). *Family Kaleidoscope.* Cambridge, MA: Harvard University Press.

Mirkin, M. D. (1983). The Peter Pan syndrome: Inpatient treatment of adolescent anorexia nervosa. *International Journal of Family Therapy, 5,* 179–189.

Morgenson, G. (1989). Act your age: A strategic approach to helping children change. *Journal of Strategic and Systemic Therapies, 8,* 52–55.

Papp, P. (1986). Letter to Salvador Minuchin. In S. Minuchin, H. Fishman, & B. Roseman (Eds.), *Evolving models for family change: A volume in honor of Salvador Minuchin* (p. 207). New York: Guilford.

Peeks, B. (1989). Strategies for solving children's problems understood as behavior metaphors. *Journal of Strategic and Systemic Therapies, 8,* 22–25.

Pevsner, R. (1982). Group parent training versus individual family therapy: An outcome study. *Journal of Behavior Therapy and Experimental Psychiatry, 13,* 119–122.

Piercy, F., & Sprenkle, D. (1990). Marriage and family therapy: A decade of review. *Journal of Marriage and the Family, 52*(4), 1116–1126.

Ponzetti, J. J., & Long, E. (1989). Healthy family functioning: A review and critique. *Family Therapy, 14,* 43–49.

Riley, R. (1993). Illustrating the family story: Art therapy, a lens for viewing the family's reality. *Arts in Psychotherapy, 20,* 253–264.

Rosenthal, J., & Glass, G. (1990). Comparative impacts of alternatives to adolescent placement. *Journal of Social Services Research, 13,* 19–37.

Satir, V. (1967). *Conjoint family therapy: A guide to theory and technique* (Rev. ed.). Palo Alto, CA: Science and Behavior Books.

Satir, V. (1971, January). Conjoint family therapy. In G. Gazda (Ed.), *Proceedings of a symposium on family counseling and therapy* (pp. 1–14). Athens: University of Georgia.

Satir, V. (1972). *Peoplemaking.* Palo Alto, CA: Science and Behavior Books.

Satir, V., & Baldwin, M. (1983). *Step by step.* Palo Alto, CA: Science and Behavior Books.

Satir, V., Bittner, J., & Krestensen, K. (1988). Family reconstruction: The family within—a group experience. *Journal for Specialists in Group Work, 13,* 200–208.

Satir, V., Stachowiak, J., & Taschman, H. (1975). *Helping families to change.* New York: Tiffany.

Sayger, T., Horne, A., & Glaser, B. (1993). Marital satisfaction and social learning family therapy for child conduct problems: Generalization of treatment effects. *Journal of Marital and Family Therapy, 19*(4), 393–402.

Sayger, T., Szykula, S., & Sudweeks, C. (1992). Treatment side effects: Maternal positive attributes of child-focused family therapy. *Child and Family Behavior Therapy, 14,* 1–9.

Schnitzer, P. (1993). Tales of the absent father: Applying the "story" metaphor in family therapy. *Family Process, 32,* 441–458.

Sedney, M., Baker, J., & Gross, E. (1994). "The story" of a death: Therapeutic considerations with bereaved families. *Journal of Marital and Family Therapy, 20*(3), 287–296.

Simon, R. (1984, November-December). Stranger in a strange land. *Family Networker,* 21–31, 66–68.

Soto-Fulp, S., & Delcampo, R. (1994). Structural family therapy with Mexican-American family systems. *Contemporary Family Therapy, 16*(5), 349–361.

Stack, S., & Wasserman, I. (1993). Marital status, alcohol consumption and suicide: An analysis of national data. *Journal of Marriage and the Family, 55,* 1018–1024.

Stewart, E., McKenry, P., Rudd, N., & Gavazzi, S. (1994). Family processes as mediators of depressive symptomatology among rural adolescents. *Family Relations, 43,* 38–45.

Stoddard, F., Wilberger, M., & Olafson, E. (1993). A case of functional urinary retention: The use of family play therapy. *Family Process, 32,* 279–289.

Stone, G., & Peeks, B. (1986). The use of strategic family therapy in the school setting: A case study. *Journal of Counseling and Development, 65,* 200–203.

Swartz, L. (1993). What is a family? A contemporary view. *Contemporary Family Therapy, 15*(6), 429–441.

Szapocznik, J., Kurtines, W., Foote, F., Perez-Vidal, A., & Hervis, O. (1986). Conjoint versus one-person family therapy: Further evidence for the effectiveness of conducting family therapy through one person with drug-abusing adolescents. *Journal of Consulting and Clinical Psychology, 54,* 395–397.

Szapocznik, J., Kurtines, W., Santisteban, D., & Rio, A. (1990). Interplay of advances between theory, research, and application in treatment interventions aimed at behavior problem children and adolescents. *Journal of Consulting and Clinical Psychology, 58*(6), 696–703.

Szykula, S., & Fleischman, M. (1985). Reducing out-of-home placements of abused children: Two controlled field studies. *Child Abuse and Neglect, 9,* 277–283.

Tamura, T., & Lau, A. (1992). Connectedness versus separateness: Applicability of family therapy to Japanese families. *Family Process, 31,* 319–338.

Taylor, J. W. (1984). Structured conjoint therapy for spouse abuse cases. *Social Casework, 65,* 11–18.

Thomas, M. (1992). *An introduction to marital and family therapy.* New York: Merrill (Macmillan).

Villeneuve, C., & LaRoche, C. (1993). The child's participation in family therapy: A review and a model. *Contemporary Family Therapy, 15*(2), 105–117.

Watzlawick, P., Weakland, J., & Fisch, R. (1974). *Change: Principles of problem formation and problem resolution.* New York: Norton.

Wuerffel, J., DeFrain, J., & Stinnet, N. (1990). How strong families use humor. *Family Perspective, 24,* 129–141.

Yaccarino, M. (1993). Using Minuchin's structural family therapy techniques with Italian-American families. *Contemporary Family Therapy, 15,* 459–466.

◆

PART THREE

COUNSELING WITH CHILDREN: SPECIAL TOPICS

Chapter 12

◆

Play Therapy

Play therapy can be incorporated into all counseling approaches and is a primary method for working with children ages 2 through 12 years because of their limited cognitive development and ability to verbalize their thoughts and feelings. Play is an integral part of children's lives and a natural mode of learning and relating to others (Landreth, 1982). Erikson (1950) believed that children attempt to understand the rules and regulations of the adult world through their play.

Kottman and Schaefer (1993) suggested that the "upsurge of interest in play therapy and practice over the past decade has been dramatic. Every year an ever-growing number of publications and presentations in this field appear" (p. xv).

The first clinician to use play in therapy with children was Hermine Hug-Hellmuth in the early 1900s. Anna Freud and Melanie Klein continued the work of Hug-Hellmuth and incorporated play therapy into their psychoanalytic practice. The greatest problems in applying psychoanalytic techniques to counseling children are children's relatively undeveloped verbal skills and inadequate cognitive development. Traditionally, raising unresolved and unconscious conflicts from the past to consciousness is achieved by free association and dream analysis and interpretation. Children are relatively receptive to dream analysis, as long as it is kept in the realm of metaphor. That way, it remains make-believe and thus more controlled and less threatening. Resolution of dreams involving conflict is a sign of therapeutic progress and emotional growth.

Free association is a more difficult problem. Children seem unable or unwilling to free-associate verbally. It is now largely believed that nondirective free play, particularly that involving symbolic make-believe (using dolls as particular real people, a stick as a gun, and the like) is closely analogous to free association. The assumption is that children translate their imagination into symbolic play action rather than words. Some counselors use play therapy as a necessary prelude to verbal psychoanalytic counseling and not necessarily as therapy in itself.

Child guidance clinics introduced structured play techniques in the 1920s. David Levy developed structured release therapy in 1939 to help children with

343

specific difficulties through catharsis and to gain insight (Schaefer & Cangelosi, 1993). In all of the structured approaches, the counselor takes an active role in determining the focus of the sessions from case histories and selects the play materials to use. The therapist may play with or for the child to facilitate the release of pent-up emotions.

Another development in play therapy came from the work of Otto Rank, who wrote about the significance of "birth trauma" in the person's development. Jessie Taft, Frederick Allen, and Clark Moustakas adapted Rank's theory in order to develop relationship therapy, which emphasized the counselor-child relationship and present realities rather than past events (Barnes, 1991; Landreth, 1987).

Virginia Axline (1947) modified Carl Rogers's nondirective approach to develop a play therapy model for children. Her work is described in her well-known *Dibs: In Search of Self* (1964). This nondirective, unstructured approach emphasized the importance of a warm, accepting relationship. The child must have the freedom to express his or her feelings, and the counselor's role is to reflect these feelings to enable the child to gain insight and make responsible choices. Limits are necessary only to establish reality (Barnes, 1991).

Adlerian play therapy techniques are based on the personality theory of individual psychology. Therapists choose play techniques to provide encouragement, reveal the family constellation, encourage early recollections, reveal the goals of the child's behavior, and form tentative hypotheses to help children (Kottman & Warlick, 1989). Adlerian therapy has four phases: (1) to establish and maintain a democratic relationship, (2) to discover the lifestyle of the child, (3) to interpret the lifestyle in such a way as to encourage insight by the child client, and (4) to reeducate the child. During the first step, establishing a relationship, the counselor may choose to track the behavior by giving a running account of what he or she is doing or by summarizing what the child has said. The counselor attempts to establish open communication, encourages the child, and asks for information or clarification about what is happening, the family constellation, family atmosphere, or early recollections. How the counselor negotiates limits is important at this stage. The counselor explores the family atmosphere, family constellation, and early recollections during Phase 2 by listening to the child's comments closely, attending to play involving dolls and the dollhouse representing the family, or by having the child draw his or her family. The counselor can facilitate insight through goal disclosure, using dolls or puppets to explain the goal of the behavior. The playroom can be used to teach problem-solving skills during the period of reeducation. The child is encouraged to brainstorm and think of alternative behaviors. The therapist should be very aware of the verbal content expressed by the child and how it relates to the patterns or themes expressed through play (Kottman & Johnson, 1993; Kottman & Warlick, 1989). Kottman (Kottman & Schaefer, 1993) successfully used Adlerian principles and play therapy with a child who was alternating between being verbally abusive and kind and who presented himself as the "king of rock and roll"—behaviors that exhibited his need for power and structure. Three themes emerged from sessions with the child: violence and aggression, nurturing, and singing. The child attempted to emulate his rock-and-roll–singing father if asked the purpose of his behavior or if his songs were used for their shock value. A punching bag was instrumental in helping the child vent his anger toward adults in his life; his play in the kitchen area of the playroom and his family drawings revealed an inconsistent family atmosphere and elicited his need for nurturing; game playing helped him learn to share power.

Gestalt Play Therapy

Oaklander (1993) wrote, "Gestalt therapy is a humanistic, process-oriented form of therapy that is concerned with all aspects of the person: senses, body, feelings, and intellect" (p. 281). She believed that Gestalt concepts and principles are very relevant to the child's growth and development. Oaklander focused on establishing the relationship and making sure that the child is comfortable in making contact during the first sessions of play therapy. The therapy also incorporates activities to help the child develop a greater sense of self. According to Oaklander (1993), "Healthy contact [with others and our environment] involves a feeling of security with oneself, a fearlessness of standing alone" (p. 283). The play therapist attempts to strengthen the child's sense of self and self-support, encourage emotional expression, and teach the child to nurture self. The problems that bring children to therapy are attempts to find health. Part of therapy is helping the child focus on his or her ways of being that are inappropriate and to remember and regain the strength he or she once had. As through play activities children become more aware of what they feel, who they are, and what they need, they realize they can make choices about their behaviors (Oaklander, 1993, 1994).

Cognitive-Behavioral Play Therapy

Knell (1993) said that cognitive-behavioral play therapy can effectively incorporate play techniques as well as verbal and nonverbal communication to help children change their own behavior and become participants in the treatment. The counselor involves the child in play by focusing on the child's thoughts, feelings, fantasies, and environment and teaches the child more adaptive behaviors through techniques such as modeling, role-playing, and behavioral contingencies. Knell described cognitive-behavioral play therapy to treat an electively mute child. In addition to free play, Knell used three puppets: one who wanted to make new friends, one who talked all the time, and one who did not talk, on which cognitive-behavioral techniques were modeled. In a 1990 article, Knell and Moore described cognitive-behavioral play to treat a 5-year-old with encopresis. They incorporated structured, directive behavioral interventions with nondirective play techniques that focused on a stuffed bear. The counselor used positive self-statements for the bear, allowed the animal to express feelings about the toilet, and put the bear through a contingency management program. The child began to compete with the bear for rewards and ceased his soiling behavior. The authors encouraged integrating this method of counseling, usually reserved for adults, with play techniques appropriate to the child's developmental level.

Family Play Therapy

Busby and Lufkin (1992) suggested using play in family therapy; they contended that counselors can discover important information about family relationships and identify common themes as they watch the family play together and that family play therapy can assist in bridging the gap between the adult and child worlds. However, the technique requires a counselor who can help adults break down their resistance to playing, encourage playfulness, and interpret the dynamics of this complex process. Anderson (1993) believed that family play therapy often creates the energy required for change.

> The responsibility for change is not only the parents' or the identified child's but is shared by all the family members. . . . Play helps families understand their maladaptive patterns; it opens up creative avenues, leading to new solutions; and it creates the accessibility for each member to achieve autonomy, while still remaining an intimate part of the family. (p. 463)

Anderson's therapeutic goals of family play are to change the family's emotional atmosphere, role expectations, rigid self-image, and structure.

Play therapy has now become a part of counseling programs in school settings in order to meet the developmental needs of all children. Landreth (1991) stated that play therapy is an essential tool for every school counselor and enumerated eight principles for what he called child-centered play therapy.

1. The counselor exhibits warmth, caring, and genuine interest in the child.
2. The counselor conveys unconditional acceptance of the child as is.
3. The counselor creates an atmosphere of safety to enable the child to explore and express self.
4. The counselor reflects the child's feelings in order to help the child understand himself or herself.
5. The counselor respects the child and his or her ability to solve problems.
6. The counselor trusts the child to lead the counseling relationship in the appropriate direction.
7. The counselor is patient, allowing the therapeutic process to evolve.
8. The counselor establishes only those limits in the relationship that encourage responsible behavior.

Counselors may choose a structured approach with children in play therapy, or they may prefer a nondirective mode, dependent on their orientation. Play techniques can be incorporated with most theories of counseling, including Adlerian and cognitive-behavioral.

Play techniques should be a primary method for counseling with children in the preoperational and concrete stages of cognitive development because of their limited cognitive development and ability to verbalize their thoughts and feelings. Play, a natural mode of expression and communication for children, can be valuable to the counselor in many phases of the counseling process.

According to Hellendoorn (1994), play can help therapists in the following ways:

1. Establish a therapeutic relationship
2. Provide the therapist with a clearer view of the problem and symptoms
3. Promote specific adaptive behaviors
4. Reduce maladaptive behaviors
5. Build better social contacts
6. Help the child communicate emotional expression
7. Provide methods for better ways of handling emotions
8. Reduce tensions and anxieties
9. Promote feelings of being loved and accepted
10. Assist in resolving past emotional experiences
11. Build self-regard and self-acceptance
12. Reduce blocks and facilitate development

Counselors need to consider their objectives for play and either structure the counseling session accordingly or allow the child to determine the structure of play sessions. Because each child is unique, counselors should decide client by client if the objective could be achieved more readily through counselor-directed play or through child-directed play.

Proponents of play therapy differ on the question of limits. Some counselors think children should have no limits in a playroom because they hamper expression and understanding. Others propose only limits that safeguard the welfare of the child and counselor and protect property. Still other counselors place limits on time, space, and certain behaviors. Limits that are imposed should be clearly defined and discussed with the child before play begins. Counselors who include play techniques in regular talking counseling sessions without moving to a playroom may need no discussion of limits.

In selecting play media, counselors should consider the child's age and needs and the purposes of the play therapy. Play media should be congruent with and facilitative of the therapeutic goals for the child. Dolls, dollhouses, puppets, clay, punching toys, blocks, planes, soldiers, tanks, trucks, hammers, soft balls, sand, Magic Markers, and crayons may suit younger children; games such as chess, checkers, or backgammon, electronic games, published games (Life, Monopoly, Twister), paper-and-pencil games (tic-tac-toe), drawing supplies (paper and Magic Markers, blackboard and chalk), or games that require the child to construct or solve problems may be more suitable for older children. Physical activities may be part of counseling sessions or homework assignments.

The counselor may choose to become involved in the play or simply observe the child during play. The counselor's skills of listening, observing, and detecting and reflecting feelings and thoughts are as important during play sessions as they are during regular counseling.

Landreth (1991) stated that limit setting is essential in the play therapy relationship in order for the child to feel safe and accepted. All feelings are acceptable, but not all behaviors. Landreth suggested that limits assure the physical and emotional security of children; protect the counselor, playroom, and media; facilitate the development of responsible behavior; emphasize reality; promote consistency; and contribute to a professional, ethical, and socially acceptable relationship between the child and the counselor. Landreth recommended that limits be set as needed. The counselor can acknowledge the child's feelings with a reflective statement, set the limit, and describe an acceptable alternative behavior; for example, "You are angry with your mother, but the doll is not for hitting. You may hit the plastic punching bag."

THE PLAYROOM AND MEDIA

The playroom can be a room by itself that provides a safe environment similar to that of the counselor's office, or it can be a corner of the counselor's office. Landreth (1991) stated that toys and materials should be selected to allow children to express their feelings and reactions. He suggested asking yourself if the media allow for creative and emotional expression, are interesting to children, facilitate expressive and exploratory play, allow for success or noncommittal play, and are sturdy and free of dangerous parts. He recommends crayons, newsprint, blunt scissors, plastic nursing bottle, small doll with soft body, Play-Doh, suction-cup dart gun, handcuffs, toy soldiers, play dishes, small airplane and car, mask, Nerf ball, Gumby, Popsicle sticks, pipe cleaners, cotton rope, telephone, hand puppets representing aggressive animals, doll family, cardboard house, transparent tape, costume jewelry, and, if space is available, a plastic punching toy and a plastic dishpan filled with an inch of sand.

PLAY TECHNIQUES

Schaefer and Cangelosi (1993) compiled an excellent description of a variety of play techniques for students and practitioners. Some of their suggestions, as well as those of other writers, follow.

Play Interview

In the play interview Conn (1993) described, children play freely with dolls to express their fears, hopes, or concerns. Through the dolls, the children speak for a number of persons in their lives—mother, father, brother, sister, grandparent, and others. The counselor interviews the child during the play to learn more about what is happening, who is speaking, the speaker's feelings, the meaning of the actions, what the child or person would like to know or do, and other meanings of the play. Conn (1993, p. 42) stated that the "emphasis in this procedure is placed upon the concrete difficulties which have arisen at a specific time in the child's life-situation" and that through this method the child becomes aware of and accepts his or her part and responsibility in the life situation. Conn suggested that improvement usually occurs after the first few sessions and that the child participate in the decision to terminate the play sessions, based on his or her needs.

Balloon Bursting in Structured Play Therapy

According to Hambridge (1993, p. 50), "Any new technique of treatment should result in increased economy of effort and closer approximation to the desired result." He contended that structured play therapy saves time and effort by focusing on the specific problem and not wasting time in diffuse play with no therapeutic returns. Once the relationship has been developed, the counselor "recreates in dramatic play" the situation causing pain in the child's life. Hambridge described several play situations, mainly those dealing with aggressive or sexual concerns, for example, a peer attack, genital differences, birth of a baby, and acting out a dream dealing with repressed rage.

Of particular interest is Hambridge's (1993) description of Levy's "balloon bursting" technique to help inhibited children become more assertive. The counselor presents to the child balloons of varying sizes and colors and encourages the child to break them in any way he or she wishes—by stomping, with pins, or using a hammer, for example. The first balloon should be small so that the loud popping noise does not frighten the child. If the child is very anxious, less noisy forms of release may be necessary as a beginning technique.

Hambridge (1993) stressed that counselors should avoid overinvolvement in structured play. He also advocated free play as a follow-up to structured play to obtain maximum value from the session and cautioned counselors to assess the child's ability to deal with the released emotions, to determine if the nature of the play threatens the child, and to assess the capacity of the people in the child's life to deal with changed behavior.

Playhouses

Kuhli (1993) recommended the two-house technique to help children who face traumatic changes in their family structure. The child might be allowed to play with two houses to demonstrate relationships and activities in the homes of separated or divorced parents, or the two houses might show how the child perceives the actual and ideal home. In the case of a child taken from her family because of neglect, Kuhli described how the child resolved her emotional conflicts and attempted to find a stable environment. The technique is appropriate for children entering stepparenting relationships, dealing with the birth of a new sibling, or mourning the loss of loved ones from death, divorce, or separation. The second house can be one where the child finds nurturing, or it could be a way of developing new ways of relating. This tool is also effective for children working through separation trauma, for example, children of separated or divorced parents who are visiting between homes or involved in custody litigation.

Puppets

Irwin (1993) described the "puppet assessment interview," a method for gaining information about a child's creativity, intelligibility, impulsivity, nonverbal communication, and control, as well as something about the characters, setting, plot, and theme of the child's life. The interview also provides diagnostic information about the child's conflicts and ability to cope.

Irwin recommended 15 to 20 puppets in several categories: aggressive, friendly, family puppets of different genders and races, nurse, policeman, teacher, ghost, witch, animals. The counselor asks the child to make up a story, notes which puppets the child selects or rejects for the story, and invites the child to introduce the puppets. As the story is played out, the counselor helps only as requested or needed. The counselor interviews the puppets after the story is told and asks the child about themes, characters, what the child liked or disliked, and other diagnostic, open-ended questions.

Jenkins and Beckh (1993) suggested finger puppets made of rubber balls with features cut into them, painted on, or glued on. A hole cut in the ball allows the child to insert an index finger. The thumb and middle finger act as arms for the puppet, and fourth and fifth fingers are used as legs. Although the puppet is the child's hand, the authors reported that children see puppets as separate and capable of expressing the forbidden or discussing conflicts impersonally. Jenkins and Beckh believed puppetry is a powerful tool that allows children to release feelings they are unable to express.

Telephone

Spero (1993) reported that the telephone has received only passing attention for play therapy but that children recognize it as an object for social interaction and communication. Children imitate their parents, converse with an imaginary friend, or talk to a lost loved one (by death or separation). The telephone also helps break down initial resistance to counseling.

Sandplay

Children love to play in sand and often construct a whole new world with sand and toys, as Margaret Lowenfeld discovered in 1939. She named this form of play therapy the "world technique" (Allan & Berry, 1993). Barnes (1991) noted that sandplay allows the counselor access to the world of the child, is a natural method for promoting healing, and encourages self-discovery. Carey (1990) used the sandbox as a setting for healing for a 9-year-old boy to allow him to talk about his low self-esteem, discuss frustration over his limitations, and resolve his grief and guilt over his father's death. Allan and Berry suggested two 20- × 30- × 3-inch waterproof trays—one for dry sand and one for damp sand; Barnes suggested one box, with water available. Make available many small toys to represent the child's world: little houses and furniture, trains, cars, soldiers, cowboys, and other usual play media, as well as toys of current interest such as Sesame Street characters, baseball or football players, and comic book characters. The child acts out inner conflicts and stresses through the selection and sandplay activities. Once the child has resolved the inner conflict, the play scenes change. The counselor invites the child to play in the sand and sits quietly by (typically 20 to 30 minutes). When the sandplay is complete or even during the activity, the counselor may want to ask the child to tell something about the scene or to describe what is happening. Barnes warned against interpreting and analyzing for the child during sandplay. Counselors can draw the final scene, photograph it, or videotape the session for further review or discussion of the child's progress in counseling.

Waterplay

Hartley, Frank, and Goldenson (1993) noted that the advantages of waterplay as a method of play therapy had been overlooked. Children are excited and fascinated by water, and "it is a basic material through which a child can experience early the satisfactions of mastery and achievement" (p. 126). Waterplay can be an outlet for releasing aggression or a relaxing, soothing process. The authors cautioned that waterplay is not a panacea but is helpful to children who are overly active or constricted.

Food in Play Therapy

Food, another play method not mentioned frequently in the literature, can be diagnostic and therapeutic because of its symbolic meanings and the various reactions to food, according to Haworth and Keller (1993). Of course, counselors should check for allergies or other stomach problems before using this technique. A child who hoards, refuses, gorges, throws, or smashes the cookie, candy, or other treat provides insight about his or her feelings about life. As with other techniques, the counselor then explores with the child the various reactions to food.

Finger Painting

Finger painting is a socially accepted form of playing with mud, according to Arlow and Kadis (1993), that can express feelings, overcome inhibitions, and reveal fantasies. (Woltmann [1993], in fact, recommended mud and clay as a form of play therapy.) Again, the counselor, having established the therapeutic climate, invites the child to play and, after the painting is complete, to tell the story of the painting. The counselor asks for clarification and feelings and makes no interpretation to the child. Stronach-Buschel (1990) reported using paints and clay figures (as well as a dollhouse) to help a 9-year-old girl work through posttraumatic stress after she witnessed family violence in her home.

Arlow and Kadis (1993) found that very few children choose red as the only color in their painting; that younger children age 4 to 10 years most often use several primary colors, and older children use a single color, usually an intermediate shade; and that inhibited, frightened, and insecure children usually select darker colors and may not cover the entire sheet. Aggressive children may extend their paintings beyond the edges of the paper. The writers believe that finger paintings usually reflect the child's personality and habits and therefore are diagnostic as well as therapeutic.

Squiggle Technique

Winnicott introduced the squiggle technique for play therapy as a means for establishing better communication with children (Claman, 1993). The counselor draws a squiggle (a straight, curved, or zigzag line) and asks the child to make a drawing from the squiggle. The counselor then invites the child to tell a story about the drawing and asks open-ended questions about the drawing to explore the child's thoughts and feelings. The process is then reversed. The child draws a squiggle, the counselor draws a picture from the squiggle and tells a story about the picture, and the child asks questions. The counselor's drawing and story interpret the theme from the child's activity and may suggest a solution to the presenting problem.

Art and Music Therapy

Lyons (1993) wrote that children do not realize that their artwork expresses thoughts and feelings and therefore are not defensive about their drawings. She asked parents and children to draw their own pictures of the family and then to make a joint drawing. According to Lyons, the counselor learns from this exercise "how members respond individually to both an unstructured and structured task, as well as their response to drawing together on the same piece of paper" (p. 156). By interpreting the drawings and recognizing the family dynamics, Lyons suggested that counselors can make recommendations about custody decisions.

Music can help children deal with stress, tension, and anxiety. Children are often familiar with simple songs that, sung or listened to, assist them in relaxing and working with stressful situations in a more open manner.

The Emotional Barometer

Elliott (1993) recommended an "emotional barometer" as an ice breaker and as an indication of the child's feelings at the time. The bubble at the top of the barometer contains a "smiley face" and the number 10. The bubble at the bottom of the barometer is labeled "pits" and marked with a zero. After using this emotional barometer for a while, Elliott added "super pits" and "better than great" categories. The child marks his or her feelings with a line to indicate how things are going in general or in specific (home, school, friends, other situations).

After marking the emotional barometer and telling about what is going on, the child writes the positive happenings on one end of a teetertotter drawing and the negatives on the other end. The client can see the positive and negative things going on and to decide what to work on next.

Elliott recommended these tools to counselors to establish the relationship, provide a record of good days and bad, and evaluate progress.

Role-Playing

Although role-play is typically used to help children and adults act out situations or rehearse new learning, Levenson and Herman (1993) recommended role-playing to help children "for its experiential value in promoting an internal corrective emotional experience" (p. 229). They pointed out that role-playing allows children direct participation in problem areas and discussion of them. The authors believed that role-playing permits the counselor to see how the child perceives the world and relates to others. Celano (1990) used role-plays to help sexually abused children practice prevention techniques such as assertive behavior, facilitate release of the children's feelings, stimulate group discussion, deal with anxiety, and help counselors assess the children's world. The role-play technique is simple to incorporate into counseling, and most children enjoy acting out the situations. (See chapter 8 for a more complete description of this counseling technique.)

Magic

Children are intrigued by magic, and several counselors have suggested that it provides a new means of communicating with children (Bowman, 1986; Frith & Walker, 1983). Spruill and Poidevant (1993) describe three magic activities that can be incorporated into counseling. "How to Change Big Problems into Little Ones and Keep Little Problems from Getting Bigger" is a magic effect available in stores as "The Growing Ball Outdone." Woody, the magic rabbit, which is available under the name "Rabbits, Rabbits, Rabbits," can be used to teach friendship skills and promote awareness of feelings. Rocky, a raccoon puppet, can be used to explain the role of the counselor.

Bow (1988) advised the counselor to note children's reactions to the trick (amazed, critical, passive) and how they deal with the secrecy of magic; does the child have a strong desire to know how the trick was done or just ignore that it is secret? Bow cautioned that magic should not be used with children who are paranoid, psychotic, or intellectually very limited.

Spruill and Poidevant (1993) suggested the following guidelines for using magic with children:

1. The child should be actively involved in the activity.
2. The counselor must enjoy the activity for it to be effective.
3. Counselors should use materials with visual appeal.
4. Choose magic tricks carefully and keep them brief.
5. Never reveal how you do the trick.

Ventriloquism

Bow (1988) reported that vent figures (dolls, puppets, stuffed animals, and the like) have a therapeutic value in working with children, for example, in gathering information from resistant children or those who have been abused and are reluctant to open up to the counselor. Vent figures provide a comfortable distance between the counselor and the child, or the child can identify with figures that have similar problems. Children can explore and evaluate the methods the vent figures use to solve problems. Counselors can also use vent figures to teach social skills and to discuss the consequences of appropriate or inappropriate behaviors.

Family Word Association Game

Bow (1988) also suggested the Family Word Association Game as a technique for "gathering specific and objective information about how the child views each family member" (p. 10). The child first draws a picture of everyone in the family doing something and then, using a stack of cards with descriptive words on them, places each card beside the person it best describes. The 80 or more cards have descriptors such as "mean," "lonely," "rude," "cheerful," "pretty," "happy," "gets mad easily," "cries a lot," and "mother's pet." Reasons for the selections are clarified by the child.

Board Games

Reid (1993) believed that "a game more closely matches the developmental interests and orientation toward the social world of latency-age children" (p. 527). Games used in play therapy are enjoyable but include a sense of pretense.

They may elicit emotional feelings that need to be dealt with or be used as a projective tool. Counselors may use games to build a therapeutic alliance with children, promote emotional growth through the pleasurable process of playing a game, enhance communication, help children master anxiety, or promote socialization. These games may be board games, fine-motor or gross-motor skill games, card games, and street games, according to Reid, who recommended the *Childwork/Childplay* catalogue for listings of therapeutic board games. Counselors can also develop their own therapeutic games.

Chess and checkers are often used as play media for children with self-esteem problems, antisocial or obsessive-compulsive behaviors, or a withdrawn manner. Gardner (1993b) stated that the "closer the game resembles a 'blank screen' the more likely the therapist will obtain material derived from the unconscious processes" (p. 248). Whatever game is selected, Gardner cautioned, both child and counselor must enjoy the activity. He suggested that games can teach children the lessons of life—that one is responsible for one's actions and the consequences that follow—and that games release emotional tension, but that games have little therapeutic value.

Competitive Play

Although competitive youth programs such as basketball, ballet, football, and gymnastics can have therapeutic effects and develop new skills in children, Kaforey and McKnight (1995) warned against the negative effects of competitive play. Sports or play geared to wins and losses may produce many more losers than winners, especially in self-esteem and attitude. The authors encourage parents and other adults to structure competitive play so that enjoyment of the game is more important than winning or losing. Parents may benefit from being involved in counseling with the child because parents often contribute to the stress of competing children.

Group Play Therapy

Children age 2 to 12 with similar problems or experiences that affect their behavior and interpersonal adjustment may benefit from a play group. O'Connor (1991) cautioned that these children should display a range of functioning to avoid competition for the therapist's attention and to provide opportunities for modeling. O'Connor suggested no more than 6 children per adult in the group, no more than 10 children in a group with two adults, no more than a 3-year age span among members, similar socioeconomic status and ethnic background, and no more than 15 IQ points separating the children. The advisability of mixing boys and girls in one group depends on the age of the members, the type of group, and the group goals. O'Connor (1991) stated that the role of play in a group is similar to that of individual play. The interactions between the group leader and the child's peers in the safety of a group are the curative elements.

Most of the literature on play therapy focuses on the effectiveness of the technique for one client. For this reason, counselors generalize the findings to broader populations cautiously. Obviously, counselors can conclude something about the efficacy of procedures by assessing progress toward counseling goals. Barnes (1991) suggested several criteria for assessing progress:

1. The child comes to the sessions looking more hopeful and relaxed.
2. The child appears to have increased confidence.
3. The child can summarize what has happened and what has been learned.
4. Interactions with parents appear more relaxed.
5. There are changes in play patterns, interactions, and/or body language.
6. The child openly raises a problem or concern.

Counselors may also want to seek supervision in the area or enter a consultative relationship with another professional until they feel comfortable with their ability to use play techniques effectively.

Although play therapy is well accepted as a counseling intervention in clinical settings, Campbell (1993) pointed out that some counselors question whether it should be a part of a school counseling program because of the time and counselor skills required for effective treatment. She concluded that play is incorporated into many school counseling activities, such as group guidance, group counseling, and individual counseling, and "it seems that many who work with young children can agree that the developmental level of children in terms of language and social-emotional development makes the use of play materials necessary for full communication and thus for counseling to take place" (p. 13).

◆ ◆ ◆

CASE STUDIES[1]

Chris

Chris was referred to play therapy at age 3 after being removed from his mother's custody because of issues of neglect. The mother abused alcohol and drugs and had reportedly exposed Chris to many inappropriate situations, including open sex with her boyfriends, frequent alcohol and drug use, and late parties.

The primary focus of Chris's play therapy was to allow him to express his needs and explore his frustrations and concerns about his mother. Chris chose several venues for his play therapy but seemed to enjoy most playing with Ninja Turtles,

---

[1]These case studies of children treated with play therapy techniques were contributed by Richard Pitcock, play therapist in private practice and at Harriet Cohn Mental Health Center, Clarksville, Tennessee.

Power Rangers, and other TV character toys. Chris's play was aggressive and quite hostile. He was particularly aggressive toward the female dolls and female characters represented. Chris frequently threw the mommy dolls and female characters across the room, and he broke several female toys, which he quickly said he did because he was mad at his mommy. After approximately 6 months of therapy, during which time his mother refused to make changes or involve herself in her son's therapy, social service agencies decided to deny her visitation and put Chris up for adoption. The therapist had the job of relaying this information to Chris. Chris needed an approach that would inform him that his contact with his mother was changing and that would allow him to express his frustration and other feelings about this circumstance.

The therapist chose to play a game of Cowboys and Indians. Chris chose to be the Indian, so the therapist played the part of Cowboy. Guns, ropes, bows, and play arrows were utilized, and Chris was encouraged to tie up the therapist. When tied up, the therapist began to talk about needing to be rescued by the Cavalry. A cotherapist broke in occasionally and saved the therapist from the Indian. However, Chris quickly recaptured and tied up the Cowboy as quickly as he could get away. Frequently the cotherapist did not come into the room, thus leaving the therapist abandoned in the hands of his captor. After a while Chris volunteered, "How come the Cavalry does not always come to rescue you?" The therapist explained to Chris that, like some people, the Cavalry was not always there when they were wanted and then asked, "Are people always there for you when you want them to be?" He quickly responded no and said that his mommy sometimes would come when she said she would and sometimes she would not. He also said his mommy had left him behind and that is why he had to be in foster care. Chris seemed to see the relationship between the Cavalry and Mommy. At this point, Chris was asked, "How would you feel if the Cavalry never came back for the Cowboy? What should the Cowboy do?" Chris said he was very confused about what a good Cowboy should do when the Cavalry does not come. The therapist introduced the concept "If they come, they come; if they do not, they do not" and asked him to consider that, if Mommy comes around for visits and if Mommy is involved in his life, then this is good, but if she does not, then a person has to get on with life, and life is still fun, and there are still people who care. So, in essence, if Mommy comes, she comes; if she does not, she does not. Chris did not quickly accept this idea; in fact, he said that mommies and cavalries were different and that mommies should always be there. However, he gradually accepted that his mother was not reliable or dependable and that he may have to adjust to the disappointment of seeing her only infrequently or perhaps never at all.

Chris chose to play Cavalry on several later occasions, but he soon tired of this activity. Chris seemed to realize that his mother was not going to be in his life and that he could never really count on her. The therapist noted increased levels of sadness and hopelessness. However, Chris's overall behavioral problems began to decrease. Play therapy continued to be unstructured, to allow Chris to express his needs and wants, and to utilize the play therapy room as a source of fun and happiness; he was able to put aside the worries and concerns about his mother for at least a short time each day. Chris is currently still involved in play therapy and continues to make steady progress as this book goes to press.

Tommy

Tommy was referred for play therapy at age 10 after his mother and teachers identified troublesome levels of energy and a poor attention span in the classroom. Tommy's pediatrician diagnosed attention deficit–hyperactivity disorder (ADHD), but his mother was strongly against conventional medication. Therefore, play therapy was chosen to help Tommy with his ADHD problem.

Typically, play therapy utilizes an unstructured approach in which symbolic toys help a child work through emotional needs. However, a more structured approach to play therapy utilizes games or specific activities to promote skills or develop problem-solving strategies. A structured game approach encourages clients with ADHD to develop strategies, pay attention, and sit through the game. Unlike school work, chores, or other boring activities, board games are typically fun for children.

As his game, Tommy chose checkers. He was familiar with many of the moves of the various pieces, as he had played chess with his brother, but he was unfamiliar with certain strategies such as crowning and specific approaches to playing. Tommy seemed enthralled in the play, and he easily sat through as many games as his 1-hour sessions allowed. In a 10-week program, Tommy and his therapist concentrated intently on developing checkers strategies and earning rewards. Tommy was promised intrinsic rewards such as praise, recognition, and extra time with his therapist for his successes. Typically a play therapist allows clients to succeed and win in the play therapy room. In a structured game approach, however, occasionally the therapist allows the child to lose, thus encouraging the child to do better. Tommy won most of the games, and he was frequently rewarded for these successes. After 10 weeks, the structured approach to game therapy stopped, but Tommy's family and friends continued to play chess with him and to allow him to pursue this activity. Even 6 months after these therapy sessions, Tommy's teacher continued to comment on his improved behavior, including longer attention span, and better ability to sit through activities. As a reward in the classroom, the teacher allowed Tommy and other students to begin a checkers club, which reinforced Tommy's therapeutic goals.

RESEARCH AND APPLICATIONS

On the topic of the child's right to the expressive arts, Jalongo (1990) presented four well-referenced arguments for using this medium with children. According to Jalongo, the expressive arts do the following:

1. Foster learning from the inside out and provide authentic learning that changes behavior and encourages reflection

2. Enhance the child's ability to interpret symbols; on the symbolic ability of the child, everything distinctly human develops
3. Promote growth in all areas of development
4. Place the child in the roles of meaning maker, constructor, discoverer, and embodiment of knowledge rather than that of a passive recipient of ready-made answers and advice

Counseling through the expressive arts, such as play, bibliotherapy, drama, music, puppetry, and poetry, is used frequently to compensate for children's limited verbal abilities for describing problems, feelings, and expectations. Landreth (1987) suggested that play therapy is an essential tool for counselors working with children and that counselors find the technique most rewarding. Johnson (1987) found that a computer helped an overly dependent young client to talk about painful feelings, gain self-confidence, and relieve his anxiety over losing parental support. Brand (1987) contended that writing "seems to proceed hand in hand with psychological growth, to reflect and enhance it, to deepen and extend it, and often to quicken the process" (p. 274). Irwin (1987) used drama to understand the inner world of her clients—the "symbolization, conflict, characterization, and interaction" (p. 282). Even though for the unmusical counselor, Bowman (1987) called music a powerful tool for counseling children. James and Myer (1987) described puppets used for counseling with children and offered some precautions for the novice. Allan and Berry (1987) suggested sandplay for counselors who have basic skills in play therapy. Gladding (1987) recommended incorporating poetry and poetic forms into guidance activities to give children "an appreciation for creativity and a new perception of life events" (p. 310). Mazza (1986), too, strongly recommended poetry and popular music to enhance counseling. These expressive forms of play therapy may provide counselors with additional tools that add to their effectiveness in counseling and developing treatment plans for children.

Barrows (1984) presented a case study of an 8-year-old boy with severe learning disabilities who benefited from play therapy. He was seen 4 times a week for 4 years. The play therapy was self-directed, and the activities were interpreted with insights into the child's inner conflicts. He and the counselor resolved issues sequentially as they arose, thereby facilitating conflict resolution. Conflict resolution helped to release the child's ability to use his imagination and to learn.

Barlow, Strother, and Landreth (1985) presented a case of play-therapy treatment for a 3-year-old who was pulling out her hair as a way of reacting to poor parenting practices. Treatment consisted of allowing the child to engage in self-directed play in a room filled with toys (dollhouse, family figures, furniture, animals, and so on). The counselor respected the child's capacity for self-direction and made no attempt to direct or change the child. The parents were given three sessions on how to parent the child more effectively. Although no follow-up report was presented, the authors noted that the child's hair grew back in seven sessions. Self-directed play therapy provided a valuable assessment tool as well as a therapeutic experience for the child.

Bertoia and Allan (1988), in an article on spontaneous drawings, described using the method successfully with a terminally ill 8-year-old girl. Based on the idea that the unconscious exists and that it can express itself through spontaneous or impromptu drawings, the authors described the counselor's role in helping children communicate through their drawings. The first step is to build rapport and create the safe, nonjudgmental climate. Children have the choice of what to draw. If a child is short on ideas, the counselor asks the child to draw a picture from one of his or her dreams. After the child has drawn the picture, the counselor thanks the child, acknowledges the effort, dates the picture, and asks for a title and a story. The drawings are kept in a file, and the stories are recorded on tape. The counselor's job is to help the child tell the story through active listening and summarizing remarks. The symbols in the picture relate to the child's thoughts, feelings, and expectations. The counselor can also help the child tell his or her story by pointing out the symbols and saying, "I noticed you have drawn a big bear; I wonder what the bear is thinking, feeling, and planning to do next." A follow-up statement might be, "I wonder why the bear would do that." The authors recommended sources for checking symbolic meanings of drawings (Cooper, 1978; Thompson & Allan, 1987).

In an article directed toward counseling middle school and junior high school students, Kottman (1990) pointed out the benefits of therapeutic game play, stories or metaphors, and role-play–simulations to involve these children in the counseling process. All these activities, whether one-on-one or in a group, provide diagnostic and therapeutic assistance. Even a game of checkers can provide information about a child's attitudes toward self, attitudes toward others, thoughts, feelings, and behavior patterns.

Kahn and Kahn (1990) recommended that counselors have children write their own books to help the children move through crisis periods in their lives. Through a process of expressive writing, children describe the origins, experiences, and adjustment strategies involved in coping with their own difficulties. The books can be illustrated in any art forms the children choose. The main point children learn from the experience is that feelings that are written down and understood become less frightening.

Any of the expressive arts (mutual storytelling, doll play, drawing, painting, or puppet play) can help children work through unresolved psychic trauma or conflict without addressing their own problems directly. The key to the process may be selecting the medium most comfortable to the child and the counselor.

Although the theory, techniques, and literature review of play therapy included in this chapter have focused on children age 2 to 12. A growing body of evidence indicates that play therapy can be an effective counseling intervention for clients of all ages, including adolescents, couples, employed people, and geriatric clients.

REFERENCES

Allan, J., & Berry, P. (1993). Sandplay. In C. E. Schaefer & D. M. Cangelosi (Eds.), *Play therapy techniques* (pp. 117–123). Northvale, NJ: Jason Aronson.

Allan J., & Berry, P. (1987). Sandplay. *Elementary School Guidance and Counseling, 21,* 300–306.

Anderson, R. (1993). As the child plays, so grows the family tree: Family play therapy. In T. Kottman & C. Schaefer (Eds.), *Play therapy in action* (pp. 457–483). Northvale, NJ: Jason Aronson.

Arlow, J., & Kadis, A. (1993). Finger painting. In C. E. Schaefer & D. M. Cangelosi (Eds.), *Play therapy techniques* (pp. 161–175). Northvale, NJ: Jason Aronson.

Axline, V. (1947). *Play therapy.* Boston: Houghton Mifflin.

Axline, V. (1964). *Dibs: In search of self.* Boston: Houghton Mifflin.

Barlow, K., Strother, J., & Landreth, G. (1985). Child-centered play therapy: Nancy from baldness to curls. *School Counselor, 32,* 347–363.

Barnes, M. (1991). *The magic of play therapy: A workshop on specialized therapeutic skills with children.* Ontario: Mandala Therapeutic Services.

Barrows, K. (1984). A child's difficulty in using his gifts and imagination. *Journal of Child Psychotherapy, 10,* 15–26.

Bertoia, J., & Allan, J. (1988). Counseling seriously ill children: Use of spontaneous drawings. *Elementary School Guidance and Counseling, 22,* 206–221.

Bow, J. (1988). Treating resistant children. *Child and Adolescent Social Work, 5*(1), 3–15.

Bowman, R. (1986). The magic counselor: The elementary school counselor's role. *Elementary School Guidance and Counseling, 21,* 128–138.

Bowman, R. (1987). Approaches for counseling children through music. *Elementary School Guidance and Counseling, 21,* 284–291.

Brand, A. (1987). Writing as counseling. *Elementary School Guidance and Counseling, 21,* 266–275.

Busby, D. M., & Lufkin, A. C. (1992). Tigers are something else: A case for family play. *Contemporary Family Therapy, 14*(6), 437–453.

Campbell, C. (1993). Play, the fabric of elementary school counseling programs. *Elementary School Guidance and Counseling, 28,* 10–15.

Carey, L. (1990). Sandplay therapy with a troubled child. *Arts in Psychotherapy, 17,* 197–209.

Celano, M. P. (1990). Activities and games for group psychotherapy with sexually abused children. *International Journal of Group Psychotherapy, 40,* 419–429.

Claman, L. (1993). The squiggle-drawing game. In C. E. Schaefer & D. M. Cangelosi (Eds.), *Play therapy techniques* (pp. 177–189). Northvale, NJ: Jason Aronson.

Conn, J. H. (1993). The play-interview. In C. E. Schaefer & D. M. Cangelosi (Eds.), *Play therapy techniques* (pp. 9–44). Northvale, NJ: Jason Aronson.

Cooper, J. C. (1978). *An illustrated encyclopedia of traditional symbols.* London: Thames and Hudson.

Elliott, S. (1993). The emotional barometer. In C. E. Schaefer & D. M. Cangelosi (Eds.), *Play therapy techniques* (pp. 191–196). Northvale, NJ: Jason Aronson.

Erikson, E. (1950). *Childhood and society.* New York: Norton.

Frith, G. H., & Walker, J. C. (1983). Magic is a motivation for handicapped students. *Teaching Exceptional Children, 15,* 108–110.

Gardner, R. A. (1993a). Mutual storytelling. In C. E. Schaefer & D. M. Cangelosi (Eds.), *Play therapy techniques* (pp. 199–209). Northvale, NJ: Jason Aronson.

Gardner, R. A. (1993b). Checkers. In C. E. Schaefer & D. M. Cangelosi (Eds.), *Play therapy techniques* (pp. 247–262). Northvale, NJ: Jason Aronson.

Gladding, S. (1987). Poetic expression: A counseling art in elementary schools. *Elementary School Guidance and Counseling, 21,* 307–311.

Hall, C. (1954). *A primer of Freudian psychology.* New York: Mentor.

Hambridge, G. (1993). Structured play therapy. In C. E. Schaefer & D. M. Cangelosi (Eds.), *Play therapy techniques* (pp. 45–61). Northvale, NJ: Jason Aronson.

Hartley, R. E., Frank, L. K., & Goldenson, R. M. (1993). Water play. In C. E. Schaefer & D. M. Cangelosi (Eds.), *Play therapy techniques* (pp. 125–130). Northvale, NJ: Jason Aronson.

Haworth, M. R., & Keller, M. J. (1993). The use of food in therapy. In C. E. Schaefer & D. M. Cangelosi (Eds.), *Play therapy techniques* (pp. 131–139). Northvale, NJ: Jason Aronson.

Hellendoorn, J. (1994). Play therapy with mentally retarded children. In K. O'Connor & C. Schaefer (Eds.), *Handbook of play therapy: Vol. 2. Advances and innovations* (pp. 349–370). New York: John Wiley & Sons.

Irwin, E. (1987). Drama: The play's the thing. *Elementary School Guidance and Counseling, 21,* 276–283.

Irwin, E. (1993). Using puppets for assessment. In C. E. Schaefer & D. M. Cangelosi (Eds.), *Play therapy techniques* (pp. 69–81). Northvale, NJ: Jason Aronson.

Jalongo, M. (1990). The child's right to the expressive arts: Nurturing the imagination as well as the intellect. *Childhood Education, 66,* 195–201.

James, R., & Myer, R. (1987). Puppets: The elementary school counselor's right or left arm. *Elementary School Guidance and Counseling, 21,* 292–299.

Jenkins, R., & Beckh, E. (1993). Finger puppets and mask making. In C. E. Schaefer & D. M. Cangelosi (Eds.), *Play therapy techniques* (pp. 83–90). Northvale, NJ: Jason Aronson.

Johnson, R. (1987). Using computer art in counseling children. *Elementary School Guidance and Counseling, 21,* 262–265.

Kaforey, G., & McKnight, J. (1995). *Counseling the young competitor.* Unpublished manuscript, University of Tennessee, Knoxville.

Kahn, B., & Kahn, W. (1990). I am the author books (ITABS). *Elementary School Guidance and Counseling, 25,* 153–157.

Knell, S. (1993). To show and not tell: Cognitive-behavioral play therapy. In T. Kottman & C. Schaefer (Eds.), *Play therapy in action* (pp. 169–208). Northvale, NJ: Jason Aronson.

Knell, S., & Moore, D. (1990). Cognitive-behavioral play therapy in the treatment of encopresis. *Journal of Clinical Child Psychology, 19*(1), 55–60.

Kottman, T. (1990). Counseling middle school students: Techniques that work. *Elementary School Guidance and Counseling, 25,* 138–145.

Kottman, T. (1993). The king of rock and roll: An application of Adlerian play therapy. In T. Kottman & C. Schaefer (Eds.), *Play therapy in action* (pp. 133–167). Northvale, NJ: Jason Aronson.

Kottman, T., & Johnson, V. (1993). Adlerian play therapy: A tool for school counselors. *Elementary School Guidance and Counseling, 28,* 42–51.

Kottman, T., & Schaefer, C. (Eds.). (1993). *Play therapy in action.* Northvale, NJ: Jason Aronson.

Kottman, T., & Warlick, J. (1989). Adlerian play therapy: Practical considerations. *Individual Psychology, 45*(4), 433–445.

Kuhli, L. (1993). The use of two houses in play therapy. In C. E. Schaefer & D. M. Cangelosi (Eds.), *Play therapy techniques* (pp. 63–68). Northvale, NJ: Jason Aronson.

Landreth, G. (1987). Play therapy: Facilitative use of child's play in elementary school counseling. *Elementary School Guidance and Counseling, 21*(4), 253–261.

Landreth, G. (1991). *Play therapy: The art of the relationship.* Muncie, IN: Accelerated Development.

Landreth, G. (Ed.). (1982). *Play therapy: Dynamics of the process of counseling with children.* Springfield, IL: Charles C. Thomas.

Levenson, R.., Jr. & Herman, J. (1993). Role playing. In C. E. Schaefer & D. M. Cangelosi (Eds.), *Play therapy techniques* (pp. 225–236). Northvale, NJ: Jason Aronson.

Lyons, S. (1993). Art psychotherapy evaluations of children in custody disputes. *Arts in Psychotherapy, 20,* 153–159.

Mazza, N. (1986). Poetry and popular music in social work education: The liberal arts perspective. *Arts in Psychotherapy, 13,* 293–299.

Oaklander, V. (1993). From meek to bold: A case study of Gestalt play therapy. In T. Kottman & C. Schaefer (Eds.), *Play therapy in action: A casebook for practitioners* (pp. 281–300). Northvale, NJ: Jason Aronson.

Oaklander, V. (1994). Gestalt play therapy. T. Kottman & C. Schaefer (Eds.), In *Play therapy: A casebook for practitioners* (pp. 143–156). Northvale, NJ: Jason Aronson.

O'Connor, K. (1991). The practice of group play therapy. In *The play therapy primer: An integration of theories and techniques* (pp. 323–330). New York: John Wiley & Sons.

Reid, S. (1993). It's all in the game: Game play therapy. In T. Kottman & C. Schaefer (Eds.), *Play therapy in action: A casebook for practitioners* (pp. 527–560). Northvale, NJ: Jason Aronson.

Schaefer, C. (1994). Play therapy for psychic trauma in children. In K. O'Connor & C. Schaefer (Eds.), *Handbook of play therapy: Vol. 2. Advances and innovations* (pp. 297–318). New York: John Wiley & Sons.

Schaefer, C. E., & Cangelosi, D. M. (Eds.). (1993). *Play therapy techniques.* Northvale, NJ: Jason Aronson.

Spero, M. (1993). Use of the telephone in play therapy. In C. E. Schaefer & D. M. Cangelosi (Eds.), *Play therapy techniques* (pp. 101–108). Northvale, NJ: Jason Aronson.

Spruill, D., & Poidevant, J. (1993). Magic and the school counselor. *Elementary School Guidance and Counseling, 27,* 228–233.

Stronach-Buschel, B. (1990). Trauma, children and art. *American Journal of Art Therapy, 29,* 48–52.

Thompson, F., & Allan, J. (1987). Common symbols of children in art counseling. *Guidance and Counseling, 2*(5), 24–32.

Woltmann, A. (1993). Mud and clay. In C. E. Schaefer & D. M. Cangelosi (Eds.), *Play therapy techniques* (pp. 141–157). Northvale, NJ: Jason Aronson.

Chapter 13

◆

Consultation

HISTORICAL PERSPECTIVE AND DEFINITION

Kurpius and Fuqua (1993) pointed out that the definition of *consultation* and the role of the consultant have evolved over the years from that of one-on-one content expert to process helper to today's collaborative consultation. Consulting was first reported in the literature as a responsibility of counselors in the late 1960s and early 1970s (Jackson & Hayes, 1993). Kurpius and Robinson (1978) wrote that the practice of consultation appeared shortly after World War II. In 1979, Kahnweiler reviewed the literature in four major American Personnel and Guidance Association (now the American Counseling Association) journals to examine the history of consultation. The first articles on the counselor as a consultant appeared in 1957 and focused on consultation as an alternative to direct-service counseling. Models for consultation did not appear until several years later, and many of the early models were vague and abstract (Kahnweiler, 1979).

According to Dougherty (1990), consultation in the mental health field began in the late 1940s with the passage of legislation that established the National Institute of Mental Health (NIMH). Because the need for mental health services exceeded the availability of such services, consultation became a method of providing preventive treatment in an attempt to meet mental health needs. Dougherty (1990) described the consultant as "a person, typically a human service professional, who delivers direct service to another person (consultee) who has a work-related or care-taking problem with a person, group, organization, or community (client system)" (p. 12).

A 1992 issue of the *Consulting Psychology Journal* reported that seven "experts" in consultation provided very similar definitions, but each had a unique aspect, as seen from the following excerpted statements (Kurpius & Fuqua, 1993, p. 598):

1. Provide information, advice, or help
2. Provide an outside gestalt

3. Provide a theory of process and organizational functioning
4. Rely on the use of multiple models
5. Require a strong conceptual process
6. Create a foundation for understanding interrelationships among the different ways to view organizational phenomena
7. Show how generic knowledge is transmitted from consultant to the consultee system

Kurpius and Fuqua (1993) summarized: "In general, consultants help consultees to think of their immediate problem as part of the larger system, and not only to understand how problems are solved but also to understand how they were developed, maintained, or avoided" (p. 598). Much of what is written concerning consultation refers to the process as it occurs in an organization rather than in a school or mental health setting.

SCHOOL CONSULTATION MODEL

According to Glosoff and Koprowicz (1990), consultation by counselors who work primarily with children typically involves the following:

- Conduct professional development workshops and discussions with teachers and other school personnel on subjects such as substance abuse or child abuse
- Assist teachers in working with individual students or groups of students
- Provide relevant materials and resources to teachers, especially relating to classroom guidance curriculum
- Help to identify and develop programs for students with special needs
- Participate in school committees that address substance abuse, human growth and development, school climate, and other guidance-related areas
- Design and conduct parent-education classes
- Interpret student information, such as results of standardized tests for students and team members
- Consult regularly with other specialists (for example, social workers, psychologists, and representatives from community agencies)

By the end of the 1960s, the literature had included models for behavioral consultation, Adlerian consultation, teacher-consultation groups, in-service training, and classroom observation (Kahnweiler, 1979).

Myrick (1987) presented three models of consultation: crisis, remedial, and developmental. According to Myrick, crisis consultation addresses urgent, critical issues; remedial consultation focuses on intervening to avert a crisis; and developmental consultation is preventive in that it sets up conditions that facilitate children's effective growth and development. (Parenting classes are an example of developmental consultation.) Myrick (1987) also defined four approaches to consultation: diagnostic-prescriptive, staff development and training, case management, and process. School psychologists probably use the *diagnostic-prescriptive* approach more than other helping professions. Information about the client/consultee is presented and analyzed, alternatives are considered, and a recommendation (prescription) is made. A school psychologist who suspects that a child has an attention-deficit disorder, for instance, presents the results of interviews with a child's parents and teacher, observations of classroom behavior, and the results of a battery of tests for a team of experts to consider. The consultants discuss various options and make a recommendation for helping the child find better ways of learning and behaving.

Myrick (1987) pointed out that often adults lack knowledge or skills to work effectively with children. He suggested the *staff development and training* consultative approach to teach school personnel new skills and to review and refine skills already present. A consultant might provide information on techniques for discipline problems, understanding developmental stages of children, teaching children with learning disabilities, classroom management, or a variety of other topics. This method of consultation could be effective for adults other than staff who work with children. Parenting classes that address developmental issues, methods for disciplining children, and ways to cope with children's special needs could help many adults, both professional and nonprofessional, who interact with children.

According to Myrick (1987), the *case-management* approach considers one particular case and is similar to the case group, or C-group, which Poppen and Thompson (1975) described as follows:

1. Brief description of the case
2. Discussion of the present situation
   a. What is happening?
   b. What behavior is helpful or hurtful?
3. How does the child view himself or herself and the situation?
   a. View of self
   b. Goals
   c. Self-evaluation of behaviors
4. How are others involved? What are their reactions?
5. What are alternatives or new behaviors?
6. What helpful resources are available?
7. Specific plan of action

This is a sharing group; there is no expert advice, diagnostic labeling or blame. Participants share feelings and experiences and help each other find new ways of coping with the presenting problem.

Myrick (1987) pointed out that children's problems are sometimes not necessarily their own problems but a function of the environment in which they live—home, classroom, or social system. In these cases, consultants can help children increase their awareness of events in the environment or values of a system, assess how the children respond, and evaluate their strength and weakness for effecting change. He called this consultative technique the *process approach.* A counselor may want to examine the child's environment with the teacher or parents to determine if it is contributing to his or her hyperactivity, stealing, aggression, poor self-image, or other problems.

Although counseling and consultation involve many of the same processes, Myrick (1987) advised considering different factors before entering a consultation relationship.

1. *Who is the client?* The answer affects the focus of discussions, interventions selected, and possibly issues of confidentiality.

2. *Which consultation approach should be used?* Would the diagnostic-prescriptive approach, staff (or parent) training, case group, or process approach or a combination of approaches be most effective?

3. *When and where does consultation happen?* Do certain conditions make individual or group consultation preferable or necessary?

4. *Who initiates the consultation?* Teachers, parents, and other adult consultees involved with the child may not be willing to discuss the case openly and without defensiveness.

5. *What are some pitfalls?* Myrick advised avoiding eliciting excessive guilt and defensiveness, giving advice freely, displaying too much self-disclosure, and other behaviors that good counselors (and good consultants) avoid.

MENTAL HEALTH CONSULTATION

Caplan's (cited in Dougherty, 1990) mental health consultation model and Bergan's (cited in Dougherty, 1990) behavioral consultation model have had wide support for a number of years (Dougherty, 1990; Dougherty, Dougherty, & Purcell, 1991; Dustin & Blocher, 1984; Meyers, 1981). Dougherty (1990) presented a detailed description of Caplan's model and its application to individual and administrative situations. Blocher (1987) cautioned that mental health consultation should not be seen as supervisory—that is, as having a more highly trained professional take over the case. Rather, the purpose is to help the consultee analyze and understand his or her interactions with the client, treatment approach and responses, and to provide support to the consultee.

Mental health consultation, according to Caplan (cited in Dougherty, 1990), focuses on primary prevention and involves helping professionals and nonprofessionals. Caplan believed that people seek consultation for four reasons: lack of understanding, lack of skills, lack of confidence, and lack of objectivity. Meyers (1981) suggested that consultants provide knowledge regarding child development, interpersonal dynamics, and abnormal psychology to help an adult understand a child. To enhance their skills, he encouraged consultants to develop the ability to observe and analyze the environment and interactions and, based on these observations, assist the adult to develop intervention skills.

For counselors interested in a more structured behavioral model, Brown, Pryzwansky, and Schulte (1991) developed general interview guidelines for noncrisis and crisis consulting. The consultant in a noncrisis situation (developmental interview) focuses on the following:

1. Establish clear general objectives.
2. Reach agreement with the consultee in the relationship between general objectives and more specific ones.
3. Generate with the consultee clearly defined, prioritized performance objectives.
4. Decide how accomplishment of performance objectives will be assessed and recorded.
5. Decide on follow-up meetings.

In a crisis or problem-centered interview, the outline focuses on the following:

1. Identify and describe problematic behavior(s) by collecting data from several sources concerning the nature of the problem.
2. Determine the conditions under which these behaviors occur, their antecedents, and their consequences; the consultant and consultee analyze either the setting or interpersonal factors that contribute to the problem or the client's skill deficits.
3. Decide on assessment procedures; the consultant and consultee design a plan to deal with the problem by identifying objectives, selecting behavioral interventions, considering barriers to be overcome, and evaluating progress.
4. Schedule future meetings. (pp. 75–76)

Combining the work of several writers in the field of consultation (Blocher, 1987; Keller, 1981; Meyers, 1981), we believe that consultation and counseling can be compared, as in Table 13-1. To enhance adult confidence, Meyers proposed that consultants listen carefully and support the adults' effective ideas. To promote objectivity, the consultant can act as a role model by objectively and calmly gathering good and bad data about the case or use an indirect technique to recognize the adult's involvement in the case, such as relating a similar interpersonal problem with the child or a story that indirectly points out the negative interaction. A direct discussion of the problem, using supportive empathy and confrontation, may also be effective (Meyers, 1981).

Behavioral consultation, as described by Bergan (1977), is indirect in process and involves a series of clearly defined steps: problem identification, problem analysis, plan implementation, and problem evaluation. According to Keller (1981), problem identification and analysis are usually accomplished by assessing or measuring behaviors in multiple settings through interview techniques, behavior checklists, rating scales, or recorded periodic observations. The plan implementation stage uses a variety of behavioral techniques, including feedback and reinforcement, self-monitoring, modeling, role-playing, and parent training.

TABLE 13-1   A comparison of counseling and consultation roles

Counseling	*Consultation*
Directly involved with client	Not directly involved with the identified client
Professionally and ethically responsible for outcome	Not directly professionally and ethically responsible for outcome
Relationship is therapeutic	Relationship is professional, not therapeutic
Establish rapport by listening and communicating understanding and respect	Establish rapport by listening and communicating understanding and respect
Identify consequences: "How does this help (or hurt) you in reaching your goal of _____?"	Identify consequences: "What happens when Jenny does this?"
Evaluate past solutions: "What have you tried to solve this?"	Evaluate past solutions: "What have you (or Jenny) tried to solve this?"
Develop alternatives by encouraging the client to brainstorm; the counselor may provide information: "What could you be doing?"	Develop alternatives by brainstorming with the client; provide information and advice: "Can you think of other things that might help?"
Contract—make a plan: "Which alternative will you choose, and when will you do this?"	Contract—make a plan. "Which alternative will you choose, and when will you do this?"
Follow up to evaluate results of the plan	Follow up to evaluate results of the plan

Evaluation is an ongoing process in behavioral consultation and the consultation is terminated when the goals established in the initial stage are accomplished (Keller, 1981). Behavioral-analysis and self-management models are presented in chapter 8, and a 10-step reality therapy model is described in chapter 4.

Blocher (1987) contended that the most frequently used model is triadic consultation, which involves a "mediator" with whom the consultant works. This mediator provides service to the ultimate client, whom the consultant may never see. Kurpius and Fuqua (1993) stated that definitions of consultation may change, but the process continues to be triadic, even though at times the consultant must work directly with the client.

THE CONSULTING PROCESS

Kurpius, Fuqua, and Rozecki (1993) contended that consultation takes place in six stages, whether the process is a short-term individual consultation or a long-term organizational consultation.

1. *Preentry:* Consultants look at themselves to see if they are right for the task and what services they can provide.

> As a consultant, how do you view humans? Are you more attracted to some than others? How do you listen and respond to leaders at the top of the organization as compared with workers at the bottom? What do you think and feel when consultees disagree with you and confront you or your ideas? What about your espoused theories versus your theories-in-use? (Kurpius, Fuqua, & Rozecki, 1993, p. 601)

The American Counseling Association (ACA), in its revision to American Counseling Association Code of Ethics and Standards of Practice (1995), addressed consultant competency: "Counselors are reasonably certain that they have or the organization represented has the necessary competencies and resources for giving the kind of consulting services needed and that appropriate referral resources are available" (Section D.2.b). Section D.2.a warns counselors to "avoid placing the consultant in a conflict of interest situation that would preclude the consultant being a proper party to the counselor's efforts to help the client."

Kurpius, Fuqua, and Rozecki (1993) also encouraged consultants to define clearly their conception of consultation.

> What models, processes, theories, and paradigms do you draw on to conceptualize your mode for helping? How do you define consultation to the consultee and consultee system? Do you see it as triadic (consultant, consultee, client) or dyadic (consultant and client)? When is visioning, looking into the future, and planning a better intervention than cause-and-effect problem solving? What about acting as a judge and evaluator of your consultee? (Kurpius, Fuqua, & Rozecki, 1993, p. 601)

2. *Entry, problem exploration, and contracting:* During the initial contact, the consultant needs to learn about the presenting problem, the persons involved, what interventions have been tried, and the expectations of the person or organization seeking consultative services. At this point the consultant must decide if he or she can be helpful and establish a contract. Kurpius, Fuqua, and Rozecki (1993) recommended for any work other than individual consultation a written contract describing the purposes, objectives, ground rules, expectations, resources needed, and time lines for consultation; individual consultation, such as between a counselor and a classroom teacher or another helping professional, should have a brief written agreement, even if it is only a memorandum of understanding.

3. *Information gathering, problem confirmation and goal setting:* Kurpius, Fuqua, and Rozecki (1993) encouraged consultants to spend enough time to gather valid and reliable data, both qualitative and quantitative, in order to assure delivering high-quality services. Accurate data are important for defining the problem and attributing of ownership—all essential steps to establishing the problem as a goal to be reached. Without agreement about the ownership of the problem (the teacher, parent, child, other child or adult), interventions the consultant suggests are not effective because no one takes responsibility.

4. *Solution searching and intervention selection:* Consultants must avoid seeing all problems in the light of their favorite paradigm or counseling theory. Pointing out that human services organizations tend to see human factors causing most problems and that industry and business most often see their problems coming from structural causes, Kurpius, Fuqua, and Rozecki (1993) suggested that consultants carefully consider both the human and structural factors (the school or other systems in the child's life) as possible causes of the problem and areas for intervention.

5. *Evaluation:* As with any counseling task, evaluation assures professional effectiveness. Kurpius, Fuqua, and Rozecki suggested asking certain questions to evaluate the outcomes of consulting services: Have the consulting goals been achieved and to what degree? How well have interventions worked? Were there unexpected outcomes and have they been addressed effectively? Evaluation should give the consultant information about how each step in the process worked.

6. *Termination:* When the consultant and consultee agree that the process should be terminated, consultant should review with the consultee each step in the process, describing what was successful or not successful. If the work was successful, this review process provides an opportunity for clarification, recognition of successes, and reflection on how the process brought about improvements. If the consultation process was not successful, the session helps all members understand the reasons for the failure.

The tasks of consultation as described by Kurpius, Fuqua, and Rozecki (1993) are, in summary, assessing one's own competency, collecting data, defining the problem, setting a goal, selecting interventions, evaluating results, and terminating the relationship—all activities with which counselors are familiar. To assure high-quality consultative services, however, counselors inexperienced in consulting ought to work with a colleague or seek supervision as they begin their consultative work, and all counselor-consultants should periodically evaluate the effectiveness of their professional services (see Evaluation of Consultation, p. 379).

CONSULTATION INTERVENTIONS

Consulting can help counselors reach more children by teaching adults (parents, teachers, and other significant persons in the children's lives) to behave in more helpful ways. Providing indirect services to children through consultation can be an important part of the counselor's role; unfortunately, few counselors are using their skills in this area. Next are techniques counselors may wish to try in their consultative efforts with the adults in the child's world. Not every technique works with every child. Each child's uniqueness and specific needs must be considered before one selects any counseling or consulting procedure.

Role Shift

Simply changing one's own behavior may elicit a behavior change in another person. Adults who change their responses to children's behaviors may cease to reinforce them or present children with an unexpected response that causes change.

Thompson and Poppen (1972) suggested asking adults to list *everything* they have tried with the child that has been ineffective. The counselor then asks them to commit themselves to never again trying any one of these ineffective techniques with this child. The list should be kept as a reminder of what not to do with the child.

When the child has behaved inappropriately, adults can stop and ask themselves, "What response does this child expect?" Does the child expect the adult to be shocked, outraged, or angry? For instance, Glen reacted to his mother's scoldings by drawing grotesque pictures of her and placing them around the house. He took great delight in watching her reactions when she found the pictures. She decided that Glen enjoyed her outrage. The next time she found a picture, she calmly commented to him, "I must have really made you angry when I scolded you for you to draw me like this." She left the picture up and went on with her work. Glen quietly removed his pictures later in the day. This technique seems to work best when the child expects to get attention, shock (as with curse words or dirty language), frustrate, anger, or get revenge.

Descriptive Discussions of Children

Many times adults are so frustrated with a child's problems that they see the child as all bad. Counselors can gain some understanding of adults' perceptions and expectations of children by asking them to describe the children and their behaviors in some detail (Thompson & Poppen, 1972). If the entire description focuses on negative traits or behaviors, the counselor might ask the adult if there is *anything* good about the child and then ask the adult to make a list of the child's strengths. Focusing on the child's positive attributes helps the adult decrease attention to the negative and increase awareness of the positive.

Listing of Behaviors

A technique similar to the descriptive discussion is listing behaviors. For instance, Mr. Jones told the counselor that Sherry was a crybaby who cried at *everything* that did not go her way. The counselor asked Mr. Jones to keep an exact count of the times that Sherry cried during the next week. The next week Mr. Jones admitted that, according to his count, Sherry had cried only 3 times that week—once when she fell, once when she was told to go to bed, and once when she was refused a request. Mr. Jones began to change his perception of Sherry as a crybaby.

Listing the number of times a behavior occurs can also provide a baseline count to determine if an intervention has reduced an inappropriate behavior or increased an appropriate one.

Logical Consequences

Proponents of Adler's individual psychology advocate allowing children to experience the natural or logical consequences of their behavior, rather than punishment, as the preferred form of discipline (see chapter 10). They suggest that adults who punish children become authority figures and lose the friendship of the child. They also point out that natural or logical consequences are reality-oriented and teach the child the rules of society, whereas punishment may teach unwanted lessons such as "power is authority."

Obviously, adults cannot allow children to experience the consequences of all their behavior; children cannot learn that busy streets are dangerous by playing in them. However, a thoughtful adult can find ways for children to see the consequences of inappropriate behavior. When Peter colors on the walls instead of on paper, for instance, Peter is responsible for using the sponge and cleanser to remove the coloring. The natural consequence of being late is to miss an event or a meal. The logical consequence of damaging someone's property is to earn enough money to replace it. The logical consequence of behaving inappropriately in a group is usually rejection by the group or isolation. Discipline with logical consequences very quickly teaches children the order and rules of society.

Isolation Techniques

At times children's behaviors become so unacceptable that they must be removed from the group (the classroom, family, or peer group). For many years, parents sent children to their rooms when they acted out. Our society isolates adults who behave inappropriately by ostracism and, in extreme cases, by imprisonment. Isolation techniques are a form of logical consequences.

Thompson and Poppen (1987) outlined four steps of isolation. Children with minor problems of maintaining attention can go to a second seat away from the group, in a quiet place but not out of sight. Children who are not attending the task of the group may be quietly reminded that their present seat, seat 1, is for working on science, participating in a group discussion, and the like and that they have to move to seat 2. Children choose to return to the group when they are ready to participate in the group activity. The success of this technique is based on the premise that children like to be part of a group and change their behavior in order to remain within the group.

The second step of isolation is the quiet corner. Some children are highly distractible and highly distracting to their peers. They must be completely screened from the group to accomplish their work. A quiet corner can be made with screens, study carrels, bookshelves (books facing outward), or large, decorated furniture cartons. The quiet corner should contain a desk, chair, books, puzzles, or other quiet materials and no windows or doors. When a child misbehaves, the adult quietly signals the child that the behavior is not appropriate and asks the child to go to the quiet corner. Children choose to return to the group when they are ready to participate more acceptably. The adult may have to impose a short time limit of 10 to 15 minutes before allowing children this choice.

Counselors can suggest a time-out room for more severe problems, when children need to be completely away from the group. Thompson and Poppen (1972) suggest that time-out be used not as a punishment but as a cooling-off time. The adult can instruct the child to make a plan for avoiding the trouble in the future while in the time-out room.

When children's problem behaviors are so severe that the first three isolation procedures have not worked, the adult can quietly ask the child to leave the premises (school, church, club, recreational center) and come back tomorrow to try again. The children should be aware of what behaviors are acceptable and unacceptable and of the conditions for remaining in the group. Because this procedure often requires the assistance of parents, school personnel, or other community workers, establish a written agreement among all parties. Many schools use in-house suspension to provide a place where children who cannot remain in the group can go for supervised study. Other community resources that provide youth services may cooperate in arranging for supervision.

At times adults may need a time-out. Dreikurs, Grunwald, and Pepper (1971) have suggested that parents who find themselves as referees in children's conflicts with others take a time-out in the bathroom. Their contention was that children try to involve adults in their conflicts to get attention, that children learn to settle their differences (and learn the consequences) more effectively without relying on adults, and that only danger of physical harm or property damage requires adult intervention.

Isolation techniques teach children the logical consequences of their behavior. Acceptable and unacceptable behaviors should be clearly defined for children. When using the procedures, adults should not nag, lecture, or scold. Isolation techniques should be viewed as a positive method of discipline rather than as punishment.

Parent Training

Gordon (1970) described a model for consulting with parents about their children's behavior in his *Parent Effectiveness Training* (PET). Based on empathetic listening and responding, PET outlines the steps for effective problem solving.

Gordon advised parents when to listen with empathy and when to assert their rights as a parent with "I" statements. He suggested techniques of active listening, nonintervention, or passive listening for children who need acceptance. He discussed roadblocks to communication such as ordering, directing, commanding, warning, threatening, giving solutions, lecturing, criticizing, ridiculing, and analyzing and showed why these typical methods of communicating with children are ineffective. When children's behaviors interfere with the rights of others, Gordon suggested that parents or other adults should use "I" statements that allow children to know how they really feel and gave examples of how to use these messages to improve communication without tearing down the child's self-esteem, talking too much, resorting to negative messages, or engaging in a power struggle.

Gordon described three ways of resolving parent-child conflict: I win–you lose, you win–I lose (both ineffective), and the effective win-win situation in which parent and child resolve the conflict and feel good about the gains. He gave case examples of why each method was ineffective or effective and demonstrated the use of good problem-solving techniques.

Gordon presented evidence to demonstrate the efficacy of his method for consulting with parents, and the popularity of PET programs across the country suggests they help parents deal with children's problems. Because the steps for communication and problem solving are outlined in an easily accessible book, it is an efficient method for helping parents.

Dinkmeyer and McKay (1976) developed a similar program. *Systematic Training for Effective Parenting* (STEP), based on Adlerian theory as popularized by Rudolf Dreikurs, emphasizes principles of logical consequences over punishment and of using cooperation rather than power as a child-rearing method. The STEP program also teaches parents to recognize the goals of misbehavior. Weekly family meetings, daily individual time with the parent, and a weekly fun activity are parts of this program.

ASSESSMENT AS A CONSULTING INTERVENTION

In their attempts to understand children's developmental and other critical problems, counselors often use a variety of tools such as self-report surveys, interviews, tests, case histories, and behavioral observations. Counselors also need to be familiar with standardized tests, understand their results, and use them effectively in counseling and in consulting with other professionals. Some of the more commonly used assessment tools are discussed in the following section.

The Interview

Counselors are usually very comfortable with interviewing their child clients and can obtain much information through this procedure. Counselors are adept not only in listening what is being said but also in noting how it is said and the accompanying behaviors. Typically, the interviewer seeks to learn something about the child (name, age, family information) and the presenting problem. While interviewing the child, the counselor has an opportunity to observe if the child can make good eye contact, is outgoing or shy, attentive or distracted, overactive or lethargic, talkative or reluctant to speak, confused or thinking clearly, anxious, or depressed. Some counselors prefer structured interviews; others allow clients to reveal themselves at their own pace. Some counselors will use self-report surveys that ask children open-ended questions (my best friend _____ ; I like it when my mother _____). Counselors can learn much through observation of appearance, behaviors, affect, and verbal and nonverbal communications of children.

Case Histories

A case history gives professionals complete biographical information about the child client. Interviewing the child and his or her parents and other family members and reviewing school records and the records of other professionals (doctors, speech therapists, special teachers, and others) working with the child provide data for the case history.

Behavioral Observations

In certain cases, the counselor will need to observe children in their work and play situations in order to understand more about their functioning and relationships with others. Personal observation can tell the counselor if a child's behavior is appropriate, any circumstances that stimulated certain responses, and how others around the child respond. Counselors may use published checklists or develop their own methods for recording behavioral observations.

Psychological and Educational Tests

Children referred for learning and behavior problems often take a battery of tests to help professionals understand more about their level of functioning. Psychologists working with the child usually decide the tests to be included in the battery.

Intelligence Tests

Intelligence is a difficult concept to define, but most agree that it is related to a person's ability to learn, especially in a school setting. Tests for children usually include some measure of knowledge, concept formation, and reasoning. Many tests tap both verbal and nonverbal abilities. Some of the more popular tests for measuring children's intelligence are the Stanford-Binet Intelligence Scale, 4th edition; the Wechsler Intelligence Scale for Children-Revised (WISC-III); the Wechsler Preschool and Primary Scale of Intelligence (WPPSI-R); the Otis-Lennon School Ability Test; and the California Test of Mental Maturity. The Stanford Binet and Wechsler scales must be administered individually by a trained professional; the Otis-Lennon and California tests can be administered in the classroom to groups in grades 1 through 12. The tests yield a numerical intelligence quotient, the IQ score, with 100 being the mean or average and a 15- to 16-point standard deviation to indicate how far above or below the mean the child scores.

A quick estimate of intelligence can be obtained with the Peabody Picture Vocabulary Test-Revised (PPVT-R). Children respond by pointing to the picture that best describes the word read by the administrator. The test taps only one area of the child's ability and therefore is not considered to be a measure of *general* intelligence.

A newer test of intelligence and achievement is the Kaufman Assessment Battery for Children (K-ABC). The developers of the K-ABC define *intelligence* in terms of a child's information-processing skills and problem-solving abilities. The test has been a helpful diagnostic tool for both normal and exceptional children.

Persons using either the PPVT-R or the K-ABC need training and supervision in the administration and interpretation of these instruments. Children are often labeled or classified by intelligence test results, and extreme care is needed to avoid harming any child through the misuse of assessment measures.

Projective Techniques

Professionals sometimes ask children to respond to an unstructured stimulus, a picture, or a story to learn more about their thoughts and feelings. One projective technique, the Children's Apperception Test (CAT), uses animals as stimuli for children age 3 to 10. An alternative form, the CAT-H, uses human figures. The administrator asks the children what they see when they are shown each card.

Trained professionals may use Machover's Draw-A-Person and the Kinetic Family Drawing tests to learn more about the child's psychological functioning. They ask children to draw a person or their family on a blank sheet of paper, and these pictures reveal how children feel about themselves and the relationships among family members.

Counselors do not ordinarily administer, score, and interpret projective instruments; however, counselors may need to be familiar with the tests to consult effectively with other professionals about their clients and their families.

Achievement Tests

Achievement tests are educational assessments that measure the accomplishment of learning. A battery of achievement tests covers more than one academic area (reading, mathematics, language, and others). Some of the more popular group tests used in kindergarten through grade 12 are the California Achievement Test, Metropolitan Achievement Test, SRA Achievement Test, and Wide Range Achievement Test. The Peabody Individual Achievement Test (PIAT) is individually administered. The results of achievement tests can be used for placement of children or to determine educational areas of strengths and weaknesses.

Aptitude Tests

These tests are similar to achievement tests but are given to predict learning or behavior, for example, school readiness or reading readiness. The Metropolitan Readiness Test (MRT) measures children's school readiness in reading and mathematics. The System of Multi-Cultural Assessment (SOMPA) was designed to be a measurement of aptitude that would be culturally fair; however, the test has been controversial, and many critics have attacked its validity.

Other Tests

Counselors may want to administer other tests, surveys, or scales to learn more about a child's interests, values, study habits, social acceptance by peers, or the age appropriateness of their behaviors. Follow-up diagnostic testing in mathematics or reading may be helpful after the results of an initial intelligence or achievement test have been obtained. Special tests are available for children with exceptional conditions—the learning disabled, the hearing or visually challenged, the mentally challenged, and others. The tests selected depend on the nature of the child's problem and the counseling objectives to be accomplished.

Before selecting any test for administration—and before accepting the results of any test—the user of assessment data should know whether the test is a good measure. At least two concepts give counselors an indication of the "goodness" of a particular instrument: validity and reliability. *Validity* is the extent to which a test measures what it is supposed to measure—intelligence, interests, achievement, or aptitude. A test that measures the child's current level of achievement in grade 2 is not a measure of the child's aptitude or intelligence; the test is valid only for measuring achievement. The *reliability* of a test indicates the consistency with which the test measures. Are the results of an intelligence test similar when the test is administered to the same child 2 days, 2 weeks, or 2 months apart? Correlation coefficients indicate the degree to which tests are valid and reliable. Counselors also need to know the type of population used in the norming process. A test with normative data for children under 5 years is not appropriate for administering to a 6-year-old. Complete information on validity and reliability as well as a description of the norm group can be found in the technical manuals that accompany tests, or the counselor can consult other references such as catalogues, journal reviews, *Tests in Print*, or *The Mental Measurement Yearbook*.

Counselors must be extremely careful in working in the area of assessment. Most are trained in interviewing, developing case histories, and behavioral observation. However, their training in assessment procedures varies, and counselors should administer and interpret only those tests for which they have received instruction. In addition, counselors can consult books such as Sattler's *Assessment of Children: Revised and Updated* (third edition) and other literature on assessment to keep current about new and revised instruments. Professionals can refer to their appropriate professional code of ethics to determine their role in assessment and appraisal.

EVALUATION OF CONSULTING

Parsons and Myers (1984) constructed the Consultee Satisfaction Form, which asks consultees to rate, on a 4-point scale, the efficacy of consultation with regard to goal definition, data gathering, and the appropriateness of the intervention plan; the consultant's expertise with regard to content and presentation; the consultant's administrative skills in using time, providing feedback, and assigning work; and the consultant's interpersonal style (good listener, pleasant, encouraging, and so on). Information from checklists or other evaluative forms helps consultants develop and maintain an effective consulting relationship.

All writers on the topic of consulting point out the need for further research to evaluate the results of consultation techniques. Dustin and Blocher (1984) concluded that "at the present time there is simply not a sufficient body of credible empirical research upon which to assess the overall effectiveness or ineffectiveness of consultation" (p. 777), but that more recent studies have been encouraging in that they have used more sophisticated research designs. Meyers (1981) and Keller (1981) also called for more carefully controlled studies to determine the efficacy of consultative models and techniques. Bundy and Poppen (1986) have found that 18 of the 21 studies of elementary school consultation they reviewed reported positive effects; of the 18 showing positive results, the two most commonly used methods were the Adlerian models and behavioral consultation. Dougherty (1990) stated that mental health consultation has "a broad and positive impact" but that "it is not without criticism" (p. 251).

SUMMARY

Although problems exist with theoretical foundations and evaluative research on consultation, we should not overlook the technique as a possible means for helping children in need. Helping techniques presented to significant people in children's lives through small groups, psychological education, outreach programs, and preventive education may reach children to whom a lone counselor's direct services would not be available. For our purposes, consultation refers to the one-to-one interaction between the counselor and a significant adult in the child's life or to a counselor-led group of significant adults, with the purpose of finding ways to assist children to function more effectively.

REFERENCES

American Counseling Association. (1995). *Ethical standards* (Rev. ed.). Alexandria, VA: Author.

Bergan, J. (1977). *Behavioral consultation.* Columbus, OH: Merrill.

Blocher, D. (1987). *The professional counselor.* New York: Macmillan.

Brown, D., Pryzwansky, W., & Schulte, A. (1991). *Psychological consultation: Introduction to theory and practice.* Boston: Allyn & Bacon.

Bundy, M., & Poppen, W. (1986). School counselors' effectiveness as consultants: A research review. *Elementary School Guidance and Counseling, 20,* 215–222.

Dinkmeyer, D., & McKay, G. (1976). *Systematic training for effective parenting.* Circle Pines, MN: American Guidance Service.

Dougherty, A. (1990). *Consultation: Practice and perspectives.* Pacific Grove, CA: Brooks/Cole.

Dougherty, A., Dougherty, L., & Purcell, D. (1991). The sources and management of resistance to consultation. *School Counselor, 38,* 178–185.

Dreikurs, R., Grunwald, B., & Pepper, F. (1971). *Maintaining sanity in the classroom.* New York: Harper & Row.

Dustin, D., & Blocher, D. (1984). Theories and models of consultation. In S. Brown & R. Lent (Eds.), *Handbook of counseling psychology* (p. 752). New York: Wiley.

Glosoff, H., & Koprowicz, C. (1990). *Children achieving potential: An introduction to elementary school counseling and state-level policies.* Washington, DC: National Conference of State Legislatures and American Association for Counseling and Development.

Gordon, T. (1970). *Parent effectiveness training.* New York: Wyden.

Jackson, D., & Hayes, D. (1993). Multicultural issues in consultation. *Journal of Counseling and Development, 7,* 144–147.

Kahnweiler, W. M. (1979). The school counselor as consultant: A historical review. *Personnel and Guidance Journal, 57,* 374–379.

Keller, H. (1981). Behavioral consultation. In J. C. Conoley (Ed.), *Consultation in schools: Theory, research, procedures* (pp. 59–89). New York: Academic Press.

Kurpius, D., & Fuqua, D. (1993). Fundamental issues in defining consultation. *Journal of Counseling and Development, 7,* 598–600.

Kurpius, D., Fuqua, D., & Rozecki, T. (1993). The consulting process: A multidimensional approach. *Journal of Counseling and Development, 7,* 601–606.

Kurpius, D., & Robinson, S. (1978). An overview of consultation. *Personnel and Guidance Journal, 56,* 321–323.

Meyers, J. (1981). Mental health consultation. In J. C. Conoley (Ed.), *Consultation in schools: Theory, research, procedures* (pp. 35–58). New York: Academic Press.

Myrick, R. (1987). *Developmental guidance and counseling: A practical approach.* Minneapolis: Educational Media.

Parsons, R., & Myers, J. (1984). *Developing consultation skills.* San Francisco: Jossey-Bass.

Poppen, W., & Thompson, C. (1975). *School counseling: Theories and concepts.* Lincoln, NE: Professional Educators.

Sattler, J. (1992). *Assessment of Children: Revised and Updated* (3rd ed.). San Diego: Author.

Thompson, C., & Poppen, W. (1972). *For those who care: Ways of relating to youth.* Columbus, OH: Merrill.

Thompson, C., & Poppen, W. (1987). *Guidance activities for counselors and teachers.* Knoxville, TN: Authors.

Chapter 14

◆

Group Processes with Children

Many counselors suggest that groups are more natural than individual counseling for working with people. Children and adults function as members of groups in their daily activities—in the family, the classroom, the work setting, or the peer group. Our beliefs and perceptions of self are formed from the feedback of significant people in groups—family, friends, and peers. Psychologists such as Alfred Adler emphasized that people are social beings and that their development is influenced significantly by the groups around them; therefore, group counseling is more reality oriented than individual counseling. Different types of groups appear to be increasing in popularity as loneliness and separation from family and friends increase in our society. At one time, group counseling was considered an effective method of counseling because the counselor could help a number of children more economically, but a more important reason is that children can unlearn inappropriate behaviors and learn new ways of relating more easily through interaction and feedback in a safe practice situation with their peers. Dyer and Vriend (1988) pointed out that in a group the number of people involved increases the helping resources.

This chapter is not intended to train counselors in conducting groups. Complete books have been written about group counseling, and most counselors have coursework and supervised practicums to help them develop skills. In this chapter an overview of the area is presented, with suggestions for those who already possess the knowledge and skills to conduct groups or who intend to pursue further training.

GROUP COUNSELING

Johnson and Johnson (1987) reviewed the literature for a definition of a *group*. They found that various definitions incorporated several components.

A group may be defined as two or more individuals who (a) interact with each other, (b) are interdependent, (c) define themselves or are defined by others as belonging to the group, (d) share norms concerning matters of common interest and participate in a system of interlocking roles, (e) influence each other, (f) find the group rewarding, and (g) pursue common goals. (p. 7)

They also said that "any effective group has three core activities: (1) accomplishing its goals, (2) maintaining itself internally, and (3) developing and changing in ways that improve its effectiveness". (p. 8)

Dyer and Vriend (1988) provided comprehensive definition and step-by-step description of group counseling:

Group counseling is a helping procedure that begins with the group members exploring their own worlds for the purpose of identifying thinking, feeling, and doing processes which are in any way self-defeating. Members determine and declare to the group what their counterproductive behaviors are and make decisions about which ones they can commit themselves to work on.

Dyer and Vriend help each member set goals, examine thoughts, behaviors, and feelings, seek positive alternatives and test them. Members complete psychological homework assignments and decide whether or not to incorporate the new behaviors into their self-systems.

Group Models

Many labels are used for the types of group work carried out in various settings. Group processes can also be described according to the type of group conducted. Some theorists differentiate between group therapy and group counseling.

Group therapy deals with unconscious motivations and seeks to effect personality changes. Group therapy is usually of longer duration and includes people who are more severely disturbed. *Group counseling* is conducted in schools, institutions, or mental health agencies and deals primarily with personal, interpersonal, educational, career, or social issues. The members of counseling groups are normal people who are experiencing some stress in their daily lives; no attempt is made to deal with severe psychological or personality disorders.

Personal-growth groups consist of healthy people who wish to function better in life. Their goals may include communicating better, learning assertion skills, improving relationship skills, developing leadership skills, learning to think positively, or acquiring other personal attitudes or abilities to adjust more effectively. Some groups are structured so that the only goal is to assist members to learn one skill (such as assertiveness or relaxation) or to cope with one type of problem (alcoholism in the family, parental divorce, sexual abuse, or eating disorders).

Self-help groups usually are not led by professionals but are structured by people who have experienced the common problem. The members share experiences and provide understanding and support for one another, and groups such as Alcoholics Anonymous, Alateen, and Weight Watchers serve an important function in our society.

Group guidance focuses on prevention of problems and is more developmental than the other groups, which are more remedial. Group guidance is conducted with large groups and is primarily didactic. It provides children with information they need to make informed decisions and adjust to the requirements of their developmental stage. Topics may include study skills, living peacefully with brothers and sisters, communicating with parents, saying no to drugs, physical and emotional changes of an age stage, or interpreting test scores on an aptitude or interest test. Group guidance is discussed in greater detail later in this chapter.

The counseling skills and techniques discussed in chapter 2 also apply to the group counseling setting. However, the group counselor has the additional tasks of directing communication traffic, facilitating the group process, blocking harmful group behaviors, connecting ideas, obtaining a consensus, moderating discussions, summarizing, and supporting children who need encouragement and reinforcement.

Theoretically Oriented Group Counseling

The number of group counseling methods almost equals the number of counseling theories. Most approaches or orientations to counseling can be adapted to a group counseling setting.

Adlerian counselors used group work in their child guidance center in the early 1900s for group discussions involving parents (see chapter 10). Because Adlerians believe that people are essentially social and need to belong to a community or group, they see group counseling as a natural environment for helping children see the reality of the situation and meet their needs through social interactions in the group.

The principles of *behavioral counseling* are also used in groups when the clients' goals are similar or members can help one another by providing feedback, support, or reinforcement to alter maladaptive behaviors, learn new behaviors, or prevent problems. Relaxation training, assertion training, modeling techniques, and self-management programs to control overeating or other negative behaviors are examples of behavioral techniques that can be used effectively in group settings.

Because *rational-emotive-behavior therapy* (REBT) attempts to teach people to think rationally about events and assume responsibility for their feelings, the techniques of this theory can be applied very effectively in groups. Members are encouraged to recognize and confront their irrational thoughts and feelings, take risks, try new behaviors, and use others' feedback to learn new social skills. Members are taught to apply REBT principles to one another.

The principles of *reality therapy* adapt effectively to group work because the group is a microcosm of the real world. The members provide feedback about the reality of their behavior and plans for change. They reinforce one another in their commitments and check on the completion of homework assignments. Reality therapy has been a popular method for helping groups of children and adolescents in schools, those confined to correctional institutions, substance abusers, and those with handicaps.

Transactional analysis (TA) is an ideal counseling method for groups; in fact, most counselors adhering to the principles of TA prefer treatment in groups. This method focuses on analysis of life scripts, games, and interactions among people, and the ideal setting for this teaching and learning is within a group that simulates life's interactions.

Gestalt therapy focuses on the here and now and on maintaining personal awareness. Some Gestalt counselors ask for volunteers and focus on one client at a time within the group; for example, the hot seat technique requires the counselor to work with one person in the presence of the other group members. Structured interaction between other group members may be encouraged at certain times.

Other counseling methods have their place in group work but do not adapt to it as readily as those already mentioned. The relationship skills set forth by *person-centered* counselors are appropriate in an individual or group setting. The therapeutic relationship is an essential ingredient for all clients to feel free enough to explore their world and make changes.

GROUP LEADERSHIP SKILLS

Dyer and Vriend (1988) listed 20 group leadership skills crucial for group counseling effectiveness.

1. *Identifying, labeling, clarifying, and reflecting feelings:* the facial expressions, body posture, movements, tone of voice, eye activity, and other behavioral indicators that are indicators of feelings.
2. *Identifying, labeling, clarifying, and reflecting behavioral data:* understanding the meaning and cause of behaviors in relation to the group process itself, the interaction of group members, and the individuals' goals.
3. *Identifying, labeling, clarifying, and reflecting cognitive data:* skills necessary to help members change their methods of thinking and communicating in order to be more effective.

4. *Questioning, drawing out, and evoking material for counseling focus:* helping counselees decide what they are willing to work on, to change, or to risk.

5. *Confronting:* identifying and pointing out discrepancies in how the group member thinks, feels, or acts, while conveying acceptance of the person.

6. *Summarizing and reviewing important material:* important for correcting distorted perceptions, to provide focus and direction, to assist members to recall important information, and to help members set goals.

7. *Interpreting* the underlying meaning of a member's statement or experience in order to correct distortions or misperceptions.

8. *Restating* the essence of a client's statements in a manner that clarifies and eliminates ambiguity. (This skill is especially important in children's groups because of their limited cognitive abilities.)

9. *Establishing connections:* attending closely in order to see relationships that help the member gain insight.

10. *Information giving:* appropriately providing "expert" information about group procedures, leader expectations, direction, and other topics important to the group.

11. *Initiating:* the ability to develop a plan of action in order to introduce appropriate material at a given moment.

12. *Reassuring, encouraging, and supporting:* to help members through difficult moments.

13. *Intervening:* interrupting when the group activity is unproductive (when a member speaks for everyone, blames others for his or her problems, or begins to ramble).

14. *Dealing with silence:* recognizing when silence can be productive and when it should be dealt with. (Silence seems to be less a problem in children's groups than in adult groups.)

15. *Recognizing and explaining nonverbal behaviors:* continually observing the nonverbal signals sent by members and using the information at the appropriate time.

16. *Using clear, concise, meaningful communication:* avoiding lectures, jargon, sarcasm, talking excessively, rambling. (Working with children requires an appropriate developmental level of language to assure that members understand what is being said.)

17. *Focusing* or staying on task. (Counselors working with children need to be very proficient in this area. Dependent on their age, children need more structure in their groups to stay involved and on track.)

18. *Restraining, subduing, and avoiding potentially explosive and divisive group happenings:* being able to determine when tensions are rising and deal with them constructively.

19. *Goal setting:* help members to set individual goals that are specific, relevant, achievable, and measurable.

20. *Facilitating closure:* effectively summarizing and planning for the end of a session or the end of the group experience.

THE GROUP COUNSELING PROCESS

Forming a Group

Because of reports of people being verbally attacked and hurt in groups that use extreme methods, parents or children may have reservations about participating in a group. Counselors should explain fully the purpose of the group and the experiences planned in order to allay fears and clarify possible misconceptions. By providing this information to children before starting the group, the counselor can inform the children of their roles and what is expected of them and explain the role and expectations of the counselor as well. Explaining the process provides the structure needed to facilitate interaction once the group is begun. Following is an example of an informative statement:

> We are forming a group made up of young people about your age in order to talk about things that bother or upset us. Many of us have similar concerns, and it is often helpful to share these worries and help each other try to find ways of solving them. Each member will be expected to talk about what bothers him or her and try to figure out what can be done about these situations. In addition, members will be expected to listen carefully to each other and to try to understand the other members' worries and help them solve their problems. The counselor, too, tries to understand what all the members are saying or feeling, to help them explain and clarify their thoughts and feelings, and to find solutions to their concerns.
>
> Most group members learn they can trust the others in the group and feel free to discuss things that worry them. Members are free to talk about anything or anyone that bothers or upsets them. However, the group will not be a gripe session, a gossip session, or a chatting session. We will be working together to find solutions to what is upsetting you. There may be very personal information or feelings that you would prefer not to discuss in the group. You should not feel pressured to disclose these feelings or thoughts to the group. Whatever is said in the group cannot be discussed with anyone except the counselor. If there is anyone you would rather not have in a group with you, discuss this with the counselor.

Intake Interview

Many group leaders prefer to hold an individual conference or intake interview with prospective members before forming the group. Other group leaders think that anyone should be eligible to join a group and that the intake interview is unnecessary. An intake interview allows the leader an opportunity to talk privately with prospective members, to learn a little about them and their concerns, and to define some possible goals. The leader also has an opportunity to determine if the child will benefit from a group experience or if individual counseling would be more helpful.

Group Membership

Some counselors, such as Adlerians, hold that anyone who wishes to participate in a group should be allowed to do so, given similar, age-related levels of interest and intellectual abilities. Other counselors attempt to select members for either heterogeneity or homogeneity. Homogeneity may be desirable for common-problems groups, such as children whose parents are divorced. However, a homogeneous group of underachievers or drug users probably would be counterproductive because no peer model and peer reinforcement for improved behaviors would be present. For children who act out or withdraw, a heterogeneous group provides active discussion and role models. Most counselors prefer a balance of boys and girls in the same group unless the presence of the opposite sex would hinder discussion, on some sex education topics, for example. The counselor should seriously consider the possible consequences of including children with highly dissimilar interests or maturity levels and extremely dominating, manipulative, gifted, or mentally retarded children. Children with extreme behaviors may be better candidates for individual counseling, especially during the initial stages of therapy.

The number of children in the group depends on age, maturity, and attention span. Children of 5 and 6 years have very short attention spans and are unable to give much attention to others' concerns. Counselors may want to limit group size at this age to three or four and to work with the children for only short periods of time at frequent intervals—for example, 20 minutes twice a week. Counselors can work with a larger number of older, more mature children for longer periods of time—for example, six children, ages 10 and 11, for 30 minutes twice a week. The maximum number of children in a group that functions effectively seems to be eight. However, the classroom meeting concept developed by Glasser (1969) has proven effective with an entire class of 30 students for periods of 20 to 30 minutes.

The Group Setting

A room away from noise and traffic is best. In addition, children should not fear being overheard if they are expected to talk openly about their concerns. Groups should be conducted with all members sitting in a circle so that everyone can see everyone else's face. Some counselors prefer to have the children sit around a circular table; others think tables are a barrier to interaction. Many counselors prefer to have groups of children sit in a circle on a carpeted floor, which provides easy access for counselors to move the group into play therapy.

The First Session

Part of the first counseling session will be devoted to establishing ground rules and agreeing on some guidelines for the group. The group or the leader determines the frequency of the meetings, the length of each meeting, the setting, and the duration of the group. Members also need to discuss confidentiality and what might be done if confidentiality is broken by a member, what to do about members who do not attend regularly, and whether to allow new members, should a member drop out.

Confidentiality is an important concept to discuss with children. They often do not understand the necessity for "keeping what is discussed in our group" and not talking to others about what happens. The leader can provide specific instances of other children asking about their group and have participants role-play their responses.

The group leader has to remind members to listen carefully to each other, to try to understand each other's feelings and thoughts, and to help one another explore possible solutions to problems. The children can be encouraged to wait until members seem to have explored and discussed their concerns thoroughly before changing the subject. The group leader can provide the role model for listening and reflecting feelings and content and then reinforce these behaviors in group members.

By establishing ground rules and structuring the group during the initial session, the group leader defines expected behaviors. When inappropriate behaviors occur, the leader can ask the group, "What was the ground rule?" or present the problem to the group for discussion and resolution. Groups are formed to help the members. The leader is the facilitator but should not take over as disciplinarian and authoritarian.

Group members may be reluctant to begin by bringing up concerns or worries for discussion, especially if the participants are not acquainted. The leader can reflect their feeling of reluctance and, if appropriate, try an icebreaker counseling technique; for example, the leader might ask members to introduce themselves and describe themselves with three adjectives, or members might be asked to introduce themselves and complete a statement such as "If I had three wishes, I would wish _____ ." Another icebreaker is to complete the statement "I am a _____ ," but I would like to be a _____ ," using animals, vegetables, automobiles, flowers, or other nonhuman categories; for instance, "I am a dandelion, but I'd like to be a long-stemmed rose." These activities can be done in the entire group or in dyads; either method eases the tension of the first session and promotes interaction.

Building cohesiveness and trust is important for counselors. Children have had little experience listening to one another and trying to help one another solve problems. Unless these behaviors are taught, the group experience is little more than unstructured play and chatter. Bergin (1989) developed a useful series of cooperative activities to build group cohesiveness: using only the sense of touch in communication, learning-to-listen activities, group planning, and cooperative physical activities.

Guidelines for the Remaining Sessions

Before the second group session, the counselor reviews thoroughly the content of the first meeting (names, behaviors, concerns, other personal information) and develops a plan for guiding the second meeting. At this point, the counselor should have tentative goals in mind for each member, based on the initial interview, and should be aware of who in the group will facilitate the group process—a good listener, encourager, problem solver—and who will distract—dominating, too talkative, silly, confrontive. The counselor may want to develop plans for dealing with distracting behaviors, should they occur. The second session opens with a brief summary of the initial meeting. If homework was assigned, the results should be shared. The group is then ready to address a member's concerns, either one that was identified earlier or a situation that occurred between meetings that is of concern to a member. If no one volunteers to discuss a problem or concern, those identified in the pregroup interviews can be suggested by the counselor: "Pam, when we talked in our interview before the first meeting of the group, you shared with me that you were worried because your younger brother is so sick all the time. Would you like to tell the group about your brother's illness?"

Just as in individual counseling, a group leader establishes a therapeutic counseling atmosphere by demonstrating the facilitative skills of empathetic understanding, genuineness, and respect for group members. Counselors can demonstrate their caring by being nonjudgmental and accepting and by providing encouragement, support, and guidance. Counselors need to be adept at identifying, labeling, clarifying, and reflecting group members' feelings and thoughts. This process becomes difficult as the group size increases. The counselor-facilitator must be concerned about and aware of the reactions of each child in the group. As the leader models facilitative behaviors, group members begin to participate in the helping process and become more effective helpers for one another.

The group counseling process closely follows the format for individual counseling:

1. Establishing a therapeutic relationship
2. Defining the problems of the member or members
3. Exploring what has been tried and whether it has hurt or helped
4. Deciding what could be done and looking at the alternatives
5. Making a plan—goal setting
6. Trying new behaviors by implementing the plan
7. Homework
8. Reporting and evaluating the results

Also as in individual counseling, the counselor-facilitator is responsible for helping children identify and define their problems and the accompanying feelings and thoughts. The process of defining what is happening in the child's life and looking at alternatives for solving the conflict is enhanced in the group setting because of the other group members. Ideally, the child has several counselors to listen, understand, and help search for solutions, while enjoying the acceptance, encouragement, support, and feedback of a number of helpers. The counselor must be skilled in facilitating these interactions and suggesting appropriate interventions. The counselor must also possess information about group dynamics and counseling skills to intervene and facilitate progress through the various steps of the counseling process.

As with individual counseling, audiotaping or videotaping the session can be helpful. Such tapes provide a record of what occurred in the session, enable the counselor to review the dynamics of the group, and help counselors evaluate their leadership skills.

The process and techniques used in individual counseling (such as role-playing, role rehearsal, play therapy, homework assignments, and contracting) are just as appropriate for group counseling. In fact, individual counseling is often conducted in groups, as the following example shows.

Karen, Susan, Peggy, Mark, Ken, and Mike are 11-year-olds in their fourth session in a counseling group.

> *Counselor:*   Last time we met, Susan told us about the misunderstanding she was having with her neighbor, Mrs. Jackson. As I remember, Susan, you were going to offer to use your allowance to replace the storm window you broke playing baseball or offer to babysit free of charge for her until the bill was paid. Can you bring us up to date on what's happened?
>
> *Susan:*   Well, she decided she would rather have me babysit for her to pay for the window. I babysat one hour last week. We are keeping a list of the times I sit and how much will go toward the cost of the window.
>
> *Counselor:*   It sounds as though you and Mrs. Jackson have worked things out to the satisfaction of both of you.
>
> *Susan:*   Yeah, she really liked the idea of my babysitting to pay for the window.
>
> *Counselor:*   Good. Is there anyone else who has something they would like to discuss today?
>
> *All six children:*   Mr. Havens!
>
> *Counselor:*   You all sound pretty angry at Mr. Havens. Could one of you tell me what's happened?
>
> *Ken:*   We were all going on a trip to the ice-skating rink next week. Yesterday, somebody broke some equipment that belonged to Mr. Havens. No one would tell who did it, so he is punishing us all by not letting us go ice-skating.
>
> *Counselor:*   You think Mr. Havens is being unfair to punish everyone because of something one person did. You'd like to find out who broke the equipment.
>
> *Karen:*   That's right. We didn't break his equipment, so why should we have to miss the trip?
>
> *Counselor:*   Have you thought of anything you could do to work this out?
>
> *Mike:*   Yeah, break the rest of his old equipment!
>
> *Counselor:*   How would that help you get to go skating?

Mark: It wouldn't. It would just make him madder.

Peggy [timidly]: We could tell him who did it.

Other five children: You know who did it? Who?

Peggy [very upset]: If I tell, I'll be called a tattler, and no one will like me. Besides, I don't want to get anyone in trouble.

Counselor: Peggy, it sounds as though you are really feeling torn apart by this. You just don't know what to do. If you don't tell, the whole group will miss the skating outing. If you do tell, you'll get someone in trouble, and your friends might think you're a tattler and not want you around.

Peggy: Yeah, I don't know what to do!

Counselor: What do you think you could do?

Peggy: Well, I could tell who did it.

Counselor: What would happen if you told? [Silence.] Let's help Peggy think of all the things that could happen if she told who broke Mr. Havens's equipment.

The group thinks of all the possible positive and negative results of Peggy's telling who broke the equipment: the group might still get to go skating, the person might beat up Peggy or try to get back at her in some other way, she might not be believed, the person could deny it and say Peggy broke the equipment, and so on.

Counselor: We've listed all the things that could happen if Peggy told. What will happen if Peggy does *not* reveal who broke the equipment?

Karen: We won't get to go skating, and the person will get away with it!

Other possibilities—such as Mr. Havens's distrust of the whole group, or the person thinking he or she "can get away with anything"—are brought out and discussed.

Counselor: Can anyone think of any alternatives to solve this other than Peggy telling or not telling Mr. Havens?

Ken: She could write him an anonymous letter telling him who did it.

Counselor: What would happen if she did?

Mike: He probably wouldn't believe an anonymous letter.

Counselor: What do the rest of you think about that?

They all agree by nodding their heads that Mike is probably right.

Counselor: Is there anything else you could do to straighten this out?

Susan: Peggy could tell you [the counselor], and you could tell Mr. Havens.

Counselor: How would my telling Mr. Havens help you all solve your problem?

Mark: Mr. Havens would believe you, and we'd get to go skating!

Counselor: I would have to tell Mr. Havens how I knew and give him some details to assure him that I was right. I really think this is the group's problem. What can you do to work it out?

Karen: Seems like it's up to Peggy, then.

Counselor: You all think it's up to Peggy to decide whether or not to tell.

The group agrees it is Peggy's decision.

Counselor: Peggy, we have looked at the consequences of your telling on the other person and not telling, and we've tried to think of other alternatives. Have you made any decision about what to do?

Peggy: No, I still don't know.

Counselor: So far, it seems that we have come up with two possible alternatives—to tell on the person or not to tell. I wonder if there are any other alternatives you can think of that might help Peggy. [Silence.] Well, our time is about up for today, but this is really important. Let's meet together tomorrow and try to help Peggy come to some decision at that time. Peggy, I wonder if you would go over the list of alternatives and think about them before tomorrow. [Peggy agrees.] How would the rest of you feel about trying to put yourselves in Peggy's place and think of what you would do if you knew who broke Mr. Havens's equipment? Also, you might think about how you would feel if you were the person who broke the equipment. What would you want Peggy to do?

The group agrees and adjourns.

The counselor checked on the results of the last homework assignment for the group, listened, and reflected the group members' angry feelings that Mr. Havens is unfair. The counselor then helped them clarify and define the problem, look at possible alternatives, and consider the consequences of these alternatives. No decision has been reached, but the group has agreed to a homework assignment of thinking further about the problem. Possibly the next session will bring new ideas and a resolution.

Research on Group Processes with Children

According to the literature, group counseling has been effective with a variety of children's concerns: divorce, bereavement, academical retention, and low-performance.

Zambelli and DeRosa (1992) advocated support groups for bereaved children to help them cope with the death of a significant person in their lives. They use group intervention techniques such as bibliotherapy, artwork, and games as well as discussion to help children understand their loss, express their thoughts and feelings in a supportive atmosphere, and learn new ways of coping with the loss.

Campbell and Myrick (1990) studied the effects of group counseling on low-performing students. Their study included four experimental groups: one group met twice a week for 3 weeks and participated in structured group activities that focused on motivation, feelings of self-control, self-concept, school attitude, and behavior; the second group met for 1 full day and participated in the same structured group activities; the third group met only to complete a "behavior-related achievement" checklist; and the fourth group only completed the instruments used for the collection of data and received no counseling. Students and teachers in the counseling groups rated the sessions favorably, and some teachers reported changes in the group counseling students' behaviors and attitudes. The marathon group approach appears to have had the most positive effect on school attitudes and classroom behavior.

Campbell and Bowman (1993) stated that small group counseling can provide support for children who have been academically retained. They developed an eight-session "Fresh Start" program to address these children's problems with self-esteem, their view of the retention, motivation, and other concerns.

Yauman (1991) reviewed the literature on school-based group counseling of children experiencing divorce in their homes. The author found that age-appropriate, structured group activities, including such interventions as biblio-therapy, movies, games, drawing, puppets, and role-playing, can stimulate discussion and problem solving.

GROUP COUNSELING STAGES

Tuckman and Jensen (1977) reviewed studies of group development and concluded that groups typically progressed through five stages: forming, storming, norming, performing, and adjourning. During the forming period, members try to learn the group's structure and rules and find their place. Tensions begin to rise during the storming phase, and resistance to accomplishing goals and tasks may arise. During the third stage, norming, group cohesiveness should grow and members should work together more easily. In the fourth stage, performing, the group begins to function effectively and move toward accomplishing tasks and solving problems. In the final stage, adjourning, the group addresses issues related to termination, breaking the emotional bond within the group, and going on with life.

Using the information developed from studies such as those of Tuckman and Jensen, Johnson and Johnson (1987) described seven stages of group development:

1. Defining and structuring procedures and becoming oriented (defining what is expected of group members and what will happen)
2. Conforming to procedures and getting acquainted (goals and procedures are leaders' rather than owned by group members)
3. Recognizing mutuality and building trust (taking responsibility for one's own learning as well as that of others; feeling freedom to discuss ideas and feelings)
4. Rebelling and differentiating (establishing their autonomy; challenging the authority of the leader)
5. Committing to and taking ownership for the goals, procedures, and other

members (ownership of the group is members' rather than leaders'; developing commitment to one another)

6. Functioning maturely and productively (all members participate in leadership and decision making)
7. Terminating (deal with separation and move toward new experiences) (pp. 363–364)

These stages may not be so apparent in children's groups, depending on the members' ages. In addition, Tuckman and Jensen reviewed groups with less directive leaders, whereas group leaders who work with children need to be more structured and directive. Nevertheless, we believe children's groups go through processes similar to those described by Tuckman and Jensen.

Johnson and Johnson (1987) stated that all groups need to set aside time to process what is occurring: (1) how well members are achieving their goals and (2) how well the group is maintaining effective working relationships among members. This processing, by reminding members of their tasks and goals and providing feedback to members about their participation and interactional skills, is intended to improve the group's effectiveness.

GROUP GUIDANCE

Gazda (1973) emphasized the preventive orientation of groups and suggested pursuing information-giving and human-development education through group processes. Through group guidance procedures, counselors can help children become more involved in school and with classmates, understand themselves and their feelings, learn to share ideas and feelings, and develop decision-making and problem-solving skills. Developing such skills promotes children's self-confidence and builds competencies for more effective functioning in daily living.

Group guidance units can present information about study skills, making friends, drugs, or any other area in which children need help to grow and develop in a healthy manner. Guidance activities designed to help children with self-concept development, peer relationships, improved adult-youth relationships, academic achievement, and career development are included in *Guidance Activities for Counselors and Teachers* by Thompson and Poppen (1987).

Poppen and Thompson (1975) described group activities that enhance self-concept by focusing on children's strengths. One such activity is to have members of the group share something about themselves, such as their favorite activity and why they enjoy it, and then have group members write all the good points observed about each member on a 3 × 5 card. Another is to have each group member draw something he or she does well and wear the drawing for the rest of the day. Children seldom have their good points recognized, and these exercises create good feelings and serve as a stimulus for group guidance activities.

Bowman (1986) described an interesting idea for facilitating group guidance. In addition to familiar attention-getting techniques such as puppets, art, music books, dramatics, humor, and yoga that are effective in working with children, he suggested magic. His review of the literature showed magic increases self-concept, eye-hand coordination, patience, attending behavior, and interpersonal skills; stimulates creative thinking and increases children's curiosity; and reinforces lessons on safety. He suggested magic to break the ice, reward or reinforce behavior, focus attention during guidance lessons, and help withdrawn or alienated children.

Classroom Meetings

Glasser (1969, 1986, 1990) contended that children's needs for love and self-worth are not being met in our society and that classroom meetings and discussions in the schools can help meet these needs. Glasser advocated three types of classroom meetings—the open-ended meeting, the problem-solving meeting, and the educational-diagnostic meeting—to help children feel loved and worthwhile. The meetings can be adapted to the age and developmental level of the children involved.

Open-ended meetings can be held to discuss anything relevant to the children's lives in order to stimulate understanding and thinking. Topics may include "What is a friend?" "What would you do if all schools closed tomorrow and you never had to go again?" and "What would you do if you inherited a million dollars today?" Open-ended meetings can also be used to discuss situations involving moral decisions and values—"What would you do if you saw your best friend cheating on a test?"—or social issues such as prejudice. The leader's job is to remain nonjudgmental and direct the discussion in a way that stimulates thinking and helps the children set goals, look at consequences, and make plans. The leader uses frequent "what," "where," "when," "who," and "how" questions and encourages members to think of what they would do in the situation under discussion. All children are encouraged to express their opinions. The leader's opinions, judgments, and criticisms are *not* interjected.

A behavior problem-solving meeting can be used to encourage the group to help one of its members solve a behavior problem or a group problem. The leader-counselor can present the problem and ask the group to think of ways to handle the conflict. Children often can decide on better methods for handling conflicts than adults can. Again, the leader's responsibility is to facilitate understanding and clarification of the problem, stimulate the children to think of alternative solutions and their consequences, and encourage commitment to a plan of action. Glasser cautioned teachers and counselors not to use the behavior problem-solving meeting too frequently because the attention a child receives from being the focus of the discussion may reinforce the unwanted behavior.

Educational-diagnostic meetings enable teachers to quickly evaluate what children have understood from a unit of learning and the relevance of the material for their lives. Glasser criticized schools for emphasizing memorization of facts rather than understanding and relevance. Educational-diagnostic meetings enable the teacher to assess how well children understand the concepts of a unit before and after the unit is taught. For example, before beginning a unit of study on photosynthesis, the teacher might ask how many of the children can define *photosynthesis* and give examples of how it works. Following the unit, a second meeting could check what the children then understand about photosynthesis.

Group Meetings: Seven Levels

Poppen (see Thompson & Poppen, 1987) suggested that children's groups work well with structured activities, provided the activities are presented in a developmental fashion that allows the children to move from easy to more difficult tasks. He proposed seven levels of group meetings:

1. *Involvement meetings:* These meetings help children participate freely and build a sense of belonging to the group. For example, children can make name tags that describe some of their favorite things and share these name tags with the group.

2. *Rules meetings:* These meetings discuss the ground rules the group needs. The meaning of rules and why they are or are not necessary may also be discussed.

3. *Thinking meetings:* These group sessions are directed toward helping children develop their cognitive skills. "What if" topics are often used. For example, children may be asked, "What if you had one pill that would allow you to live for 200 years? Would you take the pill? Why or why not? What information would you need before making your decision?" Educational-diagnostic meetings are included on this level.

4. *Values-clarification meetings:* These meetings help children examine and understand their present systems of values, not to destroy them or build new value systems. Children may be asked to write newspaper ads for themselves, describing the kind of people they are, or to vote on how well they like school and then discuss why they voted as they did.

5. *Hypothetical problem-solving meetings:* These meetings give children some group experience in solving practice problems. The primary aim in teaching group problem solving is to help children learn how to generate alternative solutions to problems. Too often children cling to one problem-solving idea, even if it is not working. A sample activity at this level is to ask three children to simultaneously play the role of a child in their age group who is having problems with his or her parents. Three students play the child's father and three students play the child's mother as the family members try to work out their difficulties; the rest of the children in the group evaluate the interaction and suggest how to play the roles better.

6. *Actual problem solving:* When children are ready for this level of group interaction, they work with actual problems. Perhaps one child has a real family- or school-related problem for the group's consideration.

7. *Group council:* The highest level in this seven-stage sequence is

the group-council procedure recommended by Adlerian psychologists. On a democratic basis a rotating three-member council that represents the entire group governs the group. This type of group uses all the skills developed in the preceding six levels of group interaction. The children bring all group problems, from discipline to next week's picnic, before the council for discussion. However, the counselor retains veto power over solutions that might endanger the children or others.

EVALUATION OF GROUP MEETINGS

Bruckner and Thompson (1987) provided a model for evaluating weekly group counseling sessions with children in the elementary school that could be adapted for use with group counseling programs in any setting. They developed an instrument containing the following six incomplete statements and two forced-choice items:

1. I think coming to the group room is _____ .
2. Some things I have enjoyed talking about in the group room are _____ .
3. Some things I would like to talk about that we have not talked about are _____ .
4. I think the counselor is _____ .
5. The counselor could be better if _____ .
6. Some things I have learned from coming to the group room are _____ .
7. If I had a choice, I (would) (would not) come to the group room with my class.
8. Have you ever talked with your parents about things that were discussed in the group? (yes) (no)

Some of these items may be used as a needs survey for future group sessions. Two independent persons rate student responses on a 5-point scale, ranging from 5 for statements showing an outright positive, accepting attitude toward the item, to a rating of 1 for statements showing an outright rejecting, negative attitude toward the item. A rating of 3 is awarded to neutral, ambivalent, or evasive responses. Limited positive and limited negative responses receive ratings of 4 and 2, respectively. Raters should reach 85% levels of agreement and generally experience little difficulty in obtaining agreement on the remaining 15%.

GROUP CRISIS INTERVENTION

Two classmates are killed in a fiery car wreck.
A 12-year-old puts a gun to his head and commits suicide.
The mother of a 9-year-old dies of cancer.

The father of a 7-year-old is murdered.

War breaks out, and the television shows bombings on 24-hour newscasts.

Economic recession hits, and many parents lose their jobs.

Reports of an earthquake forecast send feelings of fear and panic throughout the population.

A hurricane devastates an entire section of the state.

In recent years, professionals have been asked to provide crisis counseling to children in schools, churches, and clubs. Incidents such as these stimulate fear, helplessness, loss, sadness, and shock. Children worry about the loss of their parents (their security), their friends ("Could it happen to me? Why did it happen?"), and their security ("Where will I go if I lose my home?"). In some cases, their parents may be coping with their own loss or grief and be unable to help the children. In other cases, the situation may be related to the school, church, or an organizational group, and children may feel that their parents do not really understand the situation. Some parents may not realize their children are worried; some children are not able to verbalize their pain. Those who work with children recognize that young people cannot learn or perform their daily activities with these fears and concerns. They become irritable and restless, moody, or agitated. They have difficulty concentrating and sleeping. They may experience physical symptoms such as nausea or diarrhea. Someone has to help them cope, which is usually effected through group discussion and group counseling.

Gilliland and James (1988) proposed six steps for crisis counseling that are similar to the reality therapy model described in previous chapters of this book. In addition, they urged counselors to take steps to ensure the psychological, emotional, and physical safety of the client, and, as the child develops a plan, to assist him or her in identifying additional support systems, coping mechanisms, and actions to take.

Gilliland and James (1988) emphasized the need for the crisis counselor to assess the severity of the crisis subjectively (as the child views it) and objectively (as the counselor views it). They also cautioned that consideration should be given to the child's emotional state and his or her ability to cope with the problem. Suicide may be a possibility in a crisis situation, and factors in the child's family and emotional history, as well as the seriousness of the thought and plan, help counselors determine the possibilities of such an action. (See "Suicidal Behaviors" in chapter 15.) Crisis counseling is short term, and counselors should carefully consider some children's need for referrals or other arrangements to ensure that each client successfully copes with the crisis in the days and weeks to follow.

Graham (1990) presented a plan for helping children after a trauma, such as a hurricane or plane crash, that affects the families of numerous children. Incorporating ideas presented by Graham with those of Gilliland and James (1988), we suggest the following outline for group crisis counseling:

I. Introductory phase
   A. Ask members to introduce themselves and tell why they are in the group.

  B. Help members clarify their goals regarding what they would like to accomplish in the meeting.

  C. Discuss confidentiality—what group members talk about stays in the group. Get a commitment from all members to maintain confidentiality.

  D. Discuss basic rules:

   1. Take a bathroom break first because no one can leave the room after the group begins.

   2. Encourage group members to stay the entire time. The group generally runs for 2 hours; the time depends on the ages of the children.

   3. Elect or appoint a coleader or a peer leader to keep the gate (that is, not let people in or out).

   4. Remind the group that no group member holds rank over any other group member and that everyone's participation is valued equally.

 II. Fact phase

  A. Focus on discussing what happened.

  B. Encourage everyone to participate.

 III. Feeling phase

  A. Ask "What happened then?"

  B. Ask "What are you experiencing now?"

 IV. Clients' symptoms

  A. Ask "How is this affecting you?" (Is the member having trouble sleeping or studying, or is the member worrying too much?)

  B. Ask "How is this affecting your grades, your studies, your health?"

 V. Teaching phase

  A. Explore the common responses to this incident.

  B. Brainstorm about how people have been responding to the incident.

  C. Discuss how each response is helpful or not helpful to people.

 VI. Summary phase

  A. Raise questions and provide answers.

  B. Summarize what has been learned and shared.

  C. Develop action plans for individuals and/or the group if needed.

  D. Provide support for group members to ensure their physical, emotional, and psychological safety. An action plan should be made to protect any group member needing protection.

  E. Conduct a follow-up meeting in 3 to 5 days to see how well the group members are coping.

  F. Arrange individual counseling sessions for group members who need further assistance.

In conclusion, group counseling can be a highly effective method for changing children's lives or, better still, preventing excess stress and conflict in their lives. Finding their place in a group and helping one another are rewarding for children.

Watching the children grow and develop into caring, functioning group members is rewarding for the group counselor.

REFERENCES

Bergin, J. (1989). Building group cohesiveness through cooperation activities. *Elementary School Guidance and Counseling, 24,* 90–94.

Bowman, R. (1986). The magic counselor: Using magic tricks as tools to teach children guidance lessons. *Elementary School Guidance and Counseling, 21,* 128–136.

Bruckner, S., & Thompson, C. (1987). Guidance program evaluation: An example. *Elementary School Guidance and Counseling, 21,* 193–196.

Campbell, C., & Bowman, R. (1993). The "Fresh Start" support club: Small-group counseling for academically retained children. *Elementary School Guidance and Counseling, 27,* 172–185.

Campbell, C., & Myrick, R. (1990). Motivational group counseling for low-performing student. *Journal for Specialists in Group Work, 15,* 43–50.

Dyer, W., & Vriend, J. (1980). *Group counseling for personal mastery.* New York: Sovereign.

Dyer, W., & Vriend, J. (1988). *Counseling techniques that work.* Alexandria, VA: American Counseling Association.

Gazda, G. (1973). Group procedures with children: A developmental approach. In M. M. Ohlsen (Ed.), *Counseling children in groups: A forum* (pp. 118–130). New York: Holt, Rinehart & Winston.

Gilliland, B., & James, R. (1988). *Crisis intervention strategies.* Pacific Grove, CA: Brooks/Cole.

Glasser, W. (1969). *Schools without failure.* New York: Harper & Row.

Glasser, W. (1986). *Control theory in the classroom.* New York: Harper & Row.

Glasser, W. (1990). *The quality school: Managing students without coercion.* New York: Harper & Row.

Graham, C. (1990, November). *A normal response to an abnormal situation: The crisis debriefing.* Paper presented at the meeting of the Southern Association for Counselor Education and Supervision, Norfolk, VA.

Johnson, D., & Johnson, F. (1987). *Joining together: Group theory and group skills* (3rd ed.). Englewood Cliffs, NJ: Prentice-Hall.

Poppen, W., & Thompson, C. (1975). *School counseling: Theories and concepts.* Lincoln, NE: Professional Educators.

Thompson, C., & Poppen, W. (1987). *Guidance activities for counselors and teachers.* Knoxville, TN: Author.

Tuckman, B., & Jensen, M. (1977). Stages in small group development. *Group and Organizational Studies, 2,* 419–427.

Yauman, B. (1991). School-based group counseling for children of divorce: A review of the literature. *Elementary School Guidance and Counseling, 26,* 130–136.

Zambelli, G., & DeRosa, A. (1992). Bereavement support groups for school-age children: Theory, intervention, and case example. *American Journal of Orthopsychiatry, 62,* 484–493.

Chapter   15

◆

Counseling Children with
Special Concerns

In chapter 1 we described some of the difficulties inherent in our complex present-day society—difficulties with which children must cope during their major years of growth and development. Counselors obviously cannot supply all the answers to these problems; however, several concerns seem pressing and are seen frequently by counselors. In this chapter we suggest methods for working with children with these special needs and problems. The suggestions should be incorporated into a caring, accepting counseling atmosphere and modified to meet the unique needs of the child and the presenting concern. The reader may wish to refer to appendixes A and B for special procedures to handle the problem behaviors that may accompany these societal problems. The following problems are considered: child abuse, divorce, stepfamilies, single-parent homes, death and dying, cultural barriers, alcoholism, latchkey children, homeless children, suicidal behaviors, satanic cults, AIDS, and violence.

CHILD ABUSE

Congress has defined *child abuse* as the "physical or mental injury, sexual abuse, negligent treatment or maltreatment of a child under the age of 18 by a person who is responsible for the child's welfare under circumstances which indicate the child's health or welfare is harmed or threatened" (U.S. Department of Health, Education, and Welfare, 1975, p. 1). Kavanagh (1982) pointed out that most definitions of emotional abuse and neglect focus on parental fault and/or the condition of the child, with some states emphasizing parental behavior (failure to provide proper care) and other states focusing on the child's condition (the child's having been denied proper care or parental love). Kavanagh expressed concern about the diagnoses being made because of these definitions.

According to Hart, Germain, and Brassard (cited in Neese, 1989), actions associated with psychological abuse may include mental cruelty (verbal abuse, unrealistic expectations, discrimination), aspects of sexual abuse and exploitation, living in unstable or dangerous environments, drug and substance abuse condoned by adults, negative models, cultural bias or prejudice, neglect or stimulus deprivation, and institutional abuse.

The American School Counselors Association (ASCA) published a position statement on child abuse in 1988 that defined it as "the infliction by other than accidental means of physical harm upon the body of a child, continual psychological damage or denial of emotional needs" (p. 262). Examples of child abuse in the statement include extensive or patterned bruises, burns, lacerations, welts, or abrasions; injuries inconsistent with explanation; sexual abuse, molestation, or exploitation; emotional disturbances caused by friction or discord in the home or mentally ill parents; and cruel treatment. ASCA defined *child neglect* as "the failure to provide necessary food, care, clothing, shelter, supervision, or medical attention for a child" (p. 262) and described this behavior as lack of supervision or medical attention, irregular and illegal school absences, overworking or exploiting child, lack of nurturance, or abandonment (ASCA, 1988).

Abuse has been further described as psychological, physical, and/or sexual maltreatment. Moeller, Bachmann, and Moeller (1993) wrote that psychological abuse has been difficult to define; however, their review of the literature indicated six categories of emotional abuse: (1) chronic denigration of the child's qualities, capacities, desires, and emotional expressiveness; (2) isolation; (3) terrorizing; (4) excessive age-inappropriate demands; (5) witnessing extreme parental violence (including excessive use of drugs and alcohol); and (6) not providing services for a seriously emotionally handicapped child. Johnson (1990) describes physical abuse as the use of an instrument on any part of the body, tissue damage beyond simple redness from a slap, and injury from heat, caustic substances, chemicals, or drugs. The U.S. National Center on Child Abuse and Neglect has defined sexual abuse as an act perpetrated on a child by a significantly older person with the intent to stimulate the child sexually and satisfy the aggressor's sexual impulses (cited in Moeller, Bachmann, & Moeller, 1993).

Because of the differing definitions of child abuse across the nation and because many incidents of child abuse are unreported or misreported, the prevalence of child abuse is difficult to determine. The American Humane Association National Committee for the Prevention of Child Abuse reported an estimated 2,694,000 cases in 1991 or 420 per 10,000 (Bennett, 1993). Additionally, as the *Harvard Mental Health Letter* (Special Supplement, July 1993, p. 1) pointed out, "Not all families have the same rules about disciplining children or the same attitudes toward nudity, touching, and kissing." This same publication noted about 2.5 million reports of child abuse or neglect in 1989, with about 25% of these involving physical abuse, 20% sexual abuse, and 55% neglect. Most sexual abuse victims are girls. Schaefer, Briesmeister, and Fitton (1984) pointed out that child abuse occurs at all levels of social, economic, and educational status and that in 80% to 90% of the cases the offender is a male relative or friend of the family. The offender may use bribes, threats, guilt, or coercion to ensure secrecy. To protect the family and this relative or friend, the abuse may be ignored or hushed up in a variety of ways, the incidents are never reported or recorded, and the child and family never confront the issue or receive treatment.

Several hypotheses have been advanced to explain the causes of child abuse. The families are often rigid, authoritarian, and isolated from one another and the outside world. Abusers have a high incidence of alcoholism. The parents are described as often depressed and hopeless and lacking in warmth, humor, and sensitivity to their children. The abused child is usually thought of in negative terms. Some believe that child abuse should be diagnosed as an addiction because the behavior is often compulsive; the offender experiences a pattern of growing sexual tension and then sometimes disgust and remorse. Rationalization and projecting blame are also common to both child abusers and alcoholics.

Research by Germain, Brassard, and Hart (cited in Neese, 1989) reported similar findings. They found that abusers are a heterogeneous group; however, their characteristics include a low frustration tolerance, nonempathetic relationships, unmet dependency needs, power-authoritarianism problems, low self-esteem, depressed emotions, learned helplessness, and self-isolating tendencies. Abusers tend to respond to others' distress in an aversive, unsympathetic manner. From their research on the characteristics of abusers, Roehl and Burns (1985) suggested that the "abuser usually exhibits poor impulse control, immature behavior, jealousy or favoritism toward the child, rigid and authoritarian belief systems, and few social skills" (p. 20). Abusers may attempt to dominate the family, feel uncomfortable in relationships with women or anyone outside the family, possess average or above-average intelligence, and probably abuse alcohol or other drugs. Mothers in incestuous families are usually very dependent, are frequently absent from home for long periods of time, show little involvement with the family, may be disenchanted with their role as wife and mother, and may be seriously ill or disabled (Roehl & Burns, 1985).

Families in which child abuse occurs often are experiencing multiple problems (marital, financial, occupational, parent-child), but the adults lack the resources and coping skills to resolve them. Community and cultural factors—for example, economic stress, social isolation, acceptance of domestic violence and corporal punishment, socialization of men to view women as sex objects and inferior persons, and disrespect for minorities, their lifestyles, and culture—may also contribute to the incidence of child abuse (Germain et al., cited in Neese, 1989). The following characteristics are often associated with higher incidences of abuse: poverty, blue-collar employment, unemployment, two-children families, parents who were victims of abuse, families going through stressful change (moving, work, health, marital), and families that are more punitive and less empathic (Germain et al., cited in Neese, 1989). Kavanaugh, Youngblade, Reid, and Fagot (1988) found that abused children talk less than other children and that abusive parents reacted less often to the communication of their children than other parents. Abusive parents also spent less time in positive interactions with their children than did other parents. When these factors are present and abuse is suspected, the child should be considered at greater risk.

Psychological Maltreatment

Hart, Germain, and Brassard (cited in Neese, 1989) reviewed the literature to determine the destructive effects of psychological maltreatment on the lives of children. Their lists included many of the symptoms previously noted, as well as poor appetite, lying and stealing, low self-esteem, emotional instability, incompetence or underachievement, depression, prostitution, suicide, and homicide. They asserted strong evidence indicates that psychological maltreatment results in serious emotional problems, behavioral disorders, or both. Neese (1989) was also concerned about psychological maltreatment and stated that this type of abuse increases the risk of developing serious behavioral and/or emotional disorders because it affects the victim's view of self and others as well as his or her expectations for the future. For this reason, Neese advocates that "counselors and other professionals involved in the total development of children must study the aspects of prevention and intervention as they relate to psychological maltreatment" (p. 194).

Garbarino, Guttmann, and Seeley (1986) called psychological maltreatment of children a significant problem in our society. They attempted to define the issue more clearly and to link the definition to prevention and treatment. The writers suggested that psychological maltreatment "is a concerted attack by an adult on a child's development of self and social competence, a *pattern* of psychically destructive behavior" (p. 8). According to Garbarino et al., psychological maltreatment manifests itself in five forms: rejecting, isolating, terrorizing, ignoring, and/or corrupting the child. They presented numerous methods for assessing the child's situation, in addition to prevention and intervention techniques for individuals and families and ways to mobilize community resources. Counseling techniques such as marital counseling, family therapy, parent/child interventions, methods for working with socially isolated families, and educating the public are suggested and described to assist the professional working with psychological maltreatment.

Neese (1989) found suggestions in the literature that the educational system may perpetrate child psychological maltreatment. Teachers may be abusive through disparaging remarks, threats, and punishments; the curriculum may be structured to overemphasize theoretical or academic goals while neglecting social development; and school bullies are a significant factor in the psychological victimization of children (Neese, 1989). Hart, Germain, and Brassard (cited in Neese, 1989) recommended that school systems address the issue through preservice and in-service programs and through clear policy statements. Neese called attention to the AACD (now ACA) ethical standards to guide counselors in the resolution of ethical conflicts with their employing institutions and in their relationships with their child clients but pointed out that these standards do not specifically address psychological maltreatment. Counselors must keep informed about issues and legislation through continuing education (Neese, 1989).

Physical Abuse

The *Harvard Mental Health Letter* ("Child Abuse, Parts I and II," 1993) concluded that the long-term effects of physical abuse are not fully understood; the effects of abuse and those of other familial or environmental effects are difficult to distinguish. However, it (p. 3) estimated that "at least 25% of physically abused children have serious psychiatric problems, including chronic anxiety and depression and sometimes neurological damage." Kurtz, Gaudin, Wodarski, and Howing (1993) reported that the physically abused children in their study displayed an overwhelming set of problems in school, such as dropping out, teen pregnancy, institutionalization, low scores on standardized tests of language and math, and repeating one or more grades. They had lower educational aspirations and more behavior problems in the classroom than other children. Academic failure was the most obvious factor among children classified as neglected; however, this group did not experience significant behavior problems in class or display significant adjustment difficulties.

Child Sexual Abuse

According to Green (1993), reporting of sexual abuse cases in this country substantially increased during the 1980s. Data from the American Humane Association indicates that 86% of the offenses were against boys and 94% of the offenses were against girls. Sexual abuse of girls is reported more often than abuse of boys. Boys are more likely to be approached by strangers, and girls are more likely to be victims of incest ("Child Abuse, Parts I and II," 1993). Children in frequent contact with their abusers have additional problems in maintaining the relationship, as well as coping with the trauma of the abuse.

England and Thompson (1988) described a number of myths associated with childhood sexual abuse:

1. *Myth number 1: Incest rarely occurs and then mainly in lower socioeconomic, poorly educated families.* The writers' review of literature indicated that sexual abuse is *not* restricted to a social class, educational level, or ethnic group.
2. *Myth number 2: Child molesters are sexually attracted to their victims.* England and Thompson state that sexual abuse is believed to be an act of power rather than of sex. Molesters treated by one of the authors had poor interpersonal relationships, problems at work, and feelings of worthlessness. In other words, they seemed to feel they had little control in their lives; engaging in sexual behavior with children was their way of showing power and control.
3. *Myth number 3: Most child molesters are strangers (unknown) to their victims.* Unfortunately, most offenders are related to their victims; in fact, according to a 1985 Committee for Children report, the majority of offenders are persons the child loves and trusts (such as a parent), who use the child's innocence, dependence, and fear to gain control (England & Thompson, 1988).

4. *Myth number 4: Child sexual abuse is a modern phenomenon, probably resulting from the sexual revolution.* Finkelhor (1979) found children's sexual abuse by adults has been quite common throughout history. Child pornography and prostitution were readily available long before the sexual revolution and continue to flourish.

5. *Myth number 5: The sexual abuse of a child is usually a single violent incident.* The abuse is *not* usually a single incident resulting from the overuse of drugs or alcohol or loss of control for other reasons. Studies have revealed that the abuse moves through several phases unless the child reports the incidents. England and Thompson (1988) contended that most children do not "tell," and the abuse continues until the child leaves home.

6. *Myth number 6: Children frequently make up stories about engaging in sexual activities with adults.* Children tend to tell the truth in reporting sexual abuse. In fact, Finkelhor (1979) believed that most sexually abused children grow into adulthood without ever revealing their "secrets" because of guilt, threats, and the perceived consequences of such revelations. Unfortunately, a few cases of adult-reported child sexual abuse proved false (England & Thompson, 1988).

Tennant (1988) listed physical signs of possible sexual abuse such as vaginal discharge, discomfort in the genital area, difficulty walking or sitting, and venereal disease or pregnancy in a child under 13. Behavior changes may include sleep disturbances (fear, nightmares, bedwetting); eating problems; changes in school behavior, performance, or attendance; unusual sexual behavior for the child's age; sudden dependency; or fear of losing a particular person (Tennant, 1988).

In his review of the literature, Green (1993) found that short-term symptoms of sexually abused children usually include fearfulness and anxiety, sleep disturbances, insomnia, nightmares, phobic avoidance, somatic complaints, and others similar to posttraumatic stress disorder. The symptoms of sexually abused boys may include conduct disorder such as lying, stealing, vandalism, and assaults on other children ("Child Abuse, Parts I and II," 1993). Children with more severe abuse may dissociate, with early symptoms including periods of forgetfulness, excessive fantasizing and daydreaming, sleepwalking, blackout, and imaginary friends, according to Green (1993). He pointed out that multiple personality disorder appeared for the first time in children during this decade and that these children are almost always victims of severe physical or sexual abuse. Low self-esteem, depression, and suicidal behaviors may be observed in older children who have been abused. Disturbances in sexual behavior are not unusual and may take the form of acting out or sexual inhibition. Green concluded that no specific behavior patterns in children indicate sexual abuse and that some cases might show no symptoms; diagnosis must be based on a variety of data, including a history, assessment of the reliability of the child's disclosure, psychiatric evaluation, physical examination, evaluation of the child's prior psychological functioning, and assessment of the family's functioning.

The *Harvard Mental Health Letter* ("Child Abuse, Parts I and II," 1993) concluded that treatment of children who are victims of sexual or physical abuse follows no accepted formula. It suggested that crisis intervention and counseling may be helpful for a single incident, but that more severe forms require years of treatment for the child and other family members. From a review of the literature, Tennant (1988) offered the following suggestions to teachers, parents, and counselors:

1. Listen to the child carefully.
2. Be sure you understand the meaning of words used by the child and that he or she understands your meanings.
3. Discuss examples of "good" and "bad" touching.
4. Talk about the child's rights with regard to his or her body or touching someone else's body, and explain that "bad" touches can come from those close to us.
5. Teach the child to say no to inappropriate touching.
6. Discuss the importance of telling someone about any incidents that confuse the child or make him or her uncomfortable. Reassure the child that telling is appropriate and that he or she will not be blamed. (p. 51)

Sexually abused children are probably more difficult clients than physically or emotionally abused children. They, too, have learned not to trust people; they have been deeply hurt by those they love. The counselor may have a difficult time developing a relationship of trust in order to help the child.

Hollander (1989) stated that "an aware child is a safe child" (p. 184) and presented a preventive educational program that uses bibliocounseling. The program should be developed jointly by school personnel and parents. The books selected should be part of a structured curriculum and used as a follow-up to a presentation by local protective or enforcement agencies. The materials should be readily available to the children, and they should be aware that professionals in the school can answer questions that result from their reading (see the list of suggested readings at the end of this chapter). Puppets or role-playing may be used to reenact situations in books if children need help talking.

Vernon and Hay (1988) were also interested in developing a preventive approach to child sexual abuse. After reviewing the literature on sexual abuse and receiving permission from parents and the school system, they implemented activities to address accepting oneself, developing vocabularies to discuss feelings about abuse, responding to inappropriate and appropriate touching, making decisions about self-protection, using assertiveness in saying no, and finding help. They felt the response from parents and children was positive and contended that children become less vulnerable physically and psychologically when they know the issues and the methods for coping with them.

The *Harvard Mental Health Letter* ("Child Abuse, Parts I and II," 1993) was not so positive about prevention programs. It noted that the time spent on the program is short and that the concepts presented can be difficult, especially for young children. They cited studies showing only a 10% increase in the number of correct answers after a single presentation and stating that 11-year-olds were likely to give the wrong answers when asked if the abuser could be someone they knew or if breaking a promise was all right in this case. Other studies, according to the *Letter*, suggest that the children would still be too frightened or embarrassed to tell and that the programs may create anxiety. The writers concluded that no one knows how to teach children preventive techniques because abuse comes in so many different forms and because the research is so limited.

General Counseling Strategies for Working with Abused Children

Society's first priority has traditionally been to punish the offender. Until recently, society forgot the victim once medical attention had been given for the physical problem and the child had been removed from the abuser's custody. Recently, victims of abuse have gotten more assistance because of educational information in churches and schools, reporting and information provided by the news media, and the victims' increased willingness to tell their stories in the hope that they will help another victim. Courtois (1980) said that the increased attention on the victims of incest (and probably all forms of abuse) is "due to pressure from a number of sources: (1) victims who are refusing to remain silent and who, alone or with other family members, are seeking assistance in increasing numbers; (2) the Women's Movement and the attention it has brought to all forms of violence against women; and (3) the Child Welfare Movement" (p. 323). Also, empirical research on factors associated with abuse is increasing.

Recent research suggests that long-term psychological and behavioral problems may result from unresolved issues surrounding child abuse. Browne and Finkelhor (cited in Germain et al., 1985) suggested that emotional symptoms may include anger, denial, repression, fear, self-blame, self-doubts, helplessness, low self-esteem, guilt, dejection, and apathy; inappropriate behavioral symptoms may include acting out, withdrawal, somatic symptoms, nightmares, and phobias; and the child's belief system may be affected to make the world seem unpredictable and hostile. Some children are referred to counselors because they are aggressive and have behavioral problems; they model the abusive behavior of their parents. Others are referred because they are extremely withdrawn and isolated or have academic or social problems.

Abused children are not easy clients. They have learned not to trust themselves, other people, or their environment. The world and the people in it are inconsistent and hurt them. Withdrawal from this painful world is safer than chancing relationships. Building friendship and trust may be difficult.

The child needs to ventilate his or her feelings, ask questions, and replay abusive incidents in order to resolve issues. Children have been taught that caregivers and other adults in their lives act in their best interest and cannot understand that people who are supposed to love and care for them can also harm them. Their dependency on parents and other adults for care and security intensifies the conflict. Many children believe they deserve the punishment they receive. Elkind (1980) pointed out that young children in Piaget's concrete operations stage (age 7 to 11) say their parents are good parents even though they are abusive. Their view of reality is that their parents are kind and loving; they cannot verbalize their feelings because of their limited view of the world. This cognitive assumption often interferes with counseling children of abusive parents.

Specific suggestions for counseling with abused children follow.

1. In counseling all abuse victims, counselors must be prepared to become totally involved with the child client, including the child's repeated testing of their caring.

2. Counseling techniques for overcoming the feelings of worthlessness and guilt as well as methods for building self-esteem must be found. Holtgraves (1986) suggested visual imagery to help children develop positive attitudes toward life. This imagery might include situations in which they successfully encounter and resolve uncomfortable or dangerous circumstances. The emphasis should be developing strengths and positive attributes. Holtgraves reminded readers that pride in physical appearance is important for a good self-concept and recommends that children be encouraged to stand tall, make good eye contact, use a strong voice, and project an image of strength.

3. England and Thompson (1988) suggested that a playroom is a better location than an office for interviewing children suspected of experiencing abuse. The play media assist children in their efforts to communicate their feelings, and the natural environment helps the child client feel safe and in control. Gunsberg (1989) also stated that play can be used effectively to help abused or neglected children. He reported that the play behavior of these children is likely to be primitive and disorganized (making them a behavior problem), and they often see themselves as powerless to affect the behavior of others. He described a contingency play format to teach impulse control and maintain enjoyable interactions with adults.

4. Sexually abused children require extra consideration, understanding, and support from the counselor. Often the children are initially unable to discuss the problem with the counselor because of intense feelings of guilt; they believe that somehow they provoked the attack or could have done something to prevent it. They may feel worthless and ashamed of having been used or abused in such a manner. They may be more affected by the questions and reactions that follow than by the act itself, and they often feel intense guilt at having gotten a parent or other adult in trouble, in jail, or barred from the home because the child "told."

5. Ask for clarification of words or nonverbal expressions you do not understand, but avoid influencing the child's statements by asking leading or closed questions (England & Thompson, 1988).

6. Specific techniques such as bibliocounseling, role-playing, play therapy, or group counseling may be considered, depending on the child's maturity. Placing sexually abused children in groups requires caution, especially if the trauma is very recent. The child may not be ready to share intense feelings.

7. Children may need information about what is appropriate and inappropriate touching or treatment and to be assured that certain parts of their bodies are private. They may need to be told that the adult's sexual or punishing behavior

was inappropriate. Because of children's limited cognitive development and understanding, and to allay the anxiety surrounding the topic, most programs designed to teach children about child abuse use role-play, puppets, coloring books, film-strips, movies, and so on. The vocabulary used is not explicit but instead refers to *touching* and *private areas.* The programs are designed not for sex education but to give children information and strategies for coping with abusive situations. Finkelhor (1984) suggested that prevention programs are useful for children who have been abused as well as children who have not, because they give both groups information and confidence to handle situations. Those programs described earlier (Hollander, 1989; Holtgraves, 1986) may help counselors with ideas for developing preventive education presentations in their own areas.

8. Assertiveness training that focuses on how to say no or handle potentially abusive situations may be necessary. The child needs help to determine the warning signs of abuse and to plan ways for coping with the situations (for example, calling a special person when the father or mother begins to drink). Role-playing these strategies prepares children to handle such situations more effectively.

9. Encourage children to tell someone right away when an abusive situation occurs. Adults who abuse children sexually often warn the children to keep "their secret." Children need help discerning when they should tell a secret and when information should be kept confidential and in deciding whom they should tell and what to do if the adult does not believe their story.

10. Counselors must deal with issues of trust at some point in work with abused children. Developmental theorists have emphasized that children must develop trust in people and their interactions in order to live effectively, yet children receive a multitude of daily messages, designed to protect them, that imply that the world and the people in it are dangerous. Eisenberg and O'Dell (1988) recommended group discussions and activities to help children decide whom to trust and when to be cautious. They also suggested parent education programs with this theme because parental fears are extremely influential in children's lives.

11. Ratican (1992) cautioned that some models of therapy are inappropriate and perhaps harmful for abuse survivors; she quoted some writers who suggest throwing away the textbook and listening to the client! Ratican called for an eclectic combination of techniques: guided imagery, hypnosis, exploration and ventilation of feelings, journal keeping, letter writing, cognitive restructuring to correct distorted messages, empty chair technique, psychodrama, art, music, and dance.

Childhood abuse is a part of an overall pattern of abusive behavior, and the family network, as well as the personality of the abuser, must be considered. In addition, family reactions to the child who has been abused will enhance or interfere with counseling treatment and progress. Counselors ought to consider family therapy at an appropriate time in their treatment plans.

Counselors working with abused children must be prepared to provide understanding and support for all persons involved. The natural reaction is anger at anyone who hurts a child; however, these feelings must be recognized and resolved for the counselor to work effectively with the child and the family, particularly the abuser. Counselors who are overly sympathetic with abused children lose objectivity and their ability to help the child; counselors who are extremely angry and judgmental toward the family of an abused child (for allowing this to happen) or toward the abuser can never establish the relationship necessary to help these individuals. Before beginning counseling with victims of abuse, counselors may need to examine their own feelings and views about the case.

Children's Memories of Abuse

Although most professionals report a high percentage of valid child abuse reports, because of a personal experience, Spiegel (1988) has written convincingly that our society is now involved in child abuse hysteria that has resulted in "good faith but overzealous reporting, professionals looking for abuse in otherwise innocuous behaviors, and parents using accusations of sexual abuse in divorce and custody proceedings" (p. 276). Spiegel warned that the hysteria has resulted from sensationalized media reports, televised awareness programs, newspaper articles, television movies, children's programs on touching, puppet shows, lectures, and a variety of other media. He reported that a shared paranoia develops when overzealous attitudes toward abuse become prevalent and children's perceptions are directed by a biased adult eager to save the child. Spiegel summarized the body of "backlash literature" that resulted from what he described as overzealous attention to the issue of child abuse and warned counselors they can no longer simply report cases and withdraw. Spiegel believes that counselors working with children have to be aware of this hysteria and see that investigations are completed thoroughly and objectively. Sandberg, Crabbs, and Crabbs (1988), in their article on the legal issues in child abuse, also asserted that counselors have a responsibility to remain alert in cases with chronic problems but warned against a "zealous crusade." They noted an increasing number of false allegations of child abuse in divorce and custody cases but cautioned about making general assumptions about false reporting.

The accuracy of memories recalled by child abuse victims has also become a matter of concern. Freud first described how traumatic events in a person's life can be repressed from consciousness but still affect an individual's behavior in various ways. He uncovered repressed thoughts and feelings through techniques such as free association, dream analysis, and interpretation of humor or "slips of the tongue" (see chapter 3). Therapists trained in psychodynamic methods believe that clients must bring traumatic memories to consciousness and deal with them in order to get better.

Ceci, Ross, and Toglia (1987) found in their experiments that young children are particularly susceptible to suggestion or misleading information given to them after an event. They believe that this suggestibility arises in part from children's desires to please an adult.

Loftus (1993) suggested two sources that could contribute to false memories:

popular writing and counselors' suggestions. Although children may not have read the materials Loftus described, they often hear accounts of child abuse reported in news media or discussed by adults. In addition, adults may repeatedly warn them about the possibility of encountering an abuser. Loftus (1993) also reported that the therapist or counselor can unintentionally contribute to a client's false memories through suggestions made during therapy. Some counselors believe the possibility of child abuse must be discussed openly, regardless of the symptoms; others may push the client, interpret dreams as showing signs of abuse, question the client in such a manner as to suggest abuse, or reinforce their suspicions in other ways. Loftus (1993) suggested that counselors lack the tools to distinguish true memories; therefore, they should avoid zealous interventions in favor of techniques that are less potentially dangerous—clarification, compassion, empathy, and gentle confrontation.

Yapko (1993) listed guidelines for professionals working with the possibility of child abuse:

1. Do not jump to conclusions.
2. Do not ask leading questions.
3. Get external corroboration when the situation is ambiguous.
4. Be conservative in suggesting any method of limiting communication with the client's family.
5. Do not rely on your own memory, especially if sensitive information is discussed.

CHILDREN OF DIVORCE

The incidence of divorce increased rapidly in the United States during the past several decades, although there are indications of a leveling off at present. Strangeland, Pellegreno, and Lundholm (1989) report that close to one third of children under 18 are affected by the divorce of their parents. Because divorce and marital separation are emotionally comparable to losing a parent through death (Wallerstein, 1983), and because divorce, separation, and remarriage bring about rapid and multiple changes in the family (Goldman & King, 1985), the process is traumatic and painful for all involved.

Adults frequently seek help to cope with the hurt associated with divorce through individual and group counseling or through organized helping groups such as Parents Without Partners. In past years, children of divorce got little direct help; in fact, in most instances, the children were told as little as possible about family affairs and were instructed to keep the breakup secret for as long as possible. Recently, because of the noticeable effects of family separation on children, more attention has been directed to the needs of children going through this traumatic event.

The lives and relationships of children in a divorcing family are profoundly affected—socially, economically, psychologically, and even legally. Children must adjust to separation from one parent and formation of a new and different relationship with the other. A change in the family's economic status, possibly a change in the home and school environment, different parenting styles, custody battles, and sometimes a totally different lifestyle create feelings that may be positive or negative. Often, mothers who were totally involved in the care of children and home have to go to work; many are unskilled and accept low-paying jobs. Children may be torn by conflicting loyalties or learn to manipulate the parents to get their own way. Children of divorced parents may be asked to assume the role of the absent parent and to fulfill physical or emotional responsibilities beyond their maturity level. For some families, separation and divorce bring relief from tension and strife; for other families, the breakup brings more stress, pressure, and overwhelming burdens (Kupisch, Rudolph, & Weed, 1984).

Several leading researchers have pioneered the research efforts on children of divorce. Wallerstein and Kelly (1980) followed 60 divorcing families with a total of 131 children for 10 years. More recently, Wallerstein and Blakeslee (1989) conducted follow-up interviews with at least one member of 52 of these families to determine their current reactions to the prior divorce. Hetherington, Cox, and Cox (1978) studied 46 preschool children and their families for 2 years. Kurdek and Berg (1983) and Kurdek, Blisk, and Siesky (1981) are now working with 74 families. Guidubaldi (1984) and Guidubaldi, Perry, Cleminshaw, and McLoughlin (1983) are attempting to follow a national sample of elementary school children going through divorce. According to Goldman and King (1985), these major researchers in the area have gathered most of the data concerning the effects of divorce on children.

Wallerstein and Kelly (1980) noted that the "central hazard of divorce" is adverse effects on the child's development. Numerous studies have suggested that the child's developmental level is related to the reaction that follows the separation. Wallerstein and Kelly (1980) and Wallerstein and Blakeslee (1989) suggested that infants respond mainly to the emotional reactions of their caretaker; for example, mothers or fathers under stress convey their feelings to the infant through their handling and verbal communication. Very young children seem to have many of their needs met regardless of the stress of the caretaker. Very young children are dependent and demand attention to their needs. Preschoolers (age 3 to 5) have only a vague understanding of the family situation because of their limited cognitive development; thus, they often feel frightened and insecure, experience nightmares, and regress to more infantile behaviors. School-age children, who have more advanced cognitive and emotional development, see the situation more accurately. However, children age 6 to 8 often believe the divorce was their fault ("If I had not been bad, Dad would not have left"), and children at this age often hold unrealistic hopes for a family reconciliation. They may feel loss, rejection, guilt, and loyalty conflicts. Age 9 to 12 is a time when children are developing rapidly and rely on their parents for stability. They may become very angry at the parent they blame for the divorce or may take a supportive role as they worry about their troubled parents. Because of their anxiety, they may develop somatic symptoms, engage in troublesome behaviors, or experience a decline in academic achievement. The parents' divorce during children's adolescent years brings a different set of developmental problems. Young people at this age are striving for independence and exploring their own sexuality. They need structure, limits, and guidance in dealing with their sexuality. They also may worry about their own relationships and the possibility of repeating their parents' mistakes.

The results of research relating risk to age have been contradictory. Hetherington et al. (1978) believe that younger children suffer more detrimental effects of a divorce. In her 10 year follow-up, Wallerstein (1984) found that children who were very young at the time of the divorce seem to have suffered less—they remembered less about that time in their lives. A multitude of factors other than developmental level may influence the effects of divorce on the child, including the amount of tension and conflict in the home, the length of time the child has lived with the conflict, the parents' reactions to the conflict, and the parents' personal adjustment to divorce and the resumption of parenting roles.

Most researchers have reported that children, especially boys, going through a divorce experience academic problems, (Guidubaldi, 1984; Werner & Smith, 1982). School is usually a child's second most stable environment; a child whose home environment is disrupted naturally turns to the school and teachers for support and comfort. Guidubaldi et al. (1983) found that an orderly, structured, and predictable school environment was related to the resumption of student achievement. Children who were achieving well before the family disruption and who had no previous serious personality or behavioral disorder seem to resume their good adjustment within 1 to 2 years after the divorce. Children just entering school at the time of the divorce may be at greater risk academically because during these years the foundations for learning are formed. However, academic achievement is probably related more closely to other factors, such as socioeconomic status, than to the incidence of divorce.

Wallerstein (1983) and Wallerstein and Blakeslee (1989) describe "psychological tasks" that children of divorce must successfully resolve.

Acknowledging the Reality of the Marital Rupture. Young children often experience terrifying fantasies, feel abandoned, and tend to deny the reality of the family situation. Because of their own stress, parents often fail to reassure children and help them understand the situation and their future. Older children, too, may experience some fantasies of disaster, reduced ability to think and cope, and even psychosomatic symptoms indicating their anxiety. Supportive counseling techniques, including listening, reflection, clarification, and problem solving, and perhaps stress-reduction techniques such as relaxation or guided imagery are appropriate for children working through this task. Oehmen (1985) asserted that the child should be confronted with the situation quickly and forcefully and given an opportunity to discuss, process, and resolve his or her feelings about the divorce to avoid being overwhelmed by negative feelings.

Wallerstein and Blakeslee (1989) stated that the most critical factor in helping children through divorce is parental support. Both parents should talk with all the children in a group about the decision to divorce several days before one parent leaves the home. Children should be provided with a clear explanation about why their parents are divorcing, although they need not be told the details of an infidelity or other sexual problems. The parents should convey that, unfortunately, they have made a mistake in their marriage, but they remain committed to the family. The authors called understanding the divorce and its consequences the first psychological task for children of divorcing families.

Disengaging from Parental Conflict and Distress and Resuming Customary Pursuits. The resolution of this task calls for the children to distance themselves from the crisis in their household and resume their normal learning tasks, outside activities, and friendships. Parents must work to help children keep their lives in order and not let the divorce overshadow all their activities. As has been reported by other researchers, Wallerstein (1983) saw a significant decline in academic achievement in more than half of her sample of children age 7 to 11 following a marital separation. Group counseling and individual techniques directed toward improving academic achievement (for example, contingency contracting) may assist children at this level. Consultation sessions with teachers to plan for a structured class environment may bring stability to the child's life and encourage achievement.

Resolution of Loss. Divorce brings not only loss of a parent but also often loss of familiar surroundings and possibly a more comfortable lifestyle. Wallerstein (1983) noted that the task of resolving these losses may be the most difficult: "At its core this task demands that the child overcome his or her profound sense of rejection, of humiliation, of unlovability, and of powerlessness which the one parent's departure so often engenders" (p. 237). Wallerstein and Blakeslee (1989) suggested that a consistent pattern of visitation by the absent parent and an emphasis on building a new and positive relationship can help children through this stage. Unfortunately, many children do not have this relationship with the absent parent and remain disappointed for years. They feel rejected by the absent parent and thus unlovable and unworthy. Role-playing, puppetry, writing, drawing, feelings, charades, and other techniques can encourage children to express their feelings. Individual and group sessions focusing on building self-esteem may be helpful—for example, strengths testing, peer teaching, finding the child a "buddy," and the techniques of cognitive restructuring.

Resolving Anger and Self-Blame. Because divorce is a voluntary decision by one or both parents, children tend to blame them for being selfish and unresponsive to their needs, or they may blame themselves for the breakup of the family. Intense anger at one or both parents is characteristic of children of divorce, especially older children. The researchers found that the child's ability to forgive himself or herself for the divorce or lack of reconciliation was a significant step toward forgiving the parents and reconciling the relationship. Some excellent children's books can help them understand the divorce process and the reality that they are not to blame for the divorce. Most of these books emphasize that sometimes adults just cannot live together or resolve their differences. Counselors can recommend specific books for the developmental level of their clients and discuss the books with the children. The child's intense anger often results in acting-out behavior. A consistent, structured environment at home and at school provides some of the security the child needs during this period of turmoil and change. Group counseling that focuses on role-playing, play therapy, drawing, and writing can help children express their anger and feelings of guilt. Group problem-solving discussions help children find constructive ways of handling their feelings.

Accepting the Permanence of the Divorce.   Wallerstein (1983) pointed out that the fantasy of a reunited family persists tenaciously for children of divorce, even after the parents marry other partners. Whereas losing a parent through death has a finality about it, the fact that both partners are alive contributes to the continuing fantasy of restoring the intact family. Reality therapy may help the child accept the permanence of divorce. Group counseling with other children who are going through divorce or who have experienced it may also help. Drawings of the family before the divorce and at the present time, good and bad family changes since the divorce, and filmstrips and books about divorce and other family lifestyles (the stepfamily or single-parent family) often stimulate excellent discussions.

Achieving Realistic Hope Regarding Relationships.   During the adolescent years, the child of divorce must resolve issues surrounding relationships—learning to take a chance in relationships while knowing full well that they might be fulfilling or that they might fail. Doing so requires that the child feel lovable and worthy. Children often feel rejected, unlovable, and unworthy because they feel guilty over the divorce or because they believe that one or both parents rejected them and cared little about their feelings and welfare. Wallerstein and Blakeslee (1989) noted that some adolescents engage in acting-out behavior (promiscuity, alcohol or drug abuse, and the like) that indicates low self-esteem. An important task for adolescents is realizing they can love and be loved. They must learn to be open in relationships while knowing that divorce or a loss is possible. According to Wallerstein and Blakeslee, effective resolution of this last psychological task of "taking a chance on love" leads to freedom from the psychological trauma of divorce and provides second chances for children of these families. Wallerstein and Blakeslee conclude that the effects of divorce are much more pervasive and longer lasting than originally thought. In earlier research, Wallerstein and Kelly (1980) had reported that boys showed more signs of trauma from the divorce during their developmental years than girls did. Wallerstein and Blakeslee (1989) found a sleeper effect—the girls' problems became more apparent as they entered young adulthood. Twenty years after Wallerstein began her initial research, she found parents' continuing anger still a factor in their children's lives. Many of the sample of children, now adults, were underachievers or drank heavily; a few had been involved in serious crimes. One third of the girls had relationship problems.

Guidubaldi (1989) reported the results of his study on children of divorce to the National Committee for Children's Rights. He found that elementary-grade children, especially boys, experience poor academic and social adjustment after divorce and concluded that poor financial conditions and the lack of a male role model contribute to these problems. Guidubaldi suggested that special measures—including joint custody, frequent visitation rights, and the father's involvement in school activities—may help children of divorce adjust better to the breakup.

Counselors working with the parents of children involved in a divorce can be of assistance by providing consultative advice. Some of the following suggestions for parents may help:

1. Talk with the child about the divorce at his or her cognitive level (counselors may want to rehearse this with the parents). Explain what has happened at the child's level of understanding, and try to relate the experience to one that the child may have had. Emphasize that the child is not at fault. Keep the lines of communication open so the child's misconceptions or fears are recognized immediately. Avoid blaming or criticizing the other parent and relating all the unpleasant details.

2. Plan for ways to make the child's life as stable and consistent as possible, even though changes may be necessary. Household routines, school schedules, and consistent discipline help children understand that their world is not completely wrecked. Involve teachers, counselors, ministers, grandparents, and other support systems.

3. Avoid using the children as go-betweens to carry messages ("The child-support check is late!") or to find out about the other parent's life ("What does the apartment look like?"). Children love both parents and are already torn by conflicting loyalties.

4. Arrange for regular visits from the absent parent to assure the children that they are loved by both parents. Children are sometimes disappointed by absent parents who fail to call or come for a visit. Custodial parents need to provide a lot of love and reassurance at these times.

5. Talk with the children about the future. Involve them in the planning without overwhelming them with problems. They need to know what to expect.

6. Children experiencing a divorce in their family are still children at a particular developmental level. Avoid asking them to assume responsibilities beyond their capabilities—being the man of the family, babysitting younger children, or taking on excessive household chores.

Although most research cites the negative effects of divorce on children's development, Gately and Schwebel (1992) found some areas in which the children experienced favorable outcomes:

1. *Maturity,* because they tended to assume greater responsibility for chores
2. *Improved self-esteem,* because they coped effectively with their changing life's circumstances
3. *Empathy,* due to increased concern for family members
4. *Androgyny,* as a result of seeing models not confined by stereotypical sex roles

Positive factors in their lives that contributed to the development of these attributes were positive personality, supportive family environment, and supportive social environment (Gately & Schwebel, 1992).

In their comprehensive article attempting to link intervention to basic research on children of divorce, Grych and Fincham (1992) also suggested helping parents understand how their behavior affects their children's adjustment and assist them in minimizing the effect of the divorce on children.

Parents and counselors need to remember that adjustment after a divorce takes a child time and requires continuing understanding and reassurance. Parent-group meetings can help parents understand the problems their children are experiencing, learn new methods for communicating with their children, try new methods of discipline, and resolve some of their own frustration.

Omizo and Omizo (1987) found that group counseling benefited parents by encouraging a more positive child-rearing attitude, which, in turn, resulted in the children feeling more positive about themselves.

As in counseling about any problem in which values, beliefs, and attitudes may affect the counselor's objectivity, counselors may want to assess their feelings about divorce and their potential reactions to both the parents and the child. Children who are the victims of divorce have been hurt by adults they trusted and are quick to detect uneasiness, anxiety, or insincerity in the counselor's behavior.

CHILDREN IN STEPFAMILIES

For years the intact nuclear family has been considered the ideal or norm. With the present rate of divorce and the number of adults remarrying each year, this idealized view of the family must be adjusted. Kantrowitz and Wingert (1990) reported that, according to census data released in 1985, 6.8 million children lived in stepfamilies and demographers are predicting that one third of the children born in the 1980s will live with a stepparent at some point.

A stepfamily has been defined as a family in which at least one adult has had a child prior to the couple's marriage (Kupisch, 1984). Joining two families into one presents children with another set of unique problems with which to cope at a time when the effects of the biological parents' divorce may still be troublesome. Bryan, Ganong, Coleman, and Bryan (1985) concluded that, with the number of stepfamilies increasing, mental health professionals will become more involved with stepfamilies and the problems of the adults and children in these families. Kantrowitz and Wingert (1990) stated that, until the 1970s, researchers focused their attention on nuclear, intact families. Stepfamilies or single-parent families were virtually ignored, but researchers have shown that these families are very different in structure, interactional modes, and functioning from nuclear, intact families.

Because the stepfamily is not considered a "normal" family, expectations and relationships are more ambiguous and complex. Not only are cultural and social guidelines unclear, but also children who are members of two households, moving in and out, have ambiguous and complex home guidelines and schedules.

Adults and children experience changes in roles, alliances, parenting arrangements, household responsibilities, rules, expectations, and demands. For children who are attempting to regain stability after the first family breakup, this lack of structure may bring additional stresses and strains.

Kupisch (1984) contended that the stepfamily is not recognized as an equal to the ideal first-marriage family. She pointed out that some religious groups sanction only the first-marriage family and do not fully support alternative families. Legally, stepparents do not have protected parental rights; for example, they are not authorized to grant permission for medical aid to their stepchildren. Socially, stepparents are often treated as extra baggage by uncomfortable hosts at school functions, family gatherings, or parties with friends. The children in stepfamilies are often labeled maladjusted or delinquent because they have experienced divorce and the reorganization of a family. School activities are built around the intact, first-marriage family, such as Mother's Day and Father's Day. Lack of acceptance of stepfamilies—especially the children in these families—adds to the stress of coping and establishing a new and stable home life for all members.

Gardner (1984) described certain disturbances that children in stepfamilies may experience. He saw hostility and anger as extremely common, including hostility felt toward the natural parent and displaced onto the stepparent, who is a less dangerous target.

Although ordinary sibling rivalry is "fierce," according to Gardner, rivalry between stepsiblings is "even more virulent"; under ordinary circumstances, older children have an opportunity to get used to the idea of a new brother or sister, but in remarriage the stepsiblings "descend in a horde all at once."

Love in the stepfamily does not occur immediately; it takes time and work. Gardner suggested that counselors work with children to help them understand the concepts of compromise and the degrees of love—that loving one person does not take away love for another or mean that we always agree with the person we love.

Gardner included in his writings suggestions for stepmothers and stepfathers but emphasized the importance of joint counseling in the stepfamily situation. The child is a part of a family network, and the problems that concern the child are enmeshed in family interactions. Prosen and Farmer (1982), too, stressed including the stepparents in the counseling process. These authors mention outreach groups for stepparents designed to increase knowledge and acceptance of family differences, build positive attitudes toward the new family, develop competency in handling new situations, and provide support for the new family.

Summarizing findings regarding stepfamilies, Fuller (1988) reported general agreement that younger children adjust more readily to the stepfamily situation; that adolescents seem to have the most difficult time, especially if the stepparent is not the same sex as the adolescent; that children adjust better to a stepfamily after the death of a natural parent than after a divorce; and that cooperation and support among spouses and former spouses contribute to the children's adjustment. Fuller cautioned that stepfamilies' strengths are often overlooked because of the focus on problems. She suggested that being a child in a stepfamily can

(1) promote flexibility because children often must adjust to new situations, (2) provide multiple role models, (3) teach conflict-resolution skills, (4) extend the number of people who care about the child, (5) improve the child's standard of living, (6) increase the child's happiness with his or her parents, and (7) provide additional siblings for enjoyment and learning.

Zeppa and Norem (1993) tested the generally accepted conclusion that stepfamilies have more stress than do first families. While acknowledging their study's flaws the authors concluded that significantly fewer differences divide first families and stepfamilies than had been thought. Their results showed that stepfamilies experience more stress, but they suggested that the idea that stepfamilies are different from first families and have more problems may be due to socioeconomic factors or bias against stepfamilies.

Kupisch (1984) contended that counselors can facilitate a satisfactory level of functioning in a stepfamily by helping the stepfamily accomplish six critical tasks.

1. *Finding realistic, appropriate role models for stepparents.* The stepparent role is different from the parent role and must be negotiated in the new family. Both adults and children need to clarify and understand the stepparent's role.

2. *Redefining financial and social obligations.* Although a marriage may end, financial responsibility for the children does not end, nor do the social relationships that were established prior to the remarriage. Resentment over support payments or continued relationships with former friends or relatives (such as grandparents) often present problems for the new family. Children in the middle of these conflicts may be used by adults for personal gain.

3. *Arranging custody and visitation patterns.* Finding ways to allow the children to maintain "contact with both parents requires logistical planning, flexibility and continuous open communication across households," according to Kupisch (p. 41). Custody battles and arguments over visitation rights are not uncommon in stepfamilies, and the child is often the pawn.

4. *Establishing consistent leadership and discipline.* Maintaining consistency in discipline patterns with an increased number of authority figures and two households requires open communication and planning. Some research indicates that discipline controversies and divided loyalties are the most stressful conflicts for children in stepfamilies.

5. *Dispelling myths and tempering idealism.* Counselors can help new stepparents understand that the love of stepchildren is not instant but requires time and patience.

6. *Forming emotional bonds within the new family.* Developing emotional bonds for all members of a new family requires time and work. "The couple bond is particularly crucial for continuance of the stepfamily, and it is important for the children's sense of family security," according to Kupisch (p. 41).

In another article, Kupisch (1987) added a seventh task—that of dealing with sexuality in the home. The newly married adults may demonstrate more sexual behavior, which young children may model as a way to gain affection and attention.

Kupisch advocated groups as a "dynamic vehicle" for helping families as they reorganize. She presented guidelines for stepparents and stepchildren that could be used as topics for group discussions. Stepchildren are encouraged to recognize the following (p. 43):

1. They should express their feelings and thoughts honestly.
2. They should ask parents about expectancies and routines.
3. Marriage and divorce are adult decisions, and they are not responsible.
4. They do not have to divide their loyalties and choose between parent and stepparents (love can be shared).
5. They can be members of two households.
6. Love for stepkin may take time.

Kupisch (1987) also encouraged counselors to pursue issues surrounding the family constellation: the frequency and amount of significant change in the child's life; living, visitation, and custody arrangements; reactions to family disruption and remarriage; typical behavioral reactions to stress; significant emotional attachments; relationship with the absent parent and extended family; acceptance of new family members; discipline arrangements between and within both households; and other stressful life events. She suggests the kinetic family drawing as a helpful technique for understanding family dynamics.

Manning and Wooten (1987) asked 23 stepparents attending a meeting of the Stepfamily Association of Louisiana what they thought schools should know about stepfamilies. Three themes emerged from this survey. Stepfamilies wanted improved communications between the school and family and hoped for greater understanding and information about the family. The stepfamilies also asked for greater understanding from teachers concerning the amount of stress in the family. They suggested that community resources be identified so teachers could use them for referral sources. School groups for children in stepfamilies were highly praised for their helpfulness. The participants' third request was that schools be especially sensitive to including stepparents and noncustodial parents in school life (Manning & Wooten, 1987).

Diamond (1985), too, wrote about the necessity for sensitizing teachers and other school personnel to the needs of children in stepfamilies. To avoid confusion and embarrassment, for example, teachers must have information about students' living arrangements. A class list with parents' names should provide the teacher with information about the child's home. Schools, and especially teachers, should make every effort to get parents' names correct to avoid awkwardness. Special occasions and holidays can cause problems for children in stepfamilies; teachers should ask them how they wish to handle these occasions. Teachers should make every effort to respect the family's privacy and avoid embarrassing questions. Teachers are cautioned that many students in their classes live in nontraditional homes and to avoid erroneous assumptions about the child's home life and discomfort about interacting with families other than two-parent families (Diamond, 1985).

Carter (1988), in a presentation to the American Association for Marriage and Family Therapy, stated that many problems in stepfamilies stem from traditional assumptions about the woman's role in a family, for example, competition between the stepparent and stepchildren for the spouse's attention, the woman's role of being responsible for the emotional well-being of the family, and the perception that men should take financial care of the family. She recommended a "new paradigm to allow for complex relationships and roles in remarried systems," including (1) open lines of communication and permeable boundaries between households, (2) support for the parenting responsibilities of new spouses, and (3) a revision of traditional roles for men and women that allows for shared day-to-day responsibilities.

Kupisch (1984) urged counselors in both school and community mental health settings to assess their personal attitudes about all types of families and to use supportive counseling methods such as support groups, educational workshops, family therapy, and bibliotherapy to help the adults and children in these families.

Periodically, we, too, have emphasized that counselors need to examine their attitudes and beliefs about certain clients in order to maintain the highest levels of effectiveness. Visher and Visher (1979) stated that negative stereotypes of stepparents are common, and even those trained in the helping professions may not be immune to these biases. Bryan et al. (1985) attempted to investigate counselors' attitudes toward stepparents and stepchildren. The results of their study indicated that experienced counselors did not view stepfamilies and nuclear families differently; however, counselors with limited experience viewed stepparents and stepfamilies more negatively than they did members of an intact family. The researchers suggested several explanations for this difference: Inexperienced counselors may have a more unrealistically positive view of nuclear-family life, experienced counselors may not accept stereotypes as readily as inexperienced counselors do, experienced counselors may be more hesitant to make judgments about cases with only the minimal amount of data given in the experimental study, and, finally, experienced counselors may have had more frequent contact with stepfamilies in a clinical setting, thus reducing the impact of the stereotype. Bryan et al. (1985) recognized the limitations of their study but expressed concern that "if inexperienced counselors view stepfamilies significantly more negatively based on the minimal cues provided in this study, it is likely they will view their stepfamily clients somewhat negatively at the first and subsequent meetings" (p. 282). Whether the counselor is inexperienced, experienced but has had little contact with stepfamilies, or experienced with a substantial amount of contact with stepfamilies, unrecognized biases can slip into counseling practices. All of us in the helping professions need to evaluate our counseling periodically.

CHILDREN IN SINGLE-PARENT HOMES

Blum, Boyle, and Offord (1988) presented discouraging news about children in single-parent families: Of 1,800 families with children 6 to 12 years old, 304 children lived in single-parent homes. Children with conduct disorders, emotional problems, attention-deficit disorder with hyperactivity, and poor school performance were 1.7 times more likely to live in single-parent homes. Low income was also a strong factor in these homes. The researchers cautioned that their study did not indicate whether the children's disorders followed or preceded the child's living in a single-parent home. However, Shreeve, Goetter, Bunn, Norby, Stueckle, Midgley, and de Michele (1986) found that children of average intelligence earned lower grade point averages and class standings than those in two-parent households.

Since a large number of minor children live in single-parent households, Barney and Koford (1987) suggested that schools examine how they are meeting these families' needs. They asked questions designed to stimulate thinking about interactions and activities that could make members of single-parent families feel uncomfortable, including concerns about addresses of communications, timing of parent conferences, child care, teaching activities to support children in single-parent homes, and referral resources.

Richards and Schmiege (1993) were concerned that most of the literature on single-parent homes focuses on the negative effects for children experiencing divorce and not living in the ideal two-parent household. They studied 60 single-parent mothers and 11 single-parent fathers to learn more about the problems faced in the homes and the strengths identified by the parents. The single-parent mothers most often said that money was their biggest problem area, with role and task overload following. Social life and problems with their ex-spouses were rated third and fourth. Single-parent fathers rated role and task overload and problems with ex-spouses as first and second on their list of problems, with financial problems ranking last. Both single-parent mothers and single-parent fathers rated their parenting skills as their main strength. Family management (being organized, dependable, and able to coordinate schedules) was second for both groups, and good communication and personal growth were also rated as strengths by both groups. The authors suggested that, given the likelihood of young women and men living in a single-parent household, a stronger emphasis on family education is necessary. They encouraged their readers not to accept negative stereotypes and to acknowledge that single-parent homes do have strengths.

Downey (1994) compared the school performance of children from single-mother and single-father families with the performance of children living with both parents. The single fathers were better educated than single mothers in the sample, but the children of single fathers did not earn higher grades. Neither group performed in school as well as the children from two-parent families. Economic problems may be affecting the children in single-parent homes, especially single-mother households. The researchers suggested that single fathers spend less time talking to the children, and less parental involvement in the children's school and play activities may be a significant factor.

Counseling strategies to help children in single-parent homes are similar to many described for children of divorce. The counselor must deal with the child's feelings of loss, whether the loss resulted from divorce, separation, or death. Emotions must be recognized and discussed. These children need stability, security, and consistency in their lives. Therefore, counselors may want to recommend to the child's parent and other family members that they join a support group to help the family reorganize effectively after the loss. Counselors in schools can provide group activities for children of single-parent homes to help them discuss their fears, concerns, and feelings about having only one parent in the home. Crosbie-Burnett and Pulvino (1990) described a classroom guidance program for children in nontraditional families that focused on eight aspects of nontraditional families and includes topics such as having less money, feelings of anger or sadness, questions friends ask, and time alone.

As stated previously in this section, considerable research substantiates that children from single-parent homes have a higher rate of conduct disorders and other adjustment problems than children from intact homes. However, well-adjusted children live in single-parent homes. Counselors must be careful not to allow generalizations or personal bias to interfere with their objectivity in working with these children.

COUNSELING WITH CHILDREN ABOUT DEATH AND DYING

Death has been a taboo subject for discussion in our society. Asked about death or dying, most adults try to avoid the subject or excuse themselves by expressing their inadequacy to discuss such a subject with young people. Discussions about death seem to be accompanied by a great deal of adult discomfort, anxiety, vagueness, and avoidance behavior. Because of these reactions, children may become confused about the facts and emotions that accompany death and show their own grief inappropriately (Frears & Schneider, 1981). In fact, Cunningham and Hare (1989) suggested that teachers and other adults may unwittingly interfere with the grieving process by refusing to answer questions, using diverting techniques, or making negative nonverbal responses to the child's attempts to talk about death and dying.

Only recently have we begun to realize that talking about death may help us accept it as a part of life and cope with the feelings that accompany death. Every child is affected by the death of pets or grandparents, if not by loss of parents, friends, or siblings. Counselors need to be prepared to help children accept the reality of death as a part of life. To work effectively with children on the issue of death, counselors must first examine their own attitudes toward death. A counselor in conflict cannot provide the support and understanding the child needs.

Children have trouble understanding death for many reasons. As Piaget pointed out, children are limited in understanding by the stage of their cognitive development. Young children are unable to understand the finality and irreversibility of death; they feel they are immortal. They may be concerned about their own basic needs ("Who will care for me?"), or they may wonder about the needs of the deceased (Bertoia & Allan, 1988). As children grow, they begin to question death and its causes. They may recognize it as inevitable and final, but comprehending the process is still difficult for children. Children often believe that only old people die. Matter and Matter (1982) wrote an informative article, based on Piaget's work, that describes children's understanding of death at different cognitive levels of development: The preoperational child holds an egocentric view of death and uses fantasy and magical thinking to explain the occurrence. The concrete-operational child may be more specific in understanding death. According to the authors, these children note specific ways of inflicting death by act or weapon and show some interest in the details of death. Bertoia and Allan (1988) recommend that explanations be clear and specific and at a level understandable to a child in the concrete-operations stage. They suggest that explanations should be made only after listening carefully to the child for his or her thoughts. The child in the formal-thought stage "is capable of conceptualizing death in an abstract manner, and using logic in reasoning about its causes" (p. 113). At this stage the child understands that everyone dies and that death is not reversible.

Many factors in the child's environment may encourage faulty concepts concerning death. The mass media often portray death violently. Adults in the child's life may react negatively to death. Often they attempt to protect the child from death by refusing to discuss the subject and by hiding their own feelings. Understanding adult reactions may be difficult for children. They may think they caused or contributed to the death in some way or decide that death is a punishment for something bad they have done. Unfounded fears and anxieties arise out of these misunderstandings. Euphemistic explanations often cause misconceptions in children. If told that the person is "only asleep" or that "God has called her," children can learn to fear sleep or fear that God will call them away from their world.

For the most part, children have difficulty learning effective ways of handling death. Adults may not provide the answers needed or demonstrate appropriate behaviors. Unresolved grief can result in personal, interpersonal, or social problems in the future.

Segal (1984) described children's responses to loss and death in an excellent article on expressing grief through symbolic communication. He stated that, following the trauma, children may respond with denial, assume responsibility for the loss and feel guilty, internalize or act out their anger over the loss, withdraw, repress their feelings, become obsessed with fear about future losses, seek spiritual comfort ("Mom is in heaven"), feel confused about the facts, become dependent, or develop a closer relationship with a friend or sibling to gain emotional support. Segal noted that feelings are communicated nonverbally and suggested that counselors especially need to be aware of some primary modes of nonverbal communication that may indicate problems:

1. *Kinesics:* communication through body movement. The grieving or depressed child may be lethargic, rigid, or listless or may exhibit restricted movement.

2. *Oculesics:* communication through eye movements. The confused or anxious child may show involuntary eye movements, eye twitching, a blank gaze, or inability to maintain eye contact.

3. *Vocalics:* communication by tone, pitch, and rate of articulation. A grieving child may block words, stutter, or talk in low, soft tones or in a flat, colorless manner.

4. *Haptics:* communication through touch. Grieving children may withdraw from touching or kissing and distance themselves from close human relationships.

5. *Chronemics:* communication through use of time. Resistive children may come late for counseling or other appointments to distance themselves from human contact; alternatively, an anxious, insecure child may be upset at the possibility of being late for any appointment, fearing punishment or rejection.

Segal said that counselors can understand their clients more fully by attending to nonverbal communication but cautions that cultural lifestyles and family styles may also prompt these behaviors. Counselors must use care in interpreting nonverbal communication.

Segal (1984) recommended games and communication exercises to help children express feelings related to losses. He suggested passing out small blank cards and pencils to children in a group, asking them to write down a question about death or dying, and assuring them that the writer's name will not be revealed. The group leader reads the questions, and the children discuss their thoughts about the questions. Alternatively, the group leader may prefer to write the questions on cards ahead of time and ask each child to draw a card, read the question, and answer it with his or her views. Art techniques, including crayon drawings, clay, or hand puppets, may help children portray their conflicts. Children can be asked to sculpt or carve a figure representing someone for whom they have a great deal of love; usually the figure is the person they lost. These drawings, carvings, or hand puppets can express the pain of the loss more easily than the child can verbalize it. Segal described a technique for illustrating feelings with paper and music. The children draw "peaceful" views of death on one side of the paper while listening to soft music; they then draw "harsh" views of death on the other side of the sheet while listening to dissonant music. Phototherapy—having the child respond to different photographs of men, women, or children—may stimulate discussion concerning losses of loved ones. Use of all nonverbal means of communication should be followed with a discussion of their meaning and of coping strategies for the various problems revealed.

From her work with terminally ill patients, Kübler-Ross (1969) defined the stages that most patients and their families go through in facing death. The first reaction is denial: "This is not happening to me." Second, the patient and family experience anger over the situation: "Why did this have to happen to me and not to somebody else?" Third comes a stage of bargaining. People may try to make a bargain with God to be a better person if God will let them or their loved one live. When the inevitability of death must be faced and the pressures become a harsh reality, depression is common. Working these feelings through successfully enables a quiet acceptance of death.

Swander (1987) suggested there are only three stages of grief:

1. *Shock:* This stage is evident by the child's mechanical behavior and such emotional reactions as disbelief, denial, numbness, and concern for self.
2. *Suffering:* The child shows despair, depression, sadness, hurt, anger, and anxiety and may experience loss of concentration or memory, feelings of worthlessness, suicidal thoughts, fatigue, and a variety of psychosomatic symptoms.
3. *Recovery:* The child begins to look ahead and become involved with life once again but may regress into a previous stage during holidays, anniversaries, or other special reminders of the dead loved one.

Swander stated that the grieving child may move back and forth through the stages, and the duration of any stage depends on the individual and his or her relationship to the deceased.

Bertoia and Allan (1988) suggested that counselors consider four areas when they work with children coping with death or dying issues. Counselors can encourage communication with open-ended statements that reflect care, understanding, and a willingness to listen. Counselors, teachers, and others should model accepting behavior by not treating the child in a different way and by providing support. Normal routines should continue to provide structure and security, but they should be flexible enough to provide time for emotions and changes in behavior.

In summary, counseling strategies for helping children who have experienced loss through death include the following:

1. Listen carefully to children's thoughts, feelings, and concerns, and respond clearly and objectively with statements at their level of understanding. Clarify children's questions or statements that may have a double meaning or suggest a hidden concern.

2. Allow children to express their grief, talk freely, and ask questions. Play therapy, the use of puppets, role-playing, creative artwork, bibliocounseling, a visit to a nursing home, videos on dealing with loss, family drawing, relaxation and imagery, letter writing to say goodbye, the open-chair technique, and individual or group discussions may be helpful counseling techniques for working with these children. Counselors can also recommend books, pamphlets, or other resources to adults who provide support for these children. Children experiencing a loss through death may feel abandoned or insecure and need extra amounts of time, energy, and reassurance.

3. Help the child learn more about death and dying by talking about the death of an animal or a plant (Costa & Holliday, 1994).

4. Children sometimes have trouble understanding concepts such as heaven and eternity. They may be confused about why "God takes away loved ones."

Counselors may want to consult with the family's clergy for assistance in dealing with this sensitive topic.

5. Counselors are often asked if children should attend the funeral of someone who has died. The answer depends on the child's age, the kinship of the deceased, and the child's reaction to the death. Children need to learn that death is part of the natural order of life. They need the opportunity to say goodbye to a close loved one. However, consider as well the child's reaction to death and his or her concern about attending the funeral.

6. Work to reduce the stress in the child's life. Try to maintain as much familiar structure as possible. Be aware that the child may regress to behaviors of an earlier developmental stage or manifest physical symptoms of distress (Costa & Holliday, 1994).

7. Watch for triggers of grief—birthdays, holidays, the anniversary of the death (Costa & Holliday, 1994).

Little in the literature describes effective methods for counseling with children and their reactions to death and dying, especially empirical studies. Perhaps researchers avoid the subject as do parents and other adults. The severity of pain associated with the death and dying of a loved one indicates a need for study of both the short-term and long-term effects of the trauma.

COUNSELING WITH CHILDREN FROM DIFFERENT CULTURES

The child who enters the counselor's office may be African American, white, Native American, Asian American, Hispanic American, or from a number of other cultures or subcultures. The counselor is most often white and middle class. How can these two people eliminate cultural barriers and form the facilitative relationship necessary for effective counseling?

For counseling to be effective, most researchers agree, the essential ingredients of understanding and respect must be present. Counselors attempt to understand the child's world as the child perceives it, and they have faith in the child's ability to grow and fulfill his or her potential, given the proper support and guidance. In theory, counselors respect each person's uniqueness and potential. In practice, however, barriers may consciously or unconsciously interfere with this facilitative counseling relationship. Ivey (1987) cautioned counselors not to forget that they are working with a unique person in the counseling interview and suggested that counselors must be aware of cultural and group differences. Without this awareness of cultural variations, the counselor may risk offending clients because the meaning of certain behaviors such as eye contact and other attending behaviors differs among cultures. Ivey concluded that a counselor cannot really understand the individual without some degree of cultural awareness.

Lloyd (1987) was concerned that multicultural movements that emphasize differences among groups may encourage counselors to hold on to preconceived beliefs and prevent them from treating the individual as a unique person. He pointed out that differences among people within a cultural group may be greater than differences among groups. Lloyd agreed, however, that some information about different cultures is helpful in "minimizing social blunders concerning mores, religious ceremonies, and social graces" (p. 165). Hood and Arceneaux (1987) reminded readers that no one person is a sole representative of his or her cultural group. Lee and Richardson (1991) also cautioned against assuming that all people of one group are the same and that one counseling approach is appropriate for all.

Lee and Richardson (1991) defined *multicultural counseling* as "a helping process that places the emphases for counseling theory and practice equally on the cultural impressions of both the counselor and the client" (p. 3); counselors must consider differences in language, social class, and culture to be effective. They described the culturally skilled counselor as one who "uses strategies and techniques that are consistent with the life experiences and cultural values of clients" (p. 5), as well as one who is knowledgeable of the issues of cultural diversity. According to Lee and Richardson, general themes counselors should consider when working with any client of a different culture include the level of ethnic identity and acculturation, family influences, sex-role socialization, religious and spiritual influences, and the immigration experience.

Sue (1977) stated that cultural, class, and language factors discriminate against the culturally different and suggests that a "culturally competent counselor" is one who is knowledgeable of cultural and class factors and is able to use differential counseling approaches that are consistent with the client's lifestyle. Sue also advocated examining counseling process and the goals counselors hold for their clients to determine their appropriateness for the client and his or her culture.

Pederson (1994) suggested goals for the multiculturally skilled counselor:

Is aware of the other cultures

Is willing to receive information about other value systems and voluntarily selects articles and books about a different culture

Responds to instructional materials about a different culture by asking questions and offering comments

Obtains satisfaction from responding to information about another culture

Accepts the idea that knowing and understanding people of other cultures is good

Prefers the previous idea to any competing dogma, rejecting cultural isolationism

Is committed to the value of international understanding and cooperation

Conceptualizes this value into the total value system by weighing alternative international policies and practices against the standard of international understanding rather than against narrow special interest. (p. 209)

Skills and information Pederson suggests for counselors also include:

Knows much of the history, customs, language, and geography of one or more cultures other than his or her own

Knows contributions of various cultures of the world

Knows where and how to find additional information about other cultures

Demonstrates constructive ability to solve problems involving international understanding

Sees the implications in data regarding social and economic circumstances

Understands that people are more alike than different

Applies general ideas regarding culture to a popular cultural context

Analyzes a culture into component parts

Forms generalizations from cultural data and observes exceptions

Observes differences in wealth, values, and behavior between cultures and understands the reasons for the differences

Sees the necessity of world trade and the value of world travel

Understands the causes for changes in alliances among nations

Sees the implications of shortened travel and communication time between countries

Understands the nature of international interdependence

Evaluates ideas based on how they affect world harmony. (pp. 209–210)

Sue (1978, p. 451) listed the characteristics of a culturally effective counselor as follows:

1. Understanding his or her own values and philosophy concerning the nature of people and their behavior, realizing that others may differ
2. Recognizing that "no theory of counseling is politically or morally neutral"
3. Understanding that sociological and political forces external to the person have shaped culturally different persons
4. Being able to view the world as the client does, avoiding being "culturally encapsulated"
5. Being truly eclectic, drawing on techniques and methods of counseling appropriate to the culture and lifestyle of the client

Sue and Sue (1977) suggested that three cultural barriers may hinder cross-cultural counseling: language barriers, class-bound values, and culture-bound values.

1. *Language barriers.* Much traditional counseling emphasizes rapport through verbal and nonverbal communication. Children from other cultures or subcultures may be disadvantaged in their ability to communicate their thoughts or feelings accurately. Counselors often are not familiar with the informal language or slang of other cultures. The meaning of body language, such as eye contact or personal space, varies from culture to culture. These factors may make

communication between counselor and child extremely difficult and lead to misconceptions and misunderstanding.

2. *Class-bound values.* Class-bound values may hinder counseling because of conflicting attitudes and different expectations from counseling. Some of the areas of concern investigated by Wrenn (1976)—attitudes toward women, sexuality, work, and education—may be aspects of this barrier.

3. *Cultural-bound values.* Cultures hold different attitudes, values, beliefs, mores, and customs. Counselors may consciously or unconsciously communicate that the client's ways are inferior or a handicap to be overcome.

Smith (1982) stated that counseling interventions should not be selected on the basis of the client's race, but rather on the basis of other factors, such as the client's degree of acculturation, sex, socioeconomic status, and value system. In working with children, developmental and cognitive levels must be considered also.

Ponterotto and Benesch (1988) criticized multicultural counseling as fragmented and providing conceptually inadequate models for training counselors. They suggest a framework based on the work of Torrey:

1. Identify the problem; problems vary in different cultures.
2. Portray the personal qualities necessary for effective counseling; some counselors believe Rogers's core relationship conditions are universal.
3. Meet client expectations; listening, directing, giving advice, and so on also vary with the culture.
4. Seek ways to improve counselor credibility; perceptions of credible characteristics vary with culture.
5. Use appropriate counseling interventions; the effectiveness of active or passive interventions varies with culture.

According to Ponterotto and Benesch, this model provides effective guidelines for counseling white or culturally diverse clients; although these principles may apply to all races and cultures, "culture-specific knowledge is needed to accurately conceptualize and understand the client's 'place' in each stage" (p. 239).

Gibbs and Huang (1989) cautioned that ethnicity issues influence the development of minority children by shaping their belief systems about mental illness or health, the manner in which they manifest and cope with symptoms, the method they use to seek help, and the way they respond to treatment. Although minority children are vulnerable because of factors such as poverty and prejudice, they may also have available to them protective factors such as extended families, social or religious networks, or traditional sources of help within their own culture.

African American Children

Sue and Sue (1990) pointed out that many people of color are reluctant to seek counseling because they see it as a sociopolitical force. African American families are often required to go for counseling as a consequence of encounters with the law or their interactions with other community agencies. Counseling may be perceived as a punishment rather than as a helpful process. According to Allen and Majidi-Ahi (1989), the traditional clinical or medical model, which focuses on a person's weaknesses or deficits, is not appropriate for working with African American children because many of them adjust well despite poverty, prejudice, and other barriers to their development. Allen and Majidi-Ahi prefer a social-ecological approach with an emphasis on understanding how economic status, education, health care, housing, racism, and other ecological factors affect the child.

Some authors have indicated that African American children may have differences in the perception of time, differences in communication styles, and may terminate counseling earlier than other clients due to the problems of miscommunication and misunderstanding. Having been stigmatized in the past, African American children may not want to volunteer for counseling because of the possibility of another stigma.

As with all cultures, counselors need to be aware that stereotypes may interfere with their perspective of other-culture clients and strive to avoid being influenced or biased by overly generalized descriptions of individuals and groups. Children who have been reared in American cultures probably have more in common with one another than they do with other hyphenated cultures; however, counselors should not overlook possible differences between subcultures.

Richardson (1991) contended that counseling professionals must recognize nontraditional means for providing services to their clients and suggested that African American churches can be effective tools for enhancing self-esteem, self-respect, and community. Richardson provided guidelines for counselors as they attempt to develop relationships with the African American churches for the benefit of clients.

Native American Children

According to Lazarus (1982), the U.S. Office of Education estimates a total of approximately 326,000 Native American school-age children in the United States. Although these children compose a small proportion of the total population, their problems are significant. He suggested that counselors working with Native American children be aware of their particular values in order to prepare them for the difficulties of growing up in the present-day world. Each Native American tribe is different, but Lazarus (1982, p. 84) listed general guidelines for understanding values:

1. Children are respected to the same degree as adults.
2. Cooperation and harmony are valued.
3. Generosity and sharing are important, and individuals are judged on their contributions.
4. Competition is encouraged so long as it hurts no one.
5. The Native American lives in the present, with little concern for planning for tomorrow.

6. The school culture for children is strange; some behaviors are considered ill-mannered (loud talking and reprimands).
7. Older people are respected for their wisdom and knowledge.
8. Ancient legends and cultural traditions are important.
9. Peace and politeness are essential; confrontation is rude.

Lazarus suggested that counselors will have little success with "talking therapy" and that play and art may be more effective. Tribal-made materials can be incorporated into the play techniques. Rather than confrontation, Lazarus advocated communication and social control through gossip and chitchat to promote change. Counselors are cautioned to be silent and allow time for children to speak, because Native American children feel no need to fill time with idle words. Disapproval and reluctance to talk are also indicated by silence. Teachers and counselors are encouraged to avoid individual correction or praise but to recognize group efforts. The behavioral techniques of ignoring undesirable behavior and reinforcing good behavior (of the group) are effective. Because the aged are highly respected, counselors may want to consider involving them in classrooms, in the counseling process, or in working with institutionalized children.

LaFromboise and Low (1989) cautioned that Native American children may believe that going to a counselor is a sign of weakness or an avoidance of cultural values such as social responsibility, honesty, independence, kindness, and self-control. Native American cultural values may differ from traditional white values. Some tribes do not value competitiveness and individualism. LaFromboise and Low pointed out that tribal differences make generalizations difficult about counseling with Native Americans. Some researchers indicate, however, that Native American youths prefer someone who understands their culture and can help them with their lives. The writers reported that social-cognitive procedures may be effective because they tend to be less culture bound.

Herring (1991) reminded readers that the history of Native Americans is characterized by military defeat, ethnic demoralization, and forced displacement—forces that negatively influence Native American youth. The Native American family is often faced with overwhelming poverty and unemployment, family dissolution due in part to federal government policies, and educational failure. Herring cautioned that young clients evaluate the counselor from the first moment—his or her manner of greeting, appearance, communication style, and knowledge of the Native American culture. He also suggested that community and tribal leaders can be a valuable source of help in counseling Native American youth, as can bias-free media resources that show realistic, accurate portrayals of Native American culture.

Asian American Children

Asian Americans may have roots in China, Japan, Korea, Vietnam, Cambodia, or elsewhere. Although they come from different countries, Lee and Richardson

(1991) believed all Asian American groups are influenced by old religious traditions that are passed down through the generations, including issues related to moderation of behavior, self-discipline, patience, humility, honor, and respect.

Stereotypes of Asian American culture would have us believe that all adults are hardworking and successful and all children are high achieving (Sue & Sue, 1990); however, some Asian American families live in poverty and feel the stresses of discrimination (Huang & Ying, 1989). To visit a counselor for help with problems may be viewed as shameful and embarrassing and produce a sense of failure; therefore, the number of clients in treatment is low, and research on effective therapeutic interventions is limited.

Counselor credibility can be an issue with Chinese American children because it is often based not only on therapeutic skills but also on cultural roles related to age and gender. Counselors must communicate thoroughly with Chinese American families about what is going on in counseling in order to enlist their support (Huang & Ying, 1989). Sue and Sue (1990) advised counselors that "issues such as independence, the necessity of eliciting emotional reactions, and the equality of family members must be seen from a cultural perspective and not as a given" (p. 89).

Much of the Japanese culture evolved from the philosophies of Confucianism and Buddhism. These teachings continue to influence the lives of Japanese Americans and are factors that must be recognized in counseling (Tomine, 1991):

- The family is more important than the individual.
- The family roles and rules for behavior are formalized, and adherence to these roles and rules is expected in order to avoid shame and loss of face.
- The father is the leader and authority; the mother is the nurturing parent.
- Communication is usually indirect, and confrontation is avoided.
- Problems are kept within the family, and all problems are solved within the family unit.

In addition to possible enculturation concerns and problems of coping with prejudices, Japanese American children may be dealing with lingering anger over World War II internment issues in the family. They may also feel the impact of other political and economic decisions that affect American-Japanese relationships (Nagata, 1989).

Tomine (1991) cautioned counselors to attend carefully to the personal, cultural, and defensive factors that influence the coping mechanisms of Japanese Americans. The counselor needs a wide range of skills to adapt to the client's needs. Deal carefully with expression of feelings by encouraging children to express only a little more than they are comfortable with. Because of the strong family orientation, family members may serve as a nontraditional means of providing counseling, but the family may also hinder the process by preferring to solve problems within the nuclear structure.

Lee and Cynn (1991) contended that Korean Americans have cultural values similar to those of Chinese Americans and Japanese Americans. The primary adjustment problems of children from this group may be due to the rate of acculturation. Young persons adopt American values and behaviors more quickly than parents who have only recently immigrated. Lee and Cynn called on counselors to recognize this problem and the expectations both the old and new cultures place on children. Calling adjustment problems a normal part of the acculturation process can save face for the family and enable them continue counseling with a positive attitude. Counseling strategies must be consistent in degree of acculturation and stage of ethnic-identity development.

Mexican American Children

According to Baron (1991), labels have psychological meaning for groups. He used the terms *Chicano* and *Mexican American* interchangeably in his writings. Arredondo (1991) suggested that both scientific and political concerns exist about generic categories such as *Hispanic* or *Latino* and pointed out that *Hispanic* is a governmental designation. Because this section focuses on those people having ethnic origins in Mexico, the term *Mexican American* is used here.

According to Ramirez (1989), the Mexican population in the United States numbers about 12 million. Their reported income levels are significantly below those of non-Hispanic groups. These families usually have more children and less formal education than do other groups. A large number of Mexican Americans live in large cities, primarily in California, Texas, New Mexico, Arizona, Colorado, and Illinois.

Baruth and Manning (1992) pointed out that Hispanic American children tend to be less competitive to avoid standing out in their group; usually adhere to different male and female gender roles; attributes such as warmth, dignity, masculine pride, and respect for authority are important in their lives; and that these children tend to stand close to others, touch, and avoid eye contact. Counselors must also understand family behaviors of Hispanic American homes that include a strong family commitment, parental styles that emphasize obedience, and the assumption of important family responsibilities early in the child's life. Because of the Hispanic American emphasis on the family, family counseling can be an effective tool.

Because Mexican Americans are reluctant to seek mental health treatment, little information is available about the most prevalent types of problems and most effective treatment modes. However, cultural issues about which counselors need to know include the following (Ramirez, 1989):

- Mexican Americans prefer close physical contact.
- Mexican Americans tend to self-disclose very slowly and may need encouragement through storytelling, anecdotes, humor, and proverbs.
- The client needs evidence of the counselor's personal warmth and acceptance of the client's ideas and behaviors, especially in the initial phase of counseling. Ramirez recommended that counselors praise strengths and family dignity and avoid interpretations and confrontations during this stage. The treatment plan should be carefully explained and possibly involve

the family as a support system. Counselors need to be aware that the child and family may not agree with objectives or procedures but accept some aspects of the treatment plan to be polite.

Biracial Children

According to Sebring (1985),

> The stresses on an interracial marriage can be severe, and the parents' abilities to cope with these pressures can and usually do affect the lives of their children. In addition, each parent brings a racial "set" into the marriage, and there are implications here for further discord. (p. 4)

Her conclusions are relevant for counselors working with interracial children. She asserted that early formation of healthy self-esteem provides a good foundation for coping with the issues to be faced later in life. She cautioned that masculine and feminine stereotypes may become confused with racial stereotypes (such as "African American is nurturing") and suggested that role models from both races are essential. According to Sebring, the child's lack of identification with both races can lead to guilt about rejecting one parent and his or her heritage; in fact, "ambivalence over ethnic identity seems to be the most significant problem faced by interracial children" (p. 7). Suggestions for counseling children of interracial marriages include seeing the family in its culture, capitalizing on family strengths, becoming aware of the ethnic factors operating in the marriage, clarifying ambiguities, finding techniques for managing anger, and facilitating the parenting experience.

Hill and Peitzer (1982) worked with biracial families in groups to help parents raise their children with strong, positive African American identities and self-concepts. They encouraged the biracial parents of African American children to examine their own self-esteem and self-concept, to identify their own racism and that of others, and to recognize how racism influenced their lives.

In addition to having unusual characteristics and the potential for problems because of their dual ancestry, Gibbs (1989) noted that biracial children may have identity problems related to their ambiguous ethnicity. They may encounter problems with family approval, acceptance in the community, discrimination, and isolation. Gibbs enumerated their conflicts:

1. *Racial-ethnic identity:* "Who am I?"
2. *Social marginality:* "Where do I fit?"
3. *Sexuality:* "What is my sexual role?" (with regard to orientation, gender identity, and sexual activity)
4. *Autonomy:* Parents may have attempted to protect or isolate children from reality.
5. *Educational and occupational aspirations:* "Where am I going?" and whether children's expectations are realistic in the light of prejudices and discrimination

Gibbs encouraged counselors to assist children in exploring their ancestry and recognizing the impact of their heritage on themselves.

Herring (1992) also stated that biracial children may have issues in the development of self-identity. First, they must integrate two racial and cultural backgrounds while developing their own self-identity. In addition, during adolescence they must deal with the task of developing peer relations and deciding their sex roles and sex preferences. Difficulties with racial identity may lead the child to experience conflicts over separation from parents and to have concerns about career choices.

Herring advised counselors to (1) develop a positive, trusting relationship with the child; (2) understand that the child's presenting problem may cover a deeper ethnic identity concern; (3) be aware that biracial children usually identify with the minority culture, believing that the white culture is not willing to accept them; (4) become familiar with the customs of all their students in order to serve them better; (5) permit the children to ventilate their feelings about their identity and its meaning in society; (6) assist in building the children's self-esteem through supportive technique; (7) see the link between their confusion over ethnic and cultural background and other developmental concerns; and (8) involve the entire family to promote individual and family growth.

Summary

This section has discussed the characteristics and needs of some of the many cultures that professionals may encounter when they work with children. Research on the counseling needs of culturally different clients is limited. Counselor-education training programs have only begun to prepare more culturally aware professionals. Materials and resources are limited, although books, media, and special programs are beginning to appear. Myer, James, and Street (1987) published a series of lesson plans to ease the adaptation of internationally adopted children to the classroom culture. Lee and Richardson (1991) mentioned resources in their discussion of many cultures. The literature describes successful peer counseling programs. The number of minority group members living in the United States will continue to grow in the 21st century. Counselors must be prepared to bridge cultural gaps and adopt techniques and procedures to meet the needs of many different children and families.

CHILDREN IN ALCOHOLIC FAMILIES

Children living in alcoholic families receive little attention in our society. Brake (1988) noted attention paid to the fetal alcohol syndrome, adolescent alcoholics, adult children of alcoholics, and codependence, but "there continues to be a dearth of material on one of alcoholism's tragic victims, children of alcoholic parents" (p. 106). The children of alcoholics are often left out of an alcoholic parent's treatment, and agencies treating children for other problems often do not recognize alcoholism in the family (Lawson, Peterson, & Lawson, 1983). Buwick, Martin, and Martin (1988) reported that 6.5 million children under 10 live in homes with alcoholic parents. From her research review, Brake (1988) estimated that one in five children lives in an alcoholic family; thus, the lives of approximately 8 million children revolve around alcohol. Wilson and Blocher (1990) cautioned that sons of alcoholics are five times more likely to become alcoholics than others and that daughters of alcoholic mothers are three times more likely to become alcoholics than girls living in a nonalcoholic environment.

The children of alcoholic parents frequently do not have their physical or psychological needs met in the family. Money needed for food and shelter may be spent on alcohol; even if there is money, the parents may be too preoccupied with alcohol to attend to the child's physical needs. Parents who have lost control of their lives and frequently dislike themselves cannot meet the child's need for love, belonging, and security. Children who live in homes whose rules are consistently broken and whose family members cannot be relied on to provide love and nurturance cannot be expected to grow and develop into fully functioning, well-adjusted individuals.

Clinicians have identified several general characteristics to assist counselors and other helping professionals to recognize children of alcoholic families. Weddle and Wishon (1986) divided symptoms into three categories: general, physical, and emotional. These characteristics occur singularly or in combination, and children with other problems may exhibit similar symptoms; however, their presence should alert counselors to the possibility of an alcohol-related problem. Because of parental inconsistency in the home, the child may adopt certain roles such as hero, scapegoat, lost child, or mascot. Additionally, children in alcoholic families may become isolated, fearful, approval-seeking, overly responsible, overly nurturant, passive, and extremely self-critical; they may hide their feelings, fear abandonment, and show physical or nutritional neglect. All writers reviewed pointed to the extremely harmful effects of inconsistent parental attitudes, behaviors, and discipline techniques and to the lack of attention and nurturance for the children.

Newlon and Furrow (1986) added that lack of attention, trouble with concentration, growing up too soon, "walking on pins and needles," "keeping it all inside," embarrassment, shame, and guilt are conditions of children living in alcoholic families. They quote Cork's (1969) study of 113 children that indicated familial and peer relationships suffered; school achievement decreased; the children were anxious, easily upset, and lacked self-confidence; and many experienced physical problems from the stress.

Buwick, Martin, and Martin (1988) described the children in alcoholic families as angry and hostile toward their parents; as usually having lowered self-esteem, an external locus of control, and learning disabilities; and as believing they do not receive adequate affection. Buwick et al. stated that as these children grow older, they may exhibit antisocial behaviors, alcohol abuse, delinquency, or suicidal tendencies. These symptoms apparently result from the conflict and stress present in the home of alcoholics. Brake (1988), in a review of the literature, found that conflict and stress in the home affect these children less than how they perceive what is happening. They may feel guilty, believing they have done something to contribute to the alcoholism. However, Wilson and Blocher (1990) described children in alcoholic homes as under considerable stress due to family quarreling, abuse or neglect, inconsistent discipline, inadequate or unpredictable environments, disruption of family holidays or rituals, early assumption of adult roles, a denial of reality that makes understanding the real world difficult, isolation, shame, and embarrassment.

Growing up in an alcoholic family has different effects on children, according to Jones and Houts (1992). They classified families of the subjects participating in their research as "regular problem drinking," "occasional problem drinking," "minor problem drinking," or "nonproblem drinking." Young adults who grew up in homes where drinking was a regular problem felt less positive regard and less attention to their feelings from their parents. The researchers did not find significant differences among the problem-drinking groups for the parents' level of criticism of the child or emotional support. They conclude:

> Overall, the findings support our contention that in order to understand the impact of growing up in an alcoholic family, it is important to describe specific characteristics of the family and conceptualize these characteristics as interacting with problem drinking to create a family environment that influences developmental processes. At the same time, the results suggest that it is inappropriate to assume that growing up in an alcoholic family has comprehensive and maladaptive outcomes for young adult children. (p. 55)

Seilhamer, Jacob, and Dunn (1993) also pointed out that many factors can determine the effects of parental drinking on children, "including the presence and severity of other parental psychopathology, the ability of the nondrinking parent to act as a buffering influence and the availability of extra-familial sources of support" (p. 197). Additionally, the father's ability to deliver consistent discipline, a predictable environment, emotional support, and social modeling may be more important than drinking-related variables.

Reich, Earls, Frankel, and Shayka (1993) reported that children of alcoholics may be more at risk for oppositional or conduct disorders. They call for early intervention in these children's lives.

Wegscheider (1981) described extensively the roles and responses of children in alcoholic families. The roles children adopt in alcoholic families direct behavior and family interactions and form foundations that influence adult functioning. According to Wegscheider, the role assumed is often related to ordinal position. For example, the eldest child may assume the role of hero—overly responsible, overly compliant and helpful, and a parent surrogate; such a child may suffer from pervasive feelings of guilt and inadequacy. The scapegoat behaves irresponsibly, drawing attention away from the alcoholic conflict; this child is the opposite of the hero and gets attention through acting-out behavior. The lost child or loner does not ask for attention or nurturance and appears independent and self-reliant;

however, this child is confused and fearful, and feels lonely and inadequate. Lost children make no demands on anyone and therefore receive very little love, attention, and support. The mascot draws attention away from the alcoholic conflict by providing comic relief. This child gets attention by entertaining everyone, a role that inhibits the development of mature behaviors.

Black (1981) developed a similar model of descriptive roles assumed by children in alcoholic families. Her model included the "responsible" role (similar to the hero), the "adjuster" (Wegscheider's lost child), and the "placater" (comparable to both the mascot and the scapegoat). Both writers pointed out that these roles may shift over time and that no one role may fit exactly the child's pattern of behavior.

Bepko (1985) said this evolution and shifting of roles is detrimental to the child's development because it prevents the child from developing a distinct identity, thus "perpetuating the legacy of addiction" (p. 202). Goals for treatment Bepko suggested include (1) educating the child about drinking and life in an alcoholic family; (2) providing a safe environment for the expression of feelings about the alcoholic situation; (3) determining the neglect or deprivation occurring in the family, including the possibility of abuse; (4) intervening to ameliorate any symptomatic problem behaviors in the child; (5) assessing family interactional patterns, parenting styles, and the role or roles the child assumes; and (6) assisting parents in developing appropriate parenting skills and providing proper nurturance.

Bepko cautioned that when and if the parent stops drinking, the problems for the child do not cease. Roles previously assumed now become inappropriate and ineffective. Treatment goals during this period should be (1) to provide an atmosphere in which children can express their feelings about the change in the family; (2) to help the child adjust to the change and find a new, more appropriate place in the family; and (3) to provide instruction and support to the parents to help them find new ways of responding to the children and repairing the damage of the alcohol abuse period. She cautioned that children's typical reactions include anger, jealousy, competitiveness, and a sense of betrayal or abandonment. The children are divested of their power and must learn new roles, often more subordinate ones. The initial period of sobriety can be as filled with turmoil as the alcoholic phase—until new and more appropriate roles and patterns of family interaction are established.

The effects of parental alcoholism do not end when the parent assumes sobriety or the child becomes an adult. Wegscheider's (1981) research suggested that twice as many children of alcoholics marry before they reach 16 years of age, juvenile delinquency is higher in alcoholic families, mental illness is twice as likely in children with alcoholic families, and the suicide rate is higher than that of disadvantaged children. According to Newlon and Furrow (1986), "children who come from alcoholic environments suffer from a high incidence of behavioral, emotional, and psychological problems, not to mention the high risk of becoming 'problem drinkers' themselves or choosing an alcoholic spouse" (p. 287). They noted that the logical place to provide early assistance and intervention for children from alcoholic homes is the school. They described identification procedures and step-by-step guidance lessons to help these children understand alcoholism as a family problem and the necessity for all members to seek help.

Brake (1988) stated that children of alcoholics need a counselor to help them understand they can love their parents without liking their behavior and that these children need help in feeling worthwhile as individuals. She suggested group counseling preceded by an individual session. Films and books may be needed to encourage talking because these children have learned to avoid conflict by not talking. Time and patience are required to build trust. Buwick et al. (1988) added to the preceding strategies modeling consistency to provide limits and added stability to the children's lives, responding to both positive and negative behaviors, and arranging conditions to involve children in success experiences. Wilson and Blocher (1990) suggested developmental support groups incorporating bibliotherapy, role-play of problem situations, REBT techniques for assessing behavior and coping more effectively, Gestalt activities to express feelings, assertiveness to express needs and rights, and relaxation techniques to reduce stress. O'Rourke (1990) provided an outline for a children's support group that includes attention to the preceding needs and provides information about alcoholism for young participants. These children also need activities to improve their self-esteem, assertiveness training to teach them to say no to drugs and alcohol, and help with developing problem-solving and decision-making skills. Excellent drug education programs are now available to counselors working with these children.

Lawson et al. (1983) wrote, "It is impossible to avoid the idea of prevention. Treating the behavioral or emotional problems of children who have lived with an alcoholic parent is surely a major step in preventing these high-risk children from becoming alcoholics themselves" (p. 185). They recommended that prevention procedures include either treatment centers to provide group support for the children or educational programming and support groups in the schools. They pointed out that parents have modeled drinking to get drunk or avoid reality—not responsible behaviors to teach children; therefore, parents need help in becoming more aware of the models they present to their children. Parents can be encouraged to educate their children about alcoholism and to develop effective communication skills in order to become more aware of their children's concerns about drinking. Parents need to develop new parenting strategies, assist their children in improving their self-esteem, and teach them to make good choices. Lawson et al.'s (1983) "prevention fraction" includes coping skills competence, self-esteem, and support networks.

In 1985, an Associated Press article cited a study by *Family Circle* and the Parent's Resource Institute for Drug Education to indicate that drug and alcohol abuse is spreading into grammar schools. According to this study, more than 500,000 children 10 to 13 years old admitted getting drunk once a week. Information published by Cumberland Heights Alcohol and Drug Treatment Center (n.d.) reported that more than 50% of seventh graders have tried alcohol and that 13 is the average age at which young people begin to drink. These children learned at least some of their behavior from parent models who were or are alcoholics. The problem must be addressed, and counselors are in an excellent position to help.

LATCHKEY CHILDREN

Children left at home unsupervised while parents work are called *latchkey children* because they carry a key to lock the house as they leave after their parents in the mornings and to unlock the house when they return before their parents in the afternoon. Some experts believe that 15% to 20% of young elementary school-children carry their own latchkey and that approximately 45% of late elementary schoolchildren are unsupervised for some period in the day (Peterson & Magrab, 1989). The developmental implications of children's self-care are uncertain because of the lack of research in this area.

The children's activities while on their own can be problematic because of the risk of injury, emotional reactions to being alone, and poor selection of activities (Peterson, 1989). Peterson concluded from her review of the literature that children are more likely to be injured when an adult is not present in the home, that although research is not clear on children's emotional reactions to staying alone, many experience negative feelings (anxiety, worry, fear), and that children spend their unsupervised hours watching too much television, not getting enough physical exercise, snacking inappropriately, and postponing homework and chores until later in the evening. She suggested as alternative programs for preparing children for self-care, "neighborhood mothers," activities in or near the school, and expanded child care in schools or businesses. In addition, Peterson provided a checklist for checking the home for security from strangers, from fire, from poisoning, and for safe use of equipment.

Unfortunately, most children do not know how to care for themselves adequately and need direct instruction to learn to handle situations effectively. Bundy and Boser (1987) have developed a group guidance unit to address self-care issues; focusing on how parents and children can develop a self-care plan, personal safety at home, handling emergency and nonemergency situations, and "being in charge," this unit resulted in positive effects for both parents and children.

Society has generally felt that being a latchkey child negatively affects the child's development. Peterson and Magrab (1989) pointed out that some indict "working mothers" for leaving their children but that communities must recognize the changing values and lifestyles of the present and find ways to support working families. Research by Lovko and Ullman (1989) comparing latchkey children to others indicated no differences in levels of anxiety, social ability, or behavior problems. Any variance in the two groups' adjustment levels was accounted for by the demographic and background variables of sex, income, and interaction with other children. The researchers were quick to point out their study's limitations and suggest that adjustment depends on many variables still not clearly defined.

Counseling with latchkey children may include listening for fears and anxieties about being left alone and helping the child cope with these feelings. The child may have concerns about what to say when the phone or doorbell rings, who will care for the child if he or she gets hurt or sick, or what to do about boredom or loneliness. O'Brien (1989) reported that many families make a large chart listing activities that should be carried out during unsupervised periods to overcome boredom or loneliness. Group discussions with role-play provide an opportunity for children to voice their concerns and to practice appropriate techniques for answering the door or phone, reacting to emergency and nonemergency situations, and coping with other problems that may arise.

HOMELESS CHILDREN

Many communities have concerns about the increasing number of homeless families. Eddowes and Hranitz (1989) reported Children's Defense Fund statistics indicating approximately 3 million homeless people in America, with more than a third of this number including families with children. Dail (1990) described these families, based on her review of the literature: Although most homeless people in the past were male, a growing number today are single-parent families headed by women. Approximately 50% of the women heading homeless families are between 17 and 25 years of age; the majority have never been married or are separated or divorced. Most have some high school education, and a few attended college. These mothers have few social or family support systems and tend to distrust people. About 50% of homeless children are under 5 years old. They are typically undernourished, and many show delayed development with symptoms of acting-out behavior and physical problems (Dail, 1990). They may have difficulty with language and attention to the task, physical coordination problems, and symptoms of anxiety. More than half of the children over 5 years old need mental health treatment. School performance is low because of poor attendance and confused lives. These children may be abused physically or psychologically because of their parents' stress (Dail, 1990).

Eddowes and Hranitz (1989) called denial of education the most critical problem of homeless children. These children are often prohibited from entering school because of requirements such as residency, proof of age, immunization, and school records. Eddowes and Hranitz pointed out that children who do enter school are often ridiculed by their peers and not accepted by their teachers; in addition, they receive little support from their parents.

Congress passed a law in 1987 requiring that homeless children be admitted to schools. Eddowes and Hranitz (1989) suggested that communities could also provide greater access to day care, counseling, and nutritional and educational support for homeless children.

Daniels (1992) stated that school can provide a "reprieve from the frightening realities of wandering the streets" (p. 104) as well as a sense of normalcy in a child's life. She suggested interventions based on Maslow's hierarchy of needs and the developmental guidelines of Erik Erikson (see chapter 1). Daniels developed a six-session group counseling unit to increase self-esteem and address developmental concerns; its activities include an assessment of self-esteem, drawing a family portrait of those with whom the children lives as well as where they live, drawings of feelings, sharing an accomplishment of which they are proud, identifying stress and worries in their lives, and, finally, drawing a group mural. These and other group activities can increase self-esteem and promote peer acceptance and appreciation.

Masten, Miliotis, Graham-Bermann, Ramirez, and Neemann (1993) compared 159 homeless children to 62 low-income children living in a home. As would be expected, the homeless children experienced more stress and disrupted schooling and friendships than did the low-income children in homes. The researchers concluded that homeless children's behavior problems are related more to parental distress and adversity than to housing condition or income.

Counseling tasks include facilitating the child's entrance into school, helping the child and his or her family find some kind of stability in their lives, assisting the child in overcoming excessive fears and distrust of people, and being alert to the possibility of abuse. Counselors need a variety of referral resources to help the child meet physical needs such as shelter, food, and medical care. Assessing the child's educational level and helping him or her develop social skills require time, energy, and patience.

The counselor must avoid being influenced by such generalizations about the homeless as that they are mentally ill, are unmotivated, could find a job if they wanted to, or abuse alcohol or drugs. Education is the best method for overcoming the problems of the homeless, but it requires a broad spectrum of services within the school and community. The counselor may be called on to coordinate these services and act as an advocate for the child.

SUICIDAL BEHAVIORS

The popular misconception is that children's lives are so carefree that they do not have suicidal thoughts and do not commit suicidal acts. Professionals working with children know otherwise. Herring (1990) stated that nearly 200 children younger than 14 years commit suicide each year. According to the National Center for Health Statistics (1993) 266 children between 5 and 14 years old committed suicide in the United States in 1991 (cited in Jacobsen, Rabinowitz, Popper, Solomon, Sokol, & Pfeffer, 1994, p. 439). Nelson and Crawford (1990) reported that suicide is the second most likely cause of death in 15- to 19-year-olds. In a survey Nelson and Crawford (1990) conducted, counselors in one state indicated they had made contact with 187 elementary-grade students considering suicide, 26 of whom had actually attempted the act. Most researchers question the statistics relative to the incidence of child suicide, pointing out that they are probably underestimates because of our society's reluctance to admit that our children commit suicide.

Herring (1990) suggested that child suicide attempts are often silent. Parents and physicians may conceal the suicide to avoid embarrassing the family. Many accidents are actually child suicides (Stefanowski-Harding, 1990). Children sometimes run in front of vehicles or jump off high places when they want to commit suicide (Herring, 1990). Stefanowski-Harding (1990) also reported an increasing number of children under 12 who are treated for accidental overdoses. She pointed out that children rarely leave suicide notes because they cannot write or are not in the habit of writing their communications.

Why a child attempts suicide is a complex question. Some researchers believe that suicidal children are highly sensitive, have a low tolerance for frustration, and have feelings of depression, guilt, hostility, and anger that they are unable to express (Stefanowski-Harding, 1990). Nelson and Crawford (1990) asked counselors to indicate factors they thought contributed to suicidal attempts and completions in the group they saw; they rated family problems such as divorce, separation, and parental alcoholism as highly probable contributors. Peer pressure and pressure to achieve academically were ranked second and third. Drug abuse, physical handicap, and economic stress were ranked very low. Stefanowski-Harding (1990), too, found several researchers who indicated that family problems related to death, divorce, separation, physical assault, rejection, or a suicidal parent were probably factors related to child suicide. Herring (1990) reported that children with a family history of suicide are 9 times more likely to take their own life than those who do not have this history. Boys are more likely to complete the suicidal act than girls because boys use more violent means in their attempts. Stefanowski-Harding (1990) cautioned that children with learning disabilities or other learning difficulties that cause constant frustration are more likely to attempt suicide and that gifted children may attempt suicide because their advanced intellectual ability makes relating to children their own age difficult.

Thoughts of suicide and attempts to commit it often accompany a poor self-concept and feelings of hopelessness, worthlessness, depression, or guilt. A depressed or suicidal child may be extremely quiet and withdrawn or highly active and agitated. Depression may be masked by overactivity, gaiety, or acting-out behavior. Feelings of depression leading to self-destructive attempts frequently follow the death of loved ones, significant personal or material losses, events that profoundly affect self-esteem, or other traumatic life crises. Clues may include chron ic sleeplessness, loss of appetite, withdrawal, or any extreme behavioral change.

Counselors' need to be skilled in recognizing the signs and symptoms of potential suicide cuts across all client populations and settings. Counselors also need to know how to work with their clients in developmental steps that lead to recovery. Wubbolding (1989) detailed four stages of decision making that clients need to complete to get rid of the desire to kill themselves. These stages follow the reality therapy treatment plan. In the first stage, the counselor asks several questions to determine the lethality of the decision: (1) "Are you thinking about killing yourself?" (2) "Have you previously tried to kill yourself?" (3) "Do you have a specific plan and the means available to kill yourself?" and (4) "Will you make a commitment not to kill yourself (for a specific amount of time)?" When the imminent danger has passed, the second stage can be devoted to exploring the behaviors that lead to thoughts of suicide; listening to certain kinds of music might be one example. The counselor might discuss behavior choices leading to better feelings and set short-term, attainable goals. As clients meet short-term goals, they begin to feel better and move into a third stage of more positive behaviors and feelings. Third-stage people may still entertain ideas about suicide. By monitoring their daily feelings and behaviors in a journal, however, clients become encouraged about their progress in setting and attaining larger goals. If all goes well, clients move into the fourth stage, characterized by a zest for living, no suicide ideation, and plans for attaining love, belonging, self-worth, freedom, and fun in their daily living. No comment or sign indicating depression and thoughts of self-destruction should go unnoticed.

Strategies for counselors working with suicidal children include:

1. If you feel a child could be seriously contemplating suicide, suggest to the parents that they consult a doctor or psychiatrist.

2. Never hesitate to consult with someone thoroughly trained in suicide prevention—suicide-prevention centers, clinics, or psychiatrists—or refer suicidal children to them.

3. Use techniques to enhance the self-concept of children who exhibit suicidal tendencies.

4. Children with self-destructive or self-mutilating tendencies, such as head banging, breath holding, and hair pulling, have responded to behavior modification techniques in which acceptable behaviors are rewarded and destructive tendencies punished by penalties such as withdrawing privileges or ignoring the behaviors. Children with severe tendencies usually require full-time supervision and psychotherapeutic intervention in a residential situation (Blanco, 1972).

5. Never ignore threats, hints, and continued comments about destroying oneself, "leaving this world," "you're going to miss me," or "life's not worth living." These comments may be attention-getting, but children who use these techniques to get attention need help. Follow up the threat immediately with active listening in an attempt to discover the feelings or events that brought on the self-destructive feelings.

6. At a time of crisis, listen to the child carefully in a nonjudgmental manner. Have the child tell you *everything* that has happened during the previous few hours or days. You may gain some understanding or knowledge of factors contributing to the depression.

7. Suicidal children need permission to call—and the phone number of—a person (the counselor or another close and understanding friend) they feel they can talk with in times of distress.

8. The parents of a suicidal child should be made aware of the child's feelings and thoughts and helped to understand the situation without panic or

guilt. Counsel with them about how to listen to and talk with the child. Consult with them concerning danger signals, and make a plan for handling crises, should they arise.

9. If you suspect a child has suicidal tendencies, confront the child with your thoughts and feelings. You are not placing the thought in the child's mind, but you may provide an opening and opportunity for the child to discuss the troublesome thoughts and feelings.

10. Talk with suicidal children about what has happened in their lives recently. Losses of loved ones, pets, and other significant objects in the children's lives; feelings of personal failure; feelings of extreme shame or grief; and other traumatic events contribute to suicidal thoughts. Allow children to express their feelings without being judgmental, glossing over, or denying their right to these feelings.

11. If suicidal children admit to self-destructive thoughts, ask about their plan. A well-thought-out plan is a significant danger signal.

12. Ask suicidal children to tell you about their fantasies or dreams. Ask them to draw a picture or write out their thoughts. These techniques often give the adult some insight into the child's thoughts and feelings.

13. Often children do not understand death as final and irreversible; therefore, any child who is seriously disturbed or depressed needs careful attention. Greene (1994) pointed out that preschoolers link death to separation, which is temporary. Five- to 7-year-old children begin to develop concepts related to death—irreversibility and causality—and may be able to see the final meaning of death.

14. The months following the threat are also crucial, and careful attention should be continued until the conflict is completely resolved. A sudden recovery after severe depression may be a warning signal that means the client has made a decision to end one's life.

Jacobsen et al. (1994) suggested questions such as the following, among others, to interview children about suicidal ideation and behaviors:

- Did you ever feel so upset that you wished you were not alive or wanted to die?
- Did you ever do something that you knew was so dangerous that you could get hurt or killed?
- Did you tell anyone that you wanted to die or were thinking about killing yourself?
- What would happen if you died? What would that be like?
- How do you remember feeling when you were thinking about killing yourself or trying to kill yourself?
- Has anything happened recently that has been upsetting to you or your family?
- Have you had a problem with feeling sad, having trouble sleeping, not feeling hungry, losing your temper easily, or feeling tired all of the time recently? (p. 450)

Roberts (1995) found that interventions made after a youth suicide can be preventive as well as assist the grieving process. He recommended that a "psychological autopsy" be performed to try to understand all the factors that contributed to the child's decision to commit suicide, to determine why the death occurred at a particular time, to provide information to prevent other suicides, and to aid in the grieving process. Roberts urged schools to develop "postvention" plans to deal with a child's suicide during the school year and during vacation.

Many writers in this area suggested psychological education and peer-group counseling as preventive measures. In addition to forming peer-counseling groups, Herring (1990) advocated psychological education as part of the middle school curriculum, that parents be involved in training sessions to help them understand the issue of suicide, and that counselors serve as consultants, providing information and knowledge about what to do and where to refer clients.

Siehl (1990) suggested that all schools should have a disaster plan to use in the event of a suicide, just as they have a plan for hurricanes, tornadoes, earthquakes, and other traumatic events. Some of Siehl's suggestions include:

1. Develop a team of resource people to handle the emotional crisis.
2. Present in-service training programs to the entire staff on the causes of suicide, warning signs, and sources of help for suicidal persons.
3. Establish a network to inform all faculty of the facts of the tragedy.
4. Designate special crisis centers for children needing additional help.
5. Develop a checklist of activities to be included in the classroom announcement.
6. Plan for cautions about the dangers in the days following a suicide.
7. Carry out home visits.
8. Develop guidelines for media coverage.
9. Develop procedures to continue alertness for several months.

Because helping professionals are aware that children may imitate other children who commit suicide, such a plan, along with psychological education and group counseling, is appropriate for counselors to consider.

CHILDREN IN SATANIC CULTS

Although the typical young person involved in cults or satanic rituals is usually an adolescent, Rudin (1990) noted that the satanically involved can be as young as 11 years of age. In addition, some children are born into satanic cults that have been practicing rituals for generations. The typical youth involved in devil worship is troubled and alienated from his or her significant groups. The young person who might be attracted to the drug culture is also a prime candidate for the occult.

Rudin (1990) described the typical cult member as very intelligent, idealistic, and high achieving. The young person involved in satanic worship is also intelligent and curious but is usually an underachiever with low self-esteem. These people have feelings of powerlessness, have few friends, and are often isolated from their families. They are drawn to negative groups because of their need for friendships and power. Rudin cautioned school personnel to watch for black clothing; jewelry with satanic symbols; drawings or symbols of demons, death, and mutilation; satanic literature; and other paraphernalia. Wheeler, Wood, and Hatch (1988) described such common symbols as the abbreviation DW for "devil worship," the number 666, upside-down crosses, dripping blood, candles, daggers, and a goat. Young people in satanic cults may like heavy-metal music because of its emphasis on death and destruction.

Rudin (1990) warned that child abuse is prevalent in cults because children are not valued. These children may or may not attend school. Rudin strongly recommended that school personnel learn the signs of satanic involvement and schedule educational programs for staff and students. The International Cult Education Program (P.O. Box 1232, Gracie Station, New York, NY 10028) provides speakers, literature, resource lists, and other materials to assist with educational programs.

Wheeler et al. (1988) suggested that counselors help the young person understand his or her motivation for involvement and to verbalize his or her feelings of anger, pain, frustration, or alienation. They recommended that counselors help their clients find new and better ways to feel power in their lives and to develop better personal relationships. Family counseling is helpful because most children feel alienated from parents and other family members. Children deeply involved in satanic rituals or the occult may need to be removed from all contact with their present environment and require intense, continuing efforts to improve their self-esteem, to help them to find positive relationships within their families and peer groups, and to establish some control over their lives.

Young people sometimes have a casual interest in reading about the occult; however, parents, teachers, counselors, and friends should become concerned when the young person retreats from more positive group relationships and shows changes in behavior that indicate alienation and withdrawal.

Counselors working with children involved in the occult need to be aware of their feelings of alienation, powerlessness, and low self-esteem. Counselors need to listen to such children intently to understand all the underlying reasons for their involvement.

COUNSELING CHILDREN ABOUT AIDS

Because of the widespread media coverage of concerns related to acquired immune deficiency syndrome (AIDS), Holcomb (1990) sought to ascertain how elementary schoolchildren feel about AIDS and what information they have about the issues. He asked 224 fourth-grade children questions to assess their basic knowledge and attitudes about AIDS. Holcomb's results indicated that these children knew AIDS was transmitted by direct sexual contact, by direct blood-to-blood contact, and by sharing needles with an infected person. Most knew that one does not contract AIDS by hugging or shaking hands with an infected person. They were less sure about whether people contract AIDS from toilet seats, food prepared by an AIDS-infected person, and swimming pools. Kissing was very risky, according to these children, as was drinking from the glass of an AIDS-infected person. Some expressed concern over mosquito bites and donating blood. More than 50% of the children interviewed feared or worried about AIDS, and 72% said they would be worried about a child with AIDS in their classroom. Holcomb recommended that counselors make sure AIDS education is included in their curriculum, that they determine areas of misinformation and provide correct information, and that educational groups be held for parents to help them learn to talk with their children. He also encouraged counselors to hold classroom groups to discuss fears and worries about AIDS and to form small groups for children with excessive fears and worries.

Although African American and Hispanic children comprise minority groups in school, 75% of the pediatric AIDS cases are in these two groups (Jessee, Nagy, & Poteet-Johnson, 1993). In spite of the statement by the Centers for Disease Control (CDC) that casual contact between school children poses no risk, fear of AIDS-infected children prevails among many parents. The American Academy of Pediatrics issued a statement similar to that of the CDC, recommending that children with AIDS be allowed to attend school unless they cannot control bodily functions, or have open lesions (Reed, 1988). Deputy Director of the National Association of State Boards of Education (NASBE) Brenda Welburn (1989) stated that we now know "that HIV is not transmitted through saliva or urine" and that the "possibility that the AIDS virus would be transmitted through simple exposure to blood is extremely low." Obviously, good safety precautions should be practiced at all times, but no evidence exists that HIV can be transmitted from contacts such as holding, touching, hugging, or sharing bathroom facilities (Jessee et al., 1993).

In spite of assurances that AIDS is not communicated through casual contact, fear of AIDS has caused children with the virus to be ostracized from school and playmates. Bruhn (1989) stated that public fears are unjustified in most cases because the HIV virus is fragile. These fears result from ignorance about the diesase and are present in people of all educational levels (Bruhn, 1989). Protecting children is an emotional issue that troubles parents, teachers, and other school personnel. Parents often believe their children can contact AIDS by sharing toys or school supplies or by touching a child with AIDS (Walker & Hulecki, 1989) and therefore have protested against a child identified as having AIDS in the school system. Schools interested in developing clear policies and procedures regarding attendance, confidentiality, mandatory testing, and guidelines for dealing with AIDS cases in the school may wish to contact NASBE to obtain their publication, developed in cooperation with the Centers for Disease Control.

Most writers advocate AIDS education for teachers, parents, and other children as the best way to help children with AIDS. However, AIDS education requires discussion of topics such as homosexuality, drugs, and condoms. Parents often do not want these topics discussed with their children, fearing that such discussion might encourage sexual acting-out (Kirp & Epstein, 1989). Communities that do provide educational programs usually accept children with AIDS more readily and with less fear. Bennett (1987) recommended that children should be helped to develop clear standards of right and wrong, as well as tough ways of resisting pressure to engage in dangerous activities. He also advised adults to set a good example and to teach children about AIDS. Shaffer, Godwin, and Richmond (1987) suggested that adults talking to children about AIDS should provide credible information appropriate to the age level of the children without overwhelming them with information. Books, videos, pamphlets, and other materials may be used to clarify misunderstandings and stimulate discussions.

Counselors also must be ready to deal with the feelings of children with AIDS about themselves and their disease, as well as with the range of emotions that accompany the realization that one has a fatal disease. Daily activities can be problematic for the child who is isolated from friends and not physically able to participate in games and sports. Children with AIDS need supportive counseling as well as counseling to deal with specific concerns.

As with other issues that affect children, counselors need to examine their own feeling about children with AIDS. Counselors who have not resolved their own fears about contracting AIDS or who hold values that interfere with acceptance of the child should resolve these personal issues before working with children who have AIDS.

CHILDREN AND VIOLENCE

In a 1993 commentary (Graves, Zuckerman, Marans, & Cohen), the *Journal of the American Medical Association (JAMA)* reported that more than 90% of a sample of New Orleans elementary school children had seen violence—70% had seen weapons used and 40% had seen a dead body. Los Angeles researchers believe that children see from 10% to 20% of the homicides committed in that city. In Boston, 1 of every 10 children at a Boston City Hospital clinic had seen a stabbing or shooting before the age of 6 years.

Despite medical or psychiatric causes of violence and violence that may be associated with war, poverty, oppression, or political rebellion, violence may also be learned in our culture. The *Harvard Mental Health Letter*, "Violence and Violent Patients," (1991) reported that children who watch a lot of television are more aggressive and see the world as more violent than it is. In another article in this same newsletter, Comstock (1990) concluded from research on the effects of television violence that numerous studies have clearly shown a relationship between television violence and aggression, especially in boys. Viewers are more apt to become less sensitive to violence and to begin to think of the world as more threatening.

The writers of the *JAMA* commentary on children and violence (1993) suggested that children need an opportunity to talk about the violence they witness and that mental health professionals obtain specialized training to treat children who witness violence and experience symptoms of stress. They also urged society to ensure a safe environment for children to grow and develop.

In addition to treatment, children need the tools to resolve their difficulties without resorting to violent behavior. Children who learn problem-solving skills or conflict resolution are less impulsive and aggressive and tend to be more rational and patient. The basic principles of conflict resolution are similar to the problem-solving strategies described previously: Listen objectively to the other person, identify the problem, brainstorm for alternatives, agree on common grounds, and find a win-win solution. Most programs discuss the nature of the conflicts encountered by children, incorporate rules for attacking the problem (not the person) and treating other with respect, and emphasize accepting responsibility for one's behavior. Participants may also discuss issues related to diversity, power, and anger control. Role-plays, simulations, stories, and discussions provide practice for children learning the new skills required for conflict resolution.

Peer mediators are sometimes trained to facilitate the conflict-resolution process. Lane and McWhirter (1992) described a peer mediation model for elementary and middle school children with 19 steps for the mediation. Peer mediators get very specific actions concerning introductions, listening, ascertaining "wants," and finding solutions. Peer mediators are trained in the steps and must make a complete report of all interactions at the completion of the process.

Johnson and Johnson (1994) believed that all students should learn to negotiate and mediate and have the experience of serving as a mediator. They cited studies showing that conflict-resolution and mediation training results in fewer student-to-student conflicts and increased student management of their conflicts without adult intervention.

Messing (1993) cautioned that "mediation is not a replacement for short-term counseling or crisis intervention" (p. 71) but suggested that it can be used in addition to counseling "in situations when there is not a great imbalance of power between parties or when there is no clear right and wrong position or a serious crime has not been committed" (p. 71).

SUGGESTED READINGS
FOR CONCERNS OF CHILDREN*

Annotations are derived from the following sources:

1. *Booklist.* Chicago: American Library Association, 1985–1987.
2. Colborn, C. *What do children read next? A reader's guide to fiction for children.* Detroit: Gale Research, 1994.
3. Donavin, D., ed. *Best of the best for children.* New York: Random House, 1992.
4. Dreyer, S. *The bookfinder: When kids need books.* Falls Church, VA: American Guidance Service, 1985.

---

*Sincere appreciation and gratitude are given to Lynda Hunt, Coordinator of the Learning Resource Center, Austin Peay State University, Clarksville, TN for updating the suggested readings for children.

5. *The elementary school library collection: A guide to books and other media.* Williamsport, PA: Brodart, 1984.

6. Gillespie, J., and Naden, C. (1990). *Best books for children preschool through grade 6* (4th ed.). New Providence, NJ: R. R. Bowker.

7. Yaakov, J. (1987). Goldberg, J. (1988-89). *Children's catalog: 1987, 1988, 1989 supplements to the fifteenth edition.* New York: H. W. Wilson.

8. Yaakov, J. (1991). *Children's catalog: Sixteenth edition.* New York: H. W. Wilson.

9. Price, A., & Yaakov, J. (1992, 1993, 1994). *Children's catalog: 1992, 1993, and 1994 supplements to sixteenth edition.* New York: H. W. Wilson.

Abandonment

Byars, Betsy. *The house of wings.* Illustrated by Daniel Schwartz. New York: Viking Press, 1972. A wounded crane and the care an old man gives it teach Sammy to love the grandfather he could not understand before. Ages 10–12.

Hahn, Mary Downing. *Tallahassee Higgins.* New York: Clarion Books, 1987. Tallahassee Higgins has come to grips with a new lifestyle after her mother, Liz, leaves her with an aunt and uncle in Maryland so Liz can pursue a career in Hollywood. Ages 11+.

Howard, Ellen. *Edith herself.* New York: Atheneum, 1987. After her mother's death, Edith goes to live with her elder sister and dour brother-in-law. Their stern Christian household makes it difficult for her to adjust, and her epileptic seizures seem to be recurring. Ages 10–12.

Townsend, John Rowe. *Dan alone.* Philadelphia: Lippincott, 1983. Setting is industrial England in the 1920s. After his mother abandons him, having never known his father, young Dan spends time among scoundrels, but finally finds the real family of his fantasies. Ages 11+.

Voight, Cynthia. *Homecoming.* New York: Atheneum, 1981. When their momma abandons them in a shopping center, Dicey Tillerman and her three younger brothers and sisters set out on their own to find family in Connecticut, where life turns out not to be successful. They journey then to Maryland in search of their grandmother and happiness. Ages 11+.

Adoption/Foster Homes

Banish, Roslyn. *A forever family.* Illustrated by author and Jennifer Jordan-Wong. New York: Harper Collins, 1992. Eight-year-old Jennifer Jordan-Wong describes her adoption after 4 years of living as a foster child with many different families. Ages 5–8.

Caines, Jeannette Franklin. *Abby.* Illustrated by Steven Kellogg. New York: Harper & Row, 1973. Abby, an adopted black preschooler, loves to see and hear about her adoption. A temporary crisis arises when her adopted brother does not want to bother with a girl, but all ends well. Ages 5–7.

Howard, Ellen. *Her own song.* New York: Atheneum, 1988. Teased by classmates for being adopted, Mellie is friendless and lonely. Because her adoptive mother is dead, Mellie is raised by her father, Bill, a stern man, and her aunt. Befriending a Chinese laundry man helps her gain a new sense of self-worth. Ages 10+.

Hughes, Dean. *Family pose.* New York: Atheneum, 1989. David runs away from his uncaring foster family and ends up sleeping in a warm hallway of the Hotel Jefferson. Hotel workers befriend David and consult Social Services about his future. Ages 10+.

Keller, Holly. *Horace*. New York: Greenwillow, 1991. Horace is adopted and is also spotted. He is loved and cared for by his adoptive parents, who are striped. Horace feels the need to search for his roots, finding a brood like him physically, but comes to realize the love of a true family. Ages 5–7.

Krementz, Jill. *How it feels to be adopted.* New York: Knopf, 1982. Interviews with adopted children and adoptive families about their experiences and feelings concerning adoption. Ages 8–12.

Myers, Walter Dean. *Me, Mop and the Moondance Kid.* New York: Delacorte Press, 1988. Eleven-year old T.J. and his younger brother, Billy, the Moondance Kid, have lived happily for 6 months with adoptive parents. Their worry is their friend Mop, fear of her having to go to an orphanage, and hope that their coach might want to adopt her. Ages 10–12.

Thesman, Jean. *When the road ends.* Houghton Mifflin, 1992. Sent to spend the summer in the country three foster children and an older woman recovering from a serious accident are abandoned by their slovenly caretaker and must try to survive on their own. Ages 10+.

Child Abuse

Anderson, Deborah, and Martha Finne. *Robin's story: Physical abuse and seeing the doctor.* Minneapolis, MN: Dillon, 1986. Robin's mother hits her, causing a serious wound; the two are sent to counseling to improve their relationship. Ages 7–9.

Anderson, Deborah, and Martha Finne. *Michael's story: Emotional abuse and working with a counselor.* Minneapolis, MN: Dillon, 1986. Because his parents continually berate him, Michael considers himself stupid as well as unloved. A school counselor suggests family counseling. Ages 7–10.

Bawden, Nina. *Squib*. Illustrated by Hank Blaustein. New York: Lothrop, Lee & Shepard, 1982. When a shy, pale boy appears on the playground, 12-year-old Kate is haunted by his looks and compelled to discover his origins. Thinking he might be her lost brother, she discovers ways to save Squib from his abusive parents. Ages 10+.

Boegehold, Betty. *You can say "no": A book about protecting yourself.* Illustrated by Carolyn Bracken. Racine, WI: Western, 1985. Good text on the subject of child abuse. Ages 5–7.

Byars, Betsy Cromer. *Cracker Jackson.* New York: Viking/Kestrel, 1985. Young Jackson discovers that his ex-baby-sitter has been beaten by her husband; spurred by affection for her, the boy enlists his friend Goat to help drive her to a home for battered women. Ages 10+.

Kehoe, Patricia. *Something happened and I'm scared to tell.* Seattle: Parenting Press, 1987. This book is designed to encourage child victims to speak out and to give them concepts to help their recovery. Ages 3–7.

Park, Angela. *Child abuse.* New York: Gloucester, 1988. Case studies and statistics back up this discussion of a sensitive subject. Ages 10–13.

Ross, Ramon Royal. *Harper & Moon.* New York: Atheneum, 1993. Although 12-year-old Harper has always liked Moon, an abused, orphaned older boy, their friendship is tested by a discovery Harper makes when Moon joins the army. Ages 11+.

Children's Worries

Conrad, Pam. *Staying nine.* New York: HarperCollins, 1988. Heather does not want to turn 10 and takes it to the extreme. It takes her Uncle Lou's girlfriend to convince her that all grown-ups are not "grown up" and to give 10 a try. Ages 9–11.

Cooper, Ilene. *Choosing*. New York: Morrow, 1990. The attitudes, lingo, and worries of this age group abound. The focus is on Jon Rossi, whose father is so thrilled that his son is on the basketball team that the boy hesitates to follow his own instinct to quit. Ages 10–12.

Fenner, Carol. *Randall's wall*. McElderry, 1991. No one comes near fifth-grader Randall Lord. He's filthy. He lives in a home without running water. Randall hides his artistic talent and his growing loneliness behind an invisible wall. Wanting but not having friends changes when he defends Jean from a bully. Ages 10–12.

Kunz, Roxane Brown, and Judy Harris Swenson. *What should I do? Learning to make choices*. Minneapolis, MN: Dillon, 1986. A little girl describes some decision-making concepts and helps young readers learn to make choices. Ages 9–11.

Lewis, Barbara A. *The kids guide to social action: How to solve the social problems you choose and turn creative thinking into positive action*. Minneapolis, MN: Free Spirit, 1991. Good text on social problem-solving for young readers. Ages 8–12.

Little, Jean. *Different dragons*. New York: Viking/Kestrel, 1987. Ben faces many challenges on his first stay away from home without his family. Challenges he faces are "mean" Aunt Rose, sleeping alone, a bossy girl next door, and a big dog. Ages 9–11.

McPhail, David. *Something special*. Cambridge, MA: Little, 1988. Everyone in the family does something special—except Sam. Ages 5–7.

O'Donnell, Elizabeth Lee. *Maggie doesn't want to move*. Illustrated by Amy Schwartz. New York: Macmillan, 1987. Simon, with young sister Maggie in tow, hides at a neighbor's house when it's time to move. Ages 5–7.

Rosenberg, Maxine. *Living in two worlds*. Illustrated with photographs by George Ancona. New York: Lothrop, 1986. Children of biracial heritage are depicted, and their experiences are used to explain notions of race and describe common attitudes toward racial mixing. Ages 8–12.

Shaw, Diana. *Make the most of a good thing: You!* Boston: Atlantic Monthly, 1986. Shaw addresses preteen girls on the basics of taking good care of themselves as they pass into their teenage years. Ages 11–14.

Snyder, Zilpha Keatley. *Fool's gold*. New York: Delacorte, 1993. Reluctant to admit that he suffers from claustrophobia and anxious not to alienate his friends, Rudy tries to find a way to distract them from pursuing their plan of exploring an abandoned gold mine. Ages 10+.

Stolz, Mary. *Storm in the night*. New York: Harper & Row, 1988. Thomas, his grandfather, and Ringo the cat go out on the porch after a power failure during a thunderstorm. Grandfather's story helps him overcome his fear. Ages 6–9.

Teague, Mark. *The field beyond the outfield*. New York: Scholastic, 1992. Ludlow Grebe sees monsters everywhere. His worried parents urge him to try Little League. While playing outfield, his fantasies take over. Ages 6–9.

Viorst, Judith. *The good-bye book*. New York: Atheneum, 1988. Full-color pictures show parents going about the business of getting ready for an evening out as their small boy throws a tantrum in the foreground. Ages 6–8.

Children/Aids

Aiello, Barbara, and Jeffrey Shulman. *Friends for life*. Illustrated by Loel Barr. New York: Twenty-first Century, 1989. AIDS is the subject in this look at the "Kids on the Block" puppets from the stage show. Ages 7–9.

Hausherr, Rosmarie. *Children and the AIDS virus: A book for children, par-

ents, and teachers. New York: Clarion, 1989. The author examines the lives of two children who have AIDS. She seeks to explain what a virus is, how the AIDS virus affects the body, and how it is contracted. Ages 6–9.

Jordan, MaryKate. *Losing Uncle Tim.* Illustrated by Judith Friedman. Morton Grove, IL: Whitman, 1989. When his beloved Uncle Tim dies of AIDS, Daniel struggles to find reassurance and understand ing and finds that his favorite grown-up has left him a legacy of joy and courage. Ages 7–9.

Death

Bauer, Marion Dane. *On my honor.* New York: Clarion, 1986. In this powerful, soul-stirring novel, Joel comes to understand the power of choice after his daredevil friend drowns in a forbidden, raging river. Ages 10–13.

Bruchac, Joseph. *Fox song.* Illustrated by Paul Morin. Philomel Books, 1993. After the death of her Abenaki Indian great-grandmother, Jamie remembers the many special things the old woman shared with her about the natural world. Ages 6–9.

Clifton, Lucille. *Everett Anderson's good-bye.* Illustrated by Ann Gifalconi. New York: Holt, Rinehart & Winston, 1983. A little boy whose father has died experiences the five stages of grief. Ages 4+.

Coerr, Eleanor. *The Josefina story quilt.* Pictures by Bruce Degen. New York: Harper & Row, 1986. Soon after the family arrives in California by wagon train, Faith's pet hen, Josefina, dies. The family creates a special patchwork quilt that recalls the events of Josefina's trip. Ages 4–8.

Cohen, Miriam. *Jim's dog Muffins.* Illustrated by Lillian Hoban. New York: Greenwillow, 1984. Jim's friends exhibit a wide variety of reactions after his dog is killed by a garbage truck,

but Jim is helped in accepting the death. Ages 5–8.

Coman, Carolyn. *Tell me everything.* New York: Farrar, Straus & Giroux, 1993. After her mother, Ellie, dies in a rescue mission on a snowy mountain, 12-year-old Roz wonders if talking to God, and to the boy for whom her mother died, can help her understand what happened. Ages 11+.

Fayerweather Street School Staff. *The kid's book about death and dying: By and for kids.* Boston: Little, Brown, 1985. Based on a Yearling discussion group on death and dying with children age 11–14, this book should do much to foster learning about and acceptance of death. Ages 10–14.

Heymans, Annemie. *The princess in the kitchen garden.* New York: Farrar, Straus & Giroux, 1993. As their father becomes more absorbed in his work, Matthew and his sister, Hannah, come to terms with their mother's death in very unusual ways. Ages 5+.

Hyde, Margaret Oldroyd. *Meeting death.* New York: Walker & Co., 1989. Provides information to promote the acceptance of the concept of death, discussing such aspects as the terminally ill, suicide, grief and mourning, and the treatment of death in various cultures. Ages 10+.

Johnson, Angela. *Toning the sweep.* New York: Orchard, 1993. On a visit to her grandmother, Ola, who is dying of cancer in her house in the desert, 14-year-old Emmie hears many stories about the past and her family history and comes to a better understanding of relatives both dead and living. Ages 11+.

Krementz, Jill. *How it feels when a parent dies.* New York: Knopf, 1981. Twenty children speak openly and honestly about their experiences and emotions when one of their parents died, in a book designed to help other children

deal with their own emotional up-
heaval. Ages 8–12.

Rofes, Eric E. *The kids' book about death
and dying by and for kids.* Cambridge,
MA: Little, 1985. Based on a year-long
discussion group, 10- to 14-year-old
children discuss aspects of death and
grief. Ages 10–13.

Rogers, Fred. *When a pet dies.* New York:
Putnam, 1988. This book explores the
feelings of sadness, loneliness, and
frustration a youngster may feel when
a pet dies. Ages 5–7.

Thomas, Jane Resh. *Saying good-bye to
Grandma.* New York: Clarion, 1988.
Seven-year-old Suzie takes a trip to her
grandparents' house to attend her
grandmother's funeral. Her feelings
about her grandmother and her relationship with her grieving grandfather
are presented in this story. Ages 3–9.

Wild, Margaret. *The very best of friends.*
Illustrated by Julie Vivas. New York:
HBJ, 1990. James is William's cat;
Jessie is William's wife. When William
dies suddenly, Jessie and the cat grieve
in their own ways. Eventually they turn
to each other for support. Ages 5–8.

Wright, Betty Ren. *The cat next door.* New
York: Holiday House, 1991. After
Grandma dies, the annual visit to her
summer cabin is not the same, but the
cat next door remembers how things
used to be and cheers a grieving grand-
child. Ages 5–7.

Divorce/Separation/Blended Families/Single Parents

Bawden, Nina. *The outside child.* New
York: Lothrop, Lee & Shepard, 1989.
Thirteen-year-old Jane Tucker acci-
dentally learns that her widowed father, a ship's engineer, is remarried and
has two other children. She defies
relatives to locate her half-siblings and
sparks violence from her stepmother.
Ages 12+.

Boyd, Candy. *Chevrolet Saturdays.* New
York: Macmillan, 1993. When he enters fifth grade after his mother's remarriage, Joey, a child of a hardworking black family, has trouble adjusting
to his new teacher and his new stepfather. Ages 10+

Boyd, Lizi. *The not-so-wicked stepmother.*
New York: Viking/Kestrel, 1987.
Hessie is going to spend the summer
with her father and stepmother. She
plans to act horrible and mean because
she knows that stepmothers are supposed to be. To her surprise, hers is
kind and loving, which brings her
much confusion and conflicting feelings. Ages 6–9.

Brown, Laurene Krasny, and Marc
Brown. *Dinosaurs divorce: A guide for
changing families.* Boston: Atlantic,
1986. The text is excellent, briefly
getting to the heart of the feelings and
problems common to children during
and after divorce. Ages 3–8.

Christiansen, C. B. *My mother's house, my
father's house.* New York: Atheneum,
1989. A child of divorce tells what it is
like when she spends four days at her
mother's house and three days at her
father's house. Both houses are home,
but neither parent will visit the other.
Ages 6–9.

Christopher, John. *Takedown.* Boston:
Little, Brown, 1990. As he is helped by
an assistant referee to prepare for a
wrestling match with the neighborhood bully, Sean begins to wonder if
his mentor could be his long-lost father. Ages 11+.

Cleary, Beverly. *Strider.* Illustrated by Paul
O. Zelinsky. New York: Morrow Jun-
ior Books, 1991. Sequel to *Dear Mr.
Henshaw.* In a series of diary entries,
Leigh Botts, 14 and beginning high
school, tells how he comes to terms
with his parents' divorce. Ages 9+.

Fine, Anne. *My war with Goggle-eyes.*
Boston: Little, Brown, 1989. Kitty is
not pleased with her mother's boyfriend. Unexpected events prompt her
to help him find a place in the family.
Ages 11+.

Hodder, Elizabeth. *Stepfamilies.* New

York: Gloucester, 1990. The author discusses stepfamilies and the ways they differ from nuclear families. Ages 10+.

Katz, Welwyn Wilton. *False face*. New York: Macmillan, 1988. Laney's parents' bitter divorce has left her confused and vulnerable. An Indian ritual mask leads to problems, but others are already evident. Ages 11+.

Krementz, Jill. *How it feels when parents divorce*. New York: Knopf, 1984. Nineteen boys and girls, 8–16, share the experiences and feelings they had while adjusting to divorced families. Ages 9–14.

Mayle, Peter. *Why are we getting a divorce?* New York: Harmony, 1988. Calm, straightforward text on an emotional issue. Ages 8–11.

Park, Barbara. *My mother got married (and other disasters)*. New York: Knopf, 1989. Adjusting to a new stepfamily, 12-year-old Charles is presented with many difficult experiences. Not until a near-tragedy tempers his feelings is Charles willing to give up his anger. Ages 10–12.

Roberts, Willo Davis. *Megan's island*. New York: Atheneum, 1988. Megan and her younger brother, Sandy, are secretly moved to their grandfather's cabin in Minnesota. Secrets are learned and attempts at kidnapping fail. Ages 11+.

Rosenberg, Maxine. *Talking about stepfamilies*. New York: Bradbury, 1990. Children and adults who have become part of stepfamilies describe their experiences in coping with new stepparents and step-siblings. Ages 9+.

Slote, Alfred. *Moving in*. Philadelphia, Lippincott, 1988. Eleven-year-old Robbie and his 13-year-old sister, Peggy, plan some elaborate schemes to discourage their widowed father's budding romance. They try to persuade him to move back to their old hometown. Ages 10–12.

Smith, Robert Kimmel. *The squeaky wheel*.

New York: Delacorte, 1990. Moving to a new neighborhood following his parents' divorce, Mark has trouble making new friends and coping with his father's absence. Ages 9–11.

Williams, Vera B. *Scooter*. New York: Greenwillow, 1993. After her parents' divorce, Elana Rose Rosen and her mother relocate to an apartment in a big city housing project. Ages 8–10.

Drugs, Alcohol, and Tobacco Abuse

Christopher, Matt. *Tackle without a team*. Boston: Little, Brown, 1989. Scott was unjustly dismissed from the football team for drug possession. He learns that he can clear himself with his parents only by finding out who planted the marijuana in his duffel bag. Ages 11+.

Conly, Jane Leslie. *Crazy lady*. New York: Harper Collins, 1993. As he tries to come to terms with his mother's death, Vernon finds solace in his growing relationship with neighborhood outcasts, an alcoholic and a retarded son. Ages 10+.

Dolan, Edward F. *Drugs in sports*. New York: Watts, 1986. School counselors as well as students will be interested in this straightforward overview of a much-publicized topic. Ages 12–14.

Hyde, Margaret Oldroyd. *Alcohol: Uses and abuses*. Hillsdale, NJ: Enslow, 1988. The author describes medical and social problems that alcohol causes alcoholics and the community. Ages 12+.

Hyde, Margaret Oldroyd. *Know about smoking*. New York: Walker, 1990. Various aspects of smoking are treated in a straightforward, no-frills style. Ages 9+.

McFarland, Rhonda. *Drugs and your brothers and sisters*. New York: Rosen, 1991. When addiction takes over, the trust that exists in a family breaks down, and every member of the family is affected. The author tells children how to benefit from the positive influences of a sibling. Ages 10+.

Nielson, Nancy. *Teen alcoholism*. San Diego, CA: Lucent, 1989. Teen use and abuse of alcohol are widespread problems that destroy many young people's lives each year. This book explores the issue of the abuse and presents solutions for the future. Ages 10–13.

O'Neill, Catherine. *Focus on alcohol*. Illustrated by David Neuhaus. New York: 21st Century Books, 1990. The author discusses the history, use, and dangers of alcohol, the problems of alcoholism, and coping with the pressures to drink. Ages 8–11.

Perry, Robert Louis. *Focus on nicotine and caffeine*. Illustrated by David Neuhaus. New York: 21st Century Books, 1990. The author discusses the history, effects, social aspects, and physical dangers of using tobacco and caffeine products. Ages 8–11.

Rosenberg, Maxine B. *Not my family: Sharing the truth about alcoholism*. New York: Bradbury, 1988. The author interviewed eight youngsters referred to her through treatment centers and six adult children of alcoholics about their family experiences. Resources are included. Ages 10+.

Sexias, Judith S. *Drugs—what they do*. Illustrated by Tom Huffman. New York: Greenwillow, 1987. This book defines drugs and explains such topics as drug tolerance and the factors that can influence the effect of a drug on a person. Psychoactive drugs like stimulants and hallucinogens are included. Ages 6–8.

Woods, Geraldine. *Drug use and drug abuse* (Rev. ed.). New York: Watts, 1986. The author presents a factual introduction to drugs—both legitimate use and illegal abuse. The nature of addiction is also presented. Ages 9+.

Family

Adoff, Arnold. *Hard to be six*. Illustrated by Cheryl Hanna. New York: Lothrop,

Lee & Shepard, 1991. A 6-year-old boy, who wants to grow up fast so he can do the things that his 10-year-old sister does, learns a lesson about patience from his grandmother. Ages 6–8.

Blume, Judy. *The one in the middle is the green kangaroo* (Rev. ed.). Illustrated by Irene Trivas. New York: Bradbury, 1991. Freddy hates being the middle one in the family until he gets a part in the school play. Ages 6+.

Cameron, Eleanor. *The private worlds of Julia Redfern*. New York: Dutton, 1988. Julia is on the verge of 15. She is secure in her accomplishments as a writer and is exploring her talents as an actress. Coming to terms with family problems gives her insights about growing older. Ages 12+.

Cleary, Beverly. *Ramona forever*. Illustrated by Alan Tiegreen. New York: Morrow, 1984. Ramona is an impulsive, enthusiastic third-grader with a zest for life, yet she finds growing up can be difficult. Ages 8–12.

Cooper, Melrose. *I got a family*. Pictures by Dale Gottlieb. New York: Holt, 1993. In rhyming verses, a young girl describes how the members of her family make her feel loved. Age 5+.

Danziger, Paula. *Earth to Matthew*. New York: Delacorte, 1991. Matthew Martin finds himself on the threshold of becoming a teenager in suburban America and experiences conflicting emotions regarding his future. Ages 9–11.

Danziger, Paula. *Everyone else's parents said yes*. New York: Delacorte, 1989. Matthew is always playing practical jokes on his sister and all the girls in his class at school, so by his 11th birthday party, they have all declared war on him. Ages 10–12.

Flournoy, Valerie. *The patchwork quilt*. Illustrated by Jerry Pinkney. New York: Dial, 1985. A comforting sense of strong family bonds is at the heart of this story about a young African

American girl named Tonya and her grandmother, who decides to make Tonya a quilt. Ages 6–8.

Fox, Paula. *The village by the sea.* New York: Orchard, 1988. Emma experiences the devastating effects of envy and the power of love and forgiveness when she is sent to stay with her fractious aunt and eccentric uncle. Ages 11+.

Gauch, Patricia Lee. *Christina Katerina and the time she quit the family.* New York: Putnam, 1987. Christina Katerina has been unjustly accused of just about everything. She decides to change her name to Agnes and quit the family. Ages 6–9.

Goble, Paul. *Buffalo woman.* New York: Bradbury, 1984. Turning away from his own family, a young man joins his wife's people, the Buffalo Nation, in this stunning, stylized depiction of a Native American legend. Ages 6–9.

Heath, Amy. *Sofie's role.* Pictures by Shelia Hamanaka. New York: Four Winds, 1992. On the day before Christmas, Sofie makes her big debut serving customers in her family's busy Broadway Bakery. Ages 6–9.

Heide, Florence Parry. *Treehorn's wish.* Illustrated by Edward Gorey. New York: Holiday House, 1984. Treehorn is having a birthday. He is sure he will receive many presents this year because last year he received so few. Ages 8–13.

Hill, Elizabeth Starr. *Evan's corner.* Pictures by Sandra Speidel. New York: Viking, 1991. Needing a place to call his own, Evan is thrilled when his mother points out that their crowded apartment has eight corners, one for each family member. Ages 6–9.

Hines, Anna Grossnickle. *Daddy makes the best spaghetti.* Illustrated by Clarion Books. New York: Ticknor & Fields, 1986. Corey and his father enjoy a close relationship that is aptly demonstrated in picture and story. Youngsters may wish their own fathers were as funny as this one. Ages 3–5.

Honeycutt, Natalie. *Ask me something easy.* New York: Orchard, 1991. After her father leaves the family, Addie must cope with her increasingly hostile, distant mother, perfect older sister, and sensitive younger sister. Ages 11+.

Horvath, Polly. *An occasional cow.* New York: Farrar, Straus & Giroux, 1989. Imogene, a native New Yorker, dreads the thought of spending all summer with relatives in Iowa surrounded by all those cornfields. Her cousins gamely show her a new world. Ages 9–11.

Hurwitz, Johanna. *"E" is for Elisa.* Illustrated by Lillian Hoban. New York: Morrow Junior Books, 1991. Four-year-old Elisa wants to grow up and do the things her 8-year-old brother, Russell, does. Ages 7–9.

Hurwitz, Johanna. *Make room for Elisa.* Illustrated by Lillian Hoban. New York: Morrow Junior Books, 1993. The adventures of 5-year-old Elisa as she attends her brother Russell's recital, gets new glasses, moves to a new apartment, and welcomes the new baby. Ages 7–9.

Johnson, Angela. *One of three.* Pictures by David Soman. New York: Orchard, 1991. A series of candid reflections by the youngest of three black sisters on her daily relationships with her older sisters and other family members. Ages 6–8.

Kinsey-Warnock, Natalie. *The Canada geese quilt.* New York: Dutton, 1989. Ten-year-old Ariel is worried that the coming of a new baby and her grandmother's serious illness will change the warm, familiar life on her family's Vermont farm. Ariel combines her artistic talent and her grandmother's knowledge to make a special quilt. Ages 9–12.

LeShan, Eda. *When grownups drive you crazy.* New York: Macmillan, 1988. Explores the misunderstandings and conflicts that occur between adults and children and offers advice to youngsters on understanding and dealing with the things adults do that distress them. Ages 10+.

Levinson, Riki. *I go with my family to Grandma's.* New York: Dutton, 1986. Grandma's house embodies the ideal of a loving, secure home—a vivid celebration of long-ago family life in the city. Ages 4–6.

Lowry, Lois. *Attaboy, Sam!* Illustrated by Diane de Groat. Boston: Houghton Mifflin, 1992. Sam is able to help his sister Anastasia with the poem she is writing for their mother's birthday, but his own efforts to create a special perfume are disastrous. Ages 10–12.

Lyon, George Ella. *Borrowed children.* New York: Orchard, 1988. When her mother is bedridden after the birth of Willie, 12-year-old Amanda takes over. Set in Kentucky in the Depression, Amanda has a hard life and looks forward to visiting her grandparents and childless aunt, but soon misses the warmth of her own family. Ages 11–14.

MacLachlan, Patricia. *Journey.* New York: Delacorte, 1991. When their mother goes off, leaving her two children with their grandparents, they feel as if their past has been erased until Grandfather finds a way to restore it to them. Ages 9+.

Murphy, Jill. *Five minutes peace.* New York: Putnam, 1986. A humorous book that gives older children a chance to see their parents in a new light. Ages 9–11.

Namioka, Lensey. *Yang the youngest and his terrible ear.* Boston: Little, Brown, 1992. Recently arrived in Seattle from China, musically untalented Yingtao is faced with giving a violin performance to attract new students for his father when he would rather be working on friendships and playing baseball. Ages 9–11.

Naylor, Phyllis Reynolds. *Alice in April.* New York: Atheneum, 1993. While trying to survive seventh grade, Alice discovers that turning 13 will make her the woman of the house at home, so she starts a campaign to get more appreciation for taking care of her father and older brother. Ages 10+.

Naylor, Phyllis Reynolds. *Reluctantly Alice.* New York: Atheneum, 1991. Alice experiences the joys and embarrassments of seventh grade while advising her father and older brother on their love lives. Ages 10+.

Rosenberg, Maxine B. *Being a twin.* New York: Lothrop, 1985. Rosenberg focuses on twins' mutual support and companionship. She also presents the problems of competition for parents' and friends' attention and the difficulty of achieving separate individual identities. Ages 5–7.

Rylant, Cynthia. *The relatives came.* New York: MacMillan, 1993. Rylant captures perfectly the mayhem and glee produced by a visit from distant relatives. Ages 5–7.

Smith, Robert Kimmel. *Bobby baseball.* New York: Delacorte, 1989. Bobby is 10 years old and passionate about baseball. He is convinced he is a great player; his only problem is proving his skill to his father. Ages 9–12.

Walter, Mildred Pitts. *Justin and the best biscuits in the world.* New York: Lothrop, 1986. This warm story is especially welcome for its positive portrayal of African American family life. Justin learns that "it doesn't matter who does the work, man or woman, when it needs to be done." Ages 4–6.

Friendship/Sense of Belonging

Blume, Judy. *Just as long as we're together.* New York: Orchard, 1987. Stephanie, in her first year of junior high, is distressed by her parents' trial separation. Rachel is Stephanie's special friend, but both girls like a newcomer (Alison, a Vietnamese adoptee) enough to make it a triumvirate. Ages 11+.

Carle, Eric. *The mixed-up chameleon.* New York: Harper/Crowell, 1984. A funny story about a chameleon that tries changing into other animals but finds that it is best just to be itself. Ages 4–7.

Clifton, Lucille. *Three wishes.* New York: Delacorte, 1992. When a young girl finds a good luck penny and makes three wishes on it, she learns that friendship is her most valued possession. Ages 6–8.

Conford, Ellen. *Can do, Jenny Archer.* Boston: Little, Brown, 1991. Attempting to win a can-collecting contest, the winner of which will direct a class movie, Jenny risks losing her best friend. Ages 7–9.

Conford, Ellen. *Why me?* Boston: Little, Brown, 1985. G. G. Graffman has a crush on him? That's all Hobie needs. He is not interested in this bright, slightly nerdy girl. Their interactions form a comic romance of sorts, and Hobie winds up realizing that there is more to love than lusting after good looks. Ages 11+.

Gilson, Jamie. *Sticks and stones and skeleton bones.* Illustrated by Dee deRosa. New York: Lothrop, Lee & Shepard, 1991. Hobie, whose fifth-grade class is meeting in a shopping mall because the school was devastated by a flood, has a disagreement with his best friend, Nick, that escalates into a big fight as the day continues. Ages 9–11.

Greenwald, Shelia. *Here's Hermione: A Rosy Cole production.* Boston: Little, Brown, 1991. Eleven-year-old Hermione Wong wants to become a renowned rock cellist. Best friend and self-appointed manager Rosy Cole tries to help, but Hermione has ideas of her own. Ages 8–10.

Hartling, Peter. *Crutches.* New York: Lothrop, Lee & Shepard, 1988. A man on crutches in postwar Vienna befriends a young boy who is searching for his mother. Together they find hope for the future. Ages 11+.

Havill, Juanita. *Jamaica and Brianna.* Illustrated by Anne Sibley O'Brien. Boston: Houghton Mifflin, 1993. Jamaica hates wearing hand-me-down boots when her friend Brianna has pink fuzzy ones. Ages 4–8.

Hines, Anna Grossnickle. *Tell me your best thing.* Illustrated by Karen Ritz. New York: Dutton, 1991. Eight-year-old Sophie reluctantly joins the new club formed by Charlotte, the class bully, and finds herself being hurt when her best friend is manipulated into telling Sophie's darkest secret. Ages 7–9.

Honeycutt, Natalie. *The all new Jonah Twist.* New York: Bradbury, 1986. Jonah starts third grade determined to change his reputation for being slow and inattentive in class and to prove himself responsible enough to care for a pet at home. Ages 9–12.

Hughes, Shirley. *Wheels: A tale of Trotter Street.* New York: Lothrop, Lee & Shepard, 1991. Carlos is jealous of his friend Billy's new bicycle and desperately wants a new one of his own for his upcoming birthday. Ages 6–9.

Hurwitz, Johanna. *The cold and hot winter.* New York: Morrow Junior Books, 1988. Fifth-grader Derek and his best friend, Rory, are delighted when Bolivia, their neighbor's niece, comes for another visit. Derek begins to doubt Rory's honesty when a lot of objects are missing. Ages 9–12.

Hurwitz, Johanna. *The up & down spring.* Illustrated by Gail Owens. New York: Morrow Junior Books, 1993. While vacationing at Bolivia's house in Ithaca, New York, 11-year-old Rory tries to hide his fear of flying after Bolivia suggests a trip in her uncle's airplane. Ages 8–10.

Hutchins, Pat. *My best friend.* New York: Greenwillow, 1993. Despite differences in abilities, two little girls appreciate each other and are "best friends." Ages 5–7.

Lowry, Lois. *Number the stars.* Boston:

Houghton Mifflin, 1988. When Ellen's parents go into hiding to escape a Nazi roundup in wartime, best friends Annemarie and Ellen must pretend to be sisters. Ages 10+.

Martin, Ann M. *Rachel Parker, kindergarten show-off*. Illustrated by Nancy Poydar. New York: Holiday House, 1992. Five-year-old Olivia's new neighbor Rachel is in her kindergarten class, and they must overcome feelings of jealousy and competitiveness to be friends. Ages 5–7.

Polacco, Patricia. *Mrs. Katz and Tush*. New York: Bantam, 1992. A long-lasting friendship develops between Larnel, a young African American, and Mrs. Katz, a lonely Jewish widow, when Larnel presents Mrs. Katz with a scrawny kitten without a tail. Ages 6–9.

Raschka, Christopher. *Yo! Yes?* New York: Orchard, 1993. Two lonely characters, one black and one white, meet on the street and become friends. Ages 4–7.

Robinson, Nancy K. *Veronica meets her match*. New York: Scholastic, 1990. Veronica's fervent attempts to gain peer acceptance continue as she claims the new girl as her own special friend. Ages 9–11.

Schwartz, Amy. *Camper of the week*. New York: Orchard, 1991. Although Rosie, a model camper, does not participate in her friends' prank and is not caught and disciplined, she decides to join her friends in the punishment because she knows she helped them. Ages 7–11.

Shreve, Susan Richards. *Joshua T. Bates takes charge*. Illustrated by Dan Andreasen. New York: Knopf, 1993. Eleven-year-old Joshua, worried about fitting in at school, feels awkward when the new student he is supposed to be helping becomes the target of the fifth grade's biggest bully. Ages 8–10.

Smith, Doris Buchanan. *The pennywhistle tree*. New York: Putnam, 1991. A rift in the closeness shared by 11-year-old Jonathon and his best friends occurs when Sanders moves onto the street and insists on pushing himself into Jonathon's life. Ages 9–11.

Homeless

Berck, Judith. *No place to be: Voices of homeless children*. Boston: Houghton Mifflin, 1991. An exploration of homelessness in America, specifically New York City, incorporates quotes from 30 children from ages 9 to 18. Ages 10+.

Bunting, Eve. *Fly away home*. Illustrated by Ronald Himler. New York: Clarion, 1991. A homeless boy who lives in an airport with his father, moving from terminal to terminal and trying not to be noticed, is given hope when he sees a trapped bird find its freedom. Ages 6–9.

Fox, Paula. *Monkey island*. New York: Orchard, 1991. Forced to live on the streets of New York City after his mother disappears from their hotel room, 11-year-old Clay is befriended by two men who help him survive. Ages 10+.

Holman, Felice. *Secret City, U.S.A.* New York: Scribner, 1990. Benno and his friends are poor, living in overcrowded tenements and even the street and suffering all the consequences of a life in which the barest necessities are hard to come by. Ages 11+.

Pinkwater, Jill. *Tails of the Bronx: A tale of the Bronx*. New York: Macmillan, 1991. In their search for a group of missing cats, a group of children in the Bronx encounters the problems of homelessness firsthand. Ages 9–11.

Spinelli, Jerry. *Maniac Magee: A novel*. Boston: Little, Brown, 1990. Orphaned at 3, Jeffery Lionel Magee, after 8 unhappy years with relatives, one day takes off running. This unusual novel magically weaves timely issues of homelessness, racial prejudice, and illiteracy into an energetic story. Ages 10+.

Latchkey

Leiner, Katherine. *Both my parents work.* New York: Watts, 1986. Nine children tell about their families who work. Ages 7–9.

Saunders, Susan. *Lauren takes charge.* New York: Scholastic, 1989. Lauren's mother gets a job, so Lauren has extra responsibilities and more allowance. Ages 9–11.

Seabrooke, Brenda. *Jerry on the line.* New York: Bradbury, 1990. Aspiring soccer star Jerry starts an unusual friendship with a younger latchkey kid when she calls his phone number by accident. Ages 8–11.

Terris, Susan. *The latchkey kids.* New York: Farrar, 1986. Callie and Rex move from the suburbs to an apartment in San Francisco. They have to cope with a new home, school, and working mother and a father suffering from depression. Ages 9–12.

Relationships with Older Generations

Blos, Joan W. *The Grandpa days.* New York: Simon & Schuster, 1989. Philip spends a week with his grandfather. He has a special project they will do together, but first he has to learn the difference between wishes and good planning. Ages 6–9.

Cameron, Ann. *The most beautiful place in the world.* New York: Knopf, 1988. Seven-year-old Juan discovers the value of hard work, the joy of learning, and the location of the most beautiful place in the world as he grows up with his grandmother in a small Central American town. Ages 7–10.

Dugan, Barbara. *Loop the loop.* Pictures by James Stevenson. New York: Greenwillow, 1992. Annie and old Mrs. Simpson form a friendship that lasts even after the woman enters a nursing home. Ages 6–9.

Greene, Jacqueline Dembar. *Nathan's Hanukkah bargain.* Illustrated by Steffi Karen Rubin. Rockville, MD: Kar-Ben Copies, 1986. Greene portrays a warm relationship between grandfather and grandson and at the same time shows Nathan's dedication to the spirit of the holiday. Ages 8–11.

Greenfield, Eloise. *Grandpa's face.* Illustrated by Floyd Cooper. New York: Philomel, 1988. A story featuring a close-knit black family. Cooper's sunlit double-page spreads capture the delicate balance between the generations. Ages 5–8.

Griffith, Helen V. *Granddaddy's place.* New York: Greenwillow, 1987. Janetta takes a vacation to the country with her mother to visit her grandfather for the first time. Her trip seems doomed until her grandfather tells of some incredible incidents that happened to him on that very farm. Ages 6–9.

Guy, Rosa. *The ups and downs of Carl Davis III.* New York: Delacorte, 1989. Carl is sent to a small southern town to live with his grandmother. In a series of letters, he chronicles his initial anger, confusion and disdain, as well as his gradual change of heart about his new home. Ages 12+.

Howe, James. *Pinky and Rex and the mean old witch.* Illustrated by Melissa Sweet. New York: Atheneum, 1991. Pinky, Rex, and Amanda plot revenge on the bad-tempered old woman who lives across the street, until Pinky realizes that she is lonely and needs new friends. Ages 6–9.

Johnson, Angela. *When I am old with you.* Illustrated by David Simon. New York: Orchard, 1990. A young black child envisions herself old like granddaddy doing things they both do now: rocking on the porch, fishing, and playing cards. Ages 5–7.

Johnston, Tony. *Grandpa's song.* Pictures by Brad Sneed. New York: Dial, 1991. When a young girl's beloved, exuberant grandfather becomes forgetful, she helps him by singing their favorite song. Ages 5–7.

Levinson, Riki. *Watch the stars come out.* Illustrated by Diane Goode. New York: Dutton, 1985. A girl curls up with her grandmother to hear a true story of yesterday, when another red-haired girl and her big brother traveled to America to join their parents and elder sister. Ages 6–8.

McFarlane, Sheryl. *Waiting for the whales.* Illustrated by Ron Lightburn. New York: Philomel, 1993. A lonely old man who waits each year to see the orcas swim past his house imparts his love of the whales to his granddaughter. Ages 6–9.

Shalev, Meir. *My father always embarrasses me.* Illustrated by Yossi Abdafial. Tallahassee, FL: Wellington, 1990. With a father who stays at home and "does nothing—only hammers away at his typewriter," his son is embarrassed. His father's entry in a school bread-baking contest brings them closer together. Ages 4–8.

Smith, Robert Kimmel. *The war with Grandpa.* Illustrated by Richard Lauter. New York: Delacorte, 1984. Peter's grandfather comes to live with the family and occupies Peter's room. In spite of mixed emotions, Peter wages war but comes to realize that victory isn't what he expects. Ages 9–12.

Stolz, Mary. *Stealing home.* New York: HarperCollins, 1992. Although they still listen to baseball and go fishing, Thomas and his grandfather find life in their small house in Florida changed when Great-aunt Linzy comes to stay. Ages 9–11.

Tejima, Keizaburo. *Ho-limlim: A rabbit tale from Japan.* New York: Philomel, 1990. After one last foray far from his home, an aging rabbit decides he prefers to rest in his own garden and let his children and grandchildren bring him good things to eat. Ages 5–8.

Winthrop, Elizabeth. *Belinda's hurri-*

cane. New York: Dutton, 1984. Visiting her grandmother in Fox Island, Belinda weathers a hurricane in the company of Granny May; her cantankerous old neighbor, Mr. Fletcher; and his growling bulldog, Fishface. Ages 7–11.

Sex Education

Andry, Andrew C. *How babies are made.* Illustrated by Blake Hampton. Alexandria, VA: Time-Life, 1968. The illustrations give clear physiological information about intercourse, pregnancy, and birth, and the text moves from flowers to animals to humans in a brief commentary on each illustration. Ages 5–8.

Johnson, Eric W. *Love and sex and growing up* (New ed.). Illustrations by Vivien Cohen. New York: Bantam, 1990. Describes the process of human reproduction from fertilization to birth, explains growth and sexual maturation, and discusses sexually transmitted diseases. Ages 9+.

Johnson, Eric W. *People, love, sex, and families: Answers to questions that preteens ask.* Illustrated by David Wool. New York: Walker, 1985. This book is the result of a survey conducted by Johnson, who polled 1,000 young people on what they really wanted to know about people, love, sex, and families. Ages 10–14.

Kitzinger, Shelia. *Being born.* New York: Grosset & Dunlap, 1986. The author describes the 9 months of gestation in terms of an experience every reader has had. Ages 9–12.

Madaras, Lynda. *What's happening to my body? book for boys: A growing up guide for parents and sons.* New York: Newmarket, 1987. Frank, detailed information of the sexual and emotional changes that come with puberty presented stage by stage. Included is updated information on AIDS, sexually transmitted diseases, and birth control. Ages 12+.

Madaras, Lynda. *What's happening to my body? book for girls: A growing up guide for parents and daughters.* New York: Newmarket, 1987. This book discusses body changes, body image, menstruation, puberty, and sexuality and stresses the importance of liking and knowing one's own body. Ages 12+.

Marzollo, Jean. *Getting your period: A book about menstruation.* New York: Dial Books for Young Readers, 1988. Information on menstruation is combined with quotations from girls who tell their own concerns and experiences. Ages 11+.

Waxman, Stephanie. *What is a girl? What is a boy?* New York: Crowel, 1989. Simple text and photographs explain the biological differences between males and females and illustrate the similarities between the sexes. Ages 5–6.

Westheimer, Ruth. *Dr. Ruth talks to kids: Where you came from, how your body changes, and what sex is all about.* Illustrated by Diane deGroat. New York: Macmillan, 1993. The author discusses body development and sexuality. Ages 10+.

Sexual Abuse

Anderson, Deborah, and Martha Finne. *Margaret's story: Sexual abuse and going to court.* Minneapolis, MN: Dillon, 1986. Margaret tells her parents when a neighbor fondles her, and they go to court. Ages 7–9.

Caines, Jeannette. *Chilly stomach.* Pictures by Pat Cummings. New York: Harper & Row, 1986. "When Uncle Jim tickles me, I don't like it. Sometimes he hugs me and kisses me on the lips and I get a chilly stomach," begins the brief but convincing narrative of Sandy, an 8- or 9-year-old girl. Ages 4–8.

Girard, Linda Walvood. *My body is private.* Pictures by Rodney Pate. Morton Grove, IL: Albert Whitman, 1984. A first-person narrative by a girl who looks to be about 7 or 8. Discussion of "touching" and the right of an individual to set limits on what is comfortable for one's own body and emotions. Ages 4–8.

Hyde, Margaret Oldroyd. *Sexual abuse: Let's talk about it.* Louisville, KY: Westminster/John Knox, 1987. This edition has been revised to include additional information about treatment and prevention, as well as new material on the sexual abuse of boys. Ages 11+.

Nathanson, Laura. *The trouble with Wednesdays.* New York: Putnam/Pacer, 1986. Becky Grant, whose family is on a shoestring budget, needs braces, but the relative her parents send her to for the work turns out to be a child molester. Ages 11–14.

Terkel, Susan N., and Janice E. Rench. *Feeling safe, feeling strong: How to avoid sexual abuse and what to do if it happens to you.* Minneapolis, MN: Lerner, 1984. This book relies on fictional vignettes to present various abuse situations. Ages 9–12.

Wachter, Oralee. *No more secrets for me.* Illustrated by Jane Aaron. Boston: Little, Brown, 1983. Included are stories about children preyed upon sexually by adults: a stepfather, baby-sitter, and camp counselor. Ages 7–10.

Sex Roles

A Guide to non-sexist children's books. Chicago: Academy Chicago, 1987. Divided by age groups, each section is further divided into fiction and nonfiction. Adult.

Oneal, Zibby. *A long way to go.* Illustrated by Michael Dooling. New York: Viking, 1990. This short novel about the women's suffrage movement is told from the perspective of Lila, a 10-year-old girl living in New York City in 1917. Ages 8–10.

Spinelli, Jerry. *There's a girl in my hammerlock.* New York: Simon and

Schuster, 1991. Thirteen-year-old Maisie joins her school's formerly all-male wrestling team and tries to last through the season, despite opposition from other students, her best friend, and her own teammates. Ages 10+.

Walter, Mildred Pitts. *Justin and the best biscuits in the world*. Illustrated by Catherine Stock. New York: Lothrop, Lee & Shepard, 1986. Justin can't seem to do anything right at home. He angrily rejects "women's work." His wise grandfather helps him see it doesn't matter who does the work when it needs to be done. Ages 8–11.

Winthrop, Elizabeth. *Tough Eddie*. Illustrated by Lillian Hoban. New York: Dutton, 1985. Little Eddie loves building spaceships, wearing cowboy boots, and feeling tough around his buddies, but he really loves his secret dollhouse, too. Ages 5–8.

Zolotow, Charlotte. *William's doll*. Pictures by William Pene DuBois. New York: Harper & Row, 1972. When little William asks for a doll, the other boys scorn him and his father tries to interest him in conventional boys' playthings such as a basketball and a train. His grandmother buys him a doll so he can practice being a father. Ages 5–8.

Suicide

Hermes, Patricia. *A time to listen: Preventing youth suicide*. New York: Harcourt Brace Jovanovich, 1987. A list of the warning signs of suicide, guidelines for when and how to intervene, instructions for getting help, and ways to develop one's own listening skills are included in this highly significant, life-enhancing book. Ages 12+.

Kolehmainen, Janet, and Sandra Handwerk. *Teen suicide: A book for friends, family, and classmates*. Minneapolis, MN: Lerner, 1986. This book alerts readers to the symptoms of suicide and suggests ways of getting help for someone they fear may be suicidal. Ages 11–14.

Kunz, Roxane Brown, and Judy Harris Swenson. *Feeling down: The way back up*. Illustrated by Mary McKeek. Minneapolis, MN: Dillon, 1986. This first-person narrative is meant to educate children on the subject of suicide. Ages 8–11.

Nunes, Lygia Bojunga. *My friend, the painter*. New York: Harcourt Brace, 1991. A boy in Brazil becomes friends with the artist who lives upstairs and tries hard to understand when his friend commits suicide. Ages 10+.

REFERENCES

Allen, L., & Majidi-Ahi, S. (1989). Black American children. In J. Gibbs & L. Huang (Eds.), *Children of color: Psychological interventions with minority youth,* (pp 148-178). San Francisco: Jossey-Bass.

American School Counselors Association (1988). The school counselor and child abuse/neglect prevention. *Elementary School Guidance and Counseling, 22,* 261–263.

Arredondo, P. (1991). Counseling Latinas. In C. Lee & B. Richardson (Eds.), *Multicultural issues in counseling: New approaches to diversity.* Alexandria, VA: American Association for Counseling and Development.

Associated Press. (1985, September 2). Drug, alcohol use up in grammar schools. *Knoxville Journal,* Section A-1.

Barney, J., & Koford, J. (1987). Schools and single parents. *Education Digest, 53*(2), 40–43.

Baron, A. (1991). Counseling Chicano college students. In C. Lee & B. Richardson (Eds.), *Multicultural issues in counseling: New approaches to diversity* (pp. 171–184). Alexandria, VA: American Association for Counseling and Development.

Baruth, L., & Manning, M. (1992). Understanding and counseling Hispanic American children, *Elementary School Guidance and Counseling, 27,* 113–122.

Bennett, W. (1987). AIDS and the education of our children. *Education, 108,* 135–137.

Bennett, W. (1993). *The index of leading cultural indicators* (Vol. 1). Washington, DC: Empower America, Heritage Foundation, & Free Congress Foundation.

Bepko, C. (1985). *The responsibility trap: A blueprint for treating the alcoholic family.* New York: Free Press.

Bertoia, J., & Allan, J. (1988). School management of the bereaved child. *Elementary School Guidance and Counseling, 23,* 30–38.

Black, C. (1981). Innocent bystanders at risk: The children of alcoholics. In G. Lawson, J. Peterson, & A. Lawson (Eds.), *Alcoholism and the family.* Rockville, MD: Aspen.

Blanco, R. (1972). *Prescription for children with learning and adjustment problems.* Springfield, IL: Charles C. Thomas.

Blum, H., Boyle, M., & Offord, D. (1988). Single-parent families: Child psychiatric disorder and school performance. *Journal of the American Academy of Child and Adolescent Psychiatry, 27,* 214–219.

Brake, K. (1988). Counseling young children of alcoholics. *Elementary School Guidance and Counseling, 23,* 106–111.

Browne, A., & Finkelhor, D. (1986). Impact of child sexual abuse: A review of the research. *Psychological Bulletin, 99,* 66–77.

Bruhn, J. (1989). Counseling persons with a fear of AIDS. *Journal of Counseling and Development, 67,* 455–457.

Bryan, S. H., Ganong, L. H., Coleman, M., & Bryan, L. R. (1985). Counselor's perceptions of stepparents and stepchildren. *Journal of Counseling Psychology, 32,* 279–282.

Bundy, M., & Boser, J. (1987). Helping latchkey children: A group guidance approach. *School Counselor, 35,* 58–66.

Buwick, A., Martin, D., & Martin, M. (1988). Helping children deal with alcoholism in their families. *Elementary School Guidance and Counseling, 23,* 112–117.

Carter, B. (1988). Counseling stepfamilies effectively: Stepfamily expert identifies major problems. *Children and Teens Today, 8*(8), 1.

Ceci, S., Ross, D., & Toglia, M. (1987). Suggestibility of children's memory: Psychological implications. *Journal of Experimental Psychology, 116,* 38–49.

Child abuse, parts I and II. (1993, Special supplement). *Harvard Mental Health Letter,* 1–6.

Child abuse, part III. (1993). *Harvard Mental Health Letter, 10*(1), 1–5.

Comstock, G. (1990). Television violence: Is there enough evidence that it is harmful? *Harvard Medical School Mental Health Letter, 6*(11), 8.

Cork, M. (1969). *The forgotten children.* Toronto: Alcoholism and Drug Addiction Research Foundation.

Costa, L., & Holliday, D. (1994). Helping children cope with the death of a parent. *Elementary School Guidance and Counseling, 28,* 206–213.

Courtois, C. (1980). Studying and counseling women with past incest experience. *Victimology: An International Journal, 5,* 322–334.

Crosbie-Burnett, M., & Pulvino, C. (1990). Children in nontraditional families: A classroom guidance program. *School Counselor, 37,* 286–293.

Cumberland Heights Alcohol and Drug Treatment Center (n.d.). *Facts.* Ashland City, TN: Author.

Cunningham, B., & Hare, J. (1989). Essential elements of a teacher in-service program on child bereavement. *Elementary School Guidance and Counseling, 23,* 175–182.

Dail, P. (1990). The psychosocial context of homeless mothers with young children: Program and policy implications. *Child Welfare League of America, 69*(4), 291–307.

Daniels, J. (1992). Empowering homeless children through school counseling. *Elementary School Guidance and Counseling, 27,* 104–112.

Diamond, S. (1985). *Helping children of divorce.* New York: Schocken.

Downey, D. (1994). The school performance of children from single mother and single father families: Economic or interpersonal deprivation? *Journal of Family Issues, 15,* 129–147.

Eddowes, E., & Hranitz, J. (1989). Educating children of the homeless. *Childhood Education, 65,* 197–200.

Eisenberg, S., & O'Dell, F. (1988). Teaching children to trust in a nontrusting world. *Elementary School Guidance and Counseling, 22,* 264–267.

Elkind, D. (1980). Child development and counseling. *Personnel and Guidance Journal, 58,* 353–355.

England, L. W., & Thompson, C. L. (1988). Counseling child sexual abuse victims: Myths and realities. *Journal of Counseling and Development, 66,* 370–373.

Finkelhor, D. (1979). *Sexually victimized children.* New York: Free Press.

Finkelhor, D. (1984). *Child sexual abuse: New theory and research.* New York: Free Press.

Frears, L. H., & Schneider, J. M. (1981). Exploring loss and grief within a holistic framework. *Personnel and Guidance Journal, 22,* 341–345.

Fuller, M. (1988). Facts and fictions about stepfamilies. *Education Digest, 54*(2), 52–54.

Garbarino, J., Guttmann, E., & Seeley, J. (1986). *The psychologically battered child.* San Francisco: Jossey-Bass.

Gardner, R. A. (1984). Counseling children in stepfamilies. *Elementary School Guidance and Counseling, 19,* 40–49.

Gately, D., & Schwebel, A. (1992). Favorable outcomes in children after parental divorce. In *Divorce and the Next Generation.* Binghamton, NY: Haworth.

Germain, R., Brassard, M., & Hart, S. (1985). Crisis intervention for maltreated children. *School Psychology Review, 14,* 291–299.

Gibbs, J. (1989). Biracial adolescents. In J. Gibbs & L. Huang (Eds.), *Children of color: Psychological interventions with minority youth* (pp. 322–350). San Francisco: Jossey-Bass.

Gibbs, J., & Huang, L. (1989). *Children of color: Psychological interventions with minority youth.* San Francisco: Jossey-Bass.

Goldman, R., & King, M. (1985). Counseling children of divorce. *School Psychology Review, 14,* 280–290.

Graves, B., Zuckermann, B., Marans, S., & Cohen, D. (1993). Silent victims: Children who witness violence (Commentary). *Journal of the American Medical Association 269,* 262–264.

Green, A. (1993). Child sexual abuse: Immediate and long-term effects and intervention. *Journal of the American Academy of Child and Adolescent Psychiatry, 32,* 890–902.

Greene, D. (1994). Childhood suicide and myths surrounding it. *Social Work, 39,* 145–147.

Grych, J., & Fincham, F. (1992). Interventions for children of divorce: Toward greater integration of research and action. *Psychological Bulletin, 111,* 434–454.

Guidubaldi, J. (1984). *Differences in children's divorce adjustment across grade level and gender: A report from the NASP–Kent State nationwide project.* Kent, OH: Kent State University.

Guidubaldi, J. (1989). The poor achievement of children of divorce. *Children and Teens Today, 9*(5), 5–6.

Guidubaldi, J., Perry, J. D., Cleminshaw, H. K., & McLoughlin, C. S. (1983). The impact of parental divorce on children: Report of a nationwide NASP study. *School Psychology Review, 12,* 300–323.

Gunsberg, A. (1989). Empowering young abused and neglected children through contingency play. *Childhood Education, 66*(1), 8-10.

Herring, R. (1990). Suicide in the middle school: Who said kids will not? *Elementary School Guidance and Counseling, 25,* 129–137.

Herring, R. (1991). Counseling Native American youth. In C. Lee & B. Richardson (Eds.), *Multicultural issues in counseling: New approaches to diversity* (pp. 37–47). Alexandria, VA: American Association for Counseling and Development.

Herring, R. (1992). Biracial children: An increasing concern for elementary and middle school counselors. *Elementary School Guidance and Counseling, 27,* 123–130.

Hetherington, E., Cox, M., & Cox, R. (1978). Play and social interaction in children following divorce. *Journal of Social Issues, 35,* 26–49.

Hill, M., & Peitzer, J. (1982). A report of thirteen groups for white parents of black children. *Family Relations, 31,* 557–565.

Holcomb, T. (1990). Fourth graders' attitudes toward AIDS issues: A concern for the elementary school counselor. *Elementary School Guidance and Counseling, 25,* 83–90.

Hollander, S. (1989). Coping with child sexual abuse through children's books. *Elementary School Guidance and Counseling, 23,* 183–193.

Holtgraves, M. (1986). Help the victims of sexual abuse help themselves, *Elementary School Guidance and Counseling, 21,* 155–159.

Hood, A., & Arceneaux, C. (1987). Multicultural counseling: Will what you don't know help you? *Counselor Education and Supervision, 26,* 173–175.

Huang, L., & Ying, Y. (1989). Chinese American children and adolescents. In J. Gibbs & L. Huang (Eds.), *Children of color: Psychological interventions with minority youth* (pp. 30–66). San Francisco: Jossey-Bass.

Ivey, A. (1987). Cultural intentionality: The core of effective helping. *Counselor Education and Supervision, 26,* 168–171.

Jacobsen, L., Rabinowitz, I., Popper, M., Solomon, R., Sokol, M., & Pfeffer, C. (1994). Interviewing prepubertal children about suicidal ideation and behavior. *Journal of the American Academy of Child and Adolescent Psychiatry, 33,* 439–452.

Jessee, P., Nagy, C., & Poteet-Johnson, D. (1993). Children with AIDS. *Childhood Education, 70,* 10–14.

Johnson, C. (1990). Inflicted injury versus accidental injury. *Pediatric Clinics of North America, 37,* 791–814.

Johnson, D., & Johnson, R. (1994). Constructive conflict in the schools. *Journal of Social Issues, 50,* 117–137.

Jones, D., & Houts, R. (1992). Parental drinking, parent-child communication, and social skills in young adults. *Journal of Studies on Alcohol, 53,* 48–56.

Kantrowitz, B., & Wingert, P. (1990 Winter-Spring). Step by step. *Newsweek Special Issue, 114,* 24–28.

Kavanagh, C. (1982). Emotional abuse and mental injury: A critique of the concepts and a recommendation for practice. *Journal of the American Academy of Child Psychiatry, 21,* 171–177.

Kavanaugh, K., Youngblade, L., Reid, J., & Fagot, B. (1988). Interactions between children and abusive versus control parents. *Journal of Clinical Child Psychology, 17*(2), 137–142.

Kirp, D., & Epstein, S. (1989). AIDS in America's schoolhouses: Learning the hard lessons. *Phi Delta Kappan, 70,* 585–593.

Kübler-Ross, E. (1969). *On death and dying.* New York: Macmillan.

Kupisch, S. (1984). Stepping in—to counseling with stepfamilies. *Virginia Counselors Journal, 12,* 38–43.

Kupisch, S. (1987). Stepfamilies. In A. Thomas & J. Grimes (Eds.), *Children's needs: Psychological perspectives* (pp. 578–585). Washington, DC: National Association of School Psychologists.

Kupisch, S., Rudolph, L., & Weed, E. (1984). *The impact of the divorce process in the family,* March 1983, Southeastern Psychological Association. Presentation published in ERIC/CAPS. *Resources in Education,* January 1984 (ERIC Document Reproduction Service No. ED 233 277).

Kurdek, L. & Berg, B. (1983). Correlates of children's adjustment to their parents' divorce. In L. Kurdek (Ed.), *Children and divorce: New directions for child development series, 19* (pp. 47–60). San Francisco: Jossey-Bass.

Kurdek, L., Blisk, D., & Siesky, A. (1981). Correlates of children's long-term adjustment to their parents' divorce. *Developmental Psychology, 17,* 565–579.

Kurtz, P., Gaudin, J., Wodarski, J., & Howing, P. (1993). Maltreatment and the school-aged child: School performance consequences. *Child Abuse and Neglect, 17,* 581–589.

LaFromboise, T., & Low, K. (1989). American Indian children and adolescents. In J. Gibbs & L. Huang (Eds.), *Children of color: Psychological interventions with minority youth* (pp. 114–147). San Francisco: Jossey-Bass.

Lane, P., & McWhirter, J. (1992). A peer mediation model: Conflict resolution for elementary and middle school children. *Elementary School Guidance and Counseling, 27,* 15–23.

Lawson, G., Peterson, J., & Lawson, A. (1983). *Alcoholism and the family.* Rockville, MD: Aspen Systems.

Lazarus, P. J. (1982). Counseling the Native American child: A question of values. *Elementary School Guidance and Counseling, 17,* 83–88.

Lee, C., & Richardson, B. (Eds.). (1991). *Multicultural issues in counseling: New approaches to diversity.* Alexandria, VA: American Association for Counseling and Development.

Lee, J., & Cynn, V. (1991). Issues in counseling 1.5 generation Korean Americans. In C. Lee & B. Richardson (Eds.), *Multicultural issues in counseling: New approaches to diversity.* (pp. 127–140). Alexandria, VA: American Association for Counseling and Development.

Lloyd, A. (1987). Multicultural counseling: Does it belong in a counselor education program? *Counselor Education and Supervision, 27,* 164–167.

Loftus, E. (1993). The reality of repressed memories. *American Psychologist, 48,* 518–537.

Lovko, A., & Ullman, D. (1989). Research on the adjustment of latchkey children: Role of background/demographic and latchkey situation variables. *Journal of Clinical Child Psychology, 18,* 16–24.

Manning, D., & Wooten, M. (1987). What stepparents perceive schools should know about blended families. *Clearing House,* 230–235.

Masten, A., Miliotis, D., Graham-Bermann, S., Ramirez, M., & Neemann, J. (1993). Children in homeless families: Risks to mental health and development. *Journal of Consulting and Clinical Psychology, 61,* 335–341.

Matter, D., & Matter, R. (1982). Developmental sequences in children's understanding of death with implications for counselors. *Elementary School Guidance and Counseling, 17,* 112–118.

Messing, J. (1993). Mediation: An intervention for counselors. *Journal of Counseling & Development, 72,* 67–71.

Moeller, T., Bachman, G., & Moeller, J. (1993). The combined effects of physical, sexual, and emotional abuse during childhood: Long-term health consequences for women. *Child Abuse and Neglect, 17,* 623–640.

Myer, R., James, D., & Street, T. (1987). Counseling internationally adopted children: A classroom meeting approach. *Elementary School Guidance and Counseling, 22,* 88–94.

Nagata, D. (1989). Japanese American children and adolescents. In J. Gibbs & L. Huang (Eds.), *Children of color: Psychological interventions with minority youth* (pp. 67–113). San Francisco: Jossey-Bass.

National Center of Child Abuse and Neglect. (1978). *Child sexual abuse: Incest, assault, and sexual exploitation.* Special report. United States Department of Health, Education, and Welfare, Pub. No. (OHDDDS) 79-30166.

Neese, L. (1989). Psychological maltreatment in schools: Emerging issues for counselors. *Elementary School Guidance and Counseling, 23,* 194–200.

Nelson, R., & Crawford, B. (1990). Suicide among elementary school-aged children. *Elementary School Guidance and Counseling, 25,* 123–128.

Newlon, B., & Furrow, W. (1986). Using the classroom to identify children from alcoholic homes. *School Counselor, 33,* 286–291.

O'Brien, S. (1989, Summer). "Only the lonely": The latchkey child. *For Parents Particularly,* pp. 231–232.

Oehmen, S. (1985). Divorce and grief: Counseling and the child. *Elementary School Guidance and Counseling, 19,* 314–317.

Omizo, M., & Omizo, S. (1987). *Children and adults of divorce: Group intervention strategies.* Paper presented at the annual Hawaii Association for Counseling and Development Conference, Honolulu.

O'Rourke, K. (1990). Recapturing hope: Elementary School support groups for children of alcoholics. *Elementary School Guidance and Counseling, 25,* 107–115.

Pederson, P. (1994). *A Handbook for developing multicultural awareness.* Alexandria, VA: American Counseling Association.

Peterson, L. (1989). Latchkey children's preparation for self-care: Overestimated, underrehearsed, and unsafe. *Journal of Clinical Child Psychology, 18,* 36–43.

Peterson, L., & Magrab, P. (1989). Introduction to the special section: Children on their own. *Journal of Clinical Child Psychology, 18,* 2–7.

Ponterotto, J., & Benesch, K. (1988). An organizational framework for understanding the role of culture in counseling. *Journal of Counseling and Development, 66,* 237–241.

Prosen, S. S., & Farmer, J. H. (1982). Understanding stepfamilies: Issues and implications for counselors. *Personnel and Guidance Journal, 60,* 393–397.

Ramirez, O. (1989). Mexican American children and adolescents. In J. Gibbs & L. Huang (Eds.), *Children of color: Psychological interventions with minority youth* (pp. 224–250). San Francisco: Jossey-Bass.

Ratican, K. (1992). Sexual abuse survivors: Identifying symptoms and special treatment considerations. *Journal of Counseling & Development, 71,* 33–38.

Reed, S. (1988). Children with AIDS: How schools are handling the crisis. *Phi Delta Kappan, 70,* 1–11.

Reich, W., Earls, F., Frankel, O., & Shayka, J. (1993). Psychopathology in children of alcoholics. *Journal of the American Academy of Child and Adolescent Psychiatry, 32,* 995–1002.

Richards, L., & Schmiege, C. (1993). Problems and strengths of single-parent families: Implications for practice and policy. *Family Relations, 42,* 277–285.

Richardson, B. (1991). Utilizing the resources of the African American church: Strategies for counseling professionals. In C. Lee & B. Richardson (Eds.), *Multicultural issues in counseling: New approaches to diversity* (pp. 65–75). Alexandria, VA: American Association for Counseling and Development.

Roberts, W. Jr. (1995). Postvention and psychological autopsy in the suicide of a 14-year-old public school student. *School Counselor, 42,* 322–330.

Roehl, J., & Burns, S. (1985). Talking to sexually abused children: A guide for teachers. *Childhood Education, 62,* 19–22.

Rudin, M. (1990). Cults and satanism: Threats to teens. *NASSP Bulletin, 74*(526), 46–52.

Sandberg, D., Crabbs, S., & Crabbs, M. (1988). Legal issues in child abuse: Questions and answers for counselors. *Elementary School Guidance and Counseling, 22,* 268–273.

Schaefer, C., Briesmeister, J., & Fitton, M. (1984). *Family therapy techniques for problem behaviors of children and teenagers.* San Francisco: Jossey-Bass.

Seattle Institute for Child Advocacy, Committee for Children (1985). *Talking about touching: A personal safety curriculum.* Seattle: Author.

Sebring, D. L. (1985). Considerations in counseling interracial children. *Journal of Non-White Concerns in Personnel and Guidance, 13,* 3–9.

Segal, R. (1984). Helping children express grief through symbolic communication. *Social Casework: The Journal of Contemporary Social Work, 65,* 590–599.

Seilhamer, R., Jacob, T., & Dunn, N. (1993). The impact of alcohol consumption on parent-child relationships in families of alcoholics. *Journal of Studies on Alcohol, 54,* 189–193.

Shaffer, C., Godwin, P., & Richmond, S. (1987, December). Talking to kids about AIDS. *Changing Times,* p. 23.

Shreeve, W., Goetter, W., Bunn, A., Norby, J., Stueckle, A., Midgley, T., & de Michele, B. (1986). Single parents and students' achievements–a national tragedy. *Early Child Development and Care, 23,* 175–184.

Siehl, P. (1990). Suicide postvention: A new disaster plan—What a school should do when faced with a suicide. *School Counselor, 38,* 52–57.

Smith, E. (1982). Counseling psychology in the market place: The status of ethnic minorities. *Counseling Psychologist, 10,* 61–68.

Spiegel, L. (1988). Child abuse hysteria and the elementary school counselor. *Elementary School Guidance and Counseling, 22,* 275–283.

Stefanowski-Harding, S. (1990). Suicide and the school counselor. *School Counselor, 37,* 328–336.

Strangeland, C., Pellegreno, D., & Lundholm, C. (1989). Children of divorced parents: A perceptual comparison. *Elementary School Guidance and Counseling, 23,* 167–173.

Sue, D. (1977). Counseling the culturally different: A conceptual analysis. *Personnel and Guidance Journal, 55,* 422–425.

Sue, D., & Sue, D. W. (1990) *Counseling the culturally different: Theory and practice* (2nd ed.). New York: Wiley.

Sue, D. W. (1978). Counseling across cultures. *Personnel and Guidance Journal, 56,* 451.

Sue, D. W., & Sue, D. (1977). Barriers to effective cross-cultural counseling. *Journal of Counseling Psychology, 24,* 420–429.

Swander, K. (1987, January). *Death and dealing with children's grief.* Paper presented to the Smokey Mountain Association for Counseling and Development, University of Tennessee, Knoxville,

Television violence: is there enough evidence that it is harmful? (1990). *Harvard Mental Health Letter, 6*(11), 8.

Tennant, C. (1988). Preventive sexual abuse programs: Problems and possibilities. *Elementary School Guidance and Counseling, 23,* 48–53.

Tomine, S. (1991). Counseling Japanese Americans: From internment to reparation. In C. Lee & B. Richardson (Eds.), *Multicultural issues in counseling: New approaches to diversity* (pp. 91–105). Alexandria, VA: American Association for Counseling and Development.

U.S. Department of Health, Education, and Welfare. (1975). *Child abuse and neglect: A report on the status of research. Washington, DC: U.S. Government Printing Office.*

Vernon, A., & Hay, J. (1988). A preventative approach to child sexual abuse. *Elementary School Guidance and Counseling, 22,* 306–327.

Violence and violent patients: Part 1. *Harvard Mental Health Letter, 7*(12), 1–4.

Visher, E., & Visher, J. (1979). *Stepfamilies: A guide to working with stepparents and stepchildren.* New York: Brunner/Mazel.

Walker, D., & Hulecki, M. (1989). Is AIDS a biasing factor in teacher judgment? *Exceptional Children, 55*(4), 342–345.

Wallerstein, J. (1983). Children of divorce: The psychological tasks of the child. *American Journal of Orthopsychiatry, 53,* 230–243.

Wallerstein, J. (1984). Children of divorce: Ten-year follow-up of young children. *American Journal of Orthopsychiatry, 54,* 444–458.

Wallerstein, J., & Blakeslee, S. (1989). *Second chances.* New York: Ticknor & Fields.

Wallerstein, J., & Kelly, J. (1980). *Surviving the breakup: How children and parents cope with divorce.* New York: Basic Books.

Weddle, C., & Wishon, P. (1986, January/February). Children of alcoholics: What we should know; how we can help. *Children Today,* 8–12.

Wegscheider, S. (1981). *Another chance: Hope and health for the alcoholic family.* Palo Alto, CA: Science and Behavior Books.

Welburn, B. (1989). Someone at school has AIDS: A guide to developing policies for students and staff members who are infected with HIV. In I. Rosofsky (Ed.), *Children and teens today, 9*(14), (p. 5). New York: ATCOM.

Werner, E. E., & Smith, R. S. (1982). *Vulnerable but invincible: A study of resilient children.* New York: McGraw-Hill.

Wheeler, B., Wood, S., & Hatch, R. (1988). Assessment and interventions with adolescents involved in satanism. *Social Work, 33,* 547–550.

Wilson, J., & Blocher, L. (1990). The counselor's role in assisting children of alcoholics. *Elementary School Guidance and Counseling, 25,* 98–106.

Wrenn, C. G. (1976). Values and counseling in different countries and cultures. *School Counselor, 24,* 6–14.

Wubbolding, R. (1989). Professional issues: Four stages of decision making in suicidal recovery. *Journal of Reality Therapy, 8*(2), 57–61.

Yapko, M. (1993). Suggested guidelines for professional counselors. *Guidepost, 36,* 11.

Zeppa, A., & Norem, R. (1993). Stressors, manifestations of stress, and first-family/stepfamily group membership. *Journal of Divorce and Remarriage, 19,* 3–23.

Chapter 16

◆

Counseling with
Exceptional Children

THE SITUATION
OF EXCEPTIONAL CHILDREN

Exceptional children are different in some way from their peers. They deviate from what is considered to be normal or average in physical appearance, learning abilities, or behavior. They may be exceptionally gifted, or they may be exceptionally limited in their abilities to learn or to function in life.

Unfortunately, many societies throughout history have not readily accepted people with disabilities and instead viewed them as evil omens, demons, or even witches. At one point in history, people with disabilities were court jesters or on display in public streets or parks. In our not-too-distant history, people with disabilities were hidden in institutions that provided inadequate care. During the Middle Ages especially, a mentally or physically "defective" person was often considered possessed by evil spirits. Some have felt that children with disabilities were God's punishment for the sins of the parents. Some Native American tribes murdered children who had disabilities; other tribes, however, worshiped them as gods, loving and protecting them. In recent years, society is recognizing the special needs of these children and treating people with disabilities more humanely. It has placed more emphasis on meeting these children's physical, psychological, and educational needs in a nonrestrictive environment (outside an institution) and on providing support for the families through groups, associations, and legislation.

Although all of us deviate from the average to some degree—in height or weight, introversion or extroversion, the amount of happiness or sadness in our lives—myths concerning exceptional individuals still pervade our society. These individuals continue to be stereotyped, shunned, rejected, pitied, hidden in the closet, or wrongfully institutionalized. Buscaglia (1975) stated:

Though they may not be aware of it at the time, the infant born with a birth defect and the adult who is crippled later in life will be limited not so much by the actual disability as much as by society's attitude regarding the disability. It is society, for the most part, that will define the disability as a handicap and it is the individual who will suffer from this definition. (p. 11)

Too often, counseling with the exceptional child has been limited to assessment, assigning a vague diagnosis, and perhaps suggesting a prognosis. Parents and children then cope with the developmental and adjustment problems as best they can. Usually, the parents or children get no thorough explanation of the condition. They do not learn what to expect in terms of learning, social, or behavior problems, and counselors do not help the parents and children adjust to and cope with the handicapping condition. Doctors, nurses, teachers, and counselors are inadequately prepared to work with the problems of being different in a society that has little tolerance for and understanding of the different.

Being a special child presents problems to both the parents and the special child. Parents are confused about the disability. They have fears concerning their child's present and future life. They may experience feelings of guilt ("Did I cause this?"), self-pity ("Why did it have to happen to me?"), or even self-hate. Parents who are confronted with the fact that their child is disabled do not all react in the same manner. Hardman, Drew, Egan, and Wolf (1993) suggested that most parents initially react with shock, which may be accompanied by feelings of anxiety, guilt, numbness, confusion, helplessness, anger, disbelief, or denial. Realization follows and may be characterized by self-pity or self-hate and withdrawal. The parent may enter a defensive retreat stage in order to avoid facing reality. When parents move on to the acknowledgment stage, they are able to participate in the treatment process and may even become an advocate for the cause (Hardman et al., 1993). Having special children necessitates paying for medical specialists, diagnostic tests, special schools or teachers, and special therapies. Having special children causes a strain on personal resources and family relationships. Often the children must have extra attention and care. The time and energy required may take away the pleasure that could be derived from relationships with husband or wife, other children, or friends.

What will happen to the special child when he or she grows up? Will this child be self-supporting and able to find happiness, or will the child be rejected by the world, require institutionalization, or possibly become a criminal? These and many other worries, frustrations, fears, and questions plague the parent of the exceptional child.

What are the personal thoughts and concerns of the special child? From an early age, these children begin to realize they are different in some manner. This difference is often interpreted to mean "not as good as" other children. They cannot ride a bike like the kid next door; they look different from the child down the street; they do not understand jokes or what is going on in their surroundings; they are not accepted by the gang and are called *weirdo*, *dumb*, *retard*, or a multitude of other hurtful names. Even gifted children bear the burden of nicknames such as *weirdo* or *brain* and may feel rejection because of their exceptionality. The same messages are sometimes subtly conveyed to the children by parents and other significant adults. From verbal and nonverbal signals and interactions, the children are soon assured by the world that being different means being odd, inferior, or worthless.

Growth and maturity bring special problems to both child and parents. Upon entering school, some exceptional children have academic problems. The child may compensate for problems by withdrawing from the school world physically or psychologically, or the child may become a behavior problem. After all, better that others think "I do not want to learn" than "I cannot learn." Social relationships may be a disaster; peers often do not understand the exceptionality. No one discusses exceptionalities with other children because society is uncomfortable with the idea of difference. This lack of understanding interferes with friendship, and classmates tend to isolate, reject, and taunt the special child. School can be a very painful place.

At home, things may not be much better, especially at report card time and when notes come home from the teacher or principal: "Johnny is not doing well in school; he must study harder." "Johnny is misbehaving in class; we simply cannot tolerate disruptive behavior." No one seems to understand that these learning and behavior problems may have underlying causes. Because most parents are ego-involved with their children's academic achievement, they may pressure the child to study harder or behave more appropriately. Perhaps Johnny has been working hard but still cannot meet the expectations of parents and school. He may decide, "What's the use? I can't please them no matter how hard I try." Unless someone intervenes, society may have lost the opportunity to help Johnny become a productive citizen and a happy adult.

Progress toward helping exceptional children become accepted members of society has been slow. The 1880s saw the first steps toward recognizing the needs of persons with disabilities: the establishment of the first schools for the deaf and the blind. In the mid-1930s, Congress passed the Crippled Children Act, authorizing financial aid to families of the orthopedically handicapped. President Franklin D. Roosevelt, a victim of polio and having a disability himself, undoubtedly gave impetus to this legislation. President John F. Kennedy, who had a mentally retarded sister, urged that attention be given to children's developmental disabilities, including mental retardation and learning disabilities. In 1961, a President's Panel on Mental Retardation was established, and in 1963 a National Institute of Child Health and Human Development was founded.

The child advocacy movement of the late 1960s and early 1970s resulted in the formation of the National Center for Child Advocacy. During the 1970s and 1980s, legislative appropriations and federal committees and agencies increased. In 1975, President Ford signed the Education for All Handicapped Children Act, Public Law 94-142. This law provided that all handicapped children receive free educational experiences designed to meet their particular needs. It described specific procedures for identification and placement and for designing educational programs for children with certain disabling conditions. In 1977, the Education of the Handicapped Act was amended to define *learning disabilities,* and in 1978 the Gifted and Talented Children's Education Act provided money to states for planning, training, program development, and research. Amendments in 1983 extended the act to provide additional services to secondary school students and children from birth to 3 years (Wolf & Stephens, 1986). The Education for All Handicapped Children Act was renamed Individuals with Disabilities Act (IDEA) in 1990, and two new categories of disability were added: autism and traumatic brain injury (Hardman et al., 1993). Smith and Luckasson (1995) reported that 4,994,169 children and youth from birth through age 21 studied in programs under IDEA in the 1991–92 school year. In 1990 President Bush extended the 1973 Rehabilitation Act (section 504), which prohibited discrimination against qualified individuals in federally funded programs and protected the rights of students with disabilities to free and appropriate public education, when he signed the Americans with Disabilities Act (ADA), which prohibits discrimination against persons with disabilities in employment, transportation, public services, public accommodations, and telecommunications, regardless of federal funding (Smith & Luckasson, 1995; Hardman et al., 1993).

Children with disabilities and their families face considerable stress in their daily living, an area of special need that must be addressed by helping professionals. One wonders how many of the 4,994,169 children and youth served by special education programs in 1991–92 also received the services of a counselor to help them deal with their daily developmental needs and stresses.

Parette and Holder-Brown (1992) stated that counselor involvement with school-age children with disabilities is mandated by Public Law 94-142, the Education for All Handicapped Children Act of 1975 (now IDEA). They pointed out that counselors are required by law to participate with multidisciplinary teams to develop individualized educational plans (IEPs). Collaboration with families is required by Public Law 99-457 of the Education of the Handicapped Act (EHA) of 1986 to implement an individualized family service plan (IFSP).

We have defined *counseling* as a therapeutic relationship, a problem-solving process, a reeducation, and a method for changing behavior. We have also discussed counseling as a method for helping children cope with developmental problems and as a preventive process. Who more than exceptional children, constantly faced with rejection and failure, need an accepting relationship, someone to listen, assistance in setting present and future goals, guidance for improving interpersonal relationships, and, perhaps most important, help in building a strong self-concept and confidence? Counseling with the exceptional child requires no magic formula; however, it does require counselor dedication to the philosophy that all individuals are unique and capable of growth to reach their potential.

Counseling literature has suggested many ways of counseling with children's developmental and behavioral problems, but not enough research has been conducted in the area of counseling with the special problems of exceptional children. Even less research has been done with families of exceptional children.

METHODS FOR COUNSELING
WITH EXCEPTIONAL CHILDREN

Some recent literature has covered the topic of counseling the exceptional child. However, the results of much of this research are inconclusive, many studies contain methodological problems, and many of the articles offer opinions or suggest methods of counseling without citing research to support their efficacy. A few articles focus on counseling with the families of exceptional children; others suggest methods for working with children who are gifted or who have learning disabilities or behavioral disorders. The suggestions for counseling exceptional children in this chapter are a combination of research and theory published in the literature. As is true with most counseling methods, the counseling strategies should be incorporated into a positive, accepting counseling relationship.

To understand the world of the exceptional child, counselors need to have a basic knowledge of the disabling condition. What are the symptoms and general characteristics of a child with this exceptionality? What are the child's limitations? What are the child's strengths and potentials? All children have some developmental and psychological needs in common, but are other needs specific to the exceptional condition that must be considered? The counselor does not need to become an expert in the teaching techniques of special education, but knowledge of the needs and characteristics of these children is necessary for effective counseling.

Perhaps the primary concern of the counselor working with exceptional children should be the child's self-concept. Bailey and Winton (1986) called the school years particularly difficult for the handicapped child because the self-concept may be eroded.

> It may be during this period that a younger sibling matches or exceeds the handicapped child's academic performance. Furthermore, it is during the school-age years, when children's peer relations are so critical, that handicapped children are more likely to experience rejection or overt teasing or hostility from their nonhandicapped peers. (pp. 89–90)

Although the authors were writing about the need for parents to help their child develop and maintain a positive self-concept, this task would certainly need to be addressed by counselors who work with children with disabilities.

A person's self-concept begins to form early in life based on the feedback of significant persons in the child's world. In daily interactions, parents, friends, teachers, and peers send verbal and nonverbal messages to children about their worth and abilities. Exceptional children, even the gifted, often receive negative messages about their worth. Loeb and Jay (1987) found that gifted boys in the elementary grades have a more negative self-image than other boys because they do not conform to the stereotype of the traditional ideal male. Parents of children with disabilities may feel guilty or overprotective, friends and peers may pity these children or see them as a burden, and teachers may resent having to work with them. "Normal" people feel uncomfortable with "different" children for a variety of reasons. Because most exceptional children experience some type of rejection and failure, that many have negative self-concepts is not surprising.

In professional's attempts to diagnose and find help for a child with special problems, the child as a person is sometimes forgotten in the proliferation of testing, diagnosing, and planning. These procedures that are designed to aid the child may increase self-doubts and fears. Testing, diagnosing, and planning are necessary, but they cannot replace a good relationship—one in which the child feels free to express fears, anxieties, doubts, and insecurities. Being listened to is being respected. It may begin the process of developing or restoring a more positive self-evaluation. Building a better self-concept includes helping exceptional children see themselves as people who can and do perform and accomplish goals. Unfortunately, most people tend to focus on such children's limitations rather than emphasize their strengths and what they can do, encourage them to take responsibility for decisions about their own lives, and assist them in finding ways to live productive lives.

CATEGORIES OF EXCEPTIONALITY

A controversy exists over the categorizing or labeling of children as *learning disabled, mentally retarded, deaf,* and so on. Hobbs (1975) pointed out that children who are so categorized may be permanently stigmatized, rejected, or prevented from developing in a healthy manner. These children, especially if they are minority children, may be assigned to inferior educational programs, institutionalized, or sterilized because of poor diagnoses. Minority children, those most often categorized or labeled exceptional, are often the very children who need special attention or educational services to encourage their achievement. Furthermore, classification of a child can encourage the behaviors characteristic of the label.

Lerner (1989) cautioned that labels may stigmatize but they may help professionals communicate. She suggested labels may be necessary because removal of one term leads to a new categorical label to take its place. Classification is also necessary to obtain services for exceptional children. Children who do not neatly fit categories may have trouble obtaining diagnostic services and treatment.

Smith, Price, and Marsh (1986) argued, however, for adoption of a noncategorical or generic approach to serving children with disabilities in that categorical descriptions are meaningless in a system that is moving to meet the needs of mildly disabling conditions, such as those of the educable mentally retarded, the learning disabled, and the mildly emotionally disturbed or behavioral disordered. The definitions and descriptions of these disorders are often similar and overlapping. In addition, the authors pointed out that these children are more likely to be educationally served in a school resource room that does not differentiate handicapping conditions. They concluded that the similarities among children with disabilities are greater than the differences and contended that institutional methods do not differ significantly. Therefore, Smith et al. seek ways to serve an inclusive category of "mildly handicapped" individuals rather than discretely labeled groups of children.

Smith and Luckasson (1995) noted that a classification system for special education "enables us to name disabilities, to differentiate one from another, and to communicate in a meaningful and efficient way about a specific disability" (p. 9–10). In addition, a classification system is useful because it is necessary for research, for lobbying for improved services, and for relating specific treatments to specific disabilities.

Despite differences of opinion about categorization, the U.S. Department of Education reports the number of children receiving special education services for specific disabilities each year. Discussing each exceptionality individually is beyond the scope of this chapter; therefore, this chapter includes a general discussion of gifted, mentally retarded, learning-disabled, and physically handicapped children and children categorized as having behavioral disorders. These conditions seem to be the most generally recognized exceptionalities and the conditions counselors are most apt to encounter daily. Although attention-deficit disorders are not among the exceptional conditions listed by the U.S. Department of Education as special education services provided, this condition is included here because of its increasing diagnosis.

The Gifted Child

Much of the discussion so far focused on children with disabilities or some handicapping condition. However, children who are gifted are also considered exceptional, and they, too, face unique problems related to their exceptionality. Hallahan and Kauffman (1986) noted that giftedness should be fostered but that the gifted child who appears intellectually superior or achieving risks stigma and rejection. They also believe that most of us feel a moral obligation to help disadvantaged or handicapped children but are unsure of our obligation to help those children who already have so much.

The definition of giftedness accepted by the U.S. Department of Education in 1978 is as follows:

> Gifted and talented children means children, and whenever applicable, youth, who are identified at the preschool, elementary, or secondary level as possessing demonstrated or potential abilities that give evidence of high performance capability in areas such as intellectual, creative, specific academic, or leadership ability, or in the performing and visual arts, and who by reason thereof require services or activities not ordinarily provided by the school. (Congressional Record, 1978, H-12179, cited in Wolf & Stephens, 1986, pp. 438–439)

Note that the definition includes not only intellectual ability but also creative, leadership, and performing ability and other outstanding characteristics. Hallahan and Kauffman (1986) emphasized that many definitions of giftedness developed during the last two decades have included "exceptional academic ability, exceptional creativity, existence of special talents, superior achievement beyond peers in any value line of activity, [and] inclusion in the top *x* percent of children according to any criterion of giftedness" (p. 388). They believe that these defini- tions still include some children erroneously and exclude others who are gifted. The incidence of gifted and talented children is difficult to determine because of the variety of criteria various states have adopted, but most estimates range around 3% to 5% of the population; some estimates go as high as 20%. According to Smith and Luckasson (1995), the states do not report to the federal government the number of gifted children receiving services (in that this category is not funded by IDEA), and no other national reporting mechanism exists. In addition, not all school systems provide programs for the gifted. Hardman, et al. (1993) reported that from 3% to 15% of students in school may be described as gifted.

Describing all the characteristics of a person considered gifted is difficult. Terman and Oden (1947) attempted to describe the characteristics of the gifted in their studies during the early 1930s. They dispelled many of the myths concerning the gifted, but their studies focused primarily on the academically gifted. The characteristics identified do not seem adequate to describe the gifted or talented child of today. Because the definition of giftedness covers many different areas, a restrictive list of traits that could screen out a gifted student or talented child seems unfair. Wolf and Stephens (1986) pointed out that identifying gifted and talented children is difficult because they are an extremely heterogeneous group and because certain kinds of giftedness are hard to identify. Schools often use intelligence and achievement tests, tests of creativity, teacher recommendations, and parent, peer, and self-referrals. Although none of these methods alone is adequate, used in combination, they contribute to the identification process.

Because schools see gifted and talented children as outstanding in many ways (especially academically), teachers have not recognized that these children, too, may need the counselor's intervention to cope with social or emotional problems. Most people believe that the bright can solve almost any problem and find their way without help; they forget that the bright child may have problems in relationships with friends because of advanced intellectual or creative interests. Some writers (Allen & Fox, 1979; Betts, 1986) have suggested that gifted children's potential, many talents, and attention from others may obscure their emotional and social problems. The gifted often feel isolated and alienated and experience low self-esteem and underachievement. Strong, Lynch, and Smith (1987) stated that school personnel should help parents find programs, services, and financial resources for gifted children, especially gifted children from minority or other cultural groups. They also contended that career planning assistance is essential. Alexander and Muia (1982) suggested that gifted and talented youngsters need the counselor's help in recognizing the variety of career options open to them. Such children possess knowledge beyond their years but lack the physical and emotional ability to cope with this knowledge. The pressures parents, teachers, peers, and society place on gifted and talented children may be strong and overwhelming.

Wolf and Penrod (1980) cited bibliotherapy as an effective counseling technique for gifted and talented children. These children are often avid readers who can be helped to solve problems in their lives through guided reading. As with other clients, the counselor should discuss the reading with the child and assist him or her in finding an appropriate solution for the situation.

Culross (1982) stated that the guidance and counseling needs of the gifted include the need to recognize and accept one's own abilities, interests, and limitations; the need to recognize and accept the abilities, interests, and limitations of others; the need for adequate social relationships; the need to explore, discover, and create; the need for appropriate problem-solving skills; the need to develop one's abilities without regard to race, sex, or ethnic group; the need to work independently and to participate in decision making; the need to understand the attitudes of parents or teachers; the need to set realistic goals and to evaluate realistically; and the need to be challenged (p. 25). She suggested a number of services to form a core of support for gifted and talented children.

The counselor may want gifted or talented children in heterogeneous groups of peers to develop relationship skills or discuss concerns of mutual interest, or a homogeneous group of gifted and talented youngsters may want to meet to discuss their particular concerns. Barnette (1989) found that a 3-week group workshop for gifted and talented adolescents that included structured activities, community meetings, singing, meditating, poetry, and metaphorical readings "appeared to be successful in stimulating growth in personal worth and interpersonal relationships as well as growth of special gifts and talents" (p. 527).

Counseling with gifted and talented children presents a challenge to the counselor. These children are often very independent and want to solve their own problems. They are also bright enough to compensate or to disguise many of their concerns. They are perceptive and recognize insensitivity or inconsistencies immediately.

According to Smith and Luckasson (1995), the gifted child may exhibit the ability to reason abstractly, conceptualize, process information well, solve problems, and learn quickly. The child may exhibit intellectual curiosity, show wide interests, avoid drill and routine, demonstrate unevenness at times in learning, generalize learning, remember large amounts of material, demonstrate high levels of verbal ability, and tend to prefer learning in a quiet environment. Socially and emotionally, the gifted child criticizes self, empathizes, plays with older friends, persists, is sensitive to others' feelings, exhibits individualism, has strength of character, shows leadership qualities, is concerned about ethical issues, takes risks, is independent and autonomous, has a mature sense of humor, and is nonconforming, characteristics that can be of help to a gifted child. Because of their gifts and talents, gifted children can be responsive clients.

Children with Emotional or Behavioral Disorders

Problems exist in defining an emotionally disturbed (ED) child or one considered to have a behavioral disorder (BD). Cullinan and Epstein (1986) noted that one issue in attempting to define ED and BD is the subjectivity of standards that can vary by age, sex, subculture, community, politics, and economic conditions. An additional problem, they suggested, is that too few assessment tools are available to measure the social, emotional, and behavioral problems of children. Smith and Luckasson (1995) reported that IDEA has adopted the term "serious emotional disturbance" to describe children with behavioral disorders and emotional disturbance. "Serious emotional disturbance" means that a child exhibits inability to learn that cannot be explained by other factors such as intellectual, sensory, or health problems; an inability to form satisfactory interpersonal relationships with peers and teachers; inappropriate displays of feelings or behavior; pervasive unhappiness or depression; or the development of physical symptoms associated with personal or school problems. The condition must have been present to a marked extent over a period of time and must substantially interfere with the child's educational achievement. The term includes schizophrenic children but excludes those whose problems result from social maladjustment.

Because of the definitions' lack of clarity, estimates of the prevalence of ED and BD vary widely; however, most estimate that 3% to 6% of the population have some kind of ED or BD. Professionals in the helping professions estimate that 19% to 22% of children have some type of emotional problem and should be referred for help (Smith & Luckasson, 1995). Brandenburg, Friedman, and Silver (1990) suggested that the number of children in this category receiving special education is less than one third of those who need such programs, probably because of the ambiguity of the criteria and definition.

Historically, emotional and behavior disorders were attributed to causes ranging from evil spirits to subconscious factors, but recent researchers have focused on "inappropriate learning and complex interactions that take place between individuals and their environments" (Hardman et al., 1993, p. 147) and biological causes such as biochemical substances, brain abnormalities or injuries, and chromosomal problems. Hardman et al. suggested insight therapy, play therapy, group counseling, behavior therapy, marital and family therapy, and drug therapy; the counselor must be ready to coordinate services from many specialists in order to serve ED-BD children effectively.

Emotional disturbances or behavioral disorders also may be classified according to degree.* Severe disorders (psychoses) such as childhood schizophrenia and autism usually require treatment by psychiatrists and possibly institutionalization. Children with mild to moderate problems, those discussed in this section, ordinarily function relatively well in the home environment and are educated in the public schools. Their behaviors may include cruelty, fighting, extreme tantrums, disobedience, hyperactivity, impulsivity, social maladjustment, anxiety, low self-confidence, withdrawal, and low intellectual performance and achievement (Cullinan & Epstein, 1986). Again, counselors are cautioned to note the frequency and intensity of such behaviors to make sure they are extreme and not a part of normal childhood development.

---

* Counselors may wish to refer to the DSM-IV for classifications or to Appendixes A and B which describe specific behavior problems with appropriate DSM-IV classifications.

Smith and Luckasson (1995) listed the possible indicators of behavioral and emotional disorders as few or no friends, problems with family relations, problems with teacher relationships, hyperactive behavior, aggression to self or others, impulsivity, immature social skills, feelings of depression and unhappiness, withdrawal into self, anxiety or fearfulness, expression of ideas of suicide, distractibility, and inability to pay attention for an appropriate length of time. Further, the authors stated that the children usually have lower academic performance than expected for their age and social skills deficits, as well as the obvious behavior problems and internal conflicts described. They recommended behavior modification strategies, individual and family counseling, moral education, and character training. The counselor should be in contact with other professionals working with these children—teachers, medical doctors, specialists, and others—in order to coordinate all services for the ED-BD child.

The disturbance or behavior could be due to physiological causes or environmental factors. Children are expected to learn what is acceptable behavior and unacceptable behavior from socialization agents such as parents and schools. Right and wrong are taught through a system of rewards and punishments meted out by adults. Children depend less on these external reinforcements as the conscience, or internal control, develops. Because of individual differences, children vary in reaction to this training and their willingness to adapt to adult standards.

Cullinan and Epstein (1986) stated that behavioral disorders are often discerned from observing and interpreting behaviors that indicate mental or emotional problems; from the frequency and/or intensity of behaviors that deviate from the "normal"; from impaired functioning that may include self-deprecating remarks, excessive anxiety, sadness or depression, a lack of academic skills, short attention span, or outwardly aggressive behaviors; and from other disorders such as hyperactivity, social problems, or other learning disorderrs. These symptoms can have biological or psychological causes.

These children need love and understanding, and they need a counselor who can provide security and stability. The counselor who is effective with ED-BD children can detect and reflect the feelings and frustrations of the children, discuss these feelings, and decide how to manage them effectively. Much of the success achieved from working with the emotionally disturbed has been due to the relationship between adult and child as well as to the technique used. These children have often experienced inconsistency in their relationships and may be suspicious of adults because of past experiences with hurtful people. The counselor needs to be strong enough to place consistent limits on the children and require them to assume responsibility for their behavior.

To bring consistency and stability to the life of the ED-BD child, the counselor can discuss expected and appropriate behaviors with the child. Writing out what is considered inappropriate and the consequences of this behavior is often helpful. The counselor can define expected behaviors by such methods as contracting. The counselor, parents, teachers, and all significant people in the child's life must be willing to set limits and consistently maintain the rules. Behavior modification techniques emphasizing positive reinforcement have been effective. Relaxation exercises, talking therapy, physical activities, writing, drawing, or games may be scheduled into the child's day to provide outlets for tension and other emotions. Changes in the environment, expectations, stimulation, and conflicts should be as minimal as possible. Peer groups can be effective reinforcers who provide models for appropriate behavior.

Drug therapy was used widely in the mid-1900s to treat behavioral-disordered–emotionally disturbed children, especially those with acting-out behaviors or attention disorders. Smith et al. (1986) expressed reservations about this treatment and preferred behavioral techniques. They summarized the literature on the effectiveness of drug therapy by reporting that findings do not necessarily show improved learning and behavior and that drugs sometimes cause negative side effects. The researchers also found that, despite the variety of techniques available for treating this disorder, drugs are often used as a first treatment rather than as a last resort.

The tasks of the counselor of an ED-BD child can be summarized as (1) forming a counseling relationship with the child that includes well-defined responsibilities and limits; (2) working to change the child's image and expectations through counseling and consultation with family and other significant people in the child's world; (3) conducting individual and group counseling to deal with feelings and behaviors, teach social skills, and improve academic performance; and (4) assisting parents and teachers in structuring the child's physical environment and schedule, establishing rules for behavior, and providing encouragement, reinforcement, and logical consequences for misbehavior.

The Learning-Disabled Child

According to Lerner (1989), the term *learning disabilities* was first introduced in 1963 by a group of parents of children with various disorders labeled as neurological. The various definitions of learning disabilities (LD) that have been proposed over the years have been ambiguous in many cases and quite controversial.

The Education for All Handicapped Children Act, Public Law 94-142, which was passed in 1975 and became effective in 1977 (now IDEA), defined learning disabilities as follows:

"Specific learning disability" means a disorder in one or more of the basic psychological processes involved in understanding or in using language, spoken or written, which may manifest itself in an imperfect ability to listen, think, speak, read, write, spell, or to do mathematical calculations. The term includes such conditions as perceptual handicaps, brain injury, minimal brain dysfunction, dyslexia, and developmental aphasia. The term does not include children who have learning problems which are primarily the result of visual, hearing, or motor handicaps, or mental retardation, or emotional disturbance, or of environmental, cultural, or economic disadvantage. (U.S. Office of Education, 1992, cited in Smith & Luckasson, 1995)

The National Joint Committee on Learning Disabilities proposed a slightly different definition of learning disabilities that is not as medically oriented.

> "Learning disabilities" is a general term that refers to a heterogeneous group of disorders manifested by significant difficulties in the acquisition and use of listening, speaking, reading, writing, reasoning or mathematical abilities. These disorders are intrinsic to the individual, presumed to be due to central nervous system dysfunction, and may occur across the life span. Problems in the self-regulatory behaviors, social perception, and social interaction may exist with learning disabilities but do not by themselves constitute a learning disability. Although learning disabilities may occur concomitantly with other handicapping conditions (for example, sensory impairment, mental retardation, serious emotional disturbance) or with extrinsic influences (such as cultural differences or insufficient or inappropriate instruction), they are not the result of those conditions or influences. (National Joint Committee on Learning Disabilities, 1988; cited in Smith & Luckasson, 1995, p. 246)

Children with learning disabilities usually have a measured intelligence in the normal range but are achieving academically well below an expected level. This discrepancy is not due to a visual, hearing, or motor handicap; mental retardation; emotional disturbance; or environmental, cultural, or economic disadvantages. In general, the literature in this area has cited as indicators of a learning disability such characteristics as hyperactivity, distractibility, impulsiveness, motor problems, poor problem-solving skills, poor motivation, over-reliance on others for help with class assignments, poor language skills, immature social skills, and a general disorganization in learning approaches (Smith & Luckasson, 1995). A learning disability is primarily an academic problem that may not be detected and diagnosed until the child encounters problems in school (Mercer, 1986).

Although the specific causes of learning disabilities are not known, researchers believe they include biological, genetic, and environmental factors. Biological factors include a variety of causes such as minimal brain dysfunction, biochemical disturbances (allergies to certain food, for instance), developmental delay of the nervous system, and nutrition. Some evidence suggests that heredity is a factor in the prevalence of LD, and some educators now feel that a poor or inadequate learning environment may contribute to LD problems (Mercer, 1986). Smith and Luckasson (1995) reported that about 5% of the school-age population have been classified as learning disabled.

As in counseling with other exceptional children, the counselor begins by recognizing and reflecting the feelings of the LD child. Because their characteristics tend to create an unstable world, these children have often experienced failure, rejection, isolation, and confusion. Perceptions of their world change, their visual perception plays tricks on them, their impulsivity causes them trouble with authority figures, they may have communication difficulties because of poor auditory or language skills, and they are often clumsy and awkward. These and the other behaviors that accompany their disability do not endear them to teachers, parents, or peers, and emotional problems often result.

Some LD children lack social perception and skills and perform poorly in social situations. They may lack good judgment and appear to be insensitive tattlers. They may have trouble making friends and forming good relationships in their families. Lerner (1989) presented numerous activities for building body image and self-perception, sensitivity to other people, social maturity and skills, self-esteem, and emotional well-being.

Rosen (1989) has produced a learning-disability workshop to help teachers, parents, and others understand the frustration, anxiety, and tension the LD child experiences. He stated that these children experience frustration and anxiety when adults use sarcasm at their expense, move so rapidly that the children have trouble keeping up, or become intimidating and demanding in their communication with LD children. His suggestions for adults include the following:

- Move less rapidly in giving directions and information.
- Recognize that lack of participation in the group may be related to fear of risk taking.
- Avoid urging the child to try harder—he or she is already having trouble understanding the world.
- Be aware that visual or auditory misperceptions can lead the child to respond inappropriately.
- Reexamine what is fair to ensure that the child's needs are not being overlooked.

Rosen's videotaped workshop materials can help counselors assist those who live and work with LD children.

One task of a counselor working with an LD child may be to coordinate diagnostic services in order to pinpoint the child's specific strengths and weaknesses and plan an educational program based on these findings. A typical diagnostic evaluation includes physical, educational, and psychological assessments and perhaps the opinions of other specialists, such as speech pathologists or ophthalmologists. These data must be shared with all those working with the child to ensure a well-organized remediation plan and to avoid overlap or omission of services.

Emotional problems, due primarily to feelings of failure and worthlessness, often compound the learning problems of LD children. Any program planned for LD children should include individual or group counseling. Counseling for the entire family may be necessary to deal with the feelings and reactions of all family members. Behavior modification procedures, implemented both in the home and in school, provide structure and stability that help LD children navigate in a world of turmoil. Relaxation training can help LD children cope with tensions and anxieties; talking therapy can provide an outlet for expression of pent-up feelings and exploration of doubts. The counselor's job is to build an improved self-concept, help the children to learn social skills, assist them in learning to cope with environmental demands, and guide them in planning ways to realize their potential.

In recent years, medical specialists have used drugs to control the attention span, distractibility, and behavior of LD children. The practice is extremely controversial, and the counselor is involved only in observing the effects of the drug and reporting these effects to the parents. Other therapies, such as diet control, megavitamins, and motor training, are still highly controversial. Most have little research support for their use in helping LD children.

Hallahan and Kauffman (1986) suggested that LD children need a structured learning program with clear instructions, directed primarily by the teacher until the children are educated to make effective decisions, as well as an environment in which stimuli have been reduced (perhaps a learning cubicle to reduce noise and light). Hallahan and Kauffman recommended cognitive behavior modification techniques to teach self-initiative, problem solving, increased attention, and reduction of impulsivity.

Rudolph (1978) summarized the tasks of counselors working with LD children:

1. Recognize the characteristics of learning disabilities, including those that may be masked by behaviors such as withdrawal or acting out.
2. Become familiar with the assessment instruments used to determine learning disabilities in order to understand and communicate to others these children's learning problems.
3. Coordinate the activities of the professionals (resource teachers, school psychologists, medical doctors, special therapists) working with LD children.
4. Counsel and consult with parents in order to promote understanding and facilitate growth.
5. Counsel with LD children who have their own unique learning, social, or emotional problems.
6. Counsel and consult with school personnel to promote their understanding of LD children's learning, social, and/or behavioral problems.

Attention-Deficit Hyperactivity Disorder (ADHD)

The cluster of problems known as attention-deficit hyperactivity disorder (ADHD) forms an extremely complex childhood problem and elicits the most frequent referrals for professional help, according to Goldstein and Goldstein (1990). They summarized the symptoms of this disorder as including inattention, overarousal, hyperactivity, impulsivity, and difficulty with delay of gratification. However, the American Psychiatric Association's (1994) diagnostic criteria in the *Diagnostic and Statistical Manual of Mental Disorders* (fourth edition, *DSM-IV*) included other specific behaviors such as fidgeting, having difficulty remaining in a seat or awaiting a turn, blurting out, interrupting, losing things, and engaging in physically dangerous activities without awareness of the consequences.

Lerner (1989) described ADHD children as

> impulsive; driven; and unable to stay on task, focus attention, and complete work. They give the impression that they are not listening. . . . They are easily distracted, racing from one idea or interest to another. Their work is sloppy and carelessly performed. (p. 210)

Goldstein and Goldstein (1990) presented a "commonsense definition" that included four components: inattention and distractibility, overarousal, impulsivity, and difficulty with gratification.

Smith and Luckasson (1995) stated that the condition is confusing in that not all children diagnosed as having attention deficit disorders (ADD) are in special education programs, some are diagnosed as learning disabled, and others may be classified as having behavior disorders, emotional disturbance, or other disabilities.

Henker and Whalen (1989) reported that learning disabilities often occur in conjunction with ADHD, as well as with two other conditions described by *DSM-IIIR:* conduct disorder and oppositional defiant disorder. Lerner (1989) quotes others in estimating that 33% to 80% of children with learning disabilities have symptoms of hyperactivity and/or attention-deficit disorders. Goldstein and Goldstein (1990) saw a reasonable incidence rate for attention deficit as only about 1% to 6%. They pointed out that the disorder occurs more frequently in lower socioeconomic areas (which may be a result rather than a cause of the disorder) and occurs 5 to 9 times more often in boys than girls, although the latter finding is being questioned.

Goldstein and Goldstein (1990) argued that attention-deficit disorder with and without hyperactivity are different disorders and cited research that children with attention deficits and hyperactivity are more aggressive and unpopular and have greater trouble with their behavior. Other researchers have found attention-deficit children without hyperactivity to be shy, socially withdrawn, not very popular, and not adept in sports, a state some have called "undifferentiated attention-deficit disorder."

A national nonprofit organization, Children with Attention Deficit Disorders, reports that children could have ADD if they fidget, squirm, or seem restless; have trouble remaining seated, playing quietly, waiting their turn, following instructions, or sustaining attention; talk excessively; are easily distracted; blurt out answers; shift from one uncompleted task to another; interrupt others; do not seem to listen; often lose things; frequently engage in dangerous behavior; act without thinking, have a low self-esteem; have frequent, unpredictable mood swings; and get angry and lose their temper easily (de la Cruz, 1994). However, many of these characteristics may be normal behaviors for a child's particular developmental level, or they could be characteristics of other problems. Consider the intensity and duration of the symptoms as well as how they fit into the child's overall developmental pattern.

Hardman et al. (1993) described two subcategories of ADD: attention-deficit hyperactivity disorder (ADHD) and undifferentiated attention-deficit disorder

(UADD), both of which have the primary characteristic of inability to concentrate for a long period of time. The authors reported disagreement about the causes of ADD; factors such as genetic inheritance, neurological injury during birth, vitamin deficiencies, and food additives have all been suggested.

Goldstein and Goldstein (1990) contended that common sense dictates a multidisciplinary-multitreatment model. Usually, such teams are composed of professionals such as physicians, psychologists, psychiatrists, counselors, and speech and other educational specialists.

A physical examination must be a part of the diagnostic process; then professionals must supervise medications as necessary. Medications such as Ritalin, Cylert, and Dexedrine continue to be the most common form of treatment. However, these drugs have unwanted side effects for some small children, and medication as a sole treatment is not recommended. Teachers, parents, and other adults who work with children on medication must be aware of the treatment in order to provide feedback about its effects.

As with other children's problems that involve hyperactivity, overarousal, and inappropriate behaviors, behavioral techniques work well with children with ADD. They respond to a structured environment with limited stimuli and a consistent schedule. Counselors should work with parents and teachers to develop behavior modification programs and to apply rules at home and school. The children should know the rules and the consequences for not following them *before* infractions occur. All adults must remain patient, calm, and consistent while applying both positive and negative consequences. To help them deal with their activity level, ADD children may need planned physical activities at intervals, although they may not be adept at sports and other games requiring coordination. Cognitive-restructuring techniques may teach the child more positive ways of thinking as well as self-monitoring of behavior. Group counseling to teach more effective social skills may be helpful at some point during treatment; however, counselors must carefully assess the child's readiness to benefit from this interaction and to function as a group member.

For LD and ADD children, Ziegler and Holden (1988) proposed a child and family model with three therapeutic objectives: (1) increase behavioral controls and problem-solving abilities, (2) define realistic but progressive behavioral and educational goals, and (3) provide support and guidance for managing frustration. Levine (1987) stated that both children and parents need information about ADD to "demystify" the problem. He suggested nontechnical, nonaccusatory discussions using concrete examples and analogies. Optimism, the attainment of short-term goals, and responsibility for self should be emphasized. Levine also asserted that the child needs an advocate to monitor treatment, resist irresponsible treatments, and provide advice and support.

The Mentally Retarded Child

The most commonly accepted definition of *mental retardation* was developed by the American Association on Mental Retardation (AAMR):

> Mental retardation refers to substantial limitations in present functioning. It is characterized by significantly subaverage intellectual functioning, existing concurrently with related limitations in two or more of the following applicable adaptive skill areas: communication, self-care home living, social skills, community use, self-direction, health and safety, functional academics, leisure, and work. Mental retardation manifests before age 18. (Cited in Smith & Luckasson, 1995, p. 136)

Smith and Luckasson (1995) noted that this definition emphasizes three major themes: intellectual function, adaptive skill areas, and the developmental period. After the diagnoses, the child's functioning in four areas is studied: intellectual and adaptive skills; psychological and emotional concerns; physical, health, and etiology considerations; and environment. Services and support are based on the level of intensity of need. Hardman et al. (1993) suggested that the child may need help with adaptive skills such as coping in school, developing interpersonal relationships, developing language skills, coping with emotional concerns, and taking care of personal needs.

Smith and Luckasson (1995) estimated that 1% to 3% of the total population have some form of mental retardation and stated that the U.S. Department of Education reports slightly more than 1% of schoolchildren receive special education services for mental retardation. Most of these children have a form of mild retardation. Smith and Luckasson suggested that this rate is low because of a general reluctance to label a child as mentally retarded.

Although Grossman (1983) classified anyone having an IQ of approximately 50 to 70 as mildly retarded, educators have labeled those with IQs of 50 to 70 as educable mentally retarded. Most children identified fall into this group. Trainable mentally retarded score about 25 to 50 on IQ tests, and the IQs of profoundly or severely mentally retarded people fall below 20 to 25 (Hallahan & Kauffman, 1986). If no brain damage exists and no single cause for the retardation can be determined, this group may be retarded because of poor socioeconomic conditions; therefore, they can benefit from academic support services and counseling (Hallahan & Kauffman, 1986).

The old subclassification systems of mild, moderate, and severe and profound, educable mentally retarded, and trainable mentally retarded are no longer in favor, according to Smith and Luckasson (1995). They suggested that educators now "understand that all children are capable of education and have the right to education" (p. 142). They do refer to children with "severe handicaps" to describe children who required considerable care and support.

The causes of mental retardation vary. Smith and Luckasson (1995) summarized the various factors in four categories: socioeconomic and environmental factors, injury, infection and toxins, and biological causes. Poverty, with its associated factors such as pollution, poor nutrition, and inadequate health care, is the leading cause suspected in most cases with no organic basis. Head and brain injury may occur at birth or at other times (car or bicycle accidents). Mental retardation due to infection or toxin may be the result of viral infections (rubella, measles), sexually transmitted diseases (syphilis, HIV), or toxins such as alcohol, other drugs, or tobacco used by the mother during pregnancy. Down's syndrome and Tay-Sachs disease are examples of mental retardation caused by biological factors.

The behavior and potential of the mentally retarded depend on the severity of the condition. A mildly retarded individual can be educated in the regular classroom with some special help. Vocational skills, independent living skills, and work-study programs are often a part of the educational plan. Mildly retarded individuals may be able to live independent lives and hold jobs, and some have satisfactory marriages and relationships with others.

The moderately retarded child is usually educated in a self-contained classroom, with instruction focused on taking care of personal needs, performing daily tasks, and getting along with others. Supervision in work or in the performance of other activities may be necessary.

Severely or profoundly retarded individuals usually are institutionalized and require constant care and supervision. Many are confined to bed and cannot care for even their most basic needs. Recent studies have indicated that the severely or profoundly retarded respond to behavior modification techniques for learning and improving behavior.

The counseling techniques in this section are geared to mildly or moderately retarded children, the groups most likely to face societal problems and pressures. These children have physical and psychological needs similar to those of other children, but the added handicap of their exceptionality interferes with their adjustment. Patton and Payne (1986) suggested that the areas most likely to be problematic are assuming self-direction and responsibility, developing social skills, and maintaining good interpersonal relationships. The counselor can concentrate efforts on promoting self-reliance and self-esteem and teaching appropriate standards, values, and behavior. Peer feedback and peer modeling can be highly effective counseling techniques. Group counseling can help the child learn and rehearse effective ways of behaving. Behavior modification techniques, such as the token system or contingency contracting, have been found to work effectively with the mentally retarded.

Counselors will need to work with the parents and other significant people in the child's life to help them understand and encourage the child's abilities. Focus special attention on teaching the child independent living skills as well as personal and social skills. The child and parents also need guidance and assistance in planning for the child's educational and vocational future.

Studies about the value of counseling and psychotherapy for the mentally retarded are inconclusive; obviously however, the counselor can provide valuable services in personal and social development and in helping the family deal effectively with adjustment and behavior problems.

The Child with a Physical Disability

Hardman et al. (1993) described physical disorders as "impairments that may interfere with an individual's mobility and coordination. They may also affect his or her capacity to communicate, learn, and adjust" (p. 340). They may include cerebral palsy, spina bifida, spinal cord injuries, amputations, muscular dystrophy, epilepsy, diabetes, cystic fibrosis, sickle cell anemia, adolescent pregnancy, and cocaine addiction.

Many children have more than one disability, and some conditions have overlapping symptoms. Knowing the characteristics, physical problems, symptoms, and prognosis of the child with a physical disability helps counselors understand the child's world. Counselors also want to know the child's strengths. Lack of knowledge and fear of the unknown can make the counselor apprehensive, which the child can sense.

Smith and Luckasson (1995) reported that the research indicates that teachers do not feel prepared to work with children with disabilities in the classroom. They requested help most often with classroom management techniques. Because teachers' attitudes are critical to the success of children with disabilities, counselors should be prepared to work with them in a consultative manner to alleviate their personal concerns and anxieties about teaching disabled children and assist them in developing whatever skills are needed.

The child may have anxiety, fears, shame, or other negative feelings because of his or her disability. These reactions usually reflect how the child has been treated by others, especially family. Family problems increase when a child has a disability; the demands for energy, time, and financial resources add a heavy burden of stress (Hallahan & Kauffman, 1986). The children's perceptions of self and their abilities are also determined by the child's age at the time the disabling condition occurred and the severity of the condition.

The counselor who works with children who have disabilities needs to be able to work with all agencies, professionals, parents, and other significant persons in the child's life. Coordinating services, rearranging physical environments, removing barriers and inconveniences, and securing special equipment and materials may be only the first step to meeting the needs of those with physical disabilities. The counselor should focus on building feelings of self-worth and healthy attitudes. The child may need to be encouraged to express and recognize his or her feelings toward the disability, helped to learn social or personal skills, counseled in the area of independent living, and assisted in making vocational plans for the future. More important than the physical limitation is the fact that each child is a unique individual who has capabilities and potential; the counselor's role is to facilitate growth toward reaching this potential.

Summary

The tasks of the counselor working with any type of exceptional child might include the following:

1. Working toward an understanding of the child's specific exceptionality and the unique social, learning, or behavioral problems that may accompany this exceptionality
2. Counseling to enhance self-concept

3. Facilitating adjustment to exceptionality
4. Coordinating the services of other professionals or agencies working with the exceptional child
5. Helping the significant people in the child's life (parents and teachers especially) to understand the child's exceptionality, strengths and limitations, and special problems
6. Assisting in the development of effective, independent living skills
7. Encouraging recreational skills and hobbies
8. Teaching personal and social skills
9. Assisting in educational planning and possibly securing needed educational aids and equipment for the child
10. Counseling with the parents
11. Acquiring a knowledge of and working relationship with professional and referral agencies

Buscaglia (1975) best summarized the ethical code and guidelines for the counselor working with an exceptional child. Each child should be allowed to be his or her own person, unique and individual; these children are *people* first, and they have the same needs (love, self-actualization, and so on) and the same rights (even to fail) as other children. Our responsibility is to listen, encourage, and facilitate their growth by supplying guidance and other resources. We must allow them to be themselves and to make choices about their lives without imposing our ideas, values, and attitudes on them. Buscaglia ends his summary by reminding us:

> And this above all—remember that the disabled need the best *you* possible. In order for them to be themselves, growing, free, learning, changing, developing, experiencing persons—*you* must be all of these things. You can only teach what you are. If you are growing, free to learn, change, develop and experience, you will allow *them* to be. (pp. 20–21)

COUNSELING WITH PARENTS OF EXCEPTIONAL CHILDREN

Seligman (1985) pointed out that parents need the help of a mental health professional to assist them with the problems they face:

> (a) The stress of having a handicapped child in the family, which may be more than the family can bear physically, financially, and psychologically; (b) siblings who may be at risk for psychological problems when there is a handicapped brother or sister in the family; (c) the differentiated roles and reactions of mothers and fathers to a handicapped child; (d) insensitive parent-professional encounters that leave long-term scars on the family; and (e) the reactions of extended family members, friends, and those in the immediate community, which affect family adaptation. (p. 274)

Seligman chided counselors for their lack of interest and research in the area of the problems children with disabilities and their families face, noting that with their sensitivity, skills, and knowledge, counselors are in an excellent position to assist these families.

Many parents are able to accept and adjust to their child's condition in a healthy manner; others, even though they love their child, may have trouble dealing with their feelings and the situation. Parents may experience a range of emotions; grief, shock, and disbelief; fear and anxiety about the child's future; helplessness because they cannot change the condition; and disappointment because theirs is not the perfect child they expected. They may resent the burdens the child's disability placed on the family. Whatever the feeling, the counselor needs to help the parents work through them. Parents are the child's main support system, and they must be free to accept and support the child in his or her growth and development.

Parents of exceptional children who are gifted do not experience the shame, guilt, or helplessness that parents of other exceptional children may feel. However, they may wish their child was ordinary because coping with the creativity, advanced intellectual development, and precociousness of their child is so hard. Finding adequate, stimulating educational facilities may be frustrating and possibly financially draining.

Conroy (1987) asserted that the parents of gifted children also are plagued by myths, stereotypes, and misunderstandings that confuse them about their role and responsibilities. She suggested a "partnership approach" to provide information to make decisions and deal with their feelings. Conroy developed a three-session parent-education group to address definition and identification, needs and problems, and resources to give parents a better understanding of what it means to be gifted; a clear awareness of the needs and problems of their children, especially as they relate to being gifted; a realization that procedures for rearing gifted children are not very different from other child-rearing techniques; and, finally, assistance with resources and referral services for the gifted.

West, Hosie, and Mathews (1989) stated that the presence of a gifted child can be stressful to the family because "this situation (a) alters normal family roles, (b) affects parents' feelings about themselves, (c) requires the family to make several adaptations, and (d) often produces special family-neighborhood and family-school issues" (p. 121).

Switzer (1990) identified four family factors that affect the progress of learning-disabled children: level of acceptance of the problem, family engagement with achievement behavior, parental discipline method, and the role of the identified child. The family's reaction to the child's learning disability can affect appropriate identification of the problem and the child's expectations and achievement. Switzer described a case in which the family was helped to change their perception of the learning-disabled child.

Lerner (1989) stated that the first step in counseling parents of LD children is to help them get over their initial feelings—mourning, misunderstanding, guilt, self-deprecation, possibly shame—about having a child with a disability. Parents may withdraw in confusion or aggressively try to "break down doors to get things done" (p. 155). Lerner recommended group counseling to help parents understand and accept their child's problem, share problems and solutions, and discuss issues of everyday living such as discipline, behavioral management, advocacy, legislation, and other relevant concerns.

Goldstein and Goldstein (1990) recommended parent training for caretakers of ADD children. This training should be based on learning principles, especially methods for changing the environment to reduce the possibilities of inappropriate behavior. The writers contended that the child's activity negatively affects parental behavior and that efforts to normalize relationships benefit both the parent and child. They recommend that a variety of techniques to improve the parent-child interactional style and communication.

Parents may overprotect children with disabilities from a world that is cold and hurtful. They may be overwhelmed with pity and express this feeling by becoming a servant to the child's needs. Some become martyrs, giving up their lives and their own needs to devote themselves totally to the child. The children of overprotective parents get the idea that they are not capable of doing anything for themselves because their parents have never allowed them the opportunity.

Parents often need to work through their own guilt feelings about the exceptionality. Mothers often feel that a handicap is the result of something they did while pregnant, such as horseback riding, tennis, or a fall. The parent may see the child's problem as a consequence or punishment for the parent's wrong behavior.

Shame concerning the exceptionality may be the parents' primary reaction: "What will other people think?" Parents are often afraid that other people will gossip, accuse, or ridicule. Parents continue to have vague uncertainties about the causes of disabilities and may suspect that neighbors are blaming them for bad genes, poor health care, or ignorance.

Some controversy exists in the literature as to whether parents of children with disabilities go through a mourning process, similar to grieving after a loss, after diagnosis of the disabling condition. Fortier and Wanlass (1984) described a stage model of families in crisis in which families initially react with anxiety and disorganization—the impact stage. The denial stage follows, with family members refusing to accept the diagnosis, shopping for cures, fictionalizing explanations, or engaging in wishful thinking. Grief is the third stage: Family members express anger, blaming, questioning, sadness, helplessness, self-doubt, guilt, and aloneness. During the fourth stage, focusing outward, coping begins. The family begins to accept the reality of the situation, seek information, evaluate alternatives, and plan for the future. Fortier and Wanlass suggested that what these families need first in the way of counseling is a good listener—a chance to verbalize their feelings. Later they need information about how to work with their child's disability and plan for the future, as well as help in understanding the diagnosis and prognosis and in forming realistic expectations for the child's development.

Widerstrom and Dudley-Marling (1986) attempted to dispel some of the myths about living with a child with a disability. From their review of the literature, they concluded that earlier studies indicated that families who have children with disabilities had more trouble coping with daily stresses and that more recent research does not confirm this stereotype. Coping and adjustment depend on many factors, among them, the severity of the handicap, the support services received, and the family's adaptability and adjustment level. Although earlier studies indicated a higher rate of divorce in families with handicapped children, Widerstrom and Dudley-Marling concluded that some marriages may be negatively affected, but not all or even most. The marriage may be at greater risk because of the added stress, but the deciding factor seemed to be the stability of the marriage before the birth of the child. Widerstrom and Dudley-Marling also addressed the myth that fathers seem less able than mothers to cope with a child with a disability; they concluded that the father's involvement with the child's daily care and the support of family and friends contribute to acceptance by the father.

Counseling tasks for the counselor working with the parents of exceptional children include the following:

1. Encouraging and helping parents to gain knowledge about their child's exceptionality, prognosis, strengths and limitations
2. Assisting the parents in working through feelings and attitudes that may inhibit the child's progress
3. Advising parents concerning state, federal, or community resources available for educational, medical, emotional, or financial assistance
4. Assisting the parents in setting realistic expectations for their child
5. Encouraging the parents to view their child as a unique individual with rights and potentials and the ability to make choices about his or her own life

Of the excellent books available to help both children and parents understand the characteristics of an exceptionality and the future of children with a particular exceptionality, those of R. A. Gardner contain a section written to the parents about the disability and a section written for children to explain the disability in terms they can understand. Some books to help children understand some of these exceptionalities (giftedness, learning disabilities, and physical, mental, and emotional handicaps) are listed at the end of this chapter.

Parent groups are probably a good way of helping parents of exceptional youngsters. Through sharing, the parents learn that others have the feelings and problems they are experiencing. They realize they are not alone in their plight; many other parents have children who are different. Parents not only share their feelings in groups but also share methods for problem solving. Others may have lived through the particular crisis one set of parents is facing, and solutions can be discussed. Parent groups provide an atmosphere of understanding, acceptance, and support; they reassure troubled parents that they are not alone and that others care.

Counselors also may want to explore the possibilities of family therapy. Families of exceptional children often experience considerable financial, psychological, and physical stress. Family sessions could explore feelings of anger, frustration, and shame; tendencies to scapegoat, exclude, or overprotect; communication styles or blocks; and effective and ineffective interactions and other problems of families not functioning effectively.

SUMMARY

The needs of special children and their families have been ignored for too many years. Stereotypes and societal attitudes must change. We need further research to counsel special children more effectively. We need money and resources to provide means for helping these children become productive citizens. Exceptional children can learn, enjoy life, be independent and productive, and fulfill their individual potential whether they are exceptionally gifted or have disabilities. Exceptional children are unique individuals just as "normal" children are unique. They have the same rights to respect and growth as other children and have the same needs. The challenge is there for counselors.

SUGGESTED READINGS
FOR EXCEPTIONAL CHILDREN*

Annotations are derived from the following sources:

1. *Booklist.* Chicago: American Library Association, 1985–1987.
2. Dreyer, S. *The bookfinder: When kids need books.* Detroit: American Guidance Service, 1985.
3. *The elementary school library collection: A guide to books and other media.* Williamsport, PA: Brodart, 1984.
4. Gillespie, J., and C. Naden. *Best books for children preschool through grade 6* (4th ed.) New Providence, NJ: R. R. Bowker, 1990.
5. Yaakov, J., Goldberg, J. 1990. *Children's catalog: 1987, 1988, 1989 supplements to the fifteenth edition.* New York: H. W. Wilson, 1987; 1988–89.
6. Yaakov, J. *Children's catalog: sixteenth edition.* New York: H. W. Wilson, 1991.
7. Price, A., and J. Yaakov. *Children's catalog: 1993 and 1994 supplements to sixteenth edition.* New York: H. W. Wilson, 1993, 1994.

Children with Emotional Disabilities

Anderson, Deborah, and Martha Finne. *Michael's story: Emotional abuse and working with a counselor.* Minneapolis, MN: Dillon, 1986. Michael's parents continually berate him. He considers himself "stupid" as well as unloved, and his behavior reflects his feelings. Ages 7–9.

Heide, Florence Parry. *Growing anyway up.* New York: Harper, 1976. A seriously disturbed girl is alienated from her mother and finds difficulty adjusting to her new private school. Ages 10–12.

Konisburg, E. L. George. New York: Macmillan, 1970. George lives inside Ben and in times of mental stress

* Sincere appreciation and gratitude are given to Lynda Hunt, Coordinator of the Learning Resource Center, Austin Peay State University, Clarksville, TN for updating the suggested readings for children.

emerges as the dark side of Ben's personality. Ages 10–13.

Lisle, Janet Taylor. *Afternoon of the elves.* New York: Orchard, 1989. Nine-year-old Hillary has a happy home life and befriends 11-year-old Sara-Kate, who is an outcast, poorly dressed girl. Sara-Kate has an elf village that Hillary enjoys, but not Sara-Kate's stormy moods and prickly pride. Eventually, Hillary learns of her friend's mentally ill mother. Ages 9–11.

Martin, Ann M. *Inside out.* New York: Holiday House, 1984. Eleven-year-old Jon and 8-year-old Lizzie have a younger brother, James, who is a real terror. When the family learns that James is autistic, they combine their efforts toward coping with the illness. Ages 9–12.

Children with Mental Disabilities

Bergman, Thomas. *We laugh, we love, we cry: Children living with mental retardation.* Milwaukee, WI: Gareth Stevens, 1989. The home life, physiotherapy, and schooling of two mentally retarded sisters is described. Ages 6–9.

Carrick, Carol. *Stay away from Simon!* Pictures by Donald Carrick. New York: Clarion, 1985. Simon, a youth with a mental disability, is too slow to attend regular school, and the students alternately fear and make fun of the strange boy, who has the reputation of being dangerous. Ages 9–12.

Flemming, Virginia. *Be good to Eddie Lee.* Pictures by Floyd Cooper. New York: Philomel, 1993. Although Christy considered him a pest, when Eddie Lee, a boy with Down syndrome, follows her into the woods, he shares several special discoveries with her.

Laird, Elizabeth. *Loving Ben.* New York: Delacorte, 1988. Anna's teen years bring maturity and fulfillment as she experiences the birth and death of a loved and loving hydrocephalic brother, changing ideas about character in friends, and working with a child with Down's syndrome. Ages 11+.

Levinson, Marilyn. *And don't bring Jeremy.* New York: Henry Holt, 1985. In an effort to placate his new friend Eddie, Adam ignores his neurologically impaired older brother until Eddie tries to accuse him of vandalism. Ages 9–12.

Rabe, Berniece. *Where's Chimpy?* Pictures by Diane Schmidt. Morton Grove, IL: Whitman, 1988. A little girl with Down's syndrome asks for Chimpy, her missing toy monkey, before she can go to sleep. Ages 5–7.

Sobol, Harriet Langsam. *My brother Steven is retarded.* Photographs by Patricia Agre. New York: Macmillan, 1977. An 11-year-old girl talks about the mixed feelings she has for her older, mentally retarded brother. Ages 6–12.

Children with Physical Disabilities

Adler, Carole S. *Eddie's blue-winged dragon.* New York: Putnam, 1988. Eleven-year-old Eddie, who has cerebral palsy, finds the blue-winged dragon becoming a weapon of revenge against bully Darrin. Ages 10–13.

Aiello, Barbara, and Jeffrey Shulman. Pictures by Noel Barr. *Business is looking up.* New York: Twenty-first Century, 1989. The problem of blindness is explored in this book about the Kids on the Block, puppets from the stage show. Ages 7–9.

Baker, Pamela I. *My first book of sign.* Gallaudet University Press, 1986. Children are pictured forming 150 words in sign language, which are alphabetically arranged. It includes a discussion of finger spelling and the rules of signing. Ages 5–9.

Bergman, Thomas. *Finding a common language: Children living with deafness.* Milwaukee, WI: Gareth Stevens,

1989. The activities of a 6-year-old Swedish girl are followed as she attends nursery school for the deaf. Ages 5–9.

Bergman, Thomas. *Seeing in special ways: Children living with blindness.* Milwaukee, WI: Gareth Stevens, 1989. A group of blind and partially sighted children in Sweden reveal their feelings about their disability and the ways they use their other senses to help them see. Ages 6–9.

Butler, Beverly. *Maggie by my side.* New York: Dodd, Mead, 1987. Butler, who lost her sight at 14, is forced to find a new dog when her latest dog dies. Maggie's fulfills her need, and the author explains about guide dogs and the training needed. Ages 10+.

Charlip, Remy. *Handbook birthday: A number and story book in sign language.* New York: Four Winds, 1987. Mary Beth is celebrating a birthday. Sign language vocabulary is introduced by her guesses about what is in her gifts. Finger spelling and signing tell the story. Ages 5–9.

Christian, Mary Blount. *Mystery at Camp Triumph.* Morton Grove, IL: Whitman, 1986. Blinded in a car accident, Angie resents going to a camp for the disabled, where she becomes involved in a mystery and builds confidence and independence. Ages 9–12.

Drimmer, Frederick. *Born different: Amazing stories of very special people.* New York: Atheneum, 1988. A collective biography of seven people whose anatomical anomalies made them prominent; among them, Tom Thumb, Robert Wadlow, and the "elephant man." Ages 11+.

Gorman, Carol. *Chelsey and the green-haired kid.* Boston: Houghton Mifflin, 1987. Chelsey is a spunky 13-year-old who happens to be a paraplegic, and her friend Jack just happens to have green hair. A mystery intertwines their lives. Ages 11+.

Herman, Helen, and Bill Herman. *Jenny's magic wand.* New York: Watts, 1988. A photo essay of Jenny who is blind and about to enter public school. Ages 7–9.

Howard, Ellen. *Edith.* New York: Macmillan, 1987. In the 1890s young Edith is sent to live with her married sister when their mother dies; her life is complicated by epileptic seizures. Ages 10–13.

Jensen, Virginia Allen. *Catching: A book for blind and sighted children with pictures to feel as well as to see.* New York: Philomel, 1984. When Little Rough and his friends play tag, they discover they can avoid being caught by changing into different shapes and colors. Visually impaired children can recognize the various characters by touching the assortment of textures. Ages 6–8.

Johnston, Julie. *Hero of lesser causes.* Boston: Little, Brown, 1993. In 1946 12-year-old Keely is devastated when her older brother, Patrick, is paralyzed by polio, and she starts a campaign to reawaken his waning interest in life. Age 10+.

Krementz, Jill. *How it feels to live with a physical disability.* New York: Simon and Schuster, 1992. The book introduces readers to 12 young people, age 6 to 16, who have been challenged by physical disabilities. A chapter is devoted to each and is in first person from the child's point of view. Age 9+.

Kuklin, Susan. *Thinking big.* New York: Lothrop, Lee, and Shepard Books, 1986. Captivating photographs tell the story of Jaime Osborne, a dwarf, and describe the daily frustrations of being short and different. Ages 6–9.

Meddaugh, Susan. *Too short Fred.* Boston: Houghton, 1985. Fred masters situations despite his small stature. Ages 6–8.

Meltzer, Milton. *Dorothea Lange: Life through the camera.* Pictures by Donna Diamond. New York: Viking/Kestrel,

1985. As a result of childhood polio, Dorothea Lange walked with a limp, but this disability did not keep her from pursuing a rewarding career as a photographer. Ages 7–11.

Powers, Mary Ellen. *Our teacher's in a wheelchair.* Morton Grove, IL: Albert Whitman, 1986. This picture book photo essay introduces a young man named Brian Hanson, whose wheelchair doesn't stop him from teaching at a day-care center. Ages 4–6.

Rabe, Berniece. *Margaret's moves.* New York: Dutton, 1987. Margaret wants a new wheelchair, but it costs $1,000, which her parents do not have, so she decides to earn the money. Ages 9–12.

Roberts, Willo Davis. *Sugar isn't everything: A support book in fiction form, for the young diabetic.* New York: Atheneum, 1987. Eleven-year-old Amy manages to conceal her continual hunger, thirst, and need to use the bathroom until she collapses and is diagnosed as diabetic. Amy's acceptance of the disease is highlighted, along with information about it. Ages 10+.

Rosenberg, Maxine B. *Finding a way: Living with exceptional brothers and sisters.* New York: Lothrop, Lee, and Shepard Books, 1988. Rosenberg's book presents what it is like to be the brother or sister of a child with special physical problems. The positive is emphasized as well as common needs shared by all children. Ages 7–10.

Roy, Ron. *Move over, wheelchairs coming through!* Photographs by Rosemarie Hausherr. New York: Clarion, 1985. Lizzy, Jeff, Mark, and Jose are all confined to wheelchairs. Their joys and frustrations are shared in pictures and interviews. Ages 9–12.

Slepian, Jan. *The Alfred summer.* New York: Macmillan, 1980. Fourteen-year-old Lester deals with cerebral palsy and resentment of overprotective parents. He befriends retarded Alfred,

who accepts him completely, and Myron. All three build a boat and much more.

Southall, Ivan. *Let the balloon go.* New York: Bradbury, 1985. A sensitive story about a boy with cerebral palsy. Ages 10–13.

Ward, Brian R. *Overcoming disability.* New York: Watts, 1989. Discussing the most common disabilities of childhood—from poor eyesight to you name it.

Gifted Children

Blume, Judy. *Here's to you, Rachel Robinson.* New York: Orchard, 1993. Expelled from boarding school, Charles's presence at home proves disruptive, especially for sister Rachel, a gifted seventh-grader juggling friendships and school activities. Ages 10+.

Gilson, Jamie. *Double dog dare.* New York: Lothrop, Lee, and Shepard Books, 1988. A new program for talented and gifted children creates tension among classmates in Hobie's fifth-grade class. In the midst of the turmoil, Hobie plays a clever trick that defuses the issue of what it means to be gifted and helps them all see that there are many ways in which individuals are special. Ages 9–12.

Hermes, Patricia. *I hate being gifted.* New York: Putnam, 1990. Being in the sixth grade is difficult enough, but when KT is placed in the gifted program and gets the weirdest teacher in school, she feels her life is falling apart. Ages 10+.

Hurwitz, Johanna. *Class clown.* New York: Morrow, 1987. Although extremely bright, Lucas Cott is a problem child in class. He acts out involuntarily at the most inopportune moments. Things go wrong even when he is trying his best to do assignments properly. Ages 7–10.

Sebestyen, Ouida. *Words by heart.* Boston: Little, Brown, 1979. This is the story of a young African American girl who has a "magic mind" and her courage in trying to make a better life for her family and herself. Ages 9–13.

Learning-Disabled Children

Aiello, Barbara, and Jeffrey Shulman. *Secrets aren't always for keeps.* New York: Twenty-first Century, 1989. The "Kids on the Block" puppets from the stage show tackle learning disabilities. Ages 7–9.

Bethancourt, Jeanne. *My name is brain Brian.* New York: Scholastic, 1993. Although he is helped by his new sixth-grade teacher after being diagnosed as dyslexic, Brian still has some problems with school and with people he thought were his friends. Ages 9–12.

Cassedy, Sylvia. *M. E. and Morton.* New York: Thomas Y. Crowell, 1987. M. E. (short for Mary Ellen) is an excellent student at the private school she attends on scholarship. Because she is ashamed of her learning-disabled brother, she has few friends. A new friendship brings a summer filled with imaginative games. Ages 12+.

DeClements, Barthe. *Sixth grade can really kill you.* New York: Viking Kestrel, 1985. Helen dreads the first day in sixth grade. Good in math and gifted on the pitcher's mound, she is a non-reader diagnosed as a behavior problem. Ages 10+.

Fisher, Gary L. *The survival guide for kids with LD.* Minneapolis, MN: Free Spirit, 1990. This book discusses different types of disorders, programs at school, coping with negative feelings, and making friends. Ages 10–12.

Gilson, Jamie. *Do bananas chew gum?* New York: Lothrop, Lee, and Shepard Books, 1980. Sam thinks he is stupid because he reads and writes on the second-grade level. He is afraid for anyone to know about his problem but is elated to discover that something can be done to help him. Ages 9–12.

Hansen, Joyce. *Yellow Bird and me.* New York: Clarion, 1986. As Doris reluctantly helps Yellow Bird, the clown, with his homework, she realizes his frustration with reading: he reverses words and letters. Ages 9–12.

Smith, Doris Buchanan. *Kelly's creek.* New York: Crowell, 1975. A learning disability blocks Kelly's progress at school. His worried parents insist that he try harder to do his exercises and improve; until he does, they make his daily sojourns to the nearby marsh off-limits. His unique knowledge of the marsh brings self-confidence. Ages 9–11.

REFERENCES

Alexander, P. A., & Muia, J. A. (1982). *Gifted education: A comprehensive roadmap.* Rockville, MD: Aspen.

Allen, S., & Fox, D. (1979). Group counseling for the gifted. *Journal of Counseling and Development, 67,* 525–528.

American Psychiatric Association (1994). *Diagnostic and statistical manual of mental disorders* (4th rev. ed.). Washington, DC: Author.

Bailey, D., & Winton, P. (1986). Families and exceptionality. In N. Haring & L. McCormick (Eds.), *Exceptional children and youth* (4th ed., pp. 71–93). Columbus, OH: Merrill.

Barnette, E. (1989). A program to meet the emotional and social needs of gifted and talented adolescents. *Journal of Counseling and Development, 67,* 525–528.

Betts, G. (1986). Development of the emotional and social needs of gifted individuals. *Journal of Counseling and Development, 67.*

Brandenburg, N., Friedman, R., & Silver, S. (1990). The epidemiology of childhood psychiatric disorder: Prevalence findings from recent studies. *Journal of the American Academy of Child and Adolescent Psychiatry, 29,* 76–83.

Buscaglia, L. (1975). *The disabled and their parents: A counseling challenge.* Thorofare, NJ: Charles B. Slack.

Conroy, E. (1987). Primary prevention for gifted students: A parent education group. *Elementary School Guidance and Counseling, 12*(2), 110–116.

Cullinan, D., & Epstein, M. (1986). Behavior disorders. In N. Haring & L. McCormick (Eds.), *Exceptional children and youth* (4th ed., pp. 161–199). Columbus, OH: Merrill.

Culross, R. R. (1982). Developing the whole child: A developmental approach to guidance with the gifted. *Roeper Review, 5,* 24–26.

De la Cruz, B. (1994, May 23). Mothers goes on attention deficit disorder crusade. *The Tennessean,* p. 4B.

Fortier, J. M., & Wanlass, R. L. (1984). Family crisis following the diagnosis of a handicapped child. *Family Relations, 33,* 13–24.

Goldstein, S., & Goldstein, M. (1990). *Managing attention disorders in children: A guide for practitioners.* New York: Wiley.

Grossman, H. (1983). Classification in mental retardation. In N. Haring & L. McCormick (Eds.) *Exceptional children and youth* (4th ed., p. 237). Columbus, OH: Merrill.

Hallahan, D., & Kauffman, J. (1986). *Exceptional children: Introduction to special education* (3rd ed). Englewood Cliffs, NJ: Prentice-Hall.

Hardman, M., Drew, C., Egan, M., & Wolf, B. (1983). *Human exceptionality: Society, school and family.* Boston: Allyn & Bacon.

Henker, B., & Whalen, C. (1989). Hyperactivity and attention deficits. *American Psychologist, 44,* 216–223.

Hobbs, N. (1975). *The future of children.* San Francisco: Jossey-Bass.

Lerner, J. (1989). *Learning disabilities, theories, diagnosis, and teaching strategies* (5th ed.). Boston: Houghton Mifflin.

Levine, M. (1987). Attention deficits: The diverse effects of weak control systems in childhood. *Pediatric Annals, 16*(2), 117–130.

Loeb, R., & Jay, G. (1987). Self-concept in gifted children: Differential impact in boys and girls. *Gifted Child Quarterly, 31,* 9–14.

Mercer, C. D. (1986). Learning disabilities. In N. Haring & L. McCormick (Eds.), *Exceptional children and youth* (4th ed., pp. 119–159). Columbus, OH: Merrill.

Parette, H., & Holder-Brown, L. (1992). The role of the school counselor in providing services to medically fragile children. *Elementary School Guidance and Counseling, 27,* 47–55.

Patton, J. R., & Payne, J. S. (1986). Mild mental retardation. In N. Haring & L. McCormick (Eds.), *Exceptional children and youth* (4th ed., pp. 233–269). Columbus, OH: Merrill.

Rosen, P. (Producer). (1989). *How difficult can this be? Understanding learning disabilities. Frustration, anxiety, tension: The f.a.t. city workshop.* Greenwich, CT: Kopel Films.

Rudolph, L. (1978). The counselor's role with the learning disabled child. *Elementary School Guidance and Counseling, 12,* 162–169.

Seligman, M. (1985). Handicapped children and their families. *Journal of Counseling and Development, 64,* 274–277.

Smith, D., & Luckasson, R. (1995). *Introduction to special education: Teaching in an age of challenge.* Meedham Heights, MA: Allyn & Bacon.

Smith, T., Price, B., & Marsh, G. (1986). *Mildly handicapped children and adults.* St. Paul, MN: West.

Strong, J., Lynch, C., & Smith, C. (1987). Educating the culturally disadvantaged, gifted student. *School Counselor, 34*(5), 336–344.

Switzer, L. (1990). Family factors associated with academic progress for children with learning disabilities. *Elementary School Guidance and Counseling, 24,* 200–206.

Terman, L., & Oden, M. (1947). *The gifted child grows up: Twenty-five years follow-up of a superior group.* Stanford, CA: Stanford University Press.

West, J., Hosie, T., & Mathews, N. (1989). Families of academically gifted children: Adaptability and cohesion. *School Counselor, 37,* 121–127.

Widerstrom, A. H., & Dudley-Marling, C. (1986). Living with a handicapped child: Myth and reality. *Childhood Education, 62,* 359–367.

Wolf, J., & Penrod, D. (1980). Bibliotherapy: A classroom approach to sensitive problems. *Gifted/Creative/Talented, 15,* 52–54.

Wolf, J., & Stephens, T. (1986). Gifted and talented. In N. Haring & L. McCormick (Eds.), *Exceptional children and youth* (4th ed., pp. 431–473). Columbus, OH: Merrill.

Ziegler, R., & Holden, L. (1988). Family therapy for learning disabled and attention-deficit disordered children. *American Journal of Orthopsychiatry, 58,* 196–209.

Chapter 17

◆

Legal and Ethical
Considerations for Counselors

Schmidt and Meara (1984) defined the differences among ethical, professional, and legal issues in counseling: Ethical issues "arise from personal and professional standards of moral duty and obligation" (p. 56); professional issues are technical, procedural, or cultural standards that members of the profession are expected to accept; and legal issues are related to federal, state, and municipal standards of practice as regulated by law.

Salo and Shumate (1993) wrote that "counseling minor clients is an ambiguous practice" (p. 1). They suggested that absolute guidelines are difficult to determine because statutes and court decisions do not always agree. The rights of the minor and the rights of the parents to serve in a "guiding role" can cause confusion. Counselors who have concerns about state laws are urged to consult with a private attorney or legal representation for their agency or school.

Talbutt (1981) summarized the role of ethical standards in three ways: "(a) They are self-imposed regulations; (b) they prevent internal disagreement; and (c) they provide protection in case of litigation" (p. 110). Talbutt noted that ethical standards are particularly important to the counselor today because of recent litigation; the standards may protect counselors from litigation if the counselor's behavior was in line with the standards and if the counselor was acting in good faith.

Mappes, Robb, and Engels (1985) reviewed the literature to determine the various functions of codes of ethics in the mental health profession. They found that the codes serve those in the helping professions by "(a) protecting clients, (b) providing guidance to professionals, (c) ensuring the autonomy of professionals, (d) increasing the prestige of the profession, (e) increasing clients' trust and faith in the members of the profession, and (f) specifying desirable conduct between professionals" (p. 246).

All the writers Mappes et al. reviewed maintained the need for a professional code of ethics for a variety of reasons, but the various codes of the helping professions have problems. A code of ethics must be general; therefore, the standards or principles are open to interpretation. Addressing this issue, Mappes et al. (1985) cited Smotherman's observation that the "most important factor related to ethical behavior remains the integrity of the practitioner" (p. 251). They also pointed out that conflicts exist between codes of ethics and the law and among the codes of ethics of different professions in some instances—for example, on the questions of advertising, confidentiality, and the client's right to see his or her file.

PRIVACY, CONFIDENTIALITY, AND PRIVILEGED COMMUNICATION

Stadler (1990) noted confusion concerning the terms *privacy, confidentiality,* and *privileged communication.* She stated that the right to privacy ensures that people may choose what others know about them, confidentiality refers to the professional responsibility to respect and limit access to clients' personal information, and privileged communication refers to the legal rights of professionals to protect clients' confidences. According to Stadler, issues of confidentiality are the ethical problems counselors most frequently encounter. She recommended that counselors be extremely careful to apprise their clients of their limits of confidentiality at the very beginning of counseling.

Various authors have mentioned confidentiality and privileged communication as areas of conflict and concern. Schmidt and Meara (1984) called privileged communication a right granted by law, protecting communication between therapist and client from disclosure; however, they emphasized that state laws vary widely in defining the extent to which professional relationships are privileged. Confidentiality is the responsibility of the counselor to protect information as dictated by that profession's code of ethics. Mappes et al. (1985) reported that all professions have a code advocating that the helper maintain confidentiality, but laws and codes differ as to the circumstances that permit confidentiality to be broken. Failure to warn a person of a threat against his or her life in California may result in liability *(Tarasoff v. Regents of the University of California).*

Confidentiality is a special problem for counselors working with children. According to Huey (1986), parents are legally responsible for the child, but the counselor has an ethical responsibility to the child—and these two may conflict.

> Ethical codes do not supersede the law, and they should never be interpreted so as to encourage conduct that violates the law. Counselors must become familiar with local, state, and federal laws, but legal knowledge is not sufficient to determine the best course of action. Each case is unique, and laws are subject to interpretation; consequently, professional judgment will always play a role. (p. 321)

An issue of confidentiality particularly troubling to counselors is child abuse. State laws now require that child abuse or neglect be reported, and most states include criminal penalties in their laws for failure to report. This obligation places the helping professional in a "double-agent" position, according to Stadler (1989); the duty to protect the child (beneficence) overrides the principles of autonomy.

Wagner (1981) conducted a survey of school counselors to determine the attitudes of elementary, middle, and secondary school counselors toward confidentiality. The counselors surveyed (347 elementary, 423 middle school, and 426 secondary school counselors) viewed the limits of confidentiality to be determined by their counseling setting as well as by the age, maturity, and problem of the child. They agreed that informal discussion of a child's problem with a person not involved was a violation of confidentiality. Elementary counselors were the least stringent about maintaining confidentiality, followed by middle school counselors; secondary counselors were the most stringent. Counselors in elementary schools were more likely to inform parents and authorities about illegal behavior such as drug possession or sales; secondary counselors were least likely to inform. Wagner pointed out that these findings parallel the counselor's perceived responsibility to parents, and also seem to reflect the counselor's assessment of the child's age, cognitive level, and maturity level. The movement of a child toward adolescence and increasing independence from the family apparently encourages counselors to work with the individual rather than bring in other individuals responsible for his or her care—parents or guardians.

Informed Consent

Salo and Shumate (1993) contended "When a child approaches a counselor without parental knowledge or consent, immediate tension arises between the child's right to privacy and the parent's right—on the child's behalf—to provide informed consent for the counseling" (p. 10). No general rule requires counselors to obtain parental consent concerning a child with the ability to make an informed decision, but obtaining parental consent is good practice for counselors unless potential danger to the minor exists. The authors pointed out that early communication with parents concerning the purpose of counseling can prevent later problems. The law generally supports parents who forbid counseling of their minor children unless there are extenuating circumstances. The law takes precedence over all codes of ethics.

Confidentiality of Files

A national survey of American Psychological Association (APA) members found that confidentiality was their highest ranked ethical dilemma (Pope & Vetter, 1992). Access to files presented another concern involving confidentiality. There appeared to be a move toward allowing clients to see their own records. The federal Family Rights and Privacy Act gives parents and students of legal age the right to inspect their records (Burcky & Childers, 1976). Counselors need to know the types of records kept in institutional files. They may not be able to maintain confidentiality if the parents of underage children request access to such files. A personal file may be kept for confidential notes because personal files do not fall under this law. However, files that have been seen by *anyone,* except a paid secretary, or have been discussed with anyone in the process of decision making, are no longer considered personal notes (Salo & Shumate, 1993).

Counselors of children are often faced with requests for information from parents concerned about what happens in the counseling interview, and Salo and Shumate (1993) asserted that the parent probably has a legal right to know. Remley (1990) suggested five ways to cope with these requests:

1. Describe to the adult the nature of the counseling relationship and the importance of confidentiality.
2. Ask the child if he or she will disclose the information to the adult.
3. Talk with the adult and child at the same time in the hope that one of them will resolve the issue.
4. Tell the child that you must disclose the information and why before you do so.
5. Refuse to disclose the information and be prepared for the possible consequences.

Salo and Shumate (1993) urged that, in cases of parental separation or divorce, the counselor always obtain permission from the custodial parent before revealing information to a noncustodial parent. They advised counselors to obtain written proof of who retains legal custody of the child.

Remley (1990) found no legal or ethical requirement for counselors to keep notes about their counseling sessions. For the counselor who keeps notes, he suggested that factual information concerning actual occurrences in the session should be kept separate from the subjective section in which the counselor records diagnoses and develops future treatment plans. Remley also recommended writing notes carefully, with the thought in mind that they could become public one day and that counselors may want to document questionable or controversial information.

Confidentiality in Groups

Davis (1980) was especially concerned about maintaining confidentiality in group counseling. She pointed out that leaders in the field of group counseling, such as Gazda, have asserted that confidentiality is essential to the development of trust within the group. Mappes et al. (1985) also stated that the problems of confidentiality are exacerbated in group counseling. Davis (1980), however, found that group members discuss what occurs in the group process with others; "soliciting assurances of confidentiality may not be realistic" (p. 201). She suggested that group leaders need to give accurate information about confidentiality so that members may decide how much information they want to disclose during group counseling.

Salo and Shumate (1993) also noted that "groups, by their very nature, negate the presumption of privacy" (p. 34). They advised counselors to inform all group members about the necessity for confidentiality but also to point out that privileged communication may not apply to group discussion.

Breaching Confidentiality

In court cases in states where counselors and psychologists (or other helpers) are not protected by a licensure law providing for privileged communication, they have no recourse except to reveal the information if subpoenaed. Some courts, more tolerant than others, allow the counselor to share the privileged information with the judge in private to determine if the information is necessary to the proceeding or if public disclosure would be too hurtful to those involved, such as children who are a part of the case.

Mappes et al. (1985) suggested that, when breaching confidentiality is necessary, the counselor should inform the client of the intention to do so and then invite the client to participate in the process. The counselor should explain why confidentiality must be broken, summarize what he or she must do and say, and then encourage the client to take responsibility for assisting in resolving the dilemma—perhaps by talking to the parents involved or calling an authority, whichever is appropriate. If the counselor has informed the client about the counseling process during the initial interview (as required by the ACA, APA, and NASW codes of ethics), the process of breaching confidentiality is not as easily misunderstood.

Denkowski and Denkowski (1982) stated that "the extent of confidentiality that can be assured under . . . legal limitations is not absolute and is declining" (p. 374). Mappes et al. (1985) contended that "it could be in the best interest of society and future mental health clients for the professional associations of the various mental health disciplines to join forces in lobbying for privileged communication at the state and federal level" (p. 249).

TEST YOUR ETHICAL BEHAVIOR

Although understanding ethical and legal issues is of utmost importance to those who work in the helping professions, training, research, and knowledge in the area seem seriously lacking. As a test of your general understanding of ethical and legal issues, consider the following situations and describe methods and procedures you would use in handling the incident. Many situations have no *right* solution; the final answer depends on your counseling setting, the philosophy of your supervisor, the interpretation of the law by your local or state authorities, potential advantages or disadvantages of the solution, and the risks to the counselor and client. In these situations, *our comments are only our interpretation and not necessarily the right answer.*

We refer to the 1995 Ethical Standards of ACA, the Ethical Principles of

Psychologists (APA, 1992), and the Code of Ethics for the National Association of Social Workers (1993). Although we understand that other professionals bound by other professional codes encounter these situations, we believe all codes have similarities, and the principles outlined here can be generalized to other professions.

■ **Situation 1:** Increasingly, you are receiving referrals from the school and parents asking you to work with ADHD children. Your primary practice has been with adults experiencing stress, career, or life transition problems. Do you accept these referrals?

Response: ACA Code of Ethics and Standards of Practice C.2.a states that "Counselors practice only within the boundaries of their competence, based on their education, training, supervised experience, and appropriate professional experience." APA Principle A cautions that psychologists "recognize the boundaries of their particular competencies and the limitations of their expertise. They provide only those services and use only those techniques for which they are qualified by education, training, or experience." The NASW Code of Ethics states that social workers "should accept responsibility or employment only on the basis of existing competence or the intention to acquire the necessary competence." You should not accept these referrals to counsel with ADHD children.

■ **Situation 2:** Because you have treated a number of abused children in your general practice, you are introduced at a large meeting of helping professionals as specializing in working with abused children. What would you do?

Response: ACA Code of Ethics and Standards of Practice C.3.c advises that counselors should "make reasonable efforts to ensure that statements made by others about them or the profession of counseling are accurate." APA Ethical Standard 3.02 urges psychologists to "make reasonable efforts to prevent others whom they do not control (such as employers, publishers, sponsors, organizational clients, and representatives of the print or broadcast media) from making deceptive statements concerning psychologists' practice of professional or scientific activities." The NASW Code of Ethics 1.B.2 warns that social workers "should not misrepresent professional qualifications, education, experience, or affiliations." Even though you have treated children who have been abused, you hold no specialty in this area and should correct your colleague's statement immediately.

■ **Situation 3:** You are an unmarried school counselor, dating the noncustodial divorced parent of one of the children in your school. Would this cause any problem, should the child come to you for counseling?

Response: The ACA Code of Ethics and Standards of Practice A.6.a warns counselors to "avoid dual relationships with clients that could impair professional judgment or increase the risk of harm to clients." They include examples such as familial, social, business, or close personal relationships. The APA Principles and

Ethical Code of Conduct 1.17(a) cautions psychologists to refrain "from entering into or promising another personal, scientific, professional, financial, or other relationship with such persons if it appears likely that such a relationship reasonably might impair the psychologist's objectivity." The NASW Code of Ethics II.F.4 prohibits social workers from condoning or engaging "in any dual or multiple relationships with clients or former clients in which there is a risk of exploitation of or potential harm to the client." The dating relationship could interfere with helping the child.

■ **Situation 4:** You have strong feelings about children from another culture because of a previous negative experience with an adult from this culture. A 10-year-old girl from this cultural group comes to you for counseling. She has a relationship problem with her parents. What do you do?

Response: The ACA Code of Ethics and Standards of Practice A.2.a states that counselors "do not condone or engage in discrimination" based on a multitude of factors that include culture. APA Principles advise psychologists to be "aware of cultural, individual, and role differences" due to many factors and states that psychologists should "try to eliminate the effect on their work of biases based on those factors." The NASW Code of Ethics warns social workers not to "practice, condone, facilitate or collaborate with any form of discrimination" on the basis of these same factors. This counselor needs to refer the child and seek help to resolve these cultural biases.

■ **Situation 5:** Although Mike is an expert soccer player, he wants to spend more time on his music interests. His parents talk to you about working with him to encourage his sport interest in the hope that he will be eligible for a scholarship one day. What do you say to the parents? What do you say to Mike?

Response: ACA A.3.b urges counselors to "promote the freedom of clients to choose whether to enter into a counseling relationship." APA Principle D supports the client's right to self-determination and autonomy. The NASW Code II.G also urges that social workers "foster maximum self-determination on the part of clients." You explain to the parents your role as a helping professional in the light of these codes and, with their permission, ask Mike if he would like to talk with you about these concerns. If he does choose to talk with you, you should avoid pressuring him to accept his parents' plans. He should have the right of "self-determination and autonomy."

■ **Situation 6:** You are working in a religious institution that holds beliefs about the worth of persons with which you do not agree. You are advised that these beliefs should be integrated into your counseling with children. What do you do?

Response: ACA D.1.j states that acceptance of employment implies that the counselor is in agreement with institutional policies and principles but also allows counselors to "strive to reach agreement with employers" concerning policies.

APA Principle 8.03 requires psychologists to "clarify the nature of the conflict, make known their commitment to the Ethics Code, and to the extent feasible, seek to resolve the conflict in a way that permits the fullest adherence to the Ethics Code." The NASW Code IV.L.1 states that "social workers should work to improve the employing agency's policies and procedures." If you cannot change the unacceptable policies, you should consider resignation.

■ **Situation 7:** You are asked to work with six children in the fifth grade in group counseling. Most of these children are well adjusted and only have developmental problems. Your supervisor asks that you place in the group one very unruly child who lives in a home where drugs and alcohol are frequently used and abuse is suspected. The supervisor hopes that peer pressure will help to change the child's behavior. What is your ethical responsibility?

Response: ACA A.9.a states that "counselors select members whose needs and goals are compatible with goals of the group, who will not impede the group process, and whose well-being will not be jeopardized by the group experience." The ethical codes of APA and NASW do not address the screening and selection of group participants, but generally emphasize respect for the well-being of clients. An unruly child would impede the progress of the group and appears to be a better candidate for individual counseling.

■ **Situation 8:** You are employed in the local counseling center for the purpose of treating children and families. You are going through a very bitter divorce that has taken its toll on you mentally and physically. You need time to reorganize your life but feel a financial pressure to keep working. What is the ethical thing to do?

Response: The pressure of the divorce may be affecting your counseling skills in a negative manner. Counselors should always be evaluating their effectiveness, and in this case, if effectiveness seems to be decreasing, the counselor should seriously consider a leave of absence or request other duties for a period. ACA C.2.g points out that "counselors should refrain from offering professional services when their personal problems or conflicts are likely to lead to harm to a client or others." APA 1.13 urges psychologists to "recognize that their personal problems and conflicts may interfere with their effectiveness" and to "refrain from undertaking an activity when they know or should know that their personal problems are likely to lead to harm to a patient, client, colleague, student." NASW I.A.3 also cautions a social worker "not to allow his or her own personal problems, psychosocial distress, substance abuse, or mental health difficulties to interfere with professional judgment and performance or jeopardize the best interests of those for whom the social worker has a professional responsibility.

■ **Situation 9:** You are subpoenaed to testify in a divorce case because you have been counseling with the children of the couple. You may be asked to reveal information that would be very destructive to the parent-child relationship. What would you do?

Response: ACA states that "the right to privacy belongs to the clients and may be waived by the client." If the client is unwilling to do so, B.1.d advises counselors that, when courts order the release of confidential information, "counselors request to the court that the disclosure not be required due to potential harm to the client or counseling relationship." APA and NASW do not address the situation as directly, but give guidence about maintaining the confidentiality of the counseling interview.

■ **Situation 10:**   You are a school counselor working with an 11-year-old boy, Todd. The parents visit your office, demanding to know what you and Todd are discussing. If you do not tell them, they threaten to take you to court. How would you handle this? Would you be legally required to tell them? Could they demand your counseling notes?

Response: ACA B.1.a states that "counselors respect their clients' right to privacy and take steps to avoid unwarranted disclosures of confidential information." ACA B.3 points out that "informed consent, parents or guardians may be included in the counseling process as appropriate." APA points out that "psychologists have a primary obligation and take reasonable precautions to respect the confidentiality rights of those with whom they work or consult, recognizing that confidentiality must be established by law, institutional rules, or professional or scientific relationship." NASW II.H.1 maintains that the "social worker should share with others confidences revealed by clients, without their consent, only for compelling professional reasons." Refer back to the section on confidentiality in this chapter for suggestions about handling this case.

■ **Situation 11:**   A private practice counselor with whom you work and socialize talks about clients in general conversation with others. What is your responsibility? What do you do?

Response: The rules for maintaining confidentiality are described in Situation 10. Because this counselor is behaving in an unethical manner, you should attempt to resolve the conflict in an informal manner by discussing the behavior with him or her. If this does not stop the violations of confidentiality, the counselor following the ACA Ethical Code has the obligation to report the behavior to a state or national ethics committee or to a state licensing board (H.1.d and c). APA has similar standards for reporting unethical behavior (8.04 and 8.05). NASW V.M.3 encourages the social worker to "take action through appropriate channels against unethical conduct by any other member of the profession."

■ **Situation 12:**   You are conducting research with children to learn more about their intellectual abilities at various ages of development. Several new tests are out, and you believe the results would add to your research. You have not been trained on the tests, but they are computer scored and appear to be easy to administer, so you include them in your procedures. Is this ethical?

Response: ACA E.2.a cautions counselors to "recognize the limits of their competence and perform only those testing and assessment services for which they have been trained." APA 2.06 prohibits the use of "psychological assessment techniques by unqualified persons." NASW does not address assessment.

■ **Situation 13:**   You are conducting research to determine children's different responses to certain stimuli. You have 460 subjects who have completed the treatment. You need an *n* of 500 in order to meet the requirements of your funding agency but have run out of time. Because most responses are falling in a certain range, you know that adding 40 subjects will not significantly make a statistical difference in the results. Would you do this? Why or why not?

Response: ACA G.3.b states that "Counselors do not engage in fraudulent research, distort data, misrepresent data, or deliberately bias their results." Similarly, APA 6.21 (a) maintains that "psychologists do not fabricate data or falsify results in their publications." NASW does not address research specifically.

■ **Situation 14:**   The counselor in the next office is concerned about a child who is manifesting unusual behavior. He has been seeing the child for 3 months and is concerned that there is little improvement. He asks you to consult with him on this case. How would you handle this? What precautions should be taken?

Response: ACA B.6.a points out that "information obtained during a consultation is discussed for professional purposes only with persons clearly concerned with the case" and that "every effort is made to protect client identity and avoid undue invasion of privacy." APA 5.06 prohibits psychologists from sharing confidential information that could identify the client without the client's consent and urges psychologists to reveal only necessary information. NASW II.H.1 cautions social workers to reveal information for "compelling reasons" only. Consultation with colleagues is encouraged, but every effort should be made to protect the identity of the consultee.

SUMMARY

It is difficult to recommend specific answers to the situations outlined in this chapter because situations, people, and laws vary. References are given to AACD, APA, and NASW codes of ethics to aid readers in formulating their own resolutions. We hope that readers will be stimulated to read the ethical standards thoroughly and to consider the issues in the light of presenting situations and regulations.

The foregoing situations are by no means all the ethical and legal situations encountered in counseling. Other situations and their resolutions for study appear in the casebooks prepared by ACA and APA. The situations in this chapter are intended only to give readers some indication of their own ethical knowledge and practices. Should uncertainty arise concerning interpretations of ethical practices, counselors have the option of consulting other professionals or local, state, or national professional ethics committees.

REFERENCES

American Counseling Association. (1995). *Code of ethics and standards of practice.* Alexandria, VA: Author.

American Psychological Association. (1992). *Ethical principles of psychologists and code of conduct.* Washington, DC: Author.

Burcky, W. D., & Childers, J. H. Jr. (1976). Buckley amendment: Focus of a professional dilemma. *School Counselor, 23,* 162–164.

Davis, K. (1980). Is confidentiality in group counseling realistic? *Personnel and Guidance Journal, 58,* 197–201.

Denkowski, K. M., & Denkowski, G. C. (1982). Client-counselor confidentiality: An update of rationale, legal status, and implications. *Personnel and Guidance Journal, 60,* 371–375.

Huey, W. (1986). Ethical concerns in school counseling. *Journal of Counseling and Development, 64,* 321–322.

Mappes, D., Robb, G., & Engels, D. (1985). Conflicts between ethics and law in counseling and psychotherapy. *Journal of Counseling and Development, 64,* 246–252.

National Association of Social Workers. (1993). *Code of ethics, adopted by the 1979 NASW Delegate Assembly and revised by the 1993 NASW Delegate Assembly.* Silver Spring, MD: NASW Press.

Pope, K., & Vetter, V. (1992). Ethical dilemmas encountered by members of the American Psychological Association: A national survey. *American Psychologist, 47,* 397–411.

Remley, T. (1990). Counseling records: Legal and ethical issues. In B. Herlihy & L. Golden (Eds.), *Ethical standards casebook* (pp. 162–169). Alexandria, VA: American Association for Counseling and Development.

Salo, M., & Shumate, S. (1993). Counseling minor clients. In T. Remley Jr. (Ed.). *The ACA Legal Series, Vol. 4.* Alexandria, VA: American Counseling Association.

Schmidt, L., & Meara, N. (1984). Ethical, professional, and legal issues in counseling psychology. In S. Brown & R. Lent (Eds.), *Handbook of counseling psychology* (pp. 56–96). New York: Wiley.

Stadler, H. (1989). Balancing ethical responsibility: Reporting child abuse and neglect. *Counseling Psychologist, 17,* 102–110.

Stadler, H. (1990). Confidentiality. In B. Herlihy & L. Golden (Eds.). *Ethical standards casebook* (pp. 102–110). Alexandria, VA: American Association for Counseling and Development.

Talbutt, L. (1980). Medical rights of minors: Some answered and unanswered legal questions. *School Counselor, 27,* 403–406.

Talbutt, L. (1981). Ethical standards: Assets and limitations. *Personnel and Guidance Journal, 60,* 110–112.

Talbutt, L. (1983). Current legal trends regarding abortions for minors: A dilemma for counselors. *School Counselor, 31,* 120–124.

Tarasoff v. Regents of University of California. (1974). 13c. D177; 529 p. 2D553; 118 *California Reporter, 129.*

Wagner, C. (1981). Confidentiality and the school counselor. *Personnel and Guidance Journal, 51,* 305–310.

APPENDIXES

Appendixes A and B suggest techniques for intervening with specific problem behaviors and are included to stimulate ideas. The lists, of course, are not exhaustive, but we hope they help counselors who are attempting to develop treatment plans for children. Beside each heading are *suggested DSM-IV* categories (American Psychiatric Association, 1994) to assist counselors in classifying client behaviors. Use caution in assigning classifications because the categories ordinarily describe mental disorders and are not appropriate for all problematic behaviors that are not a part of a pattern or syndrome of symptoms.

Appendixes C, D, and E present the ethical standards and guidelines for counselors as outlined by the American Counseling Association, the American Psychological Association, and the National Association of Social Workers.

Appendix A

◆

Children's Conflicts with Others
Alternatives for Intervention

The suggestions in this appendix are techniques collected from a variety of resources on counseling children with learning and social problems. Some suggestions are used directly with the child; others are consultation techniques to use with parents and teachers. In each case, the procedures must be incorporated into a therapeutic counseling or consulting atmosphere that includes caring, respect, empathic understanding, and acceptance. The techniques presented can be preventive and developmental as well as remedial; that any given technique has one application to the exclusion of others is nearly impossible to say. In any case, the techniques should be adapted to meet the unique needs of children and their behaviors.

V71.02
312.8
Fighting 312.9

Fighting is one of the most common behavioral problems of children today. Many children have not learned to settle their misunderstandings other than by physical means. Fighting may be a way of gaining attention; a learned behavior from parents, peers, or other significant people in the children's lives; or a way of striking back at a world perceived as cruel and hostile. Resolution of disagreements and conflicts by means other than fighting is a viable goal of school personnel and parents; however, fighting occurs despite the best efforts of adults. Following are various suggestions for working with fighting behavior. (See also "Destructiveness.")

   1. Examine the situation that brought on the encounter. Determine the sequence of events and any particular time, place, or situation in which fights are likely to occur. Become an environmental engineer; rearrange the time schedule or the physical environment. Intervene in the sequence of events to prevent or circumvent fight-arousing conditions.

2. Fighting can be a compensation for feelings of inadequacy, ignorance of social skills, learned behavior from the home, or a means of covering up emotional or learning problems. Investigate these possibilities by becoming a child watcher and listening actively to the child (see chapter 5).

3. Use group or family discussions to focus on how fighting helps or hurts the fighter, how others feel about fighting, the consequences of fighting, and ways in which the fighter could solve conflicts more effectively. Also encourage children to practice new behaviors before the group and use their feedback to improve relationships.

4. Determine the goal of the fighter (see chapter 10 regarding goals of misbehavior). Is the child seeking attention, power, revenge, or free time? Is the fighting a learned behavior? Could the fighting be due to a lack of social skills?

5. Contract with the fighter to not fight for a short period of time (2 hours, 4 hours, 1 day). Continue to renegotiate the contract until the behavior decreases significantly. Rewards for not fighting and consequences for fighting behavior may be included (see chapter 8 regarding contingency contracting).

6. Allow two evenly matched students to fight it out under supervision, using pillows, or styrofoam bats. In an extreme case cited by Stradley and Aspinall (1975), a school administrator set aside one night a month for chronic fighters to meet, with parents required to be present.

7. Arrange with the physical education teacher for students to work out their emotions with punching bags or other equipment under supervision. Each time students are found fighting, encourage them to go to the gym and work out for a certain period of time (perhaps 15 minutes). After a cooling-off period, the fighters should be required to write a plan for avoiding future fighting. Nonwriters may dictate or tape their contracts.

8. Have the fighters write their side of the story or tell it to a tape recorder. Ask the children to read their stories to you, or listen to the tape with them. Discussion of the stories provides a release for emotion, as well as a stimulus for evaluating the behavior and its consequences and for planning other ways to resolve such situations in the future (Collins & Collins, 1975).

9. Films, television programs, or stories can stimulate children to think more objectively about fighting and its consequences. Follow the film or story with a family or group discussion examining the causes and consequences of fighting and other ways the situation could have been resolved.

10. Children and parents or teacher may cooperatively draw up a list of ground rules concerning fighting. Each time the adult notices the child about to become involved in a fight, the adult asks, "What is the ground rule?" Have the child repeat the rule. Early and consistent intervention is necessary. A variation is to clearly define the consequences of fighting and, when fighting is about to occur, ask, "What happens when someone fights?"

11. Encouragement from friends or peers (or other kinds of peer pressure) can help the child control fighting behavior. Find the fighter a good model with whom to work or play. Ask the child to describe or list the model's behaviors. Rehearse and practice admired behaviors.

12. Have two fighting children clean a window, one on each side of the window, facing one another. Encourage them to look *really mean* and glare at each other. The first child to smile loses the game of "looking mean" but wins a hug or other reinforcement (Blanco, 1972).

13. Isolation techniques such as Seat 2, the quiet corner, and time-out rooms are effective for helping children cool off. When the children feel ready to return to the family group or classroom, they may do so without lectures or blame, provided they have a plan for staying out of fights (see chapter 8 regarding isolation techniques).

14. The adult may quietly ask the fighters to leave the room and develop a plan for solving their conflict. Because the fighters are disturbing the other activities in the room, the adult may ask them to reschedule their fight for another time and place. Usually the children react in shock and quietly join in the group or family activities.

15. Three chairs are placed in a semicircle. The adult sits between the two fighters and asks them to describe what happened. The adult repeats verbatim to Child A what Child B says, and then to B what A says. This continues until usually everyone ends up laughing. The adults limit themselves to conveying messages between A and B and refrain from making judgments or placing blame (see chapter 6). Discussion of a plan for avoiding future conflicts may follow.

16. Dreikurs, Grunwald, and Pepper (1971) suggested that parents withdraw to the bedroom or bathroom until the fighting ceases. Take precautions to prevent one child from harming the other.

17. Peer pressure, especially in small groups, is often effective in helping fighting children change their behavior. Carlin and Armstrong (1968) suggested a technique for reducing aggressiveness and rewarding cooperative group play. The adult may arrange rewards to be given to the group when they are playing or working cooperatively. The adult should present the reward to the group and tell the reason for it. Fines for the misbehavior of a member may also be levied on the group. The amount of the reward minus the fines is divided among group members at the end of the day. For the child who continually misbehaves and causes the group to be fined, isolation techniques are suggested. The misbehaving child would neither receive a portion of the reward for the time spent in isolation nor be the cause of excessive fining when in isolation.

18. Have the fighting children carry index cards and keep a record of the number of fights that occur each day. Have them role-play exactly what happened and the consequences. Discuss alternatives to fighting, rehearse how the situation could have been handled more appropriately, and develop a plan for not fighting in future situations.

19. Build self-esteem so fighting is not necessary for the child to feel good about himself or herself (see "Poor Self-Concept," Appendix B). Responsibility and praise for a job well done add to a positive self-concept—for example, "I appreciate your help in putting away the games we used during this activity."

20. If excessive punishment or brutality seems to be a factor, counsel with the parents to help them learn more effective ways of relating to the child. Books

such as Ginott's *Between Parent and Child* (1965) or Gordon's *Parent Effectiveness Training* (1970) may be helpful.

21. Strongly confront older children with the reality questions (see chapter 4), using these questions every time a fight occurs or is about to occur.

22. For very young children who have trouble with fighting, try play therapy with puppets, art, or drawings to assess feelings that stimulate fighting.

23. Relaxation techniques or music therapy may help angry or anxious children who fight often.

24. Boswell (1982) suggested helping children with their anger through a HELPING model: (1) educating the children for good *H*ealth; (2) assisting them to cope with *E*motions through play therapy, games, bibliotherapy, relaxation, and humor; (3) helping them *L*earn more about their angry feelings; (4) facilitating improvements in *P*ersonal relationships through counseling techniques such as assertiveness training, role-playing, and parent counseling; (5) using *I*magery; (6) teaching them improved cognitive control, the *N*eed to know; and (7) giving *G*uidance about actions, behaviors, and consequences.

25. Limit the student's independent movement, especially in areas where he or she might become more aggressive, and maintain constant supervision (Cummins, 1988).

26. Find a quiet place for the child to work or play away from peers. This procedure should not be a punishment but rather an opportunity for productive work (Cummins, 1988).

V71.02
312.8
Verbal Abusiveness   312.9

Most verbal abusiveness, such as rudeness, sarcasm, impoliteness, and name-calling, is a cover for feelings of inadequacy, a learned behavior from adults or other models, a call for attention, or a way of striking back at an unfriendly world. In this instance, the child needs interactions with adults who are calm, rational, and consistent and who behave maturely. Adults need to be on guard against allowing the child's verbal abusiveness to provoke the same behavior from them. Adults who resort to criticism, belittling, and name-calling have little chance of changing children's behaviors.

1. Determine the goal of the verbal abusiveness. Could it be that the child is seeking attention, revenge, or power? (See chapter 10.) Become a child watcher and listen attentively to determine these needs and goals. Having defined the goal, the adult can help the child find a more constructive means of meeting this need.

2. Meet privately with rude, sarcastic, impolite, or name-calling children. Interpret their behavior to them as a cry for help. Then discuss the reasons they feel it necessary to use verbal abusiveness. Plan with the children ways to avoid the behavior in the future.

3. Meet with the "victims" of the abuser. Explain to these victims that abuse they do not respond to is not as satisfying to the abuser, and the behavior will

decrease (Collins & Collins, 1975). Plan and rehearse their behavior when the abuser attacks.

4. Contract with abusing children to reduce verbal abrasiveness. Clearly define unacceptable behaviors and their consequences. The contract can also include rewards for appropriate responses (see chapter 8).

5. Provide opportunities for success. Praise and reinforce nonabusive behavior. Example: "I noticed how understanding you were when Tom had his accident today. That was a nice thing to say to him."

6. Role-play or use films, filmstrips, or books to demonstrate and provide stimuli for group or family discussions. Examine what has occurred and the consequences. Discuss new and better methods of interacting. Behavior rehearsal may help children practice the new behaviors.

7. Call together the parties engaged in the verbal battle and have them write their story or tell it to a tape recorder. Read the story aloud with them or play the tape, and allow the children to discuss and evaluate what has happened. Ask them to make a plan for avoiding future verbal battles.

8. Encourage the teacher, parents, or other children to ignore the verbal abuser. If the behavior becomes too unacceptable to ignore, use isolation techniques such as Seat 2, quiet corner, or the time-out room (see chapter 8).

9. Use role reversal. Have someone else play the verbal abuser and the abuser play the recipient of the verbal attack. Discuss how it feels to be in each position. Plan for better ways of handling conflicts. Role-play the alternatives and the consequences of proposed new behaviors.

10. Build self-esteem so the child need not resort to verbal abuse (see "Poor Self-Concept," Appendix B). Avoid criticism, name-calling, and belittling remarks. Praise and reinforce cooperative behavior.

11. Give reprimands quietly, firmly, and calmly. Do not attack the child as a person. Focus on the behavior, and admit how the behavior makes you feel—for example, "I get really angry when I hear students talking like that, and I would like you to stop now." Avoid modeling the behaviors for which the reprimand is given.

12. Pair the child with good role models for work and other activities. Discuss with the child the behaviors he or she sees in the models and the positive and negative consequences of these behaviors. Encourage the child to rehearse and practice these behaviors.

13. Try the satiation principle (Krumboltz & Krumboltz, 1972). Every time children use abusive language, have them go into a room alone and practice being abusive. Ask them to talk to a tape recorder in an abusive manner for a specified period of time (perhaps 5 minutes). Children soon tire of this procedure and begin to speak more carefully.

14. Put up a graffiti sheet in the child's room or private area for writing out feelings. Emphasize to the child that vulgar or derogatory language must be used in private (Stradley & Aspinall, 1975).

15. Every time a child is verbally abusive, quietly place a check on a chart or card. Contract with the child so that if a certain number of checks accumulate,

privileges are lost or other consequences previously agreed on are imposed. A child who accumulates fewer checks than the agreed number is rewarded with special privileges chosen by the child. Avoid lecturing, reminding, scolding, or nagging when recording checks as this attention reinforces to the child.

16. Teach children new and acceptable ways of expressing feelings, and suggest words to say in situations in which they tend to be verbally abusive.

17. Help older children develop a self-management plan. Work with them using thought-stopping for irrational ideas and the techniques of cognitive restructuring to stop the feelings that accompany verbal abusiveness. Help them develop an alternative plan for expressing their feelings.

18. For older children, try confrontational techniques such as "Could it be?" questions ("Could it be you want to hurt me by calling me names?") or Glasser's reality questions (see chapter 4).

19. Monitor the child's activities, especially in situations where verbal abusiveness is more likely to occur, and maintain constant supervision (Cummins, 1988).

20. Interact frequently with the child in order to monitor his or her language (Cummins, 1988).

21. Omizo, Hershberger, and Omizo (1988) presented a guidance program for teaching children to cope with anger. They recommended activities for getting to know one another and for becoming aware of feelings. Then discuss specific incidents and feelings, relating the incident to a feeling represented on the Ferris color wheel. The next sessions involve making choices and finding alternative reactions to anger, modeling the behavior, role-playing, and summarizing.

	V71.02
	312.8
Physical Abusiveness	312.9

Physical abusiveness, or bullying, can be a compensation for a poor self-concept. Children often hide fears and feelings of inadequacy behind acts of bullying. Verville (1968) suggested that bullies generally feel inferior. Children may also be responding to or modeling adult behavior they have observed. Bullying may be an attempt to strike back at an unfriendly world or seek power and attention the child cannot otherwise gain. Bullying children need calm, consistent adult-child interactions. However, because bullying behavior usually provokes anger in the adult, the child may receive only criticism and punishment—increasing the child's feelings of worthlessness and hostility.

1. Give reprimands in a quiet, adult manner without devaluing the child as a person. Focus the reprimand on the behavior. Instead of calling the child a name such as *bully*, admit your feelings to the child: "I get angry when I see you hit other children like that, and I would like you to stop."

2. Sociograms are helpful in learning who the bully likes or dislikes. Activities may be grouped with liked children and appropriate role models. Discuss with

children the behaviors they see in the models and the positive and negative consequences of these behaviors. Encourage children to rehearse and practice these behaviors.

3. Have a family or group discussion. Present to the group a hypothetical example similar to an actual incident. Use films, filmstrips, or stories to stimulate discussion. Guide the discussion to explore why children bully, how bullies feel about themselves, how other children feel about bullies, and more appropriate behaviors. Role-play and rehearse the new behaviors. Use feedback and group encouragement to promote changes in behavior.

4. Praise and reinforce friendly and cooperative behavior. For example, if the child helps another, verbally or physically, during play activities or during any social interaction, comment on the appropriate behavior. Catching children in good behavior is an effective intervention for most behavior problems.

5. Contract with the child to reduce specific acts of bullying. Clearly define unacceptable behaviors. Include rewards for success in the contract, along with negative consequences such as isolation for breaking the terms of the contract (see chapter 8).

6. Provide outlets for the child's emotions in supervised activities such as running, hammering, writing out feelings, drawing, pictures, playing games, or talking out feelings.

7. Encourage responsibility by giving children responsible jobs at which they can feel successful—for example, delivering materials or messages, watering plants, or feeding the fish. Avoid drudgery-job assignments.

8. Encourage cooperation by finding an interest or ability the bully has. Have the child pursue this interest or ability by helping others or sharing it with others (for instance, sharing a stamp or rock collection, building a science project).

9. Observe the child's environment to determine situations that provoke bullying behavior. Try to engineer the child's activities to reduce opportunities for bullying. Rearrange time schedules or the physical environment, if possible. Intervene before the opportunity for bullying occurs.

10. Determine the goal of the bullying behavior. Could the child be attempting to gain attention, power, or revenge, or to strike back at what he or she perceives to be a hostile world? (See chapter 10.) Could the bullying be a learned behavior or lack of social skills?

11. Use ideas for building a good self-concept (see Appendix B) so the child does not resort to bullying to cover feelings of inadequacy. Reinforce and praise cooperative behaviors.

12. Use role reversal. Have someone else play the bully and the bully play a victim. Discuss the feelings of each player. Allow the children to suggest more appropriate methods of behaving and to practice the new behaviors.

13. Find a quiet place for the child to work or play away from situations that may stimulate physical abusiveness. Monitor his or her behavior (Cummins, 1988).

14. Teach the child problem-solving skills so he or she can find better ways of reacting to frustrating situations (Cummins, 1988).

V71.02

Cruelty to Peers, Animals, and Others   312.8

Cruelty to people or animals is usually a sign of other problems. Extended counseling may be necessary to uncover the underlying reasons for the cruelty. Children who are cruel to peers or animals may be responding to punitive adults in their own lives. Severe cases may require intensive psychotherapy or even residential treatment (see also suggestions under "Fighting" and "Destructiveness").

1. Closely supervise the children in all activities.

2. Give the children releases for emotional tension—for example, varying quiet activities with physical activities frequently. Encourage constructive physical releases such as running, playing ball, or cycling. Writing, music, art, and talking may also help. Schedule times for releases regularly throughout the day's activities.

3. Employ group or family discussions that emphasize cooperation with others. Discuss the feelings and events that provoked the cruel acts, and plan ways for coping with these feelings.

4. Encourage cooperation, responsibility, and pursuit of interests by giving children responsible jobs that enable them to feel success—for example, delivering messages or filing materials. Do not place more responsibility on the child than the child can tolerate. Find areas of interest, and structure activities and jobs around these interests.

5. Contracting and isolation techniques may be used to control behavior to some extent (see chapter 8). Clearly define and explain acceptable and unacceptable behaviors and the rewards and penalties for each.

6. Carefully structure the child's environment and daily activities to provide little or no opportunity for unacceptable behavior. Plan each hour's activity in cooperation with the child, if possible. A daily schedule of work, play, study time, and planned leisure time can be posted in the child's room or school desk.

7. Avoid physical punishment. Strong punishment produces further anger and the likelihood of aggression. It also provides a model for cruel, aggressive behavior. Limit TV viewing to nonaggressive programs. Remove as many models of aggression and cruelty as possible. Focus on strengths, and reinforce cooperative behaviors.

8. Determine the goal of the cruel behavior. Does the child see the world as cruel? Could the child be seeking revenge or power? What needs are not being met? (See chapter 10.)

9. Diaries, play therapy, fantasy games, sentence completion, and active listening may be used as aids to understanding cruel children. Diaries and play therapy also allow children to vent their thoughts and feelings nondestructively.

10. Interpret the child's cruel behavior as a cry for help and an expression of loneliness and rejection. Ask the child to write out feelings of contempt and cruelty. Discuss the feelings, and make a plan for more constructive ways of handling them.

11. Ask the cruel child to find an admired model and to keep a list of the model's behaviors for a short time. Discuss the behaviors with the child, rehearse new behaviors, and encourage the child to try out new ways of behaving.

12. With the child, draw up a behavioral contract that sets out rewards for appropriate behaviors and the consequences of cruel behavior. Clearly define acceptable and unacceptable behaviors (see chapter 8).

13. The child who has a tendency toward cruelty needs love, attention, acceptance, encouragement, patience, active listening, clearly defined limits, and structure in the environment (Dinkmeyer & McKay, 1973).

	V71.02
	312.8
Destructiveness	312.9

Destructiveness and vandalism are problems of increasing severity in our society (see also "Fighting"). One of the counselor's first concerns is to find what is happening in the child's environment to cause such intense feelings and behavior. Is the child angry at someone or something (school, for instance) to the extent of having an intense need to strike out and hurt that person or place? Could the destructiveness be a result of frustration, feelings of failure, or feelings of revenge because the child feels no one cares? A second concern is gaining the child's trust in order to change this self-defeating behavior—a task that requires time and patience.

1. Determine the goal of the child's destructiveness. Could the motive be attention, feelings of rejection, anger, a need for power, or revenge (see chapter 10)?

2. Examine the situation that brought on the destructiveness or preceded the act. Does the destructiveness occur most often at a particular place, situation, or time. If so, become an environmental engineer, arranging the circumstances or schedule to avoid the situations.

3. Use logical consequences (see Dreikurs et al., 1971) as punishment or penalty for destructive behavior. Whatever the child destroys must be paid for or the cost worked off in some manner. Refrain from harsh punishments, which may reinforce the child's idea that the world is cruel and hostile and that destructiveness is the only way of getting back at this world.

4. Have the child write a description of the destructive act and a plan for avoiding such behavior in the future. If the act occurs in school, tell the child you have placed the description in his or her school file and will remove it at the end of a specified length of time if the act has not been repeated. If the destructiveness occurs in the home or some other environment, file the description of the act in a safe place with the understanding that it will be removed and destroyed at the end of a specified length of time if the act has not been repeated (Collins & Collins, 1975). A reward might accompany the removal of the description from the file.

5. Confront the child nonjudgmentally by interpreting the destructive behavior as a distress signal. Offer to listen and to help. An attitude of genuine

caring and interest is necessary to building a helping relationship (Collins & Collins, 1975). Help the child make a plan to avoid destructive behaviors in the future.

6. Start a campaign of "Keep our school (home) clean!" Working together to build pride in personal areas is often helpful in preventing vandalism or destructiveness, especially if the children are involved and consulted during the planning and are given some responsibilities (Collins & Collins, 1975). "We" feelings build cooperativeness and responsibility.

7. Determine the child's areas of interest and involve the destructive child in working with these interests—not busywork but productive tasks. Peer teaching, peer tutoring, or sharing the interest in another way may be helpful. Guiding the child in pursuing interests and special abilities may be a productive way of diverting the child's behavior toward more constructive actions and building feelings of success.

8. To handle the negative feelings that often accompany vandalism and destructiveness, many parents or teachers put up a large sheet of paper in the child's area or room—a "graffiti sheet" on which the child is allowed to write out feelings (Stradley & Aspinall, 1975). Emphasize to the child that writing out these feelings on other people's property is destructive.

9. Encourage children to keep a diary of their feelings and thoughts or tell them to a tape recorder. Writing or talking provides a means of catharsis and gives the adult some insight into the child's world. The adult and child can then discuss these feelings and develop a plan for coping with them.

10. Play therapy with toys, Play-Doh, music, or drawing may be used in an effort to understand the feelings underlying the child's destructiveness and as a means of catharsis (see chapter 12).

11. Hold group or family discussions focusing on the consequences of vandalism and destructiveness. Help the children look at what they are doing, the consequences, and alternative ways of behaving. Use behavior rehearsal to practice new methods of handling situations.

12. Help the destructive child find a friend and model. Encouragement and peer pressure are effective in helping vandalizing children redirect their behavior into more constructive paths. Pair destructive children with more mature role models to teach them effective ways of behaving. Discuss the behaviors of the model, and allow the children to practice and rehearse these behaviors.

13. Refrain from punishing, scolding, lecturing, moralizing, preaching, or degrading destructive children. These methods reinforce the children's thinking that the world and people are cruel and uncaring.

14. Use contracting with rewards to help the child change destructive behaviors (see chapter 8). Be certain the child understands the rules. Define appropriate and inappropriate behaviors clearly, as well as the rewards and consequences of each.

15. A resource person from a local law enforcement agency can discuss laws and penalties for destructiveness and vandalism with the children, but avoid scare techniques and threats.

16. Arrange the child's schedule to allow time during the day to work off energy. Vary the day's activities from quiet to physical. Encourage physical activities such as running, football or basketball, and bicycling, and quiet releases such as writing, music, art, or talking.

17. Work out a plan with the child and an adult authority so that a child whose intense feelings become overwhelming can signal the adult and report to some agreed-upon place to work out these feelings. For example, assisting the custodians with maintenance and cleaning might help in three ways: (1) to dissipate bad feelings, (2) to develop appreciation for the building, and (3) to create empathy for the custodian, who has to repair damage to the building.

18. Maintain supervision of all activities, and interact with the child often to monitor behaviors and discuss right and wrong methods for coping with situations (Cummins, 1988).

V71.02

Tantrums   313.81

Temper tantrums may give parents or other adults feelings of anger, frustration, and helplessness. Adults often feel they have completely lost control of the child and the situation when children throw temper tantrums. In some children, tantrums are a learned behavior for getting attention or getting their way. Some children have learned to manipulate adults by throwing tantrums; some seek revenge.

1. Determine the motive for the tantrum. Is the tantrum an effort to gain attention, to cover feelings of inadequacy, to manipulate, or to embarrass or strike out at adults? (See chapter 10.)

2. Children throw tantrums because it is a learned behavior that works for them. They get their way or what they want. The adult can stop the behavior by not allowing it to work. Ignore the behavior whenever possible; refuse to give in. The tantrum thus becomes an unrewarding behavior.

3. If ignoring the tantrum becomes impossible, quietly ask the child to leave the room and write a plan for avoiding tantrums in the future. The child should have the option of returning and behaving appropriately after a cooling-off period. Physically removing the child from the room may be necessary. Putting on the act is not as much fun for the child with no audience (see chapter 8 regarding isolation techniques).

4. Provide alternative methods of venting feelings. Ask children to keep a diary of their feelings, write them out on paper, or talk to a tape recorder. Play therapy can help, and fantasy games or storytelling may provide some catharsis and insight (see chapter 12).

5. Use active listening to understand the child's feelings and the motives behind the tantrums (see chapter 5).

6. Investigate the possibility of the tantrums being related to a physical problem if the behavior continues over a period of time. Refer the child to a pediatrician for examination.

7. Try to determine the sequence of events that brings on a tantrum or if they are most likely to occur at a particular time, place, or situation. Rearrange the environment or schedule to reduce the child's frustrations, if possible.

8. Avoid threats, lectures, scolding, and nagging, which can be reinforcing because they are forms of attention. Define the unacceptable behavior and the consequences for such behavior (see chapter 8), and consistently carry out the terms of the behavioral contract between the adult and the child.

9. Kaufman and Wagner (1972) described a "barb" technique used to cope with tantrums in male adolescents. They reported a case study in which they (1) built rapport with the adolescent, (2) identified the situations provoking the tantrum, (3) defined the adolescent's actual behaviors, and (4) defined the consequences of those behaviors. Role reversal was used to demonstrate his behavior to him. The counselor then gave the adolescent a cue that a put-down or insult was coming, and he was rewarded for appropriate responses to the barb. In later sessions, barbs were given by other people and became more subtle to help the adolescent generalize his newly learned responses. The authors caution that the technique must be used systematically; that unplanned barbs must never be used in anger; that when the tantrum is unrelated to a barb, nothing should be mentioned concerning the technique or its rewards; and that moving too slowly or too quickly through the program hampers its effectiveness.

10. Severely disturbed children often have temper tantrums because they feel insecure. Using techniques of isolation and other forms of strictness may tend to intensify these feelings. In such cases, some tantrum-throwing children become quiet when held affectionately and reassured.

11. Hare-Mustin (1975) found paradoxical intention an effective method for helping one 4-year-old boy. The child's tantrums were unpredictable and occurred anywhere. The adults with the child decided that he should continue to have the tantrums, but only in a specified place. A room was selected, and each time the child began to have a tantrum he was immediately taken to this room. If he was not at home, he agreed to wait until he could return home and go to his tantrum room. The next step was to decide on a time of day for tantrums to occur. The family selected a 2 hour period. If the child started to have a tantrum at any other time, he was reminded to wait until the appropriate hour. The author reported a dramatic reduction in, and then disappearance of, the problem behavior.

12. Peer pressure can be an effective tool for modifying children's behaviors. Group or family discussions of temper tantrums and their effects on others may help the tantrum-throwing child understand how others react to the behavior.

13. Have another child role-play tantrum behavior. Discuss how the behavior helps or hurts the child and others, and make a plan for alternative ways of behaving. Rehearse and practice the new behaviors.

14. Help the child find a mature model. Ask the child to keep a list of the model's admired behaviors and ways in which the model handles frustrations. Rehearse and practice these ways of behaving.

15. Examine with children the self-messages that make them angry enough to throw tantrums, and try to identify more rational and helpful self-messages (see chapter 7).

16. Teach the child more appropriate ways to communicate his or her unhappiness through problem-solving techniques, role-modeling, or other counseling strategies.

Chronic Complaining   316.00

Chronic complaining about feeling ill gains attention or sympathy and avoids unpleasant situations. This behavior can be manifested as an exaggeration of symptoms or fantasies of diseases: "I think I have cancer." Other kinds of hypochondria are consistent headaches, stomachaches, and muscle aches.

1. Recommend to the parents and child that the complaining child be examined by a pediatrician to rule out actual physical illness.

2. Try to determine the motive or goal of the chronic complainer. Are the complaints a result of feelings of inadequacy, fear of failure, a need for attention or sympathy, or an attempt to avoid an unpleasant task? Help the child find ways of meeting this need more effectively.

3. Enlist the cooperation of the pediatrician. Many pediatricians require the children to come straight to their office whenever they feel a pain. Children (and parents) soon tire of repeated trips to the pediatrician.

4. Actively listen to the child's complaints (see chapter 5). Do not over sympathize, but tell the child you will write a note or call the parents to suggest a trip to the doctor's office to check out the complaint.

5. Ask complaining children to write out their feelings or tell them to a tape recorder. A diary might help determine the circumstances under which the feelings occur.

6. Excessive stress and tension can provoke chronic complaining. Check with parents, teachers, and other significant persons in the child's life. The child may be under pressure from schoolwork, from problems within the home, or from peers.

7. Take precautions to ensure that the child is not ill when complaints occur; parents and other adults can then firmly insist that the complainer attend to the task or return to class. Reassure the child that, should an illness occur, help will be provided (Blanco, 1972).

8. Chronic complaining may result from a lack of interest in the world around the child—school, friends, activities. Help these children find an interest or activity in which they can feel successful. Encourage participation in groups, children's clubs or organizations, or neighborhood activities.

9. Enlist the aid of a buddy to encourage the complainer to become more involved in the world and to participate in friendships and activities.

10. Rutter (1975) suggested that "treatment consists of dealing with the stresses which gave rise to the disorder and in helping the child find a better way of dealing with stress" (pp. 238–239). Actively listen for clues to what these

stresses are, and plan with the child for more constructive means of coping with the tensions (relaxation techniques, physical activities, talking, writing, play therapy).

11. Have complaining children monitor their own behavior. Give these children an index card and ask them to check it every time they become aware that they are complaining. Catching oneself in the act often increases awareness of the behavior and reduces the incidence.

12. Try to find ways for complaining children to assume more responsibility in their lives. Feeling competent and worthwhile reduces the need to gain attention through sickness.

313.81
Tattling   V61.8

The tattler, like a gossip, is attempting to gain attention and favor, usually with an adult authority figure. Ignoring talebearers is difficult because many times they bring needed information to adults. However, the tattler is usually lonely and rejected by peers.

1. Determine the goal of tattling. Is the child attempting to gain attention or power or to seek revenge? (See chapter 10.) Confront the child with your hypothesis—for example, "Could it be that you are telling me this to get Warren in trouble?" (Dreikurs et al., 1971).

2. Meet privately with the tattler and interpret the behavior as a cry for help to gain acceptance and recognition in the group. Discuss the reasons the child tattles. Plan with the tattler for ways to avoid the behavior in the future and to gain attention and acceptance in other ways.

3. Help the tattler gain acceptance by capitalizing on special abilities and interests such as sports, hobbies, or special knowledge. Encourage the child to share these abilities and interests with others or to peer-teach or tutor another child.

4. The tattler may need help in learning social skills. Help the child find a model. Have the child list the model's admired behaviors and then rehearse and practice these new behaviors.

5. Turn your attention elsewhere when the tattler begins a tale. Say, "Rather than discussing that now, perhaps we should _____."

6. Use tattling as a topic for family or group discussions. Guide the group to look at motives for tattling and the reactions and feelings of others toward a tattler. Films, filmstrips, or stories may provide a stimulus for these discussions. List alternatives to tattling, and rehearse and practice them.

7. Use storytelling, choosing a hypothetical example similar to the child's problem, to show the consequences of tattling and the reactions of others to tattling (chapter 12). Ask the child questions about how the tattler must be feeling and how the child who is being tattled on must feel.

8. Instead of listening to the tattler, ask the child to write a brief note to you explaining what has happened.

9. Ignore the tattling behavior, but praise and reinforce appropriate behaviors. Give attention to the child for the cooperativeness.

10. When ignoring tattling becomes impossible, draw up a contract with the child with rewards for not tattling. Penalties and rewards for appropriate and inappropriate behavior may be included (see chapter 8).

11. Build self-esteem (see Appendix B) so the child does not have to resort to tattling to gain attention and acceptance.

12. Pair tattlers with good role models for work and other activities. Discuss with the tattlers the behaviors they see in the model and the positive and negative consequences of these behaviors. Encourage the child to rehearse and practice these behaviors.

13. Krumboltz and Krumboltz (1972) suggested teaching children the "discrimination principle"—identifying clues that help them know when to report an incident to adults (such as danger to property or possible personal harm), as opposed to reports that are considered tattling.

14. Have tattling children monitor their own behavior. Ask them to check an index card each time they tattle or feel the urge to tattle. Increasing awareness of the behavior may decrease the frequency.

15. Encourage tattling children to problem-solve. Rather than having the adult take over the situation and seek a resolution, say to the child, "I wonder what could be done to straighten this out." Assist the child in seeking alternatives.

16. Teach the child what information is appropriate for reporting (emergencies, fighting, cheating, and so on) and what is inappropriate (Cummins, 1988).

Swearing   313.81

Swearing may reflect a need for attention, an effort to shock others or prove to peers that the child is "big," or it may be modeling behavior. Swearing can also be a release for pent-up aggression or tension or an expression of rebellion.

1. Determine the motive for the behavior (see chapter 10). Is the goal a need for attention or power, an effort to cover feelings of inadequacy, or an emotional release? Does the swearing reflect a lack of social skills?

2. Confront the child, interpreting the swearing behavior as a need to shock or gain attention—for example, "Could it be that you want to shock me by talking in that manner?" (Dreikurs et al., 1971). Work with the child to make a plan to avoid swearing in the future.

3. Examine the child's world. Does a certain time of day, a particular situation, or a certain event provoke the swearing? If so, attempt to reduce the frustrations by rescheduling or rearranging the environment.

4. Ignore the behavior, if possible. When this becomes impossible, contract with the child to decrease the swearing systematically (see chapter 8). Build in rewards for success and consequences for unacceptable behavior. Isolation techniques may or may not be used in the contract, depending on the severity of the problem.

5. Try a type of implosive counseling, or flooding. Place the swearer in an isolated room, and ask the child to swear continually for a specified period of time, such as 5 minutes.

6. Small children may not be aware of the meaning of the words they use. Ask the child to define the word. Remind swearers that certain words are acceptable in certain places and at particular times and others are not appropriate.

7. Work with the swearer to list acceptable words to express feelings. Write a contract with the child that states that, when frustrated, the child will use these words instead of the usual swearwords. The swearer can carry the list on an index card for easy reference.

8. Dreikurs et al. (1971) suggested inviting children to show how many bad words they know. The authors further suggested that the counselor help swearing children understand why they like to use these words and what they could do instead of swearing to feel important. Discuss alternative methods of for expressing emotions (physical activities, art, games, music, new verbal responses). Rehearse these alternatives, and contract with the child to try the new methods of responding to emotions.

9. Hold a family or group discussion focused on the motives for swearing and how others feel about the swearing person. Use role-playing and role rehearsal to help children see the behavior and its effects on others. Discuss alternatives to swearing, and role-play these alternatives.

10. Use storytelling (see chapter 12) with a hypothetical example similar to the child's problem. Ask the child to react to the story.

11. If swearing seems to be a means of releasing tension or aggression, contract with the child to work off these emotions in more acceptable ways—running, writing, talking, physical exercises. Writing out feelings in a diary or talking into a tape recorder may also help the child vent feelings.

12. Aversive conditioning may help a child who wants to stop swearing. For example, every time the child says a swearword, the punishment might be for the child to snap a rubber band worn on his or her wrist.

13. Help the child find a model. Have the swearer watch the model for several days and list the ways the model reacts to frustrating situations. Rehearse and practice the new behaviors with the swearer.

14. Use cognitive restructuring to help angry children who use swearing as an outlet. They may be able to reframe the situation so it does not stimulate swearing.

15. Self-monitoring may help older children become aware of their behavior. Self-reward for *not* swearing should be included in the self-management program.

16. Teach children stress-management techniques, such as deep breathing, to help ward off the feelings that may stimulate swearing. When the child feels an urge to swear, he or she is encouraged to deep-breathe instead.

17. Use confrontational techniques such as the reality questions (chapter 4) to encourage responsible behavior.

18. Fischer and Nehs (1978) successfully reduced swearing behavior in one 11-year-old boy by setting up a chore (a mildly aversive stimulus) as a consequence of the swearing behavior.

Lying   309.3

As a part of their normal development, young children often lie because of their inability to distinguish fact from fantasy or because they fear disapproval and punishment. Habitual lying may be due to feelings of inadequacy, insecurity, or pressure from parents or other significant persons in the child's life. It could also be a learned behavior to escape responsibility or punishment.

1. Determine what needs of the child are not being met (see chapter 10). Is the child seeking attention or power? Is he or she attempting to evade reality or the consequences of misbehavior?

2. Arrange for successful experiences in learning and in daily interactions with peers. Use praise and other types of reinforcement for appropriate behaviors to build confidence and self-esteem. Lying may not be necessary if the child has self-confidence (see Appendix B). Ignore the lying or fantasy behaviors while reinforcing positive behavior.

3. Avoid trying to trap the liar. If you have positive evidence that the child is lying, be quietly direct in your confrontation—for example, "Jeff, I know that you did not do your homework." If you do not have direct knowledge of the truth, admit to the child that you are having trouble understanding all of the story and ask for more details. This response lets the child know you do not believe all that is being said and gives the child a chance to tell the truth.

4. When the child continues to tell stories that are obviously fantasies, the adult may confront the fantasizer in a nonjudgmental manner, using statements such as "You know, I have never seen or heard anything like that, and I'm really having trouble understanding what you are telling me. Could we begin again?" With this technique, you do not call the child a liar, but you convey that you simply cannot accept all that is being said as the truth.

5. Note the areas in which lying seems to occur most often. Is the child lying about schoolwork, parents, money, clothes, or aggressive abilities? If the lying occurs most frequently in one area, examine the possibilities of changing the circumstances in this area to decrease the temptation or pressure to lie.

6. Talk with parents, teachers, and others close to the child. Are the expectations and pressures placed on the child too great? Do parents expect perfect behavior and the highest school marks? Are teachers demanding too much work or work that is too difficult for the child? If so, consult with these adults concerning ways of reducing pressures on the child.

7. Ignore fantasy tales that are meaningless, or ask the child to write the story and give it to you. Caution should be exercised not to ignore the child altogether. Respond to positive behaviors.

8. If the problem seems to stem from excessive pressure, decrease the push toward competition with others and emphasize competition with self: "You did six math problems yesterday. Let's see if you can do eight today."

9. Use the technique of storytelling (see chapter 12). Choose a hypothetical example involving behaviors similar to those exhibited by the lying child. Ask the child to react to the story, and discuss these reactions.

10. Review the child's academic progress. Does lying compensate for a learning difficulty or cover some other real or imagined failure?

11. Films, filmstrips, stories, and other materials may provide stimuli for a good classroom or family discussion on lying and its consequences. Include in the discussion methods for avoiding lying and better ways of handling situations.

12. Dreikurs et al. (1971) suggested that adults not pay attention to or respond to lying behavior, fantastic stories, or something that seems exaggerated or incorrect.

13. A child who feels worthwhile, loved, and successful does not have to resort to lying (see also Appendix B). Give the child responsible jobs such as carrying messages, watering plants, or feeding fish (not drudgery work) to promote feelings of success. Use a sociogram to find admired classmates, and pair the child with these children for group activities.

14. Enlist the aid of a buddy to involve the child in activities. Ask the child to keep a record of a model's behaviors to aid in learning techniques for successful interpersonal relationships. Practice and rehearse these behaviors in a safe atmosphere. Encourage the child to try the new behaviors.

15. Contract with the child not to lie. The contract should include acceptable behaviors and their rewards and clearly define unacceptable behaviors and their consequences (see chapter 8).

16. Use self-monitoring to increase awareness of the behavior. Have children keep a record of each time they told the truth when they were tempted to lie. Build in self-reward for situations in which the child tells the truth.

17. Take no action unless there is conclusive evidence that the child is telling the truth (Cummins, 1988).

Teasing

309.3
V71.02

Teasing is attention-getting behavior with several possible motives. Children may get attention only when they misbehave, they may be showing friendship for another person, or they may have hostile motivation. Teasing is sometimes the result of a lack of knowledge about how to make friends or how to be a friend or of other social skills.

1. Determine the goal of the teasing (see chapter 10). Is the motive attention, power, or revenge, or does the teasing come from a lack of social skills? Teasing can be a way of compensating for feelings of inadequacy or a means of covering up learning or emotional problems. Become a child watcher; listen actively to investigate all possibilities (see chapter 5).

2. Examine the circumstances under which the child teases. What is the sequence of events? Does teasing occur most frequently in a particular time, place, or situation. If so, rearrange the environment or schedule to reduce provoking circumstances.

3. Group or family discussions may help the child see how teasing behavior

affects others and produce suggestions and a plan for alternative ways of behaving. Peer pressure in group situations is an effective behavior modifier.

4. Ignore the teasing behavior as long as possible. Then use an isolation technique such as Seat 2, quiet corner, or the time-out room (see chapter 8). The teaser should be free to return to the group when the child has worked out a plan for behaving more acceptably.

5. Cooperatively draw up a contract to decrease teasing behaviors. Clearly define unacceptable behavior and the consequences (see chapter 8). Rewards for appropriate behaviors may also be included.

6. Help the child find other ways to get attention or acceptance. Encourage the child to pursue liked activities, interests, or hobbies and to share them with other children. Allow the child to peer-teach or tutor another child. Assign responsible tasks to the child; avoid meaningless work or drudgery jobs.

7. Teasing is often modeling behavior. Check the child's environment to determine if the teaser is modeling an admired person. Help the child find a more appropriate model, observe the model's behaviors, and rehearse new and more acceptable ways of interacting with peers.

8. Have another child role-play a teaser to allow the child to see the behavior more clearly and observe how others respond to teasing. Use role reversal to allow the teaser to see how teasing helps or hurts personal relationships. After the role playing, discuss the feelings of the person teasing and the person being teased.

9. Talk with the people being teased. Plan ways for these children not to reinforce the aggressor's teasing behavior. Explain to the victims of the teaser that the behavior is not as much fun if the person being teased does not respond. Explain to them that the motivation of the teaser is to get attention, even though it is negative attention. Role-play situations, teaching the victims to respond with new techniques as cognitive restructuring or ignoring the teasers.

10. Albert Ellis's ideas of irrational thinking may be incorporated into counseling with the person being teased (see chapter 7 for an explanation of cognitive restructuring). Teach the victim to change internal thinking from "It is terrible to be teased" to "I don't like to be teased, but it is not the end of the world, and I can just ignore the teasing."

11. Children have little need to tease if they feel they are a part of their environment and successful in the world. Find ways of providing successful experiences. Capitalize on the child's interests and abilities. Encourage participation in activities at school, at home, or in the community.

V71.02
Disobedience, Negativism, and Resistant Behavior   313.81

Disobedience, negativism, and resistant behavior are open displays of anger and antagonism toward authority figures. Children exhibiting these behaviors are often highly critical, easily irritated, and sometimes aggressive.

1. Determine the goals of the behavior (see chapter 10). Actively listen to the child to learn about the child's feelings toward self, family interactions, and the school (see chapter 5). Children tend to strike out when their needs for love and respect are not met. Recognize the child's feelings. Admit that the child has the power to disobey or resist. Avoid threatening the child. Refuse to become involved in a conflict; tell the child you will discuss the matter later (Dreikurs et al., 1971).

2. Dreikurs et al. (1971) suggested that adults interpret the goal of the misbehavior to the child with "Could it be?" questions, but not at the time of the conflict. Later the adult might ask, "Could it be that you would like to show me that you are boss?" The question opens the door for a nonjudgmental discussion of the child's motives and for planning better ways of meeting these needs.

3. When there is no conflict, discuss with the child the consequences of the negative behavior and plan alternative behaviors. Rehearse and practice alternative behaviors.

4. Avoid open confrontations with put-downs, threats, and name-calling. Try active listening to learn the reason for the negativism or disobedience (see chapter 5).

5. Assess the environment in which the child is disobedient, negative, or resistant. Is the child receiving some reinforcement from peers or other significant persons? What circumstances provoke the behavior? Is there a time when negativism, resistance, and disobedience occur most often? Rearrangement of schedules or the environment may decrease the undesirable behavior.

6. Avoid possible conflict situations by allowing the child some choices—for example, "Do you want to complete the assignment now or after lunch?" Make a list of tasks to be done, and cooperatively plan the day's schedule with the child.

7. Specify in advance the consequences for disobedience, negativism, and resistant behavior. Hold a discussion with the child in which you draw up ground rules and the consequences for breaking the rules. Rules made in cooperation with children are carried out more readily.

8. When the child misbehaves, the inappropriate behavior should be clearly explained. Children often do not understand what they have done wrong. After defining the problem, work with the child to draw up a plan or contract to change behavior (see chapter 8). The plan may include rewards for acceptable behavior and penalties for unacceptable behavior. Rehearse and practice new behaviors to help the child meet the terms of the contract.

9. Ignore the negativism, disobedience, and resistant behavior, if possible. When ignoring the behavior becomes impossible, isolation techniques such as Seat 2, quiet corner or time-out room may be effective in changing the behavior (see chapter 8). Avoid physical punishment; it provides only a model of aggression for the child.

10. Disobedience, negativism, and resistant behaviors are often attempts to cover up a lack of self-confidence, lack of social skills, or inability to find success in school and other areas of life. Attempt to determine if the unacceptable behavior is compensatory behavior for a learning problem, a lack of self-esteem,

or some other problem. Look over the child's academic progress to determine if the behavior could be related to a learning problem. Carefully watch the child's interactions with others to determine if the problem is related to difficulties with social relationships. Listen for clues that may help you understand the child's feelings about self and others (see the discussion of active listening in chapter 5).

11. Praise, telephone calls, or notes to the child's home about good behavior, along with other positive reinforcers such as praise, privileges, or rewards, may be effective in decreasing negative behavior.

12. Barcai and Rabkin (1972) reported they were successful in changing a 13-year-old girl's undesirable behavior by "excommunication." The girl had learned to control her family by behaving inappropriately to get their attention and manipulate their interactions. The family was instructed to define appropriate and inappropriate behaviors, totally ignore her when she behaved in an unacceptable manner, and talk with and respond to her when she was behaving appropriately.

13. Suggest that parents or teachers leave the room for a few moments to remove themselves from the conflict. This arouses surprise and curiosity in the child about what the adult will do. The action also prevents the adult from entering into a conflict with the child (Dreikurs et al., 1971).

14. Encourage the child to use constructive methods for releasing negative feelings. Suggest techniques such as talking out or writing out feelings, drawing, music, or physical exercises. Arrange for periodic emotional outlets if necessary.

15. Find the negative, resistant, or disobedient child a model or friend. Ask the child to watch the model and record admired behaviors. Then rehearse and practice these behaviors with the child.

16. Encourage negative children to pursue interests, hobbies, and abilities and to become involved in activities, clubs, or other organizations in which they can feel successful. Enlist the aid of a friend or buddy to involve the child in activities.

17. Blumberg (1986) used a daily progress report and checklist to change the disruptive classroom behavior of a 13-year-old boy. The inappropriate behaviors included constant talking, interrupting teachers, and daily altercations with peers. Each teacher rated the subject daily on positive and negative behaviors. Positive behaviors were reinforced with tangible rewards at first but increasingly with intangible rewards (praise, attention from special teachers) as time passed. In conferences, the parents were encouraged to use verbal praise.

V71.02
312.8
312.9
Stealing   312.32

Children may steal because of the high value society places on material wealth, because of ignorance of ownership rights, to impress others, or for the adventure of getting away with something. Although many children try stealing once or twice during their developmental years, persistent, repeated acts of stealing indicate other problems and require an understanding of the motives and needs behind the behavior.

1. Determine the motivation or goal of the behavior (see chapter 10). Is the child seeking attention, power, or revenge? Is the behavior the result of a dare, an initiation, or peer pressure? Is this the first incidence of stealing, or is there a pattern of behavior? Actively listen to the child to try to understand of the motive (see chapter 5).

2. Temptation in all situations can be kept to a minimum to help the child control stealing. Adults can place too much temptation before even the most honest children.

3. Use logical consequences to cope with the stealing child. Have the child replace or make payment for stolen property, through work if possible.

4. Give the child an opportunity to return the stolen property anonymously to an unpoliced area at a certain time without accusing anyone.

5. Have group or family discussions about stealing, its consequences, and the rights of ownership. Films, filmstrips, books, and newspapers can stimulate such a discussion. Discuss alternatives to stealing. Plan and rehearse appropriate ways of handling situations that might tempt the child.

6. Make certain children are aware of ownership rights. Comments such as "This is school property, but it is our responsibility" remind the child of ownership rights.

7. If stealing occurs in a group, often the children can solve the problem themselves if allowed to do so. Present the situation to the group, ask them to draw up a plan for resolving the problem, and leave the room for a few moments. Upon returning, ask for a discussion of the plan, avoiding accusations and blame.

8. Avoid trying to trap the thief or making threats that cannot be carried out, such as "We are all going to stay here until the property is returned." Such threats inevitably end up with the adult having to withdraw the ultimatum.

9. If you have positive evidence that the child is stealing, be quietly direct in your confrontation. Ask the child for a plan to pay for the stolen item and to avoid stealing in the future.

10. Use behavior rehearsal to practice situations in which the child could be tempted to steal. Include instances in which peer pressure might occur. Discuss ways to handle these situations, and practice the behaviors.

11. Adults can inform children who are suspected of stealing. Discuss with the children the consequences, should the behavior continue. Avoid scare tactics.

12. Use storytelling (see chapter 12), posing a hypothetical example similar to the child's problem. Ask the child for a reaction to the story. Discuss what might happen to the story character involved in stealing.

13. Help the stealing child find a model. Have the child watch the model for several days and list admired behaviors. Rehearse and practice these behaviors with the child.

14. Children may be stealing to feel more accepted by their peers. Most children who find some success in their lives and feel they belong have no need

to behave inappropriately. Find an interest, hobby, or ability (stamp or rock collection, knowledge on a subject of particular interest to children, sports ability) the child possesses. Use this strength to help the child become involved in activities and find friendships.

15. If stealing is a prevalent or persistent behavior, ask a local law enforcement person to talk with the children about the legal consequences of stealing.

16. Encourage the child to focus on "reality, responsibility, right and wrong" through the techniques of reality therapy (see chapter 4).

17. Azrin and Wesolowski (1974) suggested an "overcorrection procedure" in which children are required to give back not only the stolen property but an additional item.

18. Miller and Klungness (1986) reviewed behavioral literature on the various approaches to the treatment of stealing behavior and suggested that aversive contingency-management techniques, including scolding, threatening, lecturing, and physical force, are ineffective because the punishment is usually delayed and because of legal constraints on school personnel. Positive contingency-management techniques (including group contingencies)—reinforcing the non-occurrence of stealing and including consequences for stealing—combined with family intervention seem to be preferred. They also recommended school prevention programs that promote prosocial alternative school activities.

19. Rosen and Rosen (1983) used a highly controlled and structured behavioral technique to eliminate a 7-year-old boy's stealing behavior. During the first phase of the study, all items in the subject's desk were marked with a green pen. His desk was checked at 15-minute intervals, and he earned points redeemable at the classroom store for having only items marked in green. Fines were levied for articles not marked. The check intervals were gradually lengthened, and the point-and-fine system phased out.

REFERENCES

American Psychiatric Association. (1994). *Diagnostic and statistical manual of mental disorders* (4th ed.). Washington, DC: Author.

Azrin, N., & Wesolowski, M. (1974). Theft reversal: An overcorrection procedure for eliminating stealing by retarded persons. *Journal of Applied Behavior Analysis, 7,* 577–581.

Barcai, A., & Rabkin, L. (1972). Excommunication as a family therapy technique. *Archives of General Psychiatry, 27,* 804–808. (Reprinted in C. Schaefer & H. Millman, Eds., *Therapies for children: A handbook of effective treatments for problem behaviors.* San Francisco: Jossey-Bass, 1977.)

Blanco, R. (1972). *Prescription for children with learning and adjustment problems.* Springfield, IL: Charles C. Thomas.

Blumberg, T. (1986). Transforming low achieving and disruptive adolescents into model students. *School Counselor, 34,* 67–72.

Boswell, J. (1982). HELPING children with their anger. *Elementary School Guidance and Counseling, 16,* 278–287.

Carlin, A., & Armstrong, H. (1968). Rewarding social responsibility in disturbed children: A group play technique. *Psychotherapy: Theory, Research and Practice, 5,* 169–174.

Collins, M., & Collins, D. (1975). *Survival kit for teachers (and parents)*. Pacific Palisades, CA: Goodyear.

Cummins, K. (1988). *The teacher's guide to behavioral interventions: Intervention strategies for behavior problems in the educational environment*. Columbia, MO: Hawthorne Educational Services.

Dinkmeyer, D., & McKay, G. (1973). *Raising a responsible child*. New York: Simon & Schuster.

Dreikurs, R., Grunwald, B., & Pepper, F. (1971). *Maintaining sanity in the classroom*. New York: Harper & Row.

Fischer, J., & Nehs, R. (1978). Use of a commonly available chore to reduce a boy's rate of swearing. *Journal of Behavior Therapy and Experimental Psychiatry, 9,* 81–83. (Reprinted in C. Schaefer, H. Millman, S. Sichel, & J. Zwilling, (Eds.), *Advances in therapies for children*. San Francisco: Jossey-Bass, 1986.)

Ginott, H. (1965). *Between parent and child*. New York: Macmillan.

Gordon, T. (1970). *Parent effectiveness training*. New York: Wyden.

Hare-Mustin, R. (1975). Treatment of temper tantrums by a paradoxical intention. *Family Processes, 14,* 481–485. (Reprinted in C. Schaefer & H. Millman, Eds., *Therapies for children: A handbook of effective treatments for problem behaviors*. San Francisco: Jossey-Bass, 1977.)

Kaufman, L., & Wagner, B. (1972). Barb: A systematic treatment technology for temper control disorders. *Behavior Therapy, 3,* 84–90.

Krumboltz, J., & Krumboltz, H. (1972). *Changing children's behavior*. Englewood Cliffs, NJ: Prentice-Hall.

Miller, G., & Klungness, L. (1986). Treatment of non-confrontative stealing in school-age children. *School Psychology Review, 15,* 24–35.

Omizo, M., Hershberger, J., & Omizo, S. (1988). Teaching children to cope with anger. *Elementary School Guidance and Counseling, 22,* 241–245.

Rosen, H., & Rosen, L. (1983). Eliminating stealing: Use of stimulus control with an elementary student. *Behavior Modification, 7,* 56–63.

Rutter, M. (1975). *Helping troubled children*. New York: Plenum.

Stradley, W., & Aspinall, R. (1975). *Discipline in the junior high/middle school*. New York: Center for Applied Research in Education.

Verville, E. (1968). *Behavior problems of children*. Philadelphia: Saunders.

Appendix B

◆

Children's Conflicts with Self
Alternatives for Intervention

As in Appendix A, the following techniques are derived from a variety of resources and methods for counseling with children. The procedures must be incorporated into a caring and accepting counseling or consulting atmosphere, and the techniques should be modified to meet the individual needs of children and their particular social, learning, or behavioral problems.

	296.xx
Self-Destructive or Suicidal Behaviors	309.0

See chapter 15 for information on suicidal behaviors and suggestions for counseling with children exhibiting these symptoms.

Poor Self-Concept	V62.81

Unfortunately, most of children's negative feelings about themselves are formed from adults' evaluations. Adults lecture, scold, moralize, nag, belittle, label, and criticize. Sometimes children decide they really are worthless, stupid, unlovable, and worthy of punishment because of the continued negative judgments adults place on them. Negative feelings about themselves can affect children's motivation, work, interpersonal relationships, and future success. Once formed, a negative self-concept is difficult to reverse; however, these children can be helped.

1. Provide opportunities for success. Praise and reinforce the child's behavior whenever possible—for example, "You did a good job picking up the paper (straightening the books, throwing that ball, and so on)." Children easily recognize artificial and forced compliments, which are ineffective.

2. Use strengths exercises with children in a group situation. Give each group member a list of the names of other group members. Each child should write a positive adjective or statement beside each name. Have each child read his or her list aloud.

3. Discuss with the children what they would like to do or accomplish. Working with the children, set up realistic goals and a step-by-step program to guide the children toward achieving their goals. Continue this guidance until the children feel they can work toward their goals alone.

4. Allow children with poor self-concepts to help someone else; arrange peer teaching or tutoring. Doing something special for someone else helps the helper feel better about himself or herself.

5. Have the adult working with the children write a list of each child's strengths to help the adult form a more positive conception of the children. Encourage the adult to capitalize on these strengths whenever possible to promote success in each child's life.

6. Ask the children to write ten positive things about themselves: friendly, can play ball well, can repair a bicycle, can play the piano, and so on. Help the children find ways to use their positive attributes to increase positive feelings about themselves.

7. Supportive counseling with significant adults in the child's life can help these adults understand the child and the inappropriate behaviors that often result from a poor self-concept. Instruction in effective parenting may also be helpful. Books such as Ginott's *Between Parent and Child* (1965) and Gordon's *Parent Effectiveness Training* (1970), discussions, role-playing, and parent groups help adults understand and relate to children.

8. Have the child list uncomfortable or difficult situations. Discuss ways of behaving in these situations, and role-play new behaviors. Encourage the child to try the new behaviors in realistic situations and report the results to you.

9. Use active listening (see chapter 5). Teach the child problem-solving skills; being able to solve one's own problems builds self-confidence.

10. Involve the child in group activities at home and at school. Encourage the child to join scouts, a church group, or a club in which he or she will feel accepted and achieve success. Adults should avoid encouraging participation in groups requiring skills the child does not possess. Give responsibilities or tasks in school and in the home at which the child can feel successful. Avoid drudgery jobs.

11. Use a contract with rewards for attempting new behaviors. Rehearse and practice the new behaviors in a safe atmosphere before trying them in a real-life situation.

12. Help the child change thoughts of "I can't" to "I will try." Examine the worst thing that could happen if the child attempted the task (see chapter 7 for a discussion of cognitive restructuring). Encourage positive thinking.

13. Accept no excuses for poor behavior. Avoid being judgmental and criticizing. Ask the child what *can* be accomplished, and negotiate a contract or a new contract if the first one was not successful (see chapter 8).

14. Children with poor self-concepts often benefit from assertiveness training (see chapter 8).

15. Use diaries, drawings, incomplete sentences, fantasy games, storytelling, and play therapy as aids to understanding the child's feelings and thoughts (see chapter 12).

16. Find an appropriate model or buddy for the child. Ask the child to describe admired behaviors of the model. Rehearse and practice these behaviors with the child.

17. Examine the family constellation (Dreikurs, Grunwald, & Pepper, 1971). Often children form poor self-concepts when they are compared to elder or younger siblings and feel they do not measure up.

18. *Guidance Activities for Counselors and Teachers* (Thompson & Poppen, 1987) offers two chapters on group techniques for improving self-concept, including several variations of strengths assessment. Also, *100 Ways to Enhance Self-Concept in the Classroom* (Canfield & Wells, 1976) is an excellent resource for helping counselors work with difficult children.

19. Oldfield (1986) found that children who practiced the relaxation response decreased their acting-out behaviors and improved their self-concepts more than those who only charted these behaviors.

20. Golub and Guerriero (1981) improved learning-disabled boys' self-esteem and peer acceptance by teaching them transactional analysis and asking them to read books. The program included demonstrations of stroking and role-playing.

21. Omizo, Cubberly, and Omizo (1985), after teaching learning-disabled children the principles of rational-emotive-behavior therapy, found improved scores on self-concept scales and locus-of-control measures. Specifically, the children learned the ABC format, acquired basic problem-solving skills, learned that feelings are influenced by thoughts and that feelings are not expressed in identical ways, transferred the learning to everyday life, and developed rational coping skills. They learned to express feelings and not generalities, to be empathetic, and to dispute irrational thoughts.

22. Chirico (1985) described three guidance programs that have helped children improve their self-image: (1) puppets with messages about rules and authority, social interactions, vandalism, divorce, and so on; (2) a student-of-the-week program that rewards a student who has tried hard both academically and behaviorally; and (3) a behavior-management program to provide constant positive reinforcement to children who need extra help.

V71.02

Cheating   V62.3

Our present school system and society strongly encourage competition and high grades—values that can contribute to cheating. Students cheat for a variety of reasons, the main one possibly the pressure to achieve. School personnel and parents can place less emphasis on competition with others and more on cooperation with others and competition with self. School personnel and parents can also let students know that they expect honesty.

1. Determine the type of pressures the child may be encountering. Talk with the child and significant adults about their expectations for the child. Often parents and teachers place unrealistic pressures on children to excel in school,

sports, or other areas. If this is the problem, consult with the adults and cooperatively plan ways to reduce the stress.

2. Determine the goal of the cheater (see chapter 10). Is the child trying to impress someone, earn recognition, please parents or teachers, or cover up a learning problem?

3. Talk with cheating children concerning their study habits and preparation for work. Better study skills may increase self-confidence and reduce cheating.

4. Encourage teachers to hold class discussions with students on cheating, explore ways to reduce cheating, and draw up guidelines for consequences, should the problem occur. A film, story, or hypothetical example may stimulate a rewarding discussion. Combine your discussion with a sociodrama, role-play, or puppet play about cheating (see Thompson & Poppen, 1987, pp. 69–74, on role-playing).

5. Consult with teachers about reducing temptations to cheat by arranging classroom desks or tables to separate students.

6. Children are often asked by their friends to cheat, and many have trouble handling the situation without losing the friend. A group or family discussion focusing on the problem with a question such as "What would you do if your best friend asked you for the answer to a question during a test?" may help children find an alternative to cheating or helping their friends cheat.

7. Consult with the teacher about testing procedures. Could an open-book test be given? Could the teacher use alternative forms of the test? Is the teacher in the room monitoring the test at all times?

8. If a child is caught cheating, remove the child's paper quietly, and confront the child privately. Tell the child what you saw, and discuss what consequences should be imposed. Ask that a plan be made to solve the present cheating problem and prevent cheating in the future.

9. Refrain from accusing a child of cheating unless there is proof. Do not attempt to force a confession. Avoid name-calling, scolding, lecturing, moralizing, and preaching.

10. Place more emphasis on cooperative behavior and less on competition in interactions with the child. Stress competing with self rather than competing with another person.

11. Dreikurs (1968) suggested that two students who are caught giving each other help on a test should each be given half the score. They will soon realize the effect of cheating on their grades.

12. Relaxation and systematic desensitization (see chapter 8) may help a cheating child if the behavior is the result of anxiety or test phobia. Suspend competitive and punitive grading practices that create test anxiety.

13. Contract with the child to avoid cheating in the future. Clearly define cheating behavior and the consequences of the behavior (see chapter 8).

14. Use the reality questions (chapter 4) to encourage responsible behavior in the cheating situation.

15. Encourage children to ask for directions, explanations, or clarification of instructions for any communication they do not understand (Cummins, 1988).

V62.3
309.3
Truancy   312.8

Truancy is defined as deliberate absence from school without a valid reason. Truants are generally telling the school that they prefer to be elsewhere. Children who do not achieve well or who have other learning problems are often truant because they find school unpleasant. Avoiding the situation is easier than facing failure, rejection, or embarrassment.

1. Pinpointing the reasons for truancy may be difficult. Determine the motive for the behavior (see chapter 10). Is the child experiencing learning problems, failure, or rejection? Does the child receive encouragement to attend school and find learning relevant? Determine when truancy seems to occur most often. Is the truancy related to family problems or needs?

2. Personal interest from school personnel may be an effective reinforcer. Actively listen to the child for clues about what is happening in the child's life (see chapter 5). Many students respond to special attention in the form of invitations from the teacher, other school personnel, or peers to come to school and participate in the activities.

3. Look over the truant's class schedule and academic progress. Determine if the classes are too difficult or the assignments beyond the child's capabilities. Might the child feel more success and find more relevance in other ways of learning?

4. Check into the home situation. Could the truancy be the result of a lack of proper clothing or lunch money or of babysitting responsibilities or other job requirements? Enlist the parents' cooperation, and devise a system for keeping in touch with them concerning days present and absent.

5. Hold a group or family discussion about truancy. Discuss with truant children how their presence or absence in school is helping or hurting them in reaching their immediate or long-term goals. Work with them to make a plan to avoid truancy in the future.

6. Contract with the student to attend school the next day. Continue to renegotiate the contract, increasing days in attendance step by step. Include a clause in the contract making the child responsible for all work missed. Rewards and/or penalties for attendance and nonattendance may be worked out cooperatively with the child (see chapter 8).

7. Older students serving as peer counselors may help devise ways to keep truant children in school. The attention of the older student also serves as a reinforcer for attending school.

8. Involve the child in school activities that require his or her presence—for example, audiovisual or physical education equipment handling, room responsibilities, or a responsibility in an interesting group project.

9. Refrain from critical, sarcastic comments such as "Glad to see you made it today" or "If you had been here, you would have had the assignment." Avoid scolding, lecturing, punishing, and preaching. Concentrate on the child's positive

behaviors. School must become a pleasant place for truant children if their behavior is to be changed.

10. Whenever possible, allow the children choices in arranging their daily school activities and learning. Adjustments might also be made in the curriculum to reflect the children's individual abilities and achievement levels.

11. For children who see little relevance in school life, hold a discussion of "What does it take to make it through life?" Ask the children to imagine themselves as adults in their jobs or daily activities. Discuss what abilities and skills they will need to succeed in their imagined adult world.

12. Out-of-school suspension for truancy is seldom effective. The child who is consistently truant does not want to be in school, and suspension is no punishment. Seek ways to make school a pleasant, rewarding place.

13. Krumboltz and Thoresen (1976) reported a case study in which an adolescent boy was encouraged to return to school and remain in attendance through the use of three techniques. First, he was asked to visualize his future and what he would like to be and do in the future if he did not go back to school. He discussed his future plans and the reasons that he should return to school with the counselor. Next, the counselor asked him to look at the self that tries to make us do what we really want to and the other self that interferes and keeps us from accomplishing those goals. Behavioral rehearsal was used to help the young person imagine going back to school and to practice coping with the problems that would arise. Finally, a behavioral contract was drawn up with his family and school authorities, placing responsibility for the boy's behavior on him and outlining contingencies and reinforcements.

14. Reframing or other cognitive-restructuring techniques may help the child see school in a different light.

15. Ask the truant to interview selected people who have dropped out of school to see how their lives were affected.

16. Allen and Gardner (1989) suggested a dropout prevention program, "Tender Loving Counseling," which involves individual and group counseling, resource speakers, tutoring, study skills development, and community involvement. Information about their program may be obtained from the National Dropout Prevention Center at Clemson University, Clemson, SC 29364.

17. Ruben (1989) used the Potential Dropout Profile to identify students at risk and presented 10 guidance sessions to address success in school, being comfortable in school, being responsible in school, listening in school, improving in school, cooperating with teachers, the bright side of school, and the bright side of the student.

V62.3
309.3
Carelessness in Work and with Property   312.8

A common complaint among teachers and parents is that children are careless with school property, books, the completion of assigned work, and personal property such as coats, sweaters, and other possessions. Lecturing, scolding, preaching, and nagging are seldom effective in changing their habits. Children need to learn responsibility for their own actions and possessions and that an adult will not always be present to assume responsibility for them. Dreikurs et al. (1971) emphasized that children should assume responsibility for property, for property rights, and for their actions to learn respect for property.

1. Determine the reason for the carelessness. Is the behavior due to a lack of interest or motivation? Could the carelessness be an attempt to cover up a learning or emotional problem or an attempt to get back at parents for some real or imagined wrong? Actively listen to the child for clues that may indicate the motivation for carelessness (see chapter 5).

2. The careless child can redo the work until it is correct. Children can pay for lost items or property with time or work. Parents should not hurriedly bring forgotten items such as lunches and tennis shoes. The logical consequence of carelessness, forgetting, or losing is that the child must assume responsibility— redo the work, replace the property, or do without the forgotten items (see chapter 10).

3. Praise and reinforce responsible behavior—for example, "That paper was well written," or "You did a good job cleaning out the basement." Consistently give attention to acceptable behavior.

4. Help the careless child find a model who behaves maturely and responsibly. Pair the child with the model for activities. Ask the child to observe the model's behaviors for several days. Discuss the behaviors of the model with the careless child. Role-play and rehearse these behaviors. Make a plan for the child to try the new learning.

5. Carelessness may be due to a lack of understanding. Give clear, specific instructions to the child for proper preparation of work and other activities. Have the careless child write down the instructions to eliminate forgetting and mistakes.

6. If carelessness with homework assignments is a problem, ask the child to write down all assignments and take them home. Talk with parents to gain their cooperation in checking assigned work each night. Discontinue the procedure when the child begins to assume responsibility for homework. The parent should be available to assist the child but not do the homework for the child.

7. If the problem seems to stem from inability to cope with the amount of work or responsibility assigned, reduce the requirements for a time, requiring quality rather than quantity. Gradually work up to the point where the child meets the expected criteria (see chapter 8).

8. Carelessness may reflect a difference in cultural values. The child's environment may not place a great value on achievement or the possession of property. Hold a group discussion focusing on the value of property and of assuming responsibility for oneself. Help the children to identify acts of carelessness and their consequences, and make a plan for avoiding careless acts.

9. Ask careless children to evaluate their work from your role or to assess consequences as they think you should. Discuss with them the reasons for their evaluations.

10. Encourage responsibility through the use of reality questions (see chapter 4). Give small assignments designed for success. Focus on statements such as "I won't do my work correctly" rather than "I can't" statements.

V62.3

Underachievement 309.4

Underachievement is usually defined as a discrepancy between the child's ability and actual achievement. It may be related to a poor self-concept, cultural deprivation, lack of family involvement and encouragement, peer pressure, learning or emotional problems, physical illness, or a lack of interest in school subjects and content.

1. Try to determine the causes contributing to underachievement. Become a child watcher, and use active listening to try to understand the child (see chapter 5). Underachievement is often related to physical problems or other learning difficulties; therefore, a psychological evaluation and checkup with a physician may provide some insight into the problem.

2. Assess the child's academic level, and help the teachers build learning and class assignments from this base. Much new learning is based on old learning; the child must be able to accomplish prerequisite skills before achieving success in new ones. Once the weak link in the chain of learning is identified—a past school experience, physical health, cultural background, or any other factor—counseling can begin, and instructional materials can be designed to promote success.

3. Contract with the child to complete at least a small amount of work each day. Build in rewards for progress. The completion of two problems or questions is better than no progress. Renegotiate the contract periodically, increasing the amount of work expected (see chapter 8).

4. Try peer teaching or peer tutoring. Students who are in an upper grade can tutor students in lower grades. They can also help peers who are having trouble in areas of their strengths. Both children learn and benefit from the relationship.

5. Capitalize on an area of interest or ability by relating the assignment to that interest or ability. Situations in math, writing, spelling, and other subjects can often be related to the child's interests, hobbies, and skills.

6. Team teaching may be helpful. Two or more teachers are often able to generate more ideas to stimulate the child. The child may also be able to cooperate with one teacher more than with another.

7. Avoid lecturing, nagging, scolding, and threatening the child. Encouragement and a positive attitude produce better results. See "Poor Self-Concept," earlier in this appendix, for additional ideas.

8. Vary school activities from physical to quiet to prevent fatigue and boredom. Involve the child in arranging the day's work. Children who have taken part in the planning are likely to cooperate and complete assigned tasks.

9. Teachers can consult with underachieving children for alternative ideas for completing learning objectives. Because children learn in different ways, the child may be the best consultant for determining methods of achieving learning objectives.

10. Special arrangements can be made for testing or for completing other class assignments. For example, if the child has problems in reading or writing, oral testing, tape recorders, or typewriters can be used.

11. Help the child find an admired friend and model. Ask the child to talk with the model about study habits and to observe the model's methods of studying. Contract with the child to practice these procedures (see chapter 8). Allow the two children to work and study together as much as possible.

12. Check on study skills, test-taking procedures, and place and time for studying. A contract incorporating a schedule for studying specific subjects at certain times and places will help the child plan study time more wisely and develop discipline for studying. Thompson and Poppen (1987) have suggested a study-habits survey.

13. If the underachievement is related to parental pressures, counsel with the parents about how to decrease this pressure. Plan with them for methods to reinforce studying without pressuring the child. Assist parents and the child in determining an appropriate place and time to study. Make a plan to avoid or cope with things that might interfere with study times (small siblings, telephone calls, peers).

14. When homework assignments are not completed at home, the logical consequence is for the child to complete the work during free time at school (see chapter 13). Avoid nagging, scolding, or lecturing.

15. Focus on and reinforce work improvements; past faults and failures should be forgotten. Emphasize the positive—for example: "Jimmy, you did part of your homework assignment, and it was done very well. I wonder if you would be willing to work on these two additional questions."

16. The parent-child relationship works better if parents do not teach or tutor their own children. If the child asks for help, a parent may provide assistance; however, someone outside the family is a more effective teacher or tutor.

17. For children with special learning problems, plan a consultation session with all resource persons and teachers involved. Cooperatively draw up a learning plan, with the role and objectives of each professional clearly defined.

18. Underachievers usually respond best to a structured environment for learning. Research by Laport and Nath (1976) indicated that underachievers need specific, hard goals. Children who were simply told to do their best set low goals and achieved below their maximum abilities. Give directions for assignments very clearly. A check or reward system may be used for completed work. Learning contracts may be helpful to the underachiever. Some underachievers require additional time to complete all assignments; continue to encourage their completion.

19. Pecaut (1979) described the underachieving personality as falling into one of four categories: trust-seeking, approval-seeking, dependence-seeking, and

independence-seeking. He believes that approximately 75% of underachievers are dependence-seekers who exhibit such characteristics as vagueness, powerlessness, dependence on others to complete their work, and fear of success (they might have to assume responsibility). To work with dependence-seekers, Pecaut recommended that adults should never feel guilty when the child does not perform (guilt is a powerful tool!); adults should not accept excuses but should learn to see through the child's tendency to blame others for his or her mistakes or failures; adults should not make things easier for dependence-seekers by giving them options of easier courses or lower expectations; adults should not fall into the trap of worrying about dependence-seekers and should resist the child's manipulative efforts for assistance; and adults should avoid giving dependence-seekers time extensions. Pecaut's suggestions fit the model of reality therapy and Adlerian methods of counseling by encouraging children to accept responsibility for their behaviors. Pecaut suggested that adults ask themselves four questions about children they are about to recommend for special classes because of poor academic work: (1) Does this student make a reasonable and consistent effort to learn? (2) Has the student requested help when he or she has not understood the material? (3) Does the student complete homework? (4) Does the student pay attention and participate in class activities? Pecaut stated that any negative answer suggests a student who may not be ready for a special class; he or she may be an underachiever.

20. Rimm and Lowe (1988) suggested methods for parents of gifted children to cope with underachievement, including cautions against too much praise and admiration, consistency in parenting, positive monitoring of home-work and study habits, modeling the value of personal careers, and encouraging reasonable standards of organization.

Daydreaming   V62.3

Daydreaming is not always bad; it sometimes clears confusion, solves problems, or is creative in other ways. However, excessive daydreaming or daydreaming at the wrong times—in school—can affect the child's academic progress. Adlerian theory suggests that daydreaming children are striving for superiority. These children have no faith in their abilities to achieve success in the real world; therefore, they create fantasies in which they are always great or superior.

1. Periodic eye contact between child and adult may decrease daydreaming. If one cannot make eye contact with the child, a light touch on the shoulder should bring the child back to reality.

2. Interrupt children's fantasies by calling them by name. Avoid embarrassing children by asking them to answer a question they obviously have not heard.

3. Try incomplete sentences, storytelling, diary, or play therapy to learn more about the child and the possible reason for daydreaming.

4. Channel daydreaming into constructive channels by having the child write out the daydream. The writing could be incorporated into a learning exercise.

5. Write a contract with the daydreamer for completion of assigned work (see

chapter 8). Contract for only the amount of work the child feels he or she can accomplish. Renegotiate contracts for additional work in a step-by-step plan.

6. Tape an index card to the child's desk. When the child is working on a task, place a check on the card and give verbal reinforcement for the accomplishment. A contract may be made with the child to earn rewards or privileges for a certain number of checks. Ignore the daydreaming; reward on-task behavior.

7. Plan the child's environment and schedule to vary activities from quiet to physical. Assess the day's schedule to determine if activities are interesting, relevant, and appropriate for the child's level of maturity, interest, and ability.

8. Find the child a friend who encourages participation in groups and other activities. Encourage the teacher to include the daydreamer in group activities and projects. Counsel with the parents to plan how to reduce daydreaming at home and encourage participation in activities.

9. Often children retreat to a daydream world because the real one is too painful. Determine if the child is having learning, social, emotional, or physical problems. A psychological evaluation and physical examination may be helpful.

10. Daydreaming may be related to a poor self-concept. See "Poor Self-Concept," earlier in this appendix, for additional ideas for working with these children.

Shyness and Withdrawal   309.4

Shyness and withdrawal are attempts to avoid participation in one's surroundings. The child may fear the situation, fear failure or criticism, lack self-confidence, or fear embarrassment or humiliation. The child may also be physically ill. Unfortunately, shy and withdrawn children are usually ignored because they cause less trouble than the attention-seeking child.

1. Try to determine the underlying cause for the reserved behavior. Use diaries, puppets, role-playing, incomplete sentences, drawing, storytelling, play therapy, or any similar technique to try to understand the child better. Children often express their feelings through these means when they will not verbalize them.

2. Work on developing trust and good rapport with the child. Try active listening to increase understanding of the child (see chapter 5).

3. Have the shy child help another student through peer teaching or peer tutoring. Capitalize on any interest or ability to promote sharing and participation.

4. Involve shy or withdrawn children in small-group activities or projects with other children they like. Often a shy child is willing to talk in small groups. Encourage and reinforce these attempts to participate. Send them on errands with another child. A sociogram may determine other liked children.

5. Give the withdrawn child responsibilities such as carrying messages, feeding the fish, watering pla nts, handing out supplies, or helping the school

secretary answer the phone and take messages. Avoid drudgery jobs, and do not ask the shy child to perform tasks that may be embarrassing (such as speaking in front of the class).

6. Make a list with the withdrawn child of things he or she would like to be able to do—for example, join a group of friends, speak to a particular person, or play a game. Have the child select one thing on the list and set a goal to accomplish this behavior. Use behavior rehearsal to help the child practice certain responses or behaviors. Contract with the child to try these new behaviors (see chapter 8).

7. Avoid embarrassing shy children by teasing them about their shyness or by calling on them to perform in front of a group without first discussing and arranging the activity with them. One technique for encouraging a child to participate in class is to plan a question and answer with the child. The teacher asks the question in class and the child agrees to answer with the response. When the child feels comfortable answering rehearsed questions, the child and teacher make a contract that the teacher will call on the child only when he or she volunteers to answer. Ask the child to volunteer at least a certain number of times per week. Renegotiate periodic contracts to encourage participation in a step-by-step progression.

8. Find a model for the shy child. Ask the child to observe the model for several days and list admired behaviors. Role-play, rehearse, and contract with the child to try the new behaviors.

9. Assertiveness training may benefit withdrawn or shy children (see chapter 8). Have the children list situations in which they would like to be more assertive. Discuss possible ways of meeting each situation. Practice the new behaviors with the children, both individually and in small groups.

10. Keat (1972) suggested using a broad spectrum of techniques with the withdrawn child, including (1) building a relationship of trust, understanding, and confidence; (2) using the techniques of assertiveness training; (3) behavioral rehearsal, with the counselor role-playing the behavior and then the child rehearsing it; (4) relaxation exercises, such as breathing exercises, isometrics, and deep muscle relaxation techniques; (5) motor coordination training (if necessary); and (6) cognitive restructuring.

11. Zimbardo (1977) pointed out that shyness has its advantages. The shy child can be selective in relationships, can observe situations cautiously, is never considered obnoxious or overly aggressive, and may be considered a good listener. If the child decides to change the behavior, Zimbardo suggested five steps: (1) understand self, (2) understand the reason for the shyness, (3) build self-esteem, (4) develop social skills, and (5) help others overcome their shyness. Gestalt counseling techniques are often used to help a child look at weaknesses as secret strengths—for example, "Being shy helps me by _____." Behavioral counseling strategies are also designed to look at the payoffs of seemingly unhelpful behaviors.

12. Use a variety of play techniques, such as hand puppets, games, art, and music, to encourage expression. Pets may be a useful adjunct to therapy.

13. Franco, Christoff, Crimmins, and Kelly (1983) developed a program to

teach extremely shy children social skills—specifically, conversational skills, including asking questions, making and responding to comments, improving eye contact, and displaying warmth. The training sessions included a presentation of the skill, modeling, and then rehearsal with videotape. Reinforcement strategies and homework assignments were used to help children acquire and maintain the behaviors.

14. Matter and Matter (1985) suggested helping the lonely, shy child by teaching specific social skills similar to those of more aggressive children, combined with changing the environment to make it less conducive to isolation (for example, reducing class size and improving relationships through shared projects). The family and home environment may need to be assessed to determine if parents should be involved in the counseling process.

15. Allan and Clark (1984) described a directed art technique in which they focus the next session or drawing on a particular portion of the previous drawing that seems to have been causing pain or a portion that required a considerable amount of time to draw. They felt that these drawings tap the unconscious and that children work through the problems by expressing their feelings pictorially.

16. Sainato, Maheady, and Shook (1986) found that appointing one child at a time as classroom manager for 2 weeks increased the frequency of social interactions and improve social status. The classroom manager led the class in highly preferred activities and made assignments for fun chores. The results of the study indicated significant increases in positive social interactions, sociometric assessments showed improved social status, and parents reported that their children talked about school more often and were more eager to attend.

17. See "Poor Self-Concept," earlier in this appendix, for other ideas to encourage more participation in learning and interpersonal situations.

Excessive Tension and Anxiety

309.24
300.00

A little tension and anxiety may motivate a child, but excessive tension and anxiety interfere with learning and performance. Excessive tension and anxiety may be situational or chronic. The symptoms include continued restlessness and movement, nail biting, tics, frequent blinking, rapid breathing, repeated throat clearing, and similar somatic complaints.

School-related tension and anxiety

1. Tell highly anxious children that they have a right to fail. Take away the pressure to excel and to be perfect. This technique may ease the anxiety and allow further exploration of conditions causing the anxiety.

2. Highly anxious children function better with a teacher who is warm and understanding but also organized and structured. Suggest that teachers use techniques such as behavioral objectives and learning contracts so that highly anxious students know exactly what is expected of them.

3. Consult with the child's parents and teachers. Determine if the anxiety is a result of pressures and perfectionistic expectations. If so, work with the child and the adults to encourage more realistic expectations.

4. Teachers and parents may help decrease children's tension and anxiety by talking quietly to them about relaxing—for example, "Relax your neck; relax your shoulders." Deep-breathing exercises may also help the child relax (see chapter 8).

5. Avoid overemphasizing the importance of success on a test or task. Many adults cause anxiety in their efforts to impress the child with the importance of doing well.

6. If the child is highly anxious about tests, use the "study buddy" system. Pair the child with a capable student who is willing to help. Developing better study skills may help reduce anxieties related to school.

7. Encourage teachers to de-emphasize tests and allow the child to demonstrate learning in other ways, such as oral tests, oral reports, projects, and papers.

8. Look over the child's schoolwork and academic progress. Anxiety is often related to learning disabilities.

9. Use cognitive-restructuring techniques to help children feel they can cope with situations. Discover the irrational, self-defeating, anxiety-provoking self-statements that the children are telling themselves and help them formulate more positive ones.

10. Use imagery techniques to help children see themselves coping with situations in a relaxed, positive manner.

11. Sycamore, Corey, and Coker (1990) outlined general strategies, similar to a game plan, for approaching test taking with confidence. They suggested that counselors advise students about good test-taking procedures such as pacing responses according to the time allotted for the test, narrowing choices by eliminating obviously wrong answers, responding first to questions to which answers are known, giving last priority to questions not known, being aware of qualifiers such as "always" and "never," and marking your place with your hand or marker.

12. Wilkinson (1990) described a guidance session with specific steps for overcoming test anxiety. The focus of the sessions is on students' feelings about tests, their preparation, their source of anxiety, and their responses to feelings of anxiety.

General anxiety

1. Some tension and anxiety may be related to fear of the unknown—for example, going to new places or being in new situations. A thorough explanation of the feared situation or a visit to a feared place with a trusted person may reduce situational anxiety.

2. Talk with anxious children and agree on methods, such as physical activity, talking, or writing, for release of these feelings. When children become highly anxious or tense, they could be allowed to signal the teacher or another adult and proceed to carry out the plan previously discussed. Counselors may suggest that anxious children come to their office when they experience intense feelings.

3. Diaries, autobiographies, drawing, puppets, and other forms of play therapy may assist in determining the causes for the anxious feelings (see chapter 12).

4. Children have less anxiety about situations if they feel competent. Discuss with the child the reasons for anxiety and ways of handling specific situations; rehearse the situations.

5. Relaxation methods and desensitization reduce tension and anxiety (see chapter 8).

6. If the anxiety appears debilitating, refer the child to a medical specialist for examination.

7. Peterson and Shigetomi (1981) reduced children's anxiety about hospitalization by teaching them the techniques of muscle relaxation, imaginal distraction, and self-talk.

8. Kraft and McNeil (1985) pointed out that stress can be caused by a number of factors, such as separation and divorce, academic pressure, or parental influences, with the resulting disorders of fighting, restlessness, temper tantrums, destructiveness, inattention, bragging, and selfishness. They suggested using play, physical exercise, active relaxation procedures (such as yoga, progressive relaxation, or story plays), or passive relaxation techniques (deep breathing, imagery, autogenic training) to help children cope with their stresses.

9. For children going through a crisis and experiencing stress or anxiety, Allan and Anderson (1986) suggested that classroom discussion can help them talk about their problems and feelings, understand that others have similar feelings, and think about coping strategies. These meetings can help teachers recognize the personal concerns of students, decide who needs to be referred for counseling, and discover how discussion can facilitate the classroom climate.

10. Angus (1989) described three approaches to stress management in children: guided fantasy, yoga and autogenic phrases, and thermal biofeedback.

Distractibility/Short Attention Span   314.00

Being able to focus one's attention on the task to be done and ignore irrelevant stimuli in the environment is necessary for learning school material and new behaviors. Although attention span and the degree of distractibility vary with the child and the situation, these learning problems seem to be increasing in today's classrooms.

1. Determine if the child is actually distracted easily and has a short attention span. The child's inattention may be the result of some other reason, such as the nature of the work the child is asked to do (boring or too difficult), noisy or more interesting surroundings (windows, TV, pictures, bulletin boards), or fatigue or physical illness.

2. Record the time when distractions and inattention seem most frequent. Rearrange the environment or schedule. Vary quiet activities with more physical

ones. Limit overstimulation and distractors, including interesting bulletin boards, teachers' clothing and jewelry, mobiles, and brightly colored pictures.

3. Use seating arrangements or some method of screening the distractible child from excessive stimuli. Consider small carrels or "offices." Bookcases, movable screens, or even large moving cartons that have been painted or decorated can be used to reduce distracting stimuli.

4. Contract for the completion of short assignments. Talk with distractible children about the amount of work they believe they can accomplish—two math problems, one paragraph of English. Write a realistic contract to ensure success. Continue to renegotiate the contract, increasing the assignments as the distractibility decreases.

5. Recommend that highly distractible children be checked by a medical specialist to determine if the behavior is a medical problem.

6. Shorten teaching time and study periods, and schedule the periods more frequently. Visual aids, games, and other teaching aids may add interest and maintain attention.

7. Acker, Oliver, Carmichael, and Ozerkevich (1975) reported a case study of a 10-year-old boy whose attention span and on-task activity were increased by rewarding the whole class for the boy's on-task behavior. Teachers periodically observed behavior, and the boy earned points for appropriate behaviors. These points were exchanged for class privileges, such as trips to the museum. The boy and the whole class decided how to spend the points. The researchers suggested that the boy's peers tended to ignore off-task behavior, which resulted in an increase in on-task behavior.

8. Douglas (1972) contended that more time needs to be spent in teaching children to "stop, look, and listen." She saw a short attention span to be like impulsiveness; therefore, methods should be implemented to decrease impulsiveness and improve attentiveness and reflectiveness—for example, teaching reflective strategies and games requiring impulse control.

9. Use techniques such as raising or lowering your voice, placing your hand on the child's shoulder, or catching the child's eye to capture the distractible child's attention and direct it back to the task.

10. Encourage children to monitor their own behavior. Have them make a check mark on an index card when they catch themselves off-task and then immediately focus on the task. Increasing awareness of the problem is often a productive technique in itself. Plan for self-reward when the child can refocus attention to the task. Christie, Hiss, and Lozanoff (1984) taught three third- and fourth-grade boys to self-record their identified inappropriate behavior. According to these researchers, self-recording behavior requires the child to become an active participant in the change plan and encourages decision making about what is appropriate and inappropriate behavior.

The reader is encouraged to refer also to the section entitled "Attention-Deficit Hyperactivity Disorder" in chapter 16.

Immaturity and Dependent Behavior V62.89

Dependency may be the result of overprotective or critical parents who have told their children in many ways that they are not capable of functioning or thinking for themselves. Immature or dependent children usually do not achieve well in school because they are not ready to learn the subject matter presented. They may have trouble with interpersonal relationships because of their immature behavior and often become social isolates or discipline problems; alternatively, they may choose their friends from a younger group.

1. Work with the parents on strategies to help them trust the child's abilities and potentials. Suggest methods to develop independent behaviors. Books such as *Between Parent and Child* (Ginott, 1965) and *Parent Effectiveness Training* (Gordon, 1970) may help parents understand their children's development and abilities.

2. Have children identify areas in which they would like to be more independent or behaviors they would like to change. Discuss these situations and alternative ways of behaving with the child, and rehearse the situations until the child feels comfortable with the new behaviors.

3. Encourage and praise attempts to become more mature and independent. Ask the child to do jobs or assume responsibilities in the home and classroom to increase his or her confidence. Avoid assigning drudgery jobs.

4. Have the child select a model and observe the model's behavior for several days. Pair children with mature models for group activities. Ask them to keep a list of the model's behaviors they particularly like. Rehearse behaviors the children would like to acquire until they feel confident.

5. Encourage immature or dependent children to join groups such as Little League, Boy or Girl Scouts, clubs, or church groups. The children need support and encouragement to take the first steps and continued counseling to learn social skills for good relationships in the groups.

6. Give children as many choices as possible—for example, whether to complete the reading or the math assignment first, or whether to wear a blue shirt or a red shirt.

7. Learn about the child's abilities, interests, and hobbies. Have the child peer-teach or tutor another student in one of these areas of expertise to build self-confidence. Both children will benefit from the teaching and the relationship.

8. Work with immature or dependent children to teach them problem-solving techniques. Counsel with parents and teachers to encourage these children to attempt to solve their own problems with adult guidance rather than depend on others for solutions.

9. Avoid reinforcing dependent behaviors. Encourage immature children to make decisions and accept responsibilities within their capabilities. Reinforce efforts toward more mature behavior with praise and encouragement.

10. Use active listening to help immature and dependent children express

their fears and other feelings (see chapter 5). Help them develop realistic goals and make a systematic plan for attaining these goals.

Perfectionistic Behavior   300.0

Compulsive and overly perfectionistic children usually perform their tasks and assignments well and therefore often overachieve. This behavior can inhibit everyday functioning; for example, the child takes too much time to complete assignments and feels that everything must be absolutely perfect. Perfectionistic behavior is often accompanied by symptoms of anxiety.

1. Perfectionistic children usually perform best in a well-structured situation where rules and expectations are clearly defined. Clearly explain all instructions, and use teaching methods such as behavioral objectives and learning contracts to reduce anxiety concerning expectations.

2. Talk with parents and teachers to determine if the pressures and expectations placed on the child are too great. Perfectionistic children often have perfectionistic adults for models. Counsel with adults about normal growth and development and the behaviors that can be expected of the child.

3. Involve the children in individual and group activities that do not require perfect performance. Techniques such as creative drawing or writing de-emphasize perfection and also allow the child to express feelings.

4. Encourage the child to relax. Teach the child breathing exercises and other relaxation techniques (see chapter 8). Encourage the child to change internal self-talk to recognize that perfection in all areas is not essential (see chapter 7). "Shoulds" and "have-tos" can be changed to "It might be better ifs"–for example, "It might be better if I make all 'A's,' but that is not required for me to be a good person."

5. Use negative rehearsal to help perfectionistic children be less rigid. Observe a situation in which the child appears to be highly perfectionistic. Role-play the same situation with the child while encouraging behavior that is less than perfect. Discuss with the child what would happen if the child was not 100% perfect in the situation. Make a plan with the child to decrease compulsiveness.

6. Allot an amount of time for the child to finish a task. Place a timer within the child's sight. When the timer rings, review the child's progress. If the child has not made sufficient progress, contract with the child to set a new goal the next time.

7. The overly perfectionistic child may be compensating for feelings of inadequacy. See "Poor Self-Concept," earlier in this appendix, for further suggestions for working with these children.

8. Plan a self-management program with the child; encourage him or her to monitor perfectionistic behavior and develop alternative ways of responding to situations. Build in self-reward for accomplishments.

9. Anxiety and tension may be related to perfectionistic behaviors. See "Excessive Tension and Anxiety," earlier in this appendix, for additional ideas.

V62.3
300.23
School Phobia   309.3

School phobia may grow out of unpleasant or embarrassing experiences in school, failure in school, fear of separation from the security of home and parents, fear of the unknown, or other experiences that may have associated bad feelings with school.

1. Actively listen to try to understand the phobic child's underlying feelings and to establish a feeling of trust and security (see chapter 5).

2. The child can be desensitized by going to school with a parent and staying for a short time, such as 15 minutes the first day, 20 minutes the second day, and 25 minutes the third day. Continue in this manner until the child can remain in school a full day.

3. The desensitization procedure may be used with rewards. Write a contract with the child to provide a reward for staying in school a certain amount of time—for example, 30 minutes (see chapter 8). Renegotiate the contract for longer periods of time as the child is able to stay in school an increasing length of time.

4. If one parent is reinforcing the child's anxiety about school, suggest that the other parent or another adult bring the child to school. A parent may unconsciously be encouraging school phobia by conveying anxiety to the child, verbally or nonverbally (for example, "Now, you call me if you get afraid while you are in school" or becoming more nervous and irritable as they approach school).

5. Avoid placing the child in any situation that may increase fear or cause embarrassment. Explain all new situations and expectations clearly. Role-playing expected behaviors may help the child feel more confident about meeting the new situation.

6. School phobia may be related to learning difficulties. Review the child's academic progress, and provide needed help. Children who find school an unpleasant place because they continually fail often become phobic.

7. Ask the teacher to involve phobic children in pleasant group projects and activities. The more pleasure the children derive from school, the more they want to attend. Successful learning, good peer relationships, pleasant teachers and other school personnel, and enjoyable activities can be positive reinforcers.

8. Allow phobic children to phone home occasionally or at specific intervals if they feel fearful or insecure. Make arrangements with the parents so that someone is available to answer and to reassure the child.

9. Many parents include something from home in the child's lunchbox or with books—a picture or some favorite object, for instance.

10. Relaxation and desensitization procedures may be necessary for the extremely phobic child (see chapter 8).

11. Blanco (1972) suggested that counselors encourage parents to (1) make persistent and continued efforts to get the child to school daily, even for a short period; (2) seek family counseling if the child is extremely anxious and phobic;

(3) have the child visit classes, playgrounds, and other areas before entering school; (4) get the child off to school in a natural way without tearful goodbyes or overemphasis on parting; and (5) enlist the aid of a pediatrician if psychosomatic ailments occur. The pediatrician should be aware of the phobic problem if it occurs with any frequency.

12. Rutter (1975) listed questions that may help the counselor understand the phobic child: (1) What is the child like when not at school—temperamentally, socially, and so forth? (2) Does the child's refusal to go to school vary with the planned curriculum or activities for that day? (3) Does the child's refusal to go to school vary with what is occurring in the home—for example, when there is illness, unhappiness, or an argument, or the mother is beginning a new job or expecting a new baby?

13. Often school phobia is the result of family interactions in which children become overly dependent on parents. Consultation with the family may provide some insight into the family system and suggestions for treatment.

14. Barlow, Strother, and Landreth (1985) suggested play therapy for the child with school phobia in order to allow the child to feel less overwhelmed and provide support while returning to school.

15. See other ideas for working with the phobic child under "Excessive Tension and Anxiety," earlier in this appendix.

REFERENCES

Acker, L., Oliver, P., Carmichael, J., & Ozerkevich, M. (1975). Interpersonal attractiveness and peer interaction during behavioral treatment of the target child. *Canadian Journal of Behavioral Science, 7*, 262–273.

Allan, J., & Anderson, E. (1986). Children and crises: A classroom guidance approach. *Elementary School Guidance and Counseling, 21*, 143–149.

Allan, J., & Clark, M. (1984). Directed art counseling. *Elementary School Guidance and Counseling, 19*, 116–124.

Allen, K., & Gardner, N. (1989). Tender loving counseling: A dropout-prevention program. *School Counselor, 36*, 389–392.

American Psychiatric Association. (1994). *Diagnostic and statistical manual of mental disorders* (4th ed.). Washington, DC: Author.

Angus, S. (1989). Three approaches to stress management for children. *Elementary School Guidance and Counseling, 23*, 228–233.

Barlow, K., Strother, J., & Landreth, G. (1985). Child-centered play therapy: Nancy from baldness to curls. *School Counselor, 32*, 347–363.

Blanco, R. (1972). *Prescription for children with learning and adjustment problems.* Springfield, IL: Charles C Thomas.

Canfield, J., & Wells, H. C. (1976). *100 ways to enhance self-concept in the classroom.* Englewood Cliffs, NJ: Prentice-Hall.

Chirico, J. (1985). Three guidance programs in Providence, Rhode Island. *School Counselor, 32*, 388–391.

Christie, D., Hiss, M., & Lozanoff, B. (1984). Modification of inattentive classroom behavior: Hyperactive children's use of self-recording with teacher guidance. *Behavior Modification, 8*, 391–406.

Cummins, K. (1988). *The teacher's guide to behavioral interventions: Intervention strategies for behavior problems in the educational environment.* Columbia, MO: Hawthorne Educational Services.

Douglas, V. (1972). Stop, look and listen: The problem of sustained attention and impulse control in hyperactive and normal children. *Canadian Journal of Behavioral Science, 4,* 259–282.

Dreikurs, R. (1968). *Psychology in the classroom* (2nd ed.). New York: Harper & Row.

Dreikurs, R., Grunwald, B., & Pepper, F. (1971). *Maintaining sanity in the classroom.* New York: Harper & Row.

Franco, D., Christoff, K., Crimmins, D., & Kelly, J. (1983). Social skills training for an extremely shy young adolescent: An empirical case study. *Behavior Therapy, 14,* 568–575. (Reprinted in C. Schaefer, H. Millman, S. Sichel, & J. Zwilling, Eds., *Advances in therapies for children.* San Francisco. Jossey-Bass, 1986.)

Ginott, H. (1965). *Between parent and child.* New York: Macmillan.

Golub, S., & Guerriero, L. (1981). The effects of a transactional analysis program on self-esteem in learning disabled boys. *Transactional Analysis Journal, 11,* 244–246.

Gordon, T. (1970). *Parent effectiveness training.* New York: Wyden.

Keat, D. (1972). Broad-spectrum behavior therapy with children: A case presentation. *Behavior Therapy, 3,* 454–459.

Kraft, R., & McNeil, A. (1985). Children and stress: Coping through physical activities. *Physical Educator, 42,* 72–75.

Krumboltz, J., & Thoresen, C. (1976). *Counseling methods.* New York: Holt, Rinehart & Winston.

Laport, R., & Nath, R. (1976). Roles of performance goals in prose learning. *Journal of Educational Psychology, 3,* 260–264.

Matter, D., & Matter, R. (1985). Children who are lonely and shy: Action steps for the counselor. Elementary School Guidance and Counseling, 20, 129–135.

Oldfield, D. (1986). The effects of the relaxation response on self-concept and acting out behaviors. *Elementary School Guidance and Counseling, 20,* 255–260.

Omizo, M., Cubberly, W., & Omizo, S. (1985). The effects of rational emotive education groups on self-concept and locus of control among learning disabled children. *Exceptional Child, 32,* 13–16.

Pecaut, L. (1979). *Understanding and influencing student motivation.* Lombard, IL: Institute for Motivational Development.

Peterson, L., & Shigetomi, C. (1981). The use of coping techniques to minimize anxiety in hospitalized children. *Behavior Therapy, 12,* 1–14.

Rimm, S., & Lowe, B. (1988). Family environments of underachieving gifted students. *Gifted Child Quarterly, 32,* 353–359.

Ruben, A. (1989). Preventing school dropouts through classroom guidance. *Elementary School Guidance and Counseling, 24,* 21–29.

Rutter, M. (1975). *Helping troubled children.* New York: Plenum.

Sainato, D., Mahèady, L., & Shook, G. (1986). The effects of a classroom manager role on the social interaction patterns and social status of withdrawn kindergarten students. *Journal of Applied Behavior Analysis, 19,* 187–195.

Sycamore, J., Corey, A., & Coker, D. (1990). Reducing test anxiety. *Elementary School Guidance and Counseling, 24,* 231–233.

Thompson, C., & Poppen, W. (1987). *Guidance activities for counselors and teachers.* Knoxville, TN: Author.

Wilkinson, C. (1990). Techniques for overcoming test anxiety. *Elementary School Guidance and Counseling, 24,* 234–235.

Zimbardo, P. (1977). *Shyness.* Reading, MA: Addison-Wesley.

Appendix C

◆

American Counseling Association Code of Ethics and Standards of Practice*

PREAMBLE

The American Counseling Association is an educational, scientific and professional organization whose members are dedicated to the enhancement of human development throughout the life span. Association members recognize diversity in our society and embrace a cross-cultural approach in support of the worth, dignity, potential, and uniqueness of each individual.

The specification of a code of ethics enables the association to clarify to current and future members, and to those served by members, the nature of the ethical responsibilities held in common by its members. As the code of ethics of the association, this document establishes principles that define the ethical behavior of association members. All members of the American Counseling Association are required to adhere to the *Code of Ethics* and the *Standards of Practice*. The Code of Ethics will serve as the basis for processing ethical complaints initiated against members of the association.

CODE OF ETHICS
SECTION A: THE COUNSELING RELATIONSHIP

A.1. Client Welfare

a. *Primary Responsibility.* The primary responsibility of counselors is to respect the dignity and to promote the welfare of clients.

b. *Positive Growth and Development.* Counselors encourage client growth and development in ways that foster the clients' interest and welfare; counselors avoid fostering dependent counseling relationships.

c. *Counseling Plans.* Counselors and their clients work jointly in devising integrated,

---

individual counseling plans that offer reasonable promise of success and are consistent with abilities and circumstances of clients. Counselors and clients regularly review counseling plans to ensure their continued viability and effectiveness, respecting clients' freedom of choice. (See A.3.b.)

d. *Family Involvement.* Counselors recognize that families are usually important in clients' lives and strive to enlist family understanding and involvement as a positive resource, when appropriate.

e. *Career and Employment Needs.* Counselors work with their clients in considering employment in jobs and circumstances that are consistent with the clients' overall abilities, vocational limitations, physical restrictions, general temperament, interest and aptitude patterns, social skills, education, general qualifications, and other relevant characteristics and needs. Counselors neither place nor participate in placing clients in positions that will result in damaging the interest and the welfare of clients, employers, or the public.

A.2. Respecting Diversity

a. *Nondiscrimination.* Counselors do not condone or engage in discrimination based on age, color, culture, disability, ethnic group, gender, race, religion, sexual orientation, marital status, or socioeconomic status. (See C.5.a., C.5.b., and D.1.i.)

b. *Respecting Differences.* Counselors will actively attempt to understand the diverse cultural backgrounds of the clients with whom they work. This includes, but is not limited to, learning how the counselor's own cultural/ethnic/racial identity impacts her/his values and beliefs about the counseling process. (See E.8. and F.2.i.)

A.3. Client Rights

a. *Disclosure to Clients.* When counseling is initiated, and throughout the counseling process as necessary, counselors inform clients of the purposes, goals, techniques, procedures, limitations, potential risks and benefits of services to be performed, and other pertinent information. Counselors take steps to ensure that clients understand the implications of diagnosis, the intended use of tests and reports, fees, and billing arrangements. Clients have the right to expect confidentiality and to be provided with an explanation of its limitations, including supervision and/or treatment team professionals; to obtain clear information about their case records; to participate in the ongoing counseling plans; and to refuse any recommended services and be advised of the consequences of such refusal. (See E.5.a. and G.2.)

b. *Freedom of Choice.* Counselors offer clients the freedom to choose whether to enter into a counseling relationship and to determine which professional(s) will provide counseling. Restrictions that limit choices of clients are fully explained. (See A.1.c.)

c. *Inability to Give Consent.* When counseling minors or persons unable to give voluntary informed consent, counselors act in these clients' best interests. (See B.3.)

A.4. Clients Served by Others. If a client is receiving services from another mental health professional, counselors, with client consent, inform the professional persons already involved and develop clear agreements to avoid confusion and conflict for the client. (See C.6.c.)

A.5. Personal Needs and Values

a. *Personal Needs.* In the counseling relationship, counselors are aware of the intimacy and responsibilities inherent in the counseling relationship, maintain respect for clients, and avoid actions that seek to meet their personal needs at the expense of clients.

b. *Personal Values.* Counselors are aware of their own values, attitudes, beliefs, and behaviors and how these apply in a diverse society, and avoid imposing their values on clients. (See C.5.a.)

A.6. Dual Relationships

a. *Avoid When Possible.* Counselors are aware of their influential positions with respect to clients, and they avoid exploiting the trust and dependency of clients. Counselors make every effort to avoid dual relationships with clients that could impair professional judgment or increase the risk of harm to clients. (Examples of such relationships include, but are not limited to, familial, social, financial, business, or close personal relationships with clients.) When a dual relationship cannot be avoided, counselors take appropriate professional precautions such as informed consent, consultation, supervision, and documentation to ensure that judgment is not impaired and no exploitation occurs. (See F.1.b.)

b. *Superior/Subordinate Relationships.* Counselors do not accept as clients superiors or subordinates with whom they have administrative, supervisory, or evaluative relationships.

A.7. Sexual Intimacies with Clients

a. *Current Clients.* Counselors do not have any type of sexual intimacies with clients and do not counsel persons with whom they have had a sexual relationship.

b. *Former Clients.* Counselors do not engage in sexual intimacies with former clients within a minimum of two years after terminating the counseling relationship. Counselors who engage in such relationship after two years following termination have the responsibility to thoroughly examine and document that such relations did not have an exploitative nature, based on factors such as duration of counseling, amount of time since counseling, termination circumstances, client's personal history and mental status, adverse impact on the client, and actions by the counselor suggesting a plan to initiate a sexual relationship with the client after termination.

A.8. Multiple Clients. When counselors agree to provide counseling services to two or more persons who have a relationship (such as husband and wife, or parents and children), counselors clarify at the outset which person or persons are clients and the nature of the relationships they will have with each involved person. If it becomes apparent that counselors may be called upon to perform potentially conflicting roles, they clarify, adjust, or withdraw from roles appropriately. (See B.2. and B.4.d.)

A.9. Group Work

a. *Screening.* Counselors screen prospective group counseling/therapy participants. To the extent possible, counselors select members whose needs and goals are compatible with goals of the group, who will not impede the group process, and whose well-being will not be jeopardized by the group experience.

b. *Protecting Clients.* In a group setting, counselors take reasonable precautions to protect clients from physical or psychological trauma.

A.10. Fees and Bartering (See D.3.a. and D.3.b.)

a. *Advance Understanding.* Counselors clearly explain to clients, prior to entering the counseling relationship, all financial arrangements related to professional services including the use of collection agencies or legal measures for nonpayment. (A.11.c.)

b. *Establishing Fees.* In establishing fees for professional counseling services, counselors consider the financial status of clients and locality. In the event that the established fee structure is inappropriate for a client, assistance is provided in attempting to find comparable services of acceptable cost. (See A.10.d., D.3.a., and D.3.b.)

c. *Bartering Discouraged.* Counselors ordinarily refrain from accepting goods or services from clients in return for counseling services because such arrangements create inherent potential for conflicts, exploitation, and distortion of the professional relationship. Counselors may participate in bartering only if the relationship is not exploitive, if the client requests it, if a clear written contract is established, and if such arrangements are an accepted practice among professionals in the community. (See A.6.a.)

d. *Pro Bono Service.* Counselors contribute to society by devoting a portion of their professional activity to services for which there is little or no financial return (pro bono).

A.11. Termination and Referral

a. *Abandonment Prohibited.* Counselors do not abandon or neglect clients in counseling. Counselors assist in making appropriate arrangements for the continuation of treatment, when necessary, during interruptions such as vacations, and following termination.

b. *Inability to Assist Clients.* If counselors determine an inability to be of professional assistance to clients, they avoid entering or immediately terminate a counseling relationship. Counselors are knowledgeable about referral resources and suggest appropriate alternatives. If clients decline the suggested referral, counselors should discontinue the relationship.

c. *Appropriate Termination.* Counselors terminate a counseling relationship, securing client agreement when possible, when it is reasonably clear that the client is no longer benefiting, when services are no longer required, when counseling no longer serves the client's needs or interests, when clients do not pay fees charged, or when agency or institution limits do not allow provision of further counseling services. (See A.10.b. and C.2.g.)

A.12. Computer Technology

a. *Use of Computers.* When computer applications are used in counseling services, counselors ensure that: (1) the client is intellectually, emotionally, and physically capable of using the computer application; (2) the computer application is appropriate for the needs of the client; (3) the client understands the purpose and operation of the computer applications; and (4) a follow-up of client use of a computer application is provided to correct possible misconceptions, discover inappropriate use, and assess subsequent needs.

b. *Explanation of Limitations.* Counselors ensure that clients are provided information as a part of the counseling relationship that adequately explains the limitations of computer technology.

c. *Access to Computer Applications.* Counselors provide for equal access to computer applications in counseling services. (See A.2.a.)

SECTION B: CONFIDENTIALITY

B.1. Right to Privacy

a. *Respect for Privacy.* Counselors respect their clients' right to privacy and avoid illegal and unwarranted disclosures of confidential information. (See A.3.a. and B.6.a.)

b. *Client Waiver.* The right to privacy may be waived by the client or their legally recognized representative.

c. *Exceptions.* The general requirement that counselors keep information confidential does not apply when disclosure is required to prevent clear and imminent danger to the client or others or when legal requirements demand that confidential information be revealed. Counselors consult with other professionals when in doubt as to the validity of an exception.

d. *Contagious, Fatal Diseases.* A counselor who receives information confirming that a client has a disease commonly known to be both communicable and fatal is justified in disclosing information to an identifiable third party, who by his or her relationship with the client is at a high risk of contracting the disease. Prior to making a disclosure the counselor should ascertain that the client has not already informed the third party about his or her disease and that the client is not intending to inform the third party in the immediate future. (See B.1.c and B.1.f.)

e. *Court Ordered Disclosure.* When court ordered to release confidential information without a client's permission, counselors request to the court that the disclosure not be required due to potential harm to the client or counseling relationship. (See B.1.c.)

f. *Minimal Disclosure.* When circumstances require the disclosure of confidential information, only essential information is revealed. To the extent possible, clients are informed before confidential information is disclosed.

g. *Explanation of Limitations.* When counseling is initiated and throughout the counseling process as necessary, counselors inform clients of the limitations of confidentiality and identify foreseeable situations in which confidentiality must be breached. (See G.2.a.)

h. *Subordinates.* Counselors make every effort to ensure that privacy and confidentiality of clients are maintained by subordinates including employees, supervisees, clerical assistants, and volunteers. (See B.1.a.)

i. *Treatment Teams.* If client treatment will involve a continued review by a treatment team, the client will be informed of the team's existence and composition.

B.2. Groups and Families

a. *Group Work.* In group work, counselors clearly define confidentiality and the parameters for the specific group being entered, explain its importance, and discuss the difficulties related to confidentiality involved in group work. The fact that confidentiality cannot be guaranteed is clearly communicated to group members.

b. *Family Counseling.* In family counseling, information about one family member cannot be disclosed to another member without permission. Counselors protect the privacy rights of each family member. (See A.8., B.3., and B.4.d.)

B.3. Minor or Incompetent Clients. When counseling clients who are minors or individuals who are unable to give voluntary, informed consent, parents or guardians may be included in the counseling process as appropriate. Counselors act in the best interests of clients and take measures to safeguard confidentiality. (See A.3.c.)

B.4. Records

a. *Requirement of Records.* Counselors maintain records necessary for rendering professional services to their clients and as required by laws, regulations, or agency or institution procedures.

b. *Confidentiality of Records.* Counselors are responsible for securing the safety and confidentiality of any counseling records they create, maintain, transfer, or destroy whether the records are written, taped, computerized, or stored in any other medium. (See B.1.a.)

c. *Permission to Record or Observe.* Counselors obtain permission from clients prior to electronically recording or observing sessions. (See A.3.a.)

d. *Client Access.* Counselors recognize that counseling records are kept for the benefit of clients, and therefore provide access to records and copies of records when requested by competent clients, unless the records contain information that may be misleading and detrimental to the client. In situations involving multiple clients, access to records is limited to those parts of records that do not include confidential information related to another client. (See A.8., B.1.a., and B.2.b.)

e. *Disclosure or Transfer.* Counselors obtain written permission from clients to disclose or transfer records to legitimate third parties unless exceptions to confidentiality exist as listed in Section B.1. Steps are taken to ensure that receivers of counseling records are sensitive to their confidential nature.

B.5. Research and Training

a. *Data Disguise Required.* Use of data derived from counseling relationships for purposes of training, research, or publication is confined to content that is disguised to ensure the anonymity of the individuals involved. (See B.1.g. and G.3.d.)

b. *Agreement for Identification.* Identification of a client in a presentation or publication is permissible only when the client has reviewed the material and has agreed to its presentation or publication. (See G.3.d.)

B.6. Consultation

a. *Respect for Privacy.* Information obtained in a consulting relationship is discussed for professional purposes only with persons clearly concerned with the case. Written and oral reports present data germane to the purposes of the consultation, and every effort is made to protect client identity and avoid undue invasion of privacy.

b. *Cooperating Agencies.* Before sharing information, counselors make efforts to ensure that there are defined policies in other agencies serving the counselor's clients that effectively protect the confidentiality of information.

SECTION C: PROFESSIONAL RESPONSIBILITY

C.1. Standards Knowledge. Counselors have a responsibility to read, understand, and follow the *Code of Ethics* and the *Standards of Practice.*

C.2. Professional Competence

a. *Boundaries of Competence.* Counselors practice only within the boundaries of their competence, based on their education, training, supervised experience, state and national professional credentials, and appropriate professional experience. Counselors will demonstrate a commitment to gain knowledge, personal awareness, sensitivity, and skills pertinent to working with a diverse client population.

b. *New Specialty Areas of Practice.* Counselors practice in specialty areas new to them only after appropriate education, training, and supervised experience. While developing skills in new specialty areas, counselors take steps to ensure the competence of their work and to protect others from possible harm.

c. *Qualified for Employment.* Counselors accept employment only for positions for which they are qualified by education, training, supervised experience, state and national professional credentials, and appropriate professional experience. Counselors hire for professional counseling positions only individuals who are qualified and competent.

d. *Monitor Effectiveness.* Counselors continually monitor their effectiveness as professionals and take steps to improve when necessary. Counselors in private practice take reasonable steps to seek out peer supervision to evaluate their efficacy as counselors.

e. *Ethical Issues Consultation.* Counselors take reasonable steps to consult with other counselors or related professionals when they have questions regarding their ethical obligations or professional practice. (See H.1)

f. *Continuing Education.* Counselors recognize the need for continuing education to maintain a reasonable level of awareness of current scientific and professional information in their fields of activity. They take steps to maintain competence in the skills they use, are open to new procedures, and keep current with the diverse and/or special populations with whom they work.

g. *Impairment.* Counselors refrain from offering or accepting professional services when their physical, mental or emotional problems are likely to harm a client or others. They are alert to the signs of impairment, seek assistance for problems, and, if necessary, limit, suspend, or terminate their professional responsibilities. (See A.11.c.)

C.3. Advertising and Soliciting Clients

a. *Accurate Advertising.* There are no restrictions on advertising by counselors except those that can be specifically justified to protect the public from deceptive practices. Counselors advertise or represent their services to the public by identifying their credentials in an accurate manner that is not false, misleading, deceptive, or fraudulent. Counselors may only advertise the highest degree earned which is in counseling or a closely related field from a college or university that was accredited when the degree was awarded by one of the regional accrediting bodies recognized by the Council on Postsecondary Accreditation.

b. *Testimonials.* Counselors who use testimonials do not solicit them from clients or other persons who, because of their particular circumstances, may be vulnerable to undue influence.

c. *Statements by Others.* Counselors make reasonable efforts to ensure that statements made by others about them or the profession of counseling are accurate.

d. *Recruiting Through Employment.* Counselors do not use their places of employment or institutional affiliation to recruit or gain clients, supervisees, or consultees for their private practices. (See C.5.e.)

e. *Products and Training Advertisements.* Counselors who develop products related to their profession or conduct workshops or training events ensure that the advertisements concerning these products or events are accurate and disclose adequate information for consumers to make informed choices.

f. *Promoting to Those Served.* Counselors do not use counseling, teaching, training, or supervisory relationships to promote their products or training events in a manner that is deceptive or would exert undue influence on individuals who may be vulnerable. Counselors may adopt textbooks they have authored for instruction purposes.

g. *Professional Association Involvement.* Counselors actively participate in local, state, and national associations that foster the development and improvement of counseling.

C.4. Credentials

a. *Credentials Claimed.* Counselors claim or imply only professional credentials possessed and are responsible for correcting any known misrepresentations of their credentials by others. Professional credentials include graduate degrees in counseling or closely related mental health fields, accreditation of graduate programs, national voluntary certifications, government-issued certifications or licenses, ACA professional membership, or any other credential that might indicate to the public specialized knowledge or expertise in counseling.

b. *ACA Professional Membership.* ACA professional members may announce to the public their membership status. Regular members may not announce their ACA membership in a manner that might imply they are credentialed counselors.

c. *Credential Guidelines.* Counselors follow the guidelines for use of credentials that have been established by the entities that issue the credentials.

d. *Misrepresentation of Credentials.* Counselors do not attribute more to their credentials than the credentials represent, and do not imply that other counselors are not qualified because they do not possess certain credentials.

e. *Doctoral Degrees From Other Fields.* Counselors who hold a master's degree in counseling or a closely related mental health field, but hold a doctoral degree from other than counseling or a closely related field do not use the title, "Dr." in their practices and do not announce to the public in relation to their practice or status as a counselor that they hold a doctorate.

C.5. Public Responsibility

a. *Nondiscrimination.* Counselors do not discriminate against clients, students, or supervisees in a manner that has a negative impact based on their age, color, culture, disability, ethnic group, gender, race, religion, sexual orientation, or socioeconomic status, or for any other reason. (See A.2.a.)

b. *Sexual Harassment.* Counselors do not engage in sexual harassment. Sexual harassment is defined as sexual solicitation, physical advances, or verbal or nonverbal conduct that is sexual in nature, that occurs in connection with professional activities or roles, and that either: (1) is unwelcome, is offensive, or creates a hostile workplace environment, and counselors know or are told this; or (2) is sufficiently severe or intense to be perceived as harassment to a reasonable person in the context. Sexual harassment can consist of a single intense or severe act or multiple persistent or pervasive acts.

c. *Reports to Third Parties.* Counselors are accurate, honest, and unbiased in reporting their professional activities and judgments to appropriate third parties including courts, health insurance companies, those who are the recipients of evaluation reports, and others. (See B.1.g.)

d. *Media Presentations.* When counselors provide advice or comment by means of public lectures, demonstrations, radio or television programs, pre-recorded tapes, printed articles, mailed material, or other media, they take reasonable precautions to ensure that (1) the statements are based on appropriate professional counseling literature and practice; (2) the statements are otherwise consistent with the *Code of Ethics* and the *Standards of Practice;* and (3) the recipients of the information are not encouraged to infer that a professional counseling relationship has been established. (See C.6.b.)

e. *Unjustified Gains.* Counselors do not use their professional positions to seek or receive unjustified personal gains, sexual favors, unfair advantage, or unearned goods or services. (See C.3.d.)

C.6. Responsibility to Other Professionals

a. *Different Approaches.* Counselors are respectful of approaches to professional counseling that differ from their own. Counselors know and take into account the traditions and practices of other professional groups with which they work.

b. *Personal Public Statements.* When making personal statements in a public context, counselors clarify that they are speaking from their personal perspectives and that they are not speaking on behalf of all counselors or the profession. (See C.5.d.)

c. *Clients Served by Others.* When counselors learn that their clients are in a professional relationship with another mental health professional, they request release from clients to inform the other professionals and strive to establish positive and collaborative professional relationships. (See A.4.)

SECTION D: RELATIONSHIPS WITH OTHER PROFESSIONALS

D.1. Relationships with Employers and Employees

a. *Role Definition.* Counselors define and describe for their employers and employees the parameters and levels of their professional roles.

b. *Agreements.* Counselors establish working agreements with supervisors, colleagues, and subordinates regarding counseling or clinical relationships, confidentiality, adherence to professional standards, distinction between public and private material, maintenance and dissemination of recorded information, workload, and accountability. Working agreements in each instance are specified and made known to those concerned.

c. *Negative Conditions.* Counselors alert their employers to conditions that may be potentially disruptive or damaging to the counselor's professional responsibilities or that may limit their effectiveness.

d. *Evaluation.* Counselors submit regularly to professional review and evaluation by their supervisor or the appropriate representative of the employer.

e. *In-Service.* Counselors are responsible for in-service development of self and staff.

f. *Goals.* Counselors inform their staff of goals and programs.

g. *Practices.* Counselors provide personnel and agency practices that respect and enhance the rights and welfare of each employee and recipient of agency services. Counselors strive to maintain the highest levels of professional services.

h. *Personnel Selection and Assignment.* Counselors select competent staff and assign responsibilities compatible with their skills and experiences.

i. *Discrimination.* Counselors, as either employers or employees, do not engage in or condone practices that are inhumane, illegal, or unjustifiable (such as considerations based on age, color, culture, disability, ethnic group, gender, race, religion, sexual orientation, or socioeconomic status) in hiring, promotion, or training. (See A.2.a. and C.5.b.)

j. *Professional Conduct.* Counselors have a responsibility both to clients and to the agency or institution within which services are performed to maintain high standards of professional conduct.

k. *Exploitive Relationships.* Counselors do not engage in exploitive relationships with individuals over whom they have supervisory, evaluative, or instructional control or authority.

l. *Employer Policies.* The acceptance of employment in an agency or institution implies that counselors are in agreement with its general policies and principles. Counselors strive to reach agreement with employers as to acceptable standards of conduct that allow for changes in institutional policy conducive to the growth and development of clients.

D.2. Consultation (See B.6.)

a. *Consultation as an Option.* Counselors may choose to consult with any other professionally competent persons about their clients. In choosing consultants, counselors avoid placing the consultant in a conflict of interest situation that would preclude the consultant being a proper party to the counselor's efforts to help the client. Should counselors be engaged in a work setting that compromises this consultation standard, they consult with other professionals whenever possible to consider justifiable alternatives.

b. *Consultant Competency.* Counselors are reasonably certain that they have or the organization represented has the necessary competencies and resources for giving the kind of consulting services needed and that appropriate referral resources are available.

c. *Understanding with Clients.* When providing consultation, counselors attempt to develop with their clients a clear understanding of problem definition, goals for change, and predicted consequences of interventions selected.

d. *Consultant Goals.* The consulting relationship is one in which client adaptability and growth toward self-direction are consistently encouraged and cultivated. (See A.1.b.)

D.3. Fees for Referral

a. *Accepting Fees from Agency Clients.* Counselors refuse a private fee or other remuneration for rendering services to persons who are entitled to such services through the counselor's employing agency or institution. The policies of a particular agency may make explicit provisions for agency clients to receive counseling services from members of its staff in private practice. In such instances, the clients must be informed of other options open to them should they seek private counseling services. (See A.10.a., A.11.b., and C.3.d.)

b. *Referral Fees.* Counselors do not accept a referral fee from other professionals.

D.4. Subcontractor Arrangements. When counselors work as subcontractors for counseling services for a third party, they have a duty to inform clients of the limitations of confidentiality that the organization may place on counselors in providing counseling services to clients. The limits of such confidentiality ordinarily are discussed as part of the intake session. (See B.1.e. and B.1.f.)

SECION E: EVALUATION, ASSESSMENT,
AND INTERPRETATION

E.1. General

a. *Appraisal Techniques.* The primary purpose of educational and psychological assessment is to provide measures that are objective and interpretable in either comparative or absolute terms. Counselors recognize the need to interpret the statements in this section as applying to the whole range of appraisal techniques, including test and nontest data.

b. *Client Welfare.* Counselors promote the welfare and best interests of the client in the development, publication, and utilization of educational and psychological assessment techniques. They do not misuse assessment results and interpretations and take reasonable steps to prevent others from misusing the information these techniques provide. They respect the client's right to know the results, the interpretations made, and the bases for their conclusions and recommendations.

E.2. Competence to Use and Interpret Tests

a. *Limits of Competence.* Counselors recognize the limits of their competence and perform only those testing and assessment services for which they have been trained. They are familiar with reliability, validity, related standardization, error of measurement, and proper application of any technique utilized. Counselors using computer-based test interpretations are trained in the construct being measured and the specific instrument being used prior to using this type of computer application. Counselors take reasonable measures to ensure the proper use of psychological assessment techniques by persons under their supervision.

b. *Appropriate Use.* Counselors are responsible for the appropriate application, scoring, interpretation, and use of assessment instruments, whether they score and interpret such tests themselves or use computerized or other services.

c. *Decisions Based on Results.* Counselors responsible for decisions involving individuals or policies that are based on assessment results have a thorough understanding of educational and psychological measurement, including validation criteria, test research, and guidelines for test development and use.

d. *Accurate Information.* Counselors provide accurate information and avoid false claims or misconceptions when making statements about assessment instruments or techniques. Special efforts are made to avoid unwarranted connotations of such terms as IQ and grade equivalent scores. (See C.5.c.)

E.3. Informed Consent

a. *Explanation to Clients.* Prior to assessment, counselors explain the nature and purposes of assessment and the specific use of results in language the client (or other legally authorized person on behalf of the client) can understand, unless an explicit exception to this right has been agreed upon in advance. Regardless of whether scoring and interpretation are completed by counselors, by assistants, or by computer or other outside services, counselors take reasonable steps to ensure that appropriate explanations are given to the client.

b. *Recipients of Results.* The examinee's welfare, explicit understanding, and prior agreement determine the recipients of test results. Counselors include accurate and appropriate interpretations with any release of individual or group test results. (See B.1.a. and C.5.c.)

E.4. Release of Information to Competent Professionals

a. *Misuse of Results.* Counselors do not misuse assessment results, including test results, and interpretations, and take reasonable steps to prevent the misuse of such by others. (See C.5.c.)

b. *Release of Raw Data.* Counselors ordinarily release data (e.g. protocols, counseling or interview notes, or questionnaires) in which the client is identified only with the consent of the client or the client's legal representative. Such data are usually released only to persons recognized by counselors as competent to interpret the data. (See B.1.a.)

E.5. Proper Diagnosis of Mental Disorders

a. *Proper Diagnosis.* Counselors take special care to provide proper diagnosis of mental disorders. Assessment techniques (including personal interview) used to determine client care (e.g., locus of treatment, type of treatment, or recommended follow-up) are carefully selected and appropriately used. (See A.3.a. and C.5.c.)

b. *Cultural Sensitivity.* Counselors recognize that culture affects the manner in which clients' problems are defined. Clients' socioeconomic and cultural experience is considered when diagnosing mental disorders.

E.6. Test Selection

a. *Appropriateness of Instruments.* Counselors carefully consider the validity, reliability, psychometric limitations, and appropriateness of instruments when selecting tests for use in a given situation or with a particular client.

b. *Culturally Diverse Populations.* Counselors are cautious when selecting tests for culturally diverse populations to avoid inappropriateness of testing that may be outside of socialized behavioral or cognitive patterns.

E.7. Conditions of Test Administration

a. *Administration Conditions.* Counselors administer tests under the same conditions that were established in their standardization. When tests are not administered under standard conditions or when unusual behavior or irregularities occur during the testing session, those conditions are noted in interpretation, and the results may be designated as invalid or of questionable validity.

b. *Computer Administration.* Counselors are responsible for ensuring that administration programs function properly to provide clients with accurate results when a computer or other electronic methods are used for test administration. (See A.12.b.)

c. *Unsupervised Test-Taking.* Counselors do not permit unsupervised or inadequately supervised use of tests or assessments unless the tests or assessments are designed, intended, and validated for self-administration and/or scoring.

d. *Disclosure of Favorable Conditions.* Prior to test administration, conditions that produce most favorable test results are made known to the examinee.

E.8. Diversity in Testing.

Counselors are cautious in using assessment techniques, making evaluations, and interpreting the performance of populations not represented in the norm group on which an instrument was standardized. They recognize the effects of age, color, culture, disability, ethnic group, gender, race, religion, sexual orientation, and socioeconomic status on test administration and interpretation and place test results in proper perspective with other relevant factors. (See A.2.a.)

E.9. Test Scoring and Interpretation

a. *Reporting Reservations.* In reporting assessment results, counselors indicate any reservations that exist regarding validity or reliability because of the circumstances of the assessment or the inappropriateness of the norms for the person tested.

b. *Research Instruments.* Counselors exercise caution when interpreting the results of research instruments possessing insufficient technical data to support respondent results. The specific purposes for the use of such instruments are stated explicitly to the examinee.

c. *Testing Services.* Counselors who provide test scoring and test interpretation services to support the assessment process confirm the validity of such interpretations. They accurately describe the purpose, norms, validity, reliability, and applications of the procedures and any special qualifications applicable to their use. The public offering of an automated test interpretations service is considered a professional-to-professional consultation. The formal responsibility of the consultant is to the consultee, but the ultimate and overriding responsibility is to the client.

E.10. Test Security.
Counselors maintain the integrity and security of tests and other assessment techniques consistent with legal and contractual obligations. Counselors do not appropriate, reproduce, or modify published tests or parts thereof without acknowledgment and permission from the publisher.

E.11. Obsolete Tests and Outdated Test Results.
Counselors do not use data or test results that are obsolete or outdated for the current purpose. Counselors make every effort to prevent the misuse of obsolete measures and test data by others.

E.12. Test Construction.
Counselors use established scientific procedures, relevant standards, and current professional knowledge for test design in the development, publication, and utilization of educational and psychological assessment techniques.

SECTION F: TEACHING, TRAINING, AND SUPERVISION

F.1. Counselor Educators and Trainers

a. *Educators as Teachers and Practitioners.* Counselors who are responsible for developing, implementing, and supervising educational programs are skilled as teachers and practitioners. They are knowledgeable regarding the ethical, legal, and regulatory aspects of the profession, are skilled in applying that knowledge, and make students and supervisees aware of their responsibilities. Counselors conduct counselor education and training programs in an ethical manner and serve as role models for professional behavior. Counselor educators should make an effort to infuse material related to human diversity into all courses and/or workshops that are designed to promote the development of professional counselors.

b. *Relationship Boundaries with Students and Supervisees.* Counselors clearly define and maintain ethical, professional, and social relationship boundaries with their students and supervisees. They are aware of the differential in power that exists and the student's or supervisee's possible incomprehension of that power differential. Counselors explain to students and supervisees the potential for the relationship to become exploitive.

c. *Sexual Relationships.* Counselors do not engage in sexual relationships with students or supervisees and do not subject them to sexual harassment. (See A.6. and C.5.b)

d. *Contributions to Research.* Counselors give credit to students or supervisees for their contributions to research and scholarly projects. Credit is given through coauthorship, acknowledgment, footnote statement, or other appropriate means, in accordance with such contributions. (See G.4.b. and G.4.c.)

e. *Close Relatives.* Counselors do not accept close relatives as students or supervisees.

f. *Supervision Preparation.* Counselors who offer clinical supervision services are adequately prepared in supervision methods and techniques. Counselors who are doctoral students serving as practicum or internship supervisors to master's level students are adequately prepared and supervised by the training program.

g. *Responsibility for Services to Clients.* Counselors who supervise the counseling services of others take reasonable measures to ensure that counseling services provided to clients are professional.

h. *Endorsement.* Counselors do not endorse students or supervisees for certification, licensure, employment, or completion of an academic or training program if they believe students or supervisees are not qualified for the endorsement. Counselors take reasonable steps to assist students or supervisees who are not qualified for endorsement to become qualified.

F.2. Counselor Education and Training Programs

a. *Orientation.* Prior to admission, counselors orient prospective students to the counselor education or training program's expectations, including but not limited to the following: (1) the type and level of skill acquisition required for successful completion of the training, (2) subject matter to be covered, (3) basis for evaluation, (4) training components that encourage self-growth or self-disclosure as part of the training process, (5) the type of supervision settings and requirements of the sites for required clinical field experiences, (6) student and supervisee evaluation and dismissal policies and procedures, and (7) up-to-date employment prospects for graduates.

b. *Integration of Study and Practice.* Counselors establish counselor education and training programs that integrate academic study and supervised practice.

c. *Evaluation.* Counselors clearly state to students and supervisees, in advance of training, the levels of competency expected, appraisal methods, and timing of evaluations for both didactic and experiential components. Counselors provide students and supervisees with periodic performance appraisal and evaluation feedback throughout the training program.

d. *Teaching Ethics.* Counselors make students and supervisees aware of the ethical responsibilities and standards of the profession and the students' and supervisees' ethical responsibilities to the profession. (See C.1. and F.3.e.)

e. *Peer Relationships.* When students or supervisees are assigned to lead counseling groups or provide clinical supervision for their peers, counselors take steps to ensure that students and supervisees placed in these roles do not have personal or adverse relationships with peers and that they understand they have the same ethical obligations as counselor educators, trainers, and supervisors. Counselors make every effort to ensure that the rights of peers are not compromised when students or supervisees are assigned to lead counseling groups or provide clinical supervision.

f. *Varied Theoretical Positions.* Counselors present varied theoretical positions so that students and supervisees may make comparisons and have opportunities to develop their own positions. Counselors provide information concerning the scientific bases of professional practice. (See C.6.a.)

g. *Field Placements.* Counselors develop clear policies within their training program regarding field placement and other clinical experiences. Counselors provide clearly stated roles and responsibilities for the student or supervisee, the site supervisor, and the program supervisor. They confirm that site supervisors are qualified to provide supervision and are informed of their professional and ethical responsibilities in this role.

h. *Dual Relationships as Supervisors.* Counselors avoid dual relationships such as performing the role of site supervisor and training program supervisor in the student's or supervisee's training program. Counselors do not accept any form of professional services, fees, commissions, reimbursement, or remuneration from a site for student or supervisee placement.

i. *Diversity in Programs.* Counselors are responsive to their institution's and program's recruitment and retention needs for training program administrators, faculty, and students with diverse backgrounds and special needs. (See A.2.a.)

F.3. Students and Supervisees

a. *Limitations.* Counselors, through ongoing evaluation and appraisal, are aware of the academic and personal limitations of students and supervisees that might impede performance. Counselors assist students and supervisees in securing remedial assistance when needed, and dismiss from the training program supervisees who are unable to provide competent service due to academic or personal limitations. Counselors seek professional consultation and document their decision to dismiss or refer students or supervisees for assistance. Counselors assure that students and supervisees have recourse to address decisions made, to require them to seek assistance, or to dismiss them.

b. *Self-Growth Experiences.* Counselors use professional judgment when designing training experiences conducted by the counselors themselves that require student and supervisee self-growth or self-disclosure. Safeguards are provided so that students and supervisees are aware of the ramifications their self-disclosure may have, on counselors whose primary role as teacher, trainer, or supervisor requires acting on ethical obligations to the profession. Evaluative components of experiential training experiences explicitly delineate predetermined academic standards that are separate and not dependent on the student's level of self-disclosure. (See A.6.)

c. *Counseling for Students and Supervisees.* If students or supervisees request counseling, supervisors or counselor educators provide them with acceptable referrals. Supervisors or counselor educators do not serve as counselor to students or supervisees over whom they hold administrative, teaching, or evaluative roles unless this is a brief role associated with a training experience. (See A.6.b.)

d. *Clients of Students and Supervisees.* Counselors make every effort to ensure that the clients at field placements are aware of the services rendered and the qualifications of the students and supervisees rendering those services. Clients receive professional disclosure information and are informed of the limits of confidentiality. Client permission is obtained in order for the students and supervisees to use any information concerning the counseling relationship in the training process. (See B.1.e.)

e. *Standards for Students and Supervisees.* Students and supervisees preparing to become counselors adhere to the *Code of Ethics* and the *Standards of Practice*. Students and supervisees have the same obligations to clients as those required of counselors. (See H.1.)

SECTION G: RESEARCH AND PUBLICATION

G.1. Research Responsibilities

a. *Use of Human Subjects.* Counselors plan, design, conduct, and report research in a manner consistent with pertinent ethical principles, federal and state laws, host institutional regulations, and scientific standards governing research with human subjects. Counselors design and conduct research that reflects cultural sensitivity appropriateness.

b. *Deviation from Standard Practices.* Counselors seek consultation and observe stringent safeguards to protect the rights of research participants when a research problem suggests a deviation from standard acceptable practices. (See B.6.)

c. *Precautions to Avoid Injury.* Counselors who conduct research with human subjects are responsible for the subjects' welfare throughout the experiment and take reasonable precautions to avoid causing injurious psychological, physical, or social effects to their subjects.

d. *Principal Researcher Responsibility.* The ultimate responsibility for ethical research practice lies with the principal researcher. All others involved in the research activities share ethical obligations and full responsibility for their own actions.

e. *Minimal Interference.* Counselors take reasonable precautions to avoid causing disruptions in subjects' lives due to participation in research.

f. *Diversity.* Counselors are sensitive to diversity and research issues with special populations. They seek consultation when appropriate. (See A.2.a. and B.6.)

G.2. Informed Consent

a. *Topics Disclosed.* In obtaining informed consent for research, counselors use language that is understandable to research participants and that: (1) accurately explains the purpose and procedures to be followed; (2) identifies any procedures that are experimental or relatively untried; (3) describes the attendant discomforts and risks; (4) describes the benefits or changes in individuals or organizations that might be reasonably expected; (5) discloses appropriate alternative procedures that would be advantageous for subjects; (6) offers to answer any inquiries concerning the procedures; (7) describes any limitations on confidentiality; and (8) instructs that subjects are free to withdraw their consent and to discontinue participation in the project at any time. (See B.1.f.)

b. *Deception.* Counselors do not conduct research involving deception unless alternative procedures are not feasible and the prospective value of the research justifies the deception. When the methodological requirements of a study necessitate concealment or deception, the investigator is required to explain clearly the reasons for this action as soon as possible.

c. *Voluntary Participation.* Participation in research is typically voluntary and without any penalty for refusal to participate. Involuntary participation is appropriate only when it can be demonstrated that participation will have no harmful effects on subjects and is essential to the investigation.

d. *Confidentiality of Information.* Information obtained about research participants during the course of an investigation is confidential. When the possibility exists that others may obtain access to such information, ethical research practice requires that the possibility, together with the plans for protecting confidentiality, be explained to participants as a part of the procedure for obtaining informed consent. (See B.1.e.)

e. *Persons Incapable of Giving Informed Consent.* When a person is incapable of giving informed consent, counselors provide an appropriate explanation, obtain agreement for participation and obtain appropriate consent from a legally authorized person.

f. *Commitments to Participants.* Counselors take reasonable measures to honor all commitments to research participants.

g. *Explanations After Data Collection.* After data are collected, counselors provide participants with full clarification of the nature of the study to remove any misconceptions. Where scientific or human values justify delaying or withholding information, counselors take reasonable measures to avoid causing harm.

h. *Agreements to Cooperate.* Counselors who agree to cooperate with another individual in research or publication incur an obligation to cooperate as promised in terms of punctuality of performance and with regard to the completeness and accuracy of the information required.

i. *Informed Consent for Sponsors.* In the pursuit of research, counselors give sponsors, institutions, and publication channels the same respect and opportunity for giving informed consent that they accord to individual research participants. Counselors are aware of their obligation to future research workers and ensure that host institutions are given feedback information and proper acknowledgment.

G.3. Reporting Results

a. *Information Affecting Outcome.* When reporting research results, counselors explicitly mention all variables and conditions known to the investigator that may have affected the outcome of a study or the interpretation of data.

b. *Accurate Results.* Counselors plan, conduct, and report research accurately and in a manner that minimizes the possibility that results will be misleading. They provide thorough discussions of the limitations of their data and alternative hypotheses. Counselors do not engage in fraudulent research, distort data, misrepresent data, or deliberately bias their results.

c. *Obligation to Report Unfavorable Results.* Counselors communicate to other counselors the results of any research judged to be of professional value. Results that reflect unfavorably on institutions, programs, services, prevailing opinions, or vested interests are not withheld.

d. *Identity of Subjects.* Counselors who supply data, aid in the research of another person, report research results, or make original data available take due care to disguise the identity of respective subjects in the absence of specific authorization from the subjects to do otherwise. (See B.1.g. and B.5.a.)

e. *Replication Studies.* Counselors are obligated to make available sufficient original research data to qualified professionals who may wish to replicate the study.

G.4. Publication

a. *Recognition of Others.* When conducting and reporting research, counselors are familiar with and give recognition to previous work on the topic, observe copyright laws, and give full credit to those to whom credit is due. (See F.1.d. and G.4.c.)

b. *Contributors.* Counselors give credit through joint authorship, acknowledgment, footnote statements, or other appropriate means to those who have contributed significantly to research or concept development in accordance with such contributions. The principal contributor is listed first and minor technical or professional contributions are acknowledged in notes or introductory statements.

c. *Student Research.* For an article that is substantially based on a student's dissertation or thesis, the student is listed as the principal author. (See F.1.d. and G.4.a.)

d. *Duplicate Submission.* Counselors submit manuscripts for consideration to only one journal at a time. Manuscripts that are published in whole or in substantial part in another journal or published work are not submitted for publication without acknowledgment and permission from the previous publication.

e. *Professional Review.* Counselors who review material submitted for publication, research, or other scholarly purposes respect the confidentiality and proprietary rights of those who submitted it.

SECTION H: RESOLVING ETHICAL ISSUES

H.1. Knowledge of Standards. Counselors are familiar with the *Code of Ethics* and the *Standards of Practice* and other applicable ethics codes from other professional organizations of which they are a member, or from certification and licensure bodies. Lack of knowledge or misunderstanding of an ethical responsibility is not a defense against a charge of unethical conduct. (See F.3.e.)

H.2. Suspected Violations

a. *Ethical Behavior Expected.* Counselors expect professional associates to adhere to Code of Ethics. When counselors possess reasonable cause that raises doubts as to whether a counselor is acting in an ethical manner, they take appropriate action. (See H.2.d. and H.2.e.)

b. *Consultation.* When uncertain as to whether a particular situation or course of action may be in violation of Code of Ethics, counselors consult with other counselors who are knowledgeable about ethics, with colleagues, or with appropriate authorities.

c. *Organization Conflicts.* If the demands of an organization with which counselors are affiliated pose a conflict with Code of Ethics, counselors specify the nature of such conflicts and express to their supervisors or other responsible officials their commitment to Code of Ethics. When possible, counselors work toward change within the organization to allow full adherence to Code of Ethics.

d. *Informal Resolution.* When counselors have reasonable cause to believe that another counselor is violating an ethical standard, they attempt to first resolve the issue informally with the other counselor if feasible, providing that such action does not violate confidentiality rights that may be involved.

e. *Reporting Suspected Violations.* When an informal resolution is not appropriate or feasible, counselors, upon reasonable cause, take action such as reporting the suspected ethical violation to state or national ethics committees, unless this action conflicts with confidentiality rights that cannot be resolved.

f. *Unwarranted Complaints.* Counselors do not initiate, participate in or encourage the filing of ethics complaints that are unwarranted or intend to harm a counselor rather than to protect clients or the public.

H.3. Cooperation with Ethics Committees. Counselors assist in the process of enforcing Code of Ethics. Counselors cooperate with investigations, proceedings, and requirements of the ACA Ethics Committee or ethics committees of other duly constituted associations or boards having jurisdiction over those charged with a violation. Counselors are familiar with the ACA Policies and Procedures and use it as a reference in assisting the enforcement of the Code of Ethics.

STANDARDS OF PRACTICE

All members of the American Counseling Association (ACA) are required to adhere to the *Standards of Practice* and the *Code of Ethics*. The *Standards of Practice* represent minimal behavioral statements of the *Code of Ethics*. Members should refer to the applicable section of the *Code of Ethics* for further interpretation and amplification of the applicable Standard of Practice.

SECTION A: THE COUNSELING RELATIONSHIP

Standard of Practice One (SP-1) Nondiscrimination. Counselors respect diversity and must not discriminate against clients because of age, color, culture, disability, ethnic group, gender, race, religion, sexual orientation, marital status, or socioeconomic status. (See A.2.a.)

Standard of Practice Two (SP-2) Disclosure to Clients. Counselors must adequately inform clients, preferably in writing, regarding the counseling process and counseling relationship at or before the time it begins and throughout the relationship. (See A.3.a.)

Standard of Practice Three (SP-3) Dual Relationships. Counselors must make every effort to avoid dual relationships with clients that could impair their professional judgment or increase the risk of harm to clients. When a dual relationship cannot be avoided, counselors must take appropriate steps to ensure that judgment is not impaired and that no exploitation occurs. (See A.6.a. and A.6.b.)

Standard of Practice Four (SP-4) Sexual Intimacies with Clients. Counselors must not engage in any type of sexual intimacies with current clients and must not engage in sexual intimacies with former clients within a minimum of two years after terminating the counseling relationship. Counselors who engage in such relationship after two years following termination have the responsibility to thoroughly examine and document that such relations did not have an exploitative nature.

Standard of Practice Five (SP-5) Protecting Clients During Group Work. Counselors must take steps to protect clients from physical or psychological trauma resulting from interactions during group work. (See A.9.b.)

Standard of Practice Six (SP-6) Advance Understanding of Fees. Counselors must explain to clients, prior to their entering the counseling relationship, financial arrangements related to professional services. (See A.10.a-d. and A.11.c.)

Standard of Practice Seven (SP-7) Termination. Counselors must assist in making appropriate arrangements for the continuation of treatment of clients, when necessary, following termination of counseling relationships. (See A.11.a.)

Standard of Practice Eight (SP-8) Inability to Assist Clients. Counselors must avoid entering or immediately terminate a counseling relationship if it is determined that they are unable to be of professional assistance to a client. The counselor may assist in making an appropriate referral for the client. (See A.11.b.)

SECTION B: CONFIDENTIALITY

Standard of Practice Nine (SP-9) Confidentiality Requirement. Counselors must keep information related to counseling services confidential unless disclosure is in the best interest of clients, is required for the welfare of others, or is required by law. When disclosure is required, only information that is essential is revealed and the client is informed of such disclosure. (See B.1.a.-f.)

Standard of Practice Ten (SP-10) Confidentiality Requirements for Subordinates. Counselors must take measures to ensure that privacy and confidentiality of clients are maintained by subordinates. (See B.1.h.)

Standard of Practice Eleven (SP-11) Confidentiality in Group Work. Counselors must clearly communicate to group members that confidentiality cannot be guaranteed in group work. (See B.2.a.)

Standard of Practice Twelve (SP-12) Confidentiality in Family Counseling. Counselors must not disclose information about one family member in counseling to another family member without prior consent. (See B.2.b.)

Standard of Practice Thirteen (SP-13) Confidentiality of Records. Counselors must maintain appropriate confidentiality in creating, storing, accessing, transferring, and disposing of counseling records. (See B.4.b.)

Standard of Practice Fourteen (SP-14) Permission to Record or Observe. Counselors must obtain prior consent from clients in order to electronically record or observe sessions. (See B.4.c.)

Standard of Practice Fifteen (SP-15) Disclosure or Transfer of Records. Counselors must obtain client consent to disclose or transfer records to third parties, unless exceptions listed in SP-9 exist. (See B.4.e.)

Standard of Practice Sixteen (SP-16) Data Disguise Required. Counselors must disguise the identity of the client when using data for training, research, or publication. (See B.5.a.)

SECTION C: PROFESSIONAL RESPONSIBILITY

Standard of Practice Seventeen (SP-17) Boundaries of Competence. Counselors must practice only within the boundaries of their competence. (See C.2.a.)

Standard of Practice Eighteen (SP-18) Continuing Education. Counselors must engage in continuing education to maintain their professional competence. (See C.2.f.)

Standard of Practice Nineteen (SP-19) Impairment of Professionals. Counselors must refrain from offering professional services when their personal problems or conflicts may cause harm to a client or others. (See C.2.g.)

Standard of Practice Twenty (SP-20) Accurate Advertising. Counselors must accurately represent their credentials and services when advertising. (See C.3.a.)

Standard of Practice Twenty-one (SP-21) Recruiting Through Employment. Counselors must not use their place of employment or institutional affiliation to recruit clients for their private practices. (See C.3.d.)

Standard of Practice Twenty-two (SP-22) Credentials Claimed. Counselors must claim or imply only professional credentials possessed and must correct any known misrepresentations of their credentials by others. (See C.4.a.)

Standard of Practice Twenty-three (SP-23) Sexual Harassment. Counselors must not engage in sexual harassment. (See C.5.b.)

Standard of Practice Twenty-four (SP-24) Unjustified Gains. Counselors must not use their professional positions to seek or receive unjustified personal gains, sexual favors, unfair advantage, or unearned goods or services. (See C.5.e.)

Standard of Practice Twenty-five (SP-25) Clients Served by Others. With the consent of the client, counselors must inform other mental health professionals serving the same client that a counseling relationship between the counselor and client exists. (See C.6.c.)

Standard of Practice Twenty-six (SP-26) Negative Employment Conditions. Counselors must alert their employers to institutional policy or conditions that may be potentially disruptive or damaging to the counselor's professional responsibilities, or that may limit their effectiveness or deny clients' rights. (See D.1.c.)

Standard of Practice Twenty-seven (SP-27) Personnel Selection and Assignment. Counselors must select competent staff and must assign responsibilities compatible with staff skills and experiences. (See D.1.h.)

Standard of Practice Twenty-eight (SP-28) Exploitive Relationships with Subordinates. Counselors must not engage in exploitive relationships with individuals over whom they have supervisory, evaluative, or instructional control or authority. (See D.1.k.)

SECTION D: RELATIONSHIP WITH OTHER PROFESSIONALS

Standard of Practice Twenty-nine (SP-29) Accepting Fees from Agency Clients. Counselors must not accept fees or other remuneration for consultation with persons entitled to such services through the counselor's employing agency or institution. (See D.3.a.)

Standard of Practice Thirty (SP-30) Referral Fees. Counselors must not accept referral fees. (See D.3.b.)

SECTION E: EVALUATION, ASSESSMENT, AND INTERPRETATION

Standard of Practice Thirty-one (SP-31) Limits of Competence. Counselors must perform only testing and assessment services for which they are competent. Counselors must not allow the use of psychological assessment techniques by unqualified persons under their supervision. (See E.2.a.)

Standard of Practice Thirty-two (SP-32) Appropriate Use of Assessment Instruments. Counselors must use assessment instruments in the manner for which they were intended. (See E.2.b.)

Standard of Practice Thirty-three (SP-33) Assessment Explanations to Clients. Counselors must provide explanations to clients prior to assessment about the nature and purposes of assessment and the specific uses of results. (See E.3.a.)

Standard of Practice Thirty-four (SP-34) Recipients of Test Results. Counselors must ensure that accurate and appropriate interpretations accompany any release of testing and assessment information. (See E.3.b.)

Standard of Practice Thirty-five (SP-35) Obsolete Tests and Outdated Test Results. Counselors must not base their assessment or intervention decisions or recommendations on data or test results that are obsolete or outdated for the current purpose. (See E.11.)

SECTION F: TEACHING, TRAINING, AND SUPERVISION

Standard of Practice Thirty-six (SP-36) Sexual Relationships with Students or Supervisees. Counselors must not engage in sexual relationships with their students and supervisees. (See F.1.c.)

Standard of Practice Thirty-seven (SP-37) Credit for Contributions to Research. Counselors must give credit to students or supervisees for their contributions to research and scholarly projects. (See F.1.d.)

Standard of Practice Thirty-eight (SP-38) Supervision Preparation. Counselors who offer clinical supervision services must be trained and prepared in supervision methods and techniques. (See F.1.f.)

Standard of Practice Thirty-nine (SP-39) Evaluation Information. Counselors must clearly state to students and supervisees in advance of training, the levels of competency expected, appraisal methods, and timing of evaluations. Counselors must provide students and supervisees with periodic performance appraisal and evaluation feedback throughout the training program. (See F.2.c.)

Standard of Practice Forty (SP-40) Peer Relationships in Training. Counselors must make every effort to ensure that the rights of peers are not violated when students and supervisees are assigned to lead counseling groups or provide clinical supervision. (See F.2.e.)

Standard of Practice Forty-one (SP-41) Limitations of Students and Supervisees. Counselors must assist students and supervisees in securing remedial assistance, when needed, and must dismiss from the training program students and supervisees who are unable to provide competent service due to academic or personal limitations. (See F.3.a.)

Standard of Practice Forty-two (SP-42) Self-Growth Experiences. Counselors who conduct experiences for students or supervisees that include self-growth or self disclosure must inform participants of counselors' ethical obligations to the profession and must not grade participants based on their nonacademic performance. (See F.3.b.)

Standard of Practice Forty-three (SP-43) Standards for Students and Supervisees. Students and supervisees preparing to become counselors must adhere to the *Code of Ethics* and the *Standards of Practice* of counselors. (See F.3.e.)

SECTION G: RESEARCH AND PUBLICATION

Standard of Practice Forty-four (SP-44) Precautions to Avoid Injury in Research. Counselors must avoid causing physical, social, or psychological harm or injury to subjects in research. (See G.1.c.)

Standard of Practice Forty-five (SP-45) Confidentiality of Research Information. Counselors must keep confidential information obtained about research participants. (See G.2.d.)

Standard of Practice Forty-six (SP-46) Information Affecting Research Outcome. Counselors must report all variables and conditions known to the investigator that may have affected research data or outcomes. (See G.3.a.)

Standard of Practice Forty-seven (SP-47) Accurate Research Results. Counselors must not distort or misrepresent research data, nor fabricate or intentionally bias research results. (See G.3.b.)

Standard of Practice Forty-eight (SP-48) Publication Contributors. Counselors must give appropriate credit to those who have contributed to research. (See G.4.a. and G.4.b.)

SECTION H: RESOLVING ETHICAL ISSUES

Standard of Practice Forty-nine (SP-49) Ethical Behavior Expected. Counselors must take appropriate action when they possess reasonable cause that raises doubts as to whether counselors or other mental health professionals are acting in an ethical manner. (See H.2.a.)

Standard of Practice Fifty (SP-50) Unwarranted Complaints. Counselors must not initiate, participate in, or encourage the filing of ethics complaints that are unwarranted or intended to harm a mental health professional rather than to protect clients or the public. (See H.2.f.)

Standard of Practice Fifty-one (SP-51) Cooperation with Ethics Committees. Counselors must cooperate with investigations, proceedings, and requirements of the ACA Ethics Committee or ethics committees of other duly constituted associations or boards having jurisdiction over those charged with a violation. (See H.3.)

Appendix D

◆

Ethical Principles of Psychologists and Code of Conduct:
American Psychological Association*

PREAMBLE

Psychologists work to develop a valid and reliable body of scientific knowledge based on research. They may apply that knowledge to human behavior in a variety of contexts. In doing so, they perform many roles, such as researcher, educator, diagnostician, therapist, supervisor, consultant, administrator, social interventionist, and expert witness. Their goal is to broaden knowledge of behavior and, where appropriate, to apply it pragmatically to improve the condition of both the individual and society. Psychologists respect the central importance of freedom of inquiry and expression in research, teaching, and publication. They also strive to help the public in developing informed judgments and choices concerning human behavior. This Ethics Code provides a common set of values upon which psychologists build their professional and scientific work.

This Code is intended to provide both the general principles and the decision rules to cover most situations encountered by psychologists. It has as its primary goal the welfare and protection of the individuals and groups with whom psychologists work. It is the individual responsibility of each psychologist to aspire to the highest possible standards of conduct. Psychologists respect and protect human and civil rights, and do not knowingly participate in or condone unfair discriminatory practices.

The development of a dynamic set of ethical standards for a psychologist's work-related conduct requires a personal commitment to a lifelong effort to act ethically; to encourage ethical behavior by students, supervisees, employees, and colleagues, as appropriate; and to consult with others, as needed, concerning ethical problems. Each psychologist supplements, but does not violate, the Ethics Code's values and rules on the basis of guidance drawn from personal values, culture, and experience.

GENERAL PRINCIPLES

Principle A: Competence. Psychologists strive to maintain high standards of competence in their work. They recognize the boundaries of their particular competencies and the

---

limitations of their expertise. They provide only those services and use only those techniques for which they are qualified by education, training, or experience. Psychologists are cognizant of the fact that the competencies required in serving, teaching, and/or studying groups of people vary with the distinctive characteristics of those groups. In those areas in which recognized professional standards do not yet exist, psychologists exercise careful judgment and take appropriate precautions to protect the welfare of those with whom they work. They maintain knowledge of relevant scientific and professional information related to the services they render, and they recognize the need for ongoing education. Psychologists make appropriate use of scientific, professional, technical, and administrative resources.

Principle B: Integrity. Psychologists seek to promote integrity in the science, teaching, and practice of psychology. In these activities psychologists are honest, fair, and respectful of others. In describing or reporting their qualifications, services, products, fees, research, or teaching, they do not make statements that are false, misleading, or deceptive. Psychologists strive to be aware of their own belief systems, values, needs, and limitations and the effect of these on their work. To the extent feasible, they attempt to clarify for relevant parties the roles they are performing and to function appropriately in accordance with those roles. Psychologists avoid improper and potentially harmful dual relationships.

Principle C: Professional and Scientific Responsibility. Psychologists uphold professional standards of conduct, clarify their professional roles and obligations, accept appropriate responsibility for their behavior, and adapt their methods to the needs of different populations. Psychologists consult with, refer to, or cooperate with other professionals and institutions to the extent needed to serve the best interests of their patients, clients, or other recipients of their services. Psychologists' moral standards and conduct are personal matters to the same degree as is true for any other person, except as psychologists' conduct may compromise their professional responsibilities or reduce the public's trust in psychology and psychologists. Psychologists are concerned about the ethical compliance of their colleagues' scientific and professional conduct. When appropriate, they consult with colleagues in order to prevent or avoid unethical conduct.

Principle D: Respect for People's Rights and Dignity. Psychologists accord appropriate respect to the fundamental rights, dignity, and worth of all people. They respect the rights of individuals to privacy, confidentiality, self-determination, and autonomy, mindful that legal and other obligations may lead to inconsistency and conflict with the exercise of these rights. Psychologists are aware of cultural, individual, and role differences, including those due to age, gender, race, ethnicity, national origin, religion, sexual orientation, disability, language, and socioeconomic status. Psychologists try to eliminate the effect on their work of biases based on those factors, and they do not knowingly participate in or condone unfair discriminatory practices.

Principle E: Concern for Others' Welfare. Psychologists seek to contribute to the welfare of those with whom they interact professionally. In their professional actions, psychologists weigh the welfare and rights of their patients or clients, students, supervisees, human research participants, and other affected persons, and the welfare of animal subjects of research. When conflicts occur among psychologists' obligations or concerns, they attempt to resolve these conflicts and to perform their roles in a responsible fashion that avoids or minimizes harm. Psychologists are sensitive to real and ascribed differences in power between themselves and others, and they do not exploit or mislead other people during or after professional relationships.

Principle F: Social Responsibility. Psychologists are aware of their professional and scientific responsibilities to the community and the society in which they work and live. They apply and make public their knowledge of psychology in order to contribute to human welfare. Psychologists are concerned about and work to mitigate the causes of human suffering. When undertaking research, they strive to advance human welfare and the science of psychology. Psychologists try to avoid misuse of their work. Psychologists comply with the law and encourage the development of law and social policy that serve the interests of their patients and clients and the public. They are encouraged to contribute a portion of their professional time for little or no personal advantage.

ETHICAL STANDARDS

1. General Standards. These General Standards are potentially applicable to the professional and scientific activities of all psychologists.

1.01 Applicability of the Ethics Code. The activity of a psychologist subject to the Ethics Code may be reviewed under these Ethical Standards only if the activity is part of his or her work-related functions or the activity is psychological in nature. Personal activities having no connection to or effect on psychological roles are not subject to the Ethics Code.

1.02 Relationship of Ethics and Law. If psychologists' ethical responsibilities conflict with law, psychologists make known their commitment to the Ethics Code and take steps to resolve the conflict in a responsible manner.

1.03 Professional and Scientific Relationship. Psychologists provide diagnostic, therapeutic, teaching, research, supervisory, consultative, or other psychological services only in the context of a defined professional or scientific relationship or role. (See also Standards 2.01, Evaluation, Diagnosis, and Interventions in Professional Context, and 7.02, Forensic Assessments.)

1.04 Boundaries of Competence. (a) Psychologists provide services, teach, and conduct research only within the boundaries of their competence, based on their education, training, supervised experience, or appropriate professional experience.

(b) Psychologists provide services, teach, or conduct research in new areas or involving new techniques only after first undertaking appropriate study, training, supervision, and/or consultation from persons who are competent in those areas or techniques.

(c) In those emerging areas in which generally recognized standards for preparatory training do not yet exist, psychologists nevertheless take reasonable steps to ensure the competence of their work and to protect patients, clients, students, research participants, and others from harm.

1.05 Maintaining Expertise. Psychologists who engage in assessment, therapy, teaching, research, organizational consulting, or other professional activities maintain a reasonable level of awareness of current scientific and professional information in their fields of activity, and undertake ongoing efforts to maintain competence in the skills they use.

1.06 Basis for Scientific and Professional Judgments. Psychologists rely on scientifically and professionally derived knowledge when making scientific or professional judgments or when engaging in scholarly or professional endeavors.

1.07 Describing the Nature and Results of Psychological Services. (a) When psychologists provide assessment, evaluation, treatment, counseling, supervision, teaching, consultation, research, or other psychological services to an individual, a group, or an organization, they provide, using language that is reasonably understandable to the recipient of those services, appropriate information beforehand about the nature of such services and appropriate information later about results and conclusions. (See also Standard 2.09, Explaining Assessment Results.)

(b) If psychologists will be precluded by law or by organizational roles from providing such information to particular individuals or groups, they so inform those individuals or groups at the outset of the service.

1.08 Human Differences. Where differences of age, gender, race, ethnicity, national origin, religion, sexual orientation, disability, language, or socioeconomic status significantly affect psychologists' work concerning particular individuals or groups, psychologists obtain the training, experience, consultation, or supervision necessary to ensure the competence of their services, or they make appropriate referrals.

1.09 Respecting Others. In their work-related activities, psychologists respect the rights of others to hold values, attitudes, and opinions that differ from their own.

1.10 Nondiscrimination. In their work-related activities, psychologists do not engage in unfair discrimination based on age, gender, race, ethnicity, national origin, religion, sexual orientation, disability, socioeconomic status, or any basis proscribed by law.

1.11 Sexual Harassment. (a) Psychologists do not engage in sexual harassment. Sexual harassment is sexual solicitation, physical advances, or verbal or nonverbal conduct that is sexual in nature, that occurs in connection with the psychologist's activities or roles as a psychologist, and that either: (1) is unwelcome, is offensive, or creates a hostile workplace environment, and the psychologist knows or is told this; or (2) is sufficiently severe or intense to be abusive to a reasonable person in the context. Sexual harassment can consist of a single intense or severe act or of multiple persistent or pervasive acts.

(b) Psychologists accord sexual-harassment complainants and respondents dignity and respect. Psychologists do not participate in denying a person academic admittance or advancement, employment, tenure, or promotion, based solely upon their having made, or their being the subject of, sexual-harassment charges. This does not preclude taking action based upon the outcome of such proceedings or consideration of other appropriate information.

1.12 Other Harassment. Psychologists do not knowingly engage in behavior that is harassing or demeaning to persons with whom they interact in their work based on factors such as those persons' age, gender, race, ethnicity, national origin, religion, sexual orientation, disability, language, or socioeconomic status.

1.13 Personal Problems and Conflicts. (a) Psychologists recognize that their personal problems and conflicts may interfere with their effectiveness. Accordingly, they refrain from undertaking an activity when they know or should know that their personal problems are likely to lead to harm to a patient, client, colleague, student, research participant, or other person to whom they may owe a professional or scientific obligation.

(b) In addition, psychologists have an obligation to be alert to signs of, and to obtain assistance for, their personal problems at an early stage, in order to prevent significantly impaired performance.

(c) When psychologists become aware of personal problems that may interfere with their performing work-related duties adequately, they take appropriate measures, such as obtaining professional consultation or assistance, and determine whether they should limit, suspend, or terminate their work-related duties.

1.14 Avoiding Harm. Psychologists take reasonable steps to avoid harming their patients or clients, research participants, students, and others with whom they work, and to minimize harm where it is foreseeable and unavoidable.

1.15 Misuse of Psychologists' Influence. Because psychologists' scientific and professional judgments and actions may affect the lives of others, they are alert to and guard against personal, financial, social, organizational, or political factors that might lead to misuse of their influence.

1.16 Misuse of Psychologists' Work. (a) Psychologists do not participate in activities in which it appears likely that their skills or data will be misused by others, unless corrective mechanisms are available. (See also Standard 7.04, Truthfulness and Candor.)

(b) If psychologists learn of misuse or misrepresentation of their work, they take reasonable steps to correct or minimize the misuse or misrepresentation.

1.17 Multiple Relationships. (a) In many communities and situations, it may not be feasible or reasonable for psychologists to avoid social or other nonprofessional contacts with persons such as patients, clients, students, supervisees, or research participants. Psychologists must always be sensitive to the potential harmful effects of other contacts on their work and on those persons with whom they deal. A psychologist refrains from entering into or promising another personal, scientific, professional, financial, or other relationship with such persons if it appears likely that such a relationship reasonably might impair the psychologist's objectivity or otherwise interfere with the psychologist's effectively performing his or her functions as a psychologist, or might harm or exploit the other party.

(b) Likewise, whenever feasible, a psychologist refrains from taking on professional or scientific obligations when preexisting relationships would create a risk of such harm.

(c) If a psychologist finds that, due to unforeseen factors, a potentially harmful multiple relationship has arisen, the psychologist attempts to resolve it with due regard for the best interests of the affected person and maximal compliance with the Ethics Code.

1.18 Barter (with Patients or Clients). Psychologists ordinarily refrain from accepting goods, services, or other nonmonetary remuneration from patients or clients in return for psychological services because such arrangements create inherent potential for conflicts, exploitation, and distortion of the professional relationship. A psychologist may participate in bartering *only* if (1) it is not clinically contraindicated, *and* (2) the relationship is not exploitative. (See also Standards 1.17, Multiple Relationships, and 1.25, Fees and Financial Arrangements.)

1.19 Exploitative Relationships. (a) Psychologists do not exploit persons over whom they have supervisory, evaluative, or other authority such as students, supervisees, employees, research participants, and clients or patients. (See also Standards 4.05-4.07 regarding sexual involvement with clients or patients.)

(b) Psychologists do not engage in sexual relationships with students or supervisees in training over whom the psychologist has evaluative or direct authority, because such relationships are so likely to impair judgment or be exploitative.

1.20 Consultations and Referrals. (a) Psychologists arrange for appropriate consultations and referrals based principally on the best interests of their patients or clients, with appropriate consent, and subject to other relevant considerations, including applicable law and contractual obligations. (See also Standards 5.01, Discussing the Limits of Confidentiality, and 5.06, Consultations.)

(b) When indicated and professionally appropriate, psychologists cooperate with other professionals in order to serve their patients or clients effectively and appropriately.

(c) Psychologists' referral practices are consistent with law.

1.21 Third-Party Requests for Services. (a) When a psychologist agrees to provide services to a person or entity at the request of a third party, the psychologist clarifies to the extent feasible, at the outset of the service, the nature of the relationship with each party. This clarification includes the role of the psychologist (such as therapist, organizational consultant, diagnostician, or expert witness), the probable uses of the services provided or the information obtained, and the fact that there may be limits to confidentiality.

(b) If there is a foreseeable risk of the psychologist's being called upon to perform conflicting roles because of the involvement of a third party, the psychologist clarifies the nature and direction of his or her responsibilities, keeps all parties appropriately informed as matters develop, and resolves the situation in accordance with this Ethics Code.

1.22 Delegation to and Supervision of Subordinates. (a) Psychologists delegate to their employees, supervisees, and research assistants only those responsibilities that such persons can reasonably be expected to perform competently, on the basis of their education, training, or experience, either independently or with the level of supervision being provided.

(b) Psychologists provide proper training and supervision to their employees or supervisees and take reasonable steps to see that such persons perform services responsibly, competently, and ethically.

(c) If institutional policies, procedures, or practices prevent fulfillment of this obligation, psychologists attempt to modify their role or to correct the situation to the extent feasible.

1.23 Documentation of Professional and Scientific Work. (a) Psychologists appropriately document their professional and scientific work in order to facilitate provision of services later by them or by other professionals, to ensure accountability, and to meet other requirements of institutions or the law.

(b) When psychologists have reason to believe that records of their professional services will be used in legal proceedings involving recipients of or participants in their work, they have a responsibility to create and maintain documentation in the kind of detail and quality that would be consistent with reasonable scrutiny in an adjudicative forum. (See also Standard 7.01, Professionalism, under Forensic Activities.)

1.24 Records and Data. Psychologists create, maintain, disseminate, store, retain, and dispose of records and data relating to their research, practice, and other work in accordance with law and in a manner that permits compliance with the requirements of this Ethics Code. (See also Standard 5.04, Maintenance of Records.)

1.25 Fees and Financial Arrangements. (a) As early as is feasible in a professional or scientific relationship, the psychologist and the patient, client, or other appropriate recipient of psychological services reach an agreement specifying the compensation and the billing arrangements.

(b) Psychologists do not exploit recipients of services or payors with respect to fees.

(c) Psychologists' fee practices are consistent with law.

(d) Psychologists do not misrepresent their fees.

(e) If limitations to services can be anticipated because of limitations in financing, this is discussed with the patient, client, or other appropriate recipient of services as early as is feasible. (See also Standard 4.08, Interruption of Services.)

(f) If the patient, client, or other recipient of services does not pay for services as agreed, and if the psychologist wishes to use collection agencies or legal measures to collect the fees, the psychologist first informs the person that such measures will be taken and provides that person an opportunity to make prompt payment. (See also Standard 5.11, Withholding Records for Nonpayment.)

1.26 Accuracy in Reports to Payors and Funding Sources. In their reports to payors for services or sources of research funding, psychologists accurately state the nature of the research or service provided, the fees or charges, and where applicable, the identity of the provider, the findings, and the diagnosis. (See also Standard 5.05, Disclosures.)

1.27 Referrals and Fees. When a psychologist pays, receives payment from, or divides fees with another professional other than in an employer-employee relationship, the payment to each is based on the services (clinical, consultative, administrative, or other) provided and is not based on the referral itself.

2. Evaluation, Assessment, or Intervention

2.01 Evaluation, Diagnosis, and Interventions in Professional Context. (a) Psychologists perform evaluations, diagnostic services, or interventions only within the context of a defined professional relationship. (See also Standard 1.03, Professional and Scientific Relationship.)

(b) Psychologists' assessments, recommendations, reports, and psychological diagnostic or evaluative statements are based on information and techniques (including personal interviews of the individual when appropriate) sufficient to provide appropriate substantiation for their findings. (See also Standard 7.02, Forensic Assessments.)

2.02 Competence and Appropriate Use of Assessments and Interventions.

(a) Psychologists who develop, administer, score, interpret, or use psychological assessment techniques, interviews, tests, or instruments do so in a manner and for purposes that are appropriate in light of the research on or evidence of the usefulness and proper application of the techniques.

(b) Psychologists refrain from misuse of assessment techniques, interventions, results, and interpretations and take reasonable steps to prevent others from misusing the information these techniques provide. This includes refraining from releasing raw test results or raw data to persons, other than to patients or clients as appropriate, who are not qualified to use such information. (See also Standards 1.02, Relationship of Ethics and Law, and 1.04, Boundaries of Competence.)

2.03 Test Construction.

Psychologists who develop and conduct research with tests and other assessment techniques use scientific procedures and current professional knowledge for test design, standardization, validation, reduction or elimination of bias, and recommendations for use.

2.04 Use of Assessment in General and With Special Populations.

(a) Psychologists who perform interventions or administer, score, interpret, or use assessment techniques are familiar with the reliability, validation, and related standardization or outcome studies of, and proper applications and uses of, the techniques they use.

(b) Psychologists recognize limits to the certainty with which diagnoses, judgments, or predictions can be made about individuals.

(c) Psychologists attempt to identify situations in which particular interventions or assessment techniques or norms may not be applicable or may require adjustment in administration or interpretation because of factors such as individuals' gender, age, race, ethnicity, national origin, religion, sexual orientation, disability, language, or socioeconomic status.

2.05 Interpreting Assessment Results.

When interpreting assessment results, including automated interpretations, psychologists take into account the various test factors and characteristics of the person being assessed that might affect psychologists' judgments or reduce the accuracy of their interpretations. They indicate any significant reservations they have about the accuracy or limitations of their interpretations.

2.06 Unqualified Persons.

Psychologists do not promote the use of psychological assessment techniques by unqualified persons. (See also Standard 1.22, Delegation to and Supervision of Subordinates.)

2.07 Obsolete Tests and Outdated Test Results.

(a) Psychologists do not base their assessment or intervention decisions or recommendations on data or test results that are outdated for the current purpose.

(b) Similarly, psychologists do not base such decisions or recommendations on tests and measures that are obsolete and not useful for the current purpose.

2.08 Test Scoring and Interpretation Services. (a) Psychologists who offer assessment or scoring procedures to other professionals accurately describe the purpose, norms, validity, reliability, and applications of the procedures and any special qualifications applicable to their use.

(b) Psychologists select scoring and interpretation services (including automated services) on the basis of evidence of the validity of the program and procedures as well as on other appropriate considerations.

(c) Psychologists retain appropriate responsibility for the appropriate application, interpretation, and use of assessment instruments, whether they score and interpret such tests themselves or use automated or other services.

2.09 Explaining Assessment Results. Unless the nature of the relationship is clearly explained to the person being assessed in advance and precludes provision of an explanation of results (such as in some organizational consulting, preemployment or security screenings, and forensic evaluations), psychologists ensure that an explanation of the results is provided using language that is reasonably understandable to the person assessed or to another legally authorized person on behalf of the client. Regardless of whether the scoring and interpretation are done by the psychologist, by assistants, or by automated or other outside services, psychologists take reasonable steps to ensure that appropriate explanations of results are given.

2.10 Maintaining Test Security. Psychologists make reasonable efforts to maintain the integrity and security of tests and other assessment techniques consistent with law, contractual obligations, and in a manner that permits compliance with the requirements of this Ethics Code. (See also Standard 1.02, Relationship of Ethics and Law.)

3. Advertising and Other Public Statements

3.01 Definition of Public Statements. Psychologists comply with this Ethics Code in public statements relating to their professional services, products, or publications or to the field of psychology. Public statements include but are not limited to paid or unpaid advertising, brochures, printed matter, directory listings, personal resumes or curricula vitae, interviews or comments for use in media, statements in legal proceedings, lectures and public oral presentations, and published materials.

3.02 Statements by Others. (a) Psychologists who engage others to create or place public statements that promote their professional practice, products, or activities retain professional responsibility for such statements.

(b) In addition, psychologists make reasonable efforts to prevent others whom they do not control (such as employers, publishers, sponsors, organizational clients, and representatives of the print or broadcast media) from making deceptive statements concerning psychologists' practice or professional or scientific activities.

(c) If psychologists learn of deceptive statements about their work made by others, psychologists make reasonable efforts to correct such statements.

(d) Psychologists do not compensate employees of press, radio, television, or other communication media in return for publicity in a news item.

(e) A paid advertisement relating to the psychologist's activities must be identified as such, unless it is already apparent from the context.

3.03 Avoidance of False or Deceptive Statements. (a) Psychologists do not make public statements that are false, deceptive, misleading, or fraudulent, either because of what they state, convey, or suggest or because of what they omit, concerning their research, practice, or other work activities or those of persons or organizations with which they are affiliated. As examples (and not in limitation) of this standard, psychologists do not make false or deceptive statements concerning (1) their training, experience, or competence; (2) their academic degrees; (3) their credentials; (4) their institutional or association affiliations; (5) their services; (6) the scientific or clinical basis for, or results or degree of success of, their services; (7) their fees; or (8) their publications or research findings. (See also Standards 6.15, Deception in Research, and 6.18, Providing Participants With Information About the Study.)

(b) Psychologists claim as credentials for their psychological work, only degrees that (1) were earned from a regionally accredited educational institution or (2) were the basis for psychology licensure by the state in which they practice.

3.04 Media Presentations. When psychologists provide advice or comment by means of public lectures, demonstrations, radio or television programs, prerecorded tapes, printed articles, mailed material, or other media, they take reasonable precautions to ensure that (1) the statements are based on appropriate psychological literature and practice, (2) the statements are otherwise consistent with this Ethics Code, and (3) the recipients of the information are not encouraged to infer that a relationship has been established with them personally.

3.05 Testimonials. Psychologists do not solicit testimonials from current psychotherapy clients or patients or other persons who because of their particular circumstances are vulnerable to undue influence.

3.06 In-Person Solicitation. Psychologists do not engage, directly or through agents, in uninvited in-person solicitation of business from actual or potential psychotherapy patients or clients or other persons who because of their particular circumstances are vulnerable to undue influence. However, this does not preclude attempting to implement appropriate collateral contacts with significant others for the purpose of benefiting an already engaged therapy patient.

4. Therapy

4.01 Structuring the Relationship. (a) Psychologists discuss with clients or patients as early as is feasible in the therapeutic relationship appropriate issues, such as the nature and anticipated course of therapy, fees, and confidentiality. (See also Standards 1.25, Fees and Financial Arrangements, and 5.01, Discussing the Limits of Confidentiality.)

(b) When the psychologist's work with clients or patients will be supervised, the above discussion includes that fact, and the name of the supervisor, when the supervisor has legal responsibility for the case.

(c) When the therapist is a student intern, the client or patient is informed of that fact.

(d) Psychologists make reasonable efforts to answer patients' questions and to avoid apparent misunderstandings about therapy. Whenever possible, psychologists provide oral and/or written information, using language that is reasonably understandable to the patient or client.

4.02 Informed Consent to Therapy. (a) Psychologists obtain appropriate informed consent to therapy or related procedures, using language that is reasonably understandable to participants. The content of informed consent will vary depending on many circumstances; however, informed consent generally implies that the person (1) has the capacity to consent, (2) has been informed of significant information concerning the procedure, (3) has freely and without undue influence expressed consent, and (4) consent has been appropriately documented.

(b) When persons are legally incapable of giving informed consent, psychologists obtain informed permission from a legally authorized person, if such substitute consent is permitted by law.

(c) In addition, psychologists (1) inform those persons who are legally incapable of giving informed consent about the proposed interventions in a manner commensurate with the persons' psychological capacities, (2) seek their assent to those interventions, and (3) consider such persons' preferences and best interests.

4.03 Couple and Family Relationships. (a) When a psychologist agrees to provide services to several persons who have a relationship (such as husband and wife or parents and children), the psychologist attempts to clarify at the outset (1) which of the individuals are patients or clients and (2) the relationship the psychologist will have with each person. This clarification includes the role of the psychologist and the probable uses of the services provided or the information obtained. (See also Standard 5.01, Discussing the Limits of Confidentiality.)

(b) As soon as it becomes apparent that the psychologist may be called on to perform potentially conflicting roles (such as marital counselor to husband and wife, and then witness for one party in a divorce proceeding), the psychologist attempts to clarify and adjust, or withdraw from, roles appropriately. (See also Standard 7.03, Clarification of Role, under Forensic Activities.)

4.04 Providing Mental Health Services to Those Served by Others. In deciding whether to offer or provide services to those already receiving mental health services elsewhere, psychologists carefully consider the treatment issues and the potential patient's or client's welfare. The psychologist discusses these issues with the patient or client, or another legally authorized person on behalf of the client, in order to minimize the risk of confusion and conflict, consults with the other service providers when appropriate, and proceeds with caution and sensitivity to the therapeutic issues.

4.05 Sexual Intimacies with Current Patients or Clients. Psychologists do not engage in sexual intimacies with current patients or clients.

4.06 Therapy with Former Sexual Partners. Psychologists do not accept as therapy patients or clients persons with whom they have engaged in sexual intimacies.

4.07 Sexual Intimacies with Former Therapy Patients. (a) Psychologists do not engage in sexual intimacies with a former therapy patient or client for at least two years after cessation or termination of professional services.

(b) Because sexual intimacies with a former therapy patient or client are so frequently harmful to the patient or client, and because such intimacies undermine public confidence in the psychology profession and thereby deter the public's use of needed services, psychologists do not engage in sexual intimacies with former therapy patients and clients even after a two-year interval except in the most unusual circumstances. The psychologist who engages in such activity after the two years following cessation or termination of treatment bears the burden of demonstrating that there has been no exploitation, in light of all relevant factors, including (1) the amount of time that has passed since therapy terminated, (2) the nature and duration of the therapy, (3) the circumstances of termination, (4) the patient's or client's personal history, (5) the patient's or client's current mental status, (6) the likelihood of adverse impact on the patient or client and others, and (7) any statements or actions made by the therapist during the course of therapy suggesting or inviting the possibility of a posttermination sexual or romantic relationship with the patient or client. (See also Standard 1.17, Multiple Relationships.)

4.08 Interruption of Services. (a) Psychologists make reasonable efforts to plan for facilitating care in the event that psychological services are interrupted by factors such as the psychologist's illness, death, unavailability, or relocation or by the client's relocation or financial limitations. (See also Standard 5.09, Preserving Records and Data.)

(b) When entering into employment or contractual relationships, psychologists provide for orderly and appropriate resolution of responsibility for patient or client care in the event that the employment or contractual relationship ends, with paramount consideration given to the welfare of the patient or client.

4.09 Terminating the Professional Relationship. (a) Psychologists do not abandon patients or clients. (See also Standard 1.25e, under Fees and Financial Arrangements.)

(b) Psychologists terminate a professional relationship when it becomes reasonably clear that the patient or client no longer needs the service, is not benefiting, or is being harmed by continued service.

(c) Prior to termination for whatever reason, except where precluded by the patient's or client's conduct, the psychologist discusses the patient's or client's views and needs, provides appropriate pretermination counseling, suggests alternative service providers as appropriate, and takes other reasonable steps to facilitate transfer of responsibility to another provider if the patient or client needs one immediately.

5. Privacy and Confidentiality. These Standards are potentially applicable to the professional and scientific activities of all psychologists.

5.01 Discussing the Limits of Confidentiality. (a) Psychologists discuss with persons and organizations with whom they establish a scientific or professional relationship (including, to the extent feasible, minors and their legal representatives) (1) the relevant limitations on confidentiality, including limitations where applicable in group, marital, and family therapy or in organizational consulting, and (2) the foreseeable uses of the information generated through their services.

(b) Unless it is not feasible or is contraindicated, the discussion of confidentiality occurs at the outset of the relationship and thereafter as new circumstances may warrant.

(c) Permission for electronic recording of interviews is secured from clients and patients.

5.02 Maintaining Confidentiality. Psychologists have a primary obligation and take reasonable precautions to respect the confidentiality rights of those with whom they work or consult, recognizing that confidentiality may be established by law, institutional rules, or professional or scientific relationships. (See also Standard 6.26, Professional Reviewers.)

5.03 Minimizing Intrusions on Privacy. (a) In order to minimize intrusions on privacy, psychologists include in written and oral reports, consultations, and the like, only information germane to the purpose for which the communication is made.

(b) Psychologists discuss confidential information obtained in clinical or consulting relationships, or evaluative data concerning patients, individual or organizational clients, students, research participants, supervisees, and employees, only for appropriate scientific or professional purposes and only with persons clearly concerned with such matters.

5.04 Maintenance of Records. Psychologists maintain appropriate confidentiality in creating, storing, accessing, transferring, and disposing of records under their control, whether these are written, automated, or in any other medium. Psychologists maintain and dispose of records in accordance with law and in a manner that permits compliance with the requirements of this Ethics Code.

5.05 Disclosures. (a) Psychologists disclose confidential information without the consent of the individual only as mandated by law, or where permitted by law for a valid purpose, such as (1) to provide needed professional services to the patient or the individual or organizational client, (2) to obtain appropriate professional consultations, (3) to protect the patient or client or others from harm, or (4) to obtain payment for services, in which instance disclosure is limited to the minimum that is necessary to achieve the purpose.

(b) Psychologists also may disclose confidential information with the appropriate consent of the patient or the individual or organizational client (or of another legally authorized person on behalf of the patient or client), unless prohibited by law.

5.06 Consultations. When consulting with colleagues, (1) psychologists do not share confidential information that reasonably could lead to the identification of a patient, client, research participant, or other person or organization with whom they have a confidential relationship unless they have obtained the prior consent of the person or organization or the disclosure cannot be avoided, and (2) they share information only to the extent necessary to achieve the purposes of the consultation. (See also Standard 5.02, Maintaining Confidentiality.)

5.07 Confidential Information in Databases. (a) If confidential information concerning recipients of psychological services is to be entered into databases or systems of records available to persons whose access has not been consented to by the recipient, then psychologists use coding or other techniques to avoid the inclusion of personal identifiers.

(b) If a research protocol approved by an institutional review board or similar body requires the inclusion of personal identifiers, such identifiers are deleted before the information is made accessible to persons other than those of whom the subject was advised.

(c) If such deletion is not feasible, then before psychologists transfer such data to others or review such data collected by others, they take reasonable steps to determine that appropriate consent of personally identifiable individuals has been obtained.

5.08 Use of Confidential Information for Didactic or Other Purposes. (a) Psychologists do not disclose in their writings, lectures, or other public media, confidential, personally identifiable information concerning their patients, individual or organizational clients, students, research participants, or other recipients of their services that they obtained during the course of their work, unless the person or organization has consented in writing or unless there is other ethical or legal authorization for doing so.

(b) Ordinarily, in such scientific and professional presentations, psychologists disguise confidential information concerning such persons or organizations so that they are not individually identifiable to others and so that discussions do not cause harm to subjects who might identify themselves.

5.09 Preserving Records and Data. A psychologist makes plans in advance so that confidentiality of records and data is protected in the event of the psychologist's death, incapacity, or withdrawal from the position or practice.

5.10 Ownership of Records and Data. Recognizing that ownership of records and data is governed by legal principles, psychologists take reasonable and lawful steps so that records and data remain available to the extent needed to serve the best interests of patients, individual or organizational clients, research participants, or appropriate others.

5.11 Withholding Records for Nonpayment. Psychologists may not withhold records under their control that are requested and imminently needed for a patient's or client's treatment solely because payment has not been received, except as otherwise provided by law.

6. Teaching, Training Supervision, Research, and Publishing

6.01 Design of Education and Training Programs. Psychologists who are responsible for education and training programs seek to ensure that the programs are competently designed, provide the proper experiences, and meet the requirements for licensure, certification, or other goals for which claims are made by the program.

6.02 Descriptions of Education and Training Programs. (a) Psychologists responsible for education and training programs seek to ensure that there is a current and accurate description of the program content, training goals and objectives, and requirements that must be met for satisfactory completion of the program. This information must be made readily available to all interested parties.

(b) Psychologists seek to ensure that statements concerning their course outlines are accurate and not misleading, particularly regarding the subject matter to be covered, bases for evaluating progress, and the nature of course experiences. (See also Standard 3.03, Avoidance of False or Deceptive Statements.)

(c) To the degree to which they exercise control, psychologists responsible for announcements, catalogs, brochures, or advertisements describing workshops, seminars, or other non-degree-granting educational programs ensure that they accurately describe the audience for which the program is intended, the educational objectives, the presenters, and the fees involved.

6.03 Accuracy and Objectivity in Teaching. (a) When engaged in teaching or training, psychologists present psychological information accurately and with a reasonable degree of objectivity.

(b) When engaged in teaching or training, psychologists recognize the power they hold over students or supervisees and therefore make reasonable efforts to avoid engaging in conduct that is personally demeaning to students or supervisees. (See also Standards 1.09, Respecting Others, and 1.12, Other Harassment.)

6.04 Limitation on Teaching. Psychologists do not teach the use of techniques or procedures that require specialized training, licensure, or expertise, including but not limited to hypnosis, biofeedback, and projective techniques, to individuals who lack the prerequisite training, legal scope of practice, or expertise.

6.05 Assessing Student and Supervisee Performance. (a) In academic and supervisory relationships, psychologists establish an appropriate process for providing feedback to students and supervisees.

(b) Psychologists evaluate students and supervisees on the basis of their actual performance on relevant and established program requirements.

6.06 Planning Research. (a) Psychologists design, conduct, and report research in accordance with recognized standards of scientific competence and ethical research.

(b) Psychologists plan their research so as to minimize the possibility that results will be misleading.

(c) In planning research, psychologists consider its ethical acceptability under the Ethics Code. If an ethical issue is unclear, psychologists seek to resolve the issue through consultation with institutional review boards, animal care and use committees, peer consultations, or other proper mechanisms.

(d) Psychologists take reasonable steps to implement appropriate protections for the rights and welfare of human participants, other persons affected by the research, and the welfare of animal subjects.

6.07 Responsibility. (a) Psychologists conduct research competently and with due concern for the dignity and welfare of the participants.

(b) Psychologists are responsible for the ethical conduct of research conducted by them or by others under their supervision or control.

(c) Researchers and assistants are permitted to perform only those tasks for which they are appropriately trained and prepared.

(d) As part of the process of development and implementation of research projects, psychologists consult those with expertise concerning any special population under investigation or most likely to be affected.

6.08 Compliance with Law and Standards. Psychologists plan and conduct research in a manner consistent with federal and state law and regulations, as well as professional standards governing the conduct of research, and particularly those standards governing research with human participants and animal subjects.

6.09 Institutional Approval. Psychologists obtain from host institutions or organizations appropriate approval prior to conducting research, and they provide accurate information about their research proposals. They conduct the research in accordance with the approved research protocol.

6.10 Research Responsibilities. Prior to conducting research (except research involving only anonymous surveys, naturalistic observations, or similar research), psychologists enter into an agreement with participants that clarifies the nature of the research and the responsibilities of each party.

6.11 Informed Consent to Research. (a) Psychologists use language that is reasonably understandable to research participants in obtaining their appropriate informed consent (except as provided in Standard 6.12, Dispensing With Informed Consent). Such informed consent is appropriately documented.

(b) Using language that is reasonably understandable to participants, psychologists inform participants of the nature of the research; they inform participants that they are free to participate or to decline to participate or to withdraw from the research; they explain the foreseeable consequences of declining or withdrawing; they inform participants of significant factors that may be expected to influence their willingness to participate (such as risks, discomfort, adverse effects, or limitations on confidentiality, except as provided in Standard 6.15, Deception in Research); and they explain other aspects about which the prospective participants inquire.

(c) When psychologists conduct research with individuals such as students or subordinates, psychologists take special care to protect the prospective participants from adverse consequences of declining or withdrawing from participation.

(d) When research participation is a course requirement or opportunity for extra credit, the prospective participant is given the choice of equitable alternative activities.

(e) For persons who are legally incapable of giving informed consent, psychologists nevertheless (1) provide an appropriate explanation, (2) obtain the participant's assent, and (3) obtain appropriate permission from a legally authorized person, if such substitute consent is permitted by law.

6.12 Dispensing with Informed Consent. Before determining that planned research (such as research involving only anonymous questionnaires, naturalistic observations, or certain kinds of archival research) does not require the informed consent of research participants, psychologists consider applicable regulations and institutional review board requirements, and they consult with colleagues as appropriate.

6.13 Informed Consent in Research Filming or Recording. Psychologists obtain informed consent from research participants prior to filming or recording them in any form, unless the research involves simply naturalistic observations in public places and it is not anticipated that the recording will be used in a manner that could cause personal identification or harm.

6.14 Offering Inducements for Research Participants. (a) In offering professional services as an inducement to obtain research participants, psychologists make clear the nature of the services, as well as the risks, obligations, and limitations. (See also Standard 1.18, Barter [With Patients or Clients].)

(b) Psychologists do not offer excessive or inappropriate financial or other inducements to obtain research participants, particularly when it might tend to coerce participation.

6.15 Deception in Research. (a) Psychologists do not conduct a study involving deception unless they have determined that the use of deceptive techniques is justified by the study's prospective scientific, educational, or applied value and that equally effective alternative procedures that do not use deception are not feasible.

(b) Psychologists never deceive research participants about significant aspects that would affect their willingness to participate, such as physical risks, discomfort, or unpleasant emotional experiences.

(c) Any other deception that is an integral feature of the design and conduct of an experiment must be explained to participants as early as is feasible, preferably at the conclusion of their participation, but no later than at the conclusion of the research. (See also Standard 6.18, Providing Participants With Information About the Study.)

6.16 Sharing and Utilizing Data. Psychologists inform research participants of their anticipated sharing or further use of personally identifiable research data and of the possibility of unanticipated future uses.

6.17 Minimizing Invasiveness. In conducting research, psychologists interfere with the participants or milieu from which data are collected only in a manner that is warranted by an appropriate research design and that is consistent with psychologists' roles as scientific investigators.

6.18 Providing Participants With Information About the Study. (a) Psychologists provide a prompt opportunity for participants to obtain appropriate information about the nature, results, and conclusions of the research, and psychologists attempt to correct any misconceptions that participants may have.

(b) If scientific or humane values justify delaying or withholding this information, psychologists take reasonable measures to reduce the risk of harm.

6.19 Honoring Commitments. Psychologists take reasonable measures to honor all commitments they have made to research participants.

6.20 Care and Use of Animals in Research. (a) Psychologists who conduct research involving animals treat them humanely.

(b) Psychologists acquire, care for, use, and dispose of animals in compliance with current federal, state, and local laws and regulations, and with professional standards.

(c) Psychologists trained in research methods and experienced in the care of laboratory animals supervise all procedures involving animals and are responsible for ensuring appropriate consideration of their comfort, health, and humane treatment.

(d) Psychologists ensure that all individuals using animals under their supervision have received instruction in research methods and in the care, maintenance, and handling of the species being used, to the extent appropriate to their role.

(e) Responsibilities and activities of individuals assisting in a research project are consistent with their respective competencies.

(f) Psychologists make reasonable efforts to minimize the discomfort, infection, illness, and pain of animal subjects.

(g) A procedure subjecting animals to pain, stress, or privation is used only when an alternative procedure is unavailable and the goal is justified by its prospective scientific, educational, or applied value.

(h) Surgical procedures are performed under appropriate anesthesia; techniques to avoid infection and minimize pain are followed during and after surgery.

(i) When it is appropriate that the animal's life be terminated, it is done rapidly, with an effort to minimize pain, and in accordance with accepted procedures.

6.21 Reporting of Results. (a) Psychologists do not fabricate data or falsify results in their publications.

(b) If psychologists discover significant errors in their published data, they take reasonable steps to correct such errors in a correction, retraction, erratum, or other appropriate publication means.

6.22 Plagiarism. Psychologists do not present substantial portions or elements of another's work or data as their own, even if the other work or data source is cited occasionally.

6.23 Publication Credit. (a) Psychologists take responsibility and credit, including authorship credit, only for work they have actually performed or to which they have contributed.

(b) Principal authorship and other publication credits accurately reflect the relative scientific or professional contributions of the individuals involved, regardless of their relative status. Mere possession of an institutional position, such as Department Chair, does not justify authorship credit. Minor contributions to the research or to the writing for publications are appropriately acknowledged, such as in footnotes or in an introductory statement.

(c) A student is usually listed as principal author on any multiple-authored article that is substantially based on the student's dissertation or thesis.

6.24 Duplicate Publication of Data. Psychologists do not publish, as original data, data that have been previously published. This does not preclude republishing data when they are accompanied by proper acknowledgment.

6.25 Sharing Data. After research results are published, psychologists do not withhold the data on which their conclusions are based from other competent professionals who seek to verify the substantive claims through reanalysis and who intend to use such data only for that purpose, provided that the confidentiality of the participants can be protected and unless legal rights concerning proprietary data preclude their release.

6.26 Professional Reviewers. Psychologists who review material submitted for publication, grant, or other research proposal review respect the confidentiality of and the proprietary rights in such information of those who submitted it.

7. Forensic Activities

7.01 Professionalism. Psychologists who perform forensic functions, such as assessments, interviews, consultations, reports, or expert testimony, must comply with all other provisions of this Ethics Code to the extent that they apply to such activities. In addition, psychologists base their forensic work on appropriate knowledge of and competence in the areas underlying such work, including specialized knowledge concerning special populations. (See also Standards 1.06, Basis for Scientific and Professional Judgments; 1.08, Human Differences; 1.15, Misuse of Psychologists' Influence; and 1.23, Documentation of Professional and Scientific Work.)

7.02 Forensic Assessments. (a) Psychologists' forensic assessments, recommendations, and reports are based on information and techniques (including personal interviews of the individual, when appropriate) sufficient to provide appropriate substantiation for their findings. (See also Standards 1.03, Professional and Scientific Relationship; 1.23, Documentation of Professional and Scientific Work; 2.01, Evaluation, Diagnosis, and Interventions in Professional Context; and 2.05, Interpreting Assessment Results.)

(b) Except as noted in (c), below, psychologists provide written or oral forensic reports or testimony of the psychological characteristics of an individual only after they have conducted an examination of the individual adequate to support their statements or conclusions.

(c) When, despite reasonable efforts, such an examination is not feasible, psychologists clarify the impact of their limited information on the reliability and validity of their reports and testimony, and they appropriately limit the nature and extent of their conclusions or recommendations.

7.03 Clarification of Role. In most circumstances, psychologists avoid performing multiple and potentially conflicting roles in forensic matters. When psychologists may be called on to serve in more than one role in a legal proceeding—for example, as consultant or expert for one party or for the court and as a fact witness—they clarify role expectations and the extent of confidentiality in advance to the extent feasible, and thereafter as changes occur, in order to avoid compromising their professional judgment and objectivity and in order to avoid misleading others regarding their role.

7.04 Truthfulness and Candor. (a) In forensic testimony and reports, psychologists testify truthfully, honestly, and candidly and, consistent with applicable legal procedures, describe fairly the bases for their testimony and conclusions.

(b) Whenever necessary to avoid misleading, psychologists acknowledge the limits of their data or conclusions.

7.05 Prior Relationships. A prior professional relationship with a party does not preclude psychologists from testifying as fact witnesses or from testifying to their services to the extent permitted by applicable law. Psychologists appropriately take into account ways in which the prior relationship might affect their professional objectivity or opinions and disclose the potential conflict to the relevant parties.

7.06 Compliance with Law and Rules. In performing forensic roles, psychologists are reasonably familiar with the rules governing their roles. Psychologists are aware of the occasionally competing demands placed upon them by these principles and the requirements of the court system, and attempt to resolve these conflicts by making known their commitment to this Ethics Code and taking steps to resolve the conflict in a responsible manner. (See also Standard 1.02, Relationship of Ethics and Law.)

8. Resolving Ethical Issues

8.01 Familiarity with Ethics Code. Psychologists have an obligation to be familiar with this Ethics Code, other applicable ethics codes, and their application to psychologists' work. Lack of awareness or misunderstanding of an ethical standard is not itself a defense to a charge of unethical conduct.

8.02 Confronting Ethical Issues. When a psychologist is uncertain whether a particular situation or course of action would violate this Ethics Code, the psychologist ordinarily consults with other psychologists knowledgeable about ethical issues, with state or national psychology ethics committees, or with other appropriate authorities in order to choose a proper response.

8.03 Conflicts Between Ethics and Organizational Demands. If the demands of an organization with which psychologists are affiliated conflict with this Ethics Code, psychologists clarify the nature of the conflict, make known their commitment to the Ethics Code, and to the extent feasible, seek to resolve the conflict in a way that permits the fullest adherence to the Ethics Code.

8.04 Informal Resolution of Ethical Violations. When psychologists believe that there may have been an ethical violation by another psychologist, they attempt to resolve the issue by bringing it to the attention of that individual if an informal resolution appears appropriate and the intervention does not violate any confidentiality rights that may be involved.

8.05 Reporting Ethical Violations. If an apparent ethical violation is not appropriate for informal resolution under Standard 8.04 or is not resolved properly in that fashion, psychologists take further action appropriate to the situation, unless such action conflicts with confidentiality rights in ways that cannot be resolved. Such action might include referral to state or national committees on professional ethics or to state licensing boards.

8.06 Cooperating With Ethics Committees. Psychologists cooperate in ethics investigations, proceedings, and resulting requirements of the APA or any affiliated state psychological association to which they belong. In doing so, they make reasonable efforts to resolve any issues as to confidentiality. Failure to cooperate is itself an ethics violation.

8.07 Improper Complaints. Psychologists do not file or encourage the filing of ethics complaints that are frivolous and are intended to harm the respondent rather than to protect the public.

Appendix E

◆

Code of Ethics:
National Association of Social Workers*

PREAMBLE

This code is intended to serve as a guide to the everyday conduct of members of the social work profession and as a basis for the adjudication of issues in ethics when the conduct of social workers is alleged to deviate from the standards expressed or implied in this code. It represents standards of ethical behavior for social workers in professional relationships with those served, with colleagues, with employers, with other individuals and professions, and with the community and society as a whole. It also embodies standards of ethical behavior governing individual conduct to the extent that such conduct is associated with an individual's status and identity as a social worker.

This code is based on the fundamental values of the social work profession that include the worth, dignity, and uniqueness of all persons as well as their rights and opportunities. It is also based on the nature of social work, which fosters conditions that promote these values.

In subscribing to and abiding by this code, the social worker is expected to view ethical responsibility in as inclusive a context as each situation demands and within which ethical judgment is required. The social worker is expected to take into consideration all the principles in this code that have a bearing upon any situation in which ethical judgment is to be exercised and professional intervention or conduct is planned. The course of action that the social worker chooses is expected to be consistent with the spirit as well as the letter of this code.

In itself, this code does not represent a set of rules that will prescribe all the behaviors of social workers in all the complexities of professional life. Rather, it offers general principles to guide conduct, and the judicious appraisal of conduct, in situations that have ethical implications. It provides the basis for making judgments about ethical actions before and after they occur. Frequently, the particular situation determines the ethical principles that apply and the manner of their application. In such cases, not only the particular ethical principles are taken into immediate consideration, but also the entire code

* Reprinted with permission of the National Association of Social Workers. Copyright NASW. No further reproduction authorized without permission of the NASW.

and its spirit. Specific applications of ethical principles must be judged within the context in which they are being considered. Ethical behavior in a given situation must satisfy not only the judgment of the individual social worker, but also the judgment of an unbiased jury of professional peers.

This code should not be used as an instrument to deprive any social worker of the opportunity or freedom to practice with complete professional integrity; nor should any disciplinary action be taken on the basis of this code without maximum provision for safeguarding the rights of the social worker affected.

The ethical behavior of social workers results not from edict, but from a personal commitment of the individual. This code is offered to affirm the will and zeal of all social workers to be ethical and to act ethically in all that they do as social workers.

The following codified ethical principles should guide social workers in the various roles and relationships and at the various levels of responsibility in which they function professionally. These principles also serve as a basis for the adjudication by the National Association of Social Workers of issues in ethics.

In subscribing to this code, social workers are required to cooperate in its implementation and abide by any disciplinary rulings based on it. They should also take adequate measures to discourage, prevent, expose, and correct the unethical conduct of colleagues. Finally, social workers should be equally ready to defend and assist colleagues unjustly charged with unethical conduct.

THE NASW CODE OF ETHICS

I. The Social Worker's Conduct and Comportment as a Social Worker

a. *Propriety.* The social worker should maintain high standards of personal conduct in the capacity or identity as social worker.

1. The private conduct of the social worker is a personal matter to the same degree as is any other person's, except when such conduct compromises the fulfillment of professional responsibilities.

2. The social worker should not participate in, condone, or be associated with dishonesty, fraud, deceit, or misrepresentation.

3. The social worker should distinguish clearly between statements and actions made as a private individual and as a representative of the social work profession or an organization or group.

b. *Competence and professional development.* The social worker should strive to become and remain proficient in professional practice and the performance of professional functions.

1. The social worker should accept responsibility or employment only on the basis of existing competence or the intention to acquire the necessary competence.

2. The social worker should not misrepresent professional qualifications, education, experience, or affiliations.

3. The social worker should not allow his or her own personal problems, psychosocial distress, substance abuse, or mental health difficulties to interfere with professional judgment and performance or jeopardize the best interests of those for whom the social worker has a professional responsibility.

4. The social worker whose personal problems, psychosocial distress, substance abuse, or mental health difficulties interfere with professional judgment and performance should

immediately seek consultation and take appropriate remedial action by seeking professional help, making adjustments in workload, terminating practice, or taking any other steps necessary to protect clients and others.

c. *Service*. The social worker should regard as primary the service obligation of the social work profession.

1. The social worker should retain ultimate responsibility for the quality and extent of the service that individual assumes, assigns, or performs.

2. The social worker should act to prevent practices that are inhumane or discriminatory against any person or group of persons.

d. *Integrity*. The social worker should act in accordance with the highest standards of professional integrity and impartiality.

1. The social worker should be alert to and resist the influences and pressures that interfere with the exercise of professional discretion and impartial judgment required for the performance of professional functions.

2. The social worker should not exploit professional relationships for personal gain.

e. *Scholarship and research*. The social worker engaged in study and research should be guided by the conventions of scholarly inquiry.

1. The social worker engaged in research should consider carefully its possible consequences for human beings.

2. The social worker engaged in research should ascertain that the consent of participants in the research is voluntary and informed, without any implied deprivation or penalty for refusal to participate, and with due regard for participants' privacy and dignity.

3. The social worker engaged in research should protect participants from unwarranted physical or mental discomfort, distress, harm, danger, or deprivation.

4. The social worker who engages in the evaluation of services or cases should discuss them only for the professional purposes and only with persons directly and professionally concerned with them.

5. Information obtained about participants in research should be treated as confidential.

6. The social worker should take credit only for work actually done in connection with scholarly and research endeavors and credit contributions made by others.

II. The Social Worker's Ethical Responsibility to Clients

f. *Primacy of clients' interests*. The social worker's primary responsibility is to clients.

1. The social worker should serve clients with devotion, loyalty, determination, and the maximum application of professional skill and competence.

2. The social worker should not exploit relationships with clients for personal advantage.

3. The social worker should not practice, condone, facilitate or collaborate with any form of discrimination on the basis of race, color, sex, sexual orientation, age, religion, national origin, marital status, political belief, mental or physical handicap, or any other preference or personal characteristic, condition or status.

4. The social worker should not condone or engage in any dual or multiple relationships with clients or former clients in which there is a risk of exploitation of or

potential harm to the client. The social worker is responsible for setting clear, appropriate, and culturally sensitive boundaries.

5. The social worker should under no circumstances engage in sexual activities with clients.

6. The social worker should provide clients with accurate and complete information regarding the extent and nature of the services available to them.

7. The social worker should apprise clients of their risks, rights, opportunities, and obligations associated with social service to them.

8. The social worker should seek advice and counsel of colleagues and supervisors whenever such consultation is in the best interest of clients.

9. The social worker should terminate service to clients, and professional relationships with them, when such service and relationships are no longer required or no longer serve the clients' needs or interests.

10. The social worker should withdraw services precipitously only under unusual circumstances, giving careful consideration to all factors in the situation and taking care to minimize possible adverse effects.

11. The social worker who anticipates the termination or interruption of service to clients should notify clients promptly and seek the transfer, referral, or continuation of service in relation to the clients' needs and preferences.

g. *Rights and prerogatives of clients.* The social worker should make every effort to foster maximum self-determination on the part of clients.

1. When the social worker must act on behalf of a client who has been adjudged legally incompetent, the social worker should safeguard the interests and rights of that client.

2. When another individual has been legally authorized to act in behalf of a client, the social worker should deal with that person always with the client's best interest in mind.

3. The social worker should not engage in any action that violates or diminishes the civil or legal rights of clients.

h. *Confidentiality and privacy.* The social worker should respect the privacy of clients and hold in confidence all information obtained in the course of professional service.

1. The social worker should share with others confidences revealed by clients, without their consent, only for compelling professional reasons.

2. The social worker should inform clients fully about the limits of confidentiality in a given situation, the purposes for which information is obtained, and how it may be used.

3. The social worker should afford clients reasonable access to any official social work records concerning them.

4. When providing clients with access to records, the social worker should take due care to protect the confidences of others contained in those records.

5. The social worker should obtain informed consent of clients before taping, recording, or permitting third party observation of their activities.

i. *Fees.* When setting fees, the social worker should ensure that they are fair, reasonable, considerate, and commensurate with the service performed and with due regard for the clients' ability to pay.

1. The social worker should not accept anything of value for making a referral.

III. The Social Worker's Ethical Responsibility to Colleagues

j. *Respect, fairness, and courtesy.* The social worker should treat colleagues with respect, courtesy, fairness, and good faith.

1. The social worker should cooperate with colleagues to promote professional interests and concerns.

2. The social worker should respect confidences shared by colleagues in the course of their professional relationships and transactions.

3. The social worker should create and maintain conditions of practice that facilitate ethical and competent professional performance by colleagues.

4. The social worker should treat with respect, and represent accurately and fairly, the qualifications, views, and findings of colleagues and use appropriate channels to express judgments on these matters.

5. The social worker who replaces or is replaced by a colleague in professional practice should act with consideration for the interest, character, and reputation of that colleague.

6. The social worker should not exploit a dispute between a colleague and employers to obtain a position or otherwise advance the social worker's interest.

7. The social worker should seek arbitration or mediation when conflicts with colleagues require resolution for compelling professional reasons.

8. The social worker should extend to colleagues of other professions the same respect and cooperation that is extended to social work colleagues.

9. The social worker who serves as an employer, supervisor, or mentor to colleagues should make orderly and explicit arrangements regarding the conditions of their continuing professional relationship.

10. The social worker who has the responsibility for employing and evaluating the performance of other staff members, should fulfill such responsibility in a fair, considerate, and equitable manner, on the basis of clearly enunciated criteria.

11. The social worker who has the responsibility for evaluating the performance of employees, supervisees, or students should share evaluations with them.

12. The social worker should not use a professional position vested with power, such as that of employer, supervisor, teacher, or consultant, to his or her advantage or to exploit others.

13. The social worker who has direct knowledge of a social work colleague's impairment due to personal problems, psychosocial distress, substance abuse, or mental health difficulties should consult with that colleague and assist the colleague in taking remedial action.

k. *Dealing with colleagues' clients.* The social worker has the responsibility to relate to the clients of colleagues with full professional consideration.

1. The social worker should not assume professional responsibility for the clients of another agency or a colleague without appropriate communication with that agency or colleague.

2. The social worker who serves the clients of colleagues, during a temporary absence or emergency, should serve those clients with the same consideration as that afforded any client.

IV. The Social Worker's Ethical Responsibility to Employers and Employing Organizations

l. *Commitments to employing organization.* The social worker should adhere to commitments made to the employing organization.

1. The social worker should work to improve the employing agency's policies and procedures, and the efficiency and effectiveness of its services.

2. The social worker should not accept employment or arrange student field placements in an organization which is currently under public sanction by NASW for violating personnel standards, or imposing limitations on or penalties for professional actions on behalf of clients.

3. The social worker should act to prevent and eliminate discrimination in the employing organization's work assignments and in its employment policies and practices.

4. The social worker should use with scrupulous regard, and only for the purpose for which they are intended, the resources of the employing organization.

V. The Social Worker's Ethical Responsibility to the Social Work Profession

m. *Maintaining the integrity of the profession.* The social worker should uphold and advance the values, ethics, knowledge, and mission of the profession.

1. The social worker should protect and enhance the dignity and integrity of the profession and should be responsible and vigorous in discussion and criticism of the profession.

2. The social worker should take action through appropriate channels against unethical conduct by any other member of the profession.

3. The social worker should act to prevent the unauthorized and unqualified practice of social work.

4. The social worker should make no misrepresentation in advertising as to qualifications, competence, service, or results to be achieved.

n. *Community service.* The social worker should assist the profession in making social services available to the general public.

1. The social worker should contribute time and professional expertise to activities that promote respect for the utility, the integrity, and the competence of the social work profession.

2. The social worker should support the formulation, development, enactment and implementation of social policies of concern to the profession.

o. *Development of knowledge.* The social worker should take responsibility for identifying, developing, and fully utilizing knowledge for professional practice.

1. The social worker should base practice upon recognized knowledge relevant to social work.

2. The social worker should critically examine, and keep current with emerging knowledge relevant to social work.

3. The social worker should contribute to the knowledge base of social work and share research knowledge and practice wisdom with colleagues.

VI. The Social Worker's Ethical Responsibility to Society

p. *Promoting the general welfare.* The social worker should promote the general welfare of society.

1. The social worker should act to prevent and eliminate discrimination against any person or group on the basis of race, color, sex, sexual orientation, age, religion, national origin, marital status, political belief, mental or physical handicap, or any other preference or personal characteristic, condition, or status.

2. The social worker should act to ensure that all persons have access to the resources, services, and opportunities which they require.

3. The social worker should act to expand choice and opportunity for all persons, with special regard for disadvantaged or oppressed groups and persons.

4. The social worker should promote conditions that encourage respect for the diversity of cultures which constitute American society.

5. The social worker should provide appropriate professional services in public emergencies.

6. The social worker should advocate changes in policy and legislation to improve social conditions and to promote social justice.

7. The social worker should encourage informed participation by the public in shaping social policies and institutions.

Name Index

Subject Index

TO THE OWNER OF THIS BOOK:

We hope that you have found *Counseling Children, Fourth Edition,* useful. So that this book can be improved in a future edition, would you take the time to complete this sheet and return it? Thank you.

School and address: _____

Department: _____

Instructor's name: _____

1. What I like most about this book is: _____

_____

_____

2. What I like least about this book is: _____

_____

_____

3. My general reaction to this book is: _____

_____

4. The name of the course in which I used this book is: _____

_____

5. Were all of the chapters of the book assigned for you to read? _____

   If not, which ones weren't? _____

6. In the space below, or on a separate sheet of paper, please write specific suggestions for improving this book and anything else you'd care to share about your experience in using the book.

_____

_____

_____

_____

_____

Brooks/Cole is dedicated to publishing quality books for the helping professions. If you would like to learn more about our publications, please use this mailer to request our catalogue.

Name: —————————————————————————————————

Street Address: —————————————————————————————

City, State, and Zip: ————————————————————————

FOLD HERE

FOLD HERE